HUMAN MEMORY

Related Titles

CogLab: 35 Experiments on the Web That Demonstrate the Phenomena of Cognitive Psychology, by Greg Francis and Ian Neath

Cognitive Psychology

Cognition: Theory and Application, 5th edition, by Steve Reed

Cognitive Psychology, 3rd edition, by Robert Sternberg

Cognitive Psychology In and Out of the Laboratory, 2nd edition, by Kathleen M. Galotti

Research Methods

Experimental Psychology: Understanding Psychological Research, 7th edition, by Barry H. Kantowitz, Henry L. Roedinger, and David G. Elmes

Research Methods in Psychology, 7th edition, by David G. Elmes, Barry H. Kantowitz, and Harry L. Roedinger, III

Neuropsychology

Principles of Neuropsychology, by Eric A. Zillmer and Mary V. Spiers

HUMAN MEMORY

An Introduction to Research, Data, and Theory

SECOND EDITION

Ian Neath
Purdue University

Aimée M. Surprenant
Purdue University

WADSWORTH
CENGAGE Learning

Australia • Brazil • Japan • Korea • Mexico • Singapore • Spain • United Kingdom • United States

WADSWORTH
CENGAGE Learning

Human Memory: An Introduction to Research, Data, and Theory, Second Edition
Ian Neath, Aimée M. Surprenant

Publisher: Vicki Knight

Sponsoring Editor: Marianne Taflinger

Editorial Assistant: Nicole Root

Technology Project Manager:
Darin Derstine

Marketing Manager: Lori Grebe

Marketing Assistant: Laurel Anderson

Advertising Project Manager:
Brian Chaffee

Project Manager, Editorial Production:
Mary Noel

Print/Media Buyer: Rebecca Cross

Permissions Editor: Elizabeth Zuber

Production Service: Scratchgravel
Publishing Services

Interior and Cover Design: Roy R. Neuhaus

Copy Editor: Margaret C. Tropp

Cover Image: Allen Wallace/Photonica

Compositor: Scratchgravel Publishing
Services

For product information and technology assistance, contact us at
Cengage Learning Customer & Sales Support, 1-800-354-9706

For permission to use material from this text or product,
submit all requests online at **www.cengage.com/permissions**
Further permissions questions can be emailed to
permissionrequest@cengage.com

Library of Congress Control Number: 2002114800

ISBN-13: 978-0-534-59562-3

ISBN-10: 0-534-59562-6

Wadsworth
10 Davis Drive
Belmont, CA 94002-3098
USA

Cengage Learning is a leading provider of customized learning solutions with office locations around the globe, including Singapore, the United Kingdom, Australia, Mexico, Brazil, and Japan. Locate your local office at:
international.cengage.com/region

Cengage Learning products are represented in Canada by Nelson Education, Ltd.

For your course and learning solutions, visit **academic.cengage.com**

Purchase any of our products at your local college store or at our preferred online store **www.ichapters.com**

Printed in Canada
8 9 10 11 12 13 11 10 09 08

To H. T. G.

In Memoriam: R. T. G.

Brief Contents

Contents

CHAPTER
ELEVEN

Imagery   245

CHAPTER
TWELVE

Reconstructive Processes in Memory   264

CHAPTER
THIRTEEN

Memory for When   291

CHAPTER FOURTEEN	Memory Development	315

CHAPTER FIFTEEN	Mnemonics	343

Preface

The first edition of this text was written because there were no books on memory that were really appropriate for the courses that we teach at Purdue. We used to use Zechmeister and Nyberg's *Human Memory* (1982), but it is out of date, and the authors unfortunately have not offered a revised edition. Other books typically suffer from one of two problems: Either their scope is too limited for a full semester course on human memory, or their scope is too inclusive, including material that at Purdue is covered by a separate course on animal learning. Thus, this book encompasses most of what we cover in our classes, although not all of the material is used in all of the courses and additional readings are also assigned.

The major changes from the first edition include a completely rewritten and expanded chapter on neuropsychology (Chapter 8), an expanded coverage of the effects of aging on memory (Chapter 14), and placement of the detailed discussion of quantitative memory models in an optional chapter while retaining verbal descriptions within the original chapter. This will allow instructors of undergraduate courses to cover important models at a purely verbal level, whereas instructors of graduate courses can still delve into the architecture and operation of the models. Some of the later chapters have been reordered, so that reconstructive aspects of memory (Chapter 12) are covered before the issue of how people remember when something occurred (Chapter 13), which then leads into memory over the life span (Chapter 14).

Less obvious changes in this second edition include the updating of the material within each chapter. In particular, we have added much new material, such as the expanded coverage of different accounts of working memory (Chapter 4), the role of working memory in visual imagery (Chapter 11), and a substantial section on autobiographical memory (Chapter 13). Many chapters may look the same as those in the first edition, but closer inspection will find the inclusion of much recent research. We have tried to maintain the balance between historically significant findings and current "state-of-the-art" research; as a consequence we have also added quite a bit of older work as well.

The book retains its emphasis on the relationships among research, data, and theory. Following the lead of Zechmeister and Nyberg (1982), we feature in each chapter (with the exception of the developmental chapter) a classic or otherwise important experiment that students can easily conduct. In this second edition, we now offer two types of experiments. The original experiments require nothing more complex than pencil and paper. However, many studies (for example, those on iconic memory or mental rotation) require precise control over the presentation of stimuli. For these, the text provides links to the CogLab Web site, where students can conduct experiments online.

There are still many important topics that are not covered or that receive only minimal attention. The primary reason is the same as before: Memory plays so central a role in cognitive functioning that almost all areas of experimental psychology could legitimately be included in a memory textbook. We hope that this book reflects a reasonably fair summary of the major areas of mainstream memory research.

A Guide to the Book

Each chapter in this book is, to a large extent, self-contained, and the chapters can be read in any order. Several features help this modular design, including defining the same concept in more than one chapter and providing numerous cross-references to other chapters. Nonetheless, one set of chapters will be easier to understand if read in sequence: Chapters 5, 6, and 7 should be read in order, and Chapter 12 should be read before Chapters 13 and 14. Chapter 15 can serve either as a review or as an introduction.

Chapter 1 introduces the relationship among research, data, and theory and situates current research within a larger historical perspective. Included is a brief overview of the contribution of philosophy to psychology's early history, as well as a discussion of the pioneering work of Hermann Ebbinghaus. The experiment replicates Ebbinghaus's famous forgetting function.

Chapter 2 reviews work on sensory memory with an emphasis on whether there is evidence to support the idea that there exist separate memory systems for sensory information. Most of the chapter concerns visual and auditory modalities, but there is also a brief discussion of memory for odors, a sensory modality that has been rather understudied. The experiment examines the stimulus suffix effect, and there is a link to the CogLab demo that recreate Sperling's (1960) partial report technique.

Chapter 3 presents the common multistore, or modal, model of memory, with an indepth examination of the evidence used to support a distinction between short-term store and long-term store. The chapter also discusses in some detail the classic work of Broadbent; Miller; Peterson and Peterson; Waugh and Norman; and Atkinson and Shiffrin. It includes a critical examination of the strengths and weakness of this classic approach. The experiment compares short-term recency effects with long-term recency effects, and there are links to CogLab experiments on absolute identification, the Brown-Peterson task, and Sternberg's memory scanning paradigm.

Chapter 4 compares three current perspectives of working memory: Baddeley's (2001) working memory, Cowan's (1999) activation view, and Engle's (2001) working memory capacity view. An alternate conception of working memory, Nairne's (1990) feature model, contrasts with the working memory approaches. All of these views are presented in some detail to illustrate how theorists explain the huge amount of information we have about memory performance. The experiment demonstrates the syllable-based word-length effect—better recall of short compared to long words—and there are links to CogLab demos on memory span and operation span.

Chapter 5 focuses on processing, including both levels of processing and transfer appropriate processing. The relationship between the processing performed at study and the processing required at test is examined in detail, and the chapter concludes with presentation of Jacoby's (1991) processing dissociation framework, a technique designed to evaluate the contributions of different processes. The experiment illustrates Craik and

Lockhart's (1972) levels of processing framework, and there is a link to the CogLab demo on encoding specificity.

Chapter 6 examines three main views of forgetting, consolidation, decay, and interference. Decay and interference explanations are compared, and the experiment examines the buildup and release from proactive interference in the Brown-Peterson task. The CogLab link is to a demo of the von Restorff effect and the role of distinctiveness in memory.

Chapter 7 looks at implicit and explicit memory, particularly as they bear on the important issue of whether there are multiple memory systems. The experiment is a demonstration of repetition priming, the data most often used to support a distinction between implicit and explicit memory, and the CogLab link is to an implicit learning demonstration. The chapter compares the multiple systems view of Schacter and Tulving (1994), the transfer appropriate processing view of Roediger (1990), and the bias interpretation of Ratcliff and McKoon (1996).

Chapter 8 completes the discussion of multiple memory systems by presenting an overview of the biological bases of memory, including a discussion of various techniques. The experiment illustrates a simple behavioral measure for examining underlying neurological structure, as does the CogLab link. There is extended discussion of amnesia and memory problems associated with Alzheimer's disease.

Chapter 9 examines recognition memory, including a discussion of signal detection theory and how this can be used to assess discrimination and estimate response bias. The experiment details how to apply a signal detection analysis to recognition data, including a manipulation of response bias. Also included are discussions of the role of familiarity and recollection, the mirror effect, and an overview of face recognition. The CogLab link is to a demonstration of the remember/know paradigm.

Chapters 10 and 11 examine the issue of representation. Chapter 10 focuses on knowledge and thus emphasizes a primarily propositional form of representation. The chapter includes both spreading activation accounts of semantic priming as well as the current compound cue theories, which extend the global memory models presented in the optional chapter. The experiment examines typicality effects based on knowledge, and the CogLab link is to a lexical decision experiment.

Chapter 11 concentrates on visual imagery, arguing the need for an analog form of representation. This chapter includes the early work of Paivio and Brooks, as well as the more recent work of Kosslyn, Shepard, and Logie. Chapter 11 also discusses the issue of reality monitoring, including the Perky effect showing the difficulty in distinguishing between real and imagined stimuli. The experiment examines a prediction of Paivo's dual-coding theory, and there is a link to the CogLab mental rotation demo. The chapter concludes with a brief discussion of auditory and odor imagery.

Chapter 12 concentrates on reconstructive processes in memory, including the role of schemas and general knowledge. The chapter includes a suggestion for making the concept of a schema less vague and capable of making predictions, and it presents a detailed presentation of memory illusions. Chapter 12 also explores the consequences of reconstructive memory for evaluating the memory of eyewitnesses, including the role of misinformation, hypnosis, and the cognitive interview and how factors such as emotion and arousal can affect accuracy. The chapter includes a discussion of implanting memories and the so-called recovered memory debate. The experiment and the CogLab link both illustrate the phenomenon of memory for words not presented.

Chapter 13 presents an overview of memory for "when," including a discussion of how people remember when particular events occurred, a section on autobiographical memory, and a comparison of various theories of dating events. Two models are compared in some detail, with an emphasis on how they account for both laboratory and real world data. The chapter ends with a discussion of autobiographical memory. The experiment and the CogLab demo assess memory for when items were presented, which illustrates many of the same properties as memory for autobiographical events.

Chapter 14 looks at developmental issues, emphasizing qualitative differences in processing when infants, children, and healthy older adults are compared to college students. Because of the difficulty of recruiting appropriate subjects, this chapter has no experiment.

Chapter 15 discusses ways to improve memory. Unlike books that focus only on the technical mnemonics, this chapter includes a much broader treatment and can serve as either a review or an introduction. The experiment duplicates a classic finding of better retention following interactive imagery as compared to no imagery, and the CogLab link is to a demo of the link word technique for foreign language acquisition. In addition, the chapter provides a critique of popular books, separating the useful and scientifically supported techniques from the useless and disproven.

The optional chapter presents detailed accounts of some of the influential models of memory. These include the three so-called global memory models (SAM, MINERVA2, and TODAM), the diffusion model, compound cue theory, the feature model, as well as an example of a connectionist model of memory, in this case a nonlinear back propagation model of recognition. Implementations of most of these models are available at http://rumpole.psych.purdue.edu/models/.

Acknowledgments

Ian Neath: Professionally, I am particularly indebted to three people: my undergraduate advisor, Michael J. Watkins of Rice University; my graduate advisor, Robert G. Crowder of Yale University; and my colleague James S. Nairne at Purdue University. I would also like to thank my parents for everything they have done for me.

Aimée Surprenant: I would like to thank both of my parents for their unwavering belief and support of me through the years. In academia, my mentors include my undergraduate advisor, Joan Gay Snodgrass; my graduate advisor, Robert G. Crowder; and my postdoctoral mentor, Charles S. Watson. All of them, at different stages of my career, have provided me with invaluable guidance, and I am grateful to each of them. In addition, my friends Richard J. Gerrig and Arthur G. Samuel were (and still are) always encouraging me.

Several reviewers read the entire manuscript, and many more read portions; each made numerous insightful and critical comments that greatly improved the manuscript. For the first edition, we thank Harriett Amster, University of Texas, Arlington; Barbara H. Basden, California State University, Fresno; Robert Campbell, Clemson University; James M. Clark, University of Winnipeg; Tim Curran, Case Western Reserve University; Ira Fischler, University of Florida; Peter Graf, University of British Columbia; Robert Greene, Case Western Reserve University; Denny C. LeCompte, Compaq Computer; Wendy V. Parr, Victoria University of Wellington; Henry L. Roediger III, Washington University; J. Scott Saults, University of Missouri–Columbia; Jennifer R. Shelton-Young,

Harvard University; and Michael A. Stadler, University of Missouri–Columbia. For the second edition, we thank Brian Bornstein, University of Nebraska; Tim Curran, University of Colorado at Boulder; Gary Gargano, Saint Joseph's University; and Arnold Lewis Glass, Rutgers, The State University of New Jersey.

We would also like to thank the staff at Wadsworth: Marianne Taflinger, Kirk Bomont, and Mary Noel were a pleasure to work with, and Margaret Tropp deserves much thanks for greatly improving the prose in the text.

We are especially fortunate that our colleagues at Purdue were willing to answer questions, provide references, and offer suggestions.

Sapiens nihil affirmat quod non probat.

Ian Neath
Aimée M. Surprenant

About the Authors

Ian Neath is currently an associate professor in the Department of Psychological Sciences at Purdue University in West Lafayette, Indiana. He received a B.A. in history and psychology from Rice University in 1987 and a Ph.D. in cognitive psychology from Yale University in 1991. At Purdue, he regularly teaches both the undergraduate and graduate courses on human memory, as well as courses on introductory psychology, cognitive psychology, and stimulation modeling. He has published many articles on memory in such professional journals as *Memory & Cognition*, *Psychonomic Bulletin & Review*, *Quarterly Journal of Experimental Psychology*, *Memory*, and *Journal of Memory and Language*. He co-edited *The Nature of Remembering: Essays in Honor of Robert G. Crowder* and also co-edited a special double issue of the *International Journal of Psychology* on short-term memory.

Aimée M. Surprenant is currently an associate professor in the Department of Psychological Sciences at Purdue University in West Lafayette, Indiana. She received a B.A. in psychology from New York University in 1988 and a Ph.D. in cognitive psychology from Yale University in 1992. She received a National Research Service Award from the National Institutes of Health for postdoctoral work at Indiana University in the Department of Speech and Hearing Sciences. Her research has been published in such journals as *Memory & Cognition*, *Perception & Psychophysics*, *Journal of the Acoustical Society of America*, *Memory*, and *Quarterly Journal of Experimental Psychology*. She co-edited *The Nature of Remembering: Essays in Honor of Robert G. Crowder*.

Human Memory

An Introduction to Research, Data, and Theory

CHAPTER ONE

Introduction and Historical Overview

There seems something more speakingly incomprehensible in the powers, the failures, the inequalities of memory, than in any other of our intelligences. The memory is sometimes so retentive, so serviceable, so obedient—at others, so bewildered and so weak—and at others again, so tyrannic, so beyond control! We are to be sure a miracle every way—but our powers of recollecting and of forgetting, do seem peculiarly past finding out.

—Jane Austen

The Study of Memory

If we had no memory, in the broadest sense of the term, we would not be able to function. Memory is essential for all activities. When riding a bicycle, we rely on memory to provide the appropriate processes to keep our balance, keep the pedals turning, and navigate down the path. When reading, we rely on memory to provide knowledge about word definitions, facts, and concepts. We also need memory to keep track of the flow of ideas, why one sentence or paragraph of text follows another. When chatting with friends, we rely on memory to provide information about details of our own lives, what we did last week, or what happened at the ball game. When listening, we rely on memory to retain, however briefly, parts of the auditory signal so that it can be processed. When creating an image of what a room would look like with its furniture rearranged, we rely on memory to provide the structural descriptions that allow us to construct a mental picture. A person's identity

1

and definition of self rely solely on memory, both for what the person has done, thought, and believed and for what others have said. Memory plays such an important and ever-present role that it is often overlooked. The only time most people pay attention to their memory is when it fails.

The study of memory seeks to understand these and many other aspects of memory. Like most people, researchers look for situations in which memory fails. It is by comparing situations where memory is successful to ones where it fails that psychologists have discovered and documented the principles by which human memory operates. Although the research is not so far progressed that we can predict each individual's behavior in every particular situation, the accumulated knowledge does allow us to predict general memory performance in a wide range of situations. The purpose of this book is to introduce you to this accumulated knowledge, to illustrate the process of designing and conducting diagnostic research, and to present a survey of the resultant theories that summarize and explain the data and make predictions about performance in novel situations. As you will see, our powers of remembering and forgetting can indeed be found out.

Memory Metaphors

One of the central questions researchers must address when developing a theory or model is how best to think of memory. When most people think about memory—psychologists included—they typically conceive of a place where information is stored. As Roediger (1980) has noted, this spatial metaphor has dominated the study of memory: "We speak of *storing* memories, of *searching* for and *locating* them. We *organize* our thoughts; we *look* for memories that have been *lost*, and if we are fortunate, we *find* them" (p. 232).

In addition, these spatial metaphors have typically represented the newest or most important technology available. For example, Aristotle, in his *De memoria et reminiscentia*, compared memory to a wax tablet, with forming a memory like making a seal on wax with a signet ring. The durability of the memory depended on the age and temperament of the person, just as the durability of an impression depends on the age and malleability of the wax.

> Some men in the presence of considerable stimulus have no memory. . . . With them the design makes no impression because they are worn down like old walls in buildings, or because of the hardness of that which is to receive the impression. For this reason the very young and the old have poor memories; they are in a state of flux, the young because of their growth, the old because of their decay. For a similar reason neither the very quick nor the very slow appear to have good memories; the former are moister than they should be, and the latter harder; with the former the picture has no permanence, with the latter it makes no impression. (Aristotle, quoted in Yates, 1966, p. 33)

Plato compared memory to an aviary, whereas Augustine compared memory to a cave—both spatial objects. Vives compared memory to a body, claiming that both need regular exercise or they become lazy, sluggish, and inert. Francis Bacon compared the act of recollection to hunting a deer; if one cuts down the available space in which the deer can roam, the hunting is easier. Descartes, in *De homine*, used an analogy to the water-powered automata in the French royal gardens to describe simple reflexes and incorporated them into his conception of how the mind and body interact (Herrnstein & Boring, 1965). John Locke thought of memory as an empty cabinet. By the early 20th century, memory was being compared to a gramophone, an updating of the wax tablet metaphor but with a more precise description of various problems (Pear, 1922).

By the mid-1950s, descriptions and theories of memory were borrowing much from the telephone system and from information theory (Broadbent, 1958), only to be eclipsed by the digital computer metaphor, with the interaction of hardware and software (Feigenbaum & Simon, 1962). This metaphor led directly to what is referred to as the dual-store or modal model of memory, with separate short- and long-term stores (see Chapter 3).

Perhaps the most unusual—but still spatial—metaphor compared memory to a cow's digestive system and the passage of information through the memory system to the passage of food through the various stomachs and orifices of a cow (Hintzman, 1974a). Hintzman noted that the metaphor is invoked by phrases such as *food for thought, digesting information,* and *ruminating.* The process of forgetting was not explicitly described, but it was thought to be the reverse of "incremental learning: namely, excremental forgetting" (Hintzman, 1974a, p. 85).

In all these views, memory is a place in which memories are stored, a position called the *structural view.* Consider the following alternative to the structural view:

> Memories, like perceptions and eventually sensations, have no separate existences. The memory of what you saw yesterday has no more existence until revived than the pain you felt in your arm before it was pinched. . . . In short, for the experiencing individual, memories do not exist before they are revived or recalled. Memories are not like filed letters stored in cabinets or unhung paintings in the basement of a museum. Rather, they are like melodies realized by striking the keys on a piano. Memories are no more stored in the brain than melodies in the keys of the piano. (Wechsler, 1963, pp. 150–151)

This second view, called the *proceduralist view,* emphasizes the processes that create and re-create the memory, rather than the structure or location in which a memory might be stored (Crowder, 1993a). This idea also has long history, having been developed earlier by Bain (1855) and Hebb (1949).

Obviously, at some level, memories are stored somewhere; as we experience more and more, we remember more and more, and so structures must be important. Equally obvious, however, is that there is no one place that a memory is put. If, for example, one cell were responsible for the memory of my grandmother and that cell died (as cells do all the time), all memory for my grandmother would be permanently lost. Although neither the structuralist nor the proceduralist view can explain all memory phenomena, the field as a whole has come to emphasize process over structure. Even 25 years ago, Kintsch (1977) concluded that "many psychologists today are no longer satisfied with the box metaphor that underlies the earlier models. . . . Instead, a more dynamic conception of the memory system is evolving, with an emphasis on differential processes rather than on separate boxes" (p. 225).

A third view takes the position that discovering and enumerating general principles of memory provides an appropriate and scientifically sound mode of explanation (Neath & Surprenant, 2003a; Watkins, 2001). This approach follows in the tradition of the *functionalists* (Angell, 1907; Carr, 1930), who were concerned with answering the question "What is the function or purpose of the behavioral act?" As one example, consider the *cue overload principle* (Watkins, 1979). This principle states that the ability of a cue to elicit a particular memory can be reduced if additional items become associated with the same cue; in other words, the cue becomes overloaded and no longer functions effectively. A variety of experimental findings can be explained as instances of this general principle, and invoking the principle reduces the number of phenomena that need explanation.

No single view of human memory can explain all the phenomena of interest. Within each type of account are many different, sometimes incompatible, theories. One important goal of this book is to introduce you to these various theories of memory and to illustrate how these theories are developed and evaluated.

Memory Methodology

One problem with studying memory is that everyone has one and has experience with how it works. When a cognitive psychologist reports the results of a study, a common reaction is to exclaim, "My grandmother could've told me that!" However, the psychologist conducts experiments to determine, as objectively as possible, how memory works. An experimental psychologist uses an established set of procedures that may or may not confirm your grandmother's own experience but that do produce reliable and replicable results. As a rule, experimental psychologists are particularly wary of any unsubstantiated claim, and this may be why it seems that a reference is cited for almost every statement made (Neath & Surprenant, 2003b, Chap. 1).

The primary reason for this reliance on experimentation is that although many conventional beliefs about memory are correct, many are not. For example, many people believe that photographic memory exists, and the majority of college students believe that hypnosis will recover repressed memories (Klatzky, 1984); neither appears to be the case (see Chapters 11 and 12, respectively). A properly conducted experiment—or more usually, a series of experiments—will provide evidence that either confirms or disconfirms such statements. Citing a research study ensures that theories are based on scientifically gathered data rather than on general, untested speculations. Although many of the results may indeed be things that your grandmother knows, there is an important difference between basing conclusions on sound scientific research and untested folk wisdom.

A working definition of *memory* might be that it is the ability to use or revive information that was previously encoded or processed. Memory is never directly observed, and we need not even be aware of its influence; rather, its existence is inferred from some particular behavior or some change in level of performance. Therefore, the type of evidence needed to support the claim of memory versus no memory for a particular event requires special attention.

Another goal of this text is to give you an appreciation for experimental design. Almost every chapter has a description of the procedures necessary to conduct a classic memory study in one of two ways. The first type requires no unusual or expensive equipment and all the necessary stimuli are included in the Appendix. The second type requires only a computer, a networked connection to the Internet, and a recent Web browser. Having conducted an experiment, you will be in a better position to appreciate the arguments that surround its theoretical interpretation.

When people first become acquainted with how experiments are designed and conducted, a common reaction is to wonder whether such artificial-looking procedures can say anything interesting about memory in ordinary, everyday situations. Many researchers have similar concerns, and a debate over ecological validity regularly resurfaces. *Ecological validity* in this context refers to the extent to which an experiment in a controlled laboratory setting reflects what happens in ordinary, uncontrolled settings, usually dubbed "the real world." This recurring debate began again most recently when Ulric Neisser (1978) wrote, "If X is an interesting or socially significant aspect of memory, then psychologists have hardly ever studied X" (p. 4). He further claimed that most experimental findings were obvious or trivial and, most important, they failed to generalize outside the laboratory. According to this view, research in the tradition of Bartlett (1932), whom we will discuss in Chapter 12, has fostered more important findings than has research in the tradition of Ebbinghaus (1885), whom we discuss later in this chapter. For example, Bartlett used sentences and prose passages in his research rather than the nonsense syllables that Ebbinghaus used, and Bartlett examined memory in social settings whereas Ebbinghaus tested only himself.

Two rebuttals to Neisser's critique were offered. Roediger (1990a) pointed out that Neisser's claim is based on a rather limited review of the experimental literature. Many people Neisser cited as prime contributors to the "thundering silence" on practical issues actually spent a large portion of their careers studying practical aspects of memory. A good example is John McGeoch (see Crowder, 1992b, for a brief biography). Although best known for his interference theory of forgetting (see Chapter 6) and his 1942 textbook, McGeoch also contributed substantially to what would now be called applied memory research. In addition, Neisser overlooked the many laboratory findings that do generalize to the real world. For example, research that used artificial stimuli (nonsense syllables) in an artificial task (paired-associate learning) in an artificial setting (the laboratory) consistently found that distributed rather than massed practice produces better memory: If you allot 2 hours for practice, your memory will be better if you separate the practice into several smaller chunks (say, four half-hour blocks) than if you mass all the practice into one 2-hour block. These results have consistently generalized to the "real world": Information is retained longer if it is learned in several shorter sessions than in one longer session (for example, see Herrmann, Weingartner, Searleman, & McEvoy, 1992; Singh, Mishra, Bendapudi, & Linville, 1994). In fact, changing your study habits from massed study to distributed study is perhaps the easiest and most effective way to enhance your retention of information (see Chapter 15). It should not really be surprising that results do generalize from the laboratory to real life. As McGeoch and Irion (1952) put it, "Life in the laboratory is just as 'real' as life may be anywhere else" (p. 8).

An earlier statement by Moore (1910, p. 116) nicely captures the relation between laboratory research and behavior in "real world" conditions:

> It is very seldom, if at all, possible to reproduce in the laboratory the exact conditions of real life. Most of our experiments can only approximate more or less closely the actual occurrences in the external world. This is not, however, an insurmountable difficulty for the experimental psychology. We have not one mind for the laboratory and another for the world. The same mental processes that take place in the world are observed in the laboratory, but under different conditions. The change in conditions is in the direction of greater simplification. The mental process of the laboratory is, as it were, a purified product and its true properties can therefore be more easily determined.

As an interesting side note, the work of Ebbinghaus, done in the "ecologically invalid" way, has consistently been replicated, whereas many of Bartlett's best-known findings, done in a more "ecologically valid" way, have not. For example, the general shape of the forgetting function is the same as Ebbinghaus reported regardless of whether the stimuli are words or sentences (Slamecka & McElree, 1983) or television shows (Squire, 1989). Other examples are the difference between massed and distributed rehearsal cited

Table 1.1   A two-by-two array of approaches
to scientific research

		Ecological Validity of Method	
		Low	High
Generalizability	Low	Cell 1	Cell 2
of results	High	Cell 3	Cell 4

SOURCE: Based on Banaji & Crowder (1989).

earlier, and the effects of the time of day on memory (Petros, Beckwith, & Anderson, 1990). In contrast to this tradition of successful replication are some of Bartlett's best-known findings. Bartlett had his subjects read a Native American folk tale called the "War of the Ghosts." Because his subjects were British, they had almost no knowledge of Native American customs, traditions, and symbolism, and the story was particularly difficult for them to understand and recall. Bartlett reported that over successive recall attempts, more and more distortions were introduced. Although this result is presented in most texts, there are actually no successful replications of this result (see Gauld & Stephenson, 1967; Roediger, Wheeler, & Rajaram, 1993; Wheeler & Roediger, 1992). Of course, many of Bartlett's other studies on memory are easy to replicate, but these show patterns of results similar to those reported by Ebbinghaus.

A different critique of Neisser's thesis was offered by Banaji and Crowder (1989). Their main point was that experiments (in any area) can be classified into one of four categories. The generalizability of the results—the degree to which the results apply widely across a broad range of situations—can be either high or low, and the ecological validity of the method can be either high or low. These four possibilities are shown in Table 1.1.

Banaji and Crowder noted that Cell 4, which represents high ecological validity and high generalizability of results, represents the ideal; Cell 1, which represents contrived, artificial methods with no generalizable findings, is the least desirable situation. Banaji and Crowder disagreed with Neisser in that they opted for Cell 3 (low ecological validity but high generalizability of results) as a better compromise than Cell 2 (high ecological validity but low generalizability of results). As support for their contention, they cited many studies with apparently low ecological validity of methods (such as displaying letters and words for 1/20th of a second) that have had an enormous impact on important everyday behaviors (such as reading).

Unfortunately, many experiments that fall within Cells 1 and 2 (low generalizability of results) have been conducted and published. These studies contribute little to our knowledge of memory, and they can even hinder progress if methodological flaws have led to incorrect conclusions. Part of your job, as a student of memory, is to learn how to distinguish between those studies in Cells 1 and 2 and those in Cells 3 and 4.

Memory Terminology

In 1972, Underwood posed the following question to researchers studying human behavior: "Are we overloading memory?" Part of the problem, as he saw it, was the large number of different types of memory. If anything, the number of terms has proliferated since his article. Although Underwood was referring to overloading the subject's memory with

Table 1.2 Theory-neutral and theory-specific terms for various kinds of memory.

Type of Information	Theory-Neutral Term	Theory-Specific Term(s)
Sensations	Sensory memory	Iconic memory Echoic memory Precategorical acoustic store (PAS)
Information to be retained only briefly	Immediate memory	Short-term store Short-term memory Primary memory Working memory
Information to be retained indefinitely	Generic memory	Long-term store Long-term memory Secondary memory
Personal history	Autobiographical memory	Episodic memory
Knowledge	Generic memory	Semantic memory

Terms in the far right column entail specific assumptions, especially about the division of memory, whereas terms in the middle column are intended to be neutral.

all the different types of processing that could occur, he could also have been referring to the student of memory, who must try to retain the important distinctions among the many different proposed systems and subsystems. Table 1.2 lists some of the memory terms that will be encountered frequently.

In this text, when referring to a specific theory, we will use the terms listed in the far right column of Table 1.2. When referring to the same type of memory but without wishing to invoke a particular theory, we will use the terms listed in the middle column. The theory-specific terms carry with them particular assumptions, whereas the theory-neutral terms (as much as possible) do not. For example, the terms *episodic* and *semantic* usually imply separate memory systems along the lines proposed by Tulving (1972, 1983). In contrast, the terms *autobiographical memory* and *generic memory* refer to remembering the same kind of information as episodic and semantic memory, respectively, but are neutral on whether the systems are separate and on the presumed underlying processes. Similarly, *working memory* is usually taken as implying Baddeley's (1986) proposal, whereas *immediate memory* is the neutral equivalent, implying neither separate memory stores nor a monistic view. The terms *implicit* and *explicit memory* are not included in the table; the definitions for these terms are rather complex and will be provided in Chapter 7.

Understanding the Study of Memory

As you read through this text, keep in mind that understanding memory involves an awareness of the relationships among research, data, and theory. The experiments that are provided (both paper-and-pencil and the Web-based CogLab experiments) will give you an appreciation for experimental design. Having conducted an experiment, you will be in a better position to appreciate the arguments that surround its theoretical interpretation. You should also be able to distinguish between experiments whose results are generalizable and can be applied widely across a broad range of situations and those whose results are limited to particular situations (see Table 1.1). You should not be surprised if the results confirm something you already know, but you should also be willing to change your mind when the results disconfirm something you believe. Finally, you should see how theories are developed and evaluated. In a sense, every theory of memory is wrong. The process of conducting research, collecting data, and evaluating theories is designed to continually refine theories.

A Short History of Research on Memory

Hermann Ebbinghaus is quoted as saying that "psychology has a long past, but only a short history" (Boring, 1950, p. ix). What he meant was that although inquiries into the nature of memory began centuries ago, the early researchers lacked an appropriate set of rules, methods, and procedures for studying memory, and as a result the scientific study of memory is barely over 100 years old. Researchers did not begin to build a sound body of scientific knowledge until after they had abandoned *introspection* as the main research method.

Many early researchers believed that, just as people can be trained to observe external events accurately (judges at gymnastics or diving competitions, for example), so could people be trained to observe their internal cognitive events. Introspectionists were trained to "observe" their own mental functioning and to make repeated observations before coming to any conclusions. The main problem with introspection, as Karl Marbe (1869–1953), a leading researcher at Würzburg, quickly found out, was that similar observers performing the same act often gave very different descriptions. In one of Marbe's experiments, subjects were asked to judge which of two objects was heavier; although his subjects were quite accurate at identifying the heavier object, they could not agree on the process whereby they made this decision. (Marbe's disenchantment with introspection precipitated his change from experimental to applied psychology, where he developed aptitude tests for business and studied accident proneness with an eye to prevention; see Zusne, 1975.) As a method of inquiry, introspection has had a "dismal record of failure" in psychology (Bower & Clapper, 1989, p. 245). Although the earliest philosophers and researchers did gain many valuable insights through introspection, it should be noted that they made numerous errors as well.

Antiquity and the Middle Ages

Many ancient cultures had gods or goddesses associated specifically with memory. In Egypt in 4000 BCE, Thoth was the god of learning, memory, and wisdom; in Greece in 1000 BCE, Mnemosyne (from whom we get terms such as *mnemonic* and *mnemonist*), mother of the muses, was the goddess of memory (Herrmann & Chaffin, 1988). Although there were undoubtedly many works on how to improve memory, the earliest surviving example dates from about 400 BCE. This fragment, known as the *Dialexeis* (Yates, 1966, pp. 29–30), suggests that the three most important factors in remembering are paying attention, rehearsing, and using a formal mnemonic device, the *method of loci* (see Chapter 15).

The first real memory theorists were Plato (427–347 BCE) and Aristotle (384–322 BCE). Plato believed that all essential truths are stored in memory and that learning is simply the process of recollecting these truths. He offered three metaphors for memory. First, he likened memory to impressions formed on a wax tablet: A person might have a more or less retentive memory depending on the age of the wax, the hardness of the wax, the depth of the impression, and so forth. Second, he compared knowledge to birds in an aviary, with each different species of bird being a different piece of knowledge. A particular bird might be in the aviary but off in a distant part and not immediately accessible. Third, he likened memory to the recording of experience by a scribe, and therefore subject to the whims of the scribe: "When the inscribing feeling writes truly, then true opinion and true propositions are formed within us in consequence of its work—but when the scribe within us writes falsely, the result is false" (Herrmann & Chaffin, 1988, p. 55).

Most of Aristotle's writing on memory is found in a brief essay called *De Memoria et Reminiscentia* ("On Memory and Reminiscences"). The title reflects a distinction that Plato draws in *Philebus*: Memory is the power of retention, whereas *recollection* (or reminiscence) is the power of recall. Humans are said to have both, but other animals lack recollection. Recollection is based on associations, and an *association* is simply the connection of two mental events (ideas, thoughts, beliefs, memories). Philosophers and psychologists have identified three laws of association within the works of Aristotle: Events tend to be associated when they occur close together in time or space (the law of contiguity), when they are similar (the law of similarity), and when they contrast with each other (the law of contrast).

In the Roman world, the emphasis was on practical aspects of memory rather than on theory. Both Cicero (106–43 BCE) and Quintillian (40–96 CE) emphasized the role that memory played in oratory: Cicero emphasized the importance of order as an aid, and Quintillian emphasized exercise, both mental and physical (Burnham, 1888). An anonymous work written around 86 BCE, known as *Ad Herennium,* is the most famous pragmatic work on memory from that period (Yates, 1966) and was the basis for much of the work of subsequent scholars.

The next early memory theorist was Augustine (354–430 CE). He identified two kinds of memory, sense memory and intellectual memory (Burnham, 1888). Sense memory preserves and reproduces images of objects, including sounds, odors, and touch. Intellectual memory is concerned with knowledge, including literature, science, and philosophy. He also noted the possibility of memory illusions, such as when "we fancy we remember as though we had done or seen it, what we never did or saw at all" (Burnham, 1888, p. 61). Augustine agreed with earlier scholars such as Plotinus (205–270 CE) that memory is not a simple, passive process but rather a complex series of actions that can affect the accuracy and the nature of the memory. This idea is reflected in one of Augustine's major concerns, retrieval. He compared memory to a cave in which were stored not the original events but images of the events. Whenever we attempt to recall something, we are limited by the associations of ideas. Augustine also mentioned one of the many paradoxes of memory: "We have not entirely forgotten anything if we can remember that we have forgotten it" (Herrmann & Chaffin, 1988, p. 119).

Relatively little survives from the Middle Ages, and much of the work on memory in the Renaissance concerns practical questions and mnemonic techniques (see Carruthers, 1990; Yates, 1966). Thomas Aquinas (1224–1274) generally followed the views of Aristotle; his main contribution was bringing the works of Aristotle to a wider audience, rather than adding anything new to his views on memory. Until this point, relatively little emphasis was placed on empirical testing of ideas. Most medieval scholars were more concerned with metaphysics and its relation to theology than with accumulating empirically based knowledge. A major change in attitudes is reflected in the works of Juan Luis Vives and Francis Bacon.

The Beginning of Modern Psychology

Juan Luis Vives (1492–1540), a Spanish humanist who studied in Paris and taught for a while at Corpus Christi College, Oxford, is often regarded as one of the great *empiricists* of the Renaissance. His central focus was on practical uses of knowledge, and he is well known for his many works on education. In his main writing on psychology, *De anima et vita libri tres* ("Three Books on the Soul and Life"), published in 1538, Vives called for greater attention to observation and experimentation and less reliance on ancient authorities. He discussed the association of ideas, following Aristotle's and Augustine's formulations, and discussed memory at length, including sections on a law of forgetfulness and on mnemonics. He identified three causes of forgetting: "either because the very picture in memory is erased or destroyed directly; or it is smeared and broken up; or because it escapes our searching" (Diamond, 1974, p. 256). Vives suggested writing down whatever one wanted to remember (Burnham, 1888), thus going against the strictures of Plato, who warned that writing down information "will create forgetfulness in the learners' souls, because they will not use their memories; they will trust to the external written characters and not remember of themselves" (Herrmann & Chaffin, 1988, p. 38). Vives also believed, however, that "if memory is not exercised, it grows dull, becoming slower each day, more sluggish and inert" (Diamond, 1974, p. 256).

Francis Bacon (1561–1626), too, emphasized the practical value of empirical discoveries in contrast to the results of metaphysical speculation and introspection, and his approach and ideas influenced many other prominent British thinkers. He believed that the three great powers were memory, fancy, and reason. He offered many practical insights into improving memory that have since been demonstrated as effective, such as associating the event with something concrete, studying before sleeping to reduce interference, processing information in several different ways rather than simply repeating it in rote fashion, and reducing the size of the search set. This last suggestion was accomplished by means of a "prenotion":

> By Prenotion I mean a kind of cutting off of infinity of search. For when a man desires to recall anything into his memory, if he have no prenotion or perception of that he seeks, he seeks and strives and beats about hither and thither as if in infinite space. But if he have some prenotion, this infinity is at once cut off, and the memory ranges in a narrower compass; like the hunting of a deer within an enclosure. (Bacon, quoted in Robertson, 1905, p. 168)

Bacon is also well known for his four Idols—preconceptions or *biases* that prevent or hinder the discovery of the real truth. The Idols of the Tribe are the generally agreed-upon ways of thinking; the Idols of the Den are biases created by a person's environment or education; the Idols of the Market Place are misconceptions based on loose use of vocabulary; and the Idols of the Theater are the blind acceptance of older ideas from tradition or authority. Despite his prominent role in establishing respect for the scientific method, Bacon did not think very highly of mathematics (Watson, 1968).

British Empiricism and Continental Nativism

Thomas Hobbes (1588–1679) was the first unqualified reductionist of modern times and is generally considered the first in the line of British empiricists. Recognition of his influence was delayed, however, because he was suspected of being an atheist. He served as a secretary to Bacon for a short period and was undoubtedly influenced by Bacon's ideas. Hobbes thought that memory and imagination are decaying sensations and that all of cognition is based on sensation. He argued that qualities are not properties of the object but of the perceiver: A box is not red; rather, the perceiver has the sensation of the box's being red (Watson, 1968). Sensations lead to simple ideas, and various combinations of simple ideas lead to more complex ideas. The importance of this line of reasoning is that it implies that the mind can be analyzed mechanistically, that the study of the mind can be made scientific. This belief that ideas arise from sensations, and hence from experience, also makes Hobbes an empiricist and thus in opposition to René Descartes (1596–1650).

Descartes has been called the first great psychologist of the modern era, although not the first modern psychologist. The primary reason for the designation "great" is that he attempted, for the first time since Aristotle, to create an entirely new system of thought. The basis of his system was doubt, the first principle of which was the famous *cogito, ergo sum:*

> I resolved that everything that ever entered into my mind was no more true than the illusions of my dreams. But immediately afterwards I noticed that whilst I thus wished to think all things false, it was absolutely essential that the "I" who thought this should be somewhat, and remarking that this truth "I think, therefore I am" was so certain and so assured that all the most extravagant suppositions brought forward by the sceptics were incapable of shaking it, I came to the conclusion that I could receive it without scruple as the first principle of the Philosophy for which I was seeking. (Descartes, quoted in Watson, 1968, p. 152)

The essence of man, for Descartes, was a mind, a "thing which thinks." The mind is contrasted with the body, and this separating of mind and body into two different aspects came to be known as *Cartesian dualism.* The mind and body can interact (Descartes localized the point of interaction as the pineal gland), but the mind can also act independently, as when it considers innate ideas. Whereas Hobbes concluded that the mind can be understood in mechanistic terms, Descartes argued that it cannot; only the body is amenable to such understanding. Whereas Hobbes believed in the accumulation of knowledge through sensations and experience, Descartes held that the most important ideas are innate. Innate ideas comprise the set of universal truths, and they are innate because they arise from consciousness alone and not from objects in the world. External objects may remind us of ideas, but ideas do not come to us from sensation (Watson, 1968).

Bacon's strong stance on using the experimental method for discovering knowledge was the basis for much of the work of John Locke (1632–1704). Locke is often mistakenly called the founder of associationism, but it was not until the fourth edition of his *Essay Concerning Human Understanding* (published in 1700) that he used the phrase "association of ideas" (Diamond, 1974; Watson, 1968). His entire philosophy, therefore, was formed without the need for the associationist ideas, and he mentions neither Hobbes nor Aristotle. Locke's importance comes more deservedly from his empirical approach and his conception of the mind as a tabula rasa (clean slate) or "the yet empty cabinet" (Watson, 1968, p. 184). This idea, present in Aristotle's work, claims that experience rather than innate or inborn factors is of most importance. Locke went even further, suggesting that when something is not currently being contemplated, it no longer exists:

> But our ideas being nothing but actual perceptions in the mind, which cease to be anything when there is no perception of them, this laying up of our ideas in the repository of the memory signifies no more but this, that the mind has a power in many cases to revive perceptions which it has once had. . . . And in this sense it is that our ideas are said to be in our memories, when indeed they are actually nowhere. (quoted in Burnham, 1888, pp. 70–71)

Locke did much to refine introspection and to set bounds on what could and could not be understood about human nature with his empirical method. Also, following Hobbes, he thought of ideas as comprising elements that could be studied and analyzed.

Gottfried Wilhelm Leibniz (1646–1716) not only rejected Locke's empiricism but also disagreed with the notion that ideas had no existence when not being contemplated. He argued that if nothing remained when one ceased to think about a certain idea, it would not be possible to recollect the idea at a later time. Instead, Leibniz argued that traces of ideas remain even when they are not being thought of, although they are unconscious.

The empiricism of Locke prevailed in Britain, however. David Hartley (1705–1757), who also believed that the mind is blank at birth and that sensations give rise to ideas, systematized the views of the British empiricists and associationists. For Hartley, memory is "that faculty by which traces of sensations and ideas recur or are recalled in the same order and proportion, accurately or nearly, as they were once actually presented" (Burnham, 1888, p. 83). He distinguished between "true" memories, or recollections, and illusions of memory, or reveries: "All men are sometimes at a loss to know whether clusters of ideas that strike the fancy strongly, and succeed each other readily and immediately, be recollections or mere reveries. And the more they agitate the matter in the mind, the more does the reverie appear like a recollection" (Burnham, 1888, p. 84).

David Hume's (1711–1776) approach was to combine the experimental approach of Isaac Newton with Bacon's and Locke's study of the human mind, the ultimate goal being an experimental science of the mind. Indeed, the subtitle of Hume's *Treatise of Human Nature* is *An Attempt to Introduce the Experimental Method of Reasoning into Moral Subjects*. Hume noted that "the chief exercise of the memory is not to preserve the simple ideas, but their order and position" (Herrmann & Chaffin, 1988, p. 173). He also rediscovered two of Aristotle's principles of association—similarity and contiguity—but emphasized that his own third principle, cause and effect, was the most important. Hume recognized that associations are not automatic, and he used an analogy with gravitation to suggest the character of an association: "Here is a kind of Attraction, which in the mental world will be found to have as extraordinary effects as in the natural, and to shew itself in as many and as various forms" (Herrnstein & Boring, 1965, p. 348).

Immanuel Kant (1724–1804) distinguished three kinds of memorizing. The mechanical *(mechanisch)* method, which involves only frequent, literal repetition; the method of clever devices *(ingeniös)*, which involves forming associations between items; and the method of reflection *(judiciös)*, the best kind, which involves classification (Burnham, 1888). Kant has also been cited as a forerunner of connectionism (Van de Vijver, 1990). His *Kritik der reinen Vernunft* ("Critique of Pure Reason") attacked the empiricism of Hume; Kant went so far as to say that "it was the warning voice of David Hume that first, years ago, roused me from dogmatic slumbers" (Herrnstein & Boring, 1965, p. 586). In trying to refute empiricism, Kant argued that humans are born with certain innate properties, and this nativistic approach contributed a highly influential philosophical background for psychological schools such as the Gestalt movement in perception. The conflicts between Locke and Descartes are echoed in the opposition between Hume and Kant, and, later, that between Helmholtz and Hering (Herrnstein & Boring, 1965).

James Mill (1773–1836), in his *Analysis of the Phenomena of the Human Mind*, published in 1829, presents a thoroughly associationist view of memory but with several important insights. "In memory there is not only the idea of the thing remembered; there is also the idea of my having seen it. Now these two—1, the idea of the thing, 2, the idea of my having seen it—combined, make up, it will not be doubted, the whole of that state of consciousness which we call memory." The "idea of my having seen it" is also made up of two components, "the idea of my present self, the remembering self, and the idea of my past self, the remembered or witnessing self" (Burnham, 1888, p. 241).

Mill's son, John Stuart Mill (1806–1873), disagreed with his father's view of an infinite compounding of associations. Rather, he introduced the term *mental chemistry* to indicate that in combining simple elements, something new is created. Just as the properties of water are different from the properties of hydrogen and oxygen, the properties of a complex element may be different from those of the root elements. Mill thus anticipated Wundt and the Gestalt psychologists. Because of this view, Mill advocated studying complex ideas empirically rather than relying on observations of simpler elements.

Marie François Pierre Gonthier de Biran (1766–1824) was a French philosopher who took the name Maine de Biran, from an estate named Le Maine that belonged to his father. A member of Louis XVI's royal guards, he was injured defending the king in 1789 at Versailles. On the subject of memory, his important work is *Influence de l'habitude sur la faculté de penser* ("Influence of Habit on the Faculty of Thinking"), first published—without his name attached—in 1802 (Copleston, 1985). Although in his early works Maine de Biran followed such thinkers as Condillac and Bonnet, he later criticized and moved away from the empiricist school and became more of a Platonist (Copleston, 1985). He was careful to distinguish three types of memory systems: mechanical memory, which is concerned with motor tasks and operates largely at a nonconscious level; sensitive (or sensory) memory, which is concerned with feelings, affect, and fleeting sensations; and representative memory, which is concerned with conscious recollection of ideas and events (Schacter & Tulving, 1994).

Through Jean Gaspard Félix Ravaisson-Mollien (1813–1900), Maine de Biran's thought influenced the French philosopher Henri Bergson (1859–1941) (Copleston, 1985). Although best known for his work on topics other than memory—especially his *L'Évolution créatrice* ("Creative Evolution") published in 1907—Bergson gave an extended treatment to the idea of fundamentally different kinds of memory in *Matière et mémoire* ("Matter and Memory"), published in 1896. Like Maine de Biran, Bergson distinguished between two different memory systems. First, there is "a closed system of automatic movements which succeed one another in the same order and occupy the same time" (Copleston, 1985, p. 190). This form is similar to walking—a bodily habit—and is the type of memory that animals have, such as that possessed by a parrot taught to recite a passage of a poem. The second type is "pure memory," which represents and records "all the events of our daily life" (Copleston, 1985, p. 190). Because memory records everything, the function of the brain is to inhibit the majority of memories so that only those relevant or related to ongoing thought or action are recalled to consciousness. Bergson also argued that the brain is not a storehouse of memories but rather functions more as a telephone exchange. The neurological mechanisms permit various movements but do not themselves store memory (Copleston, 1985).

Alexander Bain (1818–1903) marks a transition. He belonged to the outgoing British associationist school early in his career but moved closer to the emerging German scientific psychology toward the end of the century (Zusne, 1975). He is noted for his attempts to connect psychology and physiology and, in particular, for his doctrine that "the renewed feeling occupies the very same parts and in the same manner as the original feeling" (Burnham, 1888, p. 243), a forerunner of the current proceduralist view of memory.

For example, the recollection of language, according to this view, is suppressed articulation. Bain was also the founder of the influential British journal *Mind* in 1876.

Ernst Heinrich Weber (1795–1878) had a medical degree rather than a doctorate in philosophy, but his experiments to determine the smallest detectable difference between two weights set the groundwork for scientific psychology. Although he found that the absolute magnitude of the difference varied depending on the size of the weights, he noted that the difference had a constant relationship to the weight: For an increment in a stimulus to be just noticeably different, the size of the increment had to be a certain proportion of the stimulus. This formulation, known as *Weber's Law*, might have gone unnoticed had it not been for Fechner (Diamond, 1974).

Scientific Psychology

Gustav Theodor Fechner (1801–1887) was the first scientific psychologist. Although he had a medical degree, his first interest was physics. Combining his interests in physics and philosophy, he initiated the field of *psychophysics*. He believed that the mind and body were aspects of the same unity (in contrast to Cartesian dualism). According to Fechner, it was on the morning of October 22, 1850, while still in bed, that he realized how to connect the body and the mind (Watson, 1968). The key, as he wrote ten years later in his *Elemente der Psychophysik* ("Elements of Psychophysics"), published in Leipzig in 1860, was finding the quantitative relation between a mental sensation and the physical stimulus:

> Just as, in order to measure space, we need a physical yardstick which is contained in space, so, in order to measure the psychic, we will need something physical which underlies it. But insofar as we cannot directly observe the psychophysical activity which does directly underlie it, the stimulus which evokes that activity, and with which it waxes and wanes in regular fashion, will be able to serve in place of the yardstick. (Diamond, 1974, p. 685)

Based on Weber's Law, *Fechner's Law* held that sensation (S) is directly proportional to the logarithm of the magnitude of the physical stimulus (P) multiplied by a constant, k:

$$S = k \log P \hspace{4cm} 1.1$$

This formulation of psychophysics directly inspired Hermann Ebbinghaus to apply similar methods to the study of a higher mental process, memory. It is interesting that Ebbinghaus worked outside of the influence of Wundt, the giant of 19th-century psychology. Wilhelm Wundt (1832–1920) offered the first formal academic course in psychology, in 1867 at the University of Heidelberg, and founded the first psychology laboratory, at the University of Leipzig in 1875 or 1879 (depending on the criteria). Watson (1968) suggests that the latter date is notable only for the appearance of the first student to do publishable research.

The scientific study of memory, then, did not begin until the latter part of the 19th century and had as its roots Aristotle's associationism, the philosophical orientation of the British empiricists, and the precision of Fechner's emerging psychophysics.

Hermann Ebbinghaus

Hermann Ebbinghaus (1850–1909), generally identified as the first major scientific researcher of memory, received his doctoral degree in philosophy at Bonn in 1873 after serving in the army during the Franco-Prussian war. Although his dissertation concerned

Hartmann's philosophy of the unconscious, Ebbinghaus also had an interest in history and philology (the study of literature and of relevant disciplines such as linguistics, language, and speech). After completing his dissertation, he spent seven years traveling around Europe and Britain. During this time, he came upon a copy of Fechner's *Elemente der Psychophysik* at a secondhand bookshop in Paris and became acquainted with and influenced by the empiricist tradition in Britain (Boring, 1950).

Ebbinghaus's contribution to the study of memory, published in 1885, was called *Über das Gedächtnis: Untersuchungen zur experimentellen Psychologie* ("Memory: A Contribution to Experimental Psychology"). In it, he combined the techniques that Fechner had applied to the study of sensation with the topic of memory, long an important consideration of the British associationists. Although he is generally noted for being his only subject and for inventing nonsense syllables as his stimuli, these factors are neither problematic nor particularly important. Rather, Ebbinghaus's far more significant and lasting contribution was that he was the first experimental psychologist, outside of psychophysicists, who understood and used the concepts of (1) measurement error, (2) distributions of observations around a mean, and (3) the importance of evaluating differences between two conditions in light of error associated with the respective means (Crowder, 1976). He is also well known for his forgetting function, which will be described later.

As befits the first scientific investigator of memory, Ebbinghaus reported what is perhaps the first true experiment on memory: He outlined two possible theories, derived a testable prediction that could distinguish between the two possibilities, and then conducted the experiment to evaluate the hypothesis. Indeed, the basic idea that came out of this research still has currency and serves as the basis for Johnson's (1991) distinctiveness model of serial learning.

The idea of an association between items had been pervasive in philosophy for hundreds of years. However, there was still uncertainty about whether there existed only direct associations, or whether there were also remote associations (see Figure 1.1).

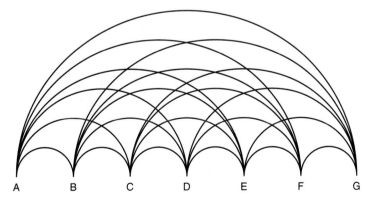

Figure 1.1   An illustration of the possible associations among seven items in a list. According to Ebbinghaus, the first item, A, can be associated with item B through a direct association, and with items C, D, E, F, and G through remote associations. The less direct the association, the weaker the link.

Experiment   *The Forgetting Function*

Purpose: To demonstrate the classic forgetting function using the method of savings

Subjects: Thirty subjects are recommended. Ten should be assigned to the 1-hour group, ten to the 1-day group, and ten to the 1-week group.

Materials: Table A in the Appendix lists 24 nonsense syllables with approximately equal association values. Create a list of 13 nonsense syllables by randomly selecting the syllables from the table. Write each syllable in large, clear form on a notecard. Each subject should get a different random ordering of items.

Design: Because each subject experiences only one condition, delay is a between-subjects factor.

Procedure: Inform the subjects that in this experiment they will be asked to learn a list of nonsense syllables. Show the subject the list of syllables at a rate of approximately 1 syllable every 2 seconds. Then, ask the subjects to repeat the list. Record the subject's responses. Then show the subject the same list again, and ask the subject to repeat the list. Keep doing this until the subject can recall the list in order without making an error. Most subjects will require several trials before they recall the list. Keep track of how many trials are required to learn the list. Have the subjects in the 1-hour group return after 1 hour, the subjects in the 1-day group return after 1 day, and the subjects in the 1-week group return after 1 week. Repeat the procedure, being careful to ensure that each subject receives the exact list in the same order during the second phase. Also, be careful not to tell the subjects what will happen during Phase 2.

Instructions for Phase 1:   "This experiment has two phases. In the first phase, you will be asked to learn a list of nonsense syllables. I will show the items, written on notecards, one at a time. After I have shown you all 13 items, I will ask you to recall the items in order. We will continue until you are able to recall all the items in order. Once you have recalled the items correctly, that will be the end of the first phase."

Instructions for Phase 2:   "For the second phase, I will ask you to relearn the list of items you originally learned 1 hour ago/1 day ago/1 week ago. We will follow the same procedure. I will show the items, written on notecards, one at a time. After I have shown you all 13 items, I will ask you to recall the items in order. We will continue until you are able to recall all of the items in order. Once you have recalled the items correctly, that will be the end of the experiment."

Scoring and Analysis: For each subject, count the number of trials required to learn the list the first time and the number of trials to relearn the list. To calculate percent savings, subtract the number of trials to relearn the list from the number of trials to learn the list originally. Then divide this value by the number of trials to learn the list originally. For example, if it takes a subject 12 trials originally and 8 trials to relearn, the percent savings is 4/12 or 33%. The *x*-axis should show the delay condition, and the *y*-axis should show the number of lists. The graph should look similar to Figure 1.2, even though savings is plotted in terms of time rather than trials.

Optional Enhancements: Include more delay conditions, increase the number of subjects, and measure the time needed to learn and relearn the lists rather than just the number of trials.

Source: Based on an experiment by Ebbinghaus (1885).

Ebbinghaus (1885) conducted a series of experiments designed to demonstrate the existence of both direct and remote associations. He learned lists of 16 syllables until he reached a certain criterion; in this case, he kept learning until he could repeat the list without error. After a delay, he measured his retention of the lists with the *method of savings*. In this method, a previously learned list is relearned and the difference between the time needed to learn the list to criterion the second time and the time it took to learn it originally represents the savings due to remembering.

Ebbinghaus then constructed "derived" lists, in which item 2 of the original list would be displaced one, two, three, or seven positions. For example, if the original list were I1, I2, I3, . . . , I16, then the derived list, skipping one syllable, would be I1, I3, I5, . . . , I2, I4, . . . , I16. If item I1 can serve as a cue, via a remote association, for item I3 in a derived list with one skipped syllable, and if it can serve as a cue, via a more remote association, for item I4 in a derived list with two skipped syllables, then learning one of these derived lists should take less time than learning a control list. If, on the other hand, there are only direct associations between adjacent items, a derived list will have no advantage over a control list because in both cases the direct association has been severed.

Ebbinghaus found a mean savings of 33.3% in relearning the original list, a 10.8% saving when skipping one syllable, 7.0% when skipping two syllables, 5.8% when skipping three syllables, and 3.3% when skipping seven syllables. In a control condition containing the same syllables but in random order, there was a savings of only 0.5%. According to Ebbinghaus, these findings support the idea of remote associations.

Ebbinghaus is probably best known for the *forgetting function*, the first systematic investigation of forgetting. He first measured the amount of time required to learn (two errorless recitations) a list of 13 nonsense syllables. Then, he waited a specific period of time before relearning the same material and measured how long it took to relearn the lists. He reported the results in terms of percent savings. For example, in 12 tests it took Ebbinghaus an average of 1081 seconds to learn a 13-item list of nonsense syllables. After a delay of 19 minutes, it took him an average of 498 seconds to relearn each list, a difference of 583. The formula (Ebbinghaus, 1885, p. 68) is

$$Q = \frac{100\Delta}{L - 85} \qquad\qquad 1.2$$

where Q is the percent savings, L is the time of first learning (including the two errorless recitations), Δ is the difference between L and the second learning (both including the two errorless recitations), and 85 is the time (in seconds) needed to say the two errorless recitations. The reason for subtracting this value is that Ebbinghaus was interested only in the savings of learning. In the example given above, he "saved" 58.5% of the time:

$$Q = \frac{100(1081 - 498)}{1081 - 85} = \frac{58300}{996} = 58.53 \qquad\qquad 1.3$$

Although the exact nature of the forgetting function can vary depending on the type of materials, the type of processing, the type of test, and so on, the basic shape appears relatively constant: The largest drop in performance occurs during the period immediately after the test (see Rubin & Wenzel, 1996). As shown in Figure 1.2, Ebbinghaus would have been at 100% at Time 0; waiting only 19 minutes resulted in a substantial drop in performance. By comparison, there is little overall loss from 2 days to 31 days.

Two points should be emphasized here. First, although Ebbinghaus is (rightly) viewed as the preeminent figure in the early study of memory, some scientific research on memory occurred before his book (see, for example, Burnham, 1888; Murray, 1976; Schacter, Eich, & Tulving, 1978). Second, although the majority of his studies can be faulted for using

Figure 1.2   Retention of lists of nonsense syllables learned by Ebbinghaus as measured by the method of savings.
SOURCE: Based on data from Ebbinghaus (1885).

only himself as a subject or for using nonsense syllables, all of his important findings replicate and have been at the center of much of the research and theory of the ensuing 100 years (Slamecka, 1985).

Research After Ebbinghaus

Memory research is central to the field of study known as *cognitive psychology*, the area of psychology that studies perception, thought, language, and speech. The field did not really exist until the late 1950s.

In the United States, the two major approaches to research until the 1950s were behaviorism and Gestalt psychology. *Behaviorism*, as propounded by John B. Watson (1913), was both a methodological movement that rejected introspection and a theoretical framework that emphasized the conditioned reflex as the foundation of behavior. Watson took the position that unobservable constructs such as memory, imagery, and consciousness could not be studied rigorously and thus were not appropriate topics for scientific study. Although this did not completely preclude the study of memory, it did severely restrict theoretical development. Behaviorism was gradually replaced with neobehaviorism (e.g., Hull, 1943), the major difference being the acceptance of unobservable mediators between the observable stimulus and the observable response.

Gestalt psychology began in Frankfurt in 1911 with a meeting of Max Wertheimer, Kurt Koffka, and Wolfgang Köhler (Ash, 1995). By 1933 all three held academic positions in the United States, at the New School for Social Research, Smith College, and Swarthmore College, respectively (Murray, 1988). Although most of the experimental research focused on perception, some theories were specifically applied to memory, thinking, and problem solving (see Ash, 1995; Murray, 1995). The Gestalt approach emphasizes the idea of studying the whole (*Gestalt* is German for "whole"); it is often said that this approach can be summarized as asserting that the "whole is different from the sum of its parts."

A large body of research, undertaken outside of both the behaviorist and Gestalt traditions, is usually referred to as *verbal learning*. This approach was a largely atheoretical way of studying the acquisition and retention of verbal material and shared many elements with the functional approach. Many studies from this period will be cited in later chapters, and many of the concepts identified—especially interference—play prominent roles in current theories of memory.

The study of memory, and cognitive psychology in general, underwent a major change between 1940 and 1970. One illustration of how radically things changed over this 30-year period concerns two books, both called *Cognitive Psychology*. Thomas Moore's book, published in 1939, had relatively little impact on research; Ulric Neisser's book, published in 1967, was an instant classic and had a tremendous influence (see Surprenant & Neath, 1997). One major reason for the different reactions to these books was the introduction and acceptance of the concept of information, the basic unit of cognitive processing. The idea, quite simply, is that one can think of information flowing through the cognitive system in a way similar to information flowing through a computer system. Although the original conception of information as put forth in information theory (e.g., Attneave, 1959) is no longer widely accepted, the basic idea still forms the foundation for cognitive psychology.

Chapter Summary and Further Reading

This chapter has provided only the briefest of sketches of the centuries of thought given to memory. Scientific psychology did not begin until Fechner began his research on psychophysics in the 1850s, and the scientific study of memory did not begin until Ebbinghaus began his series of studies a few years later. What distinguishes the work of Ebbinghaus from earlier researchers is that he outlined two possible theories, derived a testable prediction that could distinguish between the two possibilities, and then conducted an experiment. Since Ebbinghaus, two major approaches to the study of memory in the United States were behaviorism and Gestalt psychology, although much research was also done in what is now known as the verbal learning approach. Cognitive psychology began in earnest in the 1960s.

The following sources are recommended for a more complete understanding of the history of experimental psychology in general and of memory research in particular. Every student of memory should read Ebbinghaus (1885), and Slamecka (1985) provides an excellent assessment of Ebbinghaus's contribution. Burnham (1888) provides an historical overview of early memory research, and Murray (1976) discusses research on human memory in the 19th century. Diamond (1974), Herrmann and Chaffin (1988), and Herrnstein and Boring (1965) all provide translations of much of the early work on memory. Yates (1966) offers an excellent history and analysis of mnemonic techniques, particularly in the Middle Ages, and Carruthers (1990) examines memory in the medieval period.

The classic history of experimental psychology is by Boring (1950). Watson (1968) also serves as an excellent starting point, offering biographical, philosophical, and psychological summaries of important figures in the history of psychology and supplying translations and short extracts of original sources. Zusne (1975) offers a biographical sourcebook of people who influenced psychology, and Watson (1915) provides some biographical information on Vives, a figure much overlooked by psychologists.

Murray (1995) examines the contribution of Gestalt psychology to the cognitive revolution, and Gardner (1985) provides a history of cognitive psychology.

Sensory Memory

Each sense organ of the body may be said to have its memory; and these memories are in a measure independent of each other.

—William H. Burnham (1888)

Sensory memory is the name given to the memory system that retains purely sensory information (Crowder & Surprenant, 2000). Its study has been guided by two unassailable empirical facts: (1) Something that looks or sounds like the physical stimulus continues to be present for a short amount of time after the stimulus is no longer present, and (2) information can be extracted from a stimulus for a short amount of time after the stimulus is no longer present (Loftus & Irwin, 1998). Adapting terms proposed by Coltheart (1980), the former can be referred to as *stimulus persistence* and the latter as *information persistence*. Early research viewed these two types of persistence as two measures of the same entity, with iconic memory responsible for visual information and echoic memory responsible for auditory information. More recent research, however, has suggested that stimulus persistence and information persistence are different phenomena, with the former better explained by residual neural activity and the latter by the same type of memory used for longer-lasting information.

Iconic Memory

W. S. Jevons published a paper in 1871 describing "the power of numerical discrimination." He would toss a handful of beans into the air so that they fell into a black tray, in the middle of which was a white box. Jevons's task was to estimate, without hesitating,

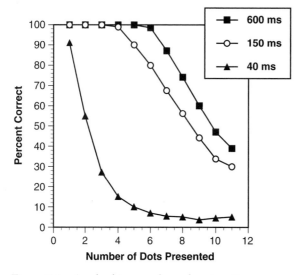

Figure 2.1 Averbach's span of apprehension. Percent correct estimates of the number of dots seen for three different exposure durations.   Source: From "The Span of Apprehension as a Function of Exposure Duration," by E. Averbach, 1963, *Journal of Verbal Learning and Verbal Behavior, 2,* 60–64. Copyright © 1963 Academic Press, Inc. Reprinted with permission.

the number of beans that fell into the white box; he recorded both his estimates and the actual number for more than 1000 trials. He found that for small numbers of beans, he was both accurate and fast in his estimates, but as the number of beans increased, his accuracy decreased. Jevons's *span of apprehension*—the number of beans that he could attend to at one time—was approximately nine: When the number of beans falling into the white box was nine or higher, he was accurate only half the time.

A more carefully controlled study was performed by Averbach (1963) using a tachistoscope, a device that presents visual information for very brief durations. Averbach varied the exposure duration—the time during which an array of black dots was visible. The number of dots that could be accurately reported depended on the exposure duration. There was a large benefit in increasing the exposure time from 40 ms to 150 ms, but very little benefit in increasing the duration from 150 ms to 600 ms (ms stands for milliseconds; there are 1000 ms in 1 second). The results are shown in Figure 2.1. It is interesting to note that Averbach's estimate for the span of apprehension is quite similar to Jevons's: When the number of stimuli is around eight or nine, estimates will be accurate only about half the time.

These two studies, using very simple stimuli (beans and dots), found similar results: For a few stimuli, people can very accurately and very quickly report the correct number; with around four to eight items, performance is a little slower and a little less accurate; and for nine items or more, accuracy quickly falls off. But what happens with more complicated items that have to be interpreted, such as letters?

George Sperling (1960) conducted a series of experiments to investigate this question. Using a 3 × 4 matrix (see Figure 2.2), he presented random arrangements of letters

F	2	T	9
3	Y	7	P
N	5	X	8

Figure 2.2 An example of a
3 × 4 matrix that might be used
in Sperling's (1960) experiment

and digits for 50 ms (1/20 s) and asked his subjects to report all the items they could see; his subjects could not report more than about four items on any one trial. The estimate of the span of apprehension for complex material, then, appeared much lower than for simple material. However, Sperling's subjects claimed that they could "see" more than the four items reported; they just could not report all of them. The subjects reported that the array seemed to fade away as time passed. This appeared consistent with the idea of iconic memory—a "single, visible, precategorical, high-capacity, quickly decaying memory that holds incoming visual stimulation for further processing" (Loftus & Irwin, 1998, p. 136). Although the subjects were introspecting, and, as we have already noted, introspection is not a reliable research method, it can generate testable hypotheses. Sperling devised a way to test this idea objectively.

When you take any kind of test, you are almost never tested for everything that you know. For example, when you take the written portion of a driving test, you may get 20 questions about motor vehicle rules and regulations. If you get 15 out of 20 correct, the agency in charge infers that you know approximately 75% of the material. Rather than examining you on every possible motor vehicle question, the motor vehicle bureau tests only a portion of your knowledge and then estimates what you know about the untested information from the partial sample.

When this approach is used in psychology experiments, it is known as the *partial report technique*. The subject is cued as to which portion of the information to recall, and then the experimenter can estimate the total number of items potentially available. What Sperling did was to cue his subjects which row of the array to recall by playing one of three tones. If a high tone was played, the subject knew to recall just the top row (F2T9 in this example); a medium tone indicated that the middle row should be recalled; and a low tone meant that the bottom row should be recalled. A trial would go as follows: The display would be presented briefly, for perhaps 50 ms. Then, following a brief interval, a tone would be played, signaling which row to recall. Sperling systematically varied the duration of the interval between the offset of the display and the onset of the tone from 0 to 1 s. There was also a condition in which the delay was –0.1 s, which means the tone was actually played 100 ms before the offset of the display. The results are shown in Figure 2.3.

Because there were three possible rows to recall and the subjects did not know until after they had heard the tone which row was the correct one, Sperling reasoned that the subjects had to attend to all of the items in all three rows. Thus, he multiplied the number of items the subjects recalled by 3 to estimate the total amount of information available. For example, if a subject heard the high-pitched tone and recalled three of the four items in the top row correctly, Sperling would estimate a total knowledge of nine items. When the tone was played 100 ms after the offset of the matrix, the estimated number of items available was about 7.2. When the tone was played 1 s after the offset of the matrix,

Figure 2.3   Estimated number of letters available when using the partial report technique (closed circles) as a function of the interval between the presentation of the letters and the presentation of the tone. The open square shows the results when using whole report.   SOURCE: Sperling (1960).

the estimated number of letters available to the subject was equal to the actual number of letters recalled in the whole report procedure. There was an advantage for partial report only if the cue to recall occurred within about 500 ms of the offset of the stimulus. If the tone was delayed further, the number of estimated items available using the partial report technique was the same as the number of items recalled using whole report.

CogLab Experiment
http://coglab.wadsworth.com/experiments/PartialReport/

Sperling (1960, 1967) concluded from these and other results that information is briefly registered in a sensory memory system and is almost totally available if accessed quickly enough. If the information is not soon attended to, however, it is rapidly lost. Although Sperling called this "visual information store," the name proposed by Ulric Neisser (1967) quickly became the dominant term: iconic memory.

The name *iconic memory* refers to the key property of the visual sensory store: Iconic memory was thought to be precategorical, meaning that it preserves information in an unanalyzed form, rather like a picture or an icon of what was seen. The stimuli have not been categorized, and there is not much processing of the image. To extract the information about what each item was, the subject must scan the icon and then translate or recode it into a more durable form. Sperling (1967) calculated that this scanning process took only about 10 ms per item. By comparison, it takes you about 250 to 300 ms to perform successive *saccades*—moving your eyes from one location to another and then focusing on the new location (Haber & Hershenson, 1973). Once the item is scanned, however, rehearsal is necessary or the information will be lost. Rehearsal is usually performed by recoding the information into its verbal name and repeating this name subvocally. Thus, when errors are made, they are likely to be based on acoustic similarity rather than on visual similarity: If the target letter is *B*, a person is more likely to say *V* than *R*.

Sperling's study examined *information persistence*—the ability of subjects to extract the identities of the letters and digits after the display was no longer present. Haber and Standing (1969) reported an experiment that examined stimulus persistence. They presented a visual stimulus (a circle) intermittently and asked subjects to report whether they perceived a continuous stimulus or whether they perceived the stimulus to completely disappear before reappearing. Of interest was the duration during which the stimulus was absent but the subjects perceived it to be present, a direct measure of visual persistence. This value was between 250 and 300 ms. At this stage of development, then, estimates of stimulus persistence and estimates of information persistence were in agreement, and both types of tasks were thought to be measuring the same thing.

One important question about iconic memory is whether it is actually memory. For example, it is conceivable that iconic memory is just an *afterimage*, a perceptual phenomenon resulting from properties of the retina. If someone takes your photograph with a flash, you see an image of the flash persist, although the afterimage is of a black (or dark) blob rather than the intense white of the flash. This persistence has to do with chemical changes of photoreceptors in your eye, rather than with memory. Similarly, if you stare at a bright red image for a minute or two and then look at a neutral wall, you will see an afterimage that has the same shape but is now green. Again, this image may persist for a minute or more. Afterimages are due to processes that occur within the eye, and some researchers have argued that iconic memory is also due to processes that occur in the eye. For example, Sakitt (1976; Sakitt & Long, 1979) has argued that the effects of iconic memory are due to activity of the rod cells in the retina.

The view that iconic memory is simply another form of afterimage makes certain predictions about how color information should be represented. Afterimages are complementary: If you stare at a red stimulus, the afterimage is green; if you stare at a blue stimulus, the afterimage is yellow. If iconic memory is an afterimage, subjects should make systematic errors when asked to report items of a certain color, reporting the green items, for example, when asked to report the red ones. However, this does not occur; subjects can select items from iconic memory based on color (Banks & Barber, 1977). This means that the original color rather than its complement is being retained, and at least some aspects of iconic memory are separate from the processes that give rise to afterimages.

More conclusive evidence comes from a study by Turvey (1973), who used brightness masking and pattern masking to distinguish between retina-based properties and memory-based properties of iconic memory. In *brightness masking*, presentation of a target letter is followed by a brighter flash of light. This bright light masks, or hides, some of the information about the target and makes identification of the target letter more difficult. In *pattern masking*, a pattern rather than a light is presented after the target letter is shown; the patterns that Turvey used looked like Chinese characters. Brightness masking occurs when both the target letter and the brightness mask are presented to the same eye. If the target is presented to the left eye and the brightness mask is presented to the right eye, there is no masking. This suggests that brightness masking works by interfering with processes that occur within the eye, at the level of the retina. In contrast, pattern masking can occur when the target and the pattern masks are presented to different eyes. If the target is shown to the left eye and the pattern mask is shown to the right eye, masking can still occur. This suggests that pattern masking occurs at some point where information from both eyes has been combined. This aspect of pattern masking implies that some of iconic memory is controlled by more central processes, such as those that may truly be memory, and not by more peripheral processes, such as those having to do with sensation.

Problems with Iconic Memory

Although it is readily apparent that some aspects of iconic memory really are memory (as opposed to retinal) phenomena, there are four serious problems with Sperling's original interpretation (see Haber, 1983). First, according to the original view, iconic memory is supposed to be precategorical; that is, it preserves an unanalyzed representation of the original physical stimulus. If this is the case, then there should be no partial report advantage when subjects are cued to recall the items by category. In the original version of the experiment, subjects were cued by a tone that indicated physical location, which requires no categorization or deep analysis of the stimuli. Merikle (1980), however, cued subjects by categories. In his experiment, subjects were asked to recall just digits, just letters, or both. One can think of this as two different partial report tests with a whole-report control condition. Merikle not only found a partial report advantage when subjects were cued by category; he also found that the advantage was similar in magnitude to that of cueing by physical location. This implies that iconic memory is not precategorical, because people could select information to be recalled on the basis of a category label, which requires knowledge about what the item is.

A second problem concerns the idea of *output interference:* The act of recalling one item can interfere with recall of the next item. Because of output interference, the more items you are required to remember, the less likely it is that you will recall the last one successfully. One important difference between partial report and whole report is that partial report reduces the amount of output interference. Sperling's original interpretation was that the icon decayed before all the information could be read off. A different interpretation might be that output interference is at least partially responsible for some of the difference. Some evidence consistent with this interpretation comes from an analysis that compared the number of times the first item in partial report was recalled correctly compared with the number of times the first item in whole report was recalled correctly. Dick (1971) found no difference between partial report and whole report for the first item, which suggests that output interference may play a large role in the advantage of partial report over whole report.

A third important concern involves the type of errors that the subjects make. It has already been noted that some of the errors are auditory confusion errors: reporting a letter that sounds like the actual target letter. In addition, different types of information seem to be available at different times, whereas if the icon is fading, all information should be lost at the same rate. Mewhort and Leppman (1985) conducted an experiment in which a row of letters was displayed for 50 ms and the subject's task was to decide if a target letter had appeared in the display. The experimenters varied the delay between the offset of the row of letters and the presentation of the probe. Subjects were equally as accurate when the delay was short as when it was long. Unlike Sperling's original study, there was no decrease in accuracy as the delay increased. Mewhort and Leppman ran a second version of the experiment in which the target was always in the display and the subject's task was to indicate the location of probe item. This time, accuracy did decrease as the delay increased, just as in Sperling's original study. Subjects appear to be forgetting location information—where an item was—rather than item information—what items were present (see also Mewhort, Campbell, Marchetti, & Campbell, 1981).

The fourth major problem involves findings that suggest stimulus persistence is different from information persistence. According to the original view of iconic memory, these should be related, not different. An experiment by Yeomans and Irwin (1985) used a procedure almost identical to that of Sperling (1960) but varied the duration of the matrix so that it was shown for either 50, 200, or 500 ms. The cue was presented after delays between 0 and 500 ms. Yoemans and Irwin found that whereas cue delay had a large effect (just like Sperling found), stimulus duration had no effect. In other words, the subjects did just as well whether the target matrix was shown for 50 ms or 500 ms. This finding that stimulus duration does not affect information persistence is problematic for the traditional view of iconic memory because stimulus duration does affect stimulus persistence (e.g., Bowen, Pola, & Matin, 1974; Di Lollo, 1980).

Loftus and Irwin (1998) directly compared performance in tasks used to measure stimulus persistence, such as a temporal integration task or subjective completeness task, and performance in tasks used to measure information persistence, such as the partial report task. The temporal integration task involves presenting a stimulus that is broken into two spatial halves. Each half is shown in succession, first one half and then the other half, and the subject is asked a question that determines whether both halves can be integrated to produce a coherent whole. The completeness rating task is similar, except that the subject is asked to provide a rating of how complete the two halves seem.

In a series of five experiments, Loftus and Irwin (1998) compared performance in temporal integration and subjective completeness tasks, and compared performance in subjective completeness tasks and a partial report task. The tasks were designed so that they would differ only in the specific question asked of the subject while all other relevant variables were held constant. Furthermore, each task involved an objective and a subjective measure. The basic idea was to present two stimuli that were separated by a variable amount of time. The objective task involved integrating the two stimuli and reporting a specific piece of information (e.g., a location or a letter). The subjective task involved rating whether the two stimuli appeared as one or as two distinct temporal events. The basic task involved a 5 × 5 matrix in which 24 dots were randomly placed; thus, one location was empty. For the objective temporal integration task, the subjects were shown two temporally distinct 12-dot halves and were asked to report the missing dot's position. In the rating task, the subject was asked to rate whether the complete combination appeared as one or two distinct events. In the partial report task, an array of letters was presented followed by a visual probe that signaled which letter was to be reported (an objective measure). The subjective measure was a rating of whether the letter array and probe appeared as one or two distinct temporal events.

In the first two experiments, the two measures of stimulus persistence—temporal integration and subjective completeness—correlated highly though not perfectly (the rank-order correlations for Experiments 1 and 2 were, respectively, $\rho = 0.977$ and 0.979). However, in Experiments 3–7, the measure of stimulus persistence, subjective completeness, did not correlate well with a measure of information persistence, partial report. Loftus and Irwin (1998, p. 189) concluded that "temporal integration and completeness rating [tasks] measure much the same thing, while partial report is the odd measure out. The traditional view of the icon . . . which assumed that all these various persistence tasks measure the same thing, is clearly incorrect."

Rather than positing a sensory memory system devoted to visual information, an emerging consensus attributes stimulus persistence to ongoing neural activity and information persistence to memory proper (Nairne, 2003). Most likely, stimulus persistence is not part of memory, as most people would define memory. Rather, it is probably the result of a particular continuing pattern of neural activity set up by the original stimulus (Di Lollo, Hogben, & Dixon, 1994). One key finding that is consistent with this view is the *inverse duration effect:* As the duration of the target stimulus increases, subjects experience less persistence (Bowen et al., 1974; Di Lollo, 1980). One explanation is that when a stimulus is presented, it begins a particular pattern of neural activity that lasts for a few hundred milliseconds. If the stimulus is removed very quickly, the neural activity continues, giving rise to stimulus persistence. If the stimulus remains for a long time, then less of the neural activity can be measured as "persistence," and little or no persistence effect is seen. Francis (1999) presents a model of how such persistence effects could be generated. The inverse duration effect also suggests that loss of information, at least for stimulus persistence effects, is not due to decay: It is hard to conceive of a form of forgetting in which the longer you are exposed to a stimulus, the faster you forget.

Information persistence effects, on the other hand, do appear to be due to memory. However, these effects are best seen not as sensory memory but rather as the same type of memory as short-term/working memory (Nairne, 2003). We examine this type of memory in subsequent chapters.

Summary of Iconic Memory

Current conceptions of iconic memory, then, have refined Sperling's original formulation. The persistence of information in iconic memory has been separated into two distinct phenomena, stimulus persistence and information persistence. The former lasts for much less time than originally thought, perhaps as little as one-fifth of the original estimate, and the latter is more properly conceived of as the same form of memory responsible for maintaining other types of information over the short term. It should not be surprising that the description of iconic memory has changed over time, nor does this reflect poorly on the original research. Rather, as we gain more information, theories need to be revised and made more precise. As we shall see, the situation is similar for echoic memory.

Echoic Memory

Echoic memory, also named by Neisser (1967), is the auditory equivalent of iconic memory. It gets its name from the idea that auditory information may persist in the form of an "echo" that can be attended to after the original stimulus is no longer present. Usually, this is most noticeable when someone says your name and you do not immediately hear it; after a brief interval, you realize that your name was said and you still seem to hear your name being spoken. Incidentally, it turns out that most people are quite poor at this. Wood and Cowan (1995; see also Conway, Cowan, & Bunting, 2001) found that people detected their name in an unattended conversation only about 30% of the time. The reason that it seems you always detect your name is because you are aware only of your successes; you do not notice your failures!

Figure 2.4   Estimated number of digits available when using the partial report technique as a function of the interval between hearing the digits and presentation of the visual signal.   SOURCE: From "An Auditory Analogue of the Sperling Partial-Report Procedure," by C. J. Darwin, M. T. Turvey, and R. G. Crowder, 1972, *Cognitive Psychology, 3,* 255–267. Copyright © 1972 Academic Press, Inc. Reprinted with permission.

Echoic memory has been studied in a variety of different ways, including an analog of Sperling's (1960) original technique. Darwin, Turvey, and Crowder (1972) presented subjects with three lists of three digits. Each list took 1 s to present. One list was played over both the left and right channels of the speakers, so to the subject it sounded as if the digits were coming from directly in front. A second list was played simultaneously but only on the left channel. The third list was also played simultaneously but only on the right channel. In the partial report conditions, a visual signal would be projected after the lists had been presented to indicate which list should be recalled. For example, if the light appeared to the left, the subject should report the list that was heard coming from the left. The researchers varied the interval between the offset of the list and the onset of the signal from 0 to 4 s. In the whole report procedure, subjects were asked to recall all of the items. The results are reproduced in Figure 2.4.

There was a partial report advantage, indicating that subjects recalled more items on average when they had to recall only one list rather than all three. Although this advantage lasted far longer, it was nowhere near as large as with the visual modality. Massaro (1976) conducted a similar experiment and found no partial report advantage. Because of the minimal effects observed, and because of certain methodological problems with this type of study (see Massaro & Loftus, 1996), many researchers began investigating echoic memory using different procedures.

One type of research investigated stimulus persistence effects for auditory information, usually tones. For example, Efron (1970a, 1970b) presented subjects with a series of brief tones that lasted from 30 to 100 ms and asked the subjects to adjust a light such that it came on exactly when the tone ended. Efron found that regardless of the actual duration of the tone, its subjective duration was about 130 ms. Based on this and many other

Figure 2.5 The modality effect in serial recall: proportion of items recalled correctly as a function of serial position when presentation modality is either reading silently (visual) or reading aloud (auditory).   SOURCE: From "Input Modality and the Serial Position Curve in Short-Term Memory," by R. Conrad and A. J. Hull, 1968, *Psychonomic Science, 10*, 135–136. Copyright © 1968. Reprinted by permission of Psychonomic Society Inc.

studies (see Cowan, 1995; Massaro & Loftus, 1996), echoic memory was divided into two distinct phenomena, roughly corresponding to stimulus persistence and information persistence. The former, which retains information for up to approximately 100–300 ms, can be thought of as ongoing neural processing.

Information persistence effects were examined using a different procedure and focused on the modality effect and the stimulus suffix (or simply suffix) effect (see Penney, 1989). These effects, although originally attributed to echoic memory, are now often seen as reflecting general memory principles rather than a separate memory system. Indeed, just as there are differences between stimulus and information persistence with visual items, there are also differences between stimulus and information persistence with auditory items (Kallman & Massaro, 1983). For the remainder of this chapter, we focus on information persistence of auditory items.

Both the modality and the suffix effects are observed when subjects are presented with a series of items, typically a random ordering of the digits 1–9, and are asked to recall them in order. This recall procedure is known as immediate serial recall, and the results are generally reported in terms of the proportion of items recalled correctly as a function of their input position. Conrad and Hull (1968) presented all the items visually but required the subject to read the items aloud in one condition and silently in the other. The results are shown in Figure 2.5. Auditory and visual presentation give rise to almost the same result with one important exception: There is a large advantage for the last one or two items in the list with auditory presentation compared to visual presentation (Corballis, 1966; Murray, 1966; Washburn, 1916, p. 74). There is usually little or no difference between reading items aloud and hearing them read (Crowder, 1970).

Theories of Echoic Memory: PAS

The modality effect has most often been accounted for by a system called *precategorical acoustic store,* or *PAS* (Crowder & Morton, 1969), which is best seen as a specific theory of echoic memory. This view assumes that auditory to-be-remembered items are stored in a relatively uncategorized code for brief periods of time, around 2 s or so, in a modality-specific sensory memory system. The store is said to be precategorical because it contains unanalyzed information, and it is acoustic because it retains only acoustic information—or, more accurately, a representation of the acoustic information. Newly entering items interfere with already present items, but only if the new items are acoustically similar to the previous items. Forgetting in PAS is thus due to a specific form of *retroactive interference:* New items interfere with items that occurred earlier. Echoic memory, according to this view, provides a source of supplementary information that can be used to identify or recall an auditory item. The modality effect arises because auditory presentation of verbal material permits information about the one or two final items to remain in PAS, from which they can be recalled. Because visual presentation, by definition, contains no acoustic information, no supplementary information is available.

PAS makes several specific predictions about the modality effect. The *modality effect* refers to the enhanced recall of the final item when the presentation modality is auditory rather than visual. This enhanced recall is known as the *recency effect,* because the most recently presented items are remembered well. PAS predicts that when serial recall is the measure, no recency effect will be observable with visual presentation. It is difficult to establish that something is not observable, because there could be many reasons for not finding a particular phenomenon. In this particular case, however, it is clear that this prediction has been confirmed: No recency effects are observed with visual presentation that are in any way comparable to those observed with auditory presentation (LeCompte, 1992).

A second prediction concerns the usefulness of the supplementary information in PAS. According to the theory, a recency effect will be observable to the extent that the acoustic information in PAS is useful for identifying the list items. There are several ways of varying the usefulness of the information. For example, if a list of homophones (such as *by, bye,* and *buy* or *pore, pour,* and *poor*) are presented, the acoustic information will be identical even though the items are different. (In studies like these, it is important to make sure that all subjects pronounce the homophones in a similar way; in some dialects of English, for example, the word *poor* can have 1 syllable or 2 syllables. If these words do not sound the same to you, think of an experiment in which the stimuli are *rite, right,* and *write.*) Crowder (1978a) verified that serial recall of homophones does not give rise to a recency effect.

Another example of varying the usefulness of the acoustic information involves differences between vowels and consonants. Vowels are typically defined by relatively long sections of steady-state information. Consonants, on the other hand—particularly the stop consonants /b/, /d/, /g/, /k/, /p/, and /t/—are distinguished primarily by very rapid bursts of dynamically changing information. Because PAS holds items with more steady-state information for longer periods than items with more transient information (Crowder, 1975), there will be more information concerning item identity in PAS when the stimuli are vowels than when they are consonants. Thus, according to this view, vowels should result in a larger recency effect than consonants because the acoustic information describing a given vowel will last longer in PAS than will the corresponding information that describes a consonant. In addition, vowels that last longer should be recalled better and should produce larger recency effects than vowels that do not last as long. Again, these predictions have been confirmed (Crowder, 1973a, 1973b; Surprenant & Neath, 1996).

Not only did PAS offer a simple, elegant explanation of the modality effect, but it also accounted for the suffix effect within the same framework. The *suffix effect* is related to the modality effect, but it applies only when the presentation modality of the to-be-remembered items is auditory. In the suffix condition, an extra item follows the last to-be-remembered item. This item is typically the word *Ready* or the digit 0; it is the same on every trial, and the subject is aware that this item need not be recalled. Even though the subject is told to ignore the suffix or to treat it merely as a sign to begin recall, the suffix dramatically reduces recall of the final items (Crowder, 1967; Dallett, 1965). As Figure 2.6 shows, when the suffix is simply a tone or a buzzer, the data look similar to those for serial recall of standard auditory lists. When the suffix is speech, however, the shape of the serial position function resembles that for visually presented items: The recency effect is greatly attenuated (Crowder, 1972).

Repeated practice with the foreknowledge that the suffix will occur and will be the same item on each trial does not reduce the effect (Balota & Engle, 1981), and although continual presentation of the suffix token throughout the entire experimental session can weaken its potency (Watkins & Sechler, 1989), a reliable suffix effect still obtains. In general, a visual suffix will have little or no effect on an auditorily presented list of items (Morton & Holloway, 1970). Although the effect of the suffix diminishes over time, with a delay of 2 s sufficient to remove most of the effect, this reduction cannot be attributed simply to delaying recall (Crowder, 1971) or to rhythmicity (Crowder, 1973c).

As Figure 2.6 shows, the suffix has a larger effect on the terminal item than on earlier list items, which has led some researchers to propose two suffix effects—one that affects only the final item and another, the so-called preterminal suffix effect, that affects the other items (see Penney, 1989; Greene, 1992). Bloom and Watkins (1999) reported a series of eight experiments in which they examined whether there are two such suffix effects. Their strategy was to carefully test all variables that were thought to affect each suffix effect differently, such as predictability of list length, rate of presentation, and practice with the task. In all eight experiments, they found no evidence of two separate effects; that is, they found no qualitative differences between preterminal and terminal suffix effects.

CogLab Experiment
http://coglab.wadsworth.com/experiments/SuffixEffect/

According to PAS, the suffix is interfering with information in echoic memory. The principles of interference during the early phases of PAS were very simple: A suffix would interfere to the extent that it was acoustically similar to the list items. For this reason, manipulations that alter acoustic factors will also affect the potency of the suffix, but manipulations that alter semantic or higher-level characteristics will not.

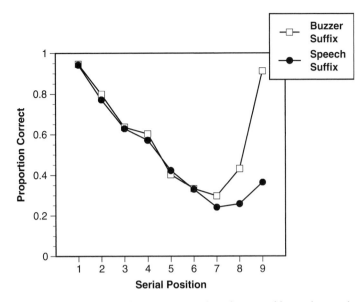

Figure 2.6 Serial recall of a nine-item list when an additional item, the suffix, is either the word *zero* or the sound made by a buzzer. SOURCE: From "Visual and Auditory Memory" by R. G. Crowder. In J. F. Kavanaugh and I. G. Mattingly (Eds.), *Language by Ear and by Eye: The Relation Betweeen Speech and Learning to Read.* Copyright © 1972 Massachusetts Institute of Technology Press. Reprinted with permission.

Morton, Crowder, and Prussin (1971) conducted the first extensive series of experiments on the suffix effect, and the main findings from their 17 experiments were consistent with the PAS interpretation. The magnitude of the suffix effect was not affected by (1) the meaning or predictability of the suffix; (2) whether the suffix was *uh* or *zero*; (3) the semantic relatedness of the suffix to list items; or (4) word frequency or emotionality of the suffix. The size of the suffix effect was reduced (1) when the acoustic properties of the suffix (such as its apparent spatial location, timbre, and pitch) were altered relative to the list items; (2) when the sex of the speaker changed from list items to suffix; and (3) when the speakers of the list items and suffix differed, even though they were of the same sex.

PAS offered a simple and elegant account of the effects described above, but evidence soon accumulated that this view had problems. In particular, three lines of evidence falsify the PAS account of suffix and modality effects. The first questions the precategorical nature of echoic memory by demonstrating that a stimulus's potency to function as a suffix depends on the context in which it is perceived (Ayres, Jonides, Reitman, Egan, & Howard, 1979; Neath, Surprenant, & Crowder, 1993). The second questions whether the store is sensitive only to acoustic information by demonstrating modality and suffix effects with clearly nonacoustic stimuli (e.g., Campbell & Dodd, 1980; Greene & Crowder, 1984; Nairne & Crowder, 1982; Nairne & Walters, 1983; Shand & Klima, 1981; Spoehr & Corin, 1978). The third involves demonstrations of modality and suffix effects when information in PAS should not be available (Conway & Gathercole, 1987; Gardiner & Gregg, 1979).

Ayres et al. (1979) challenged the precategorical interpretation of PAS by reporting an experiment in which the same, acoustically identical suffix reduced recall of the final

Experiment   *The Stimulus Suffix Effect*

Purpose: To demonstrate the effect of a redundant item (the suffix) on immediate serial recall.

Subjects: Twenty-four subjects are recommended. Twelve should be assigned to the suffix condition, and 12 to the control condition. Subject 1 should be in the suffix condition, Subject 2 in the control condition, Subject 3 in the suffix condition, and so on.

Materials: Table B in the Appendix contains lists of the digits 1–9 in random order. For each subject, select 11 lists and write them down so that the experimenter can easily read them aloud and can easily keep track of the current list. For suffix subjects, add the digit 0 at the end of each list. Also prepare answer sheets. The answer sheet should have 11 rows of boxes or blanks in which the subject will write down the responses.

Design: Because the subjects experience only one condition, the effect of the suffix is a between-subjects manipulation.

Procedure: The first list for each group is a practice list so that the subjects can familiarize themselves with the type of material, the speed of presentation, and the method of recall. The remaining 10 lists are the main trials from which data will be collected. Each list should be read aloud by the experimenter at a rate of two items per second. Try to place equal emphasis on each digit. Subjects should have approximately 20 seconds to write the digits on their answer sheet before the next trial begins.

Instructions for the Control Group: "This experiment tests your ability to recall a list of numbers in order. I will read a list of nine numbers, in random order, at a fairly quick pace. As soon as the list is over, I would like you to write down the digits in exactly the same order as you heard them. You should write down the first number in the first blank on your answer sheet, the second number in the second blank, and so on. Once you have written a number, you cannot alter it and you cannot go back and change earlier items. To be counted as correct, the digit must be in its original position. You may find that you cannot recall all of the items. If you are unsure, feel free to guess; it is better to guess than to omit an answer. The first list is a practice list." (If there are no questions following the practice list, proceed with the experimental lists. Make sure the subject is following the serial recall instructions.)

Instructions for the Suffix Group: "This experiment tests your ability to recall a list of numbers in order. I will read a list of nine numbers, in random order, at a fairly quick pace. As soon as the list is over, I would like you to write down the digits in exactly the same order as you heard them. You will know when the list is over, because you will hear the number 0. You do not have to recall this item, and you should not write it down; the number 0 will serve only as a cue to begin recalling the items. You should write down the first number in the first blank on your answer sheet, the second number in the second blank, and so on. Once you have written a number, you cannot alter it, and you cannot go back and change earlier items. To be counted as correct, the digit must be in its original position. You may find that you cannot recall all of the items. If you are unsure, feel free to guess; it is better to guess than to omit an answer. The first list is a practice list." (If there are no questions following the practice list, proceed with the experimental lists. Make sure the subject is following the serial recall instructions.)

Scoring and Analysis: The practice list is not scored. For the remaining lists, count the number of times the first number was written correctly in the first slot. This number will range from 0 to 10. Do the same for each serial position, counting the item correct only if it is the correct position. Construct two serial position functions, one for the suffix subjects and one for the control subjects. To do this, add up the individual subject data and divide by the number of subjects. To determine if the difference at the last serial position is statistically reliable, you can perform a t test for independent groups.

(continued on next page)

Experiment   *The Stimulus Suffix Effect (continued)*

Optional Enhancements: Present 21 lists to each group of subjects rather than 11. This will provide more observations, and the data will show less random error. Record the stimuli onto cassette tape and add a tone (a computer beep, a note from a piano, etc.) at the end of each list in the control condition. This will equate the time from the presentation of the ninth item until the beginning of recall in both conditions.

SOURCE: Based on an experiment by Crowder (1972).

item only when it was interpreted as human speech; when interpreted as a musical sound, this suffix did not affect recall. In a between-subjects design, three different groups received 30 seven-item lists of one-syllable words. The groups differed in which suffix was presented: either no suffix, a music suffix, or a speech suffix. The no-suffix group began serial recall of the words immediately after the seventh item, the music group heard what were labeled musical tones after the seventh item, and the speech group heard speech sounds as the suffix. The manipulation of interest was an ambiguous suffix *wa* that was presented to both suffix groups. Described as a "plunger-muted trumpet note sounding like a nasally spoken syllable" (p. 316), this suffix was referred to either as music or as speech, depending on the condition. Subjects in the speech condition were told that it was the syllable *wa*, and those in the music condition were told that it was a trumpet tone. The interesting result was that the effectiveness of the suffix depended on how the subjects were led to interpret it.

As in the Ayres et al. (1979) made a nonspeech sound act as a speech sound, Neath, Surprenant, and Crowder (1993) did the opposite, making a speech sound act as a nonspeech sound. Two real animal noises, from a cow and a dog, were obtained from a sound effects collection. In addition, recordings of a male speaker saying "woof," "moo," and the digits 1 through 9 were digitized onto a computer. Finally, the same male speaker produced a sound, nominally "baa," that resembled the sound a sheep makes. Two groups of subjects were tested: The animal group was told that "after the ninth digit, an animal noise will indicate that the list is over and that you should get ready to recall the digits, in order"; the human group was told that "after the ninth digit, the same voice will pronounce a conventional animal sound to indicate that the list is over and that you should get ready to recall the digits, in order." Because the sheep suffix was the same physical item, according to PAS, it should have the same effect in the two groups. The results are displayed in Figure 2.7.

As in the Ayres et al. (1979) study, there was a robust *context-dependent suffix effect*. The sheep suffix reduced recall only when subjects interpreted it as human speech and not when they interpreted it as an animal sound. In Experiment 2, similar effects were demonstrated in a within-subjects design (Neath, Surprenant, & Crowder, 1993). Although PAS has seen several revisions (e.g., Crowder, 1978b; Greene & Crowder, 1984), no version can account for the context-dependent suffix effect, where the subject's interpretation of the suffix critically affects the potency of the suffix.

PAS also faces problems from the many studies that demonstrate modality and suffix effects with clearly nonacoustic stimuli. Spoehr and Corin (1978) reported a suffix experiment in which the experimenter read the to-be-remembered items aloud to the subject.

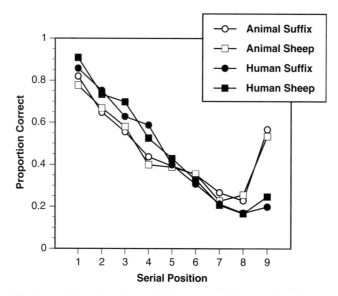

Figure 2.7   Serial recall of a nine-item list when an additional item, the suffix, is either a real animal sound (animal suffix), a real English word (human suffix), or the same speech sound described as an animal sound (animal sheep) or as an English word (human sheep).   Source: Neath, Surprenant, & Crowder (1993).

On certain trials, however, the experimenter mouthed a suffix and the subject was able to lip-read (or speech-read, to use the correct term) the item. According to PAS, this lip-read suffix should have no effect on memory, because interference in PAS occurs on the basis of acoustic similarity. Spoehr and Corin reported substantial suffix effects: A lip-read *zero* served as an effective suffix on a list of items presented aloud. Campbell and Dodd (1980) demonstrated that when subjects lip-read an entire list, a modality effect obtains; that is, lip-reading a list leads to the same excellent memory for the last item as does hearing a list. Using a single experimental setting, Nairne and Walters (1983) reported both modality and suffix effects with mouthed stimuli. In this procedure, subjects make all the gestures necessary for saying an item out loud but they make no sound. A silently mouthed suffix can also affect recall of items presented aloud (Nairne & Crowder, 1982).

   Many variations on this basic paradigm have been reported. It is important to remember that a modality effect, in this larger sense, refers to a recall advantage for the final item presented in a particular modality compared to the last item presented visually. Lip-reading and silent mouthing both produce such modality effects. In addition, Nairne and McNabb (1985) demonstrated a tactile modality effect and Watkins and Watkins (1974) demonstrated a tactile suffix effect. The basic procedure was to use a paper clip to tap subjects' fingers in a particular order. Subjects were asked to recall the order in which different parts of their hand had been touched. To impose a suffix, the experimenter would tap the subjects' knuckles (lightly) with a pen. Other modalities show similar results. For example, for deaf subjects, there is evidence of modality and suffix effects when items are presented using American Sign Language (ASL) (Shand & Klima, 1981).

Finally, PAS faces problems from demonstrations of modality and suffix effects when there should be no information available in PAS. For example, Conway and Gathercole (1987) first presented subjects with a 30-item list of words, and then presented a list of 60 words in random order, 30 from the original list and 30 distractor items. The subjects' task was to say whether each item had been in the original list. Words from the last part of an auditory list were better recognized than were words from the last part of a visual list. This is a problem for PAS because, on average, the delay between the end of the list and the testing of the last few items would be far longer than the presumed duration of PAS. Similarly, Gardiner and Gregg (1979) found a modality effect for items that had been followed by auditory distractor activity. According to PAS, the auditory distractor items should have eliminated the information in PAS about the end-of-the-list items, and so there should not have been an auditory advantage.

Similar problems arise with the PAS explanation of suffix effects. *Articulatory suppression* refers to a task in which the subject is required to say an irrelevant item out loud and continuously during list presentation. According to PAS, this irrelevant auditory information should prevent a suffix effect because the articulatory suppression should remove any contribution from PAS. However, Surprenant, LeCompte, and Neath (2000) found reliable suffix effects even when subjects were engaged in articulatory suppression.

Although it might be tempting to posit tactile and sign-language sensory memory systems and different explanations when modality and suffix effects are observed after shorter versus longer intervals, it might be more profitable to search for a single explanation for all of these phenomena. Three accounts other than PAS have been offered as explanations for modality and suffix effects.

Other Theories of Echoic Memory

The Changing-State Hypothesis   One difference between a visual and an auditory item is that a visual item can be apprehended all at once whereas an auditory item requires some sequential processing. Campbell and Dodd (1980; see also Campbell & Dodd, 1987) suggest that this difference between relatively static and relatively dynamic stimuli could serve as the basis for modality and suffix effects. Both lip-read and silently mouthed stimuli change over time, just as auditory items do, and ASL is also a dynamic mode of presentation. There are at least two problems with this view, however. First, it cannot address the modality and suffix effects observed with tactile stimuli because tactile items more closely resemble simultaneous than sequential information. Second, tests of the changing-state hypothesis have generally not been supportive. For example, Crowder (1986) presented numbers on a computer screen in such a way that, for a given number, parts of the numeral would appear sequentially. It would take approximately the same time to draw the number 7 as to say the word *seven*. There was no advantage for these items relative to visual items presented in a more traditional way.

The Primary Linguistic Code Hypothesis   Shand and Klima (1981) proposed an alternative account that disagreed about the key aspect of PAS. They claimed that speech is a primary linguistic code—that is, a preferred form of representing information in primary memory. When list items are presented in a secondary code, such as visual, the items have to be recoded to a format that is the basic code of the person. For native signers of ASL, the basic code will not be speech, but sign language. This is why ASL can give rise to modality and suffix effects. Lip-reading and silent mouthing are basically speech, but without the acoustic component.

There are problems associated with this view as well. Once again, it does not explain tactile modality and suffix effects. Second, it too has not fared well experimentally. For example, Manning, Koehler, and Hampton (1990) presented subjects with several different kinds of stimuli and forced the subjects to recode between formats. According to the primary linguistic hypothesis, recoding should interfere with modality and suffix effects, particularly when the items to be recoded are not in the primary linguistic code to begin with. Modality and suffix effects obtained, however, even though they were not primary and even though recoding was occurring.

The Multicomponent View   Cowan, Saults, Elliott, and Moreno (2002) suggested that explanations of echoic memory phenomena might be premature in that the majority of experiments have used only immediate serial recall as the test. Because the item in serial position 9 is always the last one to be recalled, it is subject to maximal output interference. On the other hand, by the time the final item is to be recalled, there is usually only one possible response to make, so the last item has the benefit of minimal response size.

To deconfound these factors, Cowan and associates used two main types of test. In their experiment, they presented the digits 1–9 in random order; the stimuli were either auditory or visual. The test was either partial recall, in which subjects were asked to recall three of the digits in serial order (the digits in positions 1–3, 4–6, or 7–9), or whole recall, in which they were asked to recall all 9 digits in order, starting with the item in position 1, position 4, or position 7. In whole recall, subjects who started recalling at position 4 or position 7 were to continue past the item in position 9 to the item in position 1 until all items were recalled. The researchers were able to examine the effect of (for example) input position while equating for output interference and response set size (see Figure 2.8).

This experiment had three important results. First, input serial position, examined when other factors were controlled, had a relatively small effect on performance and yielded small primacy and larger recency effects for both auditory and visual items. Further analysis suggested that the primacy effect usually observed in immediate serial recall is due mostly to output interference, not other factors. Second, the basic modality effect occurs because auditory items are more resistant to output interference. Confirming evidence comes from studies that varied both presentation modality and recall direction. With backward recall, the modality effect for items in the last few positions is eliminated (Madigan, 1971). Because the final visual item is the first item output, it has no interference, resulting in levels of recall equivalent to the auditory items. Third, response set size had essentially no effect.

Summary of Echoic Memory

As with iconic memory, then, no view that posits a specialized sensory memory system appears capable of explaining all the relevant data. However, there does appear to be good evidence for a separate sensory memory system for very brief intervals for both modalities (Cowan, 1995; Massaro & Loftus, 1996). For the data from longer intervals—more than 250 ms or so—some theories can explain these data, but these theories do not make recourse to sensory memory. The most successful of these theories, Nairne's (1988, 1990) feature model, attempts to explain not only modality and suffix effects but also the serial position function as a whole and many other effects associated with immediate memory. This view is presented in detail in Chapter 4.

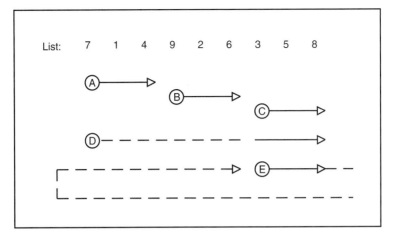

Figure 2.8 Example of how to deconfound serial recall, according to Cowan et al. (2002). The effect of input position can be observed by comparing recall of A (recall the first three items in order), B (recall the middle three items in order), and C (recall the last three items in order) because in each case the number of items output and the response set sizes are equal. The effect of output serial position can be observed by comparing recall of C to recall of D (recall all items in order). The effect of response set size can be observed by comparing recall of C to recall of E (recall all the items in order, beginning at input position 7).

One final aspect of the suffix effect is worth mentioning. Studies that explore suffix effects might seem an excellent example of research that lacks ecological validity. However, Schilling and Weaver (1983) simulated an interaction between a directory assistance operator and a telephone customer to examine the effect of a telephone company policy that directed operators to say "Have a nice day" at the end of each transaction. As expected, when the telephone numbers were followed by the phrase "Have a nice day," there were reliable reductions in the subjects' ability to recall the telephone number accurately.

Odor Memory

Studies of odor memory have lagged far behind studies of visual and auditory memory. As a result, the little that is known has not been integrated within a coherent framework. As Schab and Crowder (1995) emphasize, "too few data exist to permit broad conclusions about odor memory" (p. 10).

One aspect that parallels other forms of sensory memory is the question of whether odor memory is a separate sensory memory. Schab and Crowder (1995) take the view that recognition memory for odors follows the same principles as memory for visual or verbal stimuli. One type of study is to present a small number of odors, wait a short period, and then present a test odor; the subject's task is to say whether the target odor is one of the small set that was just presented. Although several studies have shown little forgetting of odors over 30 seconds (Engen, Kuisma, & Eimas, 1973), when the retention interval is extended to 2 minutes, there is a reliable decrease in performance (Gilmore, 1991, cited

Figure 2.9   Proportion of odors recognized correctly as a
function of serial position and whether the list was followed by
an auditory suffix or an odor suffix.   Source: Data from Miles &
Jenkins (2000).

in Schab & Crowder, 1995). Another type of study uses more stimuli and far longer retention intervals. Here, too, performance decreases with increasing retention interval (Rabin
& Cain, 1984). Elaborative rehearsal can help improve memory for odors (Lyman &
McDaniel, 1990), just as it improves memory for verbal or visual information.

Further evidence comes from research that shows suffix effects with olfactory stimuli.
For example, Miles and Jenkins (2000) first trained subjects to recognize a set of nine odors.
For list presentation, the experimenter placed a bottle under the subject's nose, then placed
a second bottle, and so on. Each odor was presented for 1 s, with a 2 s gap between items.
At the end of the list, there was a suffix: The experimenter either placed another odor (ginger) under the nose or placed an empty bottle and said the word *ginger*. The results are
shown in Figure 2.9. A subsequent experiment demonstrated that an odor suffix did not affect memory for auditory items, whereas the auditory suffix did affect those items.

One might be concerned that subjects are relying for recall on the verbal label of an
odor rather than on sensory qualities of the odor itself. Although this is possible, effects
similar to those shown in Figure 2.9 are still found when subjects engage in a verbal suppression task (Reed, 2000). If all of the memory effects were due to verbal labeling of the odors,
a verbal suppression task should have greatly reduced or even eliminated these effects.

Herz and Eich (1995) take the opposite view. They point out that many studies show
no forgetting of odors over either the short or the long term, although these studies are
generally earlier than the ones cited by Schab and Crowder (1995). Odor memory also
appears to be different in amnesic patients. For example, Mair, Harrison, and Flint (1995)
reviewed evidence suggesting that in Korsakoff patients, odor memory is preserved even
though memory for words, colors, or faces is severely impaired.

Table 2.1   The effects of proactive interference (learn A, learn B, tested on B) and retroactive interference (learn B, learn A, tested on B) for odors

	Type of Interference	
Condition	PI	RI
Control	72%	68%
Experimental	54%	68%

SOURCE: Lawless & Engen (1977).

As another example, Herz and Eich (1995) emphasize that odor information differs from verbal information with respect to interference. One prevalent finding with both visual and auditory information is that interference reduces performance (Underwood, 1957). In particular, memory for a particular item can be interfered with by information that you have already learned; this is called *proactive interference*. However, memory can also be interfered with by information that is presented after learning the key item but before the test is given; this is called *retroactive interference*. The suffix effect is a good example of retroactive interference.

With odors, Lawless and Engen (1977) found evidence of proactive interference but not retroactive interference. They asked subjects to associate a particular odor with a particular picture and, at the first test, to indicate which odor went with which picture. To create interference, the experimenters had the subjects perform two learning trials, using different pairings on the second trial. For example, on the first trial the raspberry odor might be paired with a picture of a Spanish beach, but on the second trial it might be paired with a picture of the Swiss Alps. At test, the subjects could be asked to recall the second pairing, in which case the first pairing might cause proactive interference; or subjects could be asked to recall the first pairing, in which case the second pairing might cause retroactive interference. The proportion correct for each of these groups is shown in Table 2.1, along with performance of a control group. Performance was worse for the proactive interference condition, but there was no difference between the control group and the retroactive interference condition.

Both Schab and Crowder (1995) and Herz and Eich (1995) emphasize the paucity of evidence and the need for more data. At this time, the evidence is mixed with regard to whether odor memory is a separate memory system or more nearly follows the principles of memory proper. It is likely, however, that researchers will conclude, as with visual and auditory stimuli, that there is a very brief true sensory component.

Chapter Summary

Research on sensory memory has been guided by two observations: Something that looks like or sounds like the physical stimulus continues to be present after the stimulus is no longer present (stimulus persistence), and information can be extracted from a stimulus after the stimulus is no longer present (information persistence). There is good evidence, especially for the visual and auditory modalities, that these two forms of persistence are different. Stimulus persistence lasts for perhaps 100 or 200 ms after the stimulus has been presented and is best explained as being due to the continuation of the original neural activity. Information persistence can last far longer, for as much as 30 s, and current explanations do not attribute it to a separate sensory memory that retains unanalyzed information. Rather, the sensory aspects of an item are now seen as being represented along with other information about the item in a form that does not require a separate store. Although less is known about information persistence of olfactory and tactile stimuli, it seems likely that theoretical accounts similar to those of auditory stimuli will be developed, particularly given that all these classes of stimuli give rise to suffix and modality effects.

The Modal Model

There seems to be a presence-chamber in my mind where full consciousness holds court, and where two or three ideas are at the same time in audience, and an ante-chamber full of more or less allied ideas, which is situated just beyond the full ken of consciousness. Out of this ante-chamber the ideas most readily allied to those in the presence-chamber appear to be summoned in a mechanically logical way and to have their turn of audience.

—Sir Francis Galton (1883)

Primary Memory

The publication of Broadbent's *Perception and Communication* in 1958 and of the papers by Miller (1956), Brown (1958), and Peterson and Peterson (1959) mark the beginning of the modern history of dividing memory into multiple stores with one store specialized for briefly holding information. This system has variously been called *primary memory, working memory, short-term memory,* and *short-term store.*

Memory had often been divided into multiple memory systems; for example, Burnham (1888, p. 575) documents forerunners of both iconic and echoic memory (see Chapter 2). Short-term store (STS) was based on what Exner called primary memory and Richet called elementary memory (Burnham, 1888). Although William James is usually given credit for coining the term *primary memory,* it was in fact Sigmund Exner (1846–1926), a physiological psychologist at Vienna, to whom James gives credit (James, 1890, p. 600).

Exner's contribution was published in 1879 in Leipzig in Ludimar Hermann's *Handbuch der Physiologie*.

James (1890) distinguished primary memory from secondary memory or memory proper, tracing the concept back to Wilhelm Wundt's work on *Umfang*. This German term is difficult to translate precisely as there is no real English equivalent, but it implies a kind of immediate consciousness of that which is still present. James (1890) elaborates:

> The objects we feel in this directly intuited past differ from properly recollected objects. An object which is recollected, in the proper sense of the term, is one which has been absent from consciousness altogether, and now revives anew. . . . But an object of primary memory is not thus brought back; it never was lost; its date was never cut off in consciousness from that of the immediately present moment. In fact, it comes to us as belonging to the rearward portion of the present space of time, and not to the genuine past. (pp. 608–609)

The short-term memory (STM) of the late 1950s and early 1960s was a combination of the idea of primary memory with the computer metaphor of memory; it was of limited capacity, very short duration, primarily verbal in nature, and intended mainly as a buffer where information could be temporarily stored. And just as a computer memory "forgets" when the power is turned off, so too does STM "forget" when attention is withdrawn and the maintenance process—rehearsal—is prevented. This view became so prevalent so quickly that by 1963, Melton devoted a paper to discussing "whether single-repetition, short-term memory and multiple-repetition, long-term memory are a dichotomy or points on a continuum" (p. 3). Melton's cogent arguments against multiple stores notwithstanding, the ensuing two-store conception of memory reached its most explicit form in papers by Waugh and Norman (1965), Atkinson and Shiffrin (1968), and Glanzer (1972) and a volume edited by Norman (1970). The resultant *modal model,* so termed by Murdock (1974), became the dominating, albeit not unanimous, view of memory. In this chapter, we will examine the various forms this model took.

Broadbent's Model

The most influential of the early approaches to primary memory was that of Donald Broadbent (1958). He characterized the human processor as a series of systems through which information flows, much as it does in electronic and communication systems. Information from the environment is received through the senses and is held temporarily in a preattentive sensory store (the S-system), the forerunner of iconic and echoic memory. From the S-system, information is filtered and arrives in a limited capacity store, the P-system, the site of conscious awareness. For Broadbent, the combination of the S- and P-systems constituted immediate or primary memory. Note how these systems were foreshadowed by Galton (1883), as indicated by the opening quotation for this chapter. For information to remain in primary memory, it had to be rehearsed; without rehearsal, information was assumed to fade. Secondary or long-term memory was believed to be a third, more permanent memory system, and it was thought that information passes through primary memory on its way to more or less permanent storage.

Three assumptions of Broadbent's view were retained by almost all subsequent models: (1) Primary and secondary memory involve separate memory systems. (2) Primary memory has a limited capacity. (3) Because information fades quickly in primary memory, information is retained only when it is actively rehearsed.

Recall that Sperling (1960) suggested that information in iconic memory needs to be recoded if it is to be maintained. Rather than store information in a form identical to its actual physical features, as sensory memory systems do, primary memory stores information in a speechlike code. Two early experiments by Conrad (1964) and Wickelgren (1965) quickly established that the main code or form of representation in primary memory was acoustic or sound-based. Conrad (1964) presented subjects with lists of letters, some that looked similar but sounded quite different (such as V and X) and others that looked quite different but sounded almost identical (such as V and C). Some subjects read the letters silently, and others heard the letters pronounced aloud. Surprisingly, Conrad found that regardless of whether the subjects had seen or heard the letters, any errors that were made tended to be based on acoustic similarity rather than on visual similarity. Both he and Wickelgren (1965) argued that the main code in primary memory is acoustic, suggesting that subjects are remembering the sound of the to-be-remembered items using some form of inner speech.

Baddeley (1966) found comparable results. He presented subjects with four types of lists. In the phonologically similar list, the words sounded very similar, such as *man*, *mad*, *cap*, *can*, and *map*. The control list had words of similar frequency but different sounds: *pen*, *rig*, *day*, *bar*, and *sup*. In the semantically similar list, the words all meant the same thing: *big*, *huge*, *broad*, *long*, and *tall*. Here the control list was *old*, *late*, *thin*, *wet*, and *hot*. The results of the study are shown in Figure 3.1. Similarity of meaning had very little effect, but similarity of sound resulted in very poor performance. These results are entirely consistent with other studies that show that in primary memory the dominant code appears to be acoustic, a form of inner speech.

One way of testing the idea that information in primary memory uses inner speech is to prevent subjects from rehearsing the items subvocally. If this is done successfully, the errors should no longer be based on acoustic similarity. Murray (1967) was the first to use a procedure known as *articulatory suppression* to prevent subvocal rehearsal. Throughout

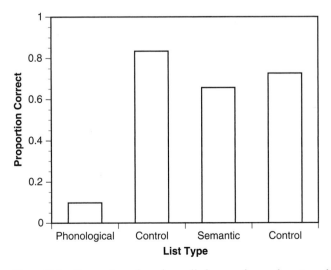

Figure 3.1   Proportion of words recalled correctly as a function of list type.   SOURCE: Baddeley (1966).

the presentation of the list items, subjects were required to say the word *the* over and over, out loud. In the articulatory suppression condition, subjects were able to recall correctly about two-thirds of the items that they had seen, but the errors they made were now different. Without articulatory suppression, subjects were more likely than would be expected by chance alone to incorrectly recall an item that sounded like the target item. With articulatory suppression, this was no longer the case; acoustically similar items were no longer the most likely errors. However, visually similar items were not more likely to be errors either. Although the mode of representing the information under conditions of articulatory suppression was not known, the mode was not visual.

Despite the observation that most people use a speech code to represent information in primary memory, this is neither a universal nor an obligatory code. R. Conrad (1972; see also Cowan, Cartwright, Winterowd, & Sherk, 1987; Locke & Fehr, 1970) demonstrated that young children do not show the same patterns of acoustic errors until they are about 5 or 6 years old. Even then, it takes several more years before their performance shows the same error pattern as that of adults.

The capacity of primary memory was a key question that many researchers attempted to address. The title of George Miller's (1956) paper was the now famous phrase "The Magical Number Seven, Plus or Minus Two," reflecting the most common estimate of the limitations of information processing. Miller arrived at this estimate after examining data from a variety of different paradigms, and he began the article with a parody of Senator Joseph McCarthy:

> My problem is that I have been persecuted by an integer. For seven years this number has followed me around, has intruded in my most private data, and has assaulted me from the pages of our most public journals. This number assumes a variety of disguises, being sometimes a little larger and sometimes a little smaller than usual, but never changing so much as to be unrecognizable. The persistence with which this number plagues me is far more than a random accident. There is, to quote a famous senator, a design behind it, some pattern governing its appearances. Either there really is something unusual about the number or else I am suffering from delusions of persecution. (p. 81)

Miller described the results from a number of different paradigms, all of which seemed to converge on the idea of a central limitation on people's ability to process information. His first topic concerns a finding that rarely fails to provoke disbelief: People are unable to learn to identify a set of items that vary along only one dimension if there are more than a few items. For example, in an *absolute identification* experiment, a subject might hear a set of nine tones that vary only in frequency. On each trial, one of these tones is played for the subject, who then tries to identify it. The subject is informed whether the response is correct and, if not, what the correct response should have been. The results of such an experiment are shown in Figure 3.2. The highest and lowest frequency tones are identified quite well (around 65% correct), but the closer to the middle of the set, the worse the performance. Generally speaking, once the number of items reaches about eight or nine, subjects become unable to perform the task without errors; interestingly, errors persist regardless of the range and practice (Pollack, 1952, 1953; Shiffrin & Nosofsky, 1993).

CogLab Experiment
http://coglab.wadsworth.com/experiments/AbsoluteIdentification/

Figure 3.2 Proportion of times a particular tone was correctly identified using the method of absolute identification.
SOURCE: Neath & Knoedler (1997).

When stimuli vary along more than one dimension, identification is much better. For example, most people can easily identify the 26 letters of the alphabet, even when they are handwritten. Because the letters vary along multiple dimensions, they are easier to discriminate from one another. When there is only one dimension involved—regardless of whether that dimension is frequency, length, height, or intensity—subjects will not be able to perform accurately once the number of items exceeds about seven.

A second topic that Miller discussed was the limitations of memory span. In 1887, Joseph Jacobs published a paper discussing his interest in measuring his students' mental capacity. His measure, known as the *memory span*, was defined as the number of items (usually digits) that can be repeated immediately in order 50% of the time. When this measure is used, the span is typically the same number that haunted Miller: seven, plus or minus two. More specifically, 90% of the adult population is able to recall at least five items in order but not more than eight (Matarazzo, 1972).

A third topic of Miller's (1956) paper concerned the question of what defines an item. For example, the list 1492200118651066 has 16 digits in it. According to the limits of memory span, you should not be able to remember that many items. However, if you recode the list into the dates 1492, 2001, 1865, and 1066, you need remember only four items or "chunks" of information.

H. A. Simon (1974) expanded on Miller's ideas of a chunk, demonstrating that the number of chunks that can be recalled is variable. As shown in Table 3.1, when the stimuli comprised 1-syllable items, the number of syllables recalled was 7, the number of words recalled was also 7, and the number of chunks was also 7. However, when the stimuli comprised 3-syllable items, the number of syllables recalled increased to 18, the number of words recalled dipped slightly, and the number of chunks recalled also dropped slightly. The best performance, in terms of maximum number of syllables and words recalled, came with eight-word phrases; the worst performance, in terms of the number of chunks, was also with eight-word phrases. Cowan (2001) provides a detailed review of this issue.

Table 3.1 Memory span expressed in chunks for different kinds of material: one-, two-, or three-syllable words or two- or eight-word phrases

	Span			
Stimuli	Syllables	Words	Imputed Chunks	Syllables per Chunk
1-syllable	7	7	7	1.0
2-syllable	14	7	7	2.0
3-syllable	18	6	6	3.0
2-word	22	9	4	5.5
8-word	26	22	3	8.7

SOURCE: Simon (1974).

Thus, with an increase in the amount of information in the chunk, there was a decrease in the number of chunks that could be remembered. Although the capacity of short-term store was an important issue at that time, the answer to the question depended on both the measure and the type of stimuli used. The limit on how much information could be retained in short-term store, then, was *not* constant.

The Brown-Peterson Paradigm

Peterson and Peterson (1959) reported an experiment that used a procedure similar to one used by Brown (1958). Their purpose was to investigate the rate at which information is lost or decays in STM. The general procedure, now known as the *Brown-Peterson paradigm*, is for the experimenter to read a consonant trigram (three consonants in a row, such as DBX) to a subject and then read a three-digit number out loud. The number of items is substantially less than almost everybody's memory span. The subject's task is then to count backward by threes (or fours) from the three-digit number for a certain amount of time. At the end of this period, the subject is asked to recall the three consonants in order. The purpose of the counting backward is to prevent rehearsal while minimizing overt interference: The digits are sufficiently different from the letters that they should not interfere. Peterson and Peterson varied how long the subjects counted backward, including conditions of 3, 6, 9, 12, 15, and 18 seconds (s). The results are shown in Figure 3.3. What is most noteworthy is that after as little as 18 s of counting backward, subjects could recall only about 10% of the items.

These results, along with those reported by Murdock (1961), Hellyer (1962), and Fuchs and Melton (1974), were generally interpreted as demonstrating the very rapid decay of information in short-term memory when rehearsal is prevented. In Chapter 6, we shall see that much of the data from the Brown-Peterson paradigm is inconsistent with a decay interpretation (Capaldi & Neath, 1995); rather, the reduced performance is due to interference. Briefly, Keppel and Underwood (1962) demonstrated that if you examine performance on the very first trial of the Brown-Peterson task, there is no difference in performance in the various delay conditions: Whether subjects count backward for 3 s or 18 s, performance is equal in the two conditions. At that time, however, less was known about the task, and so most researchers explained it in terms of decay from short-term store.

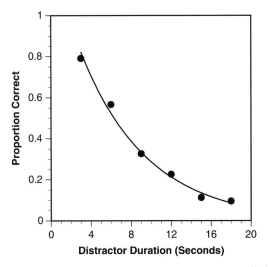

Figure 3.3   Proportion of consonant trigrams recalled correctly
as a function of the distractor task duration.
SOURCE: Peterson & Peterson (1959).

CogLab Experiment
http://coglab.wadsworth.com/experiments/BrownPeterson/

Waugh and Norman's Model

To account for these and many other observations, many researchers divided memory into
two structures. Of the many different versions, two models stand out as particularly influential. The first was developed by Waugh and Norman (1965), who specifically divided
memory into *primary* and *secondary* memory, resurrecting the terms from James (1890).
According to their model, perceived information first enters primary memory, a limited
capacity structure. From primary memory, some information is lost by displacement, as
newly arriving items "bump out" already existing items. Other information might be rehearsed and thus remain in primary memory longer. Rehearsal also causes the information
to be transferred to secondary memory, which has no capacity limitation. Recall can be
based on information in primary memory, secondary memory, or both.

   According to the model, it should be possible to measure the capacity of primary
memory. If items are continuously presented to a subject, there should be a point at which
primary memory is full and the new input has to displace the old input. At this point, recall for those items that have been displaced will depend solely on secondary memory. If
rehearsal is prevented, then there should be no memory left for the items formerly in primary memory. Preventing rehearsal will ensure that the items are not refreshed in primary
memory and are not transferred to secondary memory.

   In one of their experiments, Waugh and Norman (1965) instructed subjects not to
rehearse. To the extent that subjects followed these instructions, the items from primary

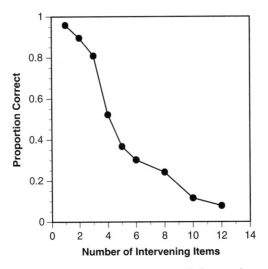

Figure 3.4 Proportion of items recalled correctly as a function of the number of intervening items. The data plotted are averaged from the two presentation rates. SOURCE: Waugh & Norman (1965).

memory should not be transferred to secondary memory. The researchers presented lists of 16 digits at a rate of either 1 digit per second or 4 digits per second. After all 16 items had been presented, a single item (a probe) was presented. The subject's task was to recall the digit that had followed the probe item in the original series. The results are replotted in Figure 3.4.

Presentation rate had only a small and inconsistent effect; memory performance depended primarily on how many items had intervened between presentation and test. The farther back in the list the probe item was, the lower the probability of correctly recalling the next item. Waugh and Norman emphasized two key aspects of their data. First, there was a very sharp drop in performance after about three or four items. Second, the asymptote of the function approached 0. This means that after a large number of items intervened, the subjects could not recall the target item. This finding reinforced the idea that the instructions not to rehearse had been obeyed and that the digits had not been transferred to secondary memory. Waugh and Norman (1965) interpreted Peterson and Peterson's (1959) results as consistent with their view. The distracting activity would have displaced the information from primary memory, but what little rehearsal there was would have transferred some of the information to secondary memory. The approximately 10% recall after 18 seconds of distracting activity would reflect the secondary memory component in the Brown-Peterson task.

Atkinson and Shiffrin's Dual-Store Model

The second model was developed in a series of papers by Richard Atkinson and Richard Shiffrin. Atkinson and Shiffrin (1968) distinguished between *structural* and *processing* components of memory. The structure is thought to be those parts of the memory system that do not change, whereas the control processes are thought to be flexible and under a person's control. Although often used as an example of a dual-store model, this model ac-

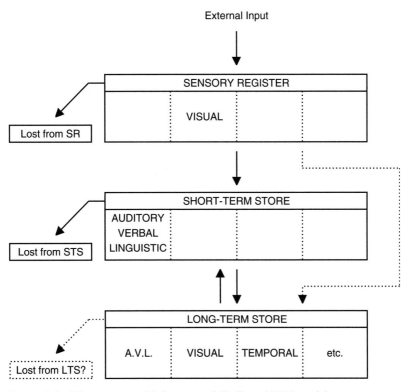

Figure 3.5 The structure of Atkinson and Shiffrin's (1968) model.
SOURCE: Adapted from Atkinson & Shiffrin (1968).

tually posits three structural components of memory (see Figure 3.5). The first structures are the *sensory registers*, one for each modality. Visual information enters a visual sensory register, auditory information enters an auditory sensory register, and haptic (touch) information enters a haptic sensory register. Atkinson and Shiffrin based their description of the visual sensory register on the work of Sperling, described in Chapter 2. Relatively little was known then about the auditory sensory register, but as the model was developed, it took on the properties of echoic memory.

Short-term store (STS) closely resembles Broadbent's P-system. It is of limited capacity, very short duration, and intended mainly as a buffer where information can be stored temporarily. Long-term store (LTS), in contrast, is a permanent, unlimited capacity store. This is where all enduring memories are stored, including knowledge, personal history, and anything else that one remembers. All information is eventually lost completely from the sensory registers and the short-term store, whereas information in the long-term store is relatively permanent (although it may be modified or rendered temporarily irretrievable as the result of other incoming information).

All information entering LTS has to go through STS (with a possible exception, discussed next, denoted by the dotted line from the sensory register), and whenever an item is retrieved from LTS it again has to enter STS. It is important to note that information is not really transferred, for that implies that the original copy is lost. Rather, information is copied from one store to the other, leaving the original item in place. (The analogy of faxing is quite useful: Usually a copy arrives at the destination, and most of the time it is legible. Some faxes do not "go through," however, and some of the information that arrives may not be readable.)

The emphasis of the Atkinson and Shiffrin (1968) model is on the control processes that manipulate the flow of information, and this flow is to a large extent under the subject's control. Control processes are "selected, constructed, and used at the option of the subject" and can be "readily modified or reprogrammed at the will of the subject" (Atkinson & Shiffrin, 1968, p. 90). Of the various control processes, the most important are rehearsal, coding, and retrieval. *Rehearsal* is necessary to preserve information in STS and copy it to LTS. The type of *coding*—what aspects of the information are registered—can determine what kinds of information will be remembered and what other information will be associated with it. *Retrieval* is most important for getting information from LTS, but the problem is more complicated than it might first appear. How does the retrieval process know what to look for, and how does it determine when to stop searching? Humans are particularly adept at knowing that they do not know something, and it is obvious that they are not performing an exhaustive search. (We will examine the retrieval process in Chapter 10.)

To make these issues a little clearer, let us follow a word through various stages of processing. A subject simultaneously hears the word *cow* spoken and sees it presented visually on a computer screen. The physical properties of each stimulus will be represented in the respective sensory stores: the shape of the letters in iconic memory, and the sound of the word in echoic memory. Control processes in each sensory store determine which portions of the information get transferred to STS. It could be the fact that an uppercase C was presented, or the whole word *cow*, or the sound of the word, or the gender of the voice that presented it, or the color of the word, or the background noise that accompanied the word, or any other similar information. Let's assume that it was the sound of the word that was transferred, so that now STS contains acoustic information that defines the word *cow*.

Rehearsal could be simple rote—merely repeating the sound—or it could be elaborative, focusing on the meaning of the word, on the image of a cow, of things associated with cows, of a distant memory of cow tipping, and so on. Such associates (for example, the word *milk*, the sound "moo," the image of a dairy cow) are copied from LTS to STS. STS, then, can store information in a variety of codes—visual, acoustic, verbal, and so on. Rehearsal is under the control of the subject, and, to a certain extent, so are the coding options. There is normally a preference for one kind of coding for a particular type of stimulus, but there is also great flexibility.

Atkinson and Shiffrin (1968) justified the division of memory into separate stores by citing several lines of converging evidence. First, they cited the papers by Miller, Broadbent, and Peterson and Peterson. They were aware of the Keppel and Underwood (1962) paper ascribing performance in the Brown-Peterson task to interference (discussed in Chapter 6), but Atkinson and Shiffrin suggested an alternative explanation. They noted that subjects in a Brown-Peterson experiment can devote attention to the to-be-remembered item for only a brief period of time before they have to begin counting backward. During this brief period, some of the information will get transferred to LTS. This explanation is supported by the observation that even after 18 s of counting backward, performance was not at 0; rather, subjects were recalling about 10% of the information. Interference occurs not in STS, according to this account, but in the search of LTS. Because of the interference in LTS, performance is determined almost entirely by STS.

Atkinson and Shiffrin (1968) assumed that the memory trace was composed of a multicomponent array consisting of a number of pieces of information, possibly redundant, correlated, or even in error. The traces do decay, but the decay rate can be affected by control processes. This explains why sometimes presentation rate does not affect estimates of decay (Waugh & Norman, 1965) and sometimes it does (Conrad & Hille, 1958).

For simplicity, Atkinson and Shiffrin focused most on the auditory-verbal-linguistic, or a-v-l, aspect of both STS and LTS. They acknowledged that other forms of information can be represented in both STS and LTS, but most work at that time had explored memory for verbal stimuli. The reason for the three terms was that it became impossible to determine whether the format was acoustic, articulatory, or some other similar form (for example, Conrad, 1964; Hintzman, 1967).

Information can be transferred from STS to LTS via rehearsal. Again, the term *transfer* is a little misleading because it implies that the original information is actually moved. Rather, Atkinson, and Shiffrin meant that a copy was made in LTS. Although transfer was seen as an unvarying feature of the system, the amount and form of transfer could be affected by the particular control processes used. Most important, they assumed that transfer began and continued during the entire time an item was in STS.

The reason for assuming that transfer occurs throughout the time that an item resides in STS was the finding that learning takes place even when the subject is not trying to remember the material. For example, Hebb (1961) presented a series of nine-item lists to 40 subjects. The lists were made up of the digits 1–9, presented in random order, and the task was to recall the items in order. Most of the lists contained novel orderings, but one list was repeated every third trial. For example, a particular subject would see the exact same list on trials 3, 6, 9, 12, and so on until trial 24. The results, shown in Figure 3.6, have been replicated by Melton (1963) and more recently by McKelvie (1987). Even when those subjects who noticed the repetition were dropped from the analysis, the effect of repetition was still present. The key finding is that simple repetition of an item, even if the subjects are unaware of the repetition, leads to better performance.

Mechanic (1964) found similar results, but in a different paradigm. According to Atkinson and Shiffrin, performance on the repeated series improved because each time the items in the series were encountered, some of the information was transferred to LTS. The amount of transfer can vary with the task, and—at least in this paradigm—several repetitions were required before there was a meaningful difference between the repeated and novel series.

We will discuss LTS in more detail later (see Chapter 10); for now, we will just sketch out the basic features. There is no universal, unchanging process of transfer. Most likely, the transfer process results in multiple copies of the original item, each of which can be either partial or complete. This assumption is based on results like those of Brown and McNeill (1966) concerning the "tip of the tongue" phenomenon. This is the situation that occurs when you cannot recall a specific piece of information, but you can provide some correct information (such as the first letter or the number of syllables) and you can accurately predict whether or not you would recognize the correct answer. According to Atkinson and Shiffrin, the reason for this situation is that you have accessed a partial trace rather than a complete trace. Some of the information is correct, but there is not enough to allow successful recall. When presented with the correct answer, another retrieval attempt is made, this time with more information, and so a complete trace is likely to be found.

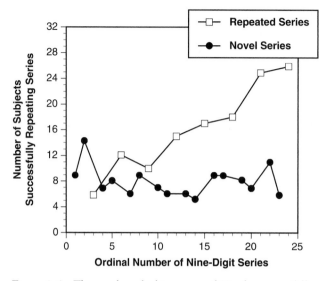

Figure 3.6   The number of subjects, out of 40, who successfully recalled a nine-digit series as a function of the position of the nine-digit series within a set of 24 trials. The repeated series was the same nine-item list repeated every third trial.   SOURCE: From "Distinctive Features of Learning in the Higher Animal," by D. O. Hebb. In J. F. Delafresnaye (Ed.), *Brain Mechanisms and Learning: A Symposium*. Copyright © 1961 Blackwell Scientific Publications Ltd. Reprinted with permission.

CogLab Experiment
http://coglab.wadsworth.com/experiments/Sternberg/

STS has two main control processes, retrieval and rehearsal. Although many theorists do not say much about retrieval from STS, Atkinson and Shiffrin emphasized the highly specialized nature of these processes. Because of decay, any retrieval process must be very fast and highly efficient. The most likely candidate comes from the work of Saul Sternberg (1966). He presented subjects with a short list of items, such as 2, 5, 3, 8, followed by a test item, or probe. A positive probe is an item that occurred in the list (such as 5 in the current example); a negative probe is an item that did not occur. Sternberg measured response time (RT), how long it took subjects to say that the probe item did or did not occur; the results are shown in Figure 3.7.

Two features of the data are noteworthy. First, the addition of an extra item in the search set results in a consistent increase in reaction time of about 40 ms. Second, the data from the positive and negative probes are almost identical. The equation of the best-fitting straight line was RT = 397 + 38 n, where n is the number of items in the search set. This can be interpreted as saying that the basic task took approximately 400 ms to perform, with an additional 40 ms to compare each item. Similar results were found for nonverbal stimuli.

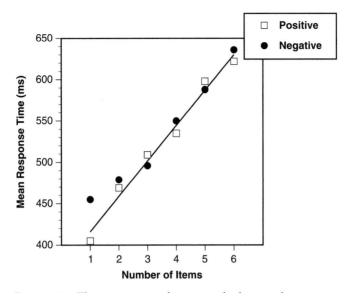

Figure 3.7 The mean time to determine whether a probe item was in the original list of items (positive probe) or was not in the original list (negative probe) as a function of the number of items in the list. SOURCE: Reprinted with permission from "High Speed Scanning in Human Memory," by S. Sternberg, 1966, *Science, 153*, 652–654. Copyright © 1966 American Association for the Advancement of Science.

Sternberg interpreted these data as supporting an *exhaustive serial scanning model*. For a negative probe, this makes sense. The probe is compared with each item in the search set, one at a time (hence *serial*). Because the probe did not occur, the search must involve comparisons with every list item (hence *exhaustive*). But the same is true when the probe is positive. An exhaustive search on a positive trial means that subjects will continue the search *after* they have found the item they were searching for. Although this may not sound very plausible, remember that we are dealing with STS, and any operation must be fast and efficient. Sternberg suggested that in order to keep the search fast, an *automatic process* is used. Once started, an automatic process must continue until completion; however, other processes can operate at the same time. Sternberg's idea is that the matching process is automatic, and, once a match is found, some note of this is made. At the end of the search, the subject examines the marker, and if it is positive, the subject presses the "yes" button; if negative, the subject presses the "no" button. Although consistent with the Atkinson and Shiffrin (1968) model, subsequent research has found the situation to be far more complex, and the simple serial exhaustive search interpretation is no longer tenable (see Van Zandt & Townsend, 1993).

The other major control process in STS is rehearsal. For the a-v-l part of STS, rehearsal was assumed to be like saying the items over and over. In certain situations, rehearsal can set up a buffer in which this rehearsal process is optimized. The buffer can be thought of as a bin that has a certain number of slots; each new item enters the rehearsal buffer and, if the buffer is already full, knocks out an item that is already there. Whether an item enters the rehearsal buffer is up to the subject, who directs the rehearsal process.

There are two possibilities for determining which items get bumped. One is a method based on the duration of the item in STS, with the oldest item getting bumped first. The second is a random method, where an item in STS is randomly selected to be bumped. The rehearsal process will be discussed in more detail in later chapters.

Many theorists proposed models similar to those of Waugh and Norman (1965) and Atkinson and Shiffrin (1968), some offering only slight modifications and others adding extra systems; however, almost all shared the same basic structures and processes. This general view became the dominant framework and was termed the *modal model* after the statistical measure *mode* (Murdock, 1974). The mode is a measure of central tendency; in a distribution of values, it is the value that occurs most frequently. Many examples of similar models can be seen in the volume edited by Norman (1970), and a paper by Glanzer (1972) critically reviews much of the evidence that supports this general conception.

Even though the models have been presented as verbal theories, one version of the Atkinson and Shiffrin (1968) model was a formal, mathematical model that made specific predictions for many different paradigms. For example, assume that it takes 1.1 s for an item in STS to decay such that it can no longer be identified. Let's further assume that it takes 0.25 s to rehearse or refresh an item and that only one item can be rehearsed at a time. (These numbers, although somewhat arbitrary, are nonetheless plausible.) The result is that no more than five items could be consistently maintained in STS without information loss. Another set of assumptions concerned the probability that an item in STS will get successfully copied into LTS. This probability is determined by the duration and the quality of the rehearsal. The final assumptions concerned the probability that an item could be recalled. Among the parameters were ones for guessing, for the buffer size (how many items could be maintained in STS), the probability of entering the buffer, the transfer rate from STS to LTS, and the decay rate of information in STS. The result was an equation that, when the parameters were estimated, could be used to make precise predictions about how much information could be recalled in a variety of situations (see Atkinson & Shiffrin 1968, p. 129).

Although the Atkinson and Shiffrin (1968) version of the modal model was very precise, many other versions were much vaguer and usually contained just the briefest description of how STS and LTS interacted. Indeed, many ignored some of the issues that Atkinson and Shiffrin had considered and discussed at great length.

The Serial Position Curve and the Modal Model

Many experiments that tested predictions of the modal model concerned the serial position function observable with *free recall*. Kirkpatrick (1894) introduced the method of free recall, noting that few students "gave the words in order, and it was quite noticeable that the first and last words were less frequently omitted than any others" (p. 606). Because free recall is really unconstrained recall, it is quite likely that different subjects are using different strategies; after all, the instructions just say, "Recall the items."

CogLab Experiment
http://coglab.wadsworth.com/experiments/SerialPosition/

Figure 3.8   Serial positions curves showing the proportion of items recalled correctly in a free recall test as a function of input position for three different list lengths.   SOURCE: Data from Murdock (1962).

Murdock (1962) reported a free recall experiment in which he presented lists of items that varied in length. Figure 3.8 shows the free recall data for lists of 10, 15, and 20 items. For all three list lengths, a typical serial position curve can be seen. For each list, there was a pronounced *recency effect,* with excellent recall of the last few items. The middle part of each list was not well recalled, but there was a *primacy effect*—better recall of the first few items. Murdock (1962, p. 485) concluded that the recency effect "appears to be essentially independent of list length" (see also Postman & Phillips, 1965).

When we examined the modality effect in Chapter 2, we saw that serial recall produced serial position curves. Free recall leads to similar-looking curves, but there are two important differences. First, in free recall, the recency effect is generally more pronounced relative to the primacy effect. Second, the recency effect in free recall can be seen with both auditory and visual presentation.

According to the modal model (e.g., Atkinson & Shiffrin, 1968; Glanzer, 1972; Waugh & Norman, 1965), primacy is due to the extra rehearsal the first few items get, which copies them into LTS, and recency is due to the dumping of items from STS. For example, when the first item in a list is presented, subjects can devote 100% of their rehearsal to this item; when the second item is presented, subjects can devote only 50% of their rehearsal to this item. Because the first item is rehearsed more, it has a greater probability of being transferred to LTS. A strong prediction of the model, then, is that if the number of rehearsals per item can be measured, they will decline as more and more items are presented.

Rundus and Atkinson (1970) examined this relationship by adopting a procedure that allowed them to measure the number of times an item was rehearsed. Subjects were told that they could rehearse whichever items they wanted to, but they must do it out

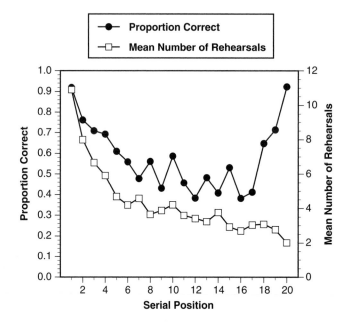

Figure 3.9   The proportion of items recalled correctly as a function of serial position and the mean number of rehearsals devoted to each item at each serial position.   SOURCE: From "Rehearsal Processes in Free Recall: A Procedure for Direct Observation," by D. Rundus and R. C. Atkinson, 1970, *Journal of Verbal Learning and Verbal Behavior, 9*, 99–105. Copyright © 1970 Academic Press, Inc. Reprinted with permission.

loud. The subjects saw lists of 20 common nouns, and each word was presented for 5 seconds. The results, shown in Figure 3.9, show the predicted relationship between the number of rehearsals (shown on the right y-axis) and the proportion correctly recalled (shown on the left y-axis). Early items received the most rehearsals and were recalled very well—the primacy effect. Items at the end of the list were also recalled well—the recency effect—but they had relatively few rehearsals. This finding is consistent with the modal model's claim that primacy is due to rehearsal and recency is due to dumping from short-term store. The middle items are not recalled well, but they also do not receive many rehearsals.

One might be concerned that the overt rehearsal procedure could introduce a confound: Overt rehearsal might place extra demands on the cognitive system, altering the number of items that can be remembered. Although an appropriate concern, it does not seem warranted; Murdock and Metcalfe (1978) directly compared memory when rehearsal was covert or overt and found few differences.

According to the modal model, the primacy effect results from extra rehearsals, which increase the probability of transferring information to long-term store, and the recency effect results from dumping from short-term store. Analysis of output order confirms that the last few items are indeed recalled first (e.g., Welch & Burnett, 1924). A strong prediction of the model, then, is that if recall is delayed, the primacy effect should remain unaltered but the recency effect should disappear. Primacy will remain because

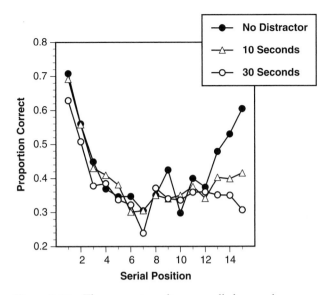

Figure 3.10   The proportion of items recalled correctly as a function of serial position in a free recall test when there is no distractor task, or when subjects are required to count backward for 10 or 30 seconds before recalling the items.   SOURCE: From "Two Storage Mechanisms in Free Recall," by M. Glanzer and A. R. Cunitz, 1966, *Journal of Verbal Learning and Verbal Behavior, 5,* 351–360. Copyright © 1966 Academic Press, Inc. Reprinted with permission.

once an item is in long-term store, it can be recalled after long delays. Recency will be eliminated because the items are not in long-term store, and items in short-term store cannot be retained for long without rehearsal.

To test this prediction, Glanzer and Cunitz (1966; see also Postman & Phillips, 1965) presented 15-item lists to subjects. In the control condition, subjects immediately recalled as many of the words as they could. In the other two conditions, subjects engaged in a distractor activity (counting backward) for either 10 or 30 seconds before recalling the items. The results are shown in Figure 3.10.

The control group showed the typical serial position function. Subjects in the two distractor groups recalled the same number of items as the control subjects, with one important exception: The longer they had to wait until recall, the fewer items from the end of the list were recalled. According to the modal model, because counting backward fills up short-term store with numbers, the words are not available for output at the time of recall. The more numbers that are processed in short-term store, the less chance there is that a to-be-remembered item survives. Recall for earlier parts of the list was not affected, because those items were recalled from long-term store.

The modal model, then, accounts for the following results: (1) The serial position curve is seen regardless of list length. (2) The first items recalled will be the last few list items, followed by the first few list items. (3) Items will be rehearsed less and less as the serial position increases. (4) The recency effect, but not the primacy effect, is abolished if recall is delayed.

Problems with the Modal Model

Although the modal model correctly predicted and accounted for numerous results from free recall experiments, a series of studies soon demonstrated that the simple ascription of the recency effect to short-term store and the primacy effect to long-term store was no longer plausible.

The first series of studies examined the so-called long-term recency effect. In the typical free recall experiment, subjects receive 12 or so list items and then recall those items immediately; a recency effect is typically observed. When Glanzer and Cunitz (1966) added 30 seconds of distractor activity at the end of the list, the recency effect was eliminated (see Figure 3.10). However, when Bjork and Whitten (1974) added distractor activity after *every* item in the list, including the final item, the recency effect re-emerged. In their procedure, a word is shown, and the subject then performs a task that involves processing sufficient information to fill STS and that is sufficiently difficult that all of the subject's resources are diverted from rehearsal and to solving the task. Then the second word is shown, followed by another period of distracting activity. This is known as the *continual distractor task* because the subjects are continually distracted from rehearsing the to-be-remembered items. This finding has been replicated numerous times (e.g., Baddeley & Hitch, 1974, 1977; Glenberg, Bradley, Kraus, & Renzaglia, 1983; Tzeng, 1973).

An experiment reported by Watkins, Neath, and Sechler (1989) illustrates the essentials of the continual distractor task. They presented a 12-item list of words to subjects for free recall. After every word, the subjects heard the digits 1 through 9 presented one at a time in random order, and they had to recall the order of presentation of the digits. Thus, the subjects heard a word, then heard and recalled nine digits in order, then heard the second item, then heard and recalled nine digits in order, and so on throughout the list. The results are shown in Figure 3.11. The most important finding is that when distracting activity occurs after every item, including the final item, there is a substantial recency effect. Recall of the digits also shows a recency effect.

Recall that when Glanzer and Cunitz (1966) added distractor activity at the end of the list, the recency effect was eliminated. The explanation was that the distractor task removed the recency items from short-term store. When distractor activity occurs after every item, including the final item, the recency effect is again observed, even though the to-be-remembered list items should have been removed from short-term memory by the distractor task. These types of results led Bjork and Whitten (1974) to conclude that "the customary two-process theoretical account of immediate free recall is certainly incomplete, if not wrong" (p. 189).

Bjork and Whitten (1974) suggested that a relatively simple rule might be operating. This rule, now known as the *ratio rule* (Glenberg et al., 1983), relates the size of the recency effect to the amount of time an item has to be remembered until recall and the amount of time that separates the items in the list. The measure of recency used is the slope of the best-fitting straight line over the last three positions. The two time measurements are the time between the presentation of list items (known as the *interitem presentation interval* or *IPI*) and the time between the presentation of the final item and the recall test (known as the *retention interval* or *RI*). Nairne and his colleagues (Nairne, Neath, Serra, & Byun, 1997) measured the size of the recency effect when the ratio of the IPI to RI varied from as large as 12:1 to as small as 1:12. The results are shown in Figure 3.12.

Experiment   *Recency Effects in Free Recall*

Purpose: To demonstrate the effect of distracting activity on the recency effect in free recall

Subjects: Thirty-six subjects are recommended; 12 should be assigned to the immediate condition, 12 to the delay condition, and 12 to the continual distractor condition. Subject 1 should be in the immediate condition, Subject 2 in the delay condition, Subject 3 in the continual distractor condition, Subject 4 in the immediate condition, and so on.

Materials: Table C in the Appendix contains a list of 96 two-syllable words randomly drawn from the Toronto word pool. For each subject, construct 8 lists, each of which contains 12 words. Table B in the Appendix contains lists of the digits 1 through 9 in random order that will be used for the distractor task. Also prepare answer sheets with 8 rows of boxes or blanks in which the subject will write down the words. Subjects in the delay condition will need an answer sheet on which to write down the digits in order 8 times, and subjects in the continual distractor condition will need an answer sheet on which to write down the digits in order 96 times.

Procedure: For the immediate group, read the list of 12 words to the subject at a rate of approximately one word every 2 s. At the end of the list, have the subject recall as many of the words as possible by writing them down, in any order, on the prepared answer sheet. The only change for the delay group is to have the subjects engage in distractor activity after the final word and before recalling the words. Read a series of digits out loud at a rate of one digit per second and have the subjects recall the digits in order; then have the subjects recall the words. The only change for the continual distractor group is to have the subjects engage in distractor activity after every list item; thus, these subjects will hear and recall 12 lists of digits before recalling the words from that list.

Instructions for the Immediate Group: "This experiment tests your ability to recall a list of words. I will read a list of 12 unrelated words, and as soon as the list is over, I would like you to write down as many words as you can remember. You can write down the words in any order, and it is better to guess than to leave a space blank. Any questions?"

Instructions for the Delayed Group: "This experiment tests your ability to recall two different lists. I will read a list of 12 unrelated words, and then I'll read a list of the digits 1 through 9 in random order. I would like you to write down the digits in order on the first line on your answer sheet and then, when I indicate, write down the words. You can write down the words in any order, but you need to write down the digits in the original presentation order. It is better to guess than to leave a space blank. Any questions?"

Instructions for the Continual Distractor Group: "This experiment tests your ability to recall two different lists. I will read a list of 12 unrelated words. After I read each word, I'll read a list of the digits 1 through 9 in random order. I would like you to write down the digits in order on the first line on your answer sheet. When you have finished, I will then read the second word on the list and then another list of digits. I will alternate reading a word and a list of digits until all 12 words have been read. At the end, I would like you to write down as many of the words as you can remember. You can write down the words in any order, but you need to write down the digits in the original presentation order. It is better to guess than to leave a space blank. Any questions?"

Scoring and Analysis: For each list, count the number of times the first word was written down; it does not matter where the word was written down as long as it appeared on the list. This number will range from 0 to 8. Do the same for each of the other serial positions. Construct three serial position functions, one for each condition. To do this, add up the individual subject data, and divide by the number of subjects.

Optional Enhancements: Score performance on the distractor task, and plot recall as individual serial positions.

Source: Based on experiments by Glanzer & Cunitz (1966), Bjork & Whitten (1974), and Watkins, Neath, & Sechler (1989).

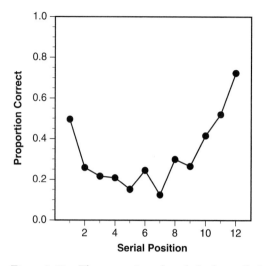

Figure 3.11 The proportion of words freely recalled as a function of serial position in the continual distractor paradigm. Each word, including the final word, was followed by a distractor task in which the subject heard nine digits presented in random order and then recalled these items.   SOURCE: From "Recency Effect in Recall of a Word List When an Immediate Memory Task Is Performed," by M. J. Watkins, I. Neath, and E. S. Sechler, 1989, *American Journal of Psychology, 102,* 265–270. Copyright © 1989 University of Illinois Press. Reprinted with permission.

The ratio rule suggests that the absolute amount of time that an item has to be remembered is not important. Instead, the recency effect should be similar when the ratios are similar: A ratio of 1 s to 1 s gives the same prediction as a ratio of 1 min to 1 min or 1 hr to 1 hr. Indeed, some recency effects have been observed when the IPI and RI are measured in weeks or years (Baddeley & Hitch, 1977; Pinto & Baddeley, 1991; Roediger & Crowder, 1976).

Some researchers have tried to save the modal model by arguing either that the long-term recency effect is somehow different from the short-term recency effect, or that different processes are used. The experimental data do not support this distinction. For example, Greene (1986) found that variables that affected recency when recall immediately followed list presentation affected recency when recall was delayed in the same way. Given both the existence of the ratio rule and empirical findings that variables affect both the short- and long-term recency effects similarly, it becomes difficult to argue that the two types of recency effects are different.

Koppenaal and Glanzer (1990) noted that in a typical continual distractor experiment, the subjects receive the same distractor task after every list item. Because of the extensive practice on the task, Koppenaal and Glanzer argued, subjects might be able to learn to time-share, alternating their processing between rehearsing the list items to keep the last few in short-term memory and performing the distractor task. If this view is correct, when the task changes, the time-sharing mechanism should be disrupted and subjects should not be able to keep the final words in short-term memory while performing the new task. Thus, if the type of distractor task is changed, the recency effect should no longer be observed.

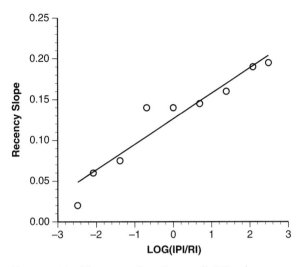

Figure 3.12 The ratio rule in free recall. IPI is the interitem presentation interval, or the time between items; RI is the retention interval, or the time between when the list ends and recall begins.
SOURCE: Data from Nairne, Neath, Serra, & Byun (1997).

They ran an experiment that had more than one kind of distractor task. The arithmetic distractor task required that subjects read a three-digit number out loud, add 1 to the number, and report the sum. The word distractor task required that subjects read six pairs of unrelated words out loud. In one condition, subjects received only the arithmetic task after every list item or only the word task after every list item. In the other condition, the distractor task that followed the final list item was different from the distractor task that followed all the other list items. Free recall in the unchanging distractor condition again yielded a recency effect, but recall in the changing distractor condition showed no recency effect.

This view makes at least three predictions. First, no changing distractor effect should be observable under incidental learning conditions. If subjects are unaware that there will be a recall test at the end of the list, there is no reason for them to rehearse and keep the final items in short-term memory; nor is there a need to develop the elaborate multitasking strategy. Without active rehearsal, the final list items should not be in short-term memory at the time of a surprise free recall test. Second, no changing distractor effect should be observable when the change in distractor activity occurs after the first list item. Koppenaal and Glanzer's (1990) account of the changing distractor effect hinges on the idea of rehearsal disruption: Encountering a novel distractor task within a list disrupts a multitasking rehearsal strategy that permits the subject to both rehearse and perform the distractor task. When the first item is presented, the subject has no way of knowing whether the list is going to be in the changing or the unchanging condition; it is only when the second item and its distractor activity are presented that the subject knows whether the first item was followed by the different distractor task. However, even at this stage, it is not until the third item and its distractor task are presented that the subject knows which distractor task—the one after the first item or the one after the second item—is the unusual one. Performance should be identical in both the unchanging and

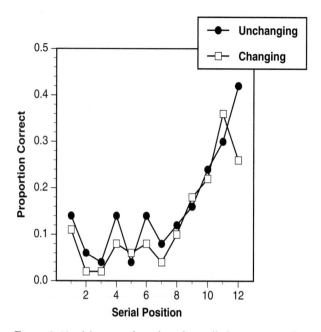

Figure 3.13   Mean number of words recalled in a surprise free recall test following incidental learning when the distractor task stays the same after every item (unchanging) and when there is a novel task after the final item (changing).   SOURCE: Neath (1993a).

changing conditions at position 1. Finally, if the distractor task changes after every list item, there should be no recency effect because there will have been no opportunity to develop the multitasking strategy.

Neath (1993a) tested these predictions. In Experiment 1, subjects were told that the experimenter was interested in what made people hesitate while reading aloud from a computer screen. Subjects were told that they would see three different kinds of stimuli that they should read as quickly and as clearly as they could. The stimuli were actually the same as those used by Koppenaal and Glanzer (1990), but subjects were unaware that a surprise recall test would occur. A surprise test was used so that it would be highly unlikely that the subjects would rehearse the list items. Each subject received only one list, and at the end of presentation subjects were asked to recall the words. Not only was there a recency effect in the unchanging distractor condition, there was a reliable changing distractor effect in the changing condition (see Figure 3.13). This result is problematic for Koppenaal and Glanzer's (1990) account because there should have been no information left in STS and thus no recency. And even if there were recency, there should be no effect of changing the distractor, because there was no rehearsal to disrupt.

A second experiment showed that recall is impaired for the first item if the first item is followed by the novel task. The effect is observable at any serial position.

In a final experiment, Neath (1993a) again used an unchanging and a changing condition, but also added a third condition in which a different distractor task occurred after every item—the continually changing condition. In this condition, each of the five list items was followed by a different distractor task. The rehearsal disruption account predicts

Table 3.2 Summary of experiments that examine the recency effect in free recall and the effect of placing various kinds of distractor tasks after various items

Manipulation	Result	Example Reference
No distractor task	Recency effect	Murdock (1962)
Distractor task after final item only	Recency disappears	Glanzer & Cunitz (1965)
Distractor after every item, including the final (continual distractor paradigm)	Recency reappears	Bjork & Whitten (1974)
Distractor task A after every item except distractor task B after final item	Recency disappeares (changing distractor effect)	Koppenaal & Glanzer (1992)
Different distractor tasks after every item	Recency reappears	Neath (1993a)

a changing distractor effect at every serial position, and thus predicts no recency. Neath did find a recency effect in the unchanging condition and no recency effect in the changing condition, but contrary to the prediction of the rehearsal disruption account, there was also a recency effect in the continually changing condition. Thus, there is a recency effect for free recall of items when there is no distractor activity; the recency effect is eliminated when distractor activity follows just the final item; the recency effect returns when there is distractor activity after every item; the recency effect is again eliminated when the distractor task changes after the final item; and the recency effect again emerges when the distractor task changes after every item. These results are clearly problematic for any view that attributes recency to the dumping of items from short-term memory (see also Thapar & Greene, 1993).

Table 3.2 summarizes much of the research on the effects of various distractor tasks on the recency portion of the serial position curve. However, both this summary and the ratio rule focus mainly on recency effects; they do not relate both primacy and recency effects together. Whereas the modal model suggests that primacy and recency effects emerge from different processes, a study by Tan and Ward (2000) suggests that primacy and recency effects might not only be related, but might be due to the same process.

Tan and Ward (2000) used a procedure in which subjects were asked to rehearse out loud. They were shown a list of 20 items and were asked to read each item out loud. The subjects were informed that they could use the interval between words to rehearse any previous items, but they should do so out loud. The data from one condition from their Experiment 1 are shown in Figure 3.14. First, the standard serial position curve is seen when the proportion of items recalled correctly is plotted as a function of the nominal serial position—the order in which the items were presented. However, Figure 3.14 also shows the same data plotted as a function of each item's *functional serial position*—a rank ordering of when each item was last rehearsed. Using this latter measure, Serial Position 20 means that item was the very last item rehearsed out loud; Serial Position 1 means that item was the very first item rehearsed out loud. What is striking about the figure is that it appears that the major determinant of the serial position function is when an item was last rehearsed.

Tan and Ward (2000) demonstrated that an extension of the ratio rule easily accommodates their findings: Rehearsal, in their scheme, reorders the items both in terms of serial position and, more important, in terms of time. They explain previous examples in which variables had different effects on primacy and recency. For example, Glanzer and

Figure 3.14   Proportion of items recalled correctly as a function of nominal (or input) serial position (white squares), and the same data replotted showing the proportion of items correctly recalled as a function of functional serial position (black circles). The functional serial position shows the ranking of when the items were last rehearsed.   SOURCE: Tan & Ward (2000).

Cuntiz (1966) found that faster presentation rates reduced recall of early list items but not of recency items. This was interpreted at the time as support for the modal model. Tan and Ward suggest that the effect of increasing the presentation rate is to prevent the early items from being rehearsed as often as with a slower rate and also to prevent them from being rehearsed near the end of the list. This will change the functional serial position of each item and will look like selective impairment of primacy items. Ward (in press) shows how this account explains the list-length effect shown in Figure 3.8. A similar way of explaining serial position effects in free recall has been offered by Brown, Neath, and Chater (2002).

Summary of the Modal Model

The modal model turns out not to explain the serial position effect in free recall very well. Instead, the ratio rule, perhaps operating in the way described by Tan and Ward (2000), offers a more parsimonious account. There are several other problems—some empirical and some logical—with most versions of the modal model.

First, as Crowder (1976) pointed out, items in sensory memory must be postcategorical because they already have their names. Because these names and other, similar kinds of information presumably reside in secondary memory, there must be some overlap. Although Atkinson and Shiffrin (1968) assume some contact of this sort (see the dotted line in Figure 3.3), most versions do not. Unless information from sensory memory makes contact with long-term store prior to entry into short-term store, there will be no way of identifying or categorizing the information. If information has gone from sensory register to long-term store, does it then go back to sensory register or to short-term store? Why not just stay in long-term store?

A second logical problem also concerns the flow of information between the systems. As Nairne (1996) points out, given the architecture of almost all versions of the modal model, there will always be contamination of one presumed store with the other. Information recalled from long-term memory has to pass through short-term memory on the way in and on the way out. Information in primary memory has to be linked to information in secondary memory so that it can be identified and categorized in the first place. Any response from any task should reflect both stores, and because of this inherent contamination, it would seem impossible to separate the types of codes.

This observation calls into question the general proposal that primary memory codes information on the basis of phonological or acoustic information and secondary memory codes items according to semantic information (Kintsch & Buschke, 1969). Indeed, there is evidence of both acoustic interference in long-term memory (Dale & McGlaughlin, 1971) and semantic confusion errors in primary memory (Shulman, 1970, 1972; Walker & Hulme, 1999).

We have described the development of the modal model, a structural account of short-term memory, in some detail. The two reasons for this in-depth explanation are that (1) the modal model has exerted more influence on memory research for a longer time than any other view, and (2) the modal model is far more sophisticated than many descriptions suggest, with several formal mathematical versions. Nonetheless, the modal model cannot account for (1) the results from the continual distractor paradigm, (2) the related ratio rule, and (3) the changing distractor effect. Furthermore, it suffers two major logical problems, already noted.

Chapter Summary

William James proposed a distinction between primary memory and secondary memory (memory proper). Memory proper occurs when an item is absent for some time from consciousness and has to be revived; in contrast, primary memory concerns items that remain in conscious awareness continuously from their presentation. It was not until the 1950s, however, that most memory researchers proposed distinct systems for storing information over the short and long term. The typical model assumed that (1) short- and long-term memory involve separate memory systems, (2) STM has a limited capacity, and (3) information in STM decays quickly unless actively rehearsed. Much of the evidence supporting the distinction came from studying the serial position function observed with free recall, although data from the Brown-Peterson paradigm were also important. Researchers have long noted empirical and logical problems with this distinction (e.g., Melton, 1963; Crowder, 1982a), most notably the inability to explain recency effects in general. The majority of memory researchers abandoned this approach for ones that emphasized memory processes more than memory structures, as detailed in the next chapter.

Working Memory

While simple qualitative conceptual models have proved very useful, one eventually reaches a point at which some form of detailed and preferably quantitative model is necessary if the concepts are to develop.

—Alan Baddeley (1994)

The previous chapter chronicled the development of the idea of separate memory stores, one devoted to memory for the short term and one for memory for the long term. In this chapter, we examine current views of short-term memory in some detail. The term *working memory* was first introduced by Miller, Galanter, and Pribram (1960, p. 65; see also Atkinson & Shiffrin, 1968, p. 92). It has long been used to reflect the idea that information often has to be retained briefly in a highly accessible state while performing cognitive tasks. One problem is that different researchers use the term in very different ways. Indeed, Kintsch, Healy, Hegarty, Pennington, and Salthouse (1999, p. 436) conclude that "it is rather difficult to identify a common core in terms of the phenomena under consideration" across theories that address working memory.

Three major uses of the term can be identified, however. Alan Baddeley's (1986) working memory is perhaps the single most influential current model of immediate memory. Although initially a theory of memory for the short term, it has been extended to other areas such as reading and language comprehension (see Gathercole & Baddeley, 1993). The second approach characterizes immediate memory as the subset of information that currently has a heightened state of activation (e.g., Cowan, 1988, 1993, 1995; Schneider & Detweiler, 1987; Shiffrin & Schneider, 1977). Although this view is quite similar to Baddeley's conception, there are several major differences. A third view (Engle, Kane, & Tuholski , 1999) uses the term *working memory capacity* to reflect attention rather than memory per se. In contrast to these various working memory views, we finish the chapter with a functional account of the same data, Nairne's (1988, 1990, 2001) feature model.

Baddeley's Working Memory

Alan Baddeley and his colleagues (see Baddeley, 1986, 2000; Baddeley & Hitch, 1974; Baddeley & Logie, 1999) have developed what is currently the most influential view of working memory. Part of their goal was to examine more closely the idea of immediate memory as a place where many basic cognitive operations are carried out—hence the name of the system. The modal model (discussed in the previous chapter) was seen as too limited and restrictive. In contrast, working memory is seen as the combination of a central executive—a controlling attentional mechanism—and a number of subsidiary slave systems (see Figure 4.1). The central executive coordinates activities within the slave systems, two of which have been studied extensively. (We will postpone discussion of the visuo-spatial sketch pad, which sets up and manipulates visual images, until the chapter on imagery.) The slave system known as the phonological loop will be of primary concern, as this is the system that handles the phenomena previously attributed to short-term store.

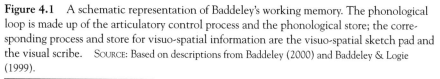

Figure 4.1 A schematic representation of Baddeley's working memory. The phonological loop is made up of the articulatory control process and the phonological store; the corresponding process and store for visuo-spatial information are the visuo-spatial sketch pad and the visual scribe. SOURCE: Based on descriptions from Baddeley (2000) and Baddeley & Logie (1999).

The Phonological Loop

The *phonological loop* has two main components: the phonological store and the articulatory control process. The *phonological store* is a memory store that can retain speech-based information for a short period of time. Unless rehearsed, the traces within the store are assumed to fade and decay within about 2 seconds, after which they are no longer usable. The second component is the *articulatory control process*, which is responsible for two different functions: It translates visual information into a speech-based code and deposits it in the phonological store; and it refreshes a trace in the phonological store, offsetting the decay process. One of the fundamental assumptions of working memory is that the articulatory control process controls subvocal rehearsal, which is analogous to overt rehearsal (saying the item out loud). The amount of verbal information that can be retained is therefore a trade-off between the decay rate (which is assumed to be fixed for a given type of item) and the covert rehearsal rate (which can vary). If rehearsal of a particular item does not occur within a certain amount of time, the memory trace for that item will have decayed too far to be usable. The phonological loop was designed to explain four basic findings: the phonological similarity effect, effects of articulatory suppression, the irrelevant speech effect, and the word-length effect (Baddeley, 1986, 1992a, 1994).

Phonological Similarity   The *phonological similarity effect* refers to the finding that memory is worse for items that sound alike than for items that differ (Baddeley, 1966; R. Conrad, 1964; see Figure 3.1). The sequence PGTCD is harder to recall from memory than the sequence RHXKW because the items in the first sequence share similar sounds. The phonological similarity effect occurs for both visual and auditory presentation because, according to the working memory view, items are retained in a speech-based code in the phonological store. In this store, items interfere with other similar items through some as yet unspecified process (Baddeley, 1992b). If the items are presented aloud, then they have immediate access to the store because they are already in the appropriate, speech-based code. If the items are presented visually, however, they need to be translated into a phonological code by the articulatory control process. A strong prediction is that if we somehow prevent the visual items from being translated by the articulatory control process, then the phonological similarity effect should disappear for visually presented items because they cannot be translated into the appropriate code for deposit into the phonological store. One way of preventing translation is to have the subject engage in articulatory suppression, the second phenomenon that working memory was designed to account for.

Articulatory Suppression   When subjects engage in *articulatory suppression* (Murray, 1968), they repeatedly say a word, such as *the*, over and over out loud. According to the working memory view, this activity occupies the articulatory control process, which is needed for both overt and covert articulation. Therefore, there should be no covert rehearsal using the articulatory control process during articulatory suppression. Without covert rehearsal, visual information cannot be translated into a phonological code and so cannot be placed into the phonological store; therefore, there should be no phonological similarity effect. Auditory items, however, have direct access to the phonological store; they do not need to be recoded. Because auditory information can enter the phonological store without the articulatory control process, there should still be a phonological similarity effect for auditory items when subjects engage in articulatory suppression.

Table 4.1 The proportion of items recalled correctly as a function of presentation modality, phonological similarity, and articulatory suppression

	Silent		Articulatory Suppression	
	Dissimilar	Similar	Dissimilar	Similar
Visual	0.93	0.73	0.57	0.58
Auditory	0.82	0.32	0.45	0.19

NOTE: With no articulatory suppression, dissimilar lists are recalled better than similar lists. With articulatory suppression, there is no phonological similarity effect for visual items, but the effect remains for auditory items. Note that articulatory suppression also greatly reduces overall performance.

SOURCE: From "Some Effects of Minimizing Articulation on Short-Term Retention," by L. R. Peterson and S. T. Johnson, 1971, *Journal of Verbal Learning and Verbal Behavior, 10*, 346–354. Copyright © 1971 Academic Press, Inc. Reprinted with permission.

The results from a study by Peterson and Johnson (1971) are shown in Table 4.1. In the silent condition, recall of the dissimilar items is better than recall of the similar items for both visual and auditory presentation. In the articulatory suppression condition, recall of dissimilar and similar items is equivalent for visually presented information, but there is still an advantage for dissimilar items for auditory information (Baddeley, Lewis, & Vallar, 1984; Estes, 1973; Levy, 1971; Longoni, Richardson, & Aiello, 1993; Murray, 1968; Peterson & Johnson, 1971).

The Irrelevant Speech Effect   The third phenomenon that working memory was designed to account for is the *irrelevant speech effect*. Colle and Welsh (1976) had two groups of subjects recall visually presented consonants, but one group saw the consonants while some irrelevant speech was played in the background. Relative to the subjects in the quiet condition, subjects who heard irrelevant speech were not as successful in recalling the information. According to working memory, the phonemes from the irrelevant speech enter the phonological store and interfere with the information about the visually presented items. Given this explanation, we can make three predictions. First, articulatory suppression should remove the irrelevant speech effect because the articulation will prevent the visually presented items from entering the phonological store. Although the irrelevant speech can still enter the store, the to-be-remembered items will not. Second, because the basis is interference at the level of the phoneme, it should not matter whether the irrelevant speech is a single phoneme or a multisyllable word; what *is* important is the similarity of the phonemes in the irrelevant speech to the phonemes in the to-be-remembered items. Third, nonspeech items, such as tones, should not produce an irrelevant speech effect. Salamé and Baddeley (1982) confirmed these predictions.

The Word-Length Effect   The fourth phenomenon that working memory was designed to account for is the *word-length effect*—the finding that short words (*man, dog*) are recalled better than long words (*gentleman, canine*). Mackworth (1963) first reported the high correlation between reading rate and memory span, but because she was interested primarily in identifying limits in iconic memory (or the *visual image*, as she termed it), she did not measure word length precisely. Nonetheless, over five experiments with a variety of stimuli, including pictures, letters, digits, and colors, she found that "the amount reported

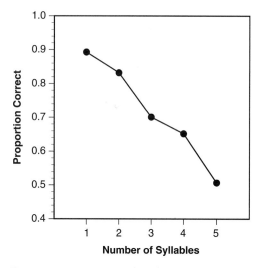

Figure 4.2   Proportion of words recalled correctly as a function of the number of syllables.   SOURCE: From "Word Length and the Structure of Short-Term Memory," by A. D. Baddeley, N. Thomson, and M. Buchanan, 1975, *Journal of Verbal Learning and Verbal Behavior, 14,* 575–589. Copyright © 1975 Academic Press, Inc. Reprinted with permission.

was proportional to the speed of reporting the individual items" (Mackworth, 1963, p. 81). Watkins (1972) and Watkins and Watkins (1973) reported effects of word length as a function of modality and serial position in both free and serial recall. In all cases, words of one syllable were recalled better than words of four syllables, and the effect was also slightly larger for visually presented items than for auditory items.

Word length can be measured in two different ways. The *syllable-based word-length effect* refers to the finding that words with fewer syllables are recalled better than equivalent words that have more syllables. The stimuli were selected so that the only important difference was the number of syllables. Each list contained the name of an animal, a disease, a country, and so forth. For example, the one-syllable list contained *stoat, mumps, Greece, Maine,* and *zinc,* and the four-syllable list contained *rhinoceros, diphtheria, Australia, Alabama,* and *uranium.* Figure 4.2 shows the results: As the number of syllables in the words increased, the proportion of words that could be recalled decreased.

Baddeley, Thomson, and Buchanan (1975) also plotted their data in a different form, measuring the reading rate of their subjects (in words per second). When this measure is used, rather than just syllables, the relationship between the time to say a word and the ability to recall a series of items becomes even more striking. These results are shown in Figure 4.3, indicating a linear relationship between how long it takes to pronounce a word and the level of recall.

The explanation of the word-length effect, according to working memory, is that the number of items that can be immediately recalled depends on how often each item can be rehearsed subvocally by the articulatory control process. This process is used to refresh the decaying traces in the phonological store. The shorter the items (in terms of pronunciation time), the more items can be rehearsed before a particular trace decays.

Figure 4.3 Proportion of words recalled correctly as a function of time required to read the words (in words per second).
Source: From "Word Length and the Structure of Short-Term Memory," by A. D. Baddeley, N. Thomson, and M. Buchanan, 1975, *Journal of Verbal Learning and Verbal Behavior, 14*, 575–589. Copyright © 1975 Academic Press, Inc. Reprinted with permission.

Baddeley, Thomson, and Buchanan (1975) explored the effect of word length in terms of pronunciation time. They demonstrated that even when items are equated for meaning and word frequency, if one set of words takes less time to pronounce than another set, memory will be better for the shorter items. The stimuli from their Experiment 3 are reproduced in Table 4.4. This word-length effect is referred to as the *time-based word-length effect* because the only systematic difference between the words is the time needed to pronounce them (Cowan, Day, Saults, Keller, Johnson, & Flores, 1992).

The time-based word-length effect is captured by a very simple equation. One critical assumption is that overt pronunciation rate is correlated with the speed that the articulatory loop can support subvocal rehearsal. Given this assumption, the relationship between memory span, s, for verbal items of type i can be described as a linear function of pronunciation rate, r, and the duration of the verbal trace, t (Schweickert, Guentert, & Hersberger, 1990):

$$s_i = r_i t \qquad\qquad\qquad (4.1)$$

Experimenters can measure both span, s in the equation, and pronunciation rate, r. They can then solve for the third variable, the duration of the trace, t. Perhaps the most compelling evidence supporting this view is the relative consistency of the estimated duration. As Schweickert and Boruff (1986) put it, "The mean of these trace duration estimates is 1.6 s. Considering the variety of methods for presenting the stimuli and measuring the spans and pronunciation rates, one is struck more by the agreement than by the differences" (p. 420). Because of the consistency of this finding, the word-length effect is seen as "the best remaining solid evidence in favor of temporary memory storage" (Cowan, 1995, p. 42).

Experiment *The Syllable-Based Word-Length Effect*

Purpose: To demonstrate the effect of word length on immediate serial recall

Subjects: Twenty subjects are recommended.

Materials: Table D in the Appendix contains eight short words and eight long words. Construct ten lists of five words each, using these words in a different random order for each subject. Each subject will need an answer sheet on which to write responses. It is useful to have five spaces marked for the subjects to write down the five responses.

Design: This is a within-subjects design, because each subject receives each level of the experimental condition, word length.

Procedure: Inform the subjects that this is an experiment on memory. Tell them that they will hear a list of five words and that they will be asked to recall the words in order. Read each list aloud at the rate of one word per second. As soon as the last word is read, the subjects should begin writing down their responses. For this experiment, serial recall is required. With serial recall, the subject must write down the first word first, the second word second, and so forth. If they cannot remember a word, have them write an X and proceed to the next word. They are not allowed to go back and change their responses. Allow about 20 seconds for recall, then read the next list.

Instructions: "This is an experiment on memory. I will read five words out loud, and then I would like you to recall them in order. Simply write the first word you heard in the first blank on your answer sheet, then write the second, and so on. It is important that you write the words in order. If you cannot remember a particular word, write an X in that blank and proceed to the next word. You are not allowed to go back and fill in a blank or change a response once you have written it down. Any questions?"

Scoring and Analysis: For each subject, count the number of words recalled in order for each word length and compute the average. A one-way analysis of variance with length as a repeated measure can be used to analyze the results.

SOURCE: Adapted from "Word Length and the Structure of Short-Term Memory," by A. D. Baddeley, N. Thomson, and M. Buchanan, 1975, *Journal of Verbal Learning and Verbal Behavior, 14*, 575–589.

This relationship, regardless of the underlying theoretical explanation, has important implications. For example, one component of many intelligence tests is a memory span task. Subjects are tested to see how many items—often digits—they can recall in order. Ellis and Hennelly (1980) showed that apparent differences in memory span and IQ between Welsh- and English-speaking subjects may be ascribed to the relatively longer time needed to say the Welsh digits compared to the English digits. The fact that it takes longer to pronounce the digits 1–9 in Welsh than in English reduces the number of items that can be recalled correctly. Bilingual Welsh-English speakers have higher memory spans and higher measures of intelligence when tested in English than when tested in Welsh. It appears that the language most optimized for digit span is Cantonese (cited in Naveh-Benjamin & Ayres, 1986), where the average digit span approaches nine or even more items, compared with seven for English.

One prediction of working memory's account of the word-length effect is that articulatory suppression should remove the effect for both auditory and visual items, because articulatory suppression prevents the items from being rehearsed with the subvocal articulatory control process. Baddeley, Thomson, and Buchanan (1975, Experiment 8) presented subjects with five-word lists for immediate serial recall. There were two word lengths (one and five syllables), two presentation modalities (auditory and visual), and two articulatory conditions (suppression and no suppression). According to the working memory view, articulatory suppression prevents subjects from registering visually presented items in the phonological store because the articulatory control process is not available. Although auditory items have automatic access to the phonological store, articulatory suppression prevents rehearsal of these items because the articulatory control process is not available. Baddeley, Thomson, and Buchanan observed appropriate effects of word length for the no suppression groups, but articulatory suppression eliminated the word-length effect *only* for the visual group; the effect of word length remained in the auditory modality with articulatory suppression group. Because articulatory suppression should remove the word-length effect regardless of presentation modality, the finding that the word-length effect remained for auditory items is problematic for the working memory view.

Baddeley (1986) argued that subjects may be rehearsing during recall, refreshing the decaying trace in the phonological store while simultaneously recalling items. This is more likely for auditory items because they are automatically registered in the phonological store and do not require conversion using the articulatory control process during presentation. If this is the case, then requiring articulatory suppression not only during presentation but also throughout recall should eliminate the word-length effect for auditory items. Baddeley, Lewis, and Vallar (1984, Experiment 4) conducted an experiment almost identical to Experiment 8 of Baddeley, Thomson, and Buchanan (1975). Five-item lists of auditory items were presented for immediate serial recall; the short words had one syllable and the long words had five syllables. The main difference was that whereas Baddeley et al. (1975) had subjects engage in articulatory suppression only during presentation, Baddeley et al. (1984) had subjects engage in articulatory suppression during both presentation and throughout the entire recall period. The data are summarized in Table 4.2. The word-length effect was present when suppression occurred only during presentation but was eliminated when suppression continued throughout the recall period. To the extent that subvocal rehearsal is prevented during both presentation and recall, there will be no word-length effect, just as working memory predicts (Baddeley, 1992a).

Another prediction concerns the interaction between word length, articulatory suppression, and phonological similarity. Articulatory suppression should remove the

Table 4.2 Percentage of short and long words recalled correctly as a function of two types of articulatory suppression

	Quiet	Suppression Presentation Only	Quiet	Suppression Presentation and Recall
Short	83.7	71.0	78.0	46.9
Long	62.0	53.7	61.0	41.7

NOTE: Articulatory suppression eliminates the word-length effect for auditory items only when it occurs during both presentation and recall.

SOURCE: Data in first and second columns from "Word Length and the Structure of Short-Term Memory," by A. D. Baddeley, N. Thomson, and M. Buchanan, 1975, *Journal of Verbal Learning and Verbal Behavior, 14,* 575–589. Copyright © 1975 Academic Press, Inc. Data in third and fourth columns from "Exploring the Articulatory Loop," by A. D. Baddeley, V. J. Lewis, and G. Vallar, 1984, *Quarterly Journal of Experimental Psychology, 36,* 233–252. Adapted with permission.

Table 4.3 The percentage of auditory items recalled correctly as a function of word length, phonological similarity, and articulatory suppression

	Silent		Articulatory Suppression	
	Dissimilar	*Similar*	*Dissimilar*	*Similar*
Short	86.2	63.2	52.0	25.0
Long	73.7	31.2	49.4	17.5

NOTE: With no articulatory suppression, dissimilar lists are recalled better than similar lists, and short lists are recalled better than long lists. With articulatory suppression, there is still a phonological similarity effect, but the word-length effect (52.0 versus 49.4 and 25.0 versus 17.5) is eliminated.

SOURCE: Data from Longoni, Richardson, & Aiello (1993).

word-length effect for both visual and auditory items, but it should remove the phonological similarity effect only for visual items, not for auditory items. We have discussed both of these findings separately. However, the working memory view predicts that, at the same time that articulatory suppression is removing the word-length effect, the phonological similarity effect should be removed for visual but remain for auditory presentation. The results from a study by Longoni, Richardson, and Aiello (1993) using auditory presentation are shown in Table 4.3.

The Episodic Buffer

One problem with early accounts of working memory is explaining how items are recalled at all when subjects engage in articulatory suppression. As the data in Tables 4.2 and 4.3 show, recall is still much higher than it should be if all rehearsal is prohibited. To address this problem, Baddeley (2000) added another system to working memory: the episodic buffer (see Figure 4.1). This component is designed to function as a "'back-up store' that is capable of supporting serial recall, and presumably of integrating phonological, visual and possibly other types of information" (Baddeley, 2000, p. 419). Given the newness of this concept, it has yet to be subjected to rigorous experimental tests.

It is possible that the episodic buffer may also alleviate some of the problems concerning the meaningfulness of stimuli. In the original account, items in the phonological store were treated as equivalent even when they varied in terms of meaningfulness. The problem for working memory was that meaningfulness is clearly an important factor in situations where working memory is invoked; for example, memory span is lower for nonwords than for words (Hulme, Maughan & Brown, 1991).

Critique of Working Memory

The major problem with working memory, particularly the phonological loop, is that recent data cast doubt on the trade-off between rehearsal and decay (see Nairne, 2002, for an extended discussion). At its core, working memory proposes that items decay unless refreshed via articulatory rehearsal. This idea, most clearly illustrated in the time-based word-length effect, serves as the heart of the verbal processing capabilities of the phonological loop.

Table 4.4 The top two rows show the short and long stimuli used by Baddeley et al. (1975); the bottom two rows show the short and long stimuli used by Lovatt, Avons, & Masterson (2000). Pronunciation times and percent recalled are from data reported by Lovatt et al. (2000).

Word Type	Stimuli	Mean Pronunciation Time	Percent Recalled
Short	bishop, pectin, ember, wicket, wiggle, pewter, tipple, hackle, decor, phallic	530 ms	70.7 %
Long	Friday, coerce, humane, harpoon, nitrate, cyclone, morphine, tycoon, voodoo, zygote	693 ms	65.5 %
Short	button, tractor, whistle, spider, pencil, pocket, shovel, candle	605 ms	60.7 %
Long	pebbles, curtains, station, needle, branches, canoes, necklace, robot	793 ms	65.1 %

Lovatt, Avons, and Masterson (2000, 2002) reported a series of experiments in which they examined recall of different sets of long and short words. One experiment used the same stimuli that Baddeley et al. (1975) had used and replicated the finding. However, a different set of words, also equated except for pronunciation time, yielded a negative or reverse word-length effect; if anything, the long words were recalled slightly better than the short words. Both sets of words, their mean pronunciation times, and the recall levels are shown in Table 4.4. Caplan, Rochon, and Waters (1992) have reported similar results with yet another set of stimuli. In their experiment, the short words took, on average, 546 ms to say and the long words took 720 ms. However, only 65.6% of the short words were recalled, compared to 76.4% of the long words. Neath, Bireta, and Surprenant (in press) report yet another set of words that vary in pronunciation time but do not produce a time-based word-length effect. Working memory unambiguously states that if an item takes longer to say, it will be recalled less well, yet these data show the opposite finding. It seems that the time-based word-length effect can be observed only with the original set of stimuli; there are now half a dozen sets of words that produce either no time-based word-length effect or even a reverse effect, but only one set that produces a positive result.

CogLab Experiment

http://coglab.wadsworth.com/experiments/MemorySpan/

A second problem concerns the interpretation of span data. Almost all of the key data come from a paradigm referred to as *immediate serial recall*. For example, memory span tests assess how many items of various kinds a person can recall correctly in order half the time. The resulting span is taken as providing critical evidence in support of a limited capacity system. Nairne and Neath (2001) reported an experiment in which the same general procedure was used: Subjects were presented with lists of items that varied in length from two to nine items and then were tested on their memory for the order. The results are shown in Figure 4.4.

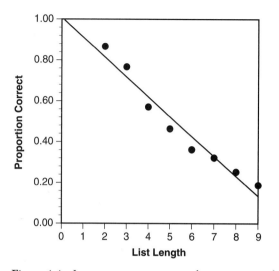

Figure 4.4   Long-term memory span: the proportion of items correctly recalled in order as a function of list length. There was a 5-minute delay between end of list presentation and recall.
Source: Nairne & Neath (2001).

Just as other researchers had found, Nairne and Neath (2001) found that span for two-syllable words was approximately 5. However, they had delayed the memory test by 5 minutes, which is well beyond the capability of short-term or working memory. There are three possible interpretations.

First, Nairne and Neath measured the span of long-term memory using the same technique that is used to measure the capacity of short-term memory and found that the capacity limit is about four or five. If this is true, you should consider carefully what you store in long-term memory: You have only five slots available at any one time! A second interpretation is that neither the long-term memory span nor the short-term memory span techniques actually measure span. Rather, the capacity limit has to do with remembering items *in a particular order*. We examine this issue in detail in Chapter 13. A third possibility is that, at least within the working memory framework of Baddeley, performance on this task is supported by the episodic buffer. If so, then the buffer has a far smaller capacity than would otherwise be useful and necessary to explain performance on other tasks (see Baddeley, 2000).

Other problems with working memory include a continuing inability to explain precisely how items in the phonological store interfere (Baddeley, 1992b). Because there is no specific interference mechanism, the phonological similarity effect is not really explained. With regard to the irrelevant speech effect, several studies have been unable to replicate the key finding that the magnitude of the irrelevant speech effect is related to the phonological similarity between the relevant and irrelevant items (Jones & Macken, 1995; LeCompte & Shaibe, 1997). Moreover, it has been shown that pure tones disrupt serial recall (Jones & Macken, 1993; LeCompte, Neely, & Wilson, 1997), and thus the irrelevant speech effect may not require speech. Both of these findings contradict predictions of working memory (see also Martin, 1993; Neath, Farley, & Surprenant, 2003).

A second problem concerns several findings that involve presentation modality. Although working memory predicts some interactions involving presentation modality (for example, that articulatory suppression will eliminate the phonological similarity effect for visual but not auditory items), it does not explain the basic modality effect—the better recall of the final item in a list that is presented auditorily rather than visually (see Chapter 2). As another example, the syllable-based word-length effect is larger for visually presented items than for auditory items (Baddeley, Thomson, & Buchanan, 1975, Experiment 8; Watkins & Watkins, 1973), but working memory does not address this finding.

A third problem concerns exactly how the many subsystems of working memory, such as the phonological loop, the episodic buffer, and episodic long-term memory, interact. They need to interact to allow the model to handle findings (reviewed below) of influences of long-term memory on immediate serial recall, and also to explain where items are recalled from when subjects engage in articulatory suppression. With no detailed description of the process, it is difficult to see how this approach explains the data.

A final problem concerns how order information is retained. The majority of findings that working memory was designed to explain are observed using immediate serial recall. In these tests, subjects must not only recall the items, but must recall them in the correct order. Whereas the verbal version of working memory (e.g., Baddeley & Logie, 1999) does not explicitly state how order information is retained, some quantitative versions do. However, among these more specific models, three different accounts have been offered (Burgess & Hitch, 1999; Henson, 1998; Page & Norris, 1998).

Baddeley's version of working memory should be seen as an ongoing process in which the ideas are still being refined and more precisely specified. Given the complexity of the topic, it should not be surprising that a simple model does not fare well. It remains to be seen whether modifications can be made that will correct or resolve the problems mentioned here or whether quantitative versions, as Baddeley (1994) advocates, can be derived that give the model more precision in its operation and predictions.

Working Memory as Activation: The Embedded-Processes Model

The second current view of immediate memory is that it is a subset of information that is currently in a heightened state of activation (for example, Cowan, 1988, 1993; Shiffrin, 1993). This view is similar to Baddeley's (1986, 1994) working memory and is sometimes (confusingly) also called working memory. The main similarities between the two are the use of decay as the fundamental cause of forgetting over the short term and the role of immediate memory as the "place" where cognitive "work" is performed. The activation view differs from Baddeley's account in that (1) it does not divide immediate memory into separate subsystems, such as the visuo-spatial sketch pad or the phonological loop, and (2) it specifically includes a long-term memory contribution (Cowan, 1999). Indeed, some properties originally ascribed to working memory are now being relegated to long-term memory (see Cowan, 1999, pp. 81–82, for an example).

The activation view encompasses at least two different approaches. One has as its goal a simulation model and specifies in great detail how the proposed system operates (e.g., Schneider & Detweiler, 1987). The second approach favors simplicity: "It appears most efficient for the time being to try to stay near the most basic level of the hypothesis space until the fundamental issues are resolved, even though this results in a model too general to make specific predictions in many situations" (Cowan, 1995, p. 24). We shall examine the latter view, because the more complex versions (e.g., Anderson, 1983a; Schneider & Detweiler, 1987) can be seen as variants of the former. With the exception of providing many elaborations and subdivisions, the major difference between Anderson (1983a) and Cowan (1988) is that the former does not include sensory stores and omits mention of selective attention. The major difference between Schneider and Detweiler (1987) and Cowan (1988) is similarly the division into eight separate modules (visual, auditory, speech, lexical, semantic, motor, mood, and context), each of which is embedded in a connectionist network. Cowan's view, then, is a framework that has many possible instantiations.

In Cowan's (1999) embedded-processes model, the term *working memory* "refers to cognitive processes that retain information in an unusually accessible state" (p. 62). This view emphasizes that working memory is a set of processes that are contained within long-term memory. In Figure 4.5, the large box represents all of memory. A subset of the information in memory is in a temporarily heightened state of activation (labeled "Activated Memory"). A subset of this information is the current focus of attention and is the information that is available to conscious awareness. Thus, an item can be activated but not the focus of attention; all items that are in the focus of attention, however, are activated.

The sensory store retains items for only a few hundred milliseconds (see Chapter 2). Information in the sensory store that is activated can undergo both sensory and semantic processing. The central executive is a set of processes that are influenced by instructions and incentives. For example, a person will attend to a stimulus that is novel, to one that has personal significance, and to those that are important for the current task. The focus of attention is limited to approximately four unrelated items (Cowan, 2001); in addition to this item-based limit, there is a time-based limit on the activation of memory of approximately 10 to 20 seconds unless the item is reactivated.

Baddeley's (1986) version of working memory addresses only phonological and visuo-spatial forms of representations, but Cowan's (1999) view emphasizes other forms, including nonverbal sounds and tactile information. Temporarily activated items will decay over time and are also subject to interference from similar items. Items can remain in the focus of attention or in a heightened state of activation thgough rehearsal, but also through other processes. For example, searching through a list of items in memory can help reactivate them. Retrieval means having the items in the focus of attention at the time they are needed. If an item is in the focus of attention, recall is almost always successful. Retrieval of items that are not in the focus of activation can fail because of both decay and interference.

The embedded-processes model accounts for many of the effects described previously in a way that is similar to that of Baddeley's (1986, 2000) version of working memory. One area in which the embedded-processes model has a distinct advantage over Baddeley's version concerns long-term memory effects on immediate memory tasks. In Cowan's (1999) model, working memory is essentially activated long-term memory; thus, long-term memory is predicted to play a substantial role in short-term memory tasks. In contrast, Baddeley's original version of working memory allowed only the phonological loop to play a major role. The episodic buffer has recently been added, but its operation and interaction with the other systems are not yet well specified.

One common finding on many long-term memory tasks is that concrete words, such as *army*, are recalled better than otherwise equivalent abstract words, such as *amount*

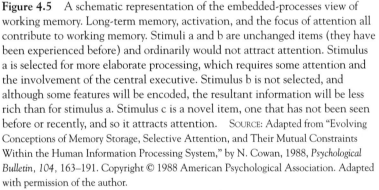

Figure 4.5 A schematic representation of the embedded-processes view of working memory. Long-term memory, activation, and the focus of attention all contribute to working memory. Stimuli a and b are unchanged items (they have been experienced before) and ordinarily would not attract attention. Stimulus a is selected for more elaborate processing, which requires some attention and the involvement of the central executive. Stimulus b is not selected, and although some features will be encoded, the resultant information will be less rich than for stimulus a. Stimulus c is a novel item, one that has not been seen before or recently, and so it attracts attention. Source: Adapted from "Evolving Conceptions of Memory Storage, Selective Attention, and Their Mutual Constraints Within the Human Information Processing System," by N. Cowan, 1988, *Psychological Bulletin, 104,* 163–191. Copyright © 1988 American Psychological Association. Adapted with permission of the author.

(Paivio, Yuille, & Madigan, 1968). The explanation of this concreteness effect is usually that concrete items have more forms of representation in long-term memory (Paivio, 1969; see Chapter 11) or more associates in semantic memory (Jones, 1988; see Chapter 10). Even though the concreteness effect has its locus in long-term memory, it is also observable on immediate serial recall tests and tests that measure memory span (Walker & Hulme, 1999). As a second example of long-term memory effects on short-term memory tasks, Roodenrys and Quinlan (2000) found that high-frequency words were recalled better on immediate serial recall tests than were low-frequency words.

The demonstration of long-term memory effects in working memory is most serious for memory span—the number of items that can be immediately recalled in order. Baddeley's (1986) version of working memory says that memory span is determined by

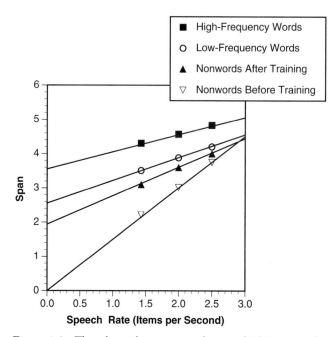

Figure 4.6   The relation between speech rate, which is assumed to be correlated with rehearsal rate, and memory span. If span is determined by decay offset by rehearsal, as in phonological loop models, then span should be 0 when the speech rate is 0. The data are hypothetical, but realistic.

how well rehearsal offsets decay within the phonological loop. If memory span is solely a function of pronunciation rate and the duration of the verbal trace, then when there is no rehearsal, span must be zero (Schweickert, Guentert, & Hersberger, 1990). When memory span is plotted as a function of speech rate (as in Figure 4.6) and the best-fitting line is calculated, the key issue is whether this line intercepts the y-axis at 0. Hulme, Maughan, and Brown (1991) did find an approximately zero intercept when they used nonwords (Italian words with subjects who knew no Italian), and both Brown and Hulme (1992) and Hulme, Roodenrys, Brown, and Mercer (1995) also found an approximately zero intercept for nonwords. However, all of these researchers found that when subjects became more familiar with the stimuli, the intercepts increased. Stuart and Hulme (2000) even found that familiarizing subjects with low-frequency words 24 hours prior to the memory span assessment improved subjects' performance.

When any stimuli other than unfamiliar nonwords are used, the predictions of the decay offset by rehearsal account are no longer accurate. There is clear evidence that information from long-term memory affects memory span. Span, then, is not be a pure measure of working memory (Nairne & Neath, 2001; Tehan & Lalor, 2000; Watkins, 1977).

A second advantage of the embedded-processes model over other versions of working memory is that it predicts that output time will have an effect on measures of span. For example, Cowan, Wood, Wood, Keller, Nugent, and Keller (1998) showed that subjects' articulation rates and the duration of pauses between items when recalling were not correlated with each other. However, both were related to span. Moreover, Dosher (1999;

Dosher & Ma, 1998) found that output time was a better predictor of recall than pronunciation time. This is readily accounted for by noting that searching through a set of items can help to reactivate them by bringing them into the focus of attention (Cowan, 1992). Thus, covert rehearsal during acquisition and search during retrieval can both maintain items and influence performance, with particular experimental factors determining the precise role each processes plays.

There are three main problems with this approach. First, the term *activation* is often not defined very precisely. Typically, researchers use operational definitions to specify what is meant by activation. For example, activation is usually defined by reference to a particular behavioral task; thus, Cowan (1993) offers one definition as "the temporary state of memory representations that would allow these representations to have a priming effect on subsequent stimuli" (p. 162). Although the concept has widespread acceptance, particularly for priming data, there are other explanations of priming (see Chapter 10). Some researchers suggest that activation corresponds to a pattern of activity across a subset of individual neurons. This suggestion runs into problems, however, as there are many instances in which the nervous system uses a change in the rate of firing, rather than activity versus no activity, to code information.

The second problem concerns the assumption of deactivation. Although the concept of decay within connectionist networks has been used without controversy (e.g., Rumelhart & McClelland, 1986), the concept has been vigorously and repeatedly rejected in the memory literature (McGeoch, 1932; Osgood, 1953; see Chapter 6). The main objection has been that time is not a causal agent: Iron rusts over time, but time does not cause rust, oxidation does. In memory, information appears lost over time, but time should not be given the causal role; some other activity (usually defined as interference) that unfolds over time should be the causal agent. The underspecification of how activated information becomes deactivated, and whether it can become inhibited, is a major omission in this view.

In defense of the activation view, its proponents (see Cowan, 1995, 1999, 2001) recognize some of these weaknesses and note that more development is necessary. It is conceivable that these problems may be solved or greatly mitigated with further theoretical work and more precise descriptions.

Working Memory Capacity

A lot of research has focused on working memory capacity—the extent to which a person can control and sustain attention in the face of interference and distraction. This capacity, which varies among individuals, reflects the ability to activate items in memory, to bring or maintain them in the focus of attention, and to ignore or disregard interfering items or distractions (Engle, Kane, & Tuholski, 1999). The reason for the interest in measures of working memory capacity is that they correlate highly with many cognitive tasks, including reading comprehension, language comprehension, spelling, vocabulary learning, writing, and reasoning (see Engle, Tuholski, Laughlin, & Conway, 1999). The assumption is that measures of working memory capacity reflect some ability that is fundamental to cognitive operations.

CogLab Experiment
http://coglab.wadsworth.com/experiments/OperationSpan/

Working memory capacity can be measured by a variety of tasks, including reading span (Daneman & Carpenter, 1980) and operation span (Turner & Engle, 1989). To measure a person's operation span, for example, subjects are asked to perform mathematical calculations and to remember the order in which a list of words was presented. They see a mathematical question, such as "Is $(4/2) - 1 = 1$?" and they are asked to respond yes or no. They then read a word, and then see another math question. After a series of problems and words have been presented, the subjects are asked to recall the words in order. For subjects who were more than 85% accurate in evaluating the math problems, the operation span is defined as the sum of sequence lengths recalled correctly. Thus, if a subject recalled a list of three words correctly in order, 3 would be added to the operation span score (see Conway & Engle, 1996).

For Engle (2001), working memory capacity is very different from capacity as used in discussions of short-term memory (i.e., 7±2) and also capacity as used in discussions of Baddeley's (1986) working memory (i.e., 2 seconds). Rather, it is about "limitations in the ability to use controlled processing to maintain information in an active, quickly retrievable state. . . . WM capacity is not about storage and processing but is about retention over a period in which there is distraction or shift of attention away from the stored information" (p. 301).

Individuals with larger working memory capacity (as measured by tasks such as operation span) are better able to ignore irrelevant but potentially distracting information. For example, Conway, Cowan, and Bunting (2001) had subjects participate in a *dichotic listening task*. In this task, subjects are asked to shadow (repeat out loud) everything they hear in one ear (referred to as the attended channel) and to ignore everything that is presented to their other ear (the unattended channel). The subjects chosen for this study were those who scored in the top 25% (high span) and the bottom 25% (low span) of the operation span task. Of key interest was the proportion of times each subject detected his or her own name when it was presented to the ear that was supposed to be ignored. Approximately 20% of the high-span subjects detected their name, compared to 65% of the low-spans. The idea is that with lower working memory capacity, the low-span subjects were less able to ignore the information in the unattended channel. In contrast, the high-span subjects, with more working memory capacity, were better able to block the distracting information (everything on the unattended channel) and so were less likely to hear their name.

The working memory capacity approach, then, is interested not so much in memory per se but rather in determining the components common over multiple tasks. Rather than emphasizing working memory as the place in which information is retained briefly in a highly accessible state while performing cognitive tasks, this view emphasizes the processing that is shared between different cognitive tasks.

The Feature Model

The feature model (Nairne, 1988, 1990) was designed to account for the major effects observed when memory is tested using immediate serial recall, including many of the phenomena described in Chapter 2, such as the recency effect, the modality effect, and the suffix effect, and phenomena described in this chapter, such as the phonological similarity effect and the effects of articulatory suppression. The model gets its name from the fact that items are assumed to be represented as a set of features, a common modeling assumption (Hintzman, 1991). In its simplest form, this assumption states that any item can be represented by a series of 1s, −1s, and 0s. As an analogy, think of a small black-and-white television set. If you look at the screen up close, you will find that each pixel can take on three values: black, white, or broken. The screen uses the same pixels to represent an ice hockey game, a debate, or a commercial. If you were to freeze the screen at any instant and write down the value of each pixel, you would be representing the information as a series of (mostly) 1s and −1s. The value of pixel number 824 is meaningless by itself; it does not tell you whether you are watching a sporting event or a disclaimer that not all plates go up in value. Rather, it is the ordered set of values that represents the particular display. In the feature model, then, no one feature in a vector is meaningful.

The feature model assumes that there are only two types of features. Modality-dependent features represent the conditions of presentation, including presentation modality; modality-independent features represent the nature of the item itself and are generated through internal processes, such as categorization and identification. This follows the distinction, proposed by the broad class of dual-coding models, between an abstract form of representation and a form that more closely represents the physical characteristics (e.g., Durlach & Braida, 1969; Fujisaki & Kawashima, 1970; Pisoni, 1973, 1975; see also Surprenant & Neath, 1996).

Regardless of whether you read the word *dog* silently to yourself or hear someone else say "dog," the modality-independent information will be the same. However, if you hear the word *dog*, the modality-dependent features may represent information such as the person's accent, whether the speaker is male or female, and so on. If you see the word *dog*, the modality-dependent feature may represent information such as whether the word is in upper- or lowercase, what color it is, and so on. Internally generated traces can contain only modality-independent features because there is no modality. There is abundant evidence for this assumption. For example, studies from the imagery literature show many differences between a percept arising from experiencing a stimulus directly and one that is created solely via internal processes (Crowder, 1989a; Nairne & Pusen, 1984; Suengas & Johnson, 1988; Surprenant, 1992).

The modality-dependent features are used to account for the effects previously attributed to echoic memory. Unlike other accounts that place the locus of echoic memory in a separate structure (Crowder & Morton, 1969), the feature model follows Watkins and Watkins (1980) in that modality-dependent information is viewed as just part of the memory representation.

The feature model also distinguishes between primary and secondary memory. Primary memory has no capacity limits, and items in primary memory do not decay. Rather, the major function of primary memory is to construct and maintain cues that may indicate which items were recently presented (see also Raaijmakers & Shiffrin, 1981). The feature model assumes that all memory is cue driven (see Watkins, 1979). The only loss of information from primary memory occurs from interference: Newly entering items can interfere with items that are already in primary memory. A simplifying assumption is that an item can interfere only with the immediately preceding item (see Figure 4.7). At the end of the presentation of a typical list, primary memory will consist of partially degraded traces. In the memory test, subjects must match the degraded primary memory traces with the appropriate intact trace in secondary memory.

For each partially degraded trace in primary memory, the subject tries to select an appropriate recall candidate by comparing the degraded trace with intact traces in the

Item Presented		Primary Memory
1	[+1 −1 +1 +1, +1 −1 +1 −1]	[+1 −1 +1 +1, +1 −1 +1 −1]
		[+1 0 0 +1, +1 0 +1 0]
2	[−1 −1 +1 −1, −1 −1 −1 −1]	[−1 −1 +1 −1, −1 −1 −1 −1]
		[+1 0 0 +1, +1 0 +1 0]
		[−1 0 +1 0, −1 −1 0 −1]
3	[+1 −1 −1 −1, +1 +1 −1 +1]	[+1 −1 −1 −1, +1 +1 −1 +1]
		[+1 0 0 +1, +1 0 +1 0]
		[−1 0 +1 0, −1 −1 0 −1]
		[+1 −1 0 0, +1 0 −1 0]
4	[−1 +1 −1 −1, −1 +1 +1 +1]	[−1 +1 −1 −1, −1 +1 +1 +1]

Figure 4.7 An example of what might happen when four items are presented, assuming perfect encoding and an overwriting probability of 1. The first four features represent modality-independent information, and the second four represent modality-dependent information. Item 1 is presented and is encoded accurately in primary memory. When item 2 is presented, any features in item 1 that overlap with features in item 2 are overwritten (set to 0). The same thing happens when item 3 is presented. Only the last item is completely intact. However, rehearsal can take place. This consists of generating an item, and a generated item can only contain modality-independent features. The rehearsed item(s) can overwrite the modality-independent features of the final item, but the modality-dependent features will remain intact.

secondary memory search set. Typically, the secondary memory search set will consist of items presented on the most recent list, but this is not necessarily always the case. For example, when the same to-be-remembered items are repeated on each list or if the items constitute a well-established group (such as the digits 1–9), the subject will use the appropriate secondary memory search group. However, when the to-be-remembered items come from a larger group (such as unique items on each trial), the search group is likely to be larger.

Even though a subject may have correctly matched a degraded primary memory trace with its intact secondary memory counterpart, the subject still may not produce the item. In general, subjects tend not to recall an item more than once, even if that item actually appeared more than once on the original list (see Hinrichs, Mewaldt, & Redding, 1973). The feature model includes this type of *output interference*. Suppose the subject is trying to find a match for primary memory trace number 2, but mistakenly selects from secondary memory the item that matches the fifth primary trace; the fifth item will be recalled (and scored as incorrect because it is in the wrong order). When it comes time to match primary memory trace number 5, the subject may select the appropriate secondary memory item. However, the subject has already produced this as a response and so is less willing to write this item down again.

Because the feature model is a computer simulation model, all details have to be specified completely. One detail that must be specified is how many features should be used. Items are assumed to have 20 modality-independent features; this number was picked solely to minimize the time required to run the simulation and has no other significance. However, it also turns out that the absolute number of features used is largely irrelevant because the rule that decides how similar two items are relies on the relative, not absolute, number of matching features.

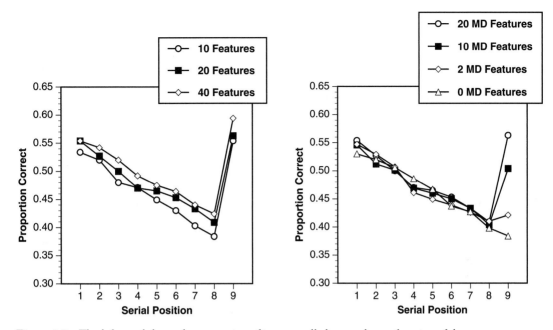

Figure 4.8 The left panel shows the proportion of items recalled correctly as a function of the number of features. The three lines show predicted performance (1) when there are 10 modality-independent and 10 modality-dependent features, (2) when there are 20 of each kind, and (3) when there are 40 of each kind. As the figure shows, there is almost no effect of increasing the absolute number of features. The right panel shows the effect of changing the number of modality-dependent features when the number of modality-independent features is held constant at 20.

The final assumption needed to get the model up and running is that different presentation modalities give rise to modality-dependent features that differ in terms of their discriminability. The key issue is how much a presentation modality differs from inner speech. It is assumed that the visual modality differs the least, the auditory modality differs the most, and other modalities, such as lip-read and mouthed, fall somewhere in between. The important assumption is that in the typical case, auditory presentation gives rise to modality-dependent features that are more useful in identifying the items that were presented than does visual presentation.

Within the model, the basic idea is the acknowledgment that primary memory traces do not exist in a vacuum; rather, they exist as part of a stream of ongoing mental activity (see Johnson & Raye, 1981; Nairne & McNabb, 1985). When interpreting a primary memory trace, the subject needs to discriminate the trace not only from other traces but also from traces that are generated internally. An extensive literature shows that visual presentation and subvocal rehearsal produce similar effects (for reviews, see Baddeley, 1986; Crowder, 1976). Thus, a visually presented item will be quite similar to an internally generated item. Because there is also evidence of differences between visually and auditorily presented items, we end up with a scheme in which auditory items have more modality-dependent features than do visual items, which in turn have more modality-dependent features than do internally generated items (Nairne, 1988, 1990; for further converging evidence, see Surprenant & Neath, 1996). The right panel of Figure 4.8

shows the effect of decreasing the number of modality-dependent features when the number of modality-independent features is held constant.

What makes the feature model seem complex is that it can simulate many different processes simultaneously. Fortunately, each individual process is simple and straightforward, and the key processes are precisely described using four simple equations (see Optional Chapter). To make things even simpler, the feature model exists as a computer program that can be used to make unambiguous predictions about what will and will not happen. An online version of the feature model that can run most of the simulations described in this chapter can be found on the Web at http://rumpole.psych.purdue.edu/models/FeatureModel.html.

Feature Model Operation

Each to-be-remembered item is made up of features. With auditory presentation, we assume there are 20 modality-independent features and 20 modality-dependent features, each of which is randomly set to a value of 1 or –1. These 40 features represent the first item presented. The second item presented also contains 40 features. Retroactive interference occurs, with features from item 2 overwriting features of item 1; specifically, if modality-independent feature number 5 of item 2 has the same value as modality-independent feature number 5 of item 1, then item 1's feature 5 is overwritten by replacing the original value with a value of 0. Then the third item is presented, then the fourth, and so on.

The final item is followed not by any external information but by rehearsal. Because subvocal rehearsal has, by definition, no modality-dependent information (there is no modality!), only the modality-independent features of the final item are subject to overwriting. At the end of list presentation, primary memory contains a trace of each of the items presented. In the typical case, these traces will be degraded because certain features will have been overwritten. The final item, however, will have its modality-dependent features intact.

The subject now tries to match each primary memory item with an intact secondary memory trace. If we are considering the case in which nine digits are presented in random order, the subject will limit the search to the representations of the nine digits in secondary memory. Beginning with the first item, each primary memory item is compared with all secondary memory items in the comparison set. In general, the secondary memory item with the fewest mismatching features will be selected as the candidate for recall. Thus, the secondary memory trace chosen as the response for a particular degraded primary memory trace will typically be that trace with the largest proportion of matching features, relative to the other choices currently available in the secondary memory search set.

Simulations Using the Feature Model

The Serial Position Function   In the feature model, recall generally declines over serial positions because of output interference; this agrees with recent empirical data (Cowan et al., 2002). Items presented later in the list have a greater chance of being mistakenly recalled early on and so are less likely to be produced even if sampled. The pronounced recency effect seen in serial recall of auditory items arises because the modality-dependent features of the last list item are not subject to overwriting. Consequently, there will be extra information available to make a better match between a degraded primary memory item and the appropriate secondary memory item. To the extent that a presentation modality provides useful modality-dependent features (for example, tactile, lip-read, mouthed), there will be a modality effect (see the right panel of Figure 4.8). To the extent that a presentation modality does not provide useful modality-dependent features, there will not be a modality effect. Because visual presentation leads to very little useful extra information, recency effects are not seen with visual presentation and serial recall (LeCompte, 1992). Another way of reducing the usefulness of the modality-dependent information is to use homophones (such as *pear, pare, pair* or *pour, poor, pore*). When a list of auditory homophones is presented, there is no recency effect (Crowder, 1978a). According to the feature model, this is because the undegraded modality-dependent features of the final item will contribute almost no useful information for matching the degraded trace to the original item; the right panel of Figure 4.8 shows these effects. Standard auditory presentation uses 20 modality-independent and 20 modality-dependent features. Standard visual presentation uses 20 modality-independent and 2 modality-dependent features. If the 20 modality-dependent features are all set to be the same (as is the case with homophones), there will be no recency effect.

The Suffix Effect   The suffix effect occurs whenever the modality-dependent features of the final item are overwritten. Two factors influence when this will occur: First, the suffix has to be perceptually grouped with the list items, and second, the stimulus has to have similar modality-dependent information. Thus, a speech suffix will overwrite some of the modality-dependent features of a list of speech items because these features are likely to be similar. Visual suffixes should have little or no effect on auditory list items, and physically similar suffixes should have far larger effects than semantically similar suffixes do (because the locus of recency lies in residual modality-dependent features). The less similar the suffix, the smaller the suffix effect (Morton, Crowder, & Prussin, 1971). If the suffix is grouped in with the list items, then there will also be a suffix effect on more than just the final items because of the increased search set (see Nairne, 1990). This approach has been used to explain the context-dependent suffix effect (see Neath, Surprenant, & Crowder, 1993), as well as modality and suffix effects that are observed in modalities with no apparent acoustic component, such as tactile (Nairne & McNabb, 1985; Watkins & Watkins, 1974) or mouthed or lip-read (Nairne & Crowder, 1982; Spoehr & Corin, 1978) stimuli. To simulate the suffix effect, an additional auditory item is presented but not recalled. Its modality-dependent features will overwrite some of the modality-dependent features of the last to-be-remembered item and will make performance roughly equivalent to a visual condition.

Grouping Effects   The feature model can predict the appropriate modality-based grouping effects. When a temporal gap is inserted in a list, performance is enhanced for auditory items, but there is little or no effect on visual items (Frankish, 1985; Ryan, 1969). A temporal gap preserves the modality-dependent features of the item immediately preceding the gap in the auditory case; thus, the auditory condition can be conceived of as two (or more) smaller lists. The reduction in the search set size provides an overall increase in performance relative to the ungrouped condition, and the removal of overwriting of the modality-dependent features of each end-boundary item produces mini serial position functions (see Nairne, 1990, Figures 11 and 12). There is almost no advantage for visual items in a grouped list, because there are far fewer modality-dependent features to be preserved.

Phonological Similarity   The feature model also accounts for the observation that phonological similarity impairs serial recall performance (Crowder, 1978). Within the model, the probability that a degraded cue will be matched to a particular secondary memory item is based on a ratio (see Equation O.33 in the optional chapter). The numerator is the similarity of the degraded cue in primary memory and the target in secondary memory. The denominator is the sum of the similarity between the cue and all the items. Any increase in similarity increases the value of the denominator relative to the numerator, resulting in overall worse performance.

Phonological similarity is simulated in the feature model by manipulating the number of overlapping features. On average, there will always be some similarity between adjacent items; phonological similarity is modeled by setting a minimum number of similar features. For example, in a control or phonologically dissimilar condition, each of the 20 modality-independent features is randomly set to be –1. Under these conditions, there will be some feature overlap, but it will be essentially random. In a phonologically similar condition, however, a certain number of features (for example, 13 out of the 20) are set to the same value—1, for example—and the remaining features (in this case, 7) are randomly set to –1. There will be at least 13 overlapping features, but some of the other 7 may also overlap.

Articulatory Suppression   When subjects engage in articulatory suppression, they repeatedly say a constant item out loud. In the feature model, this is seen as adding noise to the memory trace of each individual item (see also Murray, Rowan, & Smith, 1988) through a process known as feature adoption. Some of the modality-independent features of the item being articulated will replace some of the modality-independent features of the cues in primary memory. Because articulatory suppression affects both auditory and visual items, articulatory suppression should affect only those features that both auditory and visual items share. Because articulatory suppression does not eliminate recall of items completely, it cannot be affecting all of the modality-independent features. Thus, articulatory suppression affects half of the modality-independent features. This has the net result of decreasing the sampling probability by decreasing the similarity of the cue in primary memory to the corresponding item in secondary memory.

Irrelevant Speech   The feature model accounts for the effects of irrelevant speech in the same way as the effects of articulatory suppression, through feature adoption (Neath, 2000). Because articulatory suppression is active—the subject needs to articulate items at a particular rate—whereas irrelevant speech is passive, it is assumed that articulatory suppression requires extra resources or serves as a general distractor (see, e.g., Parkin, 1993a, p. 130) compared to irrelevant speech. The model therefore predicts that the magnitude of the disruption caused by articulatory suppression should significantly correlate with the magnitude of the disruption caused by irrelevant speech. This prediction has been confirmed (Neath, Farley, & Surprenant, in press).

Articulatory Suppression and Phonological Similarity   As Nairne (1990) has demonstrated, the feature model produces the appropriate interaction between phonological similarity effects in the two modalities when tested with and without articulatory suppression. For visual items, the phonological similarity effect is eliminated because articulatory suppression eliminates the advantage that dissimilar items have: The features in the dissimilar items that helped the cue match with the appropriate target are replaced, through feature adoption, with features from the articulated item. Visual items have so few modality-dependent features that they add essentially no information that would be useful for matching the phonologically dissimilar traces relative to the phonologically similar traces. Auditory items, however, have many more modality-dependent features, and even though the modality-independent features of the dissimilar items have been subjected to feature adoption, there remain enough intact modality-dependent features in the phonologically dissimilar condition to give an advantage over the phonologically similar items.

Word-Length Effects   The syllable-based word-length effect is implemented following an idea originally suggested by Melton (1963). The basic idea is that the more parts there are, the more opportunities there are to make a mistake. To take an extreme example, if you have a jigsaw puzzle with only 2 pieces, it is very difficult to put the pieces together incorrectly. In contrast, a 100-piece puzzle allows you to make far more mistakes in assembly. Just as a list can be divided into items, an item can be divided into segments.

The feature model assumes that words are made up of segments and that these segments have to be assembled at some stage during the recall process. For example, Caplan, Rochon, and Waters (1992) suggested that the segments could correspond to the phonological structure of the items and that the word-length effect arises when this information is being used in preparation for recall. The probability of making a segment error is the same for all segments; however, because long items have more segments than short items, there is more chance of making an error with a long than with a short item. Because word-length effects are seen with both visual and auditory presentation, segment assembly errors must affect modality-independent features.

Although some segments may undoubtedly be more critical than others to the identification of a particular item (e.g., Brown & Hulme, 1995), Neath and Nairne (1995) chose the simplifying assumption that any segment error will result in the same loss of information as any other. Regardless of the number of segment assembly errors, it seems likely that some information will remain, even if that information is only disassembled segments; thus, Neath and Nairne again chose a simplifying assumption that a segment assembly error affects half of the modality-independent features (see Neath & Nairne, 1995, for more details). The feature model predicts that there will be no difference in recall between two sets of equivalent words that differ only in pronunciation time (the so-called time-based word-length effect), which appears to be the case (Lovatt et al., 2000, 2002; Neath et al., in press). Word-length effects will be seen only when the short and long items vary in the number of segments.

Modality and Word Length   Watkins and Watkins (1973) found that the recall difference between short and long visual items was greater than the difference between short and long auditory items. The feature model correctly predicts this finding of a larger word-length effect for visual items than for auditory items (see Table 4.6). The reason is straightforward: The word-length effect is implemented in the feature model as affecting only modality-independent features. Because auditory presentation results in more modality-dependent features than does visual presentation, the effects of a word-length manipulation will affect a smaller proportion of elements in a vector that represents an auditory item, other things being equal.

Table 4.6 The predicted interaction between presentation modality and word length

	Visual	*Auditory*
Short	0.433	0.478
Long	0.322	0.414
Difference	0.111	0.064

NOTE: The word-length effect is larger (there is a larger difference between recall of short and long words) for visually presented items than for auditory items. Values come from simulations using the feature model.

Articulatory Suppression, Phonological Similarity, and Word Length   The strongest test of the feature model so far has been to see if it predicts the correct interactions among the various effects just modeled. For the most part, each main effect (word length, phonological similarity) has been modeled independently, and it could easily have been the case that when several effects were performed simultaneously within the model, it would produce inappropriate results. However, the model does predict the correct interactions. Table 4.7 shows the results of one such simulation in which the effects of word length, articulatory suppression, and phonological similarity are combined.

The silent/dissimilar condition is really the control condition, and the word-length manipulation has its effect by increasing the number of mismatches between corresponding primary and secondary memory traces. Because a long word is less likely to be assembled correctly, it is less likely to be matched correctly with the secondary memory trace. Comparing the silent/dissimilar with the silent/similar condition, the phonological similarity manipulation reduces performance by increasing the number of mismatching features between a primary memory trace and the correct secondary memory trace. The reason for this increase is that more overwriting will occur if all the items in the list are phonologically similar: Overwriting changes an element's value to 0, and the secondary memory traces do not contain any zeros. This effect is independent of the word-length manipulation; thus, word-length effects should be seen for both similar and dissimilar items.

Articulatory suppression is modeled by adopting some features from the item being said aloud. On average, these will differ from the original features in the to-be-remembered item, reducing the probability that an item will be sampled. This effect masks the word-length effect because so many features have already been changed by feature adoption that assembly errors are not detectable with standard stimuli.

Table 4.7 The predicted interaction between phonological similarity, word length, and articulatory suppression on recall of auditory items

	Silent		*Articulatory Suppression*	
	Dissimilar	*Similar*	*Dissimilar*	*Similar*
Short	0.608	0.412	0.496	0.321
Long	0.558	0.349	0.507	0.320

NOTE: Articulatory suppression eliminates the word-length effect but does not eliminate the phonological similarity effect. Similar items had a minimum of ten identical features, long items had ten segments, and short items had one segment. Compare with Table 4.4. Values come from simulations using the feature model.

Serial Recall   The feature model predicts not only which items will be recalled well, but the type of errors that will be made (Neath, 1999a). This is due to the perturbation model, which will be discussed in detail in Chapter 13.

Long-Term Effects on Memory Span   The feature model offers a natural extension to include the influence of long-term knowledge on memory span. For example, consider the finding that span is higher for concrete than abstract words. Both explanations (Paivio, 1969; Jones, 1988) suggest richer encoding, which is easily implemented by using a larger range of features. Using feature values of +1 and –1 is really the same as using feature values of +1 and +2. Thus, an abstract item might have features with values in the range of 1 to 2, whereas a concrete item might have feature values in the range 1 to 3.

Novel Predictions   The feature model allows one to generate predictions in a very precise and unambiguous way. As one example, the model was run to assess the effect of articulatory suppression on the suffix effect. According to PAS (see Chapter 2), articulatory suppression should eliminate the suffix effect because the irrelevant items being articulated should fill up PAS and thus prevent any advantage for the last item in the control condition. According to the feature model, the effects of articulatory suppression and the suffix should be independent because articulatory suppression alters modality-independent features whereas the suffix alters modality-dependent features (see Figure 4.9). This prediction has been confirmed empirically (Surprenant, LeCompte, & Neath, 2000).

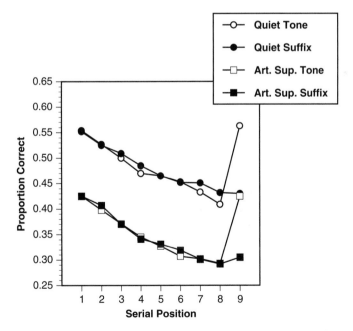

Figure 4.9   An example of a novel prediction of the feature model. Using the same parameter settings as for the previous simulations, the model predicts that a suffix effect will still be seen when subjects engage in articulatory suppression. The simulation models immediate serial recall of a list of nine digits presented auditorily and followed by either a tone or a suffix. Values come from simulations using the feature model.

Critique of the Feature Model

Although the feature model has had remarkable success in accounting for many of the basic phenomena observed when memory is assessed immediately, it has several weaknesses. The major problem with the feature model is that it does not include any specific process that models the passing of time. Many demonstrations have shown that increasing the time between the presentation of an item and recall can actually *increase* the likelihood of recall (e.g., Bjork, 2001; Glenberg, Bradley, Kraus, & Renzaglia, 1983; Neath & Crowder, 1990, 1996). Of course, there are also many demonstrations that increasing the time between presentation and test decreases the likelihood of recall. Because there is no role for time in the feature model, it cannot address these data.

A second major problem is that many experimental manipulations cannot be modeled. For example, the model addresses only serial recall, not free recall or recognition. A third problem is that the model oversimplifies the task facing the subjects: In the model, only one list is being recalled, whereas most experiments ask subjects to recall multiple lists.

The feature model does have some distinct advantages over working memory, whether Baddeley's (1986, 1994) version or Cowan's (1988, 1999) embedded-processes model. First, the feature model can address effects at different serial positions, including modality and suffix effects observable with auditory as well as tactile or olfactory stimuli, whereas the working memory and activation views cannot. Second, it can readily explain the absence of time-based word-length effects, as described above, whereas working memory has to predict that they will occur. Perhaps the most important advantage, however, is that the feature model is a precise statement of what happens during the study and retrieval process. The predictions are unambiguous because the model provides numbers that are easily compared. By this means, it also provides a check on human reasoning. It is quite easy to make an error when working through a complex set of predictions (such as those concerning the interactions among modality, word length, phonological similarity, articulatory suppression, and serial position), and it is very useful to have a computer double-check the line of reasoning.

Chapter Summary

The majority of theories currently used to explain immediate memory phenomena are based on Baddeley's (1986) "working memory" and focus on the phonological loop. This part of working memory was designed to explain the effects of word length, phonological similarity, irrelevant speech, and articulatory suppression and also to explain the interactions among these variables. Although there are many versions of the model (Martin, Shelton, & Yaffee, 1994; Miyake & Shah, 1999; Richardson, 1996), almost all maintain that some form of decay occurs and that this imposes a fundamental limit on the amount of information that can be retained. However, there is relatively little current empirical support for decay (Nairne, 2002; see also Chapter 6). Cowan's embedded-processes model views working memory as activated long-term memory, and so long-term memory is predicted to play a substantial role in short-term memory tasks. This view, although new and still incomplete, nicely handles the many results showing such long-term memory effects. It remains to be seen whether the concepts of activation and deactivation (which seems a lot like decay) can gain much empirical support. The working memory capacity approach emphasizes attention more than memory but retains many working memory components.

The feature model differs from the above views in that it does not use the concept of decay; rather, memory performance is made worse by interference. It can account for all of the phenomena that Baddeley's working memory was designed to account for, and it has predicted new findings, including that the suffix effect remains even when subjects engage in articulatory suppression. It is also the only view that directly addresses modality effects. The major problems with the feature model are that it does not include in any way the passage of time and that it has not yet been applied to as many different experimental paradigms as working memory. It remains to be seen whether the feature model can be successfully extended.

Perspectives on Processing

We soon forget what we have not deeply thought about.

—Marcel Proust

The three previous chapters have emphasized memory as a structure. For example, in the modal model, one of the most important determinants of whether an item will be recalled is the memory store that holds the item: An item stored in short-term memory will be remembered differently than will an item in long-term memory or sensory memory. During the 1970s, a different view became increasingly popular—one that shifted the emphasis from the underlying store as the most important factor to the type of processing that was performed.

Levels of Processing

Craik and Lockhart (1972) offered the first detailed view suggesting that the type of processing was more important than the underlying theoretical structure. They made four key assumptions. First, they conceptualized memory as the result of a series of analyses, each at a deeper level than the previous one, that are performed on the to-be-processed information. The level of processing should be thought of as a point on a continuum rather than as a discrete level. The continuum goes from shallow processing, which focuses on perceptual features such as how a word sounds, to deeper processing involving meaning. Second, Craik and Lockhart assumed that the deeper the level, the more durable the resulting memory. If you need to remember an item for a long time, it is better to use a deep level of processing, such as focusing on its meaning, than to use a shallower level, such as how the item sounds. Third, the levels of processing view assumes that rehearsal can be relatively unimportant. Memory improvements are due to deeper levels of analysis, not to repeating an item over and over. Rehearsal will be beneficial only to the extent that it induces a deeper level of processing. This type of rehearsal, known as Type II or *elaborative rehearsal*, will improve memory; simple rote repetition, known as Type I or *maintenance rehearsal*, will not improve memory.

The final assumption has to do with how memory should be studied rather than with specifics of the theory. Because the emphasis is on processing rather than on structure, Craik and Lockhart (1972) argued that research will be most informative when the experimenter has control over the processing. When subjects are intentionally trying to learn, they may use the processing they consider most appropriate, which may not be the processing the experimenter wants. Therefore, researchers should use an *incidental learning* procedure. In this procedure, the subject is unaware that the material being processed will be tested later on; rather, the subject simply processes the material in the way suggested by the experimenter.

> The interesting thing to do is to systematically study retention following different orienting tasks within the incidental condition, rather than to compare incidental with intentional learning. Under incidental conditions, the experimenter has a control over the processing the subject applies to the material that he does not have when the subject is merely instructed to learn and uses an unknown coding strategy. (Craik & Lockhart, 1972, p. 677)

One implication is that intent to learn is not necessarily an important variable in memory research. Indeed, Postman (1964, p. 190) had earlier concluded the same thing, that "intent per se is not a significant variable in learning."

One early experiment that seemed to support many of the assumptions of the levels of processing view, including the relative unimportance of intentionality, was reported by Hyde and Jenkins (1973). They used 22 different conditions, but we will examine only a few in detail. The to-be-remembered items were 24 common words presented auditorily. Following presentation, the subjects were asked to recall as many of these items as they could in any order they liked (free recall). The groups of subjects differed primarily in the orienting instructions given to them and in whether they were told in advance of the free recall test.

One group of subjects was given a shallow task, such as checking the words for the presence of the letter *E* or *G*. It is easy to perform this task without having to process the meaning of the words. A second group was given the slightly deeper task of identifying the part of speech, such as noun or verb. A third group was asked to rate the frequency, or how common the word was. A fourth group was asked to rate each word on how pleasant or unpleasant it was. This is thought to be a particularly deep level of processing because not only do subjects have to process the meaning of the item, but they then have to consider the meaning in relation to whether it has pleasant associations. Half the subjects in each of these groups were told that they would also need to remember the items for a later test (the intentional group); the other half were told nothing about the memory test (the incidental group). Finally, a control group was told simply to remember the words for a later free recall test. The results are shown in Figure 5.1.

There are three particularly important findings. First, looking only at the incidental groups, the deeper the level of processing, the more words were recalled. For example, those subjects performing pleasantness ratings recalled more items than did those doing

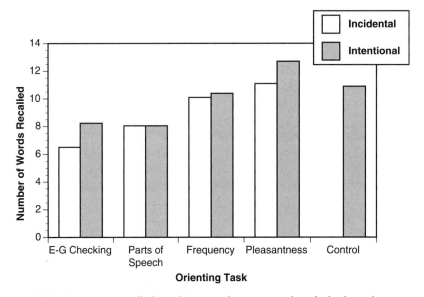

Figure 5.1   Amount recalled as a function of orienting task and whether subjects were told a memory test would be given.   Source: From "Recall of Words as a Function of Semantic, Graphic, and Syntactic Orienting Tasks," by T. S. Hyde and J. J. Jenkins, 1973, *Journal of Verbal Learning and Verbal Behavior, 12,* 471–480. Copyright © 1973 Academic Press, Inc. Reprinted with permission.

E-G checking. Second, subjects in the incidental pleasantness condition recalled as many, if not more, words than did subjects in the intentional control condition. This finding supports Postman's assertion that other factors may be more important than intent to remember. Finally, there was very little difference in performance between the incidental and intentional groups that were given the same orienting instructions. For example, those subjects performing the part of speech judgment recalled the same number of words regardless of whether they knew about the recall test.

The results from Hyde and Jenkins' (1973) study provide empirical support for many of the assumptions of Craik and Lockhart's (1972) levels of processing framework. A different set of experiments supported the idea that maintenance rehearsal has little or no effect on memory. Craik and Watkins (1973) tested the idea that maintenance rehearsal does not lead to improved memory. They induced subjects to use maintenance rehearsal by giving them special instructions. Subjects were asked to listen to a list of items and report the last word that began with a particular letter. If the critical letter was G, for example, the subject could ignore all words until one was encountered that began with G. Thus, in the list *daughter, oil, rifle, garden, grain, table, football, anchor, giraffe,* the first word the subject would rehearse would be *garden.* The subject would rehearse this item for only a moment before *grain* replaced it. *Grain* would be rehearsed for longer, because *giraffe* does not appear for a while. The operational definition of how long an item was rehearsed was termed *i,* the number of intervening words. *Garden* had an *i* value of 0, *grain* had an *i* value of 3, and some items had *i* values as large as 12. At the end of each trial, the subject would report the one item required, and the next trial would begin. The final manipulation of interest involved a surprise final recall test. Ten minutes after the final trial, Craik and Watkins asked the

---

Experiment   *Levels of Processing*

Purpose: To demonstrate the basic levels of processing phenomena.

Subjects: Forty subjects are recommended. Ten should be assigned to the intentional *E-G* group, ten to the incidental *E-G* group, ten to the intentional pleasantness group, and ten to the incidental pleasantness group.

Materials: Table E in the Appendix lists 25 common two-syllable nouns. For each subject, present these in a different random order. The orienting responses require answer sheets with numbers from 1 to 25. Additional sheets will be required for the free recall test.

Design: Because each subject experiences only one condition, both intentionality and level of processing are between-subjects factors. The basic design is a 2 × 2 factorial.

Procedure: Inform the subjects that this is an experiment on information processing. Describe the orienting task that each group will get, and explain how they will respond on the answer sheets. Do not give out the response sheets for the free recall task; it is very important that the subjects in the incidental conditions do not expect a memory test. For those subjects in the intentional conditions, inform them that they will be tested for their memory for the words later on. Read each word aloud, allowing 3 seconds for the subject's response. After reading the words, remove the first answer sheet before giving them the second. This way, they won't be able to use their previous responses as cues. Allow as much time as needed for the free recall test.

Instructions for E-G: "This is an experiment on information processing. I will read a list of 25 words, and I would like you to indicate whether there is an E or a G in the word. If the word has either an *E*, a *G*, or both, please write *Y* next to the number on the response sheet. If the word has no *E*s or *G*s, please write *N*. Please be as accurate as you can, but you will have only 3 seconds per word to make your response." To the intentional group, add, "At the end, you will be tested for your memory for the words."

Instructions for Pleasantness: "This is an experiment on information processing. I will read a list of 25 words, and I would like you to indicate whether you think the word represents something pleasant or unpleasant. If you think the word is pleasant, please write *P* next to the number on the response sheet. If the word is unpleasant, please write *U*. Please be as accurate as you can, but you will have only 3 seconds per word to make your response." To the intentional group, add, "At the end, you will be tested for your memory for the words."

Instructions for Test: "Please write down as many of the 25 words as you can remember. Feel free to write them down in any order."

Scoring and Analysis: For each subject, count the number of words recalled, and compute an average for each group. The results should be similar to those plotted in Figure 5.1. A 2 × 2 between-subjects analysis of variance can be performed on the individual subject data.

Optional Enhancements: Include a control group that receives intentional instructions but no orienting instructions.

SOURCE: Based on an experiment by Hyde & Jenkins (1973).

---

subjects to report as many of the critical items as they could—both the final ones, which they had already reported, and those that were not the final items. Craik and Watkins found that final recall was unrelated to the *i* value: Recall of an item was uncorrelated with how long it had been rehearsed using maintenance rehearsal.

This result poses a problem for the modal model because it suggests that time spent in short-term store can be unrelated to subsequent recall. Further research has generally replicated the finding of little or no effect of maintenance rehearsal. For example, Nairne (1983) replicated these results for free recall but also tested recognition. In a recognition test,

Table 5.1   Two ways of accounting for basic memory phenomena

Store	Sensory	STS	LTS
Format	Literal copy	Phonological	Semantic
Rehearsal	Not possible	Maintenance	Elaborative
Capacity	Medium	Small	Infinite
Duration	500–2000 ms	Up to 30 s	Minutes to years

NOTE: Reading the table down shows the structural view: If an item is in STS, then its format will be phonological, the capacity small, and so on. Omitting the top row shows the processing view: If an item is encoded phonologically, then the capacity is small and the duration is around 30 s. The first row becomes irrelevant.

subjects can indicate whether they do or do not recognize an item as being from a particular list. Nairne found increased "yes" responding with increased rehearsal, but this does not necessarily mean that overall memory was more accurate. Subjects were more likely to say "yes" both to items that were from the list (a correct response, known as a *hit*) and to items that were not from the list (an incorrect response known as a *false alarm*). When this tendency is taken into account, using signal detection theory and measuring accuracy with d' (see Chapter 9), there was no relation between rehearsal and performance.

Table 5.1 illustrates how the same results can be interpreted by two very different views. According to the modal model, it is the memory structure that determines the properties. If short-term store is used, the code will be phonological, the capacity will be relatively small, maintenance rehearsal will keep the item in the store, and without rehearsal, the maximum duration is about 30 s. What having levels of processing does, in effect, is eliminate the top row. According to levels of processing, if a subject processes an item at the phonological level, then the subject will not be able to remember very many items for very long.

Although levels of processing as a theoretical description can account for many experimental findings—including some findings that the modal model cannot—it has two major problems. The first major problem with levels of processing is that one of its key assumptions is *circular*. It is assumed that deeper levels of processing lead to better memory, and when there is better memory, we attribute it to a deeper level of processing. Although most researchers will concede that E-G checking is intuitively shallower than pleasantness ratings, there is no independent method for determining, before a memory experiment, whether process A is deeper or shallower than process B. Craik and Tulving (1975) reported ten experiments that attempted to define levels objectively. For example, one idea was that deeper levels of processing require more time to perform than shallower levels do. Unfortunately, they observed that it is possible to construct a situation such that a deep task requires 0.83 s to complete and leads to 82% correct, and a shallow task takes 1.70 s to complete but leads to only 57% correct.

The lack of an objective definition of a level might have been overcome had there not been a second major problem, this one concerning an omission. Levels of processing focuses almost exclusively on encoding and says relatively little about retrieval. The second major processing view developed in the 1970s, transfer appropriate processing, began as a way of rectifying this omission. Despite its major problems, however, levels of processing has had an enormous impact on the field and influenced many current theories of memory.

Transfer Appropriate Processing

The principal difference between levels of processing and transfer appropriate processing is that the latter includes retrieval. According to this view, a process leads to better performance not because it is deeper but because it is appropriate for the kind of test that will be conducted. In general, deep tasks do lead to better performance than do shallow tasks on free recall tests, but free recall is not the only way of testing memory. Morris, Bransford, and Franks (1977) demonstrated that a shallow level of processing can lead to better performance than a deep level when tested in a particular way. This demonstration clearly disconfirms an assumption of levels of processing.

Morris, Bransford, and Franks (1977) presented 32 sentences auditorily to the subjects, and in each sentence, a word was missing. In one condition, subjects judged whether a target word filled in the blank. For example, the sentence might be "The (blank) had a silver engine" and the target word might be *train*. In a different condition, subjects judged whether the target word rhymed with another. In this case, the sentence might be "(Blank) rhymes with legal" and the target word might be *eagle*. Subjects indicated "yes" or "no" to each kind of question and were unaware that a later memory test would be given. So far, this is just like a standard levels of processing experiment, with subjects performing incidental learning under two different sets of orienting instructions. But the researchers changed the paradigm by including two types of tests. One test was a standard recognition test, in which a target word was presented and subjects were asked whether it had been seen previously. The second test was a rhyming recognition test, where subjects were asked whether a word rhymed with one of the target words. In the example given above, the standard recognition test might have as a test item the word *train* or the word *eagle*. The rhyming recognition test might have as test items the word *plane* (which rhymes with *train*) and *regal* (which rhymes with *eagle*). The results are shown in Figure 5.2.

With a standard recognition test, the deeper orienting task (whether the word fit in the sentence) led to better performance than did the shallower orienting task (whether the word rhymed). However, with the rhyme recognition test, the shallow task led to better performance than did the deep task. Levels of processing assumed that deeper processing leads to better performance, but the data in Figure 5.2 show that this is true only for some kinds of tests; on other tests, shallow processing can be better than deep. Morris, Bransford, and Franks (1977) interpreted their results as supporting a theory called *transfer appropriate processing*. A type of processing will lead to better memory performance if it is appropriate for the particular test; no one type of processing is good for all tests.

One qualification should be added. Fisher and Craik (1977) replicated the results of Morris, Bransford, and Franks (1977), ruling out several uninteresting interpretations of the data. They emphasized, however, that although rhyme encoding followed by a rhyme cue led to better performance than did semantic encoding followed by a rhyme cue, semantic encoding followed by a semantic cue led to the best performance. This can be seen in the data shown in Figure 5.2. According to Fisher and Craik (1977), the reason is that semantic encoding leads to a more specific cue, which in turn leads to enhanced discriminability from competing cues. For example, there is only a limited number of possible phonemic cues, compared to an almost infinite number of semantic cues. This is related to Watkins' (1979) *cue overload principle*, which states that only so many items

Figure 5.2 Overall proportion correct on a standard or rhyme recognition memory test following either a sentence (semantic) or rhyme (nonsemantic) orienting task.   SOURCE: From "Levels of Processing Versus Transfer Appropriate Processing," by C. D. Morris, J. D. Bransford, and J. J. Franks, 1977, *Journal of Verbal Learning and Verbal Behavior, 16,* 519–533. Copyright © 1977 Academic Press, Inc. Reprinted with permission.

can be associated with a cue before the cue begins to lose its effectiveness. The more items that are associated with a cue, the less effective the cue will be in eliciting the desired item.

Organization and Distinctiveness

The levels of processing framework includes the idea that a deeper level of processing produces a more distinctive cue than does a shallow level of processing. The more distinctive an item, the more different it is from competing items (see also the discussion of distinctiveness in Chapter 6). At the same time, however, a large body of literature demonstrates that organization helps memory. When incorporating information into an organization, what matters most are the similarities. As Hunt and McDaniel (1993, p. 421) wondered, "How can both similarity and difference be beneficial to memory?"

As used in the memory field, *organization* refers to relationships among the information that is to be remembered, and it formed a cornerstone of Gestalt theory (Katona, 1940; Koffka, 1935). Subjects recall more words from a categorized list than from an uncategorized list. For example, Deese (1959a) found that subjects recalled about 49% of the words from a list that contained high associates (such as *flower, insect, bees*), compared to only 37% of the words from a random list. The effects of organization can be quite powerful. Mandler (1967) had four groups of subjects examine 52 words. Of most interest here is that subjects who were asked to sort the cards into categories of their own choosing recalled as many of the words on a surprise test as did subjects who were specifically asked to memorize the words.

A related phenomenon is called *clustering*. Bousfield (1953) presented subjects with a 60-word list made up of 15 instances of four categories (animals, names, professions, and vegetables). The words were presented in random order. Bousfield observed that subjects were likely to cluster their responses; that is, they were likely to recall two or more items from the same category sequentially even though the items were separated in the list. The lists do not need to be categorized in such a blatant fashion in order to see clustering (for example, Tulving, 1962).

One resolution has been to say the paradox that both similarity and difference helps is more apparent than real. In other words, both are important because both reflect particular types of processing. Hunt and his colleagues (Hunt & Einstein, 1981; Hunt & McDaniel, 1993) emphasize the importance of relational and item-specific processing, arguing that organization emphasizes relational processing (how the items fit together), whereas item-specific processing emphasizes the particular to-be-remembered item. Memory performance is best when both processes occur. A specific example is provided in Chapter 13 at the end of the section "Item Versus Order Information."

For now, the important point is that both relational and item-specific processing are important. Without knowledge of the to-be-remembered item itself, memory will be quite poor. Even if the item is known, however, relational processing can help provide cues that quickly produce the desired information. This interaction between the processes performed at encoding and those performed at retrieval is highlighted in our next topic, the encoding specificity principle.

The Encoding Specificity Principle

According to the *encoding specificity principle* (Tulving, 1972, 1983), the recollection of an event or a certain aspect of it depends on the interaction between the properties of the encoded event and the properties of the retrieval information. This idea is related to transfer appropriate processing in that both emphasize the interaction between the processing that occurred during encoding and the processing that occurs at retrieval. Tulving refers to the interaction as *ecphory*, from a Greek word meaning "to be made known." An ecphoric process, then, is a process by which "retrieval information is brought into interaction with stored information" (p. 178). Because it is the interaction that is important, no statements can be made about the mnemonic properties of an item, a process, or a cue (p. 239). For example, one cannot say that deeper processing leads to better recall than shallow processing because recall depends on the type of processing at retrieval. It is only when the interaction of the encoding and retrieval conditions is specified that meaningful statements can be made.

CogLab Experiment
http://coglab.wadsworth.com/experiments/EncodingSpecificity/

We have already examined one good example: The statement "deep processing at study is better than shallow processing" is inaccurate unless the statement is amended to

Table 5.2 The probability of recall when study cues and retrieval cues are varied

Study Cue	Retrieval Cue		
	None	*Weak*	*Strong*
None	0.49	0.43	0.68
Weak	0.30	0.82	0.23

SOURCE: Data from Thomson & Tulving (1970).

include a description of the test. Another example concerns the difference between a strong cue and a weak cue. A *strong cue* is a word that elicits a target word most of the time. When people hear the word *bloom*, most will respond with *flower* as the first word they think of. A *weak cue* is a word that elicits the target word only rarely. When people hear *fruit*, they respond with *flower* only about 1% of the time. You might be tempted to conclude that strong cues are better than weak cues, but this is the sort of absolute statement that Tulving (1983) argues is meaningless. The reason is that weak cues can be made more effective than strong cues depending on what happens at study and at test. In one experiment, Thomson and Tulving (1970) presented some target words alone at study, and some with a weak cue. At test, there were three cue conditions: no cue, a weak cue, or a strong cue. The results, expressed as probability of recall, are shown in Table 5.2.

In the control condition, in which there were no study cues and no retrieval cues at test, the probability of recalling the target word was 0.49. When there was no cue present at study, a strong cue at test led to better performance (0.68) than either a weak cue (0.43) or no cue (0.49). However, when there was a weak cue present at study, the weak cue at test led to better performance (0.82) than a strong cue (0.23). The important result here is that the effectiveness of even a long-standing strong cue depends crucially on the processes that occurred at study.

These results have two important implications. First, and perhaps most surprising, is that an item is not necessarily the best cue for itself. As we shall see in more detail in Chapter 9, there is a phenomenon known as *recognition failure of recallable words* in which the subject is asked to recall items that were on a list and also to recognize which items were on the list. In this paradigm (e.g., Watkins & Tulving, 1975), the subject studies a list of word pairs in which the first word in the pair is a weak cue of the second word; for example, *glue* might be paired with *chair*. Then a word that is a strong cue is given, such as *table*, and subjects are asked to write down as many words as they can that are associated with *table*. A recognition test is then given, in which a copy cue (the word *chair* itself) is used, and subjects often fail to recognize this item as one of the words on the original list. The final test is cued recall, where *glue* is the cue. Now, subjects are quite likely to recall the word they earlier failed to recognize. *Chair* is not always an effective cue when trying to remember *chair*. This finding can be explained only by theories that take into account processing at both encoding and retrieval.

The second implication is perhaps less surprising, but involves transfer appropriate processing. As Nairne (2001) has pointed out, many people have taken transfer appropriate processing to mean that performance is better when the encoding and retrieval conditions match than when they mismatch. It is true that in many cases, such as with the context-dependent memory effects discussed next, it is the match between encoding and retrieval that seems important. However, there are two things wrong with focusing on the similarity or match between the processes performed at encoding and retrieval. First, such a description is not transfer appropriate processing, but a different theory, transfer similar processing. All that transfer appropriate processing requires is that the processes be appropriate, not that they be similar. They can, of course, be similar, but that is not necessary. Second, transfer similar processing is empirically incorrect. In the Thomson and Tulving (1970) study, it is true that performance was best when there was a weak cue at study and a weak cue at test. However, there is another "match" condition: when no cues are presented at study and no cues are presented at test. Performance in this second "match" condition was worse than in the "mismatch" in which there are no cues at study and a strong cue at test. The results of Thomson and Tulving (1970) demonstrate that it is not the match that is important, but the appropriateness of the processing.

One reason many people have suggested that the match between encoding and retrieval is important is that many times similar processing is appropriate. We now examine this idea in greater depth by focusing on one paradigm.

Context and Memory

Many early experimental psychologists studied context effects or, more accurately, the change in performance when information is studied in one context and remembered in a different context (e.g., Carr, 1925; McGeoch, 1932). For example, Abernathy (1940) demonstrated that students who were tested in the same classroom in which they were taught did better on tests than did students who were tested in a different classroom. Such effects are predicted by the encoding specificity principle and, more generally, by any view of memory that emphasizes processing.

You should not be unduly worried about this result; changing classrooms from study to test often produces no decrement (e.g., Saufley, Otaka, & Bavaresco, 1985) because of at least three factors. First, most classrooms are quite similar; thus, a change from one to another will not be a very dramatic change. Second, only a limited amount of studying occurs in the first classroom, with much taking place in libraries, dorm rooms, and other locations. Third, students are taking the tests for a grade in a course, and so it should not be surprising that they do everything they can to do well. Even if you are worried, there are ways to overcome potential context effects.

Smith (1979) had subjects learn 80 words in a distinctive basement room. They were then given a recognition test on some of the words so that they would think that this phase of the experiment was over and would not rehearse the words during the next 24 hours. The next day, all subjects were given a surprise free recall test. One group was tested in the same basement room (same context), one was tested in a soundproof booth located in a computer room on the fifth floor (different context), and the third group was also tested in the booth but was given additional instructions. This third group of subjects was told to try to reinstate their memory for the basement room before trying to recall any items; they were asked to list attributes of the original room, and then try to recall the words. The same-context group recalled 18 words, on average. The different-context group recalled significantly fewer items, only 12. The third group, the different-context-plus-image group, recalled 17.2 items—almost the same number as the first group. It appears that environmental contextual information can be reinstated and can be used to compensate for a change in location.

Context has been defined in many different ways, although all share a similar distinction. For example, Wickens (1987) distinguishes between context alpha and context beta: *Context alpha* refers to "the environmental surrounds in which some event exists or occurs. . . . [There is] no implication that the context or the environment influences the event or is related to it in any significant way." *Context beta* is the "situation in which one stimulus event combines with another stimulus event to define the correct response or meaning of the event" (pp. 135–146).

The lack of an effect for changing classrooms notwithstanding, *environmental context–dependent memory* effects, in which context alpha is manipulated, are pervasive (Smith & Vela, 2001). Perhaps the most famous experiment that manipulated context alpha was reported by Godden and Baddeley (1975). Their subjects were members of a university diving club who were asked to learn a list of words either on land or 20 feet under water. They were then tested either on land or under water with four conditions: two match conditions, in which the environment (either on land or under water) was the same at both learning and testing; and two mismatch conditions, in which the environment was different at learning and testing. Regardless of where they were learning or recalling, the subjects wore their diving apparatus. There was a 4-minute interval between study and test, to allow enough time for the subjects to change environment. The results are reproduced in Figure 5.3. Subjects clearly recalled more words when the study and test environments matched than when they mismatched, regardless of whether subjects were under water or on land. When there was a mismatch, recall suffered. One practical impli-

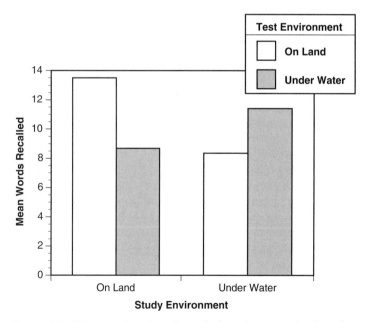

Figure 5.3   Mean number of words recalled as a function of study and test environments.   SOURCE: From "Context-Dependent Memory in Two Natural Environments," by D. R. Godden and A. D. Baddeley, 1975, *British Journal of Psychology, 66,* 325–331. Copyright © 1975 British Psychological Society. Reprinted with permission.

cation for divers is that if they memorize dive tables on land, they may not remember them very well when needed (e.g., Martin & Aggelton, 1993). A better instructional technique is to have the divers learn the material under water as well as on dry land.

One potential confound might be that the actual movement necessary to change environments was causing the memory deficit, rather than the changed environment itself. To rule out this possibility, Godden and Baddeley conducted a second experiment. Half of the subjects again learned a list of words and were then tested for recall on land. The other half also learned the list and were tested on land, but they were required to enter the pool, swim a short distance, dive to a depth of 20 feet, and then return to land prior to recall. If the movement itself was the cause of the deficit, then there should be a difference in performance between the two groups. If the change in environment caused the deficit, then there should be no difference. There was no difference; therefore, the disruption between study and test did not cause the decreased recall.

An example of context beta comes from a study by Light and Carter-Sobell (1970). They presented to subjects sentences that contained a two-word phrase that was capitalized and underlined, such as "The STRAWBERRY JAM tasted great." Subjects were told to expect a memory test for the underlined and capitalized phrases. After all the sentences had been presented, a recognition test was given. Half of the phrases were old, meaning they were ones the subjects had seen, and half were new, meaning the subjects had not seen them. Some of the old phrases contained the same noun as the original sentence, but now the noun was paired with a new adjective, such as TRAFFIC JAM. The subjects were supposed to respond on the basis of the noun. Thus, if they saw JAM, they were to indicate that it was one of the studied items, regardless of whether the adjective was the same or different. When JAM was presented in the same context, subjects correctly recognized it about 65% of the time, but when it was in a new context, they recognized it only about 25% of the time. This is an example of context beta because the adjective was essential for determining the meaning of the word.

A *context-dependent memory effect,* then, refers to the observation that memory can be worse when tested in a new or different context relative to performance in a condition in which the context remains the same. Context can be manipulated in a variety of ways. For example, Schab (1990) filled a small room with the odor of chocolate either at study, at test, or at both. Even after a 24-hour delay, subjects' performance on a surprise test was better when the odors matched. This experiment also provides empirical validation for the famous anecdote reported by Marcel Proust in the first novel of *Remembrance of Things Past.*

State-dependent memory refers to a finding similar to context-dependent memory; indeed, many theorists view them as essentially the same (e.g., Capaldi & Neath, 1995). A person's state can be changed by altering the affective or the pharmacological state from study to test. The first person to describe this concept—that what has been learned in a certain state of mind is best remembered in that state—was a French aristocrat, Marquis de Puységur, in 1809 (Eich, 1989). More recently, Morton Prince (1910) conjectured that people have difficulty remembering their dreams when awake not because they do not want to, but because of the dissimilarity of the two states. In 1934, Susukita demonstrated that something learned while calm cannot be recalled when in a state of shock, but can be recalled at a later time when calm is restored. In this particular instance, a state of shock was induced when an earthquake hit. Although the typical finding is similar, some researchers vary the environment, some the pharmacological state, and some the affective state or mood of the person.

Table 5.3   Mean number of errors of recall as a function of encoding and testing state

	Retrieval	
Encoding	Sober	Intoxicated
Sober	1.25	2.25
Intoxicated	4.58	2.50

SOURCE: Goodwin, Powell, Bremer, Hoine, & Stern (1969).

Bartlett and Santrock (1979) altered the affective state of their subjects so that they were in either a happy or a neutral mood at study, and a happy or a neutral mood at test. Performance was better when the moods matched than when they mismatched. Similar results have been reported by Bower (1981). Although there are several well-documented failures to find mood-dependent memory effects, a review by Eich (1995) goes a long way toward delineating when such effects will or will not be seen. First among these conditions is producing a strong, sincere mood.

Goodwin, Powell, Bremer, Hoine, and Stern (1969) demonstrated state-dependent memory using alcohol. Some subjects received 10 oz of 80-proof vodka either at study, at test, or at both; other subjects remained sober. Not surprisingly, performance was best when subjects were sober at both study and test. Perhaps more surprising is the finding that the worst performance was when subjects were intoxicated at study and sober during the test. In fact, subjects were worse in this condition than when the mismatch was the other way around—sober at study and intoxicated at test (see Table 5.3). Similar state-dependent memory effects have been shown using marijuana (Eich, Weingartner, Stillman, & Gillin, 1975) and nicotine (Peters & McGee, 1982).

Weingartner and Faillace (1971) conducted a state-dependent memory experiment with two different groups of subjects. One group was made up of chronic alcoholics with documented histories of long-term alcohol abuse; the other group was made up of an equal number of nonalcoholics who were closely matched to the alcoholic subjects with respect to age, education, and other demographic variables. The test session was held two days after initial learning, during which subjects tried to recall as many of the target words as they could. The subjects from both groups were either intoxicated or sober at study, and intoxicated or sober at test. In this experiment, intoxication was defined as having 1.6 ml of alcohol per kg of body weight. Both groups of subjects showed state-dependent memory effects.

State-dependent memory shows an interesting asymmetry in which a shift from intoxication to sobriety impairs memory more than a shift from sobriety to intoxication (Eich, 1989; Overton, 1984). For example, as Table 5.3 shows, there is a larger difference between recalling items encoded during intoxication while in an intoxicated state than while in a sober state (mean errors of 2.50 versus 4.58), and a smaller effect of recalling items encoded during sobriety while in a sober state than while in an intoxicated state (mean errors of 1.25 versus 2.25). As Eich (1989) points out, this asymmetry can be seen in the studies of Eich et al. (1975) with marijuana, Peters and McGee (1982) with nicotine, and Bartlett and Santrock (1979) with mood. Furthermore, it is seen in the Weingartner and Faillace (1971) study in both the alcoholic and the nonalcoholic control groups. If we label the sober state as normal for the nonalcoholics and the intoxicated state as normal for the alcoholics, then the pattern is identical: Performance is worse when switching from the unusual to normal condition than when switching from the normal to unusual condition, regardless of which condition (sober or intoxicated) is normal.

The interpretation advanced by several theorists to explain this asymmetry is actually quite simple (e.g., Barry, 1978; Capaldi & Neath, 1995; Eich, 1980). The context in which a person—or other animal, because all these context- (alpha and beta) and state-dependent memory effects can be observed in dogs, rats, and pigeons (e.g., Asratian, 1965; Bouton, 1993; Rescorla, Durlach, & Grau, 1985)—learns some information provides cues that the subject can use to remember the information (see Chapter 6 for more detail). Some N (or normal) cues will always be encoded because there will always be some aspect that is unchanged. It can be assumed that drugs add U (or unusual) cues to the representation, with N or normal state cues being little affected. For chronic alcoholics, being sober is unusual, and so the absence of the effects of alcohol provides the U cues. The N-to-N and U-to-U groups show generally good retention because the cues encoded at study (either N or U) are the cues that are useful at test. The N-to-U group shows an intermediate level of performance because some N cues were present at test as well study. The U-to-N group shows the worst performance because the U cues present at study are absent at test.

One advantage of this view is that it makes a specific prediction: In an experiment in which context is changed, the change in context can be overcome if the experimenter provides useful cues to the subject. We have already seen one example, in which the experimenter told the subject to reinstate the missing context mentally (Smith, 1979). This can be thought of as providing some of the missing U cues. Another example comes from a study reported by Eich and Birnbaum (1982), in which subjects were asked to learn a list of words in either a sober or an intoxicated state. When tested after a change in drug state, retrieval was poor, as is usually the case. However, some of the subjects in the changed-state condition were given additional cues (for example, "Think of all the flowers that you can"). Providing a category name gave the subject additional useful cues, and recall was much improved (Eich & Birnbaum, 1982).

Note that in almost all of these cases, a recall test rather than a recognition test was used. There are many reports of failures to obtain a context-dependent memory effect when recognition is used (e.g., Godden & Baddeley, 1980; Smith, Glenberg, & Bjork, 1978), as well as reports of failures to obtain mood-dependent memory effects with recognition (Eich & Metcalfe, 1989). Smith and Vela (2001) conducted an analysis of 75 experiments from 41 articles published between 1935 and 1997 and concluded that environmental context effects are reliably found, and can also be seen in recognition tests. To the extent that the processing at study and at test emphasizes noncontextual cues, or that reinstatement of the original context is encouraged, environmental context effects will be reduced.

Context-, mood-, or state-dependent memory effects, then, are larger (1) with tests such as free recall that require internally generated cues than with tests like cued recall or recognition that also have externally provided cues; and (2) when the tests emphasize conceptually driven tasks (those that focus on word meanings and relationships between words) rather than data-driven tasks (those that stress perceptual processing). This latter aspect is nicely illustrated in a series of experiments reported by Eich and Metcalfe (1989). Before describing these experiments, however, it is necessary to describe some methods and define some terms.

Johnson and Raye (1981) defined *cotemporal thought* as "the sort of elaborative and associative processes that augment, bridge, or embellish ongoing perceptual experience but that are not necessarily part of the veridical representation of perceptual experience" (p. 443). Eich and Metcalfe suggested that if a person is in a happy mood, then the cotemporal thought that occurs should lead to large mood-dependent memory effects if the cotemporal thought is allowed to be important. To test this hypothesis, they used a procedure, described first by Heller (1956) and more recently by Slamecka and Graf (1978), that gives rise to the *generation effect* (see Chapter 13 for more discussion).

In the typical generation-effect experiment, on half of the lists subjects are asked to read an item, and on the remaining trials they are asked to generate an item. For example, subjects may see a category cue followed by two words, one of which is in uppercase. Subjects are instructed that they will need to remember the uppercase word for a later memory test. In the generate condition, subjects see exactly the same display except that only the initial letter is given for the uppercase word: The subjects have to generate the word themselves. The typical finding is that generated words are remembered much better than are the read words.

Milkshake flavors: chocolate : VANILLA	[Read condition]
Milkshake flavors: chocolate : V————	[Generate condition]

Eich and Metcalfe (1989) combined a generation-effect procedure with a mood-manipulation procedure. Half of the subjects were induced to be happy at study, and half were induced to be sad. Of the happy subjects, half were induced to be happy again 24 hours later at the surprise recall test, and half were induced to be sad. Within the four groups delineated by mood, half of the subjects read the target item, and half generated the target item. Mood changes were induced by playing either happy (Mozart's *Eine Kleine Nachtmusik*) or sad (Albinoni's *Adagio in G minor*) music and instructing subjects to think either happy or sad thoughts. The results are displayed in Figure 5.4.

Subjects recalled more words when their moods matched than when the moods were mismatched, regardless of whether they read or generated the items. However, when the words were generated, not only was recall superior, but the size of the mood congruency effect was larger. These data, and others reported in the same article, support the idea that, to the extent that thoughts are important in the processing of information, there will be large effects of environment, state, and mood congruency. If thoughts are relatively unimportant, then context effects will be difficult to obtain.

Context- and state-dependent memory can be seen as examples of transfer appropriate processing. When the processing done at study (such as relying on U cues) is not appropriate for the processing required at test (generating a response based primarily on N cues), memory will be impaired. The addition of the missing cues, however, can dramatically increase the amount of information remembered. This type of finding—increased recall under one set of testing conditions relative to another set of testing conditions—has important implications for forgetting, a subject we turn to in the next chapter.

There is an important distinction between mood-dependent memory, which is shown in Figure 5.4, and mood-congruent effects. *Mood congruency* refers to the finding that a given mood tends to cue memories that are consistent with that mood, rather than memories that are inconsistent (Blaney, 1986; Hertel, 1992). For example, Teasdale and Russell (1983) had subjects learn a list of negative, neutral, or positive words. At test, subjects were induced to be either happy or sad and then were asked to recall as many words

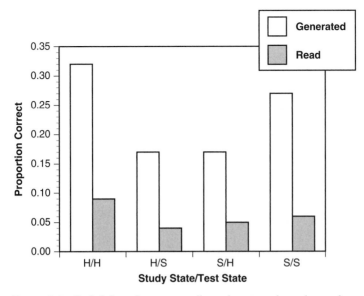

Figure 5.4   Probability of correct recall as a function of mood at study and test (happy or sad) and whether the item was generated or read.
SOURCE: From "Mood-Dependent Memory for Internal Versus External Events," by E. Eich and J. Metcalfe, 1989, *Journal of Experimental Psychology: Learning, Memory, and Cognition, 15,* 443–455. Copyright © 1989 American Psychological Association. Reprinted with permission of the author.

as they could. The sad subjects recalled more negative words than the happy subjects did, but the happy subjects recalled more positive words than the sad subjects did. The reason for mood-congruency effects is that the mood serves as a cue: Positive events are associated with positive moods, and negative events with negative moods. A particular type of mood can cue memories that are associated with that mood.

The Process Dissociation Framework

The levels of processing and transfer appropriate processing views stimulated a lot of research on the effects of different kinds of processing. One potential problem concerns how to attribute specific effects to specific processes. Several processes are used at the same time, and until quite recently it appeared difficult to separate out the effects of different operations. Jacoby (1991) has developed a technique for separating different processes that may be operating. So far, it has been applied to only a few types of processes, but it should be relatively straightforward to apply the same logic to other settings.

Jacoby and his colleagues (Jacoby, 1991; Jacoby, Toth, & Yonelinas, 1993) were interested in separating intentional retrieval processes from incidental processes. (This topic is of critical importance in the implicit memory literature and will be discussed further in Chapter 7.) On many tasks, performance improves simply because an item has been perceived a little earlier. Even though the subject may be completely unaware of this influence, performance can be enhanced. For example, if you happened to read the word *toboggan*, and a little later were doing a crossword puzzle in which *toboggan* was an answer, you would be more likely to get the answer than someone who had not recently read the word. This sort of process is sometimes termed an *automatic* or *incidental process*. By contrast, an *intentional process* is one in which the subject intentionally tries to recall an item. Because both of these processes usually contribute to test performance (Richardson-Klavehn & Bjork, 1988), it has been difficult to determine the properties and effects of each.

One way to separate them, Jacoby (1991) suggests, is to have two groups of subjects study a set of words. One group receives an inclusion test, in which both processes are allowed to contribute; the other group receives an exclusion test, in which only automatic or incidental processes can contribute. The retrieval cues available to the subject are kept constant; the sole difference between an inclusion test and an exclusion test is the instructions given to the subject. By comparing performance on the two tests, it becomes possible to separate the effects of each process.

To see how this logic works, it is easiest to follow a specific example. In Phase 1, all subjects hear a list of items. In Phase 2, more items are presented, but this time in one of two conditions. In the full-attention condition, the subjects simply read the words. In the divided-attention condition, the subjects also listen to a tape-recorded series of numbers and indicate when they hear three odd digits in a row. The divided-attention manipulation is designed to reduce the influence of the recollective process while leaving the automatic process unaffected. At test, the subjects receive a stem completion task, in which they are asked to complete the stem to make a valid English word. The stems are presented in one of two colors, green or red. If the subjects see a green stem, they are asked to use it as a cue to remember a word from either Phase 1 or Phase 2; if they cannot remember a word, they are asked to complete it with the first word that comes to mind. A green stem, then, signals an inclusion test, on which both automatic and intentional processes work together. If the subjects see a red stem, they are asked to use it as a cue to remember a word from either Phase 1 or Phase 2 but to make sure that they do *not* write any of these words as a response. A red stem signals an exclusion test, on which automatic and intentional processes work in opposition.

Table 5.4 shows the probability of responding with an old word, from two versions of this experiment. Note that in the exclusion condition, subjects were instructed not to write down any old items. In general, performance is worse under divided than under full attention, particularly for the inclusion task. Performance is equivalent for the "heard"

Table 5.4   The probability of completing the stem with a studied item on both inclusion and exclusion tests for experiments

| | Performance Component | | | |
| | Read | | Heard | |
Attention	Inclusion	Exclusion	Inclusion	Exclusion
Full	0.61	0.36	0.47	0.34
Divided	0.46	0.46	0.42	0.37

NOTE: "Read" and "Heard" correspond to whether the item came from Phase 1 or Phase 2 of presentation.

SOURCE: Jacoby, Toth, & Yonelinas (1993).

words because attention was not manipulated there. This is an important condition because it provides a check on the attention manipulation: If performance did not differ between read and heard words, we would not have confidence in the division of attention manipulation.

How can we separate the recollective process from the automatic process using these data? On an *inclusion* test, the probability of responding with a studied item (either read or heard) is the probability of conscious recollection (R) plus the probability that a word came to mind automatically (A) when there is a failure of conscious recollection (1 − R). Because the second part is a conditional probability, we need to multiply the two components together to reflect the fact that both need to occur.

$$Inclusion = R + A(1 - R) \tag{5.1}$$

For an *exclusion* test, the word will be produced only when conscious recollection fails (1 − R) and when the word automatically came to mind (A).

$$Exclusion = A(1 - R) \tag{5.2}$$

Because Equations 5.1 and 5.2 share similar terms, Equation 5.2 can be rewritten as

$$Inclusion = R + Exclusion \tag{5.3}$$

or

$$R = Inclusion - Exclusion \tag{5.4}$$

If we divide Equation 5.2 by (1 − R), we can solve for A:

$$A = \frac{Exclusion}{1 - R} \tag{5.5}$$

Using the values in Table 5.4, we can now calculate estimates of R and A for the words that were read. We focus on this condition because it was only here that the divided-attention manipulation was performed. The estimate of R for the full-attention condition in this experiment is calculated using Equation 5.4: R = 0.61 − 0.36, or 0.25. The estimate of A for the same condition is calculated using Equation 5.5: A = 0.36/(1 − 0.25), or 0.47. For the divided-attention condition, R = 0.46 − 0.46, or 0, and A = 0.46/(1 − 0), or 0.46. These values are summarized in Table 5.5.

The estimates of R and A suggest that the processing dissociation technique can separate the influences of two different processes. Divided attention was designed to minimize the effect of conscious recollective processes, because the subject was required to attend

Table 5.5 Estimates of the contribution of recollective and automatic processes for the words that were read, calculated from the data in Table 5.4

Attention	Estimate	
	Recollection	*Automatic*
Full	0.25	0.47
Divided	0.00	0.46

SOURCE: Jacoby, Toth, & Yonelinas (1993).

to the irrelevant vigilance task. As Table 5.5 shows, the contribution of R was reduced to 0. However, attention should not affect the automatic component, and indeed the estimates of A are identical in both the divided- and full-attention conditions. Jacoby, Toth, and Yonelinas (1993) performed several more replications to ensure that the results obtained here were not a fluke. In particular, in a second experiment, they again obtained an estimate of R in a divided-attention condition of 0.0.

There have been some criticisms of this approach, centering around the issue of independence of the intentional and automatic processes. For example, Richardson-Klavehn, Lee, and Joubran (1994) suggest that the two processes may operate in a symbiotic fashion: An item suggested by the automatic process may then be considered by the intentional process. The question of independence of these processes is explored in detail in an exchange between Jacoby and his colleagues (Jacoby, Begg, & Toth, 1997; Jacoby & Shrout, 1997) and Curran and Hintzman (1997; Hintzman & Curran, 1997). It is unclear at the moment whether this criticism is important or trivial; at least one study (McBride, Dosher, & Gage, 2001) found equivalent results when using a version that assumed independence and one that did not. Regardless, the usefulness of the procedure is becoming more apparent. The procedure has been used in an increasing variety of tasks, including applications to implicit learning (Destrebecqz & Cleeremans, 2001; see Chapter 7), amnesia (Verfaellie & Treadwell, 1993; Yonelinas, Kroll, Dobbins, Lazzara, & Knight, 1998; see Chapter 8), and aging (Hay & Jacoby, 1999; Jennings & Jacoby, 1993; see Chapter 14). Further confidence comes from experiments in which the estimates obtained by process dissociation agree with estimates from other procedures (Yonelinas, 2001).

What Is Encoded?

The studies on state-, mood-, and context-dependent memory suggest that even when presented with a single word, people also encode many other attributes related to their mood and their environment. Furthermore, as we shall see in the next chapter, people also seem to encode all kinds of information about the word itself, including whether it is a noun or an adjective, whether it has one or two syllables, whether it was presented in red or in green, whether it was presented in upper- or lowercase, and so on. Is this much information really being encoded? One possible answer is that an enormous amount of processing, encoding information on a large number of dimensions, occurs even in the 500 ms that a word is available for study.

There is a different way of viewing this question, however. Many of the dimensions that subjects appear to encode may be apparent at test only when particular comparisons are made. For example, describe the object in Figure 5.5A. Most people will say "a square." However, when asked to describe the same object when placed next to another item, as in Figure 5.5B, they now describe it as a small square. With two other items, as in Figure 5.5C, they describe it as a small white square.

Thus, there is a difference between a nominal stimulus and a functional stimulus. The *nominal stimulus* is what the experimenter thinks the subject is encoding, and the *functional stimulus* is what the subject actually encoded. In general, the functional stimulus is likely to include many elements of the context and many idiosyncratic associations. Taking heed of an assumption from levels of processing, memory is a by-product of processing information, and the processing can add to or subtract from the nominal stimulus.

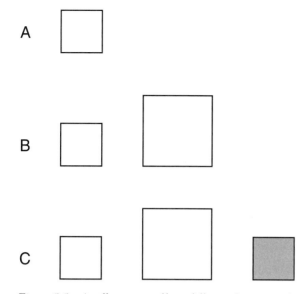

Figure 5.5   An illustration of how different dimensions become relevant. When asked to name the figure in A, the answer is a square; in B, the answer is a small square; and in C, the answer is a small white square.

One famous example of this process is the study reported by Carmichael, Hogan, and Walter (1932; see also Moore, 1910). The subjects were told that they would see a picture and would be asked to reproduce the figure as accurately as possible. As each figure was shown, the experimenter would say, "The next figure resembles . . ." and would say a name. For example, one group of subjects was told that an ambiguous figure (such as those shown in the center column of Figure 5.6) resembles "eyeglasses," and a second group was told that it resembles "dumbbells." Although the task was to reproduce the figure "as accurately as possible," most subjects changed the figure so that it more closely resembled the verbal label. Examples of some reproductions are also shown in Figure 5.6.

The point is, of course, that the nominal stimulus is the figure itself, but the functional stimulus—how the subject encoded the item—was slightly different. The subject paid attention to the verbal label, and this affected how the figure was encoded. Similar effects are observable when the labels are provided only at test (Hanawalt & Demarest, 1939). The way the information is processed at study or at test can distort the original information. (We shall examine reconstructive processes in more detail in Chapter 12.)

Chapter Summary

The levels-of-processing framework was the first detailed account of memory to argue that the type of processing was more important than the underlying theoretical structure. According to this view, items will be well remembered if they are processed deeply, regardless of factors such as intent to learn. The primary difference between levels of processing and transfer appropriate processing is that the latter specifically includes retrieval factors.

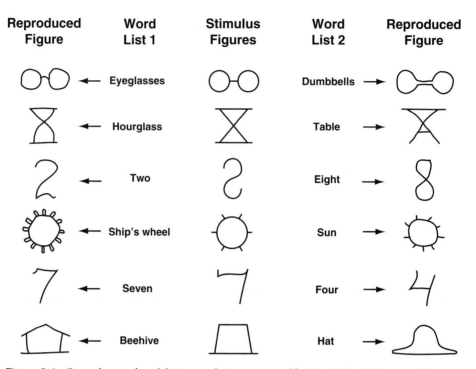

Reproduced Figure	Word List 1	Stimulus Figures	Word List 2	Reproduced Figure
	← Eyeglasses		Dumbbells →	
	← Hourglass		Table →	
	← Two		Eight →	
	← Ship's wheel		Sun →	
	← Seven		Four →	
	← Beehive		Hat →	

Figure 5.6 Several examples of the types of items presented by Carmichael, Hogan, and Walter. SOURCE: Carmichael, Hogan, & Walter (1932).

According to this view, a particular type of processing leads to better memory performance because it is appropriate for the kind of test that will be conducted. According to the related encoding specificity principle, the recollection of an event depends on the interaction between the properties of the encoded event and the properties of the retrieval information. Because it is the interaction that is important, no statements can be made about the mnemonic properties of an item, of a process, or of a cue. It is only when the interaction of the encoding and retrieval conditions is specified that meaningful statements about memory can be made. Processing approaches readily account for context-dependent (memory can be worse when tested in a new or different context) and context-congruent (a given context tends to cue memories that are consistent with that context) memory effects. Few if any tasks are process-pure. One way to separate the relative contributions of different processes is the process dissociation technique. This works by comparing performance in two conditions: one in which both processes work together and one in which they work in opposition.

Forgetting

We are told that the famous Athenian Themistocles was endowed with wisdoms and genius on a scale quite surpassing belief; and it is said that a certain learned and highly accomplished person went to him and offered to impart to him the science of mnemonics, which was then being introduced for the first time; and that when Themistocles asked what precise result that science was capable of achieving, the professor asserted that it would enable him to remember everything; and Themistocles replied that he would be doing him a greater kindness if he taught him to forget what he wanted than if he taught him to remember.

—Marcus Tullius Cicero

Historically, there have been three main views of forgetting: (1) forgetting is due primarily to initial storage problems; (2) forgetting is due primarily to decay of information between storage and retrieval; and (3) forgetting is due primarily to retrieval failures. Reflecting these three views, in this chapter we examine consolidation theory, interference theory, and a theory based on discrimination.

Consolidation Theory

Consolidation theory is not really a theory of forgetting but rather a theory of why information is not stored in the first place. Müller and Pilzecker (1900) argued that learning is not complete at the time that practice or rehearsal ends. Rather, a process known as *perseveration* occurs for a while afterward, and the longer this perseveratory period is, the stronger or more consolidated the memory trace will be. If anything occurs to interrupt this perseveration, then the trace may not have the chance to become consolidated, and recall will not be possible. This idea has substantial biological plausibility. Hebb (1949) proposed that memory involves persistent changes both (1) in the relationship between neurons (or groups of neurons, which he called cell assemblies), either through structural modification or biochemical events; and (2) within a particular neuron that affect communication with its neighbors (see Chapter 8). An obvious suggestion was that perseveration is short-term memory and the consolidated trace is long-term memory.

Any version of consolidation theory makes three key predictions. First, a period of mental inactivity (or neuronal inactivity) is more conducive to perseveration—and hence to more consolidation—than is a period of activity. Memory should be better, then, following a rest period (such as a nap) than following a period of activity (such as engaging in some distractor task). Second, if the perseveration period is interrupted, then the trace cannot be consolidated and the item will not be stored. Memory should be worse, then, following some event that prevents consolidation. Third, if consolidation is prevented, the item should *never* be recalled because the essential storage phase was not completed.

There is ample evidence for the first of these predictions. Ebbinghaus (1885) noted that forgetting is retarded by sleep or, more precisely, that the rate of forgetting is slowed when a period of sleep occurs between study and test. Jenkins and Dallenbach (1924) performed a more systematic investigation in which they had two subjects live in the lab for a period of time. The subjects learned lists of items and then were asked to recall them after 1, 2, 4, or 8 hours of sleep or wakefulness. As Figure 6.1 shows, subjects were able to recall more of the items following a period of sleep than following a period of wakefulness.

According to consolidation theory, the interpretation is simple: When the perseveration process is interrupted by other mental or neuronal activity, the trace cannot be consolidated. The longer the perseveratory process, the more the information will be consolidated and the more likely it is that it will be remembered. This interpretation is consistent with another experiment by Dallenbach, this time using cockroaches as subjects. Minami and Dallenbach (1946) investigated the effects of inactivity when sleep was not involved. They first conditioned roaches to elicit an avoidance response. Some roaches were then allowed to engage in normal activity, whereas others were wrapped in cotton wool and placed in matchboxes. The idea was to prevent the roaches from moving and to minimize stimulation. These restricted roaches showed greater retention of the avoidance response than did the roaches that were allowed to engage in normal activity.

One example often cited as supporting the second prediction of consolidation theory—that if perseveration is interrupted, then the trace cannot be consolidated and the item will not be stored—is *retrograde amnesia*. With retrograde amnesia, people cannot recall the events that occurred before a trauma. According to consolidation theory, the perseveratory activity was interrupted by the trauma, and thus the consolidation process could not be completed. Therefore, the events that occurred right before the trauma were not stored and could not be remembered.

Most experimental studies designed to test consolidation theory have used rats as subjects and induced amnesia by subjecting the rats to electroconvulsive shock (ECS). One side effect of ECS, in both humans and other animals, is retrograde amnesia. A typical study, and one that is widely cited, was performed by Duncan (1949). He first trained rats using an avoidance procedure. A rat was placed in a two-chambered box and received a mild foot shock if it did not move to the other side of the chamber within 10 seconds. Rats can learn this task rather quickly. Duncan varied the interval between completion of

Figure 6.1   Mean number of syllables recalled correctly by two subjects who either slept or remained awake for varying time intervals after learning.   Source: From "Obliviscence During Sleep and Waking," by J. G. Jenkins and K. M. Dallenbach, 1924, *American Journal of Psychology, 35*, 605–612. Copyright © 1924 University of Illinois Press. Reprinted with permission.

the avoidance response and the administration of ECS, using intervals from 20 s to 4 hr; a control group received no ECS. Consistent with consolidation theory, the longer the delay between the response and the administration of ECS—or, in terms of the theory, the longer perseveration was allowed to continue—the better was the memory for the learning episode (see Figure 6.2). The estimate of time needed for consolidation was approximately 1 hour.

One problem with this experiment is that it requires an active response on the part of the rat to demonstrate learning. There are two reasons the rat might not move after receiving ECS. First, the animal may have forgotten the avoidance response that it has learned and so does not remember to move to the other side of the chamber to avoid a foot shock. A second possibility however, is that the rats may have inadvertently been subjected to a conditioned fear experiment and may be opting for the lesser of two evils: A move to the other side of the chamber could serve as a cue for ECS, and the animal may prefer the mild foot shock to the severe ECS. Thus, the rat might remain stationary because of amnesia or because of fear.

An experiment by Chorover and Schiller (1965) tested this idea. Rather than require an active response to signify remembering, their experiment required the animal to remain stationary. The experiment involved placing a rat on a raised platform. Because the rat's natural inclination is to avoid exposed, high places, the animal quickly stepped off

Figure 6.2 Mean number of avoidance runs made by different groups of rats that differed only in the duration of the interval between the learning trial and the ECS. The x-axis is in log units. The corresponding values are 20 s, 40 s, 60 s, 4 min, 15 min, 1 hr, 4 hr, and 14 hr. The white square shows performance of animals in a control condition with no ECS.   Source: Duncan (1949).

the platform. When this happened, the rat received a mild foot shock; if the rat stayed on the platform, nothing happened. Chorover and Schiller again varied the interval between the learning episode (stepping down) and the administration of ECS. Note that this time, however, if the rat has learned fear of the ECS, it should remain on the platform; if it does not remember the foot shock, it should step down. Whereas Duncan estimated that consolidation takes 1 hour, Chorover and Schiller estimated that consolidation is complete within 10 seconds. If ECS is administered within 10 s of the learning, then there is retrograde amnesia. If ECS is delayed for more than 10 s, then memory for the learning episode will remain. This estimate of 10 s, although obtained on rats, coincided nicely with conceptions of the duration of information in short-term memory.

The third prediction of consolidation theory is that if consolidation is prevented, the item should *never* be recalled. Quartermain, McEwen, and Azmitia (1972) tested this prediction using a procedure similar to that used by Chorover and Schiller. The main difference was that whereas Chorover and Schiller tested all animals 24 hr after the administration of ECS, Quartermain and associates tested some animals 48 and 72 hr after ECS. There was evidence of amnesia in those animals tested 24 or 48 hr after ECS, but no evidence of amnesia after 72 hr. The suggestion is that in the 24- and 48-hr groups, the memory was actually stored but was rendered temporarily unavailable by the ECS; after 72 hr, the memory again became available. This finding directly contradicts the third prediction of consolidation theory: Interrupting the perseveration phase should prevent the storage of information. Quartermain et al. demonstrated that the information is stored; it is just not retrieved.

A final study reinforces this interpretation. Miller and Springer (1972) argued that if the memory is stored but temporarily unavailable, providing a reminder to the animals should remove all traces of amnesia. They followed a procedure similar to that used in the previous studies, but they gave some rats a second foot shock after ECS had been administered. The reminder foot shock was given outside the experimental chamber, so it did not constitute another learning trial. The control group, which did not receive a reminder, showed amnesia; however, the experimental group did not.

Although there is much evidence against a strong form of consolidation theory (Crowder, 1982b; Keppel, 1984; Spear & Riccio, 1994), a weaker form is undoubtedly correct: Some biological changes may indeed affect an organism's ability to store information. This weaker form, though, has yet to provide a link between the physiological processes and the cognitive consequences. As knowledge of psychobiological processes continues to grow, it may again become possible to entertain a serious version of consolidation theory. Until that time, however, several other major theories of forgetting make more accurate predictions and offer more insights into why forgetting occurs.

Interference Theory

A competing view of forgetting was also being developed during the same time as consolidation theory. Rather than suggesting that the information never entered the memory system, it proposed that other information somehow caused interference.

John McGeoch played a central role in the first stages of the development of interference theory. In 1932, he argued that time-based decay theories are not valid scientific explanations of behavior. Specifically, he argued that just as iron rusts over time, memories are forgotten over time, but in neither case is time the causal agent. For iron, it is the process of oxidation that causes rust, and this process must, of necessity, unfold over time. The same is true for forgetting: It must, of necessity, unfold over time, but something else, analogous to oxidation, occurs as time passes. McGeoch suggested that the processing of other material causes interference. Notice that the experiments by Dallenbach reported above can be interpreted as supporting an interference explanation.

Interference can be either retroactive or proactive. To illustrate, consider a hypothetical experiment. In a *paired-associate experiment*, subjects are asked to learn arbitrary pairings of two items, such as *dog* and *roof, car* and *desk*, and so forth. at test, they will be prompted with *dog* and asked to respond with the correct answer, *roof*. These item pairs are often represented as A-B, with A standing for the first item, or cue, and B standing for the second item, or target. If subjects learn a second list that contains entirely new items, C-D (such as *phone-coffee*), there will be relatively little interference. In other words, memory for the A-B relationship will not be affected very much by learning the C-D relationship. If, however, the subjects learn a list that reuses the A items but pairs them with new, D items, there will be interference. If *dog-roof* is the A-B pairing, *dog-coffee* might be the A-D pairing. When tested later for the A-B items, the A-D associations will produce what is called *retroactive interference (RI)*, because A-D interferes with something learned earlier. This is illustrated in the top part of Table 6.1. The bottom part of Table 6.1 illustrates the procedure for inducing *proactive interference (PI)*. Note that we are again testing memory of the A-B items, but subjects in the experimental group learn the A-D

Table 6.1 A schematic illustration of two experimental designs in which subjects are tested for the memory of A-B relationships

	Learn First	*Learn Second*	*Tested On*	*Interference*
Control	A-B	C-D	A-B	
Experimental	A-B	A-D	A-B	RI
Control	C-D	A-B	A-B	
Experimental	A-D	A-B	A-B	PI

NOTE: The top design produces retroactive interference; the bottom design produces proactive interference.

associations first. This will cause proactive interference because already-learned information will interfere with newer information.

Although the stimuli and methods described may seem artificial, the principles apply equally as well in real-world settings (see, for example, Bower, 1978). For example, Table 6.2 gives one example of when RI and PI might occur if a person is trying to learn both Italian and Spanish vocabulary. To take another example, as we shall see in Chapter 12, the typical experiment on the effects of misleading information on eyewitnesses is nothing more than a fancy A-B–A-D paradigm (Crowder, 1976): The original material is B, and the misleading information is D.

Underwood (1957) dramatically documented the effects of proactive interference. He combined the results of 14 studies and simply plotted them all on the same graph, shown in Figure 6.3. What he found was that the more previous trials a subject had with a particular task, the lower the performance. That is, if a person has had three previous trials and everything else is held constant, performance on the fourth trial will be worse because of interference from the first three trials. Although some suggestions were made on how to incorporate PI into interference theory, a mechanism was never really specified. This lack of a specific mechanism for PI was one major reason for the diminishing popularity of interference theory in general (Zechmeister & Nyberg, 1982). Despite this omission, however, interference theory has greatly influenced all subsequent theories of forgetting.

Consolidation theory can be seen as one form of interference theory, in which interference occurs during storage. In McGeoch's (1932, 1942) *three-factor theory of forgetting*—the initial main formulation of interference theory—the locus of interference was placed

Table 6.2 A schematic illustration of two experimental designs in which subjects are tested for Spanish vocabulary

	Learn First	*Learn Second*	*Tested On*	*Interference*
Control	Spanish vocabulary	Math	Spanish vocabulary	
Experimental	Spanish vocabulary	Italian vocabulary	Spanish vocabulary	RI
Control	Math	Spanish vocabulary	Spanish vocabulary	
Experimental	Italian vocabulary	Spanish vocabulary	Spanish vocabulary	PI

NOTE: In the top design, learning Italian vocabulary after the Spanish will produce retroactive interference, whereas in the bottom design, learning Italian vocabulary before the Spanish will produce proactive interference.

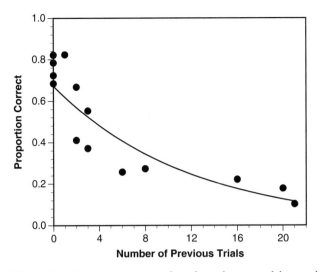

Figure 6.3   Proportion correct plotted as a function of the number of previous trials. Data were collected from 14 different studies.
SOURCE: Underwood (1957).

at retrieval. McGeoch assumed that retrieval failures occur because unwanted memories are retrieved instead of the desired memory. The A-D learning does not erase or remove the memories of the A-B learning, and the memories of the A-B pairing do not decay or fade over time; rather, both B and D coexist as memories for the correct response to A. In McGeoch's theory, there is no forgetting in the sense of loss of information; rather, forgetting is a temporary performance problem. There is no loss of information, only a lapse in retrieving it. McGeoch identified three mechanisms that can cause interference: response competition, altered stimulus conditions, and set.

Response competition occurs when two or more items are potential responses to a memory query. For example, when cued with A-?, both B and D compete as potential responses, and this competition reduces the probability that either one will be offered as a response. Much research was conducted on this aspect of interference theory; Crowder (1976) provides an excellent discussion and review. The main question concerned how best to test for the relative strength of the B and D responses so that different explanations of response competition could be further explicated. For example, Melton and Irwin (1940) used an A-B–A-D paired associate task, much like the one illustrated in Table 6.1. Subjects in the control condition learned to associate a series of items with cues, the A-B learning, and then "rested" for 30 min. Other groups had either 5, 10, 20, or 40 trials learning A-D paired associates, and then all groups were tested for the original A-B material.

If response competition were causing all of the forgetting, then all of the errors in the groups with interpolated learning should be D responses, rather than the desired B responses. Melton and Irwin demonstrated that this was not the case—that the difference in recall between the control and the experimental groups could not be attributed solely to intrusion or competition from D items. They suggested that subjects actually unlearned the original A-B material during the interpolated learning. However, the unlearning hypothesis quickly ran into the same problem that consolidation theory did: It is easy to find situations in which information that is supposed to be completely lost from the memory system reappears (Capaldi & Neath, 1995). For example, Postman and his colleagues (Postman, 1961; Postman, Stark, & Fraser, 1968) demonstrated that specific A-B–A-D associations are not actually lost, as the unlearning hypothesis predicted, but are available when different forms of testing are used.

The second of McGeoch's original three factors was *altered context* or *altered stimulus conditions*. Animal learning theorists distinguish between the nominal stimulus and the functional stimulus. For example, if a tone consistently precedes a mild foot shock, then rats will learn to avoid the shock by moving. From the experimenter's perspective, the tone is the important stimulus and nothing else. From the animal's perspective, however, the tone is only a *nominal* stimulus; additional sources of information also serve as cues. The total of all the cues that the animal attends to is the *functional* stimulus. For example, if the conditioning takes place in a white box, then the functional stimulus may be both a tone and a white environment. When the animal is placed in a black box and the tone is played, the animal may not respond. This does not mean that the animal has forgotten; rather, it could mean that the functional stimulus (white + tone) is no longer present to elicit the response.

Similar effects have long been known with humans as well (Carr, 1925; McGeoch, 1932). As discussed in the previous chapter, Abernathy (1940) demonstrated that students who were tested in the same classroom they were taught in did better than students who were tested in a different classroom. Subsequent research has consistently supported the idea that altered stimulus conditions—or more generally, contextual factors—play a major role in most kinds of forgetting.

The third factor in McGeoch's three-factor theory was set. *Set* can be thought of as a special version of context effects, with the subject using an inappropriate mind-set. The typical example is failing to recognize a friend from college when you happen to run into the person during a visit home. The idea is that, when at home, you are most likely to search through your list of "home friends" to identify a familiar face; because this person is not a "home friend," you find no match. If you had used the correct mind-set—"friends from college"—then you would have recognized the person.

A related phenomenon is known as *part-set cuing*. When people are asked to recall items from a list they have just studied or to produce examples from a well-known category, having a subset (part of a set) of those items available at recall usually does not help and can even impair performance. For example, Slamecka (1968) had subjects hear a list of words twice. The control subjects were given a blank sheet of paper and were asked to write down as many of the words as they could. The experimental subjects were given a sheet of paper that already contained 5 (or 15, or 25) of the words and were asked to supply the remaining 25 (or 15 or 5) items. The data of interest are the proportion of words recalled that were not cues. Slamecka found that the groups that had received part of the set as a cue recalled fewer items than did the control group. That is, the experimental group that received 15 words as cues could produce (on average) only 38% of the remaining words, compared to 50% for the control group. Although there is still no complete account for all of the part-set cuing data (see Nickerson, 1984), one interpretation is that the cues disrupt the normal retrieval strategy.

McGeoch's influence was so profound that no theories of forgetting from long-term memory propose decay as the main explanation. Within the realm of immediate memory, however, the most common view of forgetting has long been decay.

Decay Versus Interference in Immediate Memory

The Brown-Peterson paradigm is one area in which both a decay explanation and one based on interference were offered. Recall that in the Brown-Peterson paradigm, subjects are given three letters and are then asked to count backward (or perform some other distracting activity) for a specified amount of time. The typical finding is that after about 20 seconds of counting backward, very few people can recall the letters. Indeed, many textbooks still cite the results of Peterson and Peterson (1959) as supporting the rapid decay of information in short-term memory. We described the basic results from the Brown-Peterson paradigm in Chapter 3 and saw how they were used as evidence for a separate short-term store and for advocating a major role for decay to explain the loss of information. An enormous amount of research has been conducted in this paradigm precisely because of its importance for theories of memory. This research has generally not favored the decay explanation.

The first major challenge to the decay explanation was reported by Keppel and Underwood (1962). Remember that Underwood (1957) found that, over a large number of studies, subjects' performance decreased as they received more and more trials. Proactive interference could operate in the Brown-Peterson paradigm because all of the consonant trigrams on all of the trials were very similar: The more previous trials that subjects had seen, the worse their performance was likely to be. In fact, Peterson and Peterson were aware of this decline, and analyzed their data to see whether PI was operating. They divided the 48 trials into blocks of 12 and combined performance in the two shortest and the two longest conditions. The proportion of items recalled correctly is displayed in Table 6.3. Peterson and Peterson (1959) concluded that there was no PI because performance actually got better over blocks in the 3 s and 6 s conditions. If there were PI, performance would be expected to get worse.

The only difference between Peterson and Peterson's (1959) analysis and that of Keppel and Underwood (1962) was that the latter study examined the first four trials individually, rather than averaging over the first 12 trials. When they did so, Keppel and Underwood found substantial evidence for proactive interference. On Trial 1, there was no forgetting regardless of how long the subjects counted backward (see Figure 6.4). Forgetting was observed only on subsequent trials, and by as few as 3 trials, performance was quite poor.

The important point is that recall does not differ on the very first trial when tested after 3 s or after 18 s. Equivalent performance has been repeatedly demonstrated when the first trial is analyzed (Baddeley & Scott, 1971; Cofer & Davidson, 1968; Fuchs & Melton, 1974; Gorfein, 1987; Turvey, Brick, & Osborn, 1970; Wright, 1967). A decay explanation, such as the one usually invoked to explain the Peterson and Peterson (1959) results,

Table 6.3 Proportion of items recalled correctly, displayed as blocks of 12 trials for two different sets of delay

	Block 1	Block 2	Block 3	Block 4
3 s and 6 s	0.57	0.66	0.70	0.74
15 s and 18 s	0.08	0.15	0.09	0.12

SOURCE: Data from Peterson & Peterson (1959).

Figure 6.4   Proportion of items recalled correctly in a Brown-Peterson procedure at three different retention intervals on the first, second, and third trials.   SOURCE: From "Proactive Inhibition in Short-Term Retention of Single Items," by G. Keppel and B. J. Underwood, 1962, *Journal of Verbal Learning and Verbal Behavior, 1,* 153–161. Copyright © 1962 Academic Press, Inc. Reprinted with permission.

says that the more time that elapses, the more decay will occur. Showing equivalent performance for the 3 s and 18 s groups is inconsistent with this prediction. The reason that Peterson and Peterson (1959) did not observe PI was that it had already occurred within the 12 trials that composed Block 1.

The decay view and the interference view make different predictions. Wickens, Born, and Allen (1963; see also Wickens, 1970, 1972) tested a strong prediction of the PI interpretation of the Brown-Peterson results. Proactive interference will build up when the list items are all highly similar. If the stimulus type is changed, however, there should be less PI. Thus, on the first three trials, the researchers had subjects hear three consonants, then perform some distracting activity, and then recall the consonants. On the fourth trial, half of the subjects were switched from consonants to numbers. Performance in the switched group was much better than in the control group, regardless of the direction of the change (digits to letters or letters to digits). The PI account predicts this increase in performance when the type of stimuli is changed. The decay view, in contrast, cannot predict an increase in performance.

The amount of reduction, or *release from PI*, can be calculated easily (see Figure 6.5). If x is the difference in performance between the experimental and control groups on Trial 4, and y is the difference between the control group on Trial 4 and the control group on Trial 1, then the percent release from PI is equal to $(x/y) \times 100$. If the release is 100%, then performance on the fourth trial is the same as performance on the first trial. If it is close to 0, there is no release.

Most release from PI phenomena are symmetric; that is, the amount of release is the same when switching from consonants to numbers as it is when switching from numbers

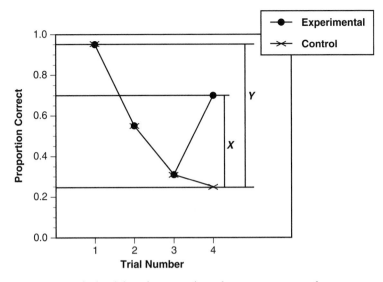

Figure 6.5   Idealized data showing release from proactive interference in the Brown-Peterson paradigm. X is the difference in performance between the experimental group (who have a different type of stimulus material on Trial 4 than on the previous trials) and the control group (who have the same type of stimulus material). Y is the difference in performance between Trial 1 and Trial 4 for the control group.

to consonants. This symmetry indicates it is the change in materials that is crucial, rather than the fact that one type of material is easier to recall than another. Switching from words to numbers gives an 85% release; switching from auditory to visual also gives about an 85% release. Changing taxonomic category (such as from types of cars to Russian novelists) gives a 65% release. Changing the number of syllables gives only a 15% release. Changing from one part of speech to another (verbs to nouns) gives less than a 5% release. One particularly interesting release concerns what is known as the *semantic differential*. If all the words on the first three trials have similar meanings, such as something pleasant (*sunny, enjoy, happy*), and the words on the last trial mean something different (*kill, death, illness*), there is about a 55% release from PI. Wickens (1972) reports many such measures.

Release from PI is not limited to the typical laboratory paradigm. Gunter, Berry, and Clifford (1981) demonstrated release from PI when testing subjects' memory for news items taped off the evening news. The news stories were classified as being either domestic or international. Subjects saw several stories from one category, and then either another from the same category or one from the other category. Subjects showed a 70% release from PI. Blumenthal and Robbins (1977) have shown buildup and release of PI when answering questions about prose passages, suggesting that this might affect performance on standardized tests. Dempster (1985) tested this idea directly, demonstrating the buildup of PI on comprehension questions like those used on the ACT and SAT.

Turvey and Egan (1970) changed two dimensions at the same time and found that performance on Trial 4 was equal to performance on Trial 1, regardless of whether the retention interval was 5 s or 15 s. Other results consistent with the proactive interference

---

Experiment   *Buildup and Release of PI*

Purpose: To demonstrate the buildup and release of proactive interference in the Brown-Peterson paradigm.

Subjects: Forty subjects are recommended; ten should be assigned to each group. Two groups receive the same type of items on all four trials, and two groups change to a different type of item on Trial 4.

Materials: Table F in the Appendix lists 32 consonant trigrams. Number trigrams can be obtained from Table B by taking the first three digits, then the second three digits, and so on. Table G lists several names of categories. For each subject, present novel items. There should also be two answer sheets: one for the category items and one for the trigrams. You will also need a stopwatch.

Design: One group of subjects will receive only letters, and one will receive only numbers. For the remaining subjects, one group will receive letters for the first three trials and numbers on the fourth, and the other group will receive numbers for the first three trials and letters on the fourth. Because each subject experiences only one condition, this is a between-subjects design.

Procedure: Inform the subjects that this is an experiment on information processing. Describe the two tasks, and explain how subjects should respond on the answer sheets. Read each trigram aloud, immediately name a category, and ask subjects to name as many examples of that category as they can. Record the examples of the category that the subject produces. After 10 s, ask the subject to report the trigram; then begin the next trial. On the fourth trial, change the type of material for half of the subjects.

Instructions: "This is an experiment on information processing. I will read three items out loud, which I will ask you to recall in order. Before you recall them, I will name a category, and I would like you to name as many examples as you can as quickly as you can. For example, if I said 'dog,' you might say 'poodle, corgi, greyhound, Pekinese, Great Dane, English setter' as quickly as you can. When I signal, you will stop and report the three items in order. Then, I'll give you the next three items and a new category. Any questions?"

Scoring and Analysis: For each subject, count the number of trigrams recalled in order, and compute an average for each group. The results from the two groups that receive only letters or only numbers can be averaged together, and the results from the two groups that experienced a change on the fourth trial can be averaged together. The results should be similar to those plotted in Figure 6.5.

Optional Enhancements: Include more subjects in each group.

SOURCE: Based on an experiment by Wickens (1972).

---

explanation were reported by Loess and Waugh (1967). If recall is being reduced by PI, then one way to decrease the amount of PI is to separate the trials. Loess and Waugh found that with very long intervals between trials (such as 300 s), there was no difference in performance as a function of trial number, even when the subjects were counting backward for 18 seconds. Subjects were about 60% accurate on Trial 1 and were still around 60% correct on Trial 4. Both results are inconsistent with an explanation that attributes forgetting to the rapid loss of information from short-term memory.

Several studies have tried to pin down the locus of the release from PI effect. An early suggestion was that when a change in stimulus properties occurs, subjects devote extra attention to the novel item. This account has two problems. One is that subjects are often unaware of the changes, particularly with the semantic differential, yet they still

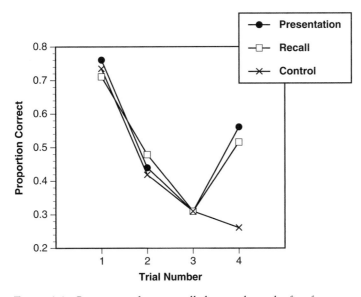

Figure 6.6   Proportion of items recalled correctly on the first four trials of a Brown-Peterson procedure as a function when the cue was presented, either before presentation (the Presentation condition) or after presentation but before recall (the Recall condition). The cue was not given to the control group.   SOURCE: From "Retrieval Cues and Release from Proactive Inhibition," by J. M. Gardiner, F. I. M. Craik, and J. Birtwistle, 1972, *Journal of Verbal Learning and Verbal Behavior, 11*, 778–783. Copyright © 1972 Academic Press, Inc. Reprinted with permission.

show release from PI. A second problem is that other manipulations designed to affect the amount of attention do not yield any release (MacLeod, 1975).

A more promising idea is that it is a retrieval effect. Gardiner, Craik, and Birtwistle (1972) examined this hypothesis using two categories of items, each of which could be divided into subgroups. Some subjects received types of games, others types of flowers. Unnoticed by the subjects, the first three trials would all be indoor games (or wildflowers), and the fourth trial would be outdoor games (or garden flowers). All subjects received this subtle change in categories, but only two of the groups were informed of the change. One group was informed prior to presentation of the fourth trial; the other group was informed after presentation of the fourth trial but prior to recall. Nothing extra was said to the control subjects. The results are shown in Figure 6.6.

The control subjects were affected by the buildup of PI, and this continued through Trial 4. If the change is unnoticed, then there will be no release from PI; but both the presentation and recall groups showed an equivalent release from PI. Gardiner and associates argued that this release must be a retrieval effect because that was the only point at which both groups had the category change information at the same time: The recall group could still take advantage of the change, even though they were unaware of this subtle change in category at encoding.

Decay explanations of the results from the Brown-Peterson paradigm do not work. A better explanation is one that views interference effects as arising from distinctiveness.

Relative Distinctiveness

Explanations of forgetting based on *relative distinctiveness* have, as their foundation, the idea that items will be well recalled to the extent that they stand out or differ in some fashion from surrounding items. A well-known example of distinctiveness is the so-called *von Restorff effect*. It turns out that what most people describe as the prototypical experiment and result of this effect differs substantially from what Hedwig von Restorff actually reported in 1933 (see Hunt, 1995). Furthermore, the results were anticipated by Calkins (1896); Wallace (1965) called it the "pre-von Restorff von Restorff effect."

What is most often meant by the von Restorff or isolation effect is the finding that if one item in a list differs from the others, it is better recalled. For example, if the item at position 6 of a 12-item list is red and all the other items are black, item 6—the red item— will be very well recalled. If, on the other hand, all the items are red, then item 6 will not be very well recalled, even though it is the same item in both cases. Pillsbury and Raush (1943) presented three-digit numbers embedded in a list of three-letter nonsense syllables. When there was only one three-digit number, recall of that number was excellent; as the number of three-digit numbers increased and the number of three-letter nonsense syllables decreased, recall of the digits decreased and recall of the nonsense syllables increased.

The most obvious explanation, that the isolated item receives more rehearsal and as a consequence is recalled better, is not borne out empirically (e.g., Einstein, Pellegrino, Mondani, & Battig, 1974). Indeed, given that the effect is observable when the isolate is in the first serial position, explanations based on increased attention to the isolated item are also ruled out.

CogLab Experiment

http://coglab.wadsworth.com/experiments/VonRestorff/

The most likely explanation of the von Restorff effect is distinctiveness. The isolated item is distinct, or stands out, from the list of items at the time of recall. This account is similar to the one used to explain the Gardiner, Craik, and Birtwistle (1972) release from PI experiment. In the typical von Restorff experiment, the isolated item will differ in distinctiveness along a size dimension or a color dimension.

Just as items can differ in terms of their distinctiveness along physical dimensions, they can also differ along other dimensions, such as time. This type of retrieval hypothesis suggests an explanation for the data reported by Turvey, Brick, and Osborn (1970). They used a Brown-Peterson task in which consonant trigrams were presented followed by various amounts of distracting activity. Although they had five conditions, we will restrict our attention to only three of them. These three conditions differed only in the duration of the retention interval (how long the subjects performed the distracting activity). One group of subjects counted backward for 10 s, one for 15 s, and one for 20 s. The proportion of items recalled correctly in each condition was equivalent on the first trial (0.85, 0.93, and 0.93, respectively). The proportion of items correctly recalled in each condition was also equivalent on the fourth trial (0.33, 0.30, and 0.30, respectively). Note that these results are already inconsistent with a decay explanation, because more decay should have occurred with the longer intervals.

On the fifth trial, Turvey and associates had every group perform the distracting activity for 15 s; thus, one group's retention interval increased, one group's remained the

Table 6.4 Three groups that receive presentation of the first item (P1) at the same time and presentation of the second item (P2) at the same time; but recall of the second item (R2) occurs after varying delays

Group	0	10	20	30	40	50	P1–R2	P2–R2	Ratio
			Time						
A	P1		P2	R2			30 s	10 s	3:1
B	P1		P2		R2		40 s	20 s	2:1
C	P1		P2			R2	50 s	30 s	1.67:1

NOTE: "Ratio" is the ratio of the time P1–R2 to the time P2–R2.

same, and the third group's retention interval decreased. On this fifth trial, performance was not equivalent: The 10 s group got worse (down to 0.20), the 15 s group remained constant (0.28), and the 20 s group got better (up to 0.38). A change in the duration of the distracting activity is not sufficient to obtain a release from PI, because one group actually performed worse after the change. However, Baddeley (1976) offered an explanation that attributes this result to the relative, rather than the absolute, duration of the distractor activity.

Imagine three groups of subjects who receive two trials in a Brown-Peterson procedure. The first item is presented at Time 0, and the second item is presented after 20 s. Up until recall of the second item, everything is the same in the three groups. The second item is recalled either 10, 20, or 30 s after it was presented, as illustrated in Table 6.4.

Baddeley (1976) calculated ratios for the times involved. The time between presentation of the first item (P1) and the test for the second item (R2) is 30 s for Group A, 40 s for Group B, and 50 s for Group C. The time between presentation of the second item (P2) and the test for the second item (R2) is 10 s for Group A, 20 s for Group B, and 30 s for Group C. These figures and the resultant ratios are shown in Table 6.4. The prediction is that the group with the largest ratio will show the best performance because, Baddeley suggested, at the time of the recall attempt for item 2, recall will be primarily determined by the subject's ability to distinguish the second item from the first item. The closer in time the recall test is to the presentation of the second item and the farther away the recall test is from the presentation of the first item, the better will be the recall of the second item. It is this idea that the ratio is capturing.

The same reasoning can be applied to the Turvey, Brick, and Osborn (1970) data, shown in Table 6.5. The fourth item is presented at Time 0 (an arbitrary starting point).

Table 6.5 Three conditions from Turvey, Brick, & Osborn (1970), represented in the same way as in Table 6.4

Group	0	5	10	15	20	25	30	35	40	P4–R5	P5–R5	Ratio
				Time								
10	P4		P5			R5				10	15	0.67
15	P4			P5			R5			15	15	1.00
20	P4				P5			R5		20	15	1.33

The fifth item is presented either 10, 15, or 20 s later, according to the group. The recall test for the fifth item occurs 15 s later. The same ratios as before are calculated, and again, the larger the ratio, the better the recall of the fifth item.

This example contains a few simplifications. The first three items are not factored in, and the time intervals are not exactly those that appeared in the experiment (we have omitted the time needed to recall). However, this analysis applies even if we factor all these things in; it is just more complex. Similar analyses based on temporal discrimination have been used to explain serial position effects observed in recognition (Neath, 1993b) and in memory for items within a sentence (Neath & Knoedler, 1994).

One particularly interesting phenomenon that this type of view emphasizes is that memory performance can get *better* as time passes (Bjork, 2001). In one experiment, Neath and Knoedler (1994) presented subjects with a series of digitized photographs of snowflakes. These stimuli were chosen because people are unable to assign verbal labels to them, and thus the stimuli cannot be rehearsed verbally (Goldstein & Chance, 1970). These flakes were presented for 1 s on a computer screen with a 1 s gap—or interstimulus interval (ISI)—between one flake and the next. The recognition test occurred after a retention interval (RI) of either 0, 2, or 5 s. For the test, the snowflake shown was either one from the immediately preceding list or one that the subjects had not seen before. Only one recognition judgment was performed after each list. The results are shown in Figure 6.7. With a short retention interval, memory for the first item is at chance levels,

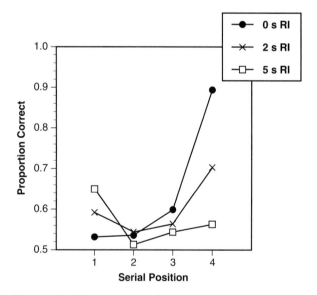

Figure 6.7 The proportion of items recognized correctly as a function of serial position and retention interval. Contrary to predictions based on decay or consolidation theories, there is an absolute increase in performance at the first serial position as the interval between presentation and test increases.   SOURCE: From "Distinctiveness and Serial Position Effects in Recognition and Sentence Processing," by I. Neath and A. J. Knoedler, 1994, *Journal of Memory and Language, 33,* 776–795. Copyright © 1994 Academic Press, Inc. Reprinted with permission.

whereas the last item is almost perfectly recognized. As the retention interval increases, performance on the last item decreases and performance on the first item increases.

A simple model based on distinctiveness explains this result. Murdock (1960) proposed the original idea, which was subsequently refined to include ideas of Baddeley (1976), Bjork and Whitten (1974), and Neath (1993b). The model defines distinctiveness as the extent to which a stimulus stands out from other stimuli, and emphasizes the relation between a given stimulus and the other members of the ensemble. The concept of distinctiveness is thus not applicable to an item in isolation, and the distinctiveness of a particular item can change depending on the other items in the list. As noted previously, for example, if the item at position 6 of a 12-item list is red and all the other items are black, item 6—the red item—will be very distinctive and very well recalled. If, on the other hand, all the items are red, then item 6 will not be very distinctive, even though it is the same item in both cases (von Restorff, 1933; Wallace, 1965).

Distinctiveness can, in principle, be calculated for any set of stimuli that vary along any dimension, whether temporal, physical, or some other dimension, although most of the work heretofore has focused on temporal (time-based) distinctiveness. In the typical memory experiment, the stimuli are equated for concreteness, length, frequency, and so on, and vary systematically only along a temporal dimension. The position of the item along the relevant dimension—here, temporal—is determined by calculating the sum of all the interstimulus intervals (ISI, in seconds) following the item in question, plus the retention interval (RI) following the final item. For example, if the RI is 1 s and each ISI is 1 s, the serial/temporal values (s) of a four-item list, beginning with the first item, would be 4, 3, 2, and 1. The final item in the list is a distance of 1 from the recaller, whereas the first item is a distance of 4 from the recaller.

These temporal values then undergo a log transformation, a process based on Weber's Law (see Chapter 1; see also Helson, 1964), yielding the preliminary discriminability of that item (d). For the example given above, the natural log values would be 1.386, 1.099, 0.693, and 0.000, respectively. A distinctiveness value of each item (δ) is calculated according to Equation 6.1, where n is the number of items in the list and k is the serial position of the current item.

$$\delta_k = \sum_{j=1}^{n} \left| d_k - d_j \right| \tag{6.1}$$

All Equation 6.1 really does is calculate a measure of how different each item is from all the other items. We take the absolute value of the difference because we do not care which number is larger, just what the size of the difference is. Thus, δ_1 is equal to (1.386 – 1.386) + (1.386 – 1.099) + (1.398 – 0.693) + (1.386 – 0.000), or 2.367. (Although all values are rounded, the values given as final results are accurate.) We then perform the same calculation for the other items and get values of 1.792, 1.792, and 3.178. (Actually, Neath, 1993b, used a slightly different equation for the middle items, but it is omitted here for the sake of simplicity.) Finally, these values are normalized. This means that they are converted to a scale that reflects the relative size of the numbers. To do this, we add up all the values, obtain a total of 9.129, and then divide each δ value by 9.129 to get the distinctiveness of each item relative to the other items on the list. The resulting values are 0.259, 0.196, 0.196, and 0.348.

What happens to the δ values when the RI is increased? Using the same example, but changing the RI to 5, we get the following serial/temporal values: 8, 7, 6, and 5. The logs of these values are 2.079, 1.946, 1.792, and 1.609. In this case, δ_1 is equal to (2.079 − 2.079) + (2.079 − 1.946) + (2.079 − 1.792) + (2.079 − 1.609), or 0.891. We then do the calculations for the other items and get values of 0.624, 0.624, and 0.989. The sum of these δ values is 3.128, and the normalized values are 0.285, 0.200, 0.200, and 0.316. Notice that with an increase in the duration of the retention interval, the model predicts that primacy will increase (0.259 becomes 0.285) and recency will decrease (0.348 becomes 0.316).

Wright and his colleagues (Wright, Santiago, Sands, Kendrick, & Cook, 1985) have shown increases in performance similar to those found by Neath and Knoedler (1994), but Wright showed that this finding holds for pigeons and monkeys. Knoedler, Hellwig, and Neath (1999) and Surprenant (2001) found that the result also holds for auditory stimuli: As the retention interval increases, memory for the items at the end of the list gets worse and memory for the items at the beginning of the list gets better. Wheeler (1995) has demonstrated, in a different paradigm, increased performance over time when there is no opportunity for further rehearsal or learning, and Bjork (2001) provides a review and extended discussion. Any theory of forgetting must explain not only why memory is often worse as time passes, but also why memory is sometimes better.

Any Evidence for Decay?

The strongest evidence against decay is finding improvement over time. Given the results just described, one might well ask whether there remains any evidence in support of decay. A strong case for decay can be made whenever absolute time has effects beyond those attributable to other sources of forgetting, such as interference.

Baddeley and Scott (1971) tested 424 undergraduates on their memory for a single spoken sequence of three, five, or seven digits after a delay of between 0 and 36 seconds. During the delay, subjects copied letters presented at a rate of 1 per second. The data are shown in the left panel of Figure 6.8.

Baddeley and Scott (1971) argued that the figure shows clear evidence of decay. Proactive interference could not have caused the forgetting, because there were no previous trials. Similarly, retroactive interference from the distractor task could not have caused the forgetting because letters and digits are sufficiently different (Wickens, Born, & Allen, 1963). The final source of interference would be intrasequence effects (Melton, 1963). Baddeley and Scott argued against this view because of the prediction that there should be faster forgetting for longer lists.

It turns out that it is easy to account for the difference in performance between the lists solely as a function of list length. According to the distinctiveness account of forgetting, the more items in the list, the less distinct any one item will be. Furthermore, performance decreases over time not because of decay, but because the memory representations become more similar, and so less distinctive. An extension of the distinctiveness model presented above (Brown, Neath, & Chater, 2002) was fitted to the Baddeley and Scott (1971) data. The right panel of Figure 6.8 shows the same data points, but the lines are those that the model predicts. Thus, these data can easily be accounted for by a model in which there is no decay.

The second study often cited as evidence for decay is one by Cowan, Saults, and Nugent (1997). On each trial, they presented two tones to subjects and asked them to judge whether the second tone was higher or lower in pitch than the first tone. The time between

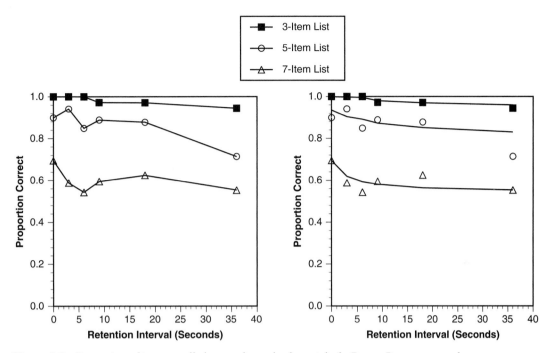

Figure 6.8 Proportion of items recalled correctly on the first trial of a Brown-Peterson procedure as a function of the number of items in the sequence and the duration of the distractor task. When the data points are simply connected, as is done in the left panel, it looks as if there is evidence for decay. The right panel shows the same data points, but this time the lines represent predictions from a distinctiveness model that attributes the forgetting to intrasequence interference: the more items in the list, the more intrasequence interference. SOURCE: Baddeley & Scott (1971).

the tones (the interitem presentation interval, or IPI) varied from 1.5 s to 12 s, and the time between trials (the intertrial interval, or ITI) also varied from 1.5 s to 12 s. With only two items, intraitem interference was minimal. They plotted their data as a function of the ratio ITI:IPI and found that for a given ratio, performance got worse over time. This suggests an effect of absolute time, and so provides evidence for decay. However, Cowan, Saults, and Nugent (2001) later reanalyzed the data, taking into account not only the role of the ITI and the IPI, but also a possible effect of tones on previous trials. They classified some of the trials from the original experiment into those in which the distinctiveness account would predict near optimal conditions, and those with suboptimal conditions. Analysis of the optimal trials found no effect of absolute time on performance. As a result, Cowan et al. (2001, p. 326) concluded that they had "failed to find clear evidence of decay in a situation that has often been viewed as one of the simplest paradigm cases for decay."

Forgetting as Discrimination

One theory of forgetting that can explain better performance as time elapses views memory and forgetting as a discrimination problem. According to Capaldi and Neath (1995), during learning the organism not only processes the material to be learned but also associates that material with a variety of internal and external contextual cues. What ends up being processed is a multidimensional complex of stimuli. Forgetting will occur if the stimulating conditions at test do not sufficiently discriminate between the desired memory and other competing memories, or if the stimuli at test elicit no memories at all. To the extent that the test cues do discriminate, the organism will remember. Thus, forgetting is simply a performance deficit resulting from inadequate stimulus conditions. This approach suggests that forgetting, in the sense of permanent loss, does not occur; there is only a failure to perform because of a difference in the stimulus conditions prevailing at encoding and at test.

The question of permanent loss versus temporary lapse is an important one, but it is difficult if not impossible to answer. If an organism learns something at Time 1, demonstrates memory for it at Time 2, but demonstrates no memory for it at Time 3, has the information been permanently lost, or is this simply a temporary retrieval deficit? In 1929, H. C. Blodgett reported an experiment demonstrating that a lack of performance was at least sometimes not a lack of learning or memory. He placed hungry rats in a complex maze and gave them food when they found their way through. These rats quickly learned the shortest route. He placed a second group of hungry rats in the maze but did not reward them. Not surprisingly, the performance of these animals did not improve over trials. With the introduction of food rewards, however, the error scores of the second group of animals plummeted to that of the first group that had been rewarded with food from the outset. This seminal study illustrates the important proposition that a lack of performance does not necessarily indicate a lack of learning—or, in memory terms, a lack of performance does not necessarily indicate a loss of previously learned information. Whenever an item is not recalled, it is possible that it is only temporarily inaccessible and that with a change in conditions or testing methods, the subject will produce it (Tulving & Pearlstone, 1966).

Loftus and Loftus (1980) took the position that there is permanent loss of information. Their evidence was mostly negative in nature, demonstrating that neither hypnosis (see Chapter 12) nor neurological studies by Wilder Penfield (see Chapter 15) supported the idea of permanent storage. The one positive line of evidence used to support their position came from the misleading eyewitness information paradigm, which we will discuss in Chapter 12. Capaldi and Neath (1995) took the opposite position. Although agreeing with Loftus and Loftus in their analysis of the hypnosis and Penfield studies, Capaldi and Neath suggested that the temporary lapse view made more predictions supported by empirical evidence than did the permanent loss view. In particular, they cited (literally) dozens of studies that demonstrated memory for information previously thought to be permanently lost (see also Miller & Grahame, 1991). To be clear, the temporary lapse view says that if a person (or animal) demonstrates memory for something at Time N, then that particular memory will be potentially available at all subsequent times as long as the retrieval cue is appropriate. The lapse view does not say that people remember everything they see or hear.

Two examples will serve here: one in which memory performance became better with the addition of a useful retrieval cue, and one in which memory for various items seems to have lasted at least 50 years. Eich and Birnbaum (1982) asked subjects to learn a list of words in either a sober or an intoxicated state. When tested after a change in drug state, retrieval was poor, as is usually the case (see Chapter 5). However, some of the subjects in the changed state condition were given an additional retrieval cue (such as "Think of all

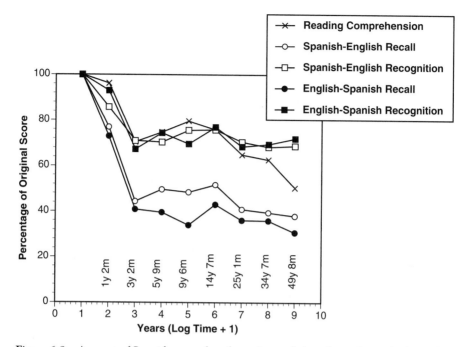

Figure 6.9 Amount of Spanish remembered over intervals from 1 year 2 months (1y 2m) to 49 years 8 months (49y 8m), expressed as a percent of original learning. Any value over 0 indicates that some material was remembered. SOURCE: Adapted from "Semantic Memory Content in Permastore: Fifty Years of Memory for Spanish Learned in School," by H. P. Bahrick, 1984, *Journal of Experimental Psychology: General, 113,* 1–29. Copyright © 1984 American Psychological Association. Adapted with permission.

the flowers that you can"). These subjects were then able to recall many of the items that they previously could not. The temporary lapse view predicts that when the appropriate retrieval cue is presented, evidence of memory—as opposed to memory loss—will be observed. The trick, of course, is finding the right retrieval cue.

The temporary lapse view also predicts that, under appropriate testing conditions, there should be evidence of retention regardless of the delay between study and test. Perhaps the most impressive data on permanent retention come from the studies reported by Harry Bahrick and his colleagues.

Bahrick, Bahrick, and Wittlinger (1975) demonstrated that although memory for people who attended the same high school more than 50 years ago may be very poor when tested with recall, when tested with a cued-recognition test, performance is surprisingly accurate. For recognition of pictures of high school classmates, accuracy remained as high as 80–90% for more than 35 years. Similar feats of retention (in what has been dubbed "the permastore") have been demonstrated in mathematics (Bahrick & Hall, 1991), for city streets and locations (Bahrick, 1983), and for the Spanish language (Bahrick, 1984a). In this last study, Bahrick tested 773 people who had taken Spanish in high school. He collected objective evidence of their original proficiency, including measures of grades, amount of practice, and years of study. He then administered a test to measure current understanding; Figure 6.9 shows the results as a percent of original performance. Although there was a substantial drop during the first three years, there was essentially no further loss over the next 50 years. Ebbinghaus (1885) reported similar results: When relearning certain stanzas from Byron's *Don Juan* after a 30-year interval, he still showed savings.

Each view, permanent loss and temporary lapse, has its proponents and detractors. For the time being, it is worthwhile to remember the basic predictions each view makes. The permanent loss view suggests the information is gone forever, whereas the temporary lapse view suggests that under different conditions with different ways of testing, the information might still be revealed. The results of the studies cited above (see also Capaldi & Neath, 1995; Miller & Grahame, 1991) are predicted by the temporary lapse view but not by the permanent loss view.

Although covered in more detail in the next chapter, results from experiments studying implicit memory also seem to support the temporary lapse view. For example, there is a paradigm known as *repetition priming*. In these experiments, subjects are typically presented with a word fragment that can be completed with only one valid word. For example, *toboggan* might be the target word, and _o_ogg_n might be the word fragment; some subjects have recently seen the word *toboggan* on a prior list, and others have not. Repetition priming refers to the finding that those subjects who have seen *toboggan* recently are more likely to complete the word fragment correctly than are those subjects who have not, even if the former subjects are unaware of their prior exposure to the word. Effects of repetition priming can be detected after a delay as long as 16 months in college students (Sloman, Hayman, Ohta, Law, & Tulving, 1988) and after a delay as long as 12 months in amnesics (Tulving, Hayman, & MacDonald, 1991). Such feats of retention after a single exposure are better explained by the temporary lapse than by the permanent loss view.

Chapter Summary

Consolidation theory attributes forgetting to problems that occur at storage. It predicts that if the memory trace is not consolidated, it will never be recalled. However, many studies show that a change in retrieval conditions is often sufficient to elicit a memory that was supposedly not consolidated. Classic interference theory attributes forgetting to response competition, altered stimulus conditions, and set. Both proactive interference (items you already have in memory can interfere with your ability to remember recently learned information) and retroactive interference (recently learned information can interfere with remembering items you already have in memory) can cause substantial decreases in memory performance. One of the few areas of memory in which decay theory is invoked is short-term/working memory. Decay theory has to predict that memory will always get worse over time. Many findings from the Brown-Peterson and other paradigms disconfirm this prediction. Current theories of forgetting view memory as a discrimination problem in which items will be recalled well if they are distinctive or stand out from competing items at the time of retrieval. This type of view is consistent with the processing accounts discussed in the previous chapter.

Implicit Memory

As has often been shown by recent writers . . . we have not memory, but memories.
—William H. Burnham

In Chapter 6, the idea was presented that memory might be fundamentally a discrimination problem. If this is the case, it should be possible to take a situation in which an organism shows no evidence of memory, change the test conditions slightly to make the discrimination task easier, and then demonstrate that the information was retained. One area of research that focuses on this type of situation, and that has attracted much attention over the past few years, is known as implicit memory.

In this chapter, we examine implicit memory and contrast it with explicit memory. We then use this analysis to shed some light on other proposed distinctions and to compare the idea of multiple memory systems to the unitary view of memory.

Implicit Versus Explicit Memory

Implicit memory is often defined as memory without awareness. In contrast, most of the research discussed in previous chapters has examined explicit memory. The key difference is that at the time of test, subjects in an implicit memory experiment are unaware that the task they are performing is related to a particular study episode.

One distinction that is made in implicit memory research is whether the subjects are aware of the relation between the study and test phases only at encoding, only at retrieval, or at both encoding and retrieval. Unfortunately, the terms used to describe these conditions and the types of test used are not standardized. For example, Roediger (Roediger, Weldon, Stadler, & Riegler, 1992) uses the terms *incidental* and *intentional* to refer to the learning task, and *implicit* and *explicit* to refer to the test; Jacoby (1984) uses *incidental* and *intentional* to refer to the test; Schacter and Tulving (1994) use *implicit* and *explicit* to refer both to the task and to the form of memory; and Johnson and Hasher (1987; see also Richardson-Klavehn & Bjork, 1988) use *indirect* and *direct* to refer to the test, and *implicit* and *explicit* to refer to the form of memory. Furthermore, there is a separate but related area of research that examines implicit learning (Reber, 1993). All of this can be quite confusing. In this text, we use *incidental* and *intentional* to refer to the learning instructions, *indirect* and *direct* to refer to the test, and *implicit* and *explicit* to refer to the type of memory used by the subject. However, we will retain the term *implicit learning* to refer to the nonconscious acquisition of structured information.

The majority of situations considered in this book so far have involved direct tests of memory following intentional learning instructions: The subject is aware that there will be a memory test and tries to memorize the information (intentional learning). At test, the subject is aware of the particular learning episode that should be recalled, and the test instructions make direct reference to the learning episode (direct test). The type of memory used in this situation is known as explicit memory.

We examined incidental learning instructions in Chapter 5 in conjunction with the orienting instructions typically given in a levels of processing experiment. Learning is incidental because the instructions require that subjects focus on some information-processing goal (such as pleasantness ratings) rather than on remembering the information. An indirect memory test, in contrast to a direct test, occurs when "the instructions refer only to the task at hand, and do not make reference to prior events" (Richardson-Klavehn & Bjork, 1988, p. 478). The type of memory used in this situation is called implicit memory.

Indirect Tests of Implicit Memory

It is important to clarify three points with respect to implicit and explicit memory. First, as Table 7.1 illustrates, there are four possible combinations of learning (incidental versus intentional) and testing (indirect versus direct). Many studies of implicit memory fall into Cell 1 of the table, meaning that subjects do not intentionally learn the items and are not aware of the relationship between the test and the study phase. Most of the studies presented in Chapters 3 and 4 fall into Cell 4: Subjects were asked to study a list of words and at test were asked to recall the list of words just studied. Many levels of processing studies

Table 7.1 Four possible ways of combining implicit and explicit study and test instructions: Learning can be incidental or intentional, and the test can be an indirect or a direct measure

| | | *Test Instructions* | |
		Indirect	*Direct*
Study Instructions	*Incidental*	Cell 1	Cell 2
	Intentional	Cell 3	Cell 4

would fall into Cell 2—implicit learning but explicit testing (for example, Postman & Phillips, 1954). In these studies, subjects are not told of the memory test prior to study, but at test they are asked to refer back to the study episode. Roediger, Weldon, Stadler, and Riegler (1992) reported an experiment that included all four cells. Although the majority of studies discussed in this chapter fit into Cell 1, it is important to note that there are other ways of assessing memory.

Second, implicit memory and implicit learning are not at all equivalent to subliminal perception. *Subliminal perception* refers to presentation of a stimulus so quickly or so quietly that it is not consciously perceived. The most famous example occurred in New Jersey in 1957, when James Vicary reported that after he flashed the message "Buy Popcorn" on the screen during a movie, popcorn sales increased by more than 50%. This is an example of subliminal perception because the theater patrons were unaware that the message had been presented. (It turns out that this episode never happened; Vicary admitted that he faked the report to try to revive his failing marketing business. See Pratkanis, 1992; Rogers, 1993.) In an implicit memory study, the subjects are aware of the stimuli as they are presented; they are simply unaware that the memory test that follows is directed toward these items.

Third, although implicit memory has received a great deal of attention during the past few years, it is not a new discovery. For example, Schacter (1989) mentions two 19th-century investigators—Dunn (1845) and Korsakoff (1889)—who accurately described implicit memory. Even Ebbinghaus (1885, p. 2; cited by Richardson-Klavehn & Bjork, 1988) claimed that prior experiences can be retained without awareness. And Claparède describes an anecdote from 1911 that conforms to an indirect test of implicit memory (Claparède, 1951; see Schacter, 1987, for an historical review).

Implicit Learning

The term *implicit learning* usually refers to "the process by which knowledge about the rule-governed complexities of the stimulus environment is acquired independently of conscious attempts to do so" (Reber, 1989, p. 219). Research on this topic has a long history; McGeoch and Irion (1952, p. 210 ff) reviewed the early research, and Reber (1993) and Stadler and Frensch (1998) have reviewed more recent work.

One common method of studying implicit learning is to examine how people learn artificial grammars. These types of studies typically have two phases. First is an acquisition phase, in which subjects are exposed to strings of letters that are consistent with the grammar; second is a testing stage, in which subjects' knowledge of the grammar is assessed.

A Markovian artificial grammar is simply a way of specifying which letters may precede and follow other letters. Figure 7.1 provides a simple example. In this system, the string PTTVPS is grammatical (it can be generated by the system), whereas the string PTTXS is not grammatical (it cannot be generated by the system). These systems are nice for studying implicit learning because they are complex enough that conscious strategies will be of little use, yet sufficiently novel that the experimenter is assured the subject enters the situation with no preexisting knowledge. In addition, the stimuli are synthetic and arbitrary. This last point is important because if implicit learning can be observed with such impoverished, artificial stimuli, it demonstrates the power and flexibility of this mode of learning (see Reber, 1993).

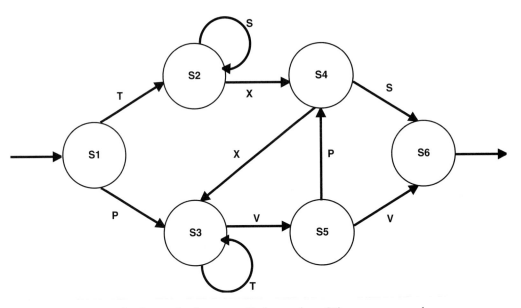

Figure 7.1   An example of an artificial grammar. Each state (e.g., S1) represents a random choice: A certain proportion of the time, the result is one direction (choose "T"); the rest of the time, the result is the other direction (choose "P"). To generate a string, one simply keeps moving through the grammar system until exiting at S6. The two shortest possible strings are TXS and PVV. Other grammatical strings include TSXXVPS, PVPS, PTVPXTVPS, and TSXS.
SOURCE: From *Implicit Learning and Tacit Knowledge: An Essay on the Cognitive Unconscious*, by A. S. Reber, p. 28. Copyright © 1993 by Oxford University Press, Inc. Used by permission of Oxford University Press, Inc.

In one study (Reber, 1967), subjects were asked to learn strings with three to eight letters in each string. Although this is intentional learning (study these lists for an upcoming test) with a direct test (recall the strings you just studied), Reber was most interested in the implicit learning that occurred. One group of subjects learned strings that were grammatical according to a Markovian artificial grammar such as the one in Figure 7.1. Another group learned random strings that conformed to no grammar. On the first trial, both groups averaged about 18 errors when recalling the strings; this demonstrates the difficulty of the task. Both groups did improve, but the group that received the grammatical strings made fewer errors than did the group with random strings. By the end of seven trials, the grammatical group was averaging fewer than 3 errors, compared to about 8 for the random group. Furthermore, subjects in the grammatical group could then use information acquired implicitly to judge quite accurately whether or not novel strings were grammatical. However, the subjects were not able to describe the rules they used to decide, and those subjects who did venture detailed accounts invariably provided rules that would not work. Implicitly learned information appears difficult to verbalize.

CogLab Experiment
      http://coglab.wadsworth.com/experiments/ImplicitLearning/

One key factor affecting whether structure can be implicitly learned is the degree of organization present in the string (cf. Garner, 1974). The stimuli do not have to be perfectly predictable; Cleeremans and McClelland (1991) demonstrated that even a noisy grammar—one in which approximately 15% of the stimuli are random—can be implicitly learned. However, changes in the organization of the sequences can affect learning.

A study reported by Stadler (1995) illustrates the complexity of the issue. Stadler's task was *implicit serial pattern learning*. An asterisk appeared in one of four locations (labeled A, B, C, and D), and the subject was prompted to press one of four corresponding keys as quickly as possible to indicate the asterisk's location. Several different sequences of locations—such as BCADBCA, DACBDAC, CDBACDB, and ABDCABD—would be repeated during the course of the experiment. Because accuracy became quite high, the dependent variable was response time. In all conditions, subjects' response times decreased systematically, illustrating learning. As the subjects learned a sequence, they became able to anticipate the next location and so could respond more quickly. Specifically, the average response time on the learned sequences was approximately 220 ms faster than on unlearned sequences.

The important data come from comparing performance in the control condition to that in three other conditions. By using three conditions, Stadler (1995) could examine several different variables and determine the relative importance of each. One condition clearly affected the organization, another clearly affected the processing demands placed on the subject, and the third did both. In the first condition (pauses), the subject responded just as the control subjects did; thus, few or no resources should have been diverted from learning. However, the time between the subject's response and the next item could vary, thus disrupting the organization of the sequence. In the second condition (memory load), subjects were asked to retain a list of seven letters over several trials. This task should require some additional processing resources compared to the control condition. However, because the letters were presented prior to a block of trials and the responses were collected after the block, the task should not interrupt processes responsible for organizing the stimuli during the block. In the final condition (tone counting), subjects were asked to count the number of times they heard a particular tone. The tone could occur after the subject made a response, thereby disrupting a sequence, and the subject also had to report the number of tones heard at the end of a block, thereby requiring additional processing resources compared to the control group.

The memory load task reduced performance; the difference in response times between learned and unlearned sequences dropped to 159 ms. However, both the tone counting and pauses conditions disrupted performance even more, down to 82 ms and 93 ms, respectively. What this means, according to Stadler (1995), is that implicit learning is affected far more by changes in the structure or organization of the information to be learned than it is by tasks that require more processing.

The issue of whether learning can occur without awareness remains controversial (Stadler & Roediger, 1998). On the one hand, subjects who have demonstrated implicit learning often cannot say what the pattern is that they have learned (Curran & Keele, 1993). On the other hand, in some studies, knowledge of the sequence appears to be available on a conscious level. For example, subjects can be given a recognition test in which they are asked to rate how sure they are that the test sequence was part of the learning sequence. Shanks and Johnstone (1999) found that subjects gave higher confidence ratings to sequences that had been seen than to ones that had not, and argued that this indicated some awareness of the sequence.

Destrebecqz and Cleeremans (2001) point out that the relation between performance on a recognition task and performance on an implicit learning task is problematic only if one insists on a "process pure" assumption. If one assumes that recognition relies only on conscious awareness, then the results are a problem. However, if one assumes that both automatic (nonconscious) and recollective processes contribute to performance on a recognition task, then the results are not necessarily problematic.

To assess the relative contributions of automatic and nonautomatic processes, Destrebecqz and Cleeremans (2001) applied Jacoby's (1991) process dissociation technique (see Chapter 5). Subjects saw a sequence of dots appear in one of four locations on a computer monitor and were asked to press one of four keys to indicate where the dot had appeared. The dots' locations were determined in a way similar to the use of a Markovian grammar described above. There were two conditions, inclusion and exclusion. The inclusion condition in the learning phase had a relatively slow presentation rate. The idea was that only with a relatively large interval between dot presentations would the subjects be able to use explicit knowledge. The exclusion condition had a faster presentation rate that did not leave enough time for subjects to use explicit knowledge. In the second phase, subjects were given a recognition test in which they were asked to rate how confident they were that a sequence of dot locations had been seen in the learning phase.

Subjects learned the sequence in both the fast (exclusion) and slow (inclusion) presentation conditions. Introduction of a different pattern slowed mean response times by 100 ms in the slow condition and by 68 ms in the fast condition; if subjects had not learned a pattern, then changing to a new one should not have disrupted performance. The mean confidence ratings from the recognition task are shown in Figure 7.2. In the slow condition, in which both implicit and explicit knowledge could play a role, the subjects were able to distinguish between old and new sequences. In the fast condition, however, in which the presentation rate was too fast to allow explicit processes to play a role, the subjects were unable to distinguish between old and new sequences. These data suggest that whether implicit learning is solely implicit or also includes some explicit information will depend on the particular experimental conditions. More important, they also suggest that learning can indeed occur in the absence of awareness.

Reber (1993) argues that such implicit learning accounts for most learning about the structure of the environment. The arguments supporting this position are too complex to be summarized here, and the reader is referred to Reber's book. Nonetheless, it is clear that highly complex structures and patterns of information can be learned largely without the subject's awareness, and in some cases, without any awareness at all.

Experimental Dissociations

To illustrate how implicit memory is assessed by an indirect test, consider the following typical experiment. There are two phases and two groups of subjects. In Phase I, the subjects are shown a long list of words (perhaps 100 or so) and are asked to perform some task, such as making pleasantness ratings. The rating task ensures that the subjects process the information. In the list of words seen by the experimental group, a small proportion will be words of interest. Thus, the experimental group may see 10 key words that the control group does not see. In Phase II, some time later, the subject is asked to complete

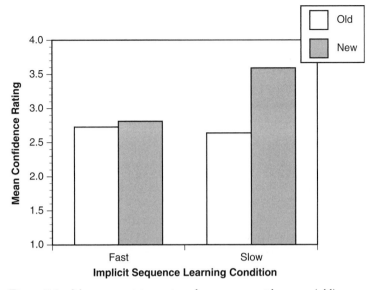

Figure 7.2   Mean recognition ratings for sequences either seen (old) or not seen (new) during an earlier implicit learning phase. A rating of 1 means the subject is certain that the item was seen during the learning phase; a rating of 6 means that the subject is certain that the item was not part of the implicit learning phase.   SOURCE: Destrebecqz & Cleeremans (2001).

another task, unrelated to the first. The subject is given a long list of word fragments— such as _o_ogg_n—and is asked to fill in the blanks to make a complete word. There is no mention of the previous list of words, and there is often a delay between the two phases. In this example, the control subjects did not see the only valid English word that completes this fragment (*toboggan*), but the experimental subjects did see this word on the list. Implicit memory is demonstrated when more experimental subjects than control subjects complete the word fragment correctly. The task is incidental because the subject was not intentionally trying to study the words during Phase I, and it is indirect because the subject was not trying to recall the list of words during Phase II.

A measure commonly used in this sort of experiment is *repetition priming*—the idea that processing something a second time benefits from its having been processed previously. (A second type of priming is *association priming*, which refers to the observation that response times are often faster if a second item is semantically related to or associated with the first item. This type of priming will be discussed in Chapter 10.) Priming is typically the difference between the mean proportion of fragments completed by the experimental group and the mean proportion completed by the control group. A priming score of 0 indicates no difference, and any positive value (such as 0.10) indicates better performance for the experimental group. A direct test of memory, in contrast, would have required the subjects to recall as many of the words from the study session as they could, or to decide whether a target item shown during the test period was one of the words studied. One of the critical issues in current memory research—the nature and number of

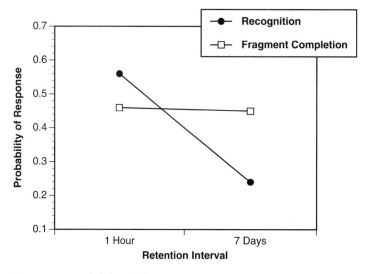

Figure 7.3 Probability of observing priming in a word-fragment completion task and probability of correctly recognizing words after a 1-hour or 1-week retention interval.   SOURCE: 'From "Priming Effects in Word-Fragment Completion Are Independent of Recognition Memory," by E. Tulving, D. L. Schacter, and H. Stark, 1982, *Journal of Experimental Psychology: Human Learning and Memory*, 8, 336–342. Copyright © 1982 American Psychological Association. Reprinted with permission.

different memory systems—has been addressed using dissociations between indirect and direct tests of memory.

A *dissociation* occurs when one variable, such as presentation modality or word frequency, is shown to affect one test differently from another. For example, when Test A is given, subjects do better with visual than with auditory presentation; when Test B is given, the opposite pattern is observed—performance is better with auditory than with visual presentation. The discovery of such a dissociation can support the idea that the two tests tap into different memory systems. Beginning in the early 1980s, several dissociations were demonstrated between indirect and direct tests, which led researchers to think that implicit and explicit memory were two different systems. Here, we consider only two dissociations.

Tulving, Schacter, and Stark (1982) conducted an experiment with three phases. In Phase I, subjects were asked to learn a list of 96 words. In Phase II, which occurred 1 hour later, subjects received a *word-fragment completion test* or a recognition test on 48 of the studied words. Phase III took place 7 days later, when the tests were given for the other 48 studied words. Of most interest is the change in memory performance over time for the direct (recognition) and indirect (fragment completion) tests; the results are shown in Figure 7.3. For the recognition test, performance declined over the retention interval; the subjects correctly recognized fewer words after 7 days than after 1 hour. For the word-fragment completion test, the measure of interest is the amount of priming—the proportion of times the fragment was accurately completed when it was a studied item compared to the number of times it was accurately completed when it was a nonstudied item. This

Experiment   *Priming Word-Fragment Completion*

Purpose: To demonstrate repetition priming effects in a word-fragment completion task.

Subjects: Twenty subjects are recommended. Ten should be assigned to the experimental group, and ten to the control group.

Materials: Table H in the Appendix lists 60 word fragments. For each subject, present 20 of these words (with no letters missing). A convenient way is to create a booklet with 1 word per page. You will also need an answer sheet containing all 60 word fragments (with the letters missing) in random order. Make sure that none of the first 10 word fragments were on the study list.

Design: The experimental group will participate in both the study and test phases; the control group will participate in only the test phase. Because each subject experiences only one condition, this is a between-subjects design.

Procedure (Phase I):   Inform the subjects in the experimental group that this is an experiment on information processing that has several parts. Tell them to read each word silently to themselves. They should look at each word for 5 seconds before turning the page and going on to the next word.

Instructions (Phase I):   "This is an experiment on information processing. On each page of your booklet, you will see a word. I would like you to read it silently to yourself. After you have seen all the words, I will give you further instructions. Please turn the page when I say the word *turn*. Any questions?"

Procedure (Phase II):   Collect all of the booklets and wait 10 minutes after subjects have processed the words before giving the test sheet. During the interval, you can have the subjects perform any other task that does not involve words (such as circling all the occurrences of the digit 6 on a sheet of paper). Then tell them the next phase consists of completing word fragments.

Instructions (Phase II):   "In this phase of the experiment, you will see a list of word fragments. For each fragment, I would like you to try to fill in the missing letters to make a valid English word. Any questions?"

Scoring and Analysis: For each subject in the control group, count the number of word fragments accurately completed. Do the same for the experimental group. Of most interest are the fragments based on words that the experimental group studied. The experimental group should have completed more words than the control group. The difference between the proportion correct for each group (experimental minus control) is the amount of priming.

Optional Enhancements: Include more subjects in each group; include another group that has a longer delay (such as 24 hours) between study and test.

SOURCE: Adapted from "Priming Effects in Word-Fragment Completion are Independent of Recognition Memory," by E. Tulving, D. L. Schacter, and H. Stark, 1982, *Journal of Experimental Psychology: Human Learning and Memory, 8,* 336–342.

value remained the same after a 1-week delay as after a 1-hour delay. These data represent a dissociation, because the independent variable—duration of the retention interval—affected the direct and indirect measures differently. The longer the retention interval, the worse the performance on the direct test; but retention interval had no measurable effect on the indirect test.

A second type of dissociation was demonstrated by Graf and Schacter (1987). Chapter 6 included a discussion of interference theory, emphasizing the prevalence of both retroactive interference (RI) and proactive interference (PI) as causes of memory failure. Graf and Schacter reported an experiment in which RI and PI affected direct tests of memory but did not affect indirect tests.

Table 7.2   Schematic representation of the conditions tested by Graf and Schacter (1987)

	Phase I	Phase II	Tested On	Interference
Control	A-B	C-D	A-B	
Experimental	A-B	A-D	A-B	RI
Control	C-D	A-B	A-B	
Experimental	A-D	A-B	A-B	PI

In Phase I, subjects studied word pairs, such as *shirt-window*. These first pairs are called A-B pairs. Subjects were asked to generate and read aloud a sentence that related the words in a meaningful manner, such as "The boy threw the shirt out of the window." This task involves incidental learning because subjects were not asked to learn the word pairs. In Phase II, the subjects performed the same processing with a second list of word pairs. In the control condition, this list (known as the C-D list) contained all new words . In the experimental condition, the second list was designed to produce interference by reusing the first words from Phase I. These interference lists, then, are called A-D lists. Both groups of subjects were then tested on the original A-B pairs. This design would lead to retroactive interference; that is, processing the A-D list could interfere with information already processed, the A-B list. Another set of subjects also experienced two learning sessions, but these were arranged so as to cause proactive interference. These subjects processed the A-D or C-D pairs in Phase I, and the A-B pairs in Phase II, and were then tested on the A-B pairs. In this case, previously processed information (the A-D pairs) could interfere with new information (the A-B pairs). The design is sketched out in Table 7.2.

The direct test was cued recall: The subject was provided with the A word and the first few letters of a B word and was asked to complete the stem with the originally studied word. This is a direct test because the subject is asked to refer back to a specific learning episode. The indirect test was word-fragment completion: The subject was provided with the A word and the stem of a B word and was asked to complete the stem with the first word that came to mind. This is an indirect test because the task can be completed without reference to the learning episode. To minimize the chance that subjects would become aware of the relationship between the word-fragment completion test and the study episode, only 12 A-B pairs were tested among 44 other items. A third, separate group of subjects received only Phase III; this group provides a baseline of how many fragments would be completed when there was no opportunity to learn. The subjects in both the control and experimental conditions performed more accurately than the baseline subjects did, confirming that memory was indeed playing a role. The other results are shown in Table 7.3.

First, consider the retroactive interference manipulation. On the direct test, the control subjects performed more accurately than the experimental subjects did (.55 versus .40), demonstrating the presence of RI. On the indirect test, however, the control and experimental subjects performed at about the same level, indicating no interference. The pattern is the same for the proactive interference condition: On the direct test, the control subjects outperformed the experimental subjects (.67 versus .45), whereas performance was equivalent on the indirect test. This represents a dissociation, because the manipulation of both RI and PI affected performance on one kind of test (direct) but had no effect on another test (indirect).

Table 7.3   The proportion of stems completed correctly in a cued recall (direct) test or word-fragment completion (indirect) test in either a retroactive or proactive interference design

Test Type	Retroactive Interference		Proactive Interference	
	Control	Experimental	Control	Experimental
Direct	.55	.40	.67	.45
Indirect	.34	.32	.32	.35

SOURCE: Based on data from Graf & Schacter (1987).

Although there are numerous other dissociations between implicit and explicit memory, there are also many situations in which parallel effects occur (Richardson-Klavehn & Bjork, 1988, p. 525). One reason for the similarities might be that no test (direct or indirect) relies solely on one type of memory, explicit or implicit. Explicit memory can be used on an indirect test, as when a subject notices that several of the word fragments can be completed with words from the pleasantness ratings task (Richardson-Klavehn & Bjork, 1988). Similarly, implicit memory can be used on a direct test, as when implicit memory facilitates encoding of recognition probes (Jacoby & Dallas, 1981). It was for this reason that Jacoby and his colleagues (Jacoby, Toth, & Yonelinas, 1993) developed the process dissociation framework presented in Chapter 5.

The process dissociation framework has been used to reexamine dissociations between implicit and explicit memory. McBride, Dosher, and Gage (2001) used the procedure to compare forgetting rates for implicit and explicit memory as measured by word-fragment completion. Subjects in the inclusion condition were asked to complete word fragments with a word they had studied; if they could not think of a word, then they were to complete the fragment with any word. Subjects in the exclusion condition were asked to avoid completing the fragment with a word they had studied. According to the process dissociation logic, both conscious (explicit) and automatic (implicit) processes can contribute to memory performance in the inclusion test, whereas only automatic processes can contribute in the exclusion test. Performance was tested at seven different retention intervals, from 1 to 45 minutes. Estimates of the relative contribution of both conscious and automatic processes were calculated at each retention interval. Results indicate that forgetting is similar for both conscious and automatic memory processes. Snodgrass and Surprenant (1989) found similar results with delays up to 14 days.

The claim the implicit memory is immune to interference has also been questioned (Lustig & Hasher, 2001a). For example, Lustig and Hasher (2001b) divided subjects into three groups: an interference group, a control group, and a baseline group. The baseline group received only word fragments and was used to determine the proportion of times a word fragment would be completed. Both the interference and control groups first saw a list of words and were asked to count the number of vowels in each word. Several filler tasks then followed before the indirect word-fragment completion test. The list of words was made up of two types of items, nontargets and targets. As in many tests of implicit memory, only 12 of the 70 word fragments corresponded to targets in the original list. The difference between the interference and control groups was that in the interference condition, the original list contained nontargets that were similar to the targets. In the control condition, the nontargets were not similar. For example, if the word fragment was *a-l--gy*, both the interference and control groups would have seen the target *allergy* in the original list; how-ever, the interference group would also have seen *analogy*, whereas the control group would have seen *urgency*. In the interference condition, then, *analogy* is sufficiently similar to *allergy* to interfere.

Priming was above baseline for both groups, but there was less priming in the interfer-ence condition than in the control condition. This result is exactly what one would expect if implicit memory is subject to interference effects. Lustig and Hasher (2001b) suggest that the reason they obtained interference effects whereas Graf and Schacter (1987) did not was because of the cues at test. In Lustig and Hasher's study, there was only one cue, the word fragment, whereas in Graf and Schacter's study, there were two cues. In the direct test, the subject was given a cue such as *shirt-win___* and was asked to complete the fragment using a word from the previously studied pair. Thus, *shirt* is relevant. In the indirect test, the cue is again *shirt-win___*, but no mention is made that *shirt* is relevant. Only *win___* is relevant; the fact that it had been paired with *shirt* or some other word had no effect.

Theoretical Accounts of Implicit Memory

There are four main accounts of the implicit memory data (for extensive reviews of data and theories, see Richardson-Klavehn & Bjork, 1988; Roediger & McDermott, 1993): the activation view (Graf & Mandler, 1984), the multiple memory systems approach (Tulving & Schacter, 1990), the transfer appropriate processing view (Roediger, Weldon, & Challis, 1989), and the bias view (Ratcliff & McKoon, 1996).

The Activation View

This account, perhaps the least popular of the four today, holds that the priming seen on indirect tests is attributable to the temporary activation of preexisting representations. This activation occurs automatically, without the need for extensive or intentional pro-cessing on the part of the subject. Because the activation is automatic and occurs without elaborative processing, no contextual information is available that would make the item appear as part of an episode. This view readily explains certain aspects of performance on indirect tests. For example, it predicts priming in the absence of elaborative processing (see Jacoby & Dallas, 1981). Furthermore, in amnesics, it predicts normal priming of in-formation that is already known, but no such priming of novel word pairs (see Cermak, Talbot, Chandler, & Wolbarst, 1985). As we will see in Chapter 8, amnesics often show impairment on tasks that require processing contextual information; according to the ac-tivation view, however, context is not important, so amnesics should still show priming for information they already know.

Several types of findings pose serious problems for the activation view, however. First is the finding that some indirect tests show priming after a delay of as long as 16 months in college students (Sloman, Hayman, Ohta, Law, & Tulving, 1988) and 12 months in amnesics (Tulving, Hayman, & MacDonald, 1991). If priming is automatic temporary ac-tivation, the time frame involved should be seconds or minutes, not months or years. Sec-ond, under certain circumstances, amnesics demonstrate priming of newly acquired infor-mation (see Graf & Schacter, 1985). This finding poses a problem because the activation view assumes that the primary cause of priming is temporary activation of preexisting representations. If newly acquired information can be primed, it calls this assumption into question. The activation explanation has not fared well of late, and it has been eclipsed by other theoretical views.

Multiple Memory Systems

The multiple memory systems view is put forward most strongly by Tulving and Schacter (1990; Schacter & Tulving, 1994; Schacter, Wagner, & Buckner, 2000). In its simplest form, it holds that many dissociations between direct and indirect tests of memory arise because the tests tap different underlying memory systems. In particular, Schacter et al. (2000) identify the *perceptual representation system (PRS)* as a separate memory system responsible for many of the effects seen on indirect tests. The PRS is a collection of nondeclarative, domain-specific modules that operate on perceptual information about the form and structure of words and objects; it is responsible for "the facilitated identification of perceptual objects from reduced cues as a consequence of a specific prior exposure to an object" (Schacter, 1994, p. 234). Before describing this proposed system more completely, we first need to define what is meant by a memory system. By necessity, the discussion begins with the assumption that there are multiple memory systems, although not all researchers agree on this point. For example, the following discussion uses a distinction between episodic and semantic memory to illustrate the requirements for proposing different systems, but many researchers question whether there is sufficient evidence to differentiate these systems (see below).

What is a system? Schacter and Tulving (1994) define a memory system by describing what it is not. First, a memory system is not a memory process: "A memory process refers to a specific operation carried out in the service of memory performance" (Schacter & Tulving, 1994, p. 12). This definition includes encoding, rehearsal, retrieval, and so forth. Second, a memory system is not a memory task. A recognition task does not imply a recognition memory system distinct from other memory systems. There is often an implicit isomorphism between certain tasks, such that most free recall tasks tap episodic memory, but this need not be the case. Except in highly unusual circumstances, a given memory task is not a pure measure of a particular memory process, let alone a particular memory system (Jacoby, 1991). Finally, implicit memory and explicit memory are not memory systems (Schacter & Tulving, 1994). Rather, these terms refer to situations in which memory is expressed without awareness (implicit) or with awareness (explicit) of the original learning episode.

Different researchers have offered different definitions of a memory system, and at least some of the confusion about what is and what is not a system is due to inconsistent or contradictory definitions. Part of the problem is that experimental research into different memory systems is relatively recent; as experimental evidence accumulates, the definitions are continually being refined and made more precise.

The most clearly defined set of criteria for what constitutes a separate memory system was offered by Sherry and Schacter (1987). In order to establish whether two memory systems, A and B, are separate, the following four properties must hold:

1. *Functional dissociations.* An independent variable that has one effect on a task thought to tap System A must have either no effect or a different effect on a task thought to tap System B.

2. *Different neural substrates.* System A must depend on different brain regions from System B.
3. *Stochastic independence.* Performance on a task that taps System A should be uncorrelated with performance on a task that taps System B.
4. *Functional incompatibility.* A function carried out by System A cannot be performed by System B.

A slightly revised set of criteria, described in the following paragraphs, was proposed by Schacter and Tulving (1994, pp. 14–20).

Class-Inclusion Operations   A memory system enables the organism to perform a very large number of tasks of a particular class or category, regardless of the specific details of the tasks. For example, one proposed memory system is episodic memory, which is the conscious recollection of personally experienced episodes. It does not matter what the personally experienced episode is; it could be a birthday party, the time your dog was nearly hit by a car, your first day at college, or any other event. All operations dealing with these types of memories occur within the episodic memory system. If there is damage to the system, then all kinds of personally experienced memories will be affected, but other cognitive operations should remain intact. Thus, certain forms of amnesia can interfere with episodic memory but not with recollection of historical facts, which are assumed to be in a different system (semantic memory).

Properties and Relations   The second criterion proposed by Schacter and Tulving (1994) is that a memory system must be described in terms of a property list: an enumeration of features and aspects by which its identity can be determined and its relation to other systems specified. These properties include the rules of operation, the kind of information that is processed, the neural substrate, and a statement about the system's evolutionary purpose. In addition to these properties, the proposed system must have a definite relationship to other systems. For example, episodic memory relies on parts of semantic memory, but semantic memory does not depend on episodic memory in any way.

Convergent Dissociations   As we have already noted, *single dissociations* occur when a particular independent variable, such as word frequency, has two different effects depending on the test—recall versus recognition. Weaker forms of dissociation occur when the independent variable has a larger effect on one test than on another, or has an effect only on one test and not on the other. Single dissociations provide no evidence for postulating a new memory system, according to Schacter and Tulving (1994). However, *convergent dissociations* are multiple single, or double, dissociations that use a variety of tasks, a variety of materials, a variety of populations, and a variety of techniques. If a proposed memory system is indeed a memory system, then these multiple dissociations will all converge on the same conclusion.

On the basis of the criteria outlined above, Schacter and Tulving (1994) propose five memory systems and nearly a dozen subsystems (see Table 7.4). The main division is between procedural and declarative memory. *Procedural memory* is involved with learning behavioral and cognitive skills and algorithms. A rule of thumb is that if you can say you know how to do something, it is a good candidate for a form of procedural memory. Sample tasks include riding a bicycle, typing (if you are a touch typist), and even performing complex skills such as solving puzzles. In contrast, *declarative memory* is involved with

Table 7.4   Major memory systems and their subsystems

System	Other Name(s)	Subsystems
Procedural	Nondeclarative	Motor skills Cognitive skills Simple conditioning Simple associative learning
Perceptual representation	Nondeclarative	Visual word form Auditory word form Structural description
Primary memory	Working memory	Visual Auditory
Semantic	Generic Factual Knowledge	Spatial Relational
Episodic	Personal Autobiographical Event memory	

SOURCE: Based on Schacter & Tulving (1994).

knowing "that" rather than knowing "how." For example, if you know that 2 plus 2 equals 4, the information is said to be declarative.

The subsystems of procedural memory include those responsible for learning motor skills, simple conditioning, and simple associative learning (Schacter & Tulving, 1994). Procedural memory is also thought to be responsible for learning about patterns and regularities in the environment that unfold over time, even quite complex ones (Reber, 1993). For example, many attributions of cause and effect have their basis, according to Reber, in implicit learning.

The perceptual representation system (PRS) mentioned before is another form of nondeclarative memory, and Schacter et al. (2000) view it as a separate memory system. This system is important in identifying words and objects but is nondeclarative in the sense that it is typically involved in nonconscious operations. The PRS encompasses three subsystems: one that handles visual input, one that handles auditory input, and one that handles descriptions of objects.

The three remaining systems belong on the declarative side, and all three involve conscious awareness. Primary memory, as we saw in Chapters 3 and 4, has had a long history, at times being called short-term store, short-term memory, or working memory. The system listed in Table 7.4 follows Baddeley's (1986) general description of two subsystems—one for visual-spatial information and another for auditory-verbal information (see Chapter 4).

The final two systems—episodic and semantic memory—take their names and general characteristics from Tulving (1972, 1983). The *semantic memory* system (also known as knowledge or generic memory) processes factual information. If you can recollect that George Washington was the first president of the United States, that information comes from your semantic memory system. *Episodic memory* (also known as autobiographical memory) differs from semantic memory in that it includes recollection of personal involvement and enables the individual to mentally "travel back" into his or her personal past (Tulving, 1998). An example will help illustrate the difference. Suppose that you know nothing about the vice presidents of the United States. One day, while waiting for an appointment, you read in an old magazine about Maine's commemoration of the 100th anniversary of the death of Hannibal Hamlin (1809–1891), Abraham Lincoln's first vice president. You immediately think of elephants crossing the Alps to fight Romans, confusing the more famous Carthaginian with the less famous Granite State native son. A few days later, you happen to watch a television quiz show and Hamlin's name occurs again. Although the bare fact that he was Lincoln's first vice president may be in semantic memory, all of the details that you recollect about the learning episode—such as the fact that you were reading an old magazine, that you thought of the more famous Hannibal, that you were so bored you were reading a magazine that was several years old, that the room was stuffy and hot—are due to episodic information. Finally, suppose that several years later, you again recollect Hamlin's name, but this time you are unaware of the source. In one sense, Hamlin has become Washington's equal; you cannot recall anything about the learning episode.

If there is some uncertainty about what constitutes a system, there is even less agreement about what distinguishes a subsystem from a system. Schacter and Tulving (1994, p. 19) define the difference as follows:

> Whereas systems are characterized by different rules of operation, as embodied in property lists and relations, subsystems, we suggest, are distinguished primarily by different kinds of information (subsystems share the principal rules of operations of their superordinate system, but they differ from one another with respect to the kinds of information each one processes) and different brain loci (although subsystems are all instantiated in the neural circuitry that defines their superordinate system, they can occupy distinct loci within the broader network). . . . Whereas postulating of full-blown systems requires satisfaction of all three of our major criteria, postulating of subsystems requires satisfaction of the first (class inclusion operations) and third (converging dissociations) but not the second (property lists and relations, with the corresponding emphasis on different rules of operation).

Despite these attempts at clarification, a major weakness of the multiple systems view is a lack of consensus among its proponents as to what the systems are, and even on what the criteria should be. For example, some researchers think of episodic and semantic memory as subsystems rather than as two distinct systems (Johnson & Chalfonte, 1994; Squire, 1994). Others propose systems not included in the Schacter and Tulving hierarchy, such as the sensory memory systems proposed by Cowan (1995). Indeed, according to some criteria, there could be as many as 25 different memory systems (Roediger, 1990b).

Transfer Appropriate Processing

The explanation of dissociations between direct and indirect tests of memory in terms of transfer appropriate processing (TAP) (see Chapter 5) has been most fully articulated by Roediger and his colleagues (see Blaxton, 1989; Roediger, Weldon, & Challis, 1989). This account proceeds from four assumptions. First, a given type of processing will lead to better memory performance if it is appropriate for the particular test (see Morris, Bransford, & Franks, 1977; Tulving & Thomson, 1973). The important point here is that different types of processing lead to good performance on different types of tests; there is no one type of processing that will lead to optimal performance on all tests. Second, direct and indirect tests of memory typically require different retrieval operations. In particular, the tasks typically chosen for direct and indirect tests differ not only in the presumed underlying memory being tapped (explicit versus implicit) but also in the type of information required. Third, most indirect tests rely primarily on perceptual processing. For example, a fragment completion task requires processing the individual letters rather than focusing on an item's meaning. Roediger calls this kind of processing *data driven*, a term introduced by Jacoby (1983). Finally, most direct tests rely primarily on the encoded meaning of concepts. For example, most subjects will focus on word meanings and relationships between the words on recall and recognition tasks. Roediger calls this kind of processing *conceptually driven* (Jacoby, 1983).

To be clear, not all indirect tests are data driven and not all direct tests are conceptually driven. Indeed, the key experiments that support the transfer appropriate processing view compare data-driven indirect tests to conceptually driven indirect tests. Another point of clarification concerns the terms *data driven* and *conceptually driven*, which represent not a dichotomy, but rather two endpoints on a continuum. In practice, most tasks will involve both data-driven and conceptually driven processes; what concerns Roediger and his colleagues is which type of processing predominates.

A study by Blaxton (1989) examined two types of indirect tests and two types of direct tests. One indirect and one direct test were predominantly data driven, and one indirect and one direct test were predominantly conceptually driven. Blaxton chose presentation modality as the key independent variable. According to dissociation logic, if indirect tests are tapping a separate system, then presentation modality should affect both indirect tests in the same way. However, if the transfer appropriate processing view is correct, then it should not matter whether the test is direct or indirect. According to this view, data-driven tasks should show one pattern of results, and conceptually driven tasks should show a different pattern.

First, all subjects saw (visual condition) or heard (auditory) a list of words; then, several different kinds of tests were administered. To illustrate the different test types, consider the target word *bashful*. The direct, data-driven test was graphemic cued recall. A grapheme, for this test, was a word that had similar letters in similar locations, such as *bushel*; subjects were instructed to recall a word from the list that had similar letters. This test is both direct (subjects are instructed to recall words from the list) and data driven (processing needs to focus on physical features rather than on meaning). The indirect, data-driven test was word-fragment completion; given the word fragment *b_sh_u_*, subjects were asked to complete the fragment with the first word that came to mind. This is an indirect test because no mention was made of the study items. The direct, conceptually driven test was free recall; subjects were simply asked to recall as many of the words as they could. The indirect, conceptually driven test was a test of general knowledge. The question was "Which of the seven dwarves comes first alphabetically?" This test is both indirect (subjects need not refer back to the learning episode) and conceptually driven (the test requires processing of meaning rather than of physical features).

The results are shown in Figure 7.4: Consistent with the transfer appropriate processing view and contrary to the multiple systems view, performance was better on data-driven tasks (the upper- and lower-left graphs) with visual presentation, and performance was equivalent or slightly better on conceptually driven tasks (upper- and lower-right graphs) with auditory presentation. The multiple systems view predicted that the two direct tasks would be similar, whereas the results showed that the two data-driven tasks were

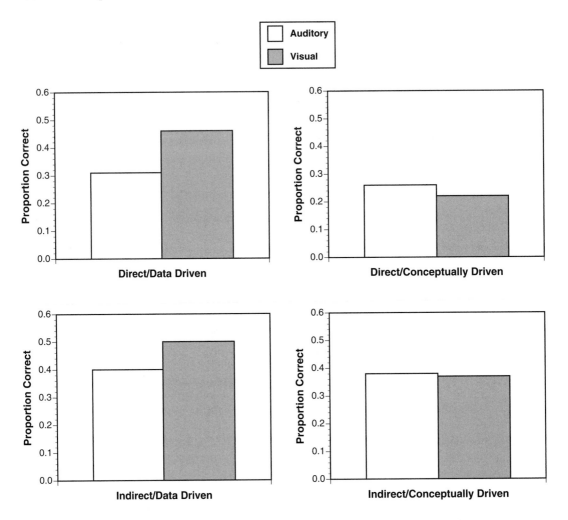

Figure 7.4 Proportion correct as a function of test type (direct or indirect), task type (data driven or conceptually driven), and presentation modality. Transfer appropriate processing predicts that type of processing is most important, whereas the multiple systems view predicts that type of test is most important.   SOURCE: From "Investigating Dissociations Among Memory Measures: Support for a Transfer-Appropriate Processing Framework," by T. A. Blaxton, 1989, *Journal of Experimental Psychology: Learning, Memory, and Cognition, 15,* 657–668. Copyright © 1989 American Psychological Association. Reprinted with permission.

similar. According to Blaxton's (1989) interpretation, the type of test (direct or indirect) did not matter as much as the predominant type of processing (data driven or conceptually driven).

The Bias View

The bias view (Ratcliff & McKoon, 1996) begins with the observation that none of the preceding views actually explains the phenomenon. In a repetition priming task, there is an increase in the probability of responding (or a decrease in the time needed to respond)

Ambiguous Woman

Old Woman   Young Woman

Figure 7.5   The ambiguous and unambiguous figures used by
Leeper (1935).   SOURCE: Adapted from Boring (1930), Leeper (1935).

when an item has been seen recently. The multiple systems view (Schacter & Tulving, 1994) explains these results by postulating three separate memory systems: one system for auditory words, one for visual words, and one for structural descriptions. However, saying that these effects occur because of the memory system responsible does not really explain them. The transfer appropriate processing view (Roediger, 1990a) also has difficulty explaining these results because of the possibility of circularity. Repetition priming will be observed when there is appropriate transfer of the study and test processing, but evidence for appropriate transfer of processing comes from observing priming.

The bias view proposes that prior presentation of an item can bias subsequent processing of the item on later presentations. Bias is seen as the result of modifications to the processes that will be used in the task, including perceptual and decision processes (Ratcliff & McKoon, 1996). At its simplest, the bias view says that, other things being equal, you are likely to interpret a stimulus in the same way as you have interpreted it in the past.

Consider an example of how an ambiguous picture might be interpreted. Leeper (1935) used a set of figures, derived from Boring (1930) and shown in Figure 7.5, known as "the wife and the mother-in-law." (Another version of this illusion, created by Botwinick, 1961, is called "the husband and the father-in-law.") First, one of the unambiguous versions was shown; two weeks later, the ambiguous version was shown. Subjects were far more likely to interpret the ambiguous picture as representing the same person as the unambiguous picture. That is, if they first saw the unambiguous old woman, they would then interpret the ambiguous picture as representing an old woman. The idea is that a person's processing becomes biased as a result of the way in which the unambiguous item was originally processed.

A central feature of the bias view is that bias entails both costs and benefits. The modifications to processing caused by the first presentation will sometimes facilitate subsequent processing and sometimes impede subsequent processing. More generally, there will be an advantage if prior processing is appropriate for the current task, but a disadvantage if prior processing is inappropriate for the current task. Many studies of repetition priming have been set up to see only benefits (such as better performance or reduced response times) because the systems view predicts only benefits. Ratcliff and McKoon (1996) surveyed several studies and reported new data that illustrate both costs and benefits in three different repetition priming paradigms, each of which had previously been attributed to separate memory systems.

Bias with Auditory Words   Ratcliff, Allbritton, and McKoon (1997) had subjects listen to two lists of words, the second of which was presented in noise to make the task difficult. Each word on the second list fell into one of three conditions: (1) It was a new word (novel); (2) it was a word that was also in the first list (repeated); or (3) it was a word that was similar to a word on the first list (similar). The measure of interest was the probability of identifying items in the second list. Novel words (the control condition) were identified correctly about 60% of the time. A repetition priming effect was seen for the repeated items, with more items identified correctly—65%—than in the control condition. Most important, there was a cost for similar items, with only 55% identified correctly. The idea is that there is no experimentally induced bias to process the control items, so they serve as a baseline. According to the bias view, the repeated items showed a benefit because the type of identification processing required had been used previously within the session. The similar items showed a cost because the processing of the similar items in the first list was inappropriate.

Bias with Visual Words   Ratcliff and McKoon (1996) reported an experiment that examined bias effects with a stem completion task. In the first phase, 32 words were presented on a computer screen, and subjects were asked to make a rating of how pleasant these words were. In the second phase, four letters appeared in the center of the screen, and subjects were asked to say, as quickly as they could, a word that began with those letters. As before, there were novel, repeated, and similar conditions. The mean response time to say a word to a novel four-letter stem was 1363 ms. Repetition priming was observed in the repeated condition, with response time decreasing to 1156 ms. In the similar condition, performance was slowest, with a mean response time of 1561 ms. Items that could take advantage of previous processing showed a decrease in response time, whereas items that could not showed an increase.

Bias with Objects   In a typical object decision experiment, subjects see a series of line drawings of possible and impossible objects (see Figure 7.6). There are two lists, and for each object, subjects are asked to decide as quickly as they can whether the object is possible. The typical finding is that only possible objects show repetition priming; there appears to be no advantage of being exposed to an impossible object during an earlier phase

Possible Objects   Impossible Objects

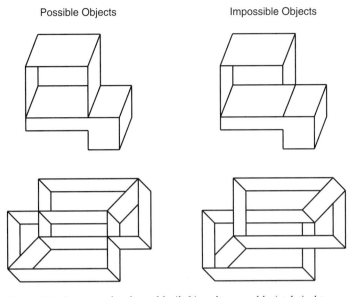

Figure 7.6 An example of possible (left) and impossible (right) objects, of the sort used in object decision experiments.   SOURCE: Adapted from "Bias in the Priming of Object Decisions," by R. Ratcliff and G. McKoon, 1995, *Journal of Experimental Psychology: Learning, Memory, and Cognition, 21,* 754–767. Copyright © 1995 American Psychological Association. Adapted with permission.

of the experiment (Schacter, Cooper, & Delaney, 1990; Schacter, Cooper, Delaney, Peterson, & Tharan, 1991). This finding of repetition priming for possible objects and no repetition priming for impossible objects is consistent with the idea of separate memory systems, one of which is devoted to processing objects.

Ratcliff and McKoon (1995a) also presented subjects with line drawings of possible or impossible objects. In their standard condition, they replicated the finding of enhanced performance for possible objects on list 2 if they had been seen previously on list 1, and no enhancement for impossible objects. According to the bias view, however, one reason for this finding may be the contribution of episodic recollection. For example, recalling that you have seen an object before biases you to say that the object is possible. This recollective process could hide the effects of repetition priming on impossible objects by biasing subjects to respond with "possible." This idea was tested by using two different ways of minimizing conscious recollection. In one version, the subjects were given a memory load; that is, they were asked to keep seven digits in memory while making their decisions. The second version implemented a *deadline procedure*, in which subjects were required to respond more quickly than usual. The idea here is that the object decision response must be made before the episodic information becomes available. The results are shown in Table 7.5.

When recollective processes were allowed (the column labeled "Replication"), the results duplicated the finding of repetition priming only for possible objects (0.67 versus 0.58) and not for impossible objects (0.42 versus 0.41). However, when the influence of the recollective processes was minimized by a deadline procedure, the results were different:

Table 7.5   The proportion of possible and impossible objects labeled "possible" in three different experiments (replication, deadline, and memory load) as a function of prior exposure

Study Form	Test Form	Proportion Labeled "Possible"		
		Replication	Deadline	Memory Load
Possible	Possible	0.67	0.64	0.66
	Possible	0.58	0.54	0.61
Impossible	Impossible	0.42	0.48	0.42
	Impossible	0.41	0.33	0.34

SOURCE: From "Bias in the Priming of Object Decisions," by R. Ratcliff and G. McKoon, 1995, *Journal of Experimental Psychology: Learning, Memory, and Cognition, 21,* 754–767. Copyright © 1995 American Psychological Association. Reprinted with permission.

Repetition priming was seen for both possible (0.64 versus 0.54) and impossible (0.48 versus 0.33) objects. The results from the memory load condition, which should also minimize the contributions of recollection, were the same as those for the deadline condition. In other words, impossible objects also have an advantage when seen a second time. Ratcliff and McKoon (1996) extend this result to show both benefits (repetition priming) and costs (worse performance) for object identification.

Not only is the bias view able to account for all these results, but more important, it actually predicts them. That is, the bias view predicts that in all instances of repetition priming (which it views as a benefit of repetition), it should be possible to show a decrement in performance (which it views as a cost of repetition). A model that allows for both qualitative and quantitative predictions within the perceptual identification paradigm has been developed (see Ratcliff & McKoon, 1997), and it seems likely that similar approaches can be made for the other paradigms.

Comparing Bias, TAP, and the Multiple Systems Views

Both the bias and transfer appropriate processing (TAP) views hold that postulating multiple memory systems is not needed to explain the currently available data. Moreover, models developed from the bias view (Ratcliff & McKoon, 1997) specify at least some of the processes that are responsible for repetition priming, and so can be seen as complementing, rather than competing with, TAP.

The major strength of the transfer appropriate processing view is the emphasis on processing information and on viewing memory as a process (see Craik & Lockhart, 1972; Kolers & Roediger, 1984), especially a discrimination process (see Capaldi & Neath, 1995). Because of this emphasis, TAP predicts dissociations based on processing rather than on the underlying memory system. For example, Blaxton (1989) predicted that her data-driven tests would benefit from visual presentation regardless of whether the test was thought to tap implicit memory (the indirect test) or explicit memory (the direct test). Similarly, Balota and his colleagues demonstrated dissociations between two tasks thought to tap semantic memory (Balota & Neely, 1980) and between two tasks thought to tap episodic memory (Balota & Chumbley, 1984). The more similarities that are found between tasks that are thought to tap different systems, the more problematic the multiple systems view becomes. Another strength of TAP is its ability to account for age-related declines in memory (see Chapter 14).

One weakness of the TAP view is that it says relatively little about the phenomenon of conscious awareness in different types of tasks. A second problem is that, although it distinguishes between perceptual and conceptual processing, the TAP approach does not yet include more fine-grained distinctions (Roediger & McDermott, 1993). It is possible that Jacoby's (1991) process dissociation framework can remedy this weakness. Thus, the TAP view cannot currently explain certain dissociations between two conceptually driven tasks (McDermott & Roediger, 1996; Tenpenny & Shoben, 1992).

Much of the evidence for multiple memory systems comes from people with various forms of brain damage. According to proponents of the multiple systems view (Tulving, 1986), it is by studying the pattern of deficits in these patients that memory researchers will be able to specify the number and type of memory systems. In the next chapter, we examine the biological basis of memory and examine the extent to which those data support the systems view.

The systems view has three major problems. First, it provides no set of criteria for determining the number of memory systems that results in just the five proposed systems listed in Table 7.4. For example, Roediger, Buckner, and McDermott (1999) show how recall and recognition meet the Sherry and Schacter (1987) criteria for being separate systems: The variable word frequency produces functional dissociations between recall and recognition (Gregg, 1976; see also Chapter 9); neuropsychological dissociations between recall and recognition are observable in amnesic subjects (Hirst, Johnson, Phelps, & Volpe, 1988); and numerous studies have found essentially no correlation between performance on the two tests (Nilsson & Gardiner, 1993). The functional incompatibility is also easy to demonstrate: Memory for taste or odors is a function that is well supported by recognition (consider the case of Marcel Proust) but not very well supported by recall. However, no theorist actually suggests that they are different (see Chapter 9).

The second major problem is that the systems view fails to account for the decline in memory performance seen when healthy people get older. One would assume that if one system were affected, then most tasks that tap that system would show deficits. However, it turns out that some tasks thought to tap episodic memory are almost unaffected by aging, whereas other episodic tasks are greatly affected (see Chapter 14).

A third major problem concerns the role that dissociations play. Not only can one find dissociations between systems, but there are also findings of dissociations within a particular memory system. As mentioned previously, Balota and his colleagues demonstrated dissociations between two tasks thought to tap semantic memory (Balota & Neely, 1980) and between two tasks thought to tap episodic memory (Balota & Chumbley, 1984). Others have shown independence between two tasks thought to tap implicit memory (Witherspoon & Moscovitch, 1989).

Neuropsychological dissociations are also problematic. As Parkin (1999) notes, many studies show that retrieval in episodic tasks involves right prefrontal activation whereas retrieval of semantic information involves left prefrontal activation. This neuropsychological dissociation, however, reverses when the two tasks are equated for difficulty: Retrieval of semantic information produces larger amounts of right frontal activation than the episodic task. In one sense, then, semantic memory under one set of conditions has a different neural substrate than semantic memory under a second set of conditions.

A final problem with dissociations is that although the system view predicts differences, it does not make a priori predictions about the precise nature of the dissociation. Consider one example that involves the *fan effect*. After learning a set of sentences that contain a fact about a person and a location, subjects are given a recognition test. The *fan effect* is the finding that response times to say that a particular sentence has been seen previously increase when the number of facts in the sentence related to the person or the location also increases (Anderson, 1974). The important point, as McKoon, Ratcliff, and Dell (1986) point out, is that this fan effect is observed in episodic tasks but not in semantic tasks. There is nothing in the distinction between episodic memory and semantic memory that would lead anyone to predict this result. Although it is a dissociation, it is not predicted; if the result had been the reverse, the distinction would still be supported! As Hintzman (1984a, p. 241) put it, "If one wants to claim that a dissociation outcome supports the episodic-semantic distinction, one must show that the dissociation is predicted by theory that embodies the distinction."

Tulving and Schacter (1990) agree that there are many similarities between tasks thought to tap one memory system and tasks thought to tap a separate system. They argue that these "'parallel effects' are theoretically uninteresting, since some similarities would be expected of all forms of memory—otherwise it would be difficult to justify their general label" (p. 305). The goal facing multiple systems theorists is to develop a theoretical account that predicts which variables will show dissociations between different systems and which variables will behave in a parallel fashion.

Chapter Summary

Implicit memory is concerned with situations in which subjects are unaware of various aspects of the learning and testing situation. Implicit serial learning examines whether people can learn structured information even though they have no awareness of what they are learning. In other implicit memory experiments, the learning instructions can be incidental (the subject is unaware that there will be a memory test) or intentional (the subject is fully aware that there will be a memory test), and the memory test can be indirect (the subject is unaware that the test is related to a particular learning episode) or direct (the subject is fully aware of the relationship between the learning episode and the test). Whereas early research found differences between implicit and explicit memory, more recent research has shown that principles of forgetting and interference apply to both. One explanation invokes separate memory systems, although there is no consensus on the exact number and type of systems. This view has difficulty accounting for the similarities between supposedly different systems and for dissociations within a single system. A second explanation is based on transfer appropriate processing and suggests that many differences arise from the relative contributions of data-driven and concept-driven processing. This view has difficulty in defining the types of processing precisely. A third view attributes the results from implicit memory tasks to bias: Prior presentation of something influences the way you process the same item a second time.

CHAPTER EIGHT

Memory, Brain, and Amnesia

Memory is no abstract property of the mind, but a universal property of nerves.
—William H. Burnham (1888)

In 1904, Richard Semon introduced the term *engram*—the set of changes in the nervous system that represents stored memory (Schacter, 1982). The next logical question one might ask is, Where is the engram? Although it seems obvious that memories must be stored in the brain, and although our knowledge of biological and physiological processes is advancing at an ever-accelerating rate, we still know relatively little about the biological basis of memory. The goal of this chapter, therefore, is to provide a general overview of what we do know about the underlying biological processes and brain structures that support memory and give an appreciation for the difficulties in conducting this kind of research. We begin with a brief overview of how neurons work, and follow with a description of the basic architecture of the brain. Then we examine memory in people with amnesia and people with Alzheimer's disease. Finally, we consider some experiments that explore how memory is implemented in the normal brain.

The Neuron

The current view is that memory involves "a persistent change in the relationship between neurons, either through structural modification or through biochemical events within neurons that change the way in which neighboring neurons communicate" (Squire, 1987, p. 7). This concept was first introduced by Ramon y Cajal (1894) and has been restated in various forms by others such as Konorski (1948), Hebb (1949), and Kandel (1977). Memory can thus be seen as a specific form of a more general biological process known as neural plasticity. *Plasticity* refers to the idea that a neuron can change as a result of experience, either structurally or functionally, in a way that is long lasting. One form of plasticity that has been of particular interest is *synaptic plasticity,* the changes that occur at and around the synapse. Although synaptic plasticity is considered necessary for memories to be formed and retrieved, the properties of memory cannot be understood with just that concept alone. A more complex level of description that gives an account of the neural circuitry of the brain and the coordinated activity of large groups of neurons must bridge the gap between the synapse and behavior. Thus, synaptic plasticity "enables memory, but does not equal it" (Martin, Grimwood, & Morris, 2000, p. 665).

The nervous system has two main types of cells, *glial cells* and *neurons.* Glia provide the basic support system for neurons and perform a variety of maintenance functions, including holding the structure together, supplying nutrients, and maintaining the chemical environment. Neurons are the cells that process information, receiving, integrating, and transmitting messages. Sensory neurons gather information that originates outside the system (such as sights and sounds), and motor neurons provide instructions to muscles that inform them when and how to move. The majority of neurons, however, are interneurons—neurons that communicate only with other neurons and not with muscles or the outside world.

Figure 8.1 shows a simplified drawing of the major parts of the prototypical interneuron. A neuron normally consists of *dendrites,* which receive information, the soma (or cell body), and an *axon,* which transmits information to another neuron or group of neurons.

Neurons can vary in size, shape, and many other properties, but their basic operation is quite clear. The neural impulse is a complex electrochemical reaction. There is a difference in electrical charge between the inside and the outside of the cell body caused by the presence, in differing amounts, of (1) sodium, potassium, or calcium for a positive charge and (2) chloride for a negative charge. The cell membrane is semipermeable; that is, at different times it will allow different types of ions to permeate, or pass through. At rest, there are more negative ions inside the cell, and more positive ions outside the cell. Thus, relative to the outside, the cell is negatively charged.

When a neuron is stimulated, either by other neurons or by a sensory event, the neuronal membrane becomes more permeable to positive ions. These positive ions rush into the cell, attracted by the large number of negative ions inside. Relative to the outside, the cell becomes less negative, creating an *action potential.* This is the name given to a brief change in the cell's electrical charge, and this voltage change is the message sent down the axon. A neural impulse is simply an electric current that flows along an axon as a result of an action potential. If the axon is insulated with a myelin sheath, the signal can travel faster. Some diseases, such as multiple sclerosis, destroy the myelin sheath, which results in loss of coordination, movement, and eventually cognitive processes. Before a neuron can fire again, the positive ions have to be pumped out of the cell, restoring the resting voltage.

Figure 8.1   The key parts of a typical interneuron. The dendrites receive information from other neurons; the soma, or cell body, contains the nucleus of the cell; and the axon transmits the information to other neurons. The axon is often covered by a myelin sheath, which serves as insulation and increases the speed at which the message is sent. The point at which the ends of the axon connect with the dendrites of the next neuron is the synapse.

Neural firing works on the all-or-none principle, like pulling a trigger on a gun. Once the trigger is pulled a certain amount, a bullet is fired. The bullet travels at the same velocity no matter how weakly or strongly the trigger is pulled. Neurons typically convey strength information not by increasing the voltage change sent down the axon but by changing the frequency of firing. For example, a stronger stimulus might cause a neuron to fire more rapidly, but each individual neural impulse will be of the same magnitude as when a weaker stimulus elicits firing.

The gap between the end of the axon of one neuron and the dendrites of another is called the *synapse*. It has been estimated that there are 6×10^{13} synapses in the human cortex (Shepard & Koch, 1990). The chemicals that transmit the neural impulse over this gap are called neurotransmitters, and they are stored in small sacs on the dendrites called synaptic vesicles. An arriving neural impulse induces a chemical reaction that releases a particular kind or set of neurotransmitters into the synapse. These molecules diffuse across the synapse (from the presynaptic membrane to the postsynaptic membrane) and reach the dendrites of the receiving neuron, attaching themselves to receptor sites on the dendrites. This generates a *postsynaptic potential* (or *PSP*), which can be one of two kinds. An excitatory PSP increases the likelihood that the receiving neuron will open the ion channels and begin the process for an action potential; an inhibitory PSP causes the voltage to remain or become even more negative, thus decreasing the likelihood of an action potential. The neurotransmitters are then either neutralized or broken down by enzymes, freeing up the receptor sites, or are taken up by the synaptic vesicles. Each neuron can have as many as 15,000 synapses receiving information from thousands of other neurons and can send signals to many thousands more; thus, neurons are more than just simple relay stations.

The Brain

The brain is an approximately 3-pound, walnut-like object that contains billions of inter-acting neurons. It has three major regions: the hindbrain, the midbrain, and the forebrain (see Figure 8.2).

The *hindbrain* is at the lower end and controls regulation of basic body functions. Connecting the brain and the spinal cord is the medulla, which is responsible for breath-ing and circulation. The pons, above the medulla, is a bulbous structure that regulates the sleep-wake cycle and includes a bridge of fibers that connects the brain stem with the rest of the brain. The cerebellum is a large structure that is critically involved in the coordina-tion of movement.

The *midbrain* lies between the hindbrain and the forebrain. Included within this re-gion is the tectum, which is involved in reflexive responses such as ducking, and part of the reticular formation, which begins in the hindbrain. This area is associated with vigi-lance and arousal; damage to this area often results in a coma. There is also an important set of dopamine-releasing neurons in the substantia nigra. Dopamine is a neurotransmit-ter often used by neurons that control smooth motor movement. Damage to these dopam-ine-producing neurons is related to Parkinson's disease, often characterized by tremors, re-duced control over voluntary movement, and muscular rigidity.

The *forebrain* is associated with complex thought and cognition. The thalamus, the hypothalamus, and the limbic system, located at the top of the brain stem, form the core of the forebrain. Over them is the cerebrum, which may contain as much as two-thirds of all the neurons within the central nervous system. The cerebrum is covered by a wrinkled surface called the *cerebral cortex*; the wrinkles make it possible for more surface area (up to approximately 1.5 square feet, or 2500 square centimeters) to fit within the skull. The elevations are called gyri, the small valleys are called sulci, and the large valleys are called fissures.

The thalamus can be thought of as a sensory relay station, integrating almost all sen-sations (with the exception of odor) before passing them on to the appropriate areas of the cortex for further processing. The hypothalamus, situated below the thalamus, is in-volved with regulating the autonomic nervous system, emotion, and what has sometimes been dubbed the four *F*s: feeding, fighting, fleeing, and reproduction. In addition, it regu-lates hormone production within the endocrine system. The limbic system, which in-cludes parts of the hypothalamus, is not a very well defined system. A group of structures that surrounds the thalamus, it includes the amygdala, the septum, and the hippocampus. The amygdala is an evaluation system that contributes to feelings of fear, anger, and so forth. Damage to the amygdala results in an inability to evaluate environmental stimuli appropriately—for example, trying to evaluate a visual stimulus by taste. The hippocam-pus has been identified as an important structure for memory and will be discussed in more detail later in this chapter.

A distinction is often made between *cortical* and *subcortical* regions. These terms refer to areas either within the cortex or below the cortex. The cortex, or cerebrum, is divided into two halves, referred to as *hemispheres*, that are separated by a central fissure. At the bottom of the fissure lies the corpus callosum, a bundle of fibers that connects the two hemispheres and allows them to communicate with each other. Each cerebral hemisphere is divided into four lobes: frontal, parietal, temporal, and occipital (see Figure 8.3). In de-scribing the brain further, neuroanatomists use directional terms. For example, the front

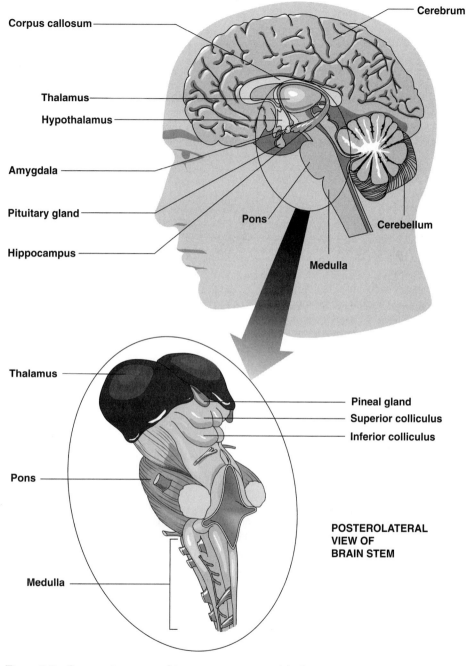

Figure 8.2   Some major areas and important structures of the brain

end of any lobe is anterior; the back is posterior. The top of the head is dorsal; the bottom is ventral. Lateral refers to left or right of the midline; medial is toward the middle. The areas of the brain have also been broken up into subdivisions called *Brodmann areas (BA)*.

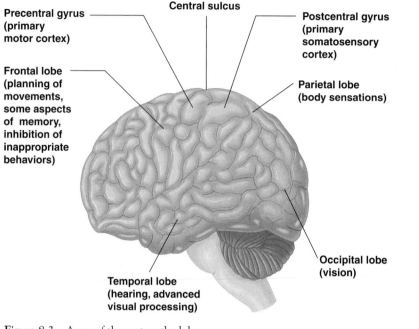

Central sulcus

**Precentral gyrus
(primary
motor cortex)**

**Postcentral gyrus
(primary
somatosensory
cortex)**

**Frontal lobe
(planning of
movements,
some aspects
of memory,
inhibition of
inappropriate
behaviors)**

**Parietal lobe
(body sensations)**

**Occipital lobe
(vision)**

**Temporal lobe
(hearing, advanced
visual processing)**

Figure 8.3   Areas of the cortex: the lobes

Korbinian Brodmann (1868–1918) was an anatomist who numbered sections of the brain based on cytoarchitecture (essentially, the appearance of the cells in a brain area under a microscope). In some instances, but not all, there is a relationship between the appearance of a region and its function. Modern forms of Brodmann's maps are often used as a common reference system for brain imaging studies. For example, the dorsolateral prefrontal cortex contains subdivisions BA 44, BA 45, BA 47, and so on.

The *frontal lobe* is responsible for motor control and contains an area called the primary motor cortex. Different parts of the motor cortex control different parts of the body, and the more precision needed for motor control (as in the fingers or the tongue), the larger the area of the motor cortex associated with it. The motor cortex occupies only a small region of the frontal lobes; the functions of the remaining areas are more speculative. Recently the frontal lobes have been shown to be important in a numerous memory functions, particularly different types of working memory functions. A summary of this research will be outlined later.

Behind the frontal lobe is the *parietal lobe*, which includes the somatosensory cortex. This region processes sensory information, including touch, temperature, and pain. As with the primary motor cortex, larger regions of the somatosensory cortex are associated with more precise sensory receivers. Below the parietal lobe is the *temporal lobe* (near the temples), which contains the primary auditory cortex and controls hearing. Finally, behind the parietal and temporal lobes is the *occipital lobe*, which contains the primary visual cortex, where most visual signals are sent and where most visual processing occurs.

Methods of Investigation

Investigations into the way in which memories are stored in the brain fall into two major categories: invasive and noninvasive. Invasive techniques involve damage (or lesions) to the brain, either through accident or, in the case of animal studies, deliberate destruction of certain areas of the brain. In addition, it is possible to take recordings from single cells or groups of brain cells using microelectrodes. Noninvasive procedures can be performed without damage to the brain and pose little risk to the experimental subjects. These include techniques to measure blood flow as well as the electrical activity of the brain.

Invasive Techniques

Lesion studies have provided much of the basic data about brain function, and both clinical patients and laboratory animals have been used. For example, when a stroke occurs in one hemisphere, it can *lesion* or destroy certain areas. By determining which areas are affected and by noting behavioral changes, a tentative assignment can be made between the area and its function. In laboratory animals, more precise lesions are possible, and appropriate control groups can be used. In many cases, however, the animal's brain function and organization can be quite different from those of humans, so great care must be taken in choosing the appropriate model.

In addition to the question of generalizing from laboratory animals to humans, another common criticism of the lesioning method is "How can the function of a complex, highly interrelated system be understood by placing a hole in the middle of it?" (Squire, 1987, p. 175). When a structure such as the hippocampus is lesioned and retention of some learned information is impaired, how do we know that it is the damage to the hippocampus, rather than to some fibers that pass through it, that caused the loss? The answer is that gross lesioning techniques cannot provide much in the way of precise answers, and most researchers do not do this. In fact, numerous technical improvements in lesioning techniques allow for selective damage to particular types of cells while leaving all the fibers that pass through the hippocampus intact (Jarrard, 1989). In addition, researchers look for converging evidence, combining data from lesion procedures with results from other paradigms to see if they all point to—or converge on—one answer. Through precision lesioning, psychologists have begun to map out the circuitry of some elementary forms of learning and memory (Byrne & Berry, 1989; Donegan, Gluck, & Thompson, 1989; McGaugh, Weinberger, & Lynch, 1990).

A great deal of the animal research on the cognitive neuroscience of memory has centered on the *hippocampal structures*. Despite some differences in overall numbers of neurons, the basic anatomy of the hippocampus is similar in rats and primates. Thus, it is thought that the results found in animal studies can be generalized to human beings. Although there has been much controversy in the literature regarding the role of the hippocampus in animal and human memory (see O'Reilly & Rudy, 2001, for a review), it is often theorized that the hippocampus is responsible for binding together the contextual features of a situation to create a unitary representation of every experience. For example, your memory of a specific event is a combination of visual, auditory, olfactory, and other stimuli, as well as the time and place of occurrence and your thoughts and impressions at the time. This information comes from different parts of the brain serving different sensory modalities, but is bound together into a single memory for an event. The hippoc-ampus is said to be instrumental in forming the contextual representations needed to con-struct an episodic memory for an event (Redish, 2001).

In the animal literature, some of the most convincing demonstrations of this binding function of the hippocampus come from studies on *negative patterning*. In these experi-ments, the subject (most often a rat) is given a food reward for responding to individual stimuli but not for responding to a combination of those same stimuli. For example, one stimulus might be a tone (A) and another a light (B). The rat is rewarded for responding when either A or B is present by itself, but is not rewarded for responding when both A and B are present at the same time. This problem requires a configural or conjunctive rep-resentation: If the subjects are learning to respond to just the features of each stimulus (A *or* B) rather than to the combination of the two stimuli (A *and* B), they cannot solve this problem correctly. Rats with hippocampal lesions are impaired compared to normal rats in both the learning and the retention of this negative patterning problem (Rudy & Sutherland, 1989).

The configural theory is an attractive one in that it can explain some of the data from amnesic subjects, reviewed later. Subsequent experiments, however, have compli-cated the picture by showing that rats with hippocampal lesions can still solve certain types of configural problems (Davidson, McKernan, & Jerrard, 1993), and researchers have suggested that other difficulties, such as an inability to inhibit responses, may ex-plain the negative patterning results without recourse to memory (Tracy, Jarrard, & Davidson, 2001). This literature is too complicated to be reviewed here, but at this point it is clear that the hippocampus is one of several medial temporal lobe structures that may support memory. Its exact function remains open to question and much debate (see, for example, Messier, 2001).

Another type of invasive technique involves recording from single neurons in the brain. Some of this research has been done using primates such as monkeys that are close to humans in terms of brain structure. Funahashi, Bruce, and Goldman-Rakic (1989) trained monkeys to fixate on the center of a display and to keep their eyes there. From time to time, a visual cue was flashed up very briefly somewhere else on the screen. After a delay ranging from 1 to 6 seconds, the monkeys were given a signal and rewarded for moving their eyes to where the cue had been. Micro-electrodes implanted in the brains of the monkeys recorded levels of activity from single groups of neurons and showed that some of these neurons seem to fire to the memory of a target in a particular location of the visual field. For example, a particular neuron's activity increased sharply after a stimulus was presented briefly at a particular location in the visual field, then remained active dur-ing the delay (in the absence of the stimulus), and then returned to baseline activation abruptly at the end of delay when the response was made. Funahashi et al. interpreted these results (and others using lesioning techniques in monkeys) as showing that areas in the prefrontal cortex are involved in a form of visual working memory necessary to hold the memory of the stimulus location and complete this task. This view, however, is not without its detractors (Rushworth, Nixon, Eacott, & Passingham, 1997).

Very few deliberately invasive techniques are used on humans, for obvious reasons. However, in certain cases where brain surgery is necessary, the surgeon needs to know which hemisphere contains certain functions (language capability, in particular). One of the techniques used in such cases is the intracarotid amobarbital perfusion test—better known as the *Wada test* after Juhn Wada, who devised it (Calvin & Ojemann, 1994). This test provides evidence about the division of functioning between the two hemispheres. A short-acting anesthetic (amobarbital) is injected into the left carotid artery, and the front two-thirds of the left hemisphere stops working for approximately 2 minutes. By noting which behavioral and cognitive operations are no longer functional, the researcher can assign those operations to the temporarily deactivated hemisphere. More detailed information can be obtained by direct stimulation of various areas of the brain during surgery. Both of these techniques are limited to clinical patients, often those with severe epilepsy or brain tumors.

Noninvasive Techniques

Because of the obvious limits of invasive techniques, a more common technique used to study the neuropsychology of human memory is imaging (see Kolb & Whishaw, 1996). Researchers use CT (computerized tomography), MRI (magnetic resonance imaging), and PET (positron emission tomography) scans. Generally, these techniques show either activity levels at various brain sites or detailed structural information.

CT scans (also known as computerized axial tomography, or CAT scans) are useful for examining brain structure. The patient's head is surrounded by a set of X-ray transmitters and receptors so that X-rays are directed through the brain along different orientations. A computer analyzes how much radiation arrives at each destination and converts this information into a photograph of the brain's structure. This technique is often used to detect gross damage caused by trauma or disease, such as degeneration caused by tumors, strokes, or advanced stages of Alzheimer's disease.

PET scans, in contrast, provide information about ongoing activity rather than about structure (see Posner & Raichle, 1994). Neurons use glucose, a form of sugar, as a source of energy; the more active neurons in the brain take up larger amounts of glucose. For a PET scan, the patient is injected with radioactive glucose, and the amount of radiation emitted by various parts of the brain is then measured and analyzed. The results are usually shown as a color map, with red representing those areas that have the most emissions—indicating that they were very active and had absorbed a relatively large amount of radioactive glucose—and colors farther along the color spectrum showing lower levels of emissions. One important detail to remember about PET scans is that the images typically displayed are computed. In a "raw" image of a PET scan, many different areas of the brain are active. The most common technique involves taking multiple scans, and subtracting one image scanned when the subject is doing one task from another image of the same subject doing a related task. In theory, the resulting image shows those areas that were more active during the second task than on the first.

For example, Tulving (1989) asked a subject to think about an autobiographical memory—an event that the person had personally experienced—or to think about something general, such as the history of astronomy, that the person had not directly experienced. The particular procedure used here was to inject a small amount of radioactive gold into the bloodstream and to use gamma-ray detectors that encircled the subject's head. Tulving (1989) found evidence of greater blood flow in the anterior portions of frontal lobe when the subject was thinking about autobiographical information, and greater blood flow in the posterior portions of the frontal lobe when thinking about generic information.

MRI is based on the effects that strong magnetic fields have on the alignment of hydrogen atoms. A computer analyzes the changes in alignment when the magnetic field is repeatedly disrupted by radio waves. Brain structure is revealed because hydrogen concentrations vary in different areas. MRIs are thought to be safe but are quite costly. More recently, the magnetic resonance imaging machinery has been used to generate a picture of the brain's activity rather than its static structure. This *functional MRI (fMRI)* is accomplished by tracking blood flow in the brain, which broadcasts a telltale signal in response to the magnetic field. The technique is based on the supposition that the more active a brain area is, the more blood flows to it. One problem with fMRI is its relative sluggishness in comparison to the speed of neural processing. For example, the fMRI signal gradually increases over about 4 to 6 seconds, even though the neural activity begins in as few as 50 to 100 milliseconds after a stimulus is presented. This severely limits the types of experiments that can be done using fMRI. A new statistical technique now being developed, called event-related fMRI, enables researchers to map short-lasting responses following single stimuli down to about 1 second, which is a little closer to the time scale of most neurophysiological processes. This technique is still in its infancy and is somewhat controversial, but shows great promise (D'Esposito, Zarahn, & Aguirre, 1999).

Although there are many difficulties and pitfalls in designing and interpreting the data in studies using such methods (see Bub, 2000, for a review), the use of these techniques in conjunction with appropriate behavioral analyses can give researchers valuable converging evidence to use in constructing theories of the cognitive neuroscience of memory.

Two other common techniques for investigating brain functioning are EEGs and ERPs. *Electroencephalograms* (EEGs) measure the pattern of electrical activity through electrodes attached to the scalp. The resulting information measures brain activity at a relatively gross level. *Event-related potentials* (ERPs) are momentary changes in the EEG associated with the presentation of a particular stimulus or with a particular type of processing (Näätänen, 1992). ERPs are analyzed in terms of positive or negative changes, relative to a baseline, within a particular time span. For example, a negative change that occurs between 300 and 500 ms after the stimulus is known as an N400 ERP.

As an example of how ERPs have been used in exploring human memory processes, Paller, Kutas, and McIsaac (1995) had subjects complete a recognition judgment (a direct test) and perform a *lexical decision task* (an indirect test). In this latter task, subjects were asked to respond as quickly as they could to indicate whether a target item was a valid word or a nonword. Prior to these tasks, the subjects were asked to perform an imagery judgment (Is the object referred to by the word larger or smaller than the computer monitor?) or a syllable judgment (Does the word have one syllable or more than one syllable?). The researchers found that subjects recognized imaged words better than words that were in the syllable judgment, but found that these tasks did not affect the lexical decision task. So far, this dissociation fits in with the type of studies reported in the previous chapter, where some measures affect direct tests of memory but do not affect indirect tests. Paller, Kutas, and McIsaac (1995) also recorded ERPs. They found that when conscious recollection was occurring, as indexed behaviorally by the improved recognition performance for the imagery words, a more positive ERP was observable between 500 and 900 ms after stimulus presentation than when the syllable words were presented. They suggested that this ERP correlates with degree of recollective processing and may be another useful way of separating automatic from recollective processes (see also Chapter 5).

All of these noninvasive techniques have their strengths and weaknesses. CT and MRI are very good techniques if the researcher is interested in the static structures of the brain, but they do not provide insight into ongoing physiological processes. PET and fMRI show activation of fairly precise areas of the brain during various types of stimulation, but they are not good for discovering how the processes might change over time. ERPs have very good temporal resolution, but the electrical activity is less easily localized to highly specific regions of the brain. Thus, researchers in cognitive neuroscience generally form their theories based on results gained using a combination of these techniques, in addition to lesion and behavioral studies.

CogLab Experiment
http://coglab.wadsworth.com/experiments/BrainAsymmetry/

Behavioral tests can be performed that rely on getting a particular hemisphere to control, or have priority in performing, some task. For example, stimuli can be presented to subjects so that they are initially processed by just the left hemisphere or just the right hemisphere. Although the information will quickly be transmitted to the other hemisphere, differences in processing time enable the researcher to infer differences in capabilities. Klatzky and Atkinson (1971) presented either pictures or letters and then had subjects make a decision about whether the stimulus had appeared in an immediately preceding list. Having subjects fixate to the left of the display area meant that the stimulus was presented in the right visual field and thence projected first to the left hemisphere; fixating to the right of the display area meant that the stimulus was presented in the left visual field and was projected to the right hemisphere first. Klatzky and Atkinson found that when the stimuli required a verbal code, right-handed subjects were faster when the stimuli were presented to the left hemisphere (856 ms) than to the right hemisphere (902 ms). When the stimuli required a spatial code, subjects were faster when the stimuli were presented to the right hemisphere (809 ms) than to the left hemisphere (828 ms). These results were obtained regardless of which hand was used for responding. Koenig, Wetzel, and Caramazza (1992) have reported similar findings.

Similar techniques have been used with other tasks. For example, Urcuioli, Klein, and Day (1981) found differences in a categorization task: Category matching relied more on the left hemisphere, but category membership tasks were less localized. Another behavioral test is to use classical conditioning and present the conditioned stimulus (CS) to one visual field or another. Using this technique, Hellige (1975) used a conditioned blink procedure and found systematic differences in speed and type of responding depending on the hemisphere that received the CS.

Kinsbourne and Cook (1971) reported a study that compared performance on a balancing task when the subject was asked either to vocalize or to remain silent. The subjects, all of whom were right-handed, first practiced balancing a wooden dowel on the left and right index fingers. They balanced the dowel for 1 minute on the left index finger and then, after a 1-minute rest, balanced the dowel for 1 minute on the right index finger. The criterion was to achieve a balancing time in excess of 5 minutes for the 20 experimental trials. The subjects then attempted to balance the dowel for as long as they could while vocalizing or while remaining silent.

As can be seen in Figure 8.4, Kinsbourne and Cook (1971) found longer balancing times with the right hand in the nonverbal condition and shorter balancing times with the right hand in the verbal condition. The reason, they suggest, is that the left hemisphere,

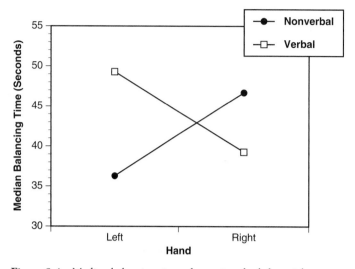

Figure 8.4   Median balancing time when using the left or right hand when concurrent vocalization was required (verbal) or not required (nonverbal).   SOURCE: Based on data from Kinsbourne & Cook (1971).

which controls the right hand, is also the seat of language. The surprising result was that the opposite pattern was observed for the left hand: longer balancing times in the verbal than in the nonverbal condition. Their interpretation is that the task of verbalizing helped performance on the left hand by distracting the subjects just enough that they did not focus too much attention on balancing. Regardless of the correct interpretation, the results do show laterality effects on a behavioral measure.

A final technique used to ascribe function to brain areas, and also to distinguish between different memory systems, is logical rather than methodological. A *dissociation* is said to have been shown when an independent variable differentially affects performance on two different tests. For example, word frequency refers to how often a word is used in written and spoken language. When the test is free recall, high-frequency words are recalled better than low-frequency words; when the test is recognition, low-frequency words are recognized better than high-frequency words (Gregg, 1976). This is an example of a single dissociation. Another example occurs when damage occurs to a specific brain area. Patients with damage to Broca's area have trouble producing fluent speech—called Broca's aphasia—whereas similar subjects without this damage do not have this difficulty. A *double dissociation* is said to have been shown when two different independent variables have opposite effects on two different tests. In neuropsychology, a double dissociation is often expressed as finding two patients of whom Patient A is impaired on Task 1 but not on Task 2, whereas Patient B is impaired on Task 2 but not on Task 1.

In practice, the logic of dissociations and double dissociations is not as simple as described above. For example, Shallice (1988) devotes three chapters to discussing what inferences may be drawn on the basis of various kinds of dissociations. Neely (1989) points out many other potential problems that may prevent the logic from being valid. In fact, he includes a set of "prescriptions" that a researcher should follow when designing an ex-

---

Experiment *Laterality of Language*

Purpose: To demonstrate the laterality of language by inducing interference on a balancing task

Subjects: Twenty right-handed subjects are recommended. Subjects should indicate that they write and throw with their right hand and that they use their right hand to brush their teeth. The reason for using right-handed subjects is that the left side of the brain is the seat of language in almost all right-handed people but in only approximately 70% of left-handed people (Corballis, 1980).

Materials: You will need a wooden rod, approximately 50 cm long, 1.5 cm in diameter, and weighing approximately 100 g. You will also need a set of sentences for the subject to verbalize (you can make these up yourself) and a stopwatch.

Procedure: Each subject should practice balancing the dowel for 1 minute on the right index finger. Allow 15 minutes for practice. Then, ten subjects should be tested on the conditions in the order RN (right-nonverbal) followed by RV (right-verbal), and ten subjects should be tested on the conditions in the order RV followed by RN.

Instructions: "We are interested in how long you can balance this rod on your index finger while standing. Try to keep the rod balanced for as long as possible, moving your whole body if necessary."

Additional Instructions for the Verbal Trials: "While you balance the rod, I would like you to repeat the following sentences out loud." (Read the sentences.)

Scoring and Analysis: For each subject, calculate the median balancing time (in seconds) for both conditions. The median is the value that is in the middle; there are an equal number of values above and below the median. Then, average the median balancing times. A paired-group *t* test can be used to test for significance. The results should replicate the data for the right hand shown in Figure 8.4.

Optional Enhancements: Include the left hand. In this case, present the conditions in the order RN, LN, RV, LV and LV, RV, LN, RN.

SOURCE: Based on an experiment by Kinsbourne & Cook (1971).

---

periment in order to avoid common interpretive difficulties. Even though both authors emphasize that dissociations can serve as a valuable tool for distinguishing different underlying systems, both also emphasize that it is very difficult to construct the appropriate series of experiments. Certainly, dissociations from a single experiment or from a single study should be looked on with skepticism. As in other areas of scientific inquiry, replication under appropriately stringent conditions is needed in order to draw firm conclusions.

Amnesia

Cognitive neuropsychologists have traditionally classified amnesia into two major categories: retrograde and anterograde. *Retrograde amnesia* refers to the case in which a person is unable to remember details that were learned prior to the event that caused the amnesia ("retro-" meaning past). Retrograde is the type of amnesia discussed in Chapter 6 in conjunction with consolidation theory. Complete retrograde amnesia, in which the person is unable to recall any events from his or her life, is relatively rare (except in soap operas), but partial retrograde amnesia is fairly common, particularly as a result of a concussion.

Usually the concussed individual will not be able to remember what happened during the few minutes or hours prior to the blow to the head. The other main form is *anterograde amnesia* ("antero-" meaning front or forward), in which a person seems unable to learn new information following some brain trauma. It is common for both kinds to be present simultaneously to differing degrees.

Within these types of amnesia, individuals are classified in three main ways: by cause, by damage, or by functional deficit. Classification by cause is most useful when giving a prognosis. For example, patients with amnesia due to chronic alcoholism are likely to have a different prognosis from those with amnesia due to viral encephalitis. This criterion is less useful for psychological purposes, though, because within a category, cases may be more or less severe. Because the degree of severity will affect the type and extent of deficits, the memory data can be ambiguous.

Some studies classify patients on the basis of the location of the brain damage. In many cases, if similar brain structures are damaged, the behavior impairment is similar regardless of the cause. The major problem with this approach is the current crudity of brain localization techniques. For example, damage to the hippocampus, a structure often implicated in memory impairment, affects not only the structure itself but also many fibers that pass through the hippocampus. With most lesions in humans, the damage is rarely localized and instead affects many different areas. Amnesia can be caused by lesions in a number of different areas of the brain, either by themselves or in combination. Figure 8.5 shows two cross-sections of the brain with the areas that have been implicated in memory and amnesia indicated by an asterisk. These areas have been found to be destroyed in individuals with Korsakoff's disease and others with memory disorders caused by tumors or stroke. Parkin and Hunkin (1993) report the case of RK, who had a tumor pressing on the mammillary bodies. The patient initially showed dense anterograde amnesia. However, as the tumor was treated and shrunk through radiation therapy, his memory performance gradually improved.

A third way of classifying amnesics is by their functional deficit. Certain patients, regardless of the etiology and localization of their deficits, have similar patterns of memory behavior. For example, one common type of deficit is known as the *amnesic syndrome*. The amnesic syndrome can arise from *Korsakoff's syndrome,* in which prolonged alcohol abuse leads to a thiamine deficiency and subsequent brain damage. It can also result from viral encephalitis, from lesions due to tumors, trauma, or surgery, or from lack of oxygen. Although pure cases are rare and there is a wide range of variability, the basic characteristics are quite robust. These patients demonstrate severe and permanent anterograde amnesia. They are unable to perform at normal levels on any direct memory test, such as recall, recognition, or paired-associate learning. They are unable to learn to recognize new faces, even ones they have seen over and over again. They have no knowledge of what they had for breakfast minutes after they have finished eating. Although they do well on learning new skills, they show no conscious knowledge that they have practiced such a skill. They seem to have no conscious knowledge of anything that has happened to them in the time since the brain injury. However, in comparison with normal individuals, they generally show preserved memory function on such tasks as digit span. They also show remarkably little impairment in previously learned general knowledge and other general measures of intelligence. Finally, they often demonstrate normal performance on skill learning, conditioning, perceptual learning, and priming (Parkin, 1997).

Figure 8.5 Cross-sections of the human brain. Those areas marked with an asterisk are known to be damaged in patients with the amnesic syndrome.   SOURCE: From *Alcoholic Korsakoff's Syndrome: An Information Processing Approach to Amnesia*, by N. Butters & L. S. Cernak. New York: Academic Press, 1980.

Wilson and Baddeley (1988) described one such case, a 59-year-old patient known as K. J. whose amnesia resulted from meningitis. On intelligence tests, K. J. performed well above average and displayed no evidence of perceptual deficits. He showed no noticeable impairment on immediate memory tasks, including the Brown-Peterson task, and his basic knowledge was unaffected. For example, he could verify sentences such as "Canaries are yellow" (true) or "Bats are birds" (false) as quickly and as accurately as appropriate control subjects. His memory for the details of his own life was well preserved, at least up until the time near his illness. His performance on implicit learning tasks was near normal. For example, he could learn to solve the Tower of Hanoi puzzle (see Figure 8.6 later in the chapter), as well as other procedural tasks such as reading reversed text. The main locus of his deficit was in retrieving episodic information. He had problems learning the names of new therapists and could not navigate in new environments or recall what he had seen on television or read in the newspaper. If tested immediately, he could recall even fairly complex paragraphs; after a short delay, however, he could recall almost nothing.

The major problem in the amnesia literature is that neither amnesia itself nor its behavioral tasks or consequents are as yet precisely described. Even within a type of amnesia (such as Korsakoff patients), there is often uncertainty about how one patient's symptoms compare with another's. For example, Weiskrantz (1985) reported on the use of the difference between the IQ score and the memory quotient (MQ) of the Weschsler Memory Scale. This difference is known as IQ-WMQ. The larger this difference, the more impaired the subject. Weiskrantz compared the IQ-WMQ scores of different types of patients and found that amnesics with the same numerical score are sometimes classified as "severe" amnesics by one researcher and as "moderate" by another. Many studies include no objective numerical assessment of the severity of the amnesia.

As one example of another problem, many reports describe only one level of task; thus, some studies report that patients can solve visual maze learning tasks, whereas other studies with apparently similar subjects report that their patients cannot. A better method is to include at least two levels of difficulty. When this method was used with H. M., a patient with profound amnesia (see the next section), it was found that he could learn the simple version of the maze but not the complex version (Milner, Corkin, & Teuber, 1968). These and other problems may have prompted Cermak (1982) to state, "Finding an amnesic to support one's thesis is neither difficult nor sufficient" (p. 44). Nonetheless, there has been an enormous amount of progress in understanding at least the character of human amnesic syndrome and related memory deficits (Parkin, 1997). Although the issues are too complex and the literature too large to be reviewed completely in one chapter, it is nonetheless possible to offer an overview.

H. M.: A Case Study

The most often cited case study of amnesia is that of H. M. (see Scoville & Milner, 1957). In 1953, when he was 27, H. M. underwent an experimental surgical procedure that bilaterally severed his hippocampus in an attempt to alleviate chronic epileptic seizures. As a result of the surgery, the previously intractable seizures became controllable by medication, and thus the surgery was partially successful. However, the surgery also produced a severe disruption of memory performance. After the operation, H. M. lived with his parents, and since 1980 has lived in a nursing home. The severity of the memory impairment and the complete disruption of his life cannot be overemphasized. For example, although his father died in 1967 and his mother in 1977, in 1986 H. M. thought he was still living with his mother and was unsure whether his father was alive (Parkin, 1993b). In general, H. M. is able to perform within the normal range on tasks that have an immediate test, but he shows almost no memory for information when the test is delayed.

Theoretical Accounts of Amnesia

The case of H. M. has been used to support (1) the role of the hippocampus in memory, (2) the distinction between long- and short-term memory, (3) the distinction between procedural and declarative memory, and (4) the distinction between implicit and explicit memory. Each of these interpretations, however, has its problems.

H. M. is often cited as evidence supporting the hypothesis that the hippocampus is critically involved in mediating memory (Milner, Corkin, & Teuber, 1968). His case also fits in nicely with the idea that the hippocampus is involved in the conjunction of features in memory, a process that is necessary to form new declarative memories. The problem with this interpretation is that the surgeon not only lesioned the hippocampus proper but also caused damage to the amygdala, the larger hippocampal formation, the surrounding cortex, the subiculum and surrounding tissue, the fornix-fimbria, and probably the thalamus (Horel, 1994; Weiskrantz, 1985; see Figure 8.5). Thus, attributing the memory deficit in H. M. solely to the hippocampus is highly questionable.

Because H. M. has a memory span well within the normal range (Wickelgren, 1968), his case has also been used as evidence for the distinction between short- and long-term memory. The problems with this argument are similar to those presented in Chapter 3 as problems with the modal model's account of memory in normal subjects. In addition, there is a further logical problem. Having normal memory for the short term and impaired memory for the long term does not necessarily imply that a normal short-term memory exists separately from an impaired long-term memory. As Crowder (1989b) put it, "evidence for (a distinct subsystem of) short-term storage is not at all the same as evidence that people . . . store things over the short term" (p. 280).

A more recent claim has been that case studies like that of H. M. support a distinction between procedural and declarative memory (Cohen & Eichenbaum, 1993; Squire, 1987). A rule of thumb is that if you can say you know *how* to do something, then it is a good candidate for a form of *procedural memory,* but if you say you know *that* something is so, it is a good candidate for *declarative memory.* H. M., as well as many other amnesics, show evidence of procedural or implicit learning. For example, Cohen, Eichenbaum, Deacedo, and Corkin (1985) found that amnesics' performance on the Tower of Hanoi problem (see Figure 8.6) is equivalent to that of matched control subjects. On the first day, the control subjects required an average of 48.6 moves, compared to 46.7 for the amnesics. By the fourth day of training (with four trials per day), both groups exhibited learning: The control subjects required only 34.1 moves, compared to 33.5 for the amnesics. Optimal performance is 31 moves. Note that the amnesics did not remember the previous trials and did not remember the rules. On each trial, the goal and rules had to be explained again.

Results from the Tower of Hanoi study, as well as many others, support the claim that procedural memory is unimpaired and declarative memory is impaired. However, this distinction is too simplistic and overlooks many problems (McCarthy & Warrington, 1990). For example, it depends on the particular definition of what constitutes procedural and what constitutes declarative memory, and many researchers disagree on which tasks tap which purported system. In addition, there are several documented cases of amnesics like H. M. who can learn new declarative information (see Glisky & Schacter, 1987; Schacter, 1985) and who are impaired on procedural tasks (see Warrington & Weiskrantz, 1974; Winocur & Weiskrantz, 1976).

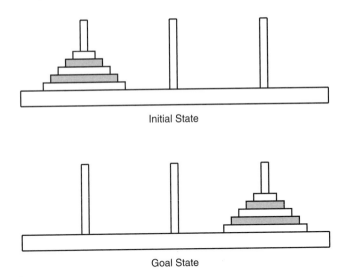

Figure 8.6   The Tower of Hanoi problem. The goal is to move five disks from the leftmost peg (top panel) to the rightmost peg (bottom panel). Only one disk may be moved at a time, and a larger disk cannot be placed on top of a smaller disk. The optimal solution requires 31 moves.

The most recent application of cases like that of H. M. has been to support the difference between implicit and explicit memory (see Chapter 7). This will be discussed below after first considering some other theoretical accounts.

Several different general explanations of amnesia have been proposed. One possibility is that amnesics do not encode information as well as control subjects do. This explanation seems unlikely, however, because Korsakoff patients show similar patterns of enhancement when coding instructions are manipulated to induce deep as compared to shallow processing (see Cermak & Reale, 1978; Meudell, Mayes, & Neary, 1980). Similar conclusions come from a more recent study that varied both encoding and retrieval conditions (Dalla-Barba & Wong, 1995).

Another possibility is that amnesics simply forget faster than control subjects do. Huppert and Piercy (1978a) tested Korsakoff patients and control subjects after equating for initial level of learning; that is, photographs were presented at a much slower rate to the amnesic subjects so that their recognition score equaled that of the control subjects. The subjects were then tested after one day and one week, and there was no evidence of faster forgetting in amnesic patients compared to controls. Similar results have been reported by others (for example, Carlesimo, Sabbadini, & Fadda, 1995; Kopelman, 1985).

Two more enduring theories have focused on retrieval problems. Warrington and Weiskrantz (1968, 1970) suggested that one important factor was interference. They used a procedure in which a list of items (words or pictures) was displayed; then, after an interval, a fragment of each item or the first letter or two was presented as a cue. Performance on both free recall and recognition tests was substantially lower for the amnesic subjects. When a fragment served as a partial cue, however, performance improved dramatically

Table 8.1 Proportion correct on three different tests for both control and amnesic subjects

Test	Control Subjects	Amnesic Subjects
Recall	48%	14%
Recognition	94%	59% (Chance = 50%)
Fragmented Words	96%	94%

SOURCE: Warrington & Weiskrantz (1970).

(see Table 8.1). Warrington and Weiskrantz (1974) also showed equivalent performance for amnesic and control subjects on a cued-recall test.

The idea is that the cue or partial fragment can help reduce interference, and overcoming this deficit restores performance to normal or near normal levels. Why, then, does recognition show a large disadvantage? On a yes-no recognition test, there is no cue to the subject that the item being presented was a studied item, whereas on a cued-recall test, the cue is part of a studied item. Consistent with this interpretation, Weiskrantz (1982) found that although amnesics are good at learning new associations where links already exist (such as *soldier–army*), they become progressively worse as the relatedness of the items decreases. To the extent that indirect tests of implicit memory usually provide as cues only studied items (see Chapter 7), this would explain why amnesics show relatively unimpaired performance on these tasks.

The second enduring theory has to do with the role of context. One of the few studies to show a qualitative rather than just a quantitative difference between amnesics and control subjects was reported by Huppert and Piercy (1978b). On Day 1, Korsakoff patients and alcoholic control subjects were shown 80 color photographs of various complex scenes. Half of these photographs were shown once, and half were shown three times. On Day 2, the subjects saw a different list of 80 photographs; again, half of the photographs were shown once, and half were shown three times. The test began 10 minutes after the end of presentation of the photographs on Day 2. The subjects were told that they would see a long series of test photographs. They were also told that they had seen all of the test photographs before, either today (Day 2) or yesterday (Day 1), and that half of the photographs had been shown once, and half had been shown three times. The subject's task was to indicate when the photograph was shown, and how many times it had been shown; the results are shown in Figure 8.7.

The control subjects were quite accurate, replicating other experiments on judgments of frequency (see Hasher & Chromiak, 1977). In the right half of Figure 8.7, the D2F1 (Day 2, Frequency 1) and D2F3 (Day 2, Frequency 3) items were accurately judged as being seen today (Day 2), and the D1F3 and D2F3 were accurately judged as being shown three times. Looking at the left half of the figure, it is evident that the Korsakoff patients showed a different pattern. They were as likely to respond with "today" for D1F3 and D2F1 pictures; furthermore, they were more likely to respond "three times" for D2F1 than D1F1. These results are consistent with the idea that the amnesic subjects were relying on familiarity, and an item could be familiar either because it occurred on the same day as the test or because it occurred three times on the previous day. Similar results have been reported by Meudell, Mayes, Ostergaard, and Pickering (1985).

Figure 8.7   Percentage of "today" and "three times" judgments for Korsakoff patients and alcoholic control subjects. D1 and D2 refer to Day 1 and Day 2, and F1 and F3 refer to frequency of presentation (once or three times).   SOURCE: From "The Role of Trace Strength in Recency and Frequency Judgments by Amnesic and Control Subjects," by F. A. Huppert and M. Piercy, 1978, *Quarterly Journal of Experimental Psychology, 30,* 347–354. Reprinted with permission of the author.

This interpretation, that the Korsakoff patients were relying on the familiarity of the memory trace to make their judgments, whereas the control subjects were relying on both familiarity and conscious recollection, gains further support from the results of a study reported by Parkin, Montaldi, Leng, and Hunkin (1990). They found that Korsakoff patients could quite accurately distinguish old from new items after a brief delay as long as the distractor (new) items had not been seen previously. When the distractors had been seen previously (in a different session), the Korsakoff patients could no longer do the task. Because they had been seen previously, the distractor items appeared to be as familiar as the test items. The amnesic syndrome, then, apparently leaves an automatic familiarity process intact but interferes with the recollective process. This interpretation also dovetails nicely with the results of Jacoby's (1991) process dissociation framework, discussed in Chapter 5.

Verfaellie and Treadwell (1993) used Jacoby's process dissociation technique to directly test the possibility that the automatic process of familiarity is intact in individuals suffering from the amnesic syndrome. They compared amnesics (mainly Korsakoff patients) and alcoholic control subjects using the inclusion and exclusion conditions described in Chapter 5. In the first phase of the experiment, subjects solved anagrams or read words presented on a computer. In the second phase, a list of words was presented auditorily. During the subsequent recognition phase, a series of words was presented on the computer monitor. In the inclusion condition, subjects were asked to call an item

Table 8.2   Proportion of "old" responses in the inclusion and exclusion conditions and estimates of recollection and fluency for the amnesics and control groups

	Type of word	Proportion of "Old" Responses		Estimates from Process Dissociation Model	
		Inclusion	Exclusion	Recollection	Fluency
Amnesics					
	Anagram	0.45	0.44	0.00	0.46
	Read	0.49	0.38	0.11	0.41
	Heard	0.40	0.41		
	New	0.32	0.27		
Controls					
	Anagram	0.67	0.34	0.33	0.50
	Read	0.45	0.33	0.11	0.36
	Heard	0.67	0.56		
	New	0.17	0.19		

SOURCE: Verfaellie & Treadwell (1993).

"old" if it had been presented in either initial phase. In the exclusion condition, subjects were instructed to call an item "old" only if it had been presented in the auditory phase. The data are shown in Table 8.2.

The control subjects demonstrated the usual effect of depth of processing in that the words that were solved as anagrams were significantly better recognized than those that were read. The amnesics, in contrast were equally likely to call anagrams and read words "old." However, recognition performance of the amnesics was significantly above chance for all three of the presentation conditions. When the contributions of conscious recollection and fluency were calculated, using Jacoby's equations, the amnesics showed virtually no recollection but did not differ from the controls in the estimation of the automatic familiarity or fluency component of the task. Thus, despite a failure to explicitly remember information about when the words were presented, amnesics nonetheless seem to have an intact automatic process of familiarity.

However, as the data in Table 8.2 show, the amnesic subjects had very high false alarm rates. They responded "old" to new items more often than the control subjects (values of 0.32 and 0.27 in the inclusion and exclusion conditions for the amnesics, compared to values of 0.17 and 0.19 for the control subjects). The particular process dissociation method used in this study did not take into account this response bias of amnesic subjects. As will be shown in Chapter 9, such response bias can be analyzed using signal detection theory. Yonelinas, Kroll, Dobbins, Lazzara, and Knight (1998), using a form of signal detection analysis, found that control subjects used both familiarity and recollection and amnesics were limited to using familiarity, but they also found that the amnesics were impaired in familiarity relative to the control subjects. The process dissociation technique used by Verfaelle and Treadwell (1993) was not able to detect this decrement in familiarity in the amnesic subjects, but the signal detection technique of Yonelinas et al. (1998) was able to demonstrate that familiarity is also significantly disrupted in patients suffering from the amnesic syndrome. So, although amnesics can use familiarity on many tasks, this use is impaired relative to controls.

Amnesia: Summary

People with amnesic syndrome will generally show normal performance whenever the task relies primarily on familiarity or fluency; these tasks are generally indirect tests of memory. However, if the test score takes into account the high false alarm rate, an impairment may be observed. Amnesics will generally show impaired performance whenever the task relies primarily on contextual discrimination; these tasks are generally direct tests of memory. The key to successful performance is determining whether a particular item occurred during a particular episode. One reason why performance on immediate memory tests, such as memory span, is unimpaired may be that contextual discrimination is not necessary. Because so little time has elapsed from the end of list presentation to the beginning of the retrieval attempt, the episodic context is unlikely to have changed and the subject is likely to be still in the original encoding state. However, if the same test is delayed, then the test is removed in context from the learning episode and performance will be impaired. From this perspective, it is not necessary to postulate multiple memory systems to explain differences between amnesic and control performance or to explain differences between direct and indirect tests. One simply has to attend to all characteristics of the learning and test situation. This position still cannot explain all of the data, but it appears more capable than others (Cermak, Verfaellie, & Chase, 1995).

Alzheimer's Disease

Named after Alöis Alzheimer, the German physician who reported the first case, in 1907, *Alzheimer's disease* is still poorly understood (see Whitehouse, Maurer, & Ballenger, 2000, for an historical review). One problem is that there are no certain symptoms; Alzheimer's disease can be conclusively diagnosed only by postmortem examination of the brain. However, a tentative diagnosis of Alzheimer-type dementia is made when there is significant cognitive decline with no other obvious cause, such as head trauma, alcoholism, or stroke. Because the damage to the brain is at the microscopic level and principally affects the synapses (see below), it is difficult to detect using structural imaging techniques such as MRI and CT scans. In some cases, however, the death of substantial groups of neurons can be seen using functional imaging techniques such as PET or fMRI. Alzheimer's disease is characterized by a slow, increasing decline in multiple areas, including memory, cognition, and the ability to perform daily tasks. Behavior problems, ranging from repeated questioning to physical violence, are quite common. The etiology is not known.

The cause of the cognitive declines in people with Alzheimer's disease is the formation of abnormal structures in the brain called amyloid plaques and neurofibrillary tangles. As these structures accumulate, nerve cell connections are interfered with, and some nerve cells are destroyed. Amyloids are protein fragments that are normally produced by the brain. For unknown reasons, the protein sometimes divides improperly, creating a substance called beta amyloid that is toxic to neurons. Plaques that consist of degenerating neurons and clumps of the amyloid proteins begin to form. The body cannot break these clumps down and dispose of them, so they build up in the brain, causing further damage.

Neurofibrillary tangles are found in the neurons themselves. They are made up of twisted fibers, consisting primarily of a protein that forms part of a structure in the neuron called a *microtubule*. The microtubules are important because, like the joists and columns of a building, they give the nerve cells structural support and shape. They also help trans-

How can I tell the difference between Alzheimer's disease and normal aging?

Although there is no single, comprehensive diagnostic test for Alzheimer's, there are some things to look for. The Alzheimer's Association and the American Academy of Neurology have published guidelines to assist in early recognition of Alzheimer's disease (Petersen et al., 2001), including a list of 10 warning signs that can help to identify the disease.

1. Memory loss that affects job skills
2. Difficulty performing familiar tasks
3. Problems with language
4. Disorientation to time and place (getting lost)
5. Poor or decreased judgment
6. Problems with abstract thinking
7. Misplacing things
8. Changes in mood or behavior
9. Changes in personality
10. Loss of initiative

People who show several of these symptoms should see their physician for a complete examination.

port nutrients from one part of the nerve cell to another. In Alzheimer's disease, abnormal proteins are formed and the microtubules twist and collapse, causing the death of the nerve cell. The fibrous tangles remain in the brain long after the dead neuron has been cleared away (for a review, see St. George-Hyslop, 2000). As the disease progresses, damage extends throughout the brain, leading to more and more problems. The average length of time from diagnosis to death is 4 to 8 years, although it can take 20 years or more for the disease to run its course.

Alzheimer's is a devastating and progressive disease that slowly, inexorably, relentlessly, erodes away the capability for conscious thought and self-awareness. In an article for *The New Yorker*, Jonathan Franzen describes his father's decline due to Alzheimer's disease as

> a prism that refracts death into a spectrum of its otherwise tightly conjoined parts—death of autonomy, death of memory, death of self-consciousness, death of personality, death of body . . . its particular sadness and horror stem from the sufferer's loss of his or her "self" long before the body dies. (Franzen, 2001, p. 89)

After his father was forced into a nursing home, Franzen and his mother found evidence of his father's secret efforts to stem the loss of memory: papers on which he had written his children's birthdays and addresses, little reminders of things that he shouldn't have forgotten. Franzen's father would pull himself together, struggling to remain himself, only to give up, "letting go, an embrace of madness in the face of unbearable emotion" (p. 89). Although it took years for his father to die, Franzen remarked that "by the time my father's heart stopped, I'd been mourning him for years" (p. 89).

It is estimated that today about 5 million Americans have Alzheimer's disease; this number could rise to as many as 15 million by the year 2050. Although individuals vary, Franzen's father's experience is fairly typical. The severity of deficit increases as the disease progresses, beginning with minor memory failures, misplacement of objects, slight disorientation, and difficulty finding words. As the disease advances, the symptoms become more pervasive; the sufferers get lost in their own homes, fail to recognize familiar people, and often lose track of the time, date, and year. Emotionally, this disease also has substantial effects on the afflicted individual as well as the caretaker. Patients often have lucid periods in which they are conscious of their mental decline. This awareness can lead to depression and bursts of anger as they see themselves gradually losing their grip on reality.

Studying memory deficits in individuals affected by Alzheimer's disease is complicated by the fact that cognitive functions other than memory are affected by the disease. In addition, as the disease progresses, more and more areas of the brain are affected. Thus, two researchers may report seemingly contradictory results as a result of studying individuals at different stages of the disease. Nonetheless, there are certain areas of consensus on which aspects of memory are affected and which are spared.

The memory deficits shown in Alzheimer's disease show some similarities to the classic amnesic syndrome described above, in that there is a deficit in delayed free recall and recognition and that primary memory, as reflected by the recency effect in free recall, may be spared. However, the deficits are more pervasive in Alzheimer's disease, often leading to difficulties in tasks such as conceptual priming and procedural learning that are relatively intact in the amnesic syndrome. The acute deficit in memory has been attributed to deficiencies in encoding and/or retrieval of information, but there is also evidence of increased susceptibility to both proactive and retroactive interference. In the following sections, we outline some of the major areas of research on memory in Alzheimer's disease, including those measured through explicit and implicit memory tasks.

Memory Span

Unlike in the case of the amnesic syndrome, memory span is impaired in individuals with Alzheimer's disease. Hulme, Lee, and Brown (1993) reported a lower memory span as well as a slower rehearsal rate for patients with Alzheimer's disease as compared to normal controls, even though the rate of spontaneous speech appears to be normal. When we look at the pattern of recall in immediate memory, it is initially the same as for control subjects. In the early stages of the disease, even though patients show greatly decreased memory performance on a free recall task, the characteristic bow shape of the serial position curve (including the primacy and recency portions) is the same as it is for age- and education-matched controls (Brandt & Rich, 1995; Mohs, 1995). (See Figure 3.8 for an example of normal serial position curves.) However, as the disease progresses, the shape of the curve starts to change. Performance on early list items (in the primacy portion of the curve) gets worse. At first glance, the recency effect also appears to diminish. However, Carlesimo, Fadda, Sabbadini, and Caltagirone (1996) showed that patients with Alzheimer's disease can recall the last two list items in a list when they start recalling from one of these two serial positions. If they start only slightly earlier in the list, the last two items are not available for recall. The finding that patients with Alzheimer's disease can show normal recall of the last one or two items in a list if they start their recall there has been used to argue that primary memory is relatively unimpaired.

Working Memory

Alzheimer's patients often show relatively normal performance on some aspects of immediate memory (Morris, 1984a). For example, Morris (1984b) measured the size of the phonological similarity effect using both auditorily and visually presented letters. He found that although overall memory span is worse, the size of the phonological similarity effect appears to be of the same magnitude as in normal controls. In addition, the size of the articulatory suppression and syllable-based word length effects have also been shown to be equivalent in controls and Alzheimer's patients (Morris, 1984b, 1992).

Some researcher's have interpreted these results using Baddeley's (1986) working memory framework (see Chapter 4) and have attributed the deficit to the central executive. The idea is that if the magnitude of the effects of phonological similarity, articulatory suppression, and word length are comparable to those observed with control subjects, the deficits cannot be in the phonological loop.

Baddeley and colleagues (Baddeley, Logie, Bressi, Della Sala, & Spinnler, 1986; Baddeley, Bressi, Della Sala, Logie, & Spinnler, 1991) have argued that a deficit in the central executive's ability to allocate attention might lead to difficulties in coordinating information from a variety of sources in individuals with Alzheimer's disease. This problem could ultimately underlie many of their cognitive processing deficits. Morris (1996) has suggested that the impairment shown by Alzheimer's patients on the Brown-Peterson task (see Chapter 6) is due to a deficit in the ability to do two tasks at the same time.

To further test this hypothesis, Baddeley et al. (1986) adjusted the difficulty of a number of tasks so that performance of the Alzheimer's patients when doing one task by itself was at the same level as that of normal age-matched and young controls. They then asked the subjects to perform each task in combination with a variety of secondary tasks. The tasks were a tracking task, requiring the subject to maintain a light pen over a moving stimulus on a computer screen; an articulatory suppression task, in which subjects were asked to repeatedly utter the digits from 1 to 5; a detection task, in which subjects were asked to press a foot pedal when a tone sounded; and a memory for digits task, adjusted in length to match the individual's memory span. These tasks were selected in order to minimize the amount of specific interference between the tasks. The patients with Alzheimer's disease were affected by the secondary tasks to a much greater degree than were the age-matched controls, who did not differ from the young controls. Figure 8.8 shows performance on the memory span task when it was the only task being performed and when it was performed with a concurrent tracking task. Although both the young and old groups were affected by performing a secondary task, the patients with Alzheimer's disease were substantially more affected by having to divide their attention. In a later study, Baddeley, Della Sala, and Spinnler (1991) showed that this difficulty in a dual-task situation worsened considerably when the same individuals were tested 6 months later. However, performance on the single task by itself did not decline over that period. Baddeley et al. (1986) argued for a particular deficit in the allocation of attentional resources.

Other experiments (Baddeley, Bressi, et al., 1991; Baddeley, Baddeley, Bucks, & Wilcock, 2001) have found that when initial performance by Alzheimer's patients and control subjects is equated, merely making a single task more difficult has no greater impact on Alzheimer's disease patients than it does on age-matched controls. This is consistent with the hypothesis that the deficit is with the coordination of resources across tasks (Della Sala & Logie, 2001).

Within the working memory framework, then, researchers have suggested that Alzheimer's patients are impaired on many tasks because of damage to the central executive. Although popular, this view is not without problems. For example, some researchers have questioned whether the central executive even exists (Parkin, 1998). Furthermore,

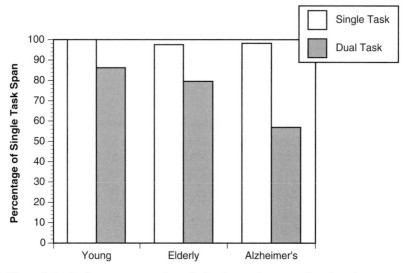

Figure 8.8   Performance on single or dual tasks as a function of single task span for healthy young adults, healthy elderly, and elderly diagnosed with Alzheimer's disease.   SOURCE: Based on data from Baddeley, Logie, Bressi, Della Sala, & Spinnler (1986).

the results showing impaired memory span but relatively normal effects of phonological similarity, articulatory suppression, and word length are predicted by the feature model (see Chapter 4).

Automatic and Controlled Processes

Patients with Alzheimer's disease show reductions in both automatic and controlled processing as measured by Jacoby's process dissociation method (see Chapter 5). However, as in the amnesic populations, automatic processing is relatively more intact than recollective processing. Smith and Knight (2002) compared performance of Alzheimer's patients, individuals with vascular dementia and alcoholic dementia (both demonstrating some amnesia and dementia), and normal controls. In Phase 1 of the study, subjects were asked to give one example for each of a group of categories (for example, name a color). In Phase 2, participants were asked to give either the same response to the category question (inclusion), or a different response from the one they had given in Phase 1 (exclusion condition). The experimenters made sure that the patients could produce at least two examples for any of the categories used. Only a 2-minute gap separated the two phases. Normal controls were at ceiling for this procedure. Performance for the Alzheimer's patients was much lower than for the vascular and alcoholic controls, with only a 50% hit rate in the inclusion condition and a 33% false alarm rate in the exclusion condition. The other two groups did not differ, with about 73% correct in the inclusion condition and 15% false alarms in the exclusion condition. Calculations of recollection were much higher for the two patient control groups than for the Alzheimer's group, but automatic processing showed equivalent scores for all three patient groups.

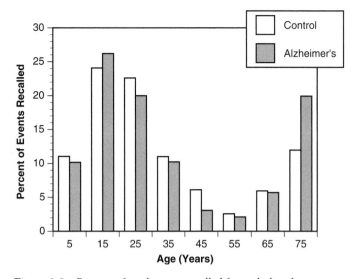

Figure 8.9 Percent of total events recalled for each decade as a function of normal or demented group. Although the absolute number of events recalled was much smaller in the demented group, the pattern of recall over time is almost identical in the two groups.   SOURCE: Based on data reported by Fromholt & Larsen (1991).

Autobiographical Memory

There are many anecdotal reports that the memory failures of Alzheimer's patients are mainly restricted to recent events and that the deficit is less noticeable when recalling incidents from further in the past. This has been used to argue for consolidation of memories over time (see Chapter 6 for a critical review of consolidation). Like many well-known facts, it is actually false. Fromholt and Larsen (1991, 1992) asked subjects to spend 15 minutes recalling events that had been important in their lives. Their subjects consisted of 30 Alzheimer's patients and 30 age- and education-matched volunteers between the ages of 70 and 90. Figure 8.9 shows the data from this experiment, plotted in terms of the percentage of total recalled memories as a function of the age of the individual at the time of the event. Although the control subjects recalled substantially more events than did the Alzheimer's patients (18 versus 8), the distribution of memories is remarkably similar for the two groups of subjects.

This study also replicates earlier studies of retrospective memory in that there is a *reminiscence bump* around ages 15–25 (Rubin, Wetzler, & Nebes, 1986). It is a fairly stable finding that people over the age of 40 recall more autobiographical memories from when they were between the ages of 15 and 25 than from earlier ages. From age 15 on, the shape of the curve looks like a typical serial position function with primacy and recency effects. There are many speculations as to why this "bump" occurs. Conway and Rubin (1993) argue that the curve is essentially a bow-shaped serial position curve with primacy occurring when the enduring sense of self has been formed. Childhood senses of self are not represented in the adult experience, and so it is more difficult to access events from that period. Thus, these data indicate that Alzheimer's patients show the same pattern of forgetting as normally aging individuals, even though their overall memory is deficient.

Semantic Memory

Alzheimer's patients are substantially worse than amnesic patients on tests of semantic or generic memory. They often have severe difficulties in naming even common objects and will often substitute and leave out words in their speech. They also do poorly in naming tests in which pictures are used, but perform better than when the task involves completely verbal materials (Chertkow, Bub, & Caplan, 1992). In addition, the organization of concepts in semantic memory can be different from normal controls. Chan et al. (1993) found that patients with Alzheimer's disease tended to represent animals in terms of concrete dimensions such as size instead of abstract dimensions such as domesticity or wildness.

Implicit Memory

Alzheimer's patients' memory impairment also differs from that of people with classic amnesic syndrome in that they show impaired performance on repetition priming tasks. As discussed above, priming and some other indirect memory tasks seem relatively unimpaired in individuals suffering from anterograde amnesia. In contrast, Alzheimer's patients are significantly impaired even on implicit memory tasks. For example, Shimamura, Salmon, Squire, and Butters (1987) performed a stem completion procedure using patients with Korsakoff's syndrome and Alzheimer's patients. Subjects were first given a list of target words, such as *motel* or *abstain*, and were asked to rate the words in terms of their likability. After a delay, the same subjects were given three-letter stems and asked to fill in the stem with the first word that came to mind. Half the stems were taken from words that had been on the studied list, and half were new. The Alzheimer's patients were significantly less likely than the amnesic controls to fill in a word from the studied list.

More recently, Fleishman and colleagues (1997) have argued that individuals with Alzheimer's disease show intact perceptual priming and show the deficit only when the task involves conceptual priming. The argument is that the areas of the brain associated with perceptual processing are still intact, but those areas of the brain that are involved in semantic processing are damaged. Thus, patients with Alzheimer's disease show normal perceptual repetition priming effects as measured by a lexical decision task but abnormal performance on a stem completion task. Beauregard, Chertkow, Gold, and Bergman (2001) manipulated the level of processing of study words to determine the effect of deep semantic encoding on stem completion in a group of Alzheimer's patients. They also measured their subjects' knowledge of each item (for example, for an animal, indicating the correct habitat, what it ate, or what it was used for). In the shallow encoding condition, they found no difference between the patients and the control group in the number of stems completed with studied words. However, in the deep processing condition, the priming effect for those words that showed "semantic degradation" was substantially smaller than the words whose concepts seemed to be intact (4.4% versus 13%). In addition, depth of processing had no effect on priming in the Alzheimer's group. The researchers concluded that the deficit in their population of patients was in conceptual, not perceptual, priming and that word stem completion is accomplished

What are the treatments for Alzheimer's disease, and are they effective?

Although there is no cure for Alzheimer's disease, certain medications and behavioral strategies can reduce the effects of the disease and improve the quality of life for those affected by it. These treatments are most effective in individuals with mild to moderate impairment. The authors of a recent large-scale review of the medical literature (Doody et al., 2001) have suggested a number of ways to manage the dementia, including medication, memory training, and behavior modification techniques.

In particular, the review showed that cholinesterase inhibitors can be of some benefit those with the disease, although the gain was small for most patients. Cholinesterase inhibitors work by inhibiting the action of acetylcholinesterase, an enzyme that breaks down the neurotransmitter acetylcholine. This neurotransmitter is predominant in areas of the brain responsible for higher-level cognitive functioning. When brain cells in this area are damaged, less acetylcholine is produced, thus affecting communication among the neurons in that part of the brain. The cholinesterase inhibitors are meant to reverse this deficit in acetylcholine by blocking the action of the enzyme responsible for breaking down the neurotransmitter. These inhibitors do not slow down the damage to the neurons, however, so they can only compensate temporarily for the loss of brain cells.

The researchers also found that large doses of vitamin E, an antioxidant, may slow the loss of brain cells and delay the worsening of the disease. The beneficial effects of other antioxidants, anti-inflammatories, and estrogen were unclear and require further study.

Environmental cues, such as clocks, calendars, and familiar objects, can help the patient with orientation. Signs pointing to the bathroom, night-lights, signs in the kitchen, and similar aids seem to help with orientation. Limiting access to one or more rooms (usually by closing a door) is a useful strategy, as is removing clutter, sharp objects, and unnecessary pieces of furniture. Other external memory aids, such as notebooks, diaries, calendars, are widely used in this area (Wilson, 1999).

Cognitive rehabilitation can include memory training and reality orientation. *Memory training* includes training in mnemonic techniques such as imagery, use of personal real-life material, self-generation of to-be-remembered items, and supplementary cues at retrieval (see Chapter 15). De Vreese, Neri, Fioravanti, Belloi, and Zanetti (2001) showed improvement in residual explicit memory functions using these techniques, particularly when paired with cholinesterase inhibitors. Another method of memory training involves the *expanding rehearsal*, or spaced retrieval, technique. In this technique, the patient repeatedly recalls information at gradually increasing time intervals (such as 5 s, 10 s, 20 s, 40 s, 75 s, 120 s, and so on). If the patient fails at one interval, the next interval is shortened to the previous level. Unlike the other memory training techniques, this one can be used by the patient alone and transferred to other situations. A third technique, called *errorless learning,* relies on the observation that learning from your mistakes only works if you remember the mistakes that you made. It is hypothesized that any errors produced during learning are strengthened through repetition, so errors during learning should be avoided.

Reality orientation operates through the presentation and repetition of orientation information that can lead to a greater sense of control in the demented patient. One particular program (Spector, Orrell, Davies, & Woods, 2001) was designed with four phases: the senses, remembering the past, people and objects, and everyday practical issues. Sessions of 45 minutes concentrated on each of these phases. In the phase focusing on the senses, patients were given multisensory stimulation. Remembering the past included remembering and talking about growing up, work and home, and recent years. People and objects included naming and using familiar objects and naming people in pictures. The final phase, everyday practical issues, included retraining on general information such as using money and finding one's way around. The program demonstrated improved cognition and reduced anxiety and depression in the participants, but little or no effect on day-to-day functional activities. Moreover, the cognitive gains were extremely modest. It is not clear that the particular program is important; very few studies have included an attention-only control, with control subjects receiving only the same amount of attention as the experimental subjects. In any case, the gains do not last much beyond the therapy, and continuous ongoing programs may be necessary.

None of these techniques or therapies can do more than slow the progression of the cognitive decline in Alzheimer's disease, and most are helpful only in the initial stages of the disease. Unfortunately, despite a great deal of research effort, the prognosis of individuals with Alzheimer's disease is extremely bleak.

using both perceptual and conceptual processing. This would also explain intact word stem completion in the amnesic syndrome, because their semantic systems appear to be intact.

Alzheimer's Disease: Summary

People with Alzheimer's disease not only show substantially more memory deficits than those with the amnesic syndrome, they also suffer from a reduced ability to switch between tasks efficiently. Alzheimer's patients are particularly impaired when two or more tasks are required.

The Frontal Lobe

Studies using a variety of brain-scanning techniques (PET, fMRI) almost universally show activation of specific regions in the frontal cortex during encoding and retrieval. Table 8.4 summarizes a number of these studies (Buckner & Wheeler, 2001). The posterior regions of the frontal cortex, particularly in the left hemisphere, seem to be involved in elaborating or rehearsing verbal information. This area is physically near Broca's area, which has been pinpointed as being fundamental in speech or language planning and production. The same area in the right hemisphere is active in retrieving nonverbal information. In addition, the posterior regions of the frontal lobe are more strongly activated as the task gets harder or requires more effort. In one study, for example, subjects studied words under conditions of either deep or shallow processing to induce easy or difficult retrieval conditions. When attempting to recall the words that were processed shallowly, subjects showed much more activation of the posterior regions of the frontal cortex than when recalling the words that were encoded in a deep manner (Buckner, Koutstaal, Schacter, Wagner, & Rosen, 1998). The assumption is that the shallowly encoded words required more effort to retrieve. Moreover, those posterior areas were activated even when retrieval was unsuccessful.

The anterior regions of the frontal lobe seems to serve a slightly different function. This region is more selective for tasks that tap actual remembering as compared with tasks

Table 8.4   Frontal regions that are active during retrieval

Frontal Region Property	Posterior (BA 44/6)	Anterior (BA 10)
Selective to remembering	No	Somewhat
Material dependent	Yes	No
Tracks amount of effort	Yes	No
Tracks retrieval success	No	Sometimes
Temporal profile	Early	Late
Sensitive to task	Somewhat	Very

NOTE: BA 44/6 and BA 10 refer to Brodmann Areas, a reference system for specifying particular brain areas. The pattern relating front lobe property to particular frontal lobe region is very complex.

SOURCE: Buckner & Wheeler (2001).

used during verbal elaboration or with processing nonverbal information, and activation is not related to the amount of effort involved in the retrieval task. Unlike the posterior cortex, this area does not show increased activity as the task becomes more difficult. This region is not specifically activated for recall of verbal material. It has been associated with the executive functioning of working memory, or at least complex problem solving and planning (Koechlin, Basso, Pietrini, Panzer, & Grafman, 1999).

The HERA Model

Recently, Endel Tulving and colleagues looked at data like those summarized in Table 8.4 and hypothesized that encoding and retrieval from episodic memory may have different and distinct underlying neural substrates (Tulving, Kapur, Craik, Moscovitch, & Houle, 1994). According to the *hemispheric encoding/retrieval asymmetry (HERA)* model, the two prefrontal cortices play different roles in the encoding and retrieval of episodic memories. According to this view, the left prefrontal cortex is involved in the encoding of information about novel happenings into episodic memory, whereas the right prefrontal cortex is involved in the retrieval of that same information from episodic memory, in free and cued recall as well as recognition (Nyberg, Cabeza, & Tulving, 1996; Cabeza et al., 1997). This is not to say that left frontal regions are never activated during retrieval or that right frontal regions are never activated during encoding, but that there is a tendency toward hemispheric asymmetry.

One might wonder why the same brain areas are not active in both encoding and retrieval phases. Craik, Govoni, Naveh-Benjamin, and Anderson (1996) showed that the control processes involved in reactivating the representation (the so-called retrieval mode or set) are different from those involved in laying down the traces. They argued that the automatic elements of encoding and retrieval are substantially the same, but the controlled or effortful elements of those processes are different. Thus, the imaging differences may be in the higher-order mind-set, not in the memory traces themselves. PET data support this idea that the activation of the right frontal regions is associated with an active retrieval strategy (Kapur et al., 1995). In addition, Nyberg et al. (1995) reported that words encoded in a shallow manner (and thus requiring more active attempts at recall) were associated with more right hemisphere activation than words encoded in a deep manner, which were associated with left hemisphere activation. Thus, both prefrontal cortices were involved in retrieval, depending on the difficulty of the retrieval effort. Further criticisms of the HERA model include suggestions that the verbal nature of the stimuli are at the core of the asymmetry and that when nonverbal stimuli such as pictures are learned, there is no asymmetry (Propper & Christman, 1999).

The Frontal Lobe: Summary

This area of research has benefited greatly from both cognitive neuroscience and cognitive psychological viewpoints. Theoretical interpretations from the neuroimaging literature have been used to guide experiments measuring behavioral responses, and vice versa. Thus, although the conclusions that can be drawn from this area are not yet firm, the progress made so far underscores the value of using both approaches in order to determine how memory works.

Where Is Memory? Local Versus Distributed Storage

There are two basic historical conceptions of where memory might be stored. A *localized view* comes from early research that showed specialized memory structures in the brain, such as Broca's area for speech production (Broca, 1861). The *distributed view* arose from the idea that mental activity was due to integrated activity of many different components of the brain. In particular, Lashley (1929) found that although the extent of the lesions in rats was positively correlated with memory impairment, there was no relationship between the location of the lesions and memory impairment. Lashley (1950) concluded that memories were not stored "anywhere" but rather were stored everywhere.

The resolution between these two views lies in the size of the area under consideration. As Squire's (1987) review shows, memory is widely distributed, but different loci store different aspects of the whole.

> Memory is distributed in that no single memory center exists, and many parts of the nervous system participate in the representation of a single event. Memory is localized in that the representation of a single event involves a limited number of brain systems and pathways, and each part of the brain contributes differently to the representation. . . . The most likely site of storage is the set of particular cortical processing systems that are engaged during the perception, processing, and analysis of the material being learned. (p. 123)

For memories such as your last Christmas Day meal, the components of the memory are distributed over a variety of areas, but within a particular area, certain cell assemblies contribute different parts of the whole picture. To further complicate matters, some of the information that you recall is clearly not from the original event but from other sources. Did you have mashed potatoes? Probably—but perhaps you are guessing about this because many people have mashed potatoes. Thus, you do not have a single place where memories are stored.

Figure 8.10 shows a summary of where activation has been found in PET/fMRI studies of episodic memory (Cabeza, 2000). What is immediately clear is that, although there is a great deal of activation in the frontal lobes, there is no single area we can point to as being the locus of memory. In fact, memory seems to be distributed over a great deal of the brain.

If much of memory is localized in the assemblies that processed the original event, and if memory is a persistent change in the way neurons communicate, an intriguing question is, Why doesn't perception also change? The answer to this question has two parts. First, perception does in fact change; but, second, it changes slowly because only a portion of cortical cells within a particular assembly are plastic (see, for example, Fuster & Jervey, 1981). This slow change is not noticed and decreases as the organism ages. For example, monkeys' capabilities to perceive touch and other sensations using their hands depend on the amount of somatosensory cortex assigned to that body part. Studies with monkeys have shown that the amount of somatosensory cortex devoted to the hand and fingers can expand and contract, depending on the experimental manipulation (Kaas, 1995). Similar changes in perception with experience and (presumably) changed neuronal communication can also be seen in humans' "higher-level" cognitive processes: Upside-down and even mirrored text can be interpreted more quickly after practice (Kolers, 1979), and chess experts perceive chess layouts differently than do novices (Chase & Simon, 1973). Indeed, the cortex seems remarkably plastic (Fuster, 1995).

Figure 8.10 Activation peaks in PET and fMRI studies of episodic memory. The top left and middle drawings represent the lateral surface of the left and right hemispheres, respectively. The bottom left and middle drawings represent the medial surface of those two hemispheres. The right two drawings represent ventral and medial temporal regions. SOURCE: Copyright 2000 from "Functional Neuroimaging of Episodic Memory Retrieval," by R. Cabeza. In E. Tulving (Ed.), *Memory, Consciousness, and the Brain: The Talinn Conference.* Reproduced by permission of Taylor & Francis, Inc., http://www.routledge-ny.com.

One of the most widespread views of the cause of amnesia is that it involves damage to the hippocampus or hippocampal formation (Squire, 1987). If this view is accurate, it supports the idea that the hippocampus and surrounding structures are critical for successful memory. Indeed, one of the most cited lines of evidence supporting the role of the hippocampus comes from studies of H. M. However, more and more researchers are suggesting that the role of the hippocampus has been overstated. There are many reasons for this change, including the fact that H. M. suffered damage not only to the hippocampus but also to a large portion of surrounding cortex (Horel, 1994; Weiskrantz, 1985), and also the finding that many lesions outside the hippocampus produce symptoms similar to the classic human amnesia syndrome (Baddeley & Wilson, 1988a; Corkin et al., 1985; De Renzi, 1982).

The imaging data show almost universal activation of the frontal lobes during intentional memory encoding and retrieval. However, only some imaging studies report activity in the hippocampus or the medial temporal lobe during these tasks. These findings seem to call into question the importance of those areas of the brain in the formation of new episodic memories. To add to the confusion, patients with frontal lobe damage often perform quite well on a variety of memory tasks such as simple recognition, whereas patients with medial temporal lobe lesions are grossly impaired on such tasks.

Buckner, Kelley, and Petersen (1999), in a recent review, have argued that when damage is limited to one hemisphere in either the hippocampus or the frontal lobes, other regions may be able to compensate for that loss. They also point out most of the studies using brain-damaged patients exclude those with verbal deficits. Buckner et al. speculate that the areas responsible for speech production in the frontal lobe may also be involved in rehearsal of verbal materials. Thus, it is possible that frontal lobe activity provides information to the temporal lobe structures, which then bind together information that has already been processed in the frontal lobe and other cortical structures. As discussed previously, the frontal lobe seems to be especially important in active retrieval processes, whereas the hippocampus may be more specialized for automatic registration and combination of features in the environment (O'Reilly & Rudy, 2001).

On evolutionary grounds, it would not be adaptive for memory functioning to rely heavily on just one structure, such as the hippocampus. Reliance on a central memory organ would be too dangerous, because damage to this one organ would eliminate all memories. Reliance on a central memory organ would also be problematic on anatomical grounds, because it would require all processing to be routed through that organ. If the hippocampus were the most important center for memory, it follows that all of the information processed must go from the perceptual processing center to the hippocampus and back again. This leads researchers who emphasize the role of the hippocampus in memory to posit what Horel (1994) calls "anatomical extension cords." For example, if damage to one area, such as the frontal lobes, produces amnesia, researchers who support the central role of the hippocampus have to argue that there must also be some damage to a connection to the hippocampus. Typically, however, only the damage to the one area (in this example, the frontal lobes) is clearly seen, and there is little evidence for damage to the hippocampus.

Although the hippocampus may be involved in some types of memory, it is not necessarily the case that the hippocampus is centrally important to all memory. Rather, it is more likely that memory is not the function of any single structure but is a part of local operations carried out in all cortical areas where the information to be remembered is processed and perceived. This view is echoed by many others (Crowder, 1993a; Roediger & Srinivas, 1993; Toth & Hunt, 1999) and makes a strong prediction: A local lesion will cause not only a loss of local function, but also a loss of memory for that function. The "anatomical extension cord" from the area of lesion to the hippocampus may not be needed.

So where is memory in the brain? As Horel (1994) observed, "Terms like 'memory' and 'perception' have truly global referents, and were invented without reference to the brain, and the brain, though exquisitely divisible, is not necessarily going to be divided according to terms that are used to divide components of intact human behavior" (p. 277).

Chapter Summary

Although it seems obvious that memories must reside in the brain, we still know relatively little about the biological underpinnings of memory. One reason for this is the complexity of the brain itself: It contains billions of interacting neurons. The brain is divided into four lobes: frontal, parietal, temporal, and occipital. The frontal lobes and the hippocampus (a structure within the temporal lobes are thought to be of critical importance in memory functioning. Techniques for studying the biology of memory include invasive methods such as lesioning and noninvasive methods such as the CT scan, PET scan, fMRI, and ERP. These noninvasive techniques give us a picture of the brain in terms of its structure or its activity. A final technique used to ascribe function to brain areas is a double dissociation, when an independent variable differentially affects performance on two different tests.

Cases in which memory is disrupted, such as amnesia, can give us some valuable insights into the structure of memory. There are two types of amnesia: Retrograde amnesia refers to the case in which a person is unable to remember details that were learned prior to the event that caused the amnesia. Anterograde amnesia refers to the situation where a person seems to be unable to learn new information following some brain trauma. Typically, persons with anterograde amnesia will show impaired performance on explicit memory tasks but be close to normal on implicit memory tasks. Individuals with Alzheimer's disease often show both anterograde and retrograde amnesia as well as exhibiting various other cognitive and behavioral symptoms. Although there has been much progress made treating the disorder, the prognosis is still rather bleak.

The fundamental question of where memory is located remains unanswered. However, it seems likely that a combination of local and distributed storage will provide the ultimate solution.

CHAPTER NINE

Recognition

A similar result comes about when a definite setting is only nascently aroused. We then feel that we have seen the object already, but when or where we cannot say, though we may seem to ourselves to be on the brink of saying it. . . . It tingles, it trembles on the verge, but does not come. Just such a tingling and trembling of unrecovered associates is the penumbra of recognition that may surround any experience and make it seem familiar, though we know not why.

—William James (1890)

People often say that although they cannot quite think of the answer, they would know it if they saw it. In other words, people believe that a recognition test is "easier" than a re-call test—although, as will be seen below, this statement is often wrong. The essential difference between recall and recognition tests was described by Hollingworth (1913): In a recall test, the experimenter provides the context and the subject has to retrieve the tar-get; in a recognition test, the experimenter provides the target and the subject has to re-trieve the context.

One classic experiment illustrates why many people think recognition is "easy." Shepard (1967) presented subjects with lengthy series of stimuli, and then at test pre-sented two stimuli. One stimulus was from the list that the subjects had just studied, and one was a similar item that had not been seen. Some subjects saw 540 words, some saw 612 sentences, some saw 1224 sentences, and some saw 612 photographs. Subjects cor-rectly recognized 88% of the words, 89% of the 612 sentences, 88% of the 1224 sen-tences, and almost 100% of the pictures. Some subjects who had seen the pictures were tested one week later, and even after that length of time, they still correctly recognized 87% of the pictures. However, if the correct cues are provided for recall tests, performance can be just as impressive. For example, Mäntylä (1986) presented subjects with 504 words, and each subject generated three properties of the word. At test, the experimenter presented the properties, and the subject had to respond with the original word. When tested immediately, subjects recalled approximately 91% of the words.

Shepard's test is known as a two alternative forced choice, or 2AFC test. In many college courses, your knowledge is assessed using a 4AFC test, in which four alternatives are provided. The advantage of this technique is that the experimenter can manipulate the type and number of distractor words. This method is very useful because it can give detailed information about the type of errors people make. For example, when adults make an error, they typically select an item that is related to the correct item by meaning (Underwood & Freund, 1968), whereas third-graders typically select an item that sounds like or is acoustically related to an old item (Bach & Underwood, 1970).

A second type of recognition test is often referred to as a *yes-no recognition test*. Subjects see a series of items, and then at test are presented with a single item, which they indicate is either from the studied list or is not from the studied list. Items that were originally presented are known as old items, and items that were not shown in the study list are known as new items. The main difference between the two types of tests is what is presented at test. With the yes-no method, only one item at a time is presented at test, and subjects have to indicate whether this item is old or new (see Table 9.1). In the forced choice procedure, two (or more) items are presented, and the subject has to indicate which one item was an old item. The new items in either test are referred to as distractors or lures.

Although the yes-no method might appear simple, it raises a very complicated issue. Subjects respond by indicating whether the item is old or new, and the test item may in fact be old or new. This means that subjects can make two types of correct responses and two types of incorrect responses.

Imagine a situation in which you are given a yes-no recognition test. The experimenter tells you that you will receive $1 for every *hit* (responding "old" when the item is old) and will be penalized only 1 cent for every *false alarm* (responding "old" when the item is new). You are likely to respond "old" on almost every trial simply to maximize the amount of money. Imagine the reverse situation, where you are penalized $1 for every

Table 9.1   Possible outcomes in a yes-no recognition test

		Subject's Response	
		Yes	*No*
Test Item	*Old*	Hit	Miss
	New	False alarm	Correct rejection

NOTE: The probability of a hit is 1 minus the probability of a miss, and the probability of a false alarm is 1 minus the probability of a correct rejection. Thus, the probability of a hit plus the probability of a miss equals 1.0. The probability of a false alarm plus the probability of a correct rejection equals 1.0. Usually, researchers report only hits and false alarms.

false alarm and rewarded with 1 cent for every hit. Now, you are likely to respond "new" on almost every trial to minimize your financial loss. Although extreme, these cases illustrate the large role that response bias can play in altering subjects' behavior, which is independent of their actual ability to tell whether an item is old or new (discrimination). Researchers have tried many different ways of correcting for guessing in the yes-no procedure, but the most common is to apply ideas from signal detection theory (Green & Swets, 1966).

Signal Detection Theory

Signal detection theory was initially developed to examine performance in perception experiments in which the subject's task was to detect the presence of a signal (a tone, for example). It is assumed that there is always some baseline neural activity, referred to as *noise*. Every so often, the experimenter plays a tone. This produces two possible situations: Either there is just noise, or there is *signal plus noise*. The task facing the subject is to distinguish between the two. The response given is based partly on the subject's true ability to discriminate the combination of signal plus noise from noise only, and partly on response bias.

A similar task confronts smoke detectors. There will always be some smoke particles in the air (perhaps from slightly burned toast or accumulated dust on a powerful lamp); the important question is whether this smoke is of sufficient concentration to indicate a fire of concern. The detector must be sensitive enough to detect smoke (detect that there are smoke particles), but it must also decide whether the smoke particles detected indicate an actual fire. Hopefully, the smoke detector will have a hit rate of 1.0, and as low a false alarm rate as possible.

Signal detection theory assumes that when you see a test item in a standard recognition test, it produces a certain amount of evidence that the item was in the study phase. Signal detection theory further assumes that this evidence is normally distributed. The normal distribution (often referred to as a bell curve) can be thought of as a frequency distribution. A frequency distribution is simply a way of plotting the number of times you observe a particular value. For example, say you flipped a coin 10 times and counted up how many heads you got and wrote this number down. Then, you flipped the coin another 10 times and counted up how many heads you got. Say you did this 1024 times. How many times did you get 5 heads out of 10? How many times did you get 9 heads out of 10? If you actually did this, you should find numbers similar to the ones in Figure 9.1, which are very close to those found in a normal distribution.

When applied to recognition, signal detection theory assumes that old and new items differ in how familiar they appear to the subject. The average new item will appear less familiar than the average old item because the old items have been processed more recently. If you were tested on all old items, and calculated the amount of evidence supporting the idea that each item was old, you could produce a graph similar to the one shown in Figure 9.1 with coins. If you also did this for all new items, you would end up with two distributions, represented in Figure 9.2.

Signal detection theory assumes that there are two normal distributions, one for old items and one for new items. On average, a new item will provide you with less evidence that it was an old item than will an old item, which is why the "old" distribution is to the

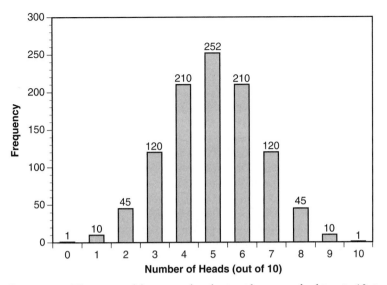

Figure 9.1   The expected frequency distribution if you tossed a fair coin 10 times, counted the number of heads, and then repeated this another 1023 times. You should find that you got only 2 heads out of 10 about 45 times, but 5 heads out of 10 about 252 times.

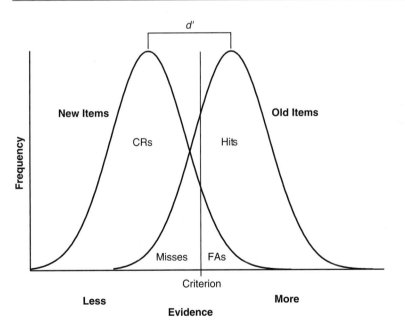

Figure 9.2   Signal detection theory as applied to yes-no recognition memory. The subject evaluates the evidence supporting the idea that the item is old or new. Old items are assumed to appear more familiar, on average, than new items, although there will often be some overlap. The distance between the means of these distributions is d', a measure of discriminability. The subject adopts a criterion, and items with more familiarity will be judged "old" (a yes response), whereas items with less familiarity will be judged "new" (a no response). Items that fall to the right of the criterion but are from the new item distribution are false alarms. Items that fall to the left of the criterion but are from the old item distribution are misses.

right of the "new" distribution. The difference between the means of these two distributions is called d' (pronounced "dee prime") and is the measure of bias-free discriminability. If old and new items appear equally familiar, then the difference between the means of the distributions will be 0. A d' of 0, then, represents the case where the distributions overlap and the subject cannot tell the difference. The greater the difference between the distributions, the larger d' is, and the more different the typical old and new items are.

How do you compute d'? It is simply the difference between the means of the two distributions divided by the standard deviation of the new distribution (noise). We cannot calculate these values directly; Figure 9.2 is a theoretical distribution. However, we can take advantage of some properties of the standard normal distribution. This is a distribution like the one shown in Figure 9.1, except that its mean is set to 0 and its standard deviation is set to 1. Any normal distribution can be converted into a standard normal distribution. In a standard normal distribution, a z score is simply the distance from the mean. So, a z score of 2 is two standard deviations above the mean; a z score of -1 is one standard deviation below the mean. Another property of the standard normal distribution is that the total area under the curve is 1.0. Half the area is above the mean, and half is below the mean. So, we find a z score such that the area above it equals the hit rate and call this z_{sn}. We also find a z score such that the area above it equals the false alarm rate and call this z_n. Then, $d' = z_n - z_{sn}$. Values of d' between 1 and 2 usually represent good yes-no recognition performance.

There are three main ways of obtaining the needed z scores. First, you can use tables that are included in most statistics textbooks. A more convenient way is to use a spreadsheet program. Most such programs have a built-in function that returns what is called "the inverse of the standard normal cumulative distribution." These functions take $1 - p(H)$ and $1 - p(FA)$ as arguments and will return z_{sn} and z_n. A third way is to use a special program. Many such programs are available on the Web, including one at http://rumpole.psych.purdue.edu/models/DPrimeCalculator.html.

If an experimenter uses a yes-no recognition test and reports only the proportion of items correctly recognized as old (hits), there is no way to assess the subjects' performance. Table 9.2 illustrates why this is the case. The first three rows all have hit rates of 90%, but d' ranges from 0 to 0.76 to 3.34. A d' of 0 means the subjects could not discriminate between old and new items, even though the hit rate is nearly perfect. Why is this the case? Because the false alarm rate is varying also. The last row shows how a hit rate of 50% can mean better discriminability than a hit rate of 90% when different false alarm

Table 9.2 Sample d' values for different hit and false alarm rates

$p(H)$	$p(FA)$	z_{sn}	z_n	d'	C
0.90	0.90	−1.282	−1.282	0.00	−1.282
0.90	0.70	−1.282	−0.524	0.76	−0.904
0.90	0.02	−1.282	2.054	3.34	0.384
0.50	0.02	0.000	2.054	2.05	1.029

NOTE: $p(H)$ is the probability of a hit, $p(FA)$ is the probability of a false alarm, z_{sn} is the z score such that the area above it equals the hit rate (sn denotes "signal + noise"), z_n is the z score such that the area above it equals the false alarm rate (n denotes "noise"), d' is $z_n - z_{sn}$, and C is $0.5(z_n + z_{sn})$.

Experiment   *Recognition and Signal Detection Theory*

Purpose: To demonstrate the use of signal detection theory in analyzing yes-no recognition tests

Subjects: Thirty subjects are recommended; 10 should be assigned to the neutral condition, 10 to the conservative condition, and 10 to the liberal condition. Subject 1 should be in the neutral condition, Subject 2 in the conservative condition, Subject 3 in the liberal condition, Subject 4 in the neutral condition, and so on.

Materials: Table C in the Appendix contains a list of 96 two-syllable words randomly drawn from the Toronto word pool. For each subject, construct a list of 48 words in random order. The answer sheet should have all 96 words (in random order) followed by OLD and NEW.

Procedure: For each group, read to the subject the first set of instructions followed by the list of 48 words, at a rate of approximately 1 word every 2 seconds. At the end of the list, read the instructions appropriate for each group. Give subjects the prepared answer sheet, and have them circle either OLD or NEW for each item.

Instructions for All Groups: "I will read you a long list of words. After I have finished reading the words, I will give you a memory test. I will tell you more about the test after I have read the words."

Instructions for the Neutral Group: "On the answer sheet, you will see a list of 96 words. Half of these words came from the list I just read, and half are new words. I would like you to circle OLD or NEW beside each word to indicate if it was on the list. Because half of the words are new, if you are unsure of your response, it is no better to guess OLD than to guess NEW because each response is equally likely to be correct. Any questions?"

Instructions for the Conservative Group: "On the answer sheet, you will see a list of 96 words; 25% of these words came from the list I just read, and 75% are new words. I would like you to circle OLD or NEW beside each word to indicate if it was on the list. Because 75% of the words are new, if you are unsure of your response, it is better to guess NEW than to guess OLD because you will be more likely to be correct. Any questions?"

Instructions for the Liberal Group: On the answer sheet, you will see a list of 96 words; 75% of these words came from the list I just read, and 25% are new words. I would like you to circle OLD or NEW beside each word to indicate if it was on the list. Because 75% of the words are old, if you are unsure of your response, it is better to guess OLD than to guess NEW because you will be more likely to be correct. Any questions?"

Scoring and Analysis: For each list, count the number of times an old pair was judged to be old (hits) and the number of times a new pair was judged to be old (false alarms). The text describes three ways to calculate d' and C.

Optional Enhancements: Include more subjects in each condition, and collect a measure of confidence. For each item, after the old/new judgment, have the subject write down a number from 1 to 6 to indicate confidence. A 1 means very low confidence; a 6 means very high confidence.

SOURCE: Based on an experiment by Knoedler (1996).

---

rates are taken into account. The measure of response bias when applying signal detection theory to recognition memory is C (see Snodgrass & Corwin, 1988, for why C is preferred to b). C is the mean of the z_n and z_{sn} values. A value greater than 0 indicates a conservative response bias, a tendency to respond "new" more often than "old." A value less than 0 indicates a liberal bias—a tendency to respond "old" more often than "new." A well-analyzed study of yes-no recognition memory will present both the hit and the false alarm rates, a measure of discriminability (d'), and a measure of response bias (C). For hit or false alarm rates of 1 or 0, there is a standard correction so that d' and C can still be calculated (see Snodgrass & Corwin, 1988).

Signal detection theory is not the only way of analyzing data from yes-no recognition tasks. It assumes that the variance of the two distributions is the same, and it also assumes that the distributions are normal. A' is a nonparametric analog of d' (Pollack & Norman, 1964) that has been shown to be highly correlated with d' (Snodgrass, Volvovitz, & Walfish, 1972). It ranges from 0 to 1, with 0.5 reflecting chance performance. Because of the way it is calculated, it allows analysis of data from subjects who have hit or false alarm rates of 0, and it does not require the assumption of homogenous variance. Snodgrass, Levy-Berger, and Haydon (1985) show how to calculate A'. The appropriate measure of bias for A' is B''_D. This measure ranges from -1 to 1, with 0 indicating no bias; a positive number indicates a conservative bias (see Donaldson, 1992).

A third method is generally referred to as the *two-high-threshold model* (see Feenan & Snodgrass, 1990). The name comes from the idea that there is a threshold for old items and a threshold for new items (hence "two thresholds"), and only items that exceed the threshold will be recognized (hence "high"). The discrimination measure is Pr, also known as the corrected recognition score. It is simply the difference between the hit and false alarm rates. The bias measure, Br, is the false alarm rate divided by 1 minus Pr. A value of Br greater than 0.5 indicates a liberal response bias; a value less than 0.5 indicates a conservative response bias.

Feenan and Snodgrass (1990) recommend reporting not only hit and false alarm rates and d' and C (or A' and B''_D, if more appropriate), but also Pr and Br. The reason is that that some effects are observable in only a subset of these measures. For example, in their Experiment 1, subjects saw line drawings and were then given a recognition test in either the same context or a different context. The hit rate was larger when the pictures were tested in the same context compared to when they were tested in a different context, but there was no difference in the false alarm rates. Similarly, there was a difference in the Pr measure of discrimination but not in d'. Both measures of bias, however, revealed a large and statistically significant effect of changing the context: With a different context, subjects responded more conservatively than when the test context was the same as the study context. Although it is better to report a complete analysis, for many of the studies reported in this section, we will focus on only one measure to make the presentation more concise.

Single Process Models

Early theories of recognition were of a class known as single process models. For example, Yntema and Trask (1963) proposed a *tagging model* of recall and recognition in which each item is tagged when it occurs. To determine whether a word had been presented on a list, the subject examines the word in generic memory and looks to see whether there is a tag. The tag encodes not only the mere fact of presentation but also the relative time of occurrence. This view explains why people are very accurate at judging which of two words occurred first (Yntema & Trask, 1963), because all they need to do is examine the tags. It also explains why distractor words that are similar to target words are often incorrectly labeled "old" (Anisfeld & Knapp, 1968). For example, seeing the word *beach* might make the subject think of ocean, and *ocean* gets tagged along with beach.

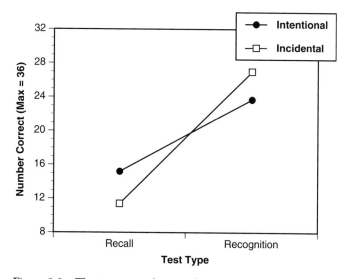

Figure 9.3   The interaction between learning instructions (intentional versus incidental) and test type (free recall or recognition).
Source: Eagle & Leiter (1964).

A second type of single process model is *strength theory* (Bahrick, 1970; Wickelgren & Norman, 1966). The basic idea is that the more recently a particular item was experienced, the stronger or more familiar it seems. Strength could be used as the dimension in a signal detection type analysis.

The key limitation in both of these models is that they contain only a single process. With only a single mechanism, the same manipulation has to have the same effect regardless of the task; there is no provision for different processes. Evidence inconsistent with both of these views comes from studies that report different effects of the same manipulation depending on whether the test is recall or recognition.

Eagle and Leiter (1964) presented one group of subjects with a list of 36 words and told them they would have to remember the words. This was the intentional learning condition. Subjects recalled 15.2 words and recognized 23.7 words. In the incidental learning condition, a different group of subjects was given the same 36 words and told to classify the words based on part of speech. When a surprise memory test was given, the subjects recalled only 11.4 words but recognized 27.0 words. The key result, shown in Figure 9.3, is that recall is higher when intentional instructions are given than when incidental instructions are given (15.2 versus 11.4), but the opposite is true for recognition: Performance is better when incidental instructions are given than when intentional instructions are given (23.7 versus 27.0). Estes and Da Polito (1967) reported similar results. One reason may be that when intentional instructions are given, subjects can engage in appropriate strategies to organize the material, and organization has larger benefits for recall than for recognition (Kintsch, 1970; Mandler, 1967; see also Hunt & Einstein, 1981).

A second result of interest is the differential effect of word frequency. High-frequency words are recalled better than low-frequency words are, but low-frequency words are recognized more accurately than are high-frequency words (Deese, 1961; Gregg, 1976; Hall, 1954). Word frequency is normally expressed as the number of times the word is likely to

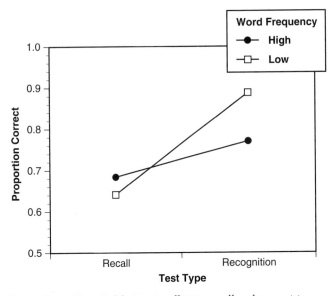

Figure 9.4   The word frequency effect in recall and recognition.
SOURCE: Based on data from Kinsbourne & George (1974).

be encountered per million words; it is computed by counting the number of occurrences in several different kinds of written documents (such as newspapers, novels, and magazines). Kinsbourne and George (1974) presented subjects with a 16-item list of words that were either of high frequency (words that occurred no fewer than 200 times per million) or of low frequency (words that occurred no more than 15 times per million). Half the subjects received a free recall test, and half received a recognition test; the results are shown in Figure 9.4. More high-frequency words than low-frequency words were recalled correctly, but more low-frequency words than high-frequency words were recognized.

Neither single process model can account for these results. With only a single process, a manipulation such as word frequency or intentionality must have the same effect on both recall and recognition. To overcome the limitations of single process models, researchers have developed a class of two-stage models known as generate-recognize models.

Generate-Recognize Models

Single process models were quickly replaced by a class of two-stage models collectively known as *generate-recognize models* (Anderson & Bower, 1972; Bahrick, 1970; Kintsch, 1970). According to these models, recall is made up of two processes, but recognition is made up of only one. In a free recall test, subjects must first generate a set of plausible candidates for recall. Once the set is generated, the subject then has to confirm whether each word is worthy of being recalled. (It is unfortunate that the second stage is called "recognition," which leads to confusion with a recognition test.) In a recognition test, the subject does not need the generation stage; the experimenter has provided the candidate. All that remains is the confirmation or recognition stage.

How would such a model explain the two findings described in the previous section? Anderson and Bower's (1973) version, called *HAM* (*human associative memory*), begins with the assumption that words are stored in an associative network of nodes (see Chapter 10, e.g., Figure 10.5). Each node represents both a word and the concept represented by the word, and the nodes are connected by pathways to related nodes. As each word is presented, the node gets tagged with a contextual marker. Contextual markers contain information about salient stimuli—for example, a clock that was ticking, a door that slammed, or a siren in the background. If one word is associated with another word, the pathway can also be tagged. This is a little like Hansel and Gretel: As they went through the forest, they left bread crumbs to mark their passage, with the hope of retracing their steps. At recall, the subject follows the contextual markers to generate a set of plausible candidates.

The second stage, recognition, examines the number of associations between the target word and the context associated with the particular list. If there is sufficient contextual evidence, the subject is willing to say "old." If there is not sufficient evidence, the subject will say "new." Thus, the signal detection analysis shown in Figure 9.2 is again applicable: Recall will be enhanced to the extent that there is a rich network and lots of pathways have been tagged, and recognition will be enhanced to the extent that individual words are associated with particular contextual elements.

The intentional/incidental learning dissociation is easily explained. When learning is incidental, the subject does not associate words in the list with each other because there is no reason to do so; this will hurt recall during the generation stage. However, because the subject focuses entirely on one word at a time, there will be a strong association between the word and the contextual elements; this will help recognition. When learning is intentional, most subjects will adopt a strategy of associating each word in the list with other words. According to HAM, this will set up a richly marked network with lots of pathways tagged, facilitating generation and thus helping recall. At the same time, this strategy of associating words with one another will result in only weak associations between a given word and context, hurting recognition.

A similar analysis explains the word frequency effect. High-frequency words tend to have more associates and thus more pathways. Subjects should be able to find a shorter, more direct path between the nodes for a given list of short items. Low-frequency words, on the other hand, have fewer associates and can take longer to read. This makes it less likely that a short path can be obtained and so hurts recall. However, because many low-frequency words are unusual looking, they can take longer to process and thus lead to more item-context associations; this helps recognition. Indeed, the more unusual looking the word, the better the recognition of the item (Zechmeister, 1972).

There is one major problem with most versions of generate-recognize models: They require that if a word can be recalled, it must also be recognized (Watkins & Gardiner, 1979). Because the second stage is the stage that both recall and recognition have in common, a successful outcome at this stage in one test means a successful outcome at this stage for the other test. The reason a word can often be recognized when it is not recalled is due to the extra preliminary stage on a test of recall: Even though the item was not generated, it was capable of being recognized. For example, you may not be able to recall the name of the actor who starred in one of your favorite films, but as soon as someone suggests the name, you can accurately recognize it. Thus, recall failure of recognizable words is quite common. Tulving and his colleagues (Tulving & Thomson, 1973; Watkins & Tulving, 1975), however, have demonstrated a phenomenon known as *recognition failure*

Table 9.3   One procedure used to demonstrate recognition failure (Step 5b)
of recallable (Step 6) words

Step	Procedure	Example
1a	List 1 presented	*badge—button*
1b	Cued recall of List 1	*badge—button*
2a	List 2 presented	*preach—rant*
2b	Cued recall of List 2	*preach—rant*
3	List 3 presented	*glue—chair*
4a	Free association stimuli presented	*table*
4b	Free association responses made	*table—chair, cloth, desk, dinner*
5a	Recognition test sheets presented	*desk top chair*
5b	Recognized items circled	*desk top chair*
6	Cued recall of list 3	*glue—chair*

SOURCE: Based on Watkins & Tulving (1975).

of recallable words. That is, contrary to the prediction of generate-recognize models, a word can be recalled under certain conditions even though it cannot be recognized.

The procedure used by Watkins and Tulving (1975) is shown in Table 9.3 (but simplified a little). The first two steps consist of a traditional paired-associate task, where the task is to recall the second word when given the first word as a cue. In Step 3, the critical list is presented, but note that it is not tested immediately. The important aspect of Step 3 is that the cue word is a weak associate of the target word (see Chapter 5). Step 4 is a free association test in which subjects are asked to generate as many associates as they can think of to a target word. Because the target word (*table*) is a strong associate of the target word in the previous step (*chair*), the subject usually provides the response term from Step 3. In Step 5, the subject is given a forced choice recognition test; this is where recognition failure can occur. The final step is the cued recall test for the list presented in Step 3. At this step, the subject often produces the word that was not recognized in the previous step. Watkins and Tulving (1975) found that 49% of the recalled items were not recognized. In Experiments 2 through 6, this value varied from a low of 16% to a high of 62%. They also determined, by using various techniques, that "the hocus pocus procedures of the early experiments turned out not to have been necessary to produce the phenomenon of recognition failure of recallable words" (p. 26). In particular, the free association step can be omitted and recognition failure can still occur.

Based on the encoding specificity idea presented in Chapter 5, the explanation of this phenomenon is quite straightforward. Contrary to the fundamental assumption of generate-recognize theory, recognition and recall both depend on the cues available at test. In the situation concocted by Watkins and Tulving, the cues available at test were better in the recall test than in the recognition test. (A more detailed account is presented in the optional chapter at the end of this book.) Recognition is not easier than recall, and recall is not easier than recognition; performance on each test depends on the cues available.

Beyond Simple Generate-Recognize Models

One change to a simple generate-recognize model that will allow it to account for recognition failure of recallable words is to have a search process occur during the recognition phase. For example, it is possible to have the same search and confirmation process operate in both recognition and recall (Jacoby & Hollingshead, 1990). The main problem with this approach is that subjects can very quickly and with a great deal of confidence correctly say that an item was not presented (Atkinson & Juola, 1974). Given the speed and confidence with which subjects reject an item, it seems unlikely that an extensive search of memory occurs every time.

Several researchers have suggested a process whereby recognition can use a search but can also rely on a simple familiarity process (Atkinson & Juola, 1973; Mandler, 1980). The idea is that a measure of familiarity is instantly computed. If this value is very large, then the subject gives a very rapid "old" response. If this value is very low, then the subject gives a very rapid "new" response. It is only for the intermediate familiarity values that a search takes place. A fundamental assumption is that the process of assessing familiarity is faster than the search process.

Mandler (1980) is careful to distinguish two types of recognition judgments: simple recognition, in which a judgment of prior occurrence is made, and identification. The former process may be accomplished solely by an evaluation of the item's familiarity, but the latter requires both familiarity and retrieval. Familiarity is related to the ease of processing the item: The more recently the item has been perceived, the easier it is to perceive the item at test. Both processes, familiarity and retrieval, are assumed to be initiated simultaneously. Although it has not been directly applied to the recognition failure of recallable words, Mandler's (1980) model has mechanisms that should allow it to produce the appropriate pattern. In the procedure detailed in Table 9.3, there is a relatively long delay between learning and the recognition test. This delay could lower the feelings of familiarity until they fall into the intermediate range, and performance must then rely more on the retrieval component. Because the target word in the recognition test is presented in a context different from the study context, the retrieval phase contains inappropriate cues. The recall test (Step 6) provides appropriate cues, so here the retrieval process will succeed. Note that this idea is similar to the encoding specificity idea presented in Chapter 5.

Mandler (1980) did report a simulation of a study of recognition that supports this analysis. Subjects studied word pairs and then received a variety of tests. For example, a subject studied the pair A-B; recognition was then assessed when just A was presented, when just B was presented, and when both A and B were presented. According to the analysis outlined above, performance will be better for the A-B items than for either A or B individually. This is exactly what Table 9.4 shows. In particular, notice that whereas both the hit rate and the false alarm rate improve when both A and B are presented at test, there is a larger difference in the false alarm rate. These results are nicely predicted by the model. Because the single A and B items are being tested in a new context, performance is worse than when tested in the old context (both items together).

Given the success on the recognition component, Mandler (1980) looked at recognition performance of B when B has been either recalled or not recalled (using data from Rabinowitz, Mandler, & Barsalou, 1977). According to the analysis presented above, the familiarity values for recognizing B should be relatively constant and in the intermediate range. This will cause more reliance on the retrieval component. When B was recalled, it

Table 9.4   Observed and predicted hit rate and false alarm rate for word pairs

	Hits		False Alarms	
Items	Observed	Predicted	Observed	Predicted
A	0.76	0.79	0.18	0.23
B	0.77	0.79	0.23	0.22
AB	0.86	0.81	0.06	0.04

SOURCE: Mandler (1980).

was recognized correctly with a probability of 0.69; when B was not recalled, it was recognized with a probability of 0.41. Despite this large difference, the estimates of the familiarity component were identical and were in the intermediate range: 0.40 and 0.39, respectively. A combination of familiarity and retrieval, then, can produce recognition failure of recallable words.

Gillund and Shiffrin (1984) conducted three experiments to test the assumption that both familiarity and a search process are important. The basic idea was to force subjects to respond very quickly or to make them wait a while. The average response time in the fast response condition was approximately 500 ms, compared to 2.5 to 3 s in the slow condition. In the fast condition, subjects should be relying more on the familiarity process, whereas in the slow condition, they should be relying more on the search process. Gillund and Shiffrin reported two main results. First, and not surprising, subjects were more accurate in the slow condition than in the fast condition. Second, and more important, there were no other differences between slow and fast responses. To the extent that the two processes are different, Gillund and Shiffrin argued, there should have been some interactions. Because they did not observe any interactions, they argued that a search process for recognition was not required and that recognition could be based solely on familiarity.

Current models of recognition are part of the so-called global memory models, such as SAM (Gillund & Shiffrin, 1984), MINERVA 2 (Hintzman, 1988), and TODAM (Murdock, 1982). These models, along with a connectionist model of recognition, are presented in the optional chapter at the end of this book. Interestingly, however, the type of view suggested by Mandler (1980) is making a comeback of sorts (see, for example, Reder et al., 2000). The mechanisms he suggested accord nicely with results from the remember/know paradigm that asks people to make distinctions more fine grained than simply whether they recognize the item.

Remember Versus Know

One relatively recent change in recognition methodology concerns the *remember/know* procedure (Gardiner, 1988; Tulving, 1985), although the ideas behind it were well articulated by Mandler (1980). In this procedure, subjects are given a recognition test and are asked to indicate whether they actually remember the information (have a conscious recollection of the information's occurrence on the study list) or just somehow know the answer (know that the item was on the list but have no conscious recollection of its actual occurrence). In Tulving's (1985) study, the first using remember/know methodology, subjects studied pairs of words in which the second word was a member of the category indicated by the first word, such as *musical instrument—viola*. The subjects then received a standard free recall test, followed by a cued recall test with the category name as a cue, and finally a cued recall test with the category name as a cue plus the first letter of the target item. The proportion of "remember" judgments decreased over the three kinds of tests and also decreased with increasing retention interval, relative to overall recognition performance.

Several other variables have been found to have different effects on remember compared to know responses; most of these have been reported by Gardiner and his colleagues. Gardiner (1988) found a levels of processing (Chapter 5) effect on remember judgments but not on know judgments, and also found a generation effect (Chapter 6) for remember judgments but not for know judgments. Gardiner and Java (1990) found the standard better recognition of low-frequency than high-frequency words for remember judgments but not for know judgments. Gardiner and Parkin (1990) had subjects engage in a secondary task during study and found that this divided attention manipulation disrupted remember judgments but not know judgments. Gardiner and Java (1991) have also shown that performance as assessed by remember judgments decreases more quickly over a 6-month period than does performance on know judgments.

CogLab **Experiment**
http://coglab.wadsworth.com/experiments/RememberKnow/

As an explanation, Gardiner (Gardiner & Parkin, 1990; Gardiner & Java, 1993) has suggested that remember judgments are influenced by conceptual and attentional factors, whereas know judgments are not; instead, they may be based on a procedural memory system, much like Schacter's (1994) PRS. This distinction sounds much like that between the factors that affect explicit memory and those that affect implicit memory (see Chapter 7).

Rajaram (1993) reported a series of experiments that examined remember/know judgments in more detail. Her first experiment replicated Gardiner's (1988) findings of a large level of processing effect on remember judgments, but no effect (if anything, a slight reversal) on know judgments (see the left panel of Figure 9.5). Her second experiment involved showing either pictures or words at study and only words at test. The task was to say whether either the word or the picture named had been seen previously. The standard picture superiority effect (Madigan, 1983) was observed for remember judgments: Performance was better for pictures than for words. However, there was again a reversal for know judgments: Performance was better for words than for pictures (see right panel of Figure 9.5). Although this finding is consistent with the idea that remember judgments are based on the explicit system and know judgments are based on implicit memory, it is also consistent with the idea that remember judgments may depend more on recollective processes whereas know judgments are based more on familiarity.

Rajaram's (1993) final experiments compared know judgments to judgments of confidence. In addition to distinguishing between remember and know judgments, Rajaram had subjects categorize their judgments in terms of whether they were sure or not sure. She again found a difference between remember and know judgments, but found no difference in confidence ratings. This important finding suggests that know judgments are not based solely on the perceived confidence of the subject. (However, see Donaldson, 1996, for an argument that remember/know differences might be attributable to a criterion shift.)

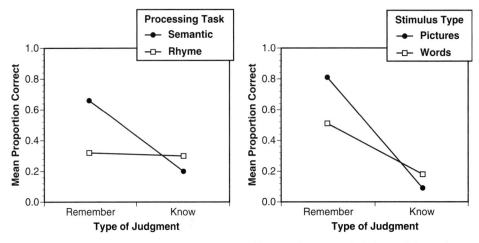

Figure 9.5 Two differences between remember and know judgments. The left panel shows the basic level of processing effect; the right panel shows the picture superiority effect, but only for remember judgments.   SOURCE: Based on data from Rajaram (1993).

Recollection and Familiarity

The data from the remember/know paradigm illustrate quite nicely the idea that recognition performance is a combination of two different types of processes (Yonelinas, 2002). In one process, usually called *recollection*, memory judgments are made on the basis of conscious recollection of information about previous events. This process is similar to that used in free recall. In the second process, usually called *familiarity*, memory judgments are made on the basis of the assessed familiarity of a particular stimulus.

In addition to the remember/know paradigm, researchers have used a variety of tests to investigate recollection and familiarity. Yonelinas (2002) distinguishes between *task dissociation* and *process dissociation* methods. Task dissociation methods compare performance on two tasks that are thought to differ in their reliance on recollection and familiarity. For example, a response deadline task forces subjects to make a response at a particular time after the stimulus is presented. The subject might see the test stimulus and be asked to respond whether the item is old or new within 500 ms or within 1000 ms. The idea is that, because familiarity is supposed to be faster than recollection, fast responses should rely more on familiarity than recollection, whereas slow responses should include a larger contribution from recollection. Process dissociation methods generally compare performance in two conditions. In one (called the *inclusion* condition), both recollection and familiarity contribute to accurate performance, whereas in the second (the *exclusion* condition), the processes are set in opposition. Chapter 5 reviews this logic in detail.

Yonelinas (2002) reviewed empirical data from studies using both task dissociation and process dissociation techniques. Table 9.5 summarizes the effects of various encoding and retrieval manipulations on recollection and familiarity. Each row describes an experimental manipulation that occurred either at encoding or at retrieval and the effects of this manipulation on the two recognition processes. The table should be read in the following way: Relative to shallow processing (focusing on the perceptual characteristics of

Table 9.5 Summary of the effects of encoding manipulations and retrieval manipulations on recollection and familiarity

	Recollection	*Familiarity*
Encoding Manipulations		
Shallow vs. Deep Processing	Larger increase	Smaller increase
Read vs. Generate	Larger increase	Smaller increase
Full vs. Divided Attention	Larger decrease	Smaller decrease
Shorter vs. Longer Study Duration	Increase	Increase
Retrieval Manipulations		
Full vs. Divided Attention	Large decrease	No effect
Same vs. Different Perceptual Match (verbal)	No effect	Large decrease
Same vs. Different Perceptual Match (nonverbal)	Decrease	Decrease
No Delay vs. Short Delay	No effect	Rapid decrease
No Delay vs. Long Delay	Decrease	Decrease
Less Fluency vs. More Fluency	No effect	Large increase
Change Response Criterion	No effect	Large effect

NOTE: "Increase" and "decrease" refer to the effect on performance relative to the appropriate control condition.

a stimulus), deep processing (focusing on the meaning of a stimulus) led to an increase for both recollection and familiarity, but the increase was larger for recollection than for familiarity. The "larger increase" and "smaller increase" terms refer to the actual numerical differences calculated by Yonelinas for the experiments he reviewed. For the deep versus shallow manipulation, deep processing led to an increase of approximately 0.30 in the probability of recollecting the item, whereas deep processing led to an increase of slightly less than 0.20 for familiarity. The table summarizes this finding as a larger increase for recollection and a smaller increase for familiarity.

In general, encoding manipulations lead to similar effects on both recollection and familiarity, although the effects are usually larger on recollection than on familiarity. Retrieval manipulations, on the other hand, produce a pattern of results consistent with the idea that the two processes are independent. Familiarity processes are faster than recollective processes. Familiarity can be accurately modeled using signal detection theory, whereas recollection is better thought of as reflecting a threshold process. Both processes are sensitive to manipulations of conceptual information, although recollection shows larger effects than familiarity. Familiarity is more automatic than is recollection, although both can be affected by dividing attention at encoding.

Based on Yonelinas's (2002) review, it is clear that recognition memory is supported by at least two processes, one based on assessing the familiarity of the test item and the other based on recollection of information about previous events. This finding reinforces the conclusion from early studies, reviewed above, that ruled out single process models of recognition. A variety of dual process models have been proposed, including Mandler's (1980, 1991) model described earlier. Others have been proposed by Atkinson and Juola (1973, 1974), Jacoby (1991), Reder et al. (2000), and Yonelinas (2001). It remains unclear whether the so-called global memory models (SAM, MINERVA2, and TODAM, discussed in the optional chapter) can account for all of the results now attributed to recollection and familiarity. On the one hand, the global memory models are single factor models in that they assess a global measure of memory. On the other hand, different types of information can be included within that assessment. Thus, SAM can account for at least some of the process dissociation results using only the global assessment measure (Ratcliff, Van Zandt, & McKoon, 1995). The establishment of two processes within recognition may also shed some light on a problem that has long posed trouble for models of recognition: the mirror effect.

The Mirror Effect

One aspect of recognition that has received much attention in recent years is the mirror effect (Brown, Lewis, & Monk, 1977; Glanzer & Adams, 1985). In its simplest form, the *mirror effect* describes a regularity when examining performance on a variety of different kinds of recognition tests (such as yes-no, forced choice, multiple choice, and rating scales). A mirror effect is observed when "The type of stimulus that is accurately recognized as old when old is also accurately recognized as new when new. The type that is poorly recognized as old when old is also poorly recognized as new when new" (Glanzer & Adams, 1985, p. 8).

One example of a mirror effect concerns the effect of word frequency on recognition memory. Generally, low-frequency words are recognized more accurately than high-frequency words are (see Table 9.6 and Figure 9.4). However, word frequency also shows a mirror effect. Both of these effects can be seen in the data shown in Table 9.6. Rao and Proctor (1984) had subjects see a list of 120 words and then presented a recognition test of 240 words. The mirror effect can be seen clearly in their data: The number of hits was higher for the low-frequency words than for the high-frequency words; at the same time, the number of false alarms was lower for the low-frequency than for the high-frequency words. The standard word frequency effect can be seen in the larger d' value for the low- compared to the high-frequency words.

One reason this finding has attracted a great deal of attention is that the mirror effect seems pervasive. Glanzer and Adams (1985) reviewed all the published recognition studies they could find in which (1) a within-subjects design was used in which two (or more) levels of the variable were assessed and (2) the authors reported sufficient data (hit rates and false alarm rates for each stimulus class) to make the study useful. The results are shown in Table 9.7.

Table 9.6   The mirror effect (higher hit rates and lower false alarm rates in low-frequency than high-frequency words) and the word frequency effect in recognition

	Word Frequency	
	High	*Low*
Hits	27.84	31.00
False Alarms	10.20	7.63
d'	1.36	1.88

SOURCE: Based on data from Rao & Proctor (1984).

Table 9.7 The number of reports (separate studies or, in the case of the pictures versus words, separate experiments) that met the criteria and the number that showed a mirror effect

Variable	Number of Reports	Number Showing a Mirror Effect
Word Frequency	24	23
Concreteness	9	8
Meaningfulness	13	9
Pictures vs. Words	8	6
Miscellaneous	26	17
Total	80	63

The one notable departure from the mirror effect comes from studies in the miscellaneous category that looked at recognition for normal as opposed to transformed text. With the transformed text studies removed, the number of mirror effects observed becomes 17 out of 22. Another possible exception is rare words (Wixted, 1992). Since the initial report, many studies have demonstrated mirror effects with other types of stimuli, including frequency discrimination (Greene & Thapar, 1994), associative information (Hockley, 1994), presentation rate (Ratcliff, Sheu, & Gronlund, 1992), age of the subject (Bäckman, 1991), and recency (Glanzer, Adams, & Iverson, 1991). It can also be seen with incidental learning (Glanzer & Adams, 1990) and when latency rather than accuracy is used as the response (Hockley, 1994). Even though they were excluded from the survey, experiments that use between-subject designs also show the mirror effect (Glanzer & Adams, 1985).

Having established the generality of the mirror effect, the next question is whether this effect is important or trivial. It could be that the mirror effect is an artifact of the way recognition data are analyzed. For example, a "mirror effect" occurs between false alarm rates and correct rejection rates. As false alarm rates increase, correct rejection rates decrease. This is an uninteresting mirror effect, however, because the false alarm rate and the correct rejection rate must add to 1.0 (see Table 9.1). Is this also the case for the mirror effect between hit rates and false alarm rates?

The consensus is that the mirror effect is not an artifact (Glanzer & Adams, 1985; Hintzman, Caulton, & Curran, 1994). One reason for this conclusion is that hit rates and false alarm rates can, in theory, vary independently; for any given hit rate, the false alarm rate can still be anywhere between 0.0 and 1.0. In the example given in the preceding paragraph, false alarm and correct rejection rates cannot vary independently; if the false alarm rate is 0.2, then the correct rejection rate must be 0.8. A second reason is that the actual pattern is not what is most likely. Let A represent a stimulus class in which old items are called "old" more often than B items, and also in which new items are called "new" more often than B items. To see a mirror effect, the distributions of these items needs to be ordered such that New A < New B < Old B < Old A. This is shown graphically in the top panel of Figure 9.6. Note, however, that this is not the only possible ordering; all old items could share a distribution, or all new items could share a distribution. In fact, given that

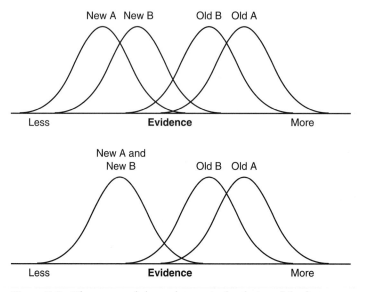

New A New B   Old B Old A

Less   **Evidence**   More

New A and
New B   Old B Old A

Less   **Evidence**   More

Figure 9.6   The top panel shows the required ordering of the four distributions of A and B stimuli according to signal detection theory if the mirror effect is to be seen. The bottom panel shows the most likely ordering of the distributions, where unstudied (new) items are unlikely to differ.   SOURCE: Adapted from "The Mirror Effect in Recognition Memory," by M. Glanzer and J. K. Adams, 1985, *Memory & Cognition, 13,* p. 8. Copyright © 1985. Adapted by permission of Psychonomic Society Inc.

none of the new items has been studied, the most reasonable pattern is that the New A and New B distributions overlap, as shown in the bottom panel of Figure 9.6. However, the mirror effect is clearly the rule and not the exception.

Given that the mirror effect is both general and important, another important issue concerns its relationship to theories of recognition. The mirror effect clearly eliminates from contention all theories of recognition based on a unidimensional conception of strength or familiarity (Brown, Lewis, & Monk, 1977; Glanzer & Adams, 1985, 1990; Hintzman, Caulton, & Curran, 1994). It is unclear whether the global memory models (SAM, MINERVA 2, and TODAM, described in the optional chapter), which all rely on a unidimensional conception of familiarity, can explain the mirror effect. Although several new models of recognition have been proposed (Glanzer, Adams, Iverson, & Kim, 1993; Greene, 1996; Hintzman, Caulton, & Curran, 1994), it now seems likely that the mirror effect can be explained by dual process models (Balota, Burgess, Cortese, & Adams, 2002; Reder, Angstadt, Cary, Erickson, & Ayers, 2002).

For example, Joordens and Hockley (2000) have suggested that the mirror effect is due to two different factors, one of which affects the false alarm rate and the other the hit rate. The idea is that the mirror effect for word frequency occurs because high-frequency words are generally more familiar and low-frequency items are generally easier to recollect. With low-frequency words, the hit rate would be high because of better recollection, but the false alarm rate would be low because they are not very familiar. With high-frequency words, the hit rate would be lower because of reduced recollection, but the false alarm rate would be higher because they are more familiar.

Table 9.8 The mirror effect (higher hit rate and lower false alarm rate for low-frequency than high-frequency words)

	New Items (False Alarms)		Old Items (Hits)	
	High	Low	High	Low
Control	0. 26	0.18	0.75	0.80
Speeded Recognition	0.41	0.34	0.69	0.71

NOTE: The mirror effect is seen when unlimited time is allowed for the recognition judgment (the control condition). When speeded judgments are required, which should reduce the contribution of recollection, the hit rate advantage is eliminated but the false alarm advantage is unaffected.
SOURCE: Based on data from Joordens & Hockley (2000).

To test this idea, they conducted an experiment in which subjects were asked to recognized low- and high-frequency words. In the control condition, the subjects were given unlimited time to make their recognition judgments. In the speeded condition, they were told to make their response within 800 ms. The logic is that requiring a speeded response should reduce the influence of the recollection process but should not affect the familiarity process, because familiarity is faster than recollection. The results are shown in Table 9.8. With unlimited time, a standard mirror effect was observed. When speeded recognition was required, the hit rate advantage of the low-frequency items was eliminated but the false alarm rate advantage remained.

Currently, this account works well for many mirror effects that are produced by stimulus characteristics, but it does yet not offer a comprehensive account. A similar account has been formalized within a computational model (Reder et al., 2000). However, other explanations are probably needed for some forms of the mirror effect. Whatever the outcome, the mirror effect will play a large role in theory development in the future.

Face Recognition

Face recognition needs to be distinguished from face identification, a more difficult task. *Face identification* is being able to supply the name (and perhaps other details) that goes with a particular face, a form of paired-associate learning. *Face recognition*, in contrast, is deciding whether a particular face has been seen before. Bahrick (1984b) reported a study in which college teachers were asked both to identify and to recognize faces of former students. One variable of particular interest was the retention interval—the time since the end of the semester in which the student was in class. Bahrick's results are shown in Table 9.9. Face identification was consistently less accurate than face recognition.

Table 9.9 Percent correct recognition and identification of students' faces by their college teachers

	11 Days	1 Year	4 Years	8 Years
Recognition	69.0	47.5	31.0	26.0
Identification	35.5	6.0	2.5	0.0

SOURCE: Based on data from Bahrick (1984b).

It turns out that people make an extraordinary number of face identification and face recognition errors. Young, Hay, and Ellis (1985) had 22 subjects keep track of all of the errors they made recognizing and identifying people over an 8-week period. They reported 1008 errors, nearly 6 errors per day per subject. Of these, 114 were failures to recognize a person. Subjects rely heavily on physical features to recognize people—especially hair, forehead, eyes, and nose (Ellis, 1975)—and when these features change, recognition can fail. A second common error was mistakenly identifying one person as another; there were 314 such incidents, the most common being thinking an unfamiliar person is a familiar one. A third common error (233 reports) involved recognizing a person but failing to identify the person (as opposed to incorrectly identifying the person). These errors typically involved a slight acquaintance in a novel context, such as meeting your dentist in the grocery store. The fourth common error (190 incidents) was failing to recall the name of a person. In most cases, other information such as occupation was recalled. This finding, the so-called *name effect*, has been replicated: McWeeny, Young, Hay, and Ellis (1987) found that it took subjects longer to provide a name than an occupation. One nice control in this study was that the names and occupations were the same; for example, one face would be described as Mr. Baker, whereas a different face would be described as that of a baker. It was easier to say the occupation "baker" than the name "Baker."

Faces of people of the same race as the subject tend to be recognized slightly more accurately than faces of people from different races. For example, O'Toole, Deffenbacher, Valentin, and Abdi (1994) had a group of Caucasian subjects and a group of Asian subjects study Caucasian and Japanese faces. They performed a signal detection analysis on the recognition data, shown in Figure 9.7. Caucasian subjects recognized Caucasian faces more accurately than they did Japanese faces, and Asian subjects recognized Japanese faces more accurately than they did Caucasian faces. Similar conclusions have been reached by Valentine and Endo (1992) and Vokey and Read (1992).

Similar to the *other-race effect* just described is the *face inversion effect*. If even a very familiar face is shown upside down, the probability of correctly identifying or recognizing the face drops precipitously (Yin, 1969; Valentine, 1988). This face inversion effect has played a large role in the question of whether face recognition is a special process (see below). A face does not have to be shown rotated a full 180° to see a decrease in performance. A change in orientation of 45° (such as full face to three-quarter view) reliably impairs performance, and a change of 90° (full face to profile) results in even worse performance (Baddeley & Woodhead, 1983).

As with words and other stimuli, a form of priming can be observed with faces. If two well-known faces that are associated with each other are presented one after the other, the second face is identified more quickly than if it were an unfamiliar face (Bruce & Valentine, 1986). Thus, presenting a picture of Abbott will make recognition of Costello faster than if Abbott were not presented. Interestingly, if subjects believe that a face they are looking at belongs to a criminal, it is remembered more accurately (Honeck, 1986). The severity of the crime does not correlate with accuracy.

Two issues concerning face recognition and identification are how to explain the various phenomena and whether they involve a special process. Ellis and Young (1989) concluded that face recognition is special but not unique; faces are not the only stimuli to take advantage of it. As evidence that face recognition is special, they noted that (1) neonates show a preference for faces over nonfaces, (2) face recognition has a different developmental history than other phenomena, (3) faces are very difficult to identify upside

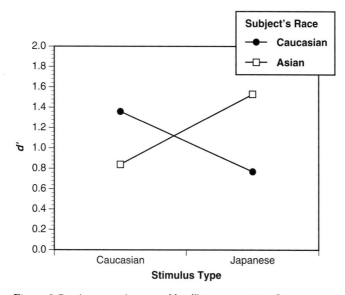

Figure 9.7 Accuracy (measured by *d'*) in recognizing Caucasian or Japanese faces as a function of the subject's race. SOURCE: Adapted from "Structural Aspects of Face Recognition and the Other-Race Effect," by A. J. O'Toole et al., 1994, *Memory & Cognition, 22,* 208–224. Copyright © 1994. Reprinted by permission of Psychonomic Society Inc.

down (the face inversion effect), and (4) there appears to be a special neural substrate that supports face recognition. Each of these factors will be discussed briefly.

The first line of evidence offered by Ellis and Young (1989) to support the conclusion that face recognition is special is the finding that newborn infants appear to display a preference for faces over nonfaces. However, the pattern of data is quite complicated. First, several studies show that face preference can disappear in infants at around 2 months of age, only to return a little later (see Maurer, 1985). Furthermore, other types of pictures show a similar privileged status; for example, infants may show a preference for pictures of normal over scrambled cars (Levine, 1989). Rather than arguing for specialness, this result could be seen as a general preference for coherence, or even for closed forms. A similar criticism has been offered regarding the second line of evidence, the special developmental history of face recognition. It turns out that this is not unique; both voice recognition and tonal memory have similar patterns of development (Carey & Diamond, 1980).

The third line of evidence concerns the face inversion effect. Diamond and Carey (1986) suggested that expertise—or, more accurately, a lack of expertise—may explain the face inversion effect. Subjects have a great deal of experience recognizing upright faces but almost no experience recognizing upside-down faces. Diamond and Carey used photographs of dogs as control stimuli for faces, and recruited experts in judging dogs. The dog experts showed a difference in recognizing upside-down versus upright dogs, just as people show a difference in recognizing inverted versus upright faces. The novices (people with little familiarity with particular dog breeds) did not show a difference. Similar explanations have been offered to explain the other-race effect.

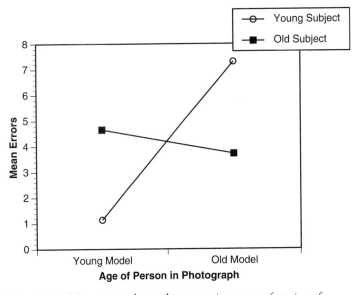

Figure 9.8   Mean errors observed in age estimates as a function of model age group and participant age group.   SOURCE: Data from Winningham (2001).

This view predicts a phenomenon called the *other-age effect*. Assuming that young people interact more with other young people and that older people interact more with other older people, one should find that people process faces better if the faces are from their own age group. Winningham (2001) asked young (mean age 19.5 years) and old (mean age 77.3 years) subjects to estimate the age of models in photographs. Half the photographs were of young models (mean age 20.1 years), and half were of old models (mean age 79.9 years). As shown in Figure 9.8, the younger subjects were more accurate in estimating the age of the young models, and the older subjects were more accurate in estimating the age of the old models.

Valentine (1988) also views face recognition as more a matter of expertise than a special process. His conclusion comes from examining studies of inverted faces; rather than saying an upside-down face disrupts the special face recognition process, he argues that people have almost no experience with the task.

Ellis and Young's (1989) final point is that there appears to be some evidence of special neural substrates supporting face recognition. For example, the right hemisphere appears to be more involved in face recognition than the left, and several researchers have found cells in monkeys that respond only when the animal looks at faces. Furthermore, there is the phenomenon termed *prosopagnosia*, which refers to the inability to recognize familiar faces after certain brain injuries. As with the other points, this line of evidence is open to alternative explanations. For example, Levine, Banich, and Koch-Weser (1988) suggest that face recognition is not special, but is similar to other tasks that tap particular processes situated in the right hemisphere. In one study, they found a similar pattern of localized neural responding when the stimuli were houses. As another example, Dalesbred sheep have cells that respond to faces of sheep, dogs, and humans (Kendrick & Baldwin,

1987); however, at least one set of cells responded to familiar Dalesbred sheep rather than to unfamiliar Dalesbred sheep. A familiarity or expertise argument could again account for these findings. (Oddly, human and dog faces were responded to by the same cells, although the interpretation of this is not clear.)

One way in which processing of faces might differ from processing of other objects is that faces seem to be processed holistically. The *holistic encoding hypothesis* says that the encoded representation of the face is a unitary psychological entity (Farah, Wilson, Drain, & Tanaka, 1998). The key claim is that there is little or no decomposition of the encoded whole into its constituent parts. For example, subjects were presented with two faces simultaneously and were asked to judge whether one particular anatomical feature (such as the nose) was same or different. Other features, irrelevant to the main task, could also be the same or different. Farah et al. found a substantial advantage when the irrelevant features were the same in the two faces, and this advantage was larger when the faces were upright than when they were inverted. This type of finding supports the idea of holistic representation because factors other than the target affect performance. It is as if the other anatomical features cannot be ignored. Wenger and Ingvalson (in press) suggest that the effect is due to decisional factors rather than to representing faces in a unitary way. In particular, it seemed as if subjects became more conservative in their judgment if irrelevant features varied but the relevant feature was same in the two faces.

Although there is still debate over whether face recognition is special, there is little evidence to support the argument that it is unique. Even such proponents as Ellis and Young think of it as only one of several special processes that have a similar set of properties. As more neurological evidence becomes available, there may be more consensus on the issue of how special face recognition is. In addition to advances in neurological study, analyses by several formal models of face recognition may also help (see, for example, Wenger & Townsend, 2001). For example, a recent connectionist model has simulated the other-race effect based solely on degree of experience with various kinds of faces (O'Toole et al., 1994).

Chapter Summary

In a standard recognition test, the stimulus can be old or new and the subject can respond yes, it is an old item, or no, it is not an old item. This results in four types of responses: hits (old item, yes), false alarms (new item, yes), misses (old item, no), and correct rejections (new item, no). Recognition performance cannot be determined unless both the hit rate and the false alarm rate are included. Several methods exist that try to determine how much of the response is due to knowledge (d', A', Pr) and how much to response bias (C, B''_D, Br).

Simple single process models of recall and recognition are ruled out by findings such as high-frequency words are recall better than low-frequency words but low-frequency words are recognized better than high-frequency words. The mirror effect also poses problems for these models. Generate-recognize models are ruled out by findings that under certain circumstances, words that cannot be recognized can be recalled. More information can be obtained by asking subjects to make remember or know judgments for all items they indicate are old. Findings from this paradigm are consistent with current views that recognition is made up of at least two processes, recollection and familiarity.

Face recognition (saying a face is familiar or not) is different from face identification (attaching a name to a face). Although people may be good at both, errors still occur. Face recognition does seem to be special but not unique; it seems closely related to expertise with processing the stimuli. For example, people are worse at processing unfamiliar kinds of faces (the face inversion effect, the other-race effect).

CHAPTER TEN

Knowledge

I consider that a man's brain originally is like a little empty attic, and you have to stock it with such furniture as you choose. . . . It is a mistake to think that the little room has elastic walls and can distend to any extent. Depend upon it there comes a time when for every addition of knowledge you forget something that you knew before.

—Sherlock Holmes

The more you put in a brain, the more it will hold.

—Nero Wolfe

Knowledge refers to what you know. You probably know the capital of Canada, the number of states in the United States, your telephone number, the number of legs on an ostrich, several types of dinosaurs, the color of carrots, the texture of sandpaper, the taste of seawater, and perhaps even the air-speed velocity of an unladen European swallow. Perhaps more surprising than the number of things you know is the number of things you know that you do not know. For example, you probably know that you do not know the name of the 44th element in the periodic table (molybdenum), the name of William McKinley's first vice president (Garret A. Hobart), or the name of the 1959 Nobel Prize winner for literature (Salvatore Quasimodo).

In this chapter, we look at various explanations for how people organize and retrieve information from semantic or generic memory. Although *semantic* memory is the most common term, a better term is Hintzman's (1978) *generic* memory, for three reasons: First, the topic is about everyday, ordinary knowledge (hence, generic); second, it includes information other than purely semantic information (having to do with words and meanings); and finally, the term *semantic memory* is usually taken as implying that semantic and episodic memory are different systems (Tulving, 1972, 1983), which should be a separate issue from the study of knowledge.

Propositions and Concepts

Before examining the most common views of generic memory, we need to define and explain some terms. The most common class of models that attempt to explain generic memory rely on concepts and propositions. A *proposition* is simply a relationship between two concepts that has a truth value. For example, a proposition might be that "A canary can sing." Singing is a concept and canary is a concept; this statement becomes a proposition because the concepts are arranged such that the truth of the statement can be verified. Even though most of the propositions we consider will be in the form of English sentences, this need not be the case. English is simply a convenient way of expressing the information, and people who speak different languages are assumed to have similar propositional representations.

A *concept*, then, is simply a mental representation of something. More technically, a concept is "an idea that includes all that is characteristically associated with it" (Medin, 1989, p. 1469). It could be a type of animal such as aardvark, a part of speech such as adjective, or an idea such as justice. Although words are frequently used to name concepts, a concept is more than a word and does not have to be a verbal entity. An analogy might be that a concept is like the entry in a dictionary that follows the word rather than the word itself.

One final point we need to consider is how best to test the models that will be described. The main problem is that everybody knows that birds fly, canaries sing, and animals eat. If we used an accuracy measure like proportion correct, everyone would score near 100% correct and there would be no observable differences. Instead of accuracy, researchers have used *latency* as their behavioral measure. Measurements of how quickly a person can respond are usually called *response times*, conveniently abbreviated as RT. The key data, therefore, will come from seeing how quickly people process various types of information. One common test is to measure how long it takes people to verify that a proposition is true or false; another is to measure how long it takes people to verify that a target item is a valid word. The former is known as a *semantic verification test* and the latter as a *lexical decision test*.

Collins and Quillian's Hierarchical Model

Collins and Quillian (1969) converted a model for storing generic information in a computer (Quillian, 1967, 1969) into a testable model of human knowledge. Figure 10.1 shows the organization and illustrates the key features. Each black dot represents a category name (or concept), arranged in a hierarchical fashion so that the most general concepts are at the top and more specific instances are further down. Thus, canaries are a type of bird, and birds are a type of animal. The properties that most animals have in common

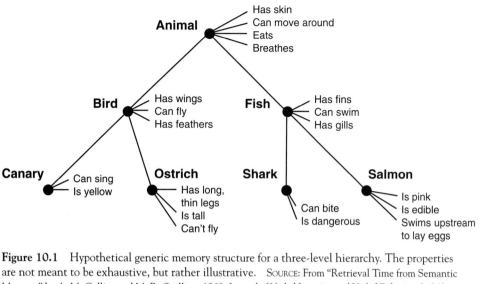

Figure 10.1 Hypothetical generic memory structure for a three-level hierarchy. The properties are not meant to be exhaustive, but rather illustrative. SOURCE: From "Retrieval Time from Semantic Memory," by A. M. Collins and M. R. Quillian, 1969, *Journal of Verbal Learning and Verbal Behavior, 8*, 240–247. Copyright © 1969 Academic Press, Inc. Reprinted with permission.

are represented at the level of the animal concept; those that birds share but that other animals do not are at the level of bird; and those that distinguish canaries from other birds are down at the level of canary. This general principle is known as *cognitive economy*, because each property is listed as few times as possible. If asked whether canaries fly, the subject responds by retrieving the knowledge that canaries are birds and that birds can fly; it can then be inferred that canaries can fly. Ostriches cannot fly, and this information is stored at the level of ostrich to prevent an incorrect inference.

How does this model make testable predictions to see whether this organization is a plausible model for how people organize knowledge? The Collins and Quillian model makes predictions about how long it will take a person to verify a sentence. Suppose a person is asked to verify two sentences: "A canary can sing" and "A canary can fly." The model shown in Figure 10.1 predicts slower responding to the second sentence than to the first. To verify the second sentence, the subject starts at the canary node but then has to move up the hierarchy one level to confirm that the desired property is there. No such metaphoric travel is necessary for the first sentence; the property is stored at the same level as the category.

To state the predictions as precisely as possible, Collins and Quillian (1969) made three assumptions. First, they assumed that both retrieving a property and traversing the hierarchy take time. Second, they assumed that the times are additive whenever one step is dependent on the completion of another. For example, to verify the sentence "A canary can fly," retrieving the property "can fly" is dependent on first moving up the hierarchy. The additive assumption simply means that the time to complete both steps is the sum of completing each step individually. Third, Collins and Quillian assumed that the time to retrieve a property is independent of the level of the hierarchy.

Collins and Quillian (1969) presented subjects with two kinds of sentences to verify. Sentences that involved properties were called P sentences, and those that involved

Figure 10.2   Mean response time to verify property or superset sentences as a function of how many levels need to be traveled.
SOURCE: From "Retrieval Time from Semantic Memory," by A. M. Collins and M. R. Quillian, 1969, *Journal of Verbal Learning and Verbal Behavior, 8,* 240–247. Copyright © 1969 Academic Press, Inc. Reprinted with permission.

superset relations were called S sentences. In addition, there were three possible levels of the hierarchy. A 0-level sentence involves properties or supersets at the same level. For example, a P0 sentence might be "A canary can sing." An S0 sentence might be "A canary is a canary." Any sentence that involved moving one level up the hierarchy was called either an S1 or P1 sentence; a sentence that involved moving two levels was called an S2 or P2 sentence. In three experiments, Collins and Quillian (1969) presented true and false sentences from knowledge bases similar to that shown in Figure 10.1. For example, a true P1 sentence from a Games knowledge base might be "Badminton has rules." A false sentence might be "Hockey is a race." Other knowledge domains tested included trees and beverages.

The model predicts two parallel lines, with the property line higher than that for superset questions. As Figure 10.2 shows, this is exactly what happens. The difference between P0 and P1, and P1 and P2 is about 75 ms, as is the difference between S1 and S2. The difference between P1 and S1 and P2 and S2 is about 225 ms. These measures can be interpreted as suggesting that it takes about 75 ms to retrieve a property, regardless of the level in the hierarchy, and that it takes about 225 ms to travel up a level. Given the simplicity of the model, it is remarkably accurate in its predictions.

There were two main problems with this version of the model. First, and most important, there is no clear way of explaining performance on the false sentences. Collins and Quillian considered three different hypotheses: (1) the contradiction hypothesis, in which search stops when a contradiction is reached; (2) the unsuccessful search hypothesis, in which search stops after a certain criterion is reached; and (3) the search and destroy hypothesis, in which search continues until all possible connections are evaluated. None gave a good account of performance.

The second main problem was that the Collins and Quillian (1969) model was proposed as a specific test of the simplest version of the model, and it made assumptions that were stricter than necessary (see Collins & Loftus, 1975). For example, although the description appears to suggest that each item is stored only once, Collins and Quillian (1969, p. 242) acknowledged there are often multiple representations and that structures may not be perfectly hierarchical.

This problem is illustrated in a study by C. Conrad (1972). She first obtained normative data on how frequently subjects produced a particular property when given a category. Properties that were mentioned by more than 50% of the subjects were called high-frequency properties; those that were mentioned by fewer than 25% of subjects were called low-frequency properties; and those that were mentioned by 25% to 50% of subjects were called moderate-frequency properties. Contrary to the predictions of the Collins and Qullian (1969) model, high-frequency properties did not show a regular increase in RT with an increase in level. Moreover, RTs were linearly related to frequency; mean RTs to high-, moderate-, and low-frequency properties were 1080, 1106, and 1140 ms, respectively. Conrad suggested that the regular linear pattern obtained by Collins and Quillian (shown in Figure 10.2) was due in part to their using high-frequency properties at Level 0, moderate-frequency properties at Level 1, and low-frequency properties at Level 2.

The Feature Overlap Model

The next major model was developed by Smith and his colleagues (Smith, Shoben, & Rips, 1974), who assumed that the meaning of a concept is not a single unit but a set of features or attributes. They posited two types of features, defining and characteristic. *Defining features* are essential, whereas *characteristic features* are typical. This relationship is not an either-or situation, however; a particular feature can be more defining or more characteristic. For example, some features of robins are that (1) they are bipeds, (2) they have wings, (3) they have red breasts, (4) they perch in trees, and (5) they are not domesticated. Feature (3) is probably the most defining, and features 1 and 5 are the least defining.

One way of obtaining evidence consistent with this idea is to have subjects rate how typical various instances of various categories are. Rips, Shoben, and Smith (1973) found that robins and sparrows were thought to be more typical birds than were chicken and geese. These judgments are consistent with the idea that subjects are using characteristic features. A more sophisticated way of representing these data is to use *multidimensional scaling*. This procedure converts similarity ratings to distance: The more similar two items are judged to be, the closer the items are when plotted. One such solution is shown in Figure 10.3. Note that goose, duck, and chicken are close together (they are similar) but are far away from robin and sparrow. Notice also that these three birds are closer (more similar) to the concept of an animal than to the concept of a bird. One implication of this view is that category membership is not all or none; rather, membership within a category is a matter of degree.

Further evidence consistent with the idea that the meaning of a concept is a set of features or attributes was reported by Rips (1975). He had subjects read a report about a fictitious island that contained several kinds of animals: geese, ducks, eagles, hawks, robins, sparrows, ostriches, and bats. As can be seen in Figure 10.3, the first three pairs are widely spaced, but each item in the pair is close to the other item. Subjects were told that

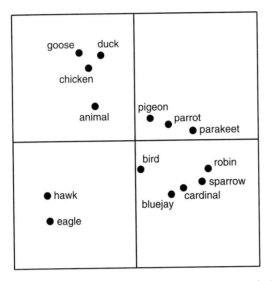

Figure 10.3   A multidimensional scaling solution for birds.
SOURCE: From "Semantic Distance and the Verification of Semantic
Relations," by L. J. Rips, E. J. Shoben, and E. E. Smith, 1973, *Journal of Verbal
Learning and Verbal Behavior, 12*, 1–20. Copyright © 1973 Academic Press,
Inc. Reprinted with permission.

one species had been diagnosed with a contagious disease, and they were asked to estimate the percentages of other animals that also had the disease. The results are shown in
Table 10.1. The species closest to the infected bird in Figure 10.3 was the species with the
highest estimated infection rate. As the species became more distant, the predicted infection rate decreased.

Rips's (1975) study is important because it provides converging evidence. Although
he used different subjects and a very different task, the results are consistent with those
from the multidimensional scaling procedure. This is called *converging evidence*, because
both sets of results converge, or point to the same answer (Garner, Hake, & Ericksen,
1956). Furthermore, it shows how information in generic memory can affect performance
on other tasks.

Table 10.1   Estimated rates of infection for five species when told that a sixth species was infected

Infected Species	Estimated Percent Infection Rate					
	Goose	Duck	Robin	Sparrow	Hawk	Eagle
Goose	—	**74**	17	18	16	13
Duck	81	—	18	18	43	35
Robin	26	30	—	**79**	35	41
Sparrow	32	27	**66**	—	49	43
Hawk	40	27	27	29	—	63
Eagle	17	16	26	29	72	—

NOTE: The boldface figures are for birds that are most similar to the infected species.
SOURCE: Based on Rips (1975).

Experiment   *Typicality Effects and Inferences*

Purpose: To demonstrate how typicality can affect inferences

Subjects: Thirty-six subjects are recommended.

Materials: Table 10.1 lists six of the eight animals needed; ostrich and bat should also be included. You will also need an answer sheet on which subjects can write their responses. This answer sheet should have all eight animal names in a different random order for each subject.

Procedure: Inform the subjects that in this experiment they will be asked to make estimates of how many animals from various species are infected by a particular disease. One-sixth of the subjects should be given sparrow as the infected species, one-sixth should be given robin, and so forth. No subjects are told that bat or ostrich is infected.

Instructions: "Imagine an island has been discovered that contains eight different species of animals. These are listed on your answer sheet. Scientists have found that the [name of infected bird]s are infected with a contagious disease. We would like you to estimate how many of the other animals are likely to be infected. On your answer sheet, please write down a number from 0% to 100% to indicate how many of each species is likely to be infected. Any questions?"

Scoring and Analysis: For each infected species, calculate the average percent infection rate for the other five species of birds. The data should look like Table 10.1.

Optional Enhancements: Increase the number of subjects, making sure to keep an even multiple of 6. Use other types of animals, or adapt the experiment to other types of materials.

SOURCE: Based on an experiment by Rips (1975).

According to the *feature overlap model*, how does a person decide whether a robin is a bird? The basic processes involved are outlined in Figure 10.4. After the proposition is presented, the first process is to retrieve the list of features for both concepts. These feature lists contain both characteristic and defining features. It is assumed that the lists are organized with the most defining features listed first, with subsequent features being less defining and more characteristic. The feature lists of the two concepts in the proposition are then compared, and an overall measure of similarity or overlap, x, is computed. What happens next depends on the value of x. There are two criteria: an upper value, c_1, and a lower value, c_0. If x is greater than c_1, there is a high degree of overlap, indicating a match, and a positive response is made quickly. If x is lower than c_0, there is very little overlap, indicating a mismatch, and a negative response is made quickly. Thus, when x has extreme values, only one decision stage is necessary. If x is greater than the lower criterion but less than the upper criterion, however, there is some overlap. In this case, an immediate "false" response cannot be given, but there is not enough overlap to give an immediate "true" response. This is where the second decision stage occurs; this second stage separates the more defining features from the characteristic features. For example, although bats have several characteristic features of birds (for example, they both fly), bats have different defining features (they are mammals whereas birds are not). Comparing all features would produce an intermediate value for x, and the defining features would then be examined. This second comparison is more analytic and slower than the first, which can be thought of as more holistic.

This model can account for all the data that the Collins and Quillian (1969) hierarchical model can, as well as for several results that the former model could not. For example, subjects verify more quickly that "A robin is a bird" than "A robin is an animal."

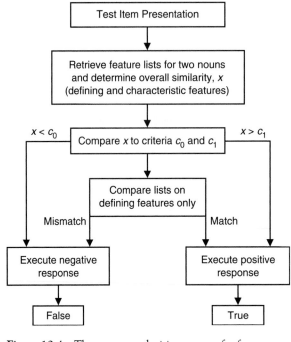

Figure 10.4   The two-stage decision process for feature comparison.   SOURCE: Smith, Shoben, & Rips (1974).

The hierarchical model says this is because there are two levels of hierarchy to travel for the second sentence, compared to only one in the first. The Smith et al. (1974) model says this is because robins share more features with the concept bird than with the concept animal. In Figure 10.3, robin is closer to bird than to animal, which indicates that there is more feature overlap between robins and birds than between robins and animals. The second finding from Collins and Quillian (1969) was that people are faster to verify sentences like "A canary can sing" than "A canary can fly." In the hierarchical model, this was because the properties were stored at different levels of the hierarchy. In the feature overlap model, this is explained by the ordering of features within the feature list. The most defining features are listed first, which in the case of a canary would be that it is yellow, can sing, and so forth. Farther down the list are features that are less defining, such as that it can fly and has wings. The farther down the list of features the particular property is, the longer it will take to verify the sentence.

The feature overlap model has two major advantages. It can handle false responses, which occur when the feature overlap between two concepts is very small. But even more important, it can handle different kinds of false responses. For example, subjects more quickly indicate that the proposition "Magnesium is an animal" is false than the proposition "A tree is an animal" (Collins & Quillian, 1970). This is because animals and trees are both living things and will have some features in common, whereas magnesium is inanimate.

The model is not without problems, the most important of which concerns the distinction between defining and characteristic features. A concept such as triangle has defining features: a three-sided, closed figure whose interior angles add to 180°. If a shape has these features, it is a triangle; if it does not, then it is not a triangle. For nontechnical concepts, though—the ones people use every day (furniture, cars, tools)—there is no such thing as a defining feature. This problem, well known in philosophy (Wittgenstein, 1953), is illustrated by asking subjects to answer a simple question: Can you name one feature that all games have in common? For every suggestion, one can easily find a game for which the feature is not true or can find something that has that feature but is not a game. The feature overlap model requires a distinction between characteristic and defining features in order to have two stages, but the distinction is probably not valid for the majority of concepts.

A second problem is that the feature overlap model restricts the kind of information that can be brought to bear on a task. Because the key decision processes are based only on feature comparison, other sources of knowledge are excluded from the categorization process. For example, another task commonly used to uncover the properties of generic memory is called *production frequency*. Here, subjects are either given a category name and asked to name an example, or given an example and asked to name the category. Depending on which item is given first, different results occur. Loftus (1973) found, for example, that although insect is often mentioned as the category for butterfly, butterfly is rarely mentioned as an example of an insect. The problem for the feature overlap model is how to explain these differences when the same set of features is recruited for each comparison.

Collins and Loftus's Spreading Activation Model

Collins and Loftus (1975) proposed a revision of the basic hierarchical model to take into account the problematic findings for both models described so far. The key idea, expanded and clarified from earlier versions, is that activation spreads from one or two concepts to all related concepts. The main differences between this model and the earlier versions are that implied or suggested constraints are explicitly disavowed. For example, the *spreading activation model* (1) is not strictly hierarchical or, to phrase the same idea slightly differently, relaxes the notion of cognitive economy so that some concepts can be represented multiple times; (2) has links between concepts that have differential travel time; and (3) explicitly allows activation to spread from both category and exemplar nodes.

Collins and Loftus list 13 assumptions about the spreading activation model's operation, including the following:

> **Assumption 1.** When a concept is processed, activation spreads out along all paths; the strength of the activation decreases as the number of paths increases.
> **Assumption 2.** Only one concept can be processed at a time, but once processed, activation can spread in parallel.
> **Assumption 3.** Activation decreases over time and/or activity.
> **Assumption 5.** The more properties two concepts have in common, the more links there are between the concepts. For example, most vehicles are very similar, so they will have many interconnecting links, but most red things share only one feature (color) and so will have very few links (see Figure 10.5).
> **Assumption 8.** The decision process requires enough evidence to exceed a positive or negative criterion. Evidence comes from examining intersections, points where activation links from different sources meet.

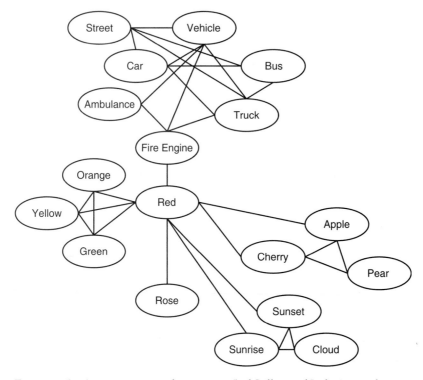

Figure 10.5   A representation of assumption 5 of Collins and Loftus's spreading activation model.   SOURCE: Collins & Loftus (1975).

Assumptions 9 through 13 detail the types of positive and negative evidence available. Intersections that involve a superordinate category, properties that match, exclusive subordinates (such as male and female), and counterexamples are all types of evidence that can be used to render a decision, either positive or negative.

Chang (1986) compared the hierarchical model and the spreading activation model in the following way: "As easy as it was to falsify the hierarchical-network model, it is just as difficult to disprove the present spreading-activation theory; but, at the same time, as easy as it was to [generate] empirical implications of the earlier model, it is just as difficult at present to derive unequivocal predictions [of the revised model]" (p. 217). Because of these problems, the Collins and Loftus (1975) version is probably best viewed as a framework rather than as a precise, testable model, and for that reason we do not provide a detailed analysis of its predictions about verifying propositions. We will examine this model in more detail in the section comparing its account of association priming with the account offered by compound cue theories.

Spreading activation quickly became the dominant explanation for theories of generic memory (Anderson, 1983a), as well as word production (Dell, 1986) and word perception (McClelland & Rumelhart, 1981; Rumelhart & McClelland, 1982). Indeed, connectionist models, which have been applied to numerous areas in psychology, can be thought of as spreading activation models. Although each of these versions is more specific and detailed than the original proposal, each is based on the same idea.

Knowing That You Don't Know

Before continuing with a discussion of the core feature of spreading activation, it is worthwhile to pause and consider how people decide that they do not know something. There has been relatively little work on this area compared to research on what people do know. For example, all of the models discussed so far have emphasized how people respond "true" or "false," with no option for a "don't know" response.

One notable exception is a series of experiments reported by Glucksberg and McCloskey (1981). In their first experiment, they had subjects memorize a set of sentences—for example, "John has a pencil. John doesn't have a shovel. Bill has a bowl. Bill doesn't have a magazine." After learning these sentences, subjects were given a variety of questions that could be answered "true," "false," or "don't know." The true sentences were the same as the studied sentences, whereas the false sentences contradicted some aspect of a studied sentence (such as "John doesn't have a pencil" or "Bill has a magazine"). The don't-know sentences contained names and objects that had been studied but in new combinations ("Bill has a pencil" or "John doesn't have a magazine"). Subjects were asked to decide true, false, or don't know as fast as they could.

Subjects took 1596 ms to correctly respond "true" to true test items and 1688 ms to correctly respond "false" to false items, but they required only 1337 ms to correctly respond "don't know." An analysis of errors illustrated the same pattern: Subjects made about 12% errors on true items and 12% errors on false items, but only 2% errors on don't-know items. People can thus be both faster and more accurate in saying they don't know than in responding with what they do know.

Glucksberg and McCloskey's (1981) second experiment tested an interesting idea. They hypothesized that people will take more time to respond "don't know" if they have explicitly stored the fact that they don't know something than if they have not explicitly stored that fact. The design was similar to the previous experiment, except that some sentences contained information about what was not known (such as "It is unknown whether John has a chair"). An explicit don't-know test item might be "John has a chair" or "John doesn't have a chair," whereas an implicit don't-know test item would be the same as in the previous experiment. The results are shown in Table 10.2. When the subjects had explicit knowledge that the information was not known, it took them longer to respond and they were less accurate than when they did not have explicit knowledge about their lack of information.

Glucksberg and McCloskey (1981) suggested that don't-know decisions are made by a two-stage process. First, the subject examines whether there are any relevant facts about the question. If there are none, then a quick "don't know" response is made. If

Table 10.2   Mean response time and mean error rate for true, false, explicitly stored uncertain, and not stored uncertain test items

	True	False	Explicit DK	Implicit DK
Response Time (ms)	1888	2093	1892	1594
Error Rate (%)	4.8	7.3	4.0	1.4

Source: Data from Glucksberg & McCloskey (1981).

there is some information available, a more detailed examination of the facts takes place (the second stage). If the information is still not sufficient to answer the question, then a slow "don't know" response is made.

Priming

Spreading activation can be reduced to one main finding: priming. Unfortunately, the term *priming* can refer to at least two different effects. In Chapter 7, we examined *repetition priming* in conjunction with implicit memory: The processing of something a second time benefits from having processed it previously. A second type of priming is *association priming*—the observation that response times are often faster if a second item is related to or associated with the first item. Thus, in repetition priming the target item is processed twice, whereas in association priming the target item is processed only once.

To give a specific example of association priming, in one experiment two strings of letters were shown, one above the other. If both were valid words, the subject was to respond "yes." If one or both strings were not words, the subject was to respond "no." The results are shown in Table 10.3.

Subjects responded approximately 85 ms faster when both strings were related words (*nurse-doctor, bread-butter*) than when they were unrelated (*doctor-butter, bread-nurse*) (Meyer & Schvaneveldt, 1971). Spreading activation models provide a simple explanation: As the first word is read, the relevant concept is activated. Activation spreads to related concepts, so that by the time the second word is read, its relevant concept is already partially active. This saves time in processing the second item and produces a decrease in response time. When the first string was a nonword, response times were also fast, but this was a result of the task: There is no need to process the second string if the first one gives sufficient information to answer the question. Subjects were slowest when the first string was a word and the second was a nonword.

CogLab Experiment
http://coglab.wadsworth.com/experiments/LexicalDecision/

Priming can also be seen when the stimuli are more complex than single words. For example, Ashcraft (1976) demonstrated priming with topics. Sentences that involved high-frequency properties, such as "A sparrow has feathers," were verified in approximately 1330 ms. If a second sentence followed on the same topic, such as "A robin can fly," response times decreased to approximately 1200 ms, indicating priming.

Table 10.3   Mean response times showing association priming

Top String	Bottom String	Example	Mean RT	% Errors
word	associated word	nurse-doctor	855	6.3
word	unassociated word	nurse-butter	940	8.7
word	nonword	bread-marb	1087	27.6
nonword	word	besk-doctor	904	7.8
nonword	nonword	besk-marb	884	2.6

Source: Data from Meyer & Schvaneveldt (1971).

Neely (1977) demonstrated that expectations can affect priming, using a lexical decision task. Subjects were asked to judge as quickly and as accurately as they could whether a target was a word or a nonword. (We will ignore the responses to nonwords; they were there primarily to keep the subjects honest.) In one condition, subjects were told that if the first word (the prime) was *bird*, then the second word (target) would be a type of bird. These subjects might see *bird* followed by *robin*. In a second condition, subjects were told that if the prime was *body*, then the target would be a building part. These subjects might see *body* followed by *door*. Neely also manipulated two other variables. One is called *stimulus onset asynchrony*, or SOA. This is simply the amount of time between the presentation of the first item and the presentation of the second: An SOA of 0 ms means the two items are presented simultaneously; an SOA of 2000 ms means presentation of the second item began 2 seconds after the presentation of the first item began. The final variable was whether the prime-target relationship was as advertised: Subjects who were expecting *bird-robin* might occasionally see *bird-arm*; subjects who were expecting a category shift (*body-door*) might occasionally see *body-arm*.

The results are shown in Figure 10.6, in terms of the amount of facilitation or inhibition compared with baseline performance. Baseline performance is simply the time taken to respond when the prime was XXX rather than a word. The left panel of Figure 10.6 shows the results for subjects who were not expecting a category shift: The open circles represent trials in which no shift occurred, and the closed squares represent trials in which a shift did

Figure 10.6   The left panel shows what happens when subjects expect a bird-related target to follow the cue *bird*, which is a preexisting relation. When subjects see the expected target, priming occurs at both short and long SOAs. When subjects see an unexpected target, there is neither facilitation nor inhibition at short SOAs, but inhibition increases as the SOA increases. The right panel shows what happens when subjects expect a building-part related target to follow the cue *body*, a relation that does not normally exist. When the expected target occurs, there is no priming at short SOAs, but priming emerges as the SOA increases. When subjects see an unexpected target that has a preexisting relation (e.g., *heart*), priming is seen at short SOAs but not at long SOAs.   SOURCE: Based on data from Neely (1977).

occur. The right panel shows the results for subjects who were expecting a category shift. At the shortest SOA, there is priming for semantically related items (*bird-robin* and *body-heart*). However, as the SOA increases, the subject's expectations come into play: *bird-robin* priming continues (left panel), but *body-heart* priming disappears (right panel). Neither *bird-arm* nor *body-robin* shows priming; indeed, as the SOA increases, inhibition increases. Neither group expected this pairing, and both pairs contain unrelated words. The final data come from the *body-door* group in the right panel. These subjects were expecting this relationship, but they show no priming with short SOAs. Because priming here is dependent on expectations, it takes some time to be observable; by 2000 ms SOA, *body* primes *door* (when expected) as well as *bird* primes *robin*.

These results are consistent with the idea that priming involves at least two components. First, there is an automatic component that is independent of the subject's intentions or expectations. This is seen in Neely's (1977) data when related items, such as *body-heart*, show priming at short SOAs even though the subject was not expecting this relationship. The second component is more strategic and reflects the subject's expectations. Thus, *body* can prime *door*, but only after a relatively long SOA; no priming is seen at short SOAs. Most models focus on the automatic aspect, because it is more likely to yield information about the basic structure of generic memory than is the intentional component, which reflects strategies the subject is currently using. It should be noted that further research (Neely, Keefe, & Ross, 1989) has revealed that the process is more complex than described here.

Spreading activation models are so dominant today that many people use the terms *priming* and *activation* as synonyms (Ratcliff & McKoon, 1988). Indeed, the concept of activation is so well accepted that it is widely used in other areas of research. For example, one current view of immediate memory uses activation and decay of activation as the key theoretical idea (see Chapter 4). Immediate memory, according to this view, is that portion of permanent knowledge that is in a heightened state of activation. Because only a very small fraction of information in memory can be active at one time, these views also need to posit some mechanism or process, usually decay, that can deactivate it.

The most fundamental findings that support a spreading activation approach are the association priming data discussed above. These results are widely considered to be the most direct evidence possible: All the subject is required to do is process one word after processing a related item. According to spreading activation, as the first word is read, the relevant concept is activated. Activation spreads to related concepts, so that by the time the second word is read, its relevant concept is already partially active.

If the spreading activation account of association priming is called into question, then spreading activation as a general concept, in theories of both immediate and generic memory, can also be called into question. Compound cue theory, a more recent explanation of association priming, does indeed call into question the fundamental assumption of spreading activation theory.

Alternatives to Spreading Activation

One relatively recent competitor to spreading activation is a class of models known as *compound cue models* (Dosher & Rosedale, 1989; Ratcliff & McKoon, 1988). The basic idea is that instead of selecting items that have been activated by spreading activation, generic memory functions more the way other forms of memory function. Ratcliff and McKoon's (1988; McKoon & Ratcliff, 1992) model, for example, is based on a process similar to that used by SAM (Gillund & Shiffrin, 1984; see the optional chapter at the end of this book), which is designed to explain both free recall and recognition data. However, Ratcliff and McKoon point out that two other models (also discussed in the optional chapter)—MINERVA 2 (Hintzman, 1986) and TODAM (Murdock, 1982)—can both implement the main idea.

In SAM (Gillund & Shiffrin, 1984), items in memory are represented as images. An *image* is an interconnected feature set that contains information about (1) the context in which the item was learned, (2) the item itself (its meaning, name, and so forth), and (3) its relation with other images. In a memory test, the subject assembles a set of cues in short-term memory and then uses these to probe various images in long-term memory. In a recognition test, the result of this probe, called *familiarity*, is used to decide whether to respond "old" or "new."

For normal recognition, the SAM model assumes that the subject uses several pieces of information to judge whether the target is an old item or a new item. Recognition tests usually involve asking whether the subject recognizes a word as one that has appeared during a specific period of time (for example, was the word on the preceding list?). One factor used by SAM is the strength of the association between the target item and context. A second factor is the strength of the association between the target item and other items. For example, during study, two words may have been rehearsed together, and so they become associated. The familiarity of an item on a recognition test, then, depends on the strength of the associations between the cues used and the target item and on the strength of the association between the target item and other items in memory.

In a typical priming study that uses a lexical decision test, one target is shown, and the subject is asked to decide whether it is a valid word. According to compound cue theory as incorporated in SAM, the difference between this test and a recognition test is that there are two cues (the prime and the target) rather than just one (the recognition probe). The model now adds a third type of association, the strength of the association between the prime and other items in memory, to the two already mentioned (the association between the target and the context and the association between the target and other items in memory). The resulting familiarity value will be a combination of the familiarity to both items that form the compound.

The main finding to be explained is why responses to *nurse* are faster when it is preceded by *doctor* than when it is preceded by an unrelated prime such as *butter*. According to compound cue theory, the reason is that the prime and the target have a large number associates in common. A large number of common associates produces a higher level of familiarity than if the prime and target have very few associates in common.

Compound cue theory, as implemented in SAM, produces a number that corresponds to a familiarity, in contrast to lexical decision tasks as measured using RT. To convert familiarity to RT, Ratcliff and McKoon (1988) used the diffusion model (Ratcliff, 1978; see the optional chapter for a detailed description). This model converts high values of familiarity to fast and accurate positive ("yes") response times, low values of familiarity to fast and accurate negative ("no") response times, and intermediate values to slower and less accurate positive and negative response times.

Comparing Spreading Activation and Compound Cue Theory

Although relatively few studies directly compare predictions of spreading activation models and compound cue models, some differences have been noted. The compound cue model referred to below is described more completely by Ratcliff and McKoon (1988, 1995b), and a spreading activation account is described by McNamara (1992a, 1992b).

Priming   *Spreading activation* models account for association priming by assuming that activation spreads from one concept to related concepts; the more directly related the concept is, the more priming will occur. *Compound cue theory* accounts for association priming by assuming that both the prime and the target form a compound cue; because they have associates in common, there is more familiarity. There is no such thing as activation within compound cue theory.

Priming Onset   Priming onset refers to how quickly priming is evident. Early versions of spreading activation theories (Collins & Quillian, 1969; Collins & Loftus, 1975) assumed that the onset of priming was a function of the number of intervening concepts, or links. These models predict that priming should take longer to see for *canary-animal* than *canary-bird*. (Do not confuse priming with sentence verification. In priming, subjects respond whether the target is a word or not. Responses to the target are facilitated when the prime is associated with it, compared to when the prime is unrelated.) The compound cue model predicts no difference in priming onset, because the same computations are performed regardless of how related the items may be. Ratcliff and McKoon (1981) varied the duration of the SOA to determine when priming was first evident and found that when words rather than sentences were used, there was no difference in response times for primes that are closer together (*canary-bird*) compared with primes that are farther apart (*canary-animal*). Spreading activation models have since been revised to account for this finding by allowing the spread of activation from concept to concept to be much faster (on the order of 5 ms per link).

Decay of Priming   As more items intervene between the prime and the target, the amount of facilitation decreases. Compound cue models account for this by having the prime replaced by the intervening item within the compound cue (Ratcliff & McKoon, 1988). Although the compound cue could include any number of items, if more than one or two nonassociated items are included, the effects of priming will be minimal. This places a limit on the model's prediction of how long the target can be delayed and still show priming. If priming is seen after ten intervening items, for example, compound cue theory is disproven. Spreading activation models, in contrast, typically have activation decrease as a function of time (Anderson, 1983b; McClelland & Rumelhart, 1981). There is nothing within the structure of these models that places a limit on how many intervening items can occur.

Multiple Meanings   There is evidence that when an ambiguous word is presented, both meanings are primed immediately, but only the appropriate meaning remains primed (Swinney, 1979). For example, the word *bank* can refer to a place where money is kept or to the side of a river; the word *bug* can refer to an insect or to a covert listening device. Spreading activation explains this priming effect by assuming that decay of activation occurs to both meanings; the "correct" meaning is kept active, however, by activation from other words compatible with the context of the sentence. The compound cue model states that no decay occurs, because no activation occurs; rather, a compound cue that contains an ambiguous word will give a high value of familiarity. When the ambiguous word is replaced in the cue by a later word, then only the appropriate meaning will have a high familiarity value.

Mediated Priming   Mediated priming refers to priming seen when two items that are unrelated (*lion* and *stripes*) can become related by a third, mediating item (here, *tiger*). According to spreading activation models, activation spreads from *lion* to *stripes* via the mediating link of *tiger*. *Lion* and *tiger* are related, and *tiger* and *stripes* are related. Compound cue theories posit that no mediation is necessary. If the two components in the compound are sufficiently familiar, then there will be priming. One measure related to familiarity should be co-occurrence: how often two words are experienced together. McKoon and Ratcliff (1992) showed that mediated priming (*lion-stripes*, presumably mediated by *tiger*) resulted in as much facilitation as nonmediated priming of words that co-occur frequently (*deer-grain*, where no obvious item associated with deer is also related to grain). Much ongoing work is currently examining mediated priming, but both views can predict the basic effect.

Strengths and Weaknesses   Given that both views are consistent with the main data, which is the better explanation? Currently, spreading activation is still the most widely accepted view of how information in generic memory is retrieved. One reason is its intuitive appeal: The basic idea of spreading activation captures the introspection of how one word or idea can lead to another.

The main weakness of the spreading activation view is its lack of specificity. Most versions (one exception is Anderson, 1983a) are so vague that it is difficult to derive a strong, a priori prediction (see Chang, 1986). Related to this is a logical problem (see Ratcliff & McKoon, 1994). Suppose each word has 20 other words associated with it; this assumption is reasonable, given data on word association norms (Postman & Keppel, 1970). Presenting one prime would activate 20 words, and each of those would activate another 20. If activation is allowed to spread, as is required to explain mediated priming (McNamara & Altarriba, 1988), then each of these 400 active words would activate another 20. From one prime, 8000 words are now active, roughly an eighth of the words that the typical adult English speaker knows. McNamara (1992b) has demonstrated mediated priming with four items (for example, *mane-stripes*, presumably mediated by *lion* and *tiger*). According to the account of mediated priming offered by spreading activation theories, 32,000 words are now active, approximately half of the typical English speaker's vocabulary.

Compound cue theory has two major advantages. First, it is better specified, in the equations that describe the processes, than spreading activation models are. Researchers easily agree on the predictions that it makes, and these predictions can be made before the experiment. Second, it uses the mechanisms and processes of the global memory models (see the optional chapter), and so relates memory performance from generic memory to performance on recall and recognition tasks.

Compound cue theory also has two main problems. First, the rules for determining which items will form a compound cue are not yet well specified. Second, there is some question about the accuracy of one of its predictions. The words *spider* and *ant* are related, but they are not associated. In other words, when people are asked to say the first thing that comes into their head when they hear the word *spider*, they do not say *ant*. Compound cue theory predicts that priming should occur because of the semantic relatedness, but some researchers (Shelton & Martin, 1992) have found no priming, whereas others (McKoon & Ratcliff, 1992) have found priming. It remains unclear how to interpret these mixed results.

How Is Generic Memory Organized?

Despite its apparent simplicity, the answer to the question of how generic memory is organized is likely to be complex, elusive, and a long way off. Categories can be organized at different levels of abstraction, some very broad (furniture), some less broad (chair), and some quite specific (rocking chair). These have been termed (respectively) *superordinate*, *basic*, and *subordinate level categories* (Rosch & Mervis, 1975). What is particularly intriguing is that basic level categories (chair, dog, car) seem to be learned first, are the level at which objects are named, and show remarkable cross-cultural consistency (Rosch, Mervis, Gray, Johnson, & Bayes-Braem, 1976). Basic level categories are neither the most inclusive nor the most specific, but they do seem to have a special status relative to other levels of categorization.

The idea that concepts are organized by similarity has intuitive appeal. People seem to group many things together on the basis of shared perceptual qualities. However, as Medin (1989) has argued, rather than being organized by similarity, concepts are organized around theories. According to this view (Murphy & Medin, 1985), the relationship between a concept and an example of that concept is similar to the relationship between theory and data. An example must have the right explanatory relationship to the concept, not merely be similar. We will examine this idea further by focusing on one particular area of research.

One currently popular approach is to examine people who have deficits in particular aspects of generic memory: They can identify certain types of items but have difficulty identifying other items. One early suggestion was that generic memory might be organized by categories, such as animate versus inanimate things.

Warrington and Shallice (1984) described four people who had recovered from herpes encephalitis but who had sustained both left and right temporal lobe damage. In one task, two subjects were asked to identify pictures of living things and nonliving things; in another task, they heard a word and were asked to provide a definition. The results are shown in Table 10.4. For example, when asked to define *ostrich*, JBR responded with "unusual." When asked to define *wasp*, SBY responded with "bird that flies." Even though these subjects were not perfect in identifying or defining all nonliving things, their perfor-

Table 10.4 Performance by two subjects with damage to both left and right temporal lobes on two generic memory tasks

Subject	Living Things		Nonliving Things
		Picture identification	
JBR	6%		90%
SBY	0%		75%
		Spoken word definition	
JBR	8%		79%
SBY	0%		52%

NOTE: Although subjects' ability to identify and define living things is grossly impaired, their ability to identify and define nonliving things is relatively intact.

SOURCE: Based on data from Warrington & Shallice (1984).

mance was much better than for living things. Similar results have been reported by other investigators (De Renzi & Lucchelli, 1994; Farah, McMullen, & Meyer, 1991; Pietrini et al., 1988; Sartori, Miozzo, & Job, 1993).

One tempting conclusion is that generic memory organizes information about living things and nonliving things differently, such that it is possible to sustain damage to one area but have the other area relatively intact. Such a simple principle quickly became more complicated, however, because there were subtypes that did not fit in with these categories. For example, De Renzi and Lucchelli (1994) reported that their subject, Felicia, had only mild impairment for naming body parts, which technically are living, but had severe impairment for professions, which are clearly not animate. Similarly, performance showed impairment for food items, of which some are living (fruits and vegetables) and others nonliving (soft drinks, spaghetti, ice cream). Thus, Warrington and Shallice (1984; Warrington & McCarthy, 1983) suggested that the relevant difference was actually based on different properties. In general, visual features are of greater importance in discriminating living things, whereas function (what it does) is more important for discriminating nonliving things.

Farah and McClelland (1991) explored this idea by constructing a simulation model and then lesioning the part of the model responsible for visual features in generic memory. The basic architecture of the model is shown in Figure 10.7. In this model, generic memory consists of two different types of knowledge: visual and functional. Input to the system can be either verbal (such as hearing a word) or visual (such as seeing a picture).

What is most intriguing are the results from simulations in which Farah and McClelland damaged part of the model. They removed the visual component of generic memory by altering the weights on the connections or, in some cases, by disconnecting

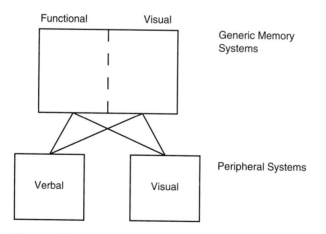

Figure 10.7   A schematic representation of the Farah and McClelland parallel distributed processing model of generic memory.   SOURCE: From "A Computational Model of Semantic Memory Impairment," by M. J. Farah and J. L. McClelland, 1991, *Journal of Experimental Psychology: General, 120,* 339–357. Copyright © 1991 American Psychological Association. Reprinted with permission.

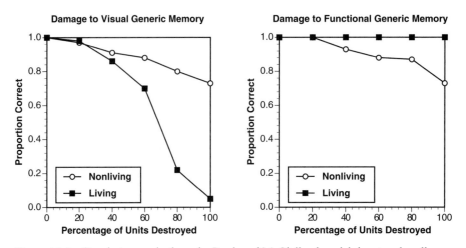

Figure 10.8 Simulation results from the Farah and McClelland model showing the effects of damaging increasing proportions of visual generic memory (left panel) or functional generic memory (right panel). SOURCE: From "A Computational Model of Semantic Memory Impairment," by M. J. Farah and J. L. McClelland, 1991, *Journal of Experimental Psychology: General, 120,* 339–357. Copyright © 1991 American Psychological Association. Reprinted with permission.

the units entirely. As the left panel of Figure 10.8 shows, when visual generic memory is damaged, performance for nonliving things declines only slightly, whereas performance for living things declines to almost 0. This pattern is similar to that seen in Table 10.4. When visual generic memory is left intact and functional generic memory is damaged, there is no deficit apparent for living things and only a slight loss for nonliving things. This is also what subjects show (De Renzi & Lucchelli, 1994).

The results of the simulation are consistent with the organizational scheme proposed by Warrington and Shallice (1984). They do not, of course, prove that the scheme is correct, or that it is the only way of organizing information. Rather, they serve as an existence proof. Can a generic memory system that distinguishes between visual or perceptual information and functional information give rise to the sorts of deficits seen in subjects with bilateral temporal lobe damage? The answer is yes, but with qualifications.

The sensory/functional view can capture the broad pattern, but it fails to produce some deficits that are very fine grained. For example, Hillis and Caramazza (1991) described two patients, PS and JJ, who had contrasting deficits: PS showed a pervasive deficit in processing animal terms, whereas JJ showed a pervasive deficit in processing all categories tested except for animals. In both cases, processing for animals, rather than all living things, was the exception. As another example, Hart, Berndt, and Caramazza (1985) described a patient, MD, whose deficit was limited to naming fruits and vegetables. This distinction cannot be captured by the sensory/functional view.

Although deficits in processing certain types of information from generic memory may suggest how it is organized, there is still no definitive view, and it is likely that this controversy will persist. Nonetheless, it is suggestive that many of the deficits described in a recent review by Caramazza, Hillis, Leek, and Miozzo (1994) correspond to basic level categories (discussed at the beginning of this section).

Capacity and Acquisition

We began this chapter with two opposing viewpoints expressed by two fictional geniuses. It turns out that Nero Wolfe is better informed than Sherlock Holmes. Two series of experiments by Voss and his colleagues (Chiesi, Spilich, & Voss, 1979; Spilich, Vesonder, Chiesi, & Voss, 1979) illustrate the point. Using the criterion of baseball knowledge, subjects were divided into two groups: those with a lot of knowledge about baseball and those with very little. All subjects heard a fictional account of half an inning of a baseball game. Subjects with more knowledge of baseball remembered more of the specific details, provided a more organized response, and included more details relevant to the outcome of the game than did those subjects with less knowledge. Finally, high-knowledge subjects were able to predict the outcome better than low-knowledge subjects were. Existing knowledge, then, allows people to interpret new information, provides structures that add meaning to events, and enables people to make predictions. The more you know about something, the easier it is to acquire new related information; in that sense, the more you know, the more you can know.

There are at least two different ideas about how generic memory develops. One simple notion might be that as new information is received, it is categorized, labeled, and assigned to the relevant location within generic memory (placed at the appropriate level of the hierarchy in Collins and Quillian's structural model, or entered with appropriate connections in spreading activation models). This structure and set of connections can be quite different from that which supports episodic memory. This view predicts that there should be differences between episodic and generic memory, and such dissociations have been found. However, as discussed in Chapter 7, this view is as yet unable to predict the precise nature of the dissociations and has a difficult time accounting for dissociations within one system.

A quite different explanation is offered by *MINERVA2* (Hintzman, 1986; see the optional chapter at the end of this book). In this model, only episodic traces are stored, with each new episode producing a new trace. Generic memory results from parallel activation of all episodic traces, with the generic information being abstracted from the summed responses of those traces that are most strongly activated by the cue. If a compound cue mechanism is added (see Ratcliff & McKoon, 1988), then MINERVA2 can account easily and parsimoniously for both episodic (recall and recognition) and generic (priming, schemas, and abstractions) memory within a single system. All dissociations, according to this view, arise from different processing requirements, because the same memory system is supporting both types of memory performance.

As this chapter has shown, people's knowledge is complex and richly organized, and its retrieval is wonderfully fast. It is the ability to draw on this resource that distinguishes human cognitive capabilities from those of other animals or machines. We will examine the functions of knowledge in other memory situations in more detail in Chapter 12, especially where they lead to systematic biases in what people perceive, encode, and recall.

Chapter Summary

Most explanations of generic memory rely on concept, a mental representation of something, and proposition, a relationship between two concepts that has a truth value. Collins and Quillian's hierarchical model used the principle of cognitive economy, storing each concept as few times as possible. The model assumed it took time to traverse the network and to retrieve property information. Its major problems were in explaining how people decide a sentence is false and in overly strict assumptions that did not allow for multiple representations and nonhierarchical structures. The feature overlap model distinguished between defining features, those that are essential, and characteristic features, those that are typical. Propositions are compared by evaluating the similarity of the features. Although it accounted well for data that the hierarchical model could not explain, the feature overlap model ran into problems with the very idea of defining features.

Spreading activation models assume that when a concept is accessed, its activation level increases and also spreads to related concepts. These models explain association priming by suggesting that activation from processing the prime spreads to the related target so that by the time the target is read, its relevant concepts is already partially active. An alternative account, compound cue theory, attributes the result to the same processes that explain recognition memory.

It is not yet clear exactly how generic memory is organized or whether there is a limit on the amount of knowledge that a person can store and retrieve. The data that we do have suggest that the more you know about something, the easier it is to acquire new related information.

Imagery

Any single Circumstance of what we have formerly seen often raises up a whole Scene of Imagery.

—Joseph Addison

Scientific research on imagery is a relatively recent development, primarily because of the emphasis that behaviorists placed on overt behavior. Imagery, by its very nature, is internal, and asking subjects about their images seemed exactly like introspection. Because introspection as a method of inquiry had been shown to have a "dismal record of failure" in psychology (Bower & Clapper, 1989, p. 245), research on imagery was out of the provenance of respectable psychologists. In the late 1960s, this attitude began to change as several researchers demonstrated that imagery could be studied objectively without recourse to introspection.

Analog Versus Propositional Representations

One common definition of a *proposition* is that it is the smallest unit of knowledge that has a truth value. Propositions are usually represented as English sentences (at least in English-speaking countries), but they are not necessarily tied to language. Rather, a proposition is a basic unit of meaning that is either true or false and cannot be made any smaller without losing its truth value. For example, a proposition might be "Chicago is

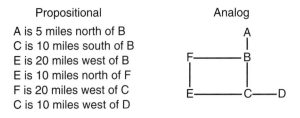

Propositional

A is 5 miles north of B
C is 10 miles south of B
E is 20 miles west of B
E is 10 miles north of F
F is 20 miles west of C
C is 10 miles west of D

Analog

Figure 11.1   A comparison of a propositional and an analog way of representing the same information about the distances between six cities

north of Indianapolis" or "A robin has wings." No part of these propositions can be removed and still leave the proposition with a truth value.

An *analog* form of representation, by contrast, is one that preserves the structure of the original information in a more or less direct manner. A map is a good example of an analog form of representation; a map preserves the spatial structure of the actual physical environment but changes many other aspects of the information. It is often convenient to use a picture as an illustration of an analog form of representation. Just as propositions are not English sentences, analog representations are not pictures. What is important is that some aspect of the physical structure is represented in an accurate way in a more or less direct manner.

A good way to see the difference between an analog and a propositional form of representation is to compare the way the same information might look in each format. In Figure 11.1, both forms contain information about the relationships between six cities. In this example, most people would prefer the analog form to the propositional form because it is more readily useful for the purpose of navigating. For some forms of information, a propositional code might be more useful, whereas for other forms of information, an analog form might be more useful.

The central issue in the visual imagery literature is whether results from visual imagery experiments require two forms of representation or whether a propositional form can account for all the results. Almost all theorists agree that propositional forms are needed for representing knowledge; the question is whether analog forms are needed for imagery. At a general level, it is convenient to think of verbal codes (particularly knowledge and sentences) as being represented by propositions. In this chapter, we will see that it is equally convenient to think of visual codes (particularly visual images) as analog representations.

The Dual-Task Method

In 1968, Lee Brooks reported a series of experiments in which he had subjects perform two tasks simultaneously. The logic behind the *dual-task method* (also known as the *method of interference*) is that people can perform multiple tasks simultaneously as long as the resources required do not overlap. For example, many people can walk and chew gum at the same time; however, probably nobody can chew gum and whistle at the same time. The obvious reason is that the same resources are required in the latter task (moving the mouth, tongue, and lips), whereas different resources are required in the former case (legs versus mouth). Brooks used one task that was designed to require verbal processing and a

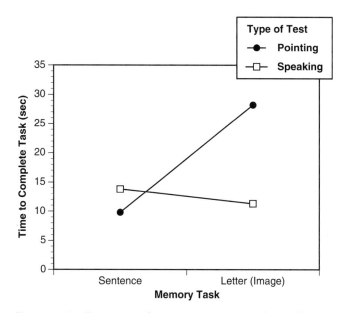

Figure 11.2   Time required to answer "yes" or "no" by speaking or pointing when the task involves processing either a sentence or an image.   SOURCE: From "Spatial and Verbal Components of the Act of Recall," by L. R. Brooks, 1968, *Canadian Journal of Psychology, 22,* 349–368. Copyright © 1968 Canadian Psychological Association. Reprinted with permission.

second task that was designed to require spatial processing. He also devised two ways of responding: One required verbal answers, and the other required the subject to point to the correct answer.

Brooks (1968) used a verbal task and a verbal response, and a spatial task and a spatial response. In the verbal task, subjects were given sentences such as "A bird in the hand is not in the bush." The task was to identify each word as being a noun (respond "yes") or not a noun (respond "no"). Responses could be either verbal (saying the answer) or spatial (pointing to the answer). For the spatial response, subjects had to point to a *Y* or an *N* printed in irregularly staggered columns on a sheet of paper. In the imagery task, the subject was asked to imagine the outline of a letter, such as the letter *F*, and then to imagine a marker beginning at the lower left and moving around the outside. At each corner, the subjects were asked to indicate if it was an extreme top or bottom corner. For the letter *F*, correct responding would be "yes," "yes," "no," "no," and so on.

The results are shown in Figure 11.2. Note that the subject had to keep either the sentence or the image of the letter in memory while performing the response. When both the task and the response mode tapped the same mode of representation (letter form and pointing, sentence and speaking), responses were slower than when the task and response mode tapped different modes of representation (letter form and speaking, sentence and pointing). These results are consistent with the idea that there are two forms of representation—one corresponding roughly to a propositional or verbal format, and the other to an analog or spatial format. In his original report, Brooks (1968) included several other experiments to eliminate other possible explanations of the data.

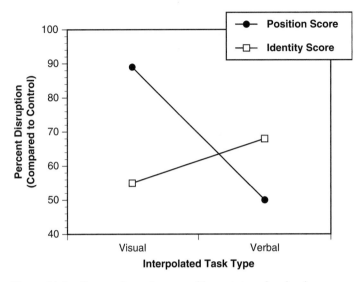

Figure 11.3   Percent disruption caused by an interpolated task compared to no interpolated task. Position scoring indicates that the correct cells were marked as having letters, regardless of whether the letter was correct. Identity scoring indicates that the correct letters were recalled regardless of which cell they were placed in. A disruption score of 0 would mean performance was the same as in the control group; larger scores mean more disruption.   SOURCE: From "Selective Loss of Visual and Verbal Information in STM by Means of Visual and Verbal Interpolated Tasks," by K. den Heyer and B. Barrett, 1971, *Psychonomic Science, 25,* 100–102. Copyright © 1971. Reprinted by permission of Psychonomic Society Inc.

Den Heyer and Barrett (1971) replicated these results, using a paradigm in which both verbal and spatial aspects came from the same stimulus. Subjects briefly saw a grid in which several letters were placed; then, they were given one of three tasks. The first was to do nothing for 10 seconds (the control group), the second was to add several two-digit numbers, and the third was to compare three small grids and decide which was the odd one out. Then the memory test was given: The original grid was displayed again, and the subject's task was to enter the appropriate letters into the appropriate cells. Two different scores were calculated. The position score indicated how many cells were marked correctly as containing a letter, regardless of whether the letter entered was the correct one. The identity score indicated how many letters were recalled correctly, regardless of whether they were placed in the correct location.

The results are shown in Figure 11.3. The scores are shown in a measure called percent disruption. This score shows how much worse performance was in the two conditions with interpolated activity than in the control condition, in which there was no activity. A score of 0% would indicate equivalent performance; the larger the score, the more the interpolated activity disrupted performance. The pattern of results is the same as in Brooks's (1968) study: A visual interpolated task affected memory for location (measured by the position score) far more than it affected memory for specific letters (measured by the identity score). Conversely, a verbal interpolated task affected memory for specific letters far more than it affected memory for location.

Segal and Fusella (1970) found analogous results using auditory and visual stimuli: If subjects were asked to image a visual stimulus, they were worse at detecting a visual stimulus than an auditory one. Conversely, if they were asked to image an auditory stimulus, they were worse at detecting an auditory stimulus than a visual one. This is a modern demonstration of the Perky effect, named after Cheves Perky (1910). These findings are consistent with the idea of two forms of representation, propositional and analog. Much of the early theoretical work was done by Allan Paivio.

Paivio's Dual-Coding Theory

According to Paivio's (1971, 1986) *dual-coding theory,* words representing concrete objects can be encoded in two different ways, whereas words representing abstract objects can be encoded in only one way. For example, *dog* can be encoded using both a verbal code (the word itself) and a visual code (an image of a dog). The word *idea,* in contrast, probably has no visual code: What would an image of an idea look like? It may be possible to generate an image that is associated with *idea,* such as a lightbulb going on over a person's head, but that is not nearly as direct a coding as an image of a dog.

Because concrete words have two potential codes, compared to only one for abstract words, the dual-coding view predicts that concrete words should be remembered better; this is exactly what happens (Paivio, 1969). Furthermore, other things being equal, pictures are remembered better than words representing those pictures—the so-called picture *superiority effect* (Madigan, 1983; Paivio, 1971). The reason for the better performance is that two types of attributes are processed for concrete items; even if one of them fails to be useful, a second code is potentially retrievable. The benefit of concrete over abstract can

---

Experiment   *Dual-Coding Theory*

Purpose: To demonstrate the advantage for concrete words over abstract words

Subjects: Twenty subjects are recommended.

Materials: Table I in the Appendix lists 80 abstract words and 80 concrete words of approximately equal word frequency and length. For each subject, create 10 lists of concrete words and 10 lists of abstract words; each list should have 8 different words. The first 10 lists should have 5 abstract and 5 concrete lists. You will also need an answer sheet on which subjects can write their responses.

Design: Because each subject experiences both conditions, concreteness is a within-subjects factor.

Procedure: Inform the subjects that in this experiment they will be asked to learn lists of words. Read each list at a rate of 1 word every 2 seconds. Then allow 30 seconds for free recall. Give a short break after 10 lists.

Instructions: "In this experiment, I will read you a list of words, and then I would like you to write down as many as you can remember on the answer sheet. Feel free to write the words in any order you like, and feel free to guess. After you have recalled each list, the next one will begin. Any questions?"

Scoring and Analysis: For each subject, count the number of concrete words recalled and the number of abstract words recalled. A paired *t* test can be used to verify that the means are different.

Optional Enhancements: Plot the data as a function of serial position.

SOURCE: Based on an experiment by Paivio (1969).

be magnified if subjects are told to image the two objects interacting in some fashion. For example, Schnorr and Atkinson (1969) found that subjects could recall more than 80% of items when given imagery instructions, compared to about 40% when rote rehearsal instructions were used. However, imagery instructions do not have to be given for the advantage to be seen. Perhaps even more surprising, the advantage is seen in a free reconstruction-of-order test. In this test, a subject sees a list of words presented and is then given the list items in a new order. The task is to reconstruct the original presentation order. Even though all the words are given back to the subject, the concrete words are still remembered more accurately than the abstract words are (Neath, 1997).

There is a fair degree of similarity between Paivio's (1971, 1986) dual-code theory and the idea of the phonological loop and the visuo-spatial sketch pad in Baddeley's (1986; Baddeley & Hitch, 1974) working memory, as well as other proposals (Potter, 1979). The major difference between the two views is that whereas dual-coding assumes multiple memory codes that are modality specific, the other views include some more generic code common to both abstract and concrete information (Marschark, 1992).

Even with the success of dual-coding theory in accounting for these and other findings, much experimental work remained to be done to confirm the analog nature of visual imagery and to investigate further the properties of this system when engaged in more active processing of the image. Thus, studies turned away from examining the structure toward an emphasis on the function or dynamic properties of the analog form of representation.

Mental Rotation

If visual imagery is represented within an analog system that preserves the structure of the physical environment, then certain physical laws should be observed in imagery tasks. For example, if you hold a cube in your hand and rotate it 180°, the cube must first be rotated 1°, and then another 1°, and so forth. In other words, the cube has to pass through all intermediate orientations before completing the full 180°. This is a physical law in the real world. If the system representing visual information is preserving the spatial structure of the real world, as the studies by Brooks (1968) and den Heyer and Barrett (1971) suggest, then the same law should hold true when subjects image a cube rotating 180°.

CogLab Experiment
http://coglab.wadsworth.com/experiments/MentalRotation/

Note that this need not be the case. In fact, in a truly efficient system it is far quicker to simply flip the image 180° than to calculate each intervening orientation. When you ask a computer graphics program to rotate an object 180°, this is exactly what the computer does: a simple flip. To demonstrate that the imagery representation system is analog, one needs to show that an image of a rotated cube passes through all intermediate orientations.

This is exactly what Roger Shepard and his colleagues demonstrated (Cooper & Shepard, 1973; Shepard & Metzler, 1971; much of the work is reprinted in Shepard & Cooper, 1983). Shepard used objects that were made out of cubes (see Figure 11.4). Two such objects were shown, one on the left (the standard) and one on the right (the target). The subject was asked to decide if the target was the same as the standard, only rotated. Although the target was often not the same as the standard, the data of interest came

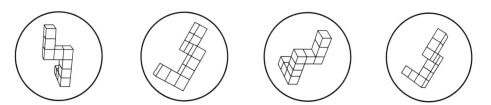

Figure 11.4   Two pairs of objects used in mental rotation studies. The subjects were shown the forms on the left and asked to decide if the form on the right was the same object, only rotated. SOURCE: From "Mental Rotation of Three-Dimensional Objects," by R. N. Shepard and J. Metzler, 1971, *Science, 171*, 701. Copyright © 1971 American Association for the Advancement of Science. Reprinted with permission.

when the target and standard were the same. In particular, Shepard was interested in how long it would take subjects to indicate that the objects were the same as a function of the degree of rotation. The results are shown in Figure 11.5.

The relationship between how far the object was rotated and the response time to decide that the two objects matched was linear, just as it would be in the real world: The further you rotate a cube in your hand, the longer it will take you, assuming the speed of rotation is constant. Notice also that it did not seem to matter which direction the rotation occurred, in either the picture plane (seeing an object rotate like the hands on a clock) or in the depth plane (seeing the top of the clock move toward you and then continue down as the bottom of the clock swings away from you and then up). Further work suggested that for a particular individual, the speed of rotation was constant (Finke, 1989).

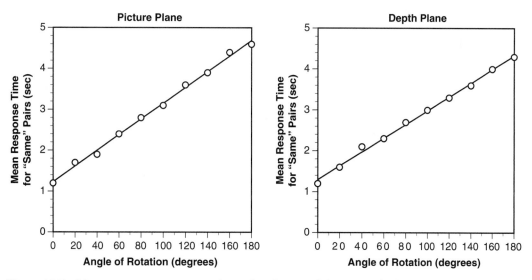

Figure 11.5   Mean response time to correctly say that the pair of objects matched as a function of the angle of rotation in degrees. The left panel shows objects that were rotated in the picture plane; the right panel shows objects that were rotated in depth.   SOURCE: From "Mental Rotation of Three-Dimensional Objects," by R. N. Shepard and J. Metzler, 1971, *Science, 171*, 701–703. Copyright © 1971 American Association for the Advancement of Science. Reprinted with permission.

Of particular interest are the reaction times for 0° and 180°. The time taken to compare the two objects when both are in the same orientation can be taken as a baseline of how long the task and response take; any extra time can be attributed to the time needed to rotate. If subjects were simply flipping the object 180°, then the response time at this angle of rotation should be quite fast; the data clearly show that it was the slowest. This finding is consistent with the idea that the subjects were rotating through all intermediate positions.

Distinguishing Propositional from Analog Representation

Kosslyn (1976) reported an experiment consistent with the idea that both propositional and analog forms of representation are available. He selected features that were either highly associated or only marginally associated with a particular object. For example, claws are highly associated with the concept of a cat, whereas heads are not highly associated, even though cats have them. In addition, one of the features was small in relation to the main object, and the other large. Kosslyn's task was to have subjects verify statements such as "Cats have claws" and "Cats have heads." He predicted that if subjects were instructed to form an image, they should respond faster to the larger feature. In an image of a cat, the head is easier to "see" than the claws. However, if subjects were not instructed to use imagery, then the subjects should respond faster to the more highly associated item. As Figure 11.6 shows, this is exactly what happened.

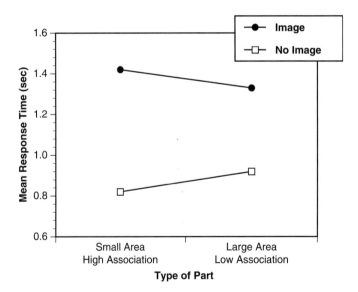

Figure 11.6   The time needed to verify a statement in which the part was either small but highly associated or large but had only a low association, as a function of instructions. Propositional theory predicts the results when no imagery instructions are given, but an analog theory better accounts for the results when imagery instructions are given.
SOURCE: 'From "Can Imagery Be Distinguished from Other Forms of Internal Representation?," by S. M. Kosslyn, 1976, Memory & Cognition, 4, p. 291–297. Copyright © 1976. Reprinted by permission of Psychonomic Society Inc.

Any theory of knowledge based on propositions would predict that subjects can retrieve information more quickly when the two concepts are highly associated than when they are less associated (Anderson, 1976). When no specific instructions are given, subjects will use a propositional form to get the answer because it is faster. Thus, subjects verified the statement "Cats have claws" faster than the statement "Cats have heads." However, when imagery instructions are given, subjects will generate an image and then answer the question based on the image. They will be able to retrieve information about a large part more quickly than a small part. Thus, subjects verified the statement "Cats have heads" faster than the statement "Cats have claws" because in the image, the head is larger than the claws.

Recall that Shepard and Metzler (1971) discovered a linear relationship between response time and degree of rotation. Kosslyn, Ball, and Reiser (1978) discovered that the same linear relationship holds for distance. They reported a study in which subjects first memorized a map of an island on which were seven objects, such as a hut, a swamp, a beach, and a well. These objects created 21 distances ranging from 2 cm to 19 cm. After subjects demonstrated that they had learned the map locations, the "mental scanning" phase of the experiment began. The subjects were asked to examine their image of the map and to focus on the named object, imagining a small speck hovering over the location. A second location was named, and the subject was asked to move the speck in a direct straight-line path and to press a button when the speck arrived at the destination. Kosslyn and his colleagues observed a linear relationship between distance scanned and response time; indeed, the correlation was 0.97.

Arguments Against Imagery

One of the most influential critics of the analog view of imagery is Zenon Pylyshyn (1973, 1979, 1981). Regardless of the outcome of the imagery debate, Pylyshyn's critiques have forced the research to become more rigorous, objective, and careful. Although his three objections are listed separately, they are not mutually exclusive, and they can operate simultaneously. Other arguments have also been offered against the need for a separate form of representation (Anderson, 1978).

One of Pylyshyn's objections is that *experimenter bias* may have determined experimental outcomes. It is well known that the expectations of the experimenter can influence how a subject responds in a particular situation (Rosenthal, 1966). For example, Intons-Peterson (1983) has shown that subtle cues provided by the experimenter can change the way the subject responds in an imagery experiment.

A second argument made by Pylyshyn is that subjects are using their tacit knowledge to guide their responses. *Tacit knowledge* is information people possess that reflects their beliefs about how things should work but that may not be verbalizable. (Tacit knowledge is often thought to be similar to implicit learning; see Chapter 7.) For example, because of interactions with the environment, people tacitly know that it takes more time to travel a long distance than a short distance at a given speed. They may not be able to formulate the equation rate × time = distance, but they are tacitly aware of this relationship. When asked to scan a visual image, subjects may assume that it should work just as physical motion does, and so their responses produce a linear relationship. The tacit knowledge point, then, says that the linear relationship between distance scanned and time to respond is due to the fact that subjects expect it to work this way.

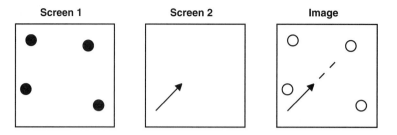

Figure 11.7 The subject saw the left panel for 5 seconds; then it disappeared. One second later, the middle panel was presented. The arrow could appear anywhere and could be in any orientation. Subjects reported deciding whether the arrow pointed to a dot by imagining they were scanning from the tip of the arrow along the direction specified until they hit a dot or a boundary. This strategy is represented in the right panel.   SOURCE: Data from "Spontaneous Imagery Scanning in Mental Extrapolation," by R. A. Finke and S. Pinker, 1982, *Journal of Experimental Psychology: Learning, Memory, and Cognition, 8,* 142–147. Copyright © 1982 American Psychological Association. Reprinted by permission of the author.

Pylyshyn's third argument suggests that task demands may be affecting the results. *Task demands* are similar to experimenter bias, except that it is the task itself, rather than any cues provided by the experimenter, that causes the subject to behave in one way rather than another. For example, when subjects are told that they are in an imagery experiment, the task is quite different from when no mention is made of the task.

To address Pylyshyn's first objection, Jolicoeur and Kosslyn (1985) conducted a replication of the Kosslyn et al. (1978) map study to see whether the experimenter's expectations affected the results. They told some of the experimenters to expect a U-shaped function between response time and distance scanned. Despite the experimenters' expectations, the usual linear function was found, and the Kosslyn et al. (1978) results were replicated. Although some results may be influenced by experimenter bias, the linear relationship between distance scanned and time to scan does not appear to be one of them.

An experiment by Finke and Pinker (1982) answered the last two criticisms. In this experiment, subjects saw a display that contained a random pattern of dots (see Figure 11.7). After 5 seconds, this display disappeared, followed 1 second later by a display that contained only an arrow. The task was to indicate whether the arrow pointed to any of the previously seen dots and to press a button to indicate yes or no.

Notice that in this experiment there is no mention of scanning, of forming an image, or even of the key variable—the distance between the tip of the arrow and the location of the dot. Nonetheless, the results were similar to those observed in other mental scanning studies: The farther the tip of the arrow was from the dot, the longer the response time. Kosslyn (1980) provides a model that addresses in detail how visual images might be constructed and manipulated.

Imagery and Perception

Despite the evidence supporting the analog view, there are still plausible theories of imagery that rely on propositional representations. For example, Humphreys and Bruce (1989) detail how both images and percepts may be built up from a common underlying propositional system. Regardless of which view ultimately explains the most data, both suggest great commonalities between the visual perception system and the visual imagery system.

Some of the most striking evidence comes from studies that tested patients with various visual deficits (reviewed by Farah, 1988). For example, Riddoch and Humphreys (1987) reported a case in which acquired cerebral color blindness (in which a patient loses the ability to perceive certain colors) was accompanied by a similar deficit in imagery for color. Levine, Warach, and Farah (1985) tested two patients, one with visual localization impairment and one with visual object identification impairment. The patient with object identification difficulties also had difficulties with tasks that required the formation of a visual image of an object. The patient with localization problems was unable to describe the relative locations of items in an image.

Another example concerns a person known as L. H. (Farah, Hammond, Levine, & Calvanio, 1988). L. H. had a perceptual deficit called agnosia; he had trouble identifying objects presented visually. He could see all the parts, such as lines, but could not assemble these parts together into whole objects. Consistent with the view that visual perception and visual imagery are related, L. H. had similar deficits with visual imagery.

A final example concerns patients with unilateral visual neglect. Patients with damage to the right parietal lobe often fail to detect stimuli presented in the left visual field, even though their basic perceptual processes are apparently normal (Posner, Walker, Friedrich, & Rafal, 1984). (Information from the left visual field goes to the right hemisphere, and information from the right visual field goes to the left hemisphere.) Patients with this disorder show a similar disorder in visual imagery tasks: Bisiach and his colleagues (Bisiach & Luzzatti, 1978; Bisiach, Luzzatti, & Perani, 1979) have demonstrated that when their patients were asked to imagine a famous square in Milan (with which the subjects were familiar), they failed to report landmarks that were in the left side of the scene. When the task was repeated, but the patients were asked to describe the square from a different side, the previously neglected information was now reported, because it was on the right side. Although unilateral neglect is usually attributable to an attentional disorder (e.g., Bisiach, 1999), the important point is that both vision and imagery are affected in a similar way. On the basis of these and other studies, Farah (1988) concluded that "for all of the types of selective visual deficits due to cortical lesions in which imagery has been examined, parallel imagery deficits have been observed" (p. 312). Farah (1989) offers one interpretation of how perception and imagery interact.

Another area of research relevant to the relationship between imagery and perception is called *memory psychophysics*. In traditional *psychophysics*, people perceive a stimulus and then make a judgment. In memory psychophysics, the same task is performed, but the judgment is made about a remembered stimulus. A standard technique is *magnitude estimation*, in which subjects rate a set of stimuli along some dimension such as size. The main restriction on the estimates is that they must preserve ratio properties. For example, if a subject sees one stimulus and rates it as a 10 and then sees another stimulus that is perceived to be twice as long, the subject should give it a 20, an estimate twice as large as the first. Typically, the estimated value (e) is related to the actual value (a) by a power function, $e = a^x$.

Kerst and Howard (1978) obtained magnitude estimations for distance (using centers of major U.S. cities) and area (of various states), and the exponents were calculated to be 1.04 and 0.79. Thus, subjects typically overestimated distance and underestimated area. Kerst and Howard also ran an imagery condition in which subjects first studied a map of the United States and then made judgments about distance and area from memory. The exponents in the imagery condition were calculated to be 1.10 and 0.60 for distance and area judgments, respectively. The important point is that the imagery exponents were the square of the perceptual exponents: $1.04 \times 1.04 = 1.08$, and $0.79 \times 0.79 = 0.62$. What this means, according to Kerst and Howard, is that in the imagery condition, the subjects were reperceiving the stimuli. There was one transformation during the encoding, when the actual distances were transformed with an exponent of 1.04. During the imagery phase of the experiment, the stimuli in memory, now an image, were reperceived and underwent a second transformation with an exponent of 1.04. These results have been replicated (Moyer, Bradley, Sorensen, Whiting, & Mansfield, 1978).

Algom and his colleagues (Algom, Wolf, & Bergman, 1985) conducted an extensive series of experiments on both perceptual and memory psychophysics that generally support the reperceptual hypothesis, at least for area judgments. The general methodology was to have subjects estimate the area of a rectangle given information about its height and width. This information could be provided entirely perceptually, entirely through memory, or in a mixture. Although the memory exponent was often close to the square of the perceptual exponent, there were several conditions under which this relationship did not hold. In all conditions, however, the memory exponent was smaller than the appropriate perceptual exponent. The researchers also found that whenever both perceptual and remembered information needed to be combined, the memory transformation dominated. Algom et al. concluded that their results support the analog view of imagery because of the "definitive evidence of second-order isomorphism between internal and external physical relations" (p. 469).

One further result consistent with the idea of some overlap between the visual imagery and visual perception systems comes from studies of visual imagery in congenitally blind subjects. These subjects, who have never seen anything, still show concreteness effects and effects attributable to visual imagery (De Beni & Cornoldi, 1988). Indeed, Kerr (1983) replicated the results of Kosslyn's map study (Kosslyn, Ball, & Reiser, 1978; Jolicoeur & Kosslyn, 1985) using blind subjects and a three-dimensional rendering of the map. These results are consistent with the idea that visual imagery is an analog form of representation that preserves spatial relationships. To the extent that the congenitally blind subjects had no deficit neurologically, then the standard visual imagery patterns should be observed.

Current Accounts of Imagery

There are two main theoretical accounts of imagery. One, usually referred to as visuo-spatial working memory (e.g., Logie, 1995), is related to Baddeley's (1986, 2000) working memory. The computational model of imagery, proposed by Kosslyn (1980, 1994), posits a system separate from memory. The two views have many similarities, but also some important differences. We focus primarily on the visuo-spatial account, as it is more integrated into theories of memory, whereas the computational model is more focused on the imagery processes of generation and transformation.

According to both views, images are generated or constructed sequentially (Kosslyn, 1994; Pearson, De Beni, & Cornoldi, 2001). This can be done either part by part or object by object, depending on what is being imaged. In general, a global image is generated first, followed by a second phase in which details are added that make the image more similar to visual experience. Images can be generated entirely from stored information, or can include information directly from perceptual experiences. Furthermore, there is more than one kind of visual image.

There is good evidence for a difference between visual imagery and spatial imagery (Farah et al., 1988). According to the visuo-spatial working memory view, the visuo-spatial sketch pad has a passive cache supported by an active spatial rehearsal mechanism called the visual scribe (Logie & Pearson, 1997). The architecture is similar to that seen in the phonological loop, where information decays within the phonological store unless rehearsed by the articulatory control process. In visuo-spatial working memory, information in the visual cache decays unless spatially rehearsed by the visual scribe. Information in the cache is also subject to retroactive interference from new items entering the cache.

The visual cache is used for retaining visual patterns, whereas the visual scribe is involved with retention of sequences of spatial movement. Evidence supporting this distinction comes from studies using the method of interference, described earlier in the chapter. For example, Logie and Marchetti (1991) found that memory for spatial patterns was disrupted by arm movements during the retention interval, whereas memory for purely visual information was not. Retention of visual information, but not spatial patterns, was disrupted when irrelevant pictures were shown during the retention interval.

Kosslyn (1994) suggests that the average duration of an image is 250 ms, which suggests that maintenance of the image is critical if the image is to be used in any kind of cognitive task. Furthermore, people seem to have difficulty maintaining an image for more than a few seconds (Cocude, Charlot, & Denis, 1997; Pazzaglia & Cornoldi, 1999). Kosslyn (1980, 1994) proposes that maintenance is an extension of generation, rather than a separate process. According to the visuo-spatial working memory view, some aspects of generation may contribute to maintenance, but other processes are also required (Logie, 1995; Pearson, De Beni, & Cornoldi, 2001)

Visuo-spatial working memory is not necessarily synonymous with visual imagery. Morton and Morris (1995) report a case study of a patient, M. G., who was impaired on typical mental imagery tasks, such as mental rotation and mental scanning, but was unimpaired on visuo-spatial working memory tasks involving the temporary maintenance of visual and spatial information. Additional evidence comes from the method of interference task. Although spatial tapping or arm movements can interfere with some mental imagery tasks, they do not always do so (Pearson, Logie, & Green, 1996; Salway & Logie, 1995). Further work is needed to understand fully the relationship between these processes and to develop a more complete theoretical account.

Real Versus Imagined Events

Given the similarities between visual imagery and visual perception, it might seem likely that the two events can sometimes be confused. The area of research that investigates how accurately people can distinguish real from imagined events is called *reality monitoring* and is related to the more general *source monitoring* (Mitchell & Johnson, 2000).

Johnson and Raye (1981) offer the most influential account of reality monitoring. According to their view, real (external) events can be distinguished from imagined (internal) events in two ways. The first is by an evaluation of qualitative attributes. Externally produced memories are likely to contain a rich representation of sensory attributes, including color, texture, intensity, and so forth. To the extent that a memory contains a rich encoding of sensory attributes and is highly detailed, it is likely to be an externally produced event. Internally generated events will lack some of this sensory information and will be less detailed and less integrated with contextual information. They often contain evidence of related cognitive processing, such as reasoning or decision making, that was necessary to generate the memory in the first place. For many memories, an evaluation of these details can determine the origin of the event, external or internal.

Many events, however—perhaps even a majority—will fall in a middle range. Although some features may indicate an external origin, a number of features may also indicate an internal origin. For these memories, Johnson and Raye (1981) propose a second kind of examination, based on plausibility and coherence. By *plausibility*, they mean that the memory must fit in with other knowledge about the world. A memory of flying by flapping one's arms is an extreme example of a lack of plausibility. *Coherence* refers to how well the memory fits in with other memories. For example, if supporting memories are available that make the memory of uncertain origin fit in with the grand scheme of things, then the uncertain memory is likely to be of a real event.

Note that these methods are not foolproof. Many sorts of memories are likely to fall into the middle category of uncertain. For example, Shepard (1984) points out that to be useful, intentions and plans need to be specific and detailed. Your memory for the plan is thus likely to have many of the attributes of an external memory, even though it was internally generated.

Many experiments support the general outline proposed by Johnson and Raye (1981). For example, Johnson, Raye, Wang, and Taylor (1979) divided subjects into two groups on the basis of their scores on a test that required them to remember details of pictures. During the experimental session, the subjects were shown pictures of common objects. Every so often, instead of a picture, the subjects saw the name of an object and were asked to create an image of the object. Johnson et al. varied the number of times each object was imaged. At the end of the session, the subjects were given an unexpected test in which they were asked to indicate the number of times they had seen a picture and to ignore the number of times they had imagined seeing it. Subjects who were deemed vivid imagers were less accurate than were subjects classified as less vivid imagers. According to Johnson et al., the rich imagery of the former group made it more difficult to distinguish instances of the imagined object from instances of the presented object.

The more similar the events in terms of their features, the more difficult it becomes to discriminate real from imagined. For example, Foley, Johnson, and Raye (1983) found that subjects were less accurate in determining whether they had spoken a word or imagined speaking the word than they were in deciding whether they had heard a word or imagined hearing the word. Similar results were reported by Anderson (1984).

Another quite systematic bias is known as the "it had to be you" effect (Anderson, 1984; Johnson & Raye, 1981). Here, the subjects appear to adopt the position that if they had really performed some action, it would be more memorable than if they had only imagined it. As a result, imagined events are more likely to be judged real than real events are to be judged imagined. Thus, memories of uncertain origins are more likely to be judged as originating externally than internally.

Further evidence comes from a study by Johnson, Kounios, and Reeder (1994), in which subjects saw some pictures and imagined others; at test, they received words and were asked to decide whether the object named had been seen, imagined, or neither.

Johnson et al. (1994) used a procedure whereby the subjects had to give a response as soon as they heard a tone. The tone could occur 300, 500, 900, or 1500 ms after the test item was displayed. At the short lags, Johnson et al. found that subjects were more accurate in determining "old" or "new" than they were in determining "seen" or "imagined." The researchers interpreted this finding as consistent with the idea that real and imagined events are made up of differing attributes and that the availability of these attributes can vary over time.

Johnson, Kahan, and Raye (1984) had subjects pair up and tell their partner about dreams they had actually dreamed, dreams they had made up, or dreams they had read about. Subjects were then given a discrimination test in which they had to decide whether a target event was one they had reported or one their partner had told them. Subjects had more difficulty with real dreams than with dreams they had read about or made up. In other words, they had difficulty recalling whether they had dreamed the dream or whether their partner had dreamed the dream. According to the reality-monitoring view, this is because dreams lack evidence of cognitive processes that are included in the memory when an event is imagined or read about. Based on this and other work, Johnson (1985) has suggested that memories generated under hypnosis may be more difficult to distinguish from real events (Dywan & Bowers, 1983) because of the extra vividness and degree of detail often present. Furthermore, such memories should lack evidence of cognitive operations because they were generated largely outside of conscious intent. According to this view, memories generated under hypnosis should be very difficult to distinguish from externally produced memories. In Chapter 12, we shall have more to say about the effects of hypnosis on memory.

Eidetic Imagery

Eidetic imagery is the technical name for *photographic memory*. The criteria for true photographic memory are very stringent. For example, a complex picture from *Alice's Adventures in Wonderland* might be shown for about 30 seconds; then, a variety of questions would be asked about specific details. The subject might be asked the number of stripes on the Cheshire Cat's tail or how many whiskers the cat had. To be truly photographic, the memory must preserve all the details that a photograph would.

The evaluation of eidetic imagery has remained constant between articles by Woodworth (1938, p. 45), Gray and Gummerman (1975), and Crowder (1992b). Eidetic images are more vivid and contain more detail than normal visual images do; they have a far longer duration than do afterimages or iconic memory; and they are found almost exclusively in preadolescent children.

Haber and Haber (1964) examined 150 preadolescent schoolchildren. The children were first shown afterimages (see Chapter 2) to get them used to talking about information not physically present. They were shown pictures for 30 seconds, and then the pictures were removed. The experimenters interviewed the children as they gazed at a blank sheet of cardboard where the picture had been. Although 84 demonstrated some evidence of imagery, only 12 (8% of the original sample) demonstrated eidetic imagery. These subjects were highly accurate and never used the past tense when answering. Furthermore, their eyes moved to the location on the blank where the target information had been displayed. Virtually no other children scanned the blank when answering.

Although the prevalence in preadolescent children is estimated at around 8% (Gray & Gummerman, 1975; Haber, 1979; Paivio & Cohen, 1979), the frequency in adults has been estimated as low as none in a million (Merrit, 1979). The notable exceptions to this are a report by Stromeyer and Psotka (1970) and one by Coltheart and Glick (1974); in the latter study, the subject could take a 10-word sentence and read off the letters backward. It is possible that the incidence of eidetic imagery is greater in elderly populations (Giray, Altkin, Vaught, & Roodin, 1985), but more data are needed on this point. Some authors assert that the famous Russian mnemonist S. used eidetic imagery. A careful reading of Luria's (1968) report, however, shows that although S. did make extensive use of visual imagery, he did not use eidetic imagery (see Chapter 15).

Many explanations have been offered for the drop in the prevalence of eidetic imagery from around 8% in preadolescent children to around 0% in normal adults, but none is universally accepted (Crowder, 1992b). One popular explanation is that as degree of literacy increases, reliance on the earlier pictorial form that gives rise to eidetic imagery decreases. However, Doob (1966) showed that degree of literacy, both within and between groups, is unrelated to prevalence of eidetic imagery. As Crowder (1992b) summarized the literature, "The most important conclusion about eidetic imagery is that it is a genuine phenomenon, capable of objective measurement and study" (pp. 155–156). Its cause and the reason for its disappearance and possible resurgence in older age are still unclear.

Other Forms of Imagery

So far, we have examined only visual imagery. More is known about both visual perception and visual imagery than about other forms of perception and imagery. Nonetheless, some research has focused on auditory imagery.

Although Perky (1910) included reports of auditory images and Seashore (1938) included a discussion in his text, much of the work on auditory imagery has been even more recent than that on visual imagery (see Reisberg, 1992). The nontemporal properties of a tone include pitch, loudness, and timbre. It is clear that the auditory image can contain information about pitch, although intensity is less reliably imaged (Intons-Peterson, 1992). Crowder (1989b) has used an interference demonstration to show that timbre can also be represented. Timbre is a potentially more interesting aspect, because it is more difficult for a subject to reproduce, physically, the unique sound of an oboe or a cello than it is to produce a sound of a particular frequency or intensity.

Crowder's (1989b) experiment involved two phases, the first demonstrating the perceptual effect and the second showing a similar effect in imagery. He presented two tones, and the subject's task was to decide whether they were the same or a different pitch. The pitches were either F, G, or A, and the timbres were of a flute, guitar, or trumpet. Subjects correctly said "same" more quickly when the pitch and timbre were identical than when only the pitches were identical and the timbres differed (see Figure 11.8). In the second phase, the tone was always a sine wave—a tone that essentially has no timbre—at one of the three pitches. After this tone was played, the subject was asked to imagine a tone of that pitch as produced by either a flute, a guitar, or a trumpet. The subject indicated when the image had been formed by pressing a button, and then the second note was played, this time by a flute, guitar, or trumpet. The task was to judge whether the pitch was the same or different, regardless of the timbre. Subjects again more quickly said "same" when the imagined and perceptual timbres matched than when they differed.

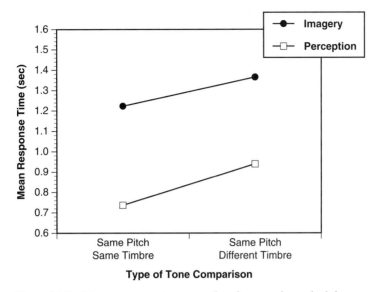

Figure 11.8   Mean response time to say that the second tone had the same pitch as the first tone when the timbre was the same or different. Subjects either heard (perception) or imaged (imagery) the timbre of the second tone.

SOURCE: From "Imagery for Musical Timbre," by R. G. Crowder, 1989, *Journal of Experimental Psychology: Human Perception and Performance, 15,* 472–478. Copyright © 1989 American Psychological Association. Reprinted with permission of the author.

Voices can also be imaged (see, for example, Geiselman & Bjork, 1980; Nairne & Pusen, 1984), although this work has been less psychophysical than has research on auditory imagery for pitch, loudness, and timbre. For example, Geiselman and Glenny (1977) had subjects listen to a tape of either a male or female voice. They then saw words and were asked to imagine these words being pronounced by the voice they had just heard. At test, the subjects again heard words spoken in a male or female voice, but their task was simply to indicate whether the word spoken was a studied word. Subjects were more accurate for imagined words if the test word was presented in the same voice as imagined. MacKay (1992) reviewed work on a related area, termed *inner speech.*

There are relatively few theories of auditory imagery; indeed, Intons-Peterson (1992) states in her review, "I have not been able to find a single model of auditory imagery, per se" (p. 65). What models exist are either general models of imagery (Hebb, 1968) or simply adaptations of accounts of visual imagery.

Relatively little work has been done on tactile imagery. However, Marchant and Malloy (1984) did find that creating a tactile image facilitated memory for word pairs that were rated high in imagibility, just as using visual imagery facilitates memory for word pairs rated high in concreteness.

Crowder and Schab (1995) have reviewed imagery for odor, which appears somewhat different from visual and auditory imagery, at least based on the results of memory psychophysics experiments. Algom and Cain (1991) first trained subjects to associate a color with a particular odor. The odors were actually all the same (amyl acetate), but they differed in intensity. To ensure accurate memory, the subject sampled an odor and then gave its name (such as red). Twenty-four hours after learning, the magnitude estimation procedure began.

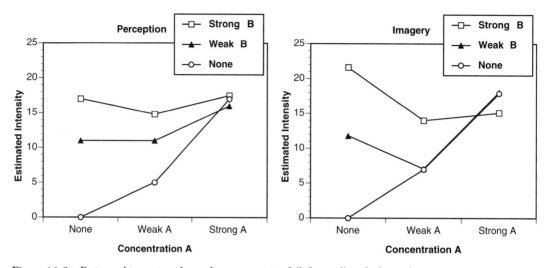

Figure 11.9   Estimated intensity when odors are perceived (left panel) and when odors are imaged (right panel).   SOURCE: From "Remembered Odor and Mental Mixtures," by D. Algom and W. S. Cain, 1991, *Journal of Experimental Psychology: Human Perception and Performance, 17,* 1104–1119. Copyright © 1991 American Psychological Association. Reprinted with permission of the author.

Contrary to findings with visual stimuli, the exponents were almost identical for both perceptual and memory conditions. Thus, imagery for odors may be quite different from imagery for visual stimuli.

The best evidence for imagery for odors comes from a study in which subjects were able to combine and manipulate images of odors. Algom and Cain (1991) found that subjects performed very similarly when giving estimations of a mixture of two odors and when giving estimates of an imagined mixture. In this latter condition, the subjects first learned the individual odors as described above; in the psychophysical phase, they were asked to judge the intensity of mixing, for example, brown with red. Even though they had no physical experience with this mixture, their estimates were very similar to those given in the perceptual condition (see Figure 11.9).

Chapter Summary

One form of representation is a proposition, the smallest unit of knowledge that has a truth value. An analog form of representation is one that preserves the structure of the original information in a more or less direct manner. Solid evidence for the existence of two forms of representation first came from experiments that used the method of selective interference and from work on dual-coding theory, the idea that words can be represented in both a verbal and a visual code. Much of the research focused on eliminating other possible explanations—such as experimenter bias, tacit knowledge, and task demands—for results obtained in mental rotation and visual imagery experiments.

Although the relation between visual perception and visual imagery is still not completely understood, there are many intriguing parallels. Disruptions in visual imagery are often mirrored with similar disruptions to visual perception. Complicating this, however, is evidence that spatial imagery differs from visual imagery.

Reality monitoring refers to the ability to tell the difference between real events and imagined events. People are more likely to misremember an imagined event as real than a real event as imagined. Eidetic memory is the technical term for what most people refer to as photographic memory. About 5%–10% of preadolescent children seem to have this ability, but no adults do, with the possible exception of very elderly adults.

Just as people can create visual images, they can also create auditory images, tactile images, and odor images, although these have been the subjects of far less research than has visual imagery.

Reconstructive Processes in Memory

> *Give us a dozen healthy memories, well-formed, and our own specified world to handle*
> *them in. And we'll guarantee to take any one at random and train it to become any*
> *type of memory that we might select—hammer, screwdriver, wrench, stop sign, yield*
> *sign, Indian chief—regardless of its origin or the brain that holds it.*
> —E. F. Loftus and H. G. Hoffman

Although Loftus and Hoffman (1989, p. 103) are parodying a famous quotation by John
B. Watson (1939, p. 104), they are making an extremely important point: Memories are
highly malleable. In this chapter, we review ways in which memories change or are constructed, usually without any awareness of the distortion. Indeed, in all the studies that
follow, we can assume that the subjects were being as honest as possible; what is most impressive—or most disturbing—is how pervasive these changes can be.

Schemas

One frequently reported characteristic of people who try to recall various events is *con-
fabulation*—supplying additional information and details that were not part of the original
episode. Rather than thinking of memory as some object that gradually becomes less clear
or more distorted, most memory researchers believe that memories change because they
are continually constructed and reconstructed. This repeated processing can change the
memory in any number of ways, depending on the schema that is active at the time of
recollection.

A *schema* is an organized knowledge structure that reflects an individual's knowledge, experience, and expectations about some aspect of the world. Information contained within a schema is usually recruited to help recall various events, especially in situations involving surprising or emotion-laden memories. Although not all researchers define schemas in the same way, most agree that a schema has five general characteristics (see Rumelhart & Norman, 1985; Rumelhart & Ortony, 1977).

First, schemas represent knowledge. This means that an individual's experience, rather than abstract or objective knowledge, is reflected in a schema; it also means that a particular schema can change with new experiences. Second, schemas can represent knowledge at all levels, from a schema of a penny (Nickerson & Adams, 1979) to a schema of social structure (Schank & Abelson, 1977). Third, schemas can be embedded within each other. A schema about buying ice cream would involve an embedded schema about a commercial transaction (handing over money, receiving change), which in turn could have an embedded schema about coins (did you get a real coin or a funny foreign one?).

The actual information within a schema is general; a restaurant schema applies to most restaurants. Information that is not common to all restaurants is represented by the fourth characteristic: Schemas have variables. One variable in a restaurant schema might be whether you seat yourself or wait to be seated. Variables can also have default values—the most common value for a variable for a particular individual. Thus, in schemas involving coffee, the default value is that the coffee is hot, even though it is not uncommon to see restaurants serving iced coffee.

The fifth characteristic is that schemas are active, dynamic, and continually changing. Schemas are used to comprehend sentences, to understand sensations, to organize information, to make predictions, and to foster expectations.

An experiment by Bransford and Johnson (1972) illustrates the usefulness of schemas in understanding. They presented subjects with a passage such as the following (Bransford & Johnson, 1972):

> The procedure is actually quite simple. First you arrange items into different groups. Of course, one pile may be sufficient depending on how much there is to do. If you have to go somewhere else due to lack of facilities that is the next step, otherwise you are pretty well set. It is important not to overdo things. That is, it is better to do too few things at once than too many. In the short run this may not seem important but complications can easily arise. A mistake can be expensive as well. At first, the whole procedure will seem complicated. Soon, however, it will become just another facet of life. It is difficult to foresee any end to the necessity for this task in the immediate future, but then one never can tell. After the procedure is completed one arranges the materials into different groups again. Then they can be put into their appropriate places. Eventually they will be used once more and the whole cycle will then have to be repeated. However, that is part of life. (p. 722)

Subjects rated the passage on a scale of 1 to 7, where 1 equals very difficult to understand and 7 means very easy to understand. Half of the subjects rated the passage as very difficult, and half rated it as very easy. Those who rated the passage as easy recalled almost twice as much as those who rated it as more difficult. The only difference between the groups was whether they had been told that the passage was about washing clothes. By giving the subjects this information, the experimenters ensured that the subjects could use the appropriate schema while reading, and thus integrate the information with knowledge they already had. At recall, the schema was again useful in providing structure: If you know the general procedure for washing clothes, then it is easy to generate the next step in the process.

Schemas can also introduce errors. Bower, Black, and Turner (1979) had subjects read 18 stories, each based on a particular generic schema. These generic schemas were identified through a series of pilot experiments. (Actually, Bower et al. were looking at scripts, which refer to certain situation-action routines. For current purposes, think of a script as one type of schema.) In their study, a particular generic schema could be the basis of 1, 2, or 3 different stories. Within a generic schema "Visiting a health professional," for example, subjects might read one story about "Going to the doctor" and another about "Going to the dentist." In this case, there would be two versions of the same generic schema.

The subjects were then given a recognition test. Some of the items on the test were schema actions that came from the stories, some were actions that had previously been identified as being in the generic schema but that did not appear in the stories, and some were novel actions that were neither in the generic schema nor in the stories. For each item on the test, the subjects gave a rating on a scale of 1 to 7, with 1 indicating "Very sure I did not read this sentence" and 7 indicating "Very sure I did read this sentence." The results are shown in Table 12.1.

Subjects gave higher ratings for sentences that were in the stories than for sentences that were not; however, sentences that were in the generic schema received higher ratings than novel actions did. Furthermore, the more stories a subject read that tapped a particular generic schema, the more likely it was that the subject would incorrectly say that an unstated sentence had been read. In other words, subjects were quite likely to falsely recognize actions as being from the passage if these actions were in their schema. Actions not in the schema (and not in the passage) were rarely falsely recognized or recalled.

If you recall the passage was about washing clothes, one action is putting in the detergent. But did this action occur in the passage, or just in the schema that was activated? Did the passage mention that sometimes you have to insert coins? Many of the details that subjects recall in flashbulb memory studies (discussed later in the chapter) fit in this category: The information recalled is attributed to the original event, but it is also information that is found in a schema of the event. Similar distortions and changes have been found by other researchers (Hasher & Griffin, 1978; Spiro, 1980).

There are numerous other examples. Sulin and Dooling (1974) found that subjects who were told that the main character of a story was Helen Keller were likely to remember reading the sentence "She was deaf, dumb, and blind," even though that sentence was not presented. Bransford, Barclay, and Franks (1972) found that subjects who read sentences such as "There is a box to the right of a tree" and "There is a chair on the box" also

Table 12.1 Average recognition ratings for three kinds of statements as a function of the number of script versions

Number of Script Versions	Stated Script Actions	Unstated Script Actions	Other Actions
1	5.46	3.91	1.71
2	5.40	4.62	1.76
3	5.59	4.81	1.86

SOURCE: Bower, Black, & Turner (1979).

remembered reading the sentence "The tree is to the left of the chair," even though that sentence was not presented.

People are also very likely to remember actually reading sentences that were not presented, if those sentences are likely inferences. Johnson, Bransford, and Solomon (1973) had subjects hear some stories in which a key sentence implied some action or consequence. The story might have been the following:

> It was late at night when the phone rang and a voice gave a frantic cry. The spy threw the secret document into the fireplace just in time since 30 seconds longer would have been too late.

At test, the subjects were asked to indicate whether a test sentence had been in the story. Subjects correctly recognized about 66% of the old sentences. However, sentences such as "The spy burned the secret document just in time since 30 seconds longer would have been too late" were incorrectly judged as being in the story approximately 63% of the time.

Although schemas can introduce errors, it is important to remember that they can also improve recall. Switching from an inappropriate to an appropriate schema can facilitate memory. Anderson and Pichert (1978) had subjects read a story about two boys skipping school, from the perspective of either a burglar or a person interested in buying a home. After recalling the story, the subjects were asked to recall the story a second time but now were asked to change perspective. On their second recall, the subjects produced more details important to the second perspective (that they had not recalled on the first attempt) and fewer details important to the first perspective (that they had recalled on the first attempt).

This basic idea is not new. Plato, in the *Theatetus*, recognized that the memory of an event is quite likely to be different now from when the event was originally experienced. More recently, Sir Frederic Bartlett (1932) proposed that new information is remembered in terms of already existing structures. In one famous experiment, he had subjects read a Native American folk tale called "War of the Ghosts." Because the story followed different narrative conventions from those previously experienced by English students, the effect was not unlike reading the laundry passage without knowing about laundry. Bartlett had his subjects recall the story after intervals ranging from immediately to several years. In general, the recalled story became shorter and, from a British perspective, more coherent; most of the supernatural elements disappeared, resulting in a more traditional story about fighting and dying. Bartlett identified three types of reconstructive errors: (1) omissions, in which unusual or unfamiliar items tended not to be reported; (2) linkages, in which subjects added made-up reasons—or rationalizations—to give the story greater coherence; and (3) transformations, in which unfamiliar names or terms were changed into more familiar ones (*canoe* became *boat*, *seal hunting* became *fishing*). These patterns were also noted in the reproduction of other stories (see Chapter 7 of Bartlett, 1932). Although some of Bartlett's results have proved difficult to replicate (Gauld & Stephenson, 1967; Roediger, Wheeler, & Rajaram, 1993; Wheeler & Roediger, 1992; see Chapter 1), the generally reconstructive nature of recollection has been consistently supported.

Specific Schemas

The most common criticism of the idea of a schema is that it is too vague to be a useful concept. It is one of those ideas that explains everything but predicts nothing. David

Figure 12.1   An illustration of how a schema can be made more precise. Instead of remembering ten pairs of items (e.g., 1 is paired with 2.9, 4 is paired with 11.5), a person could use one schema, $B = (2 \times A) + 1$, to reconstruct all of the items fairly accurately.

Rumelhart and his colleagues (Rumelhart, Smolensky, McClelland, & Hinton, 1986) have attempted to provide a more precise definition and to derive and test predictions.

The basic idea is that a schema preserves general information at the expense of particular details. A simple implementation is represented in Figure 12.1 in the form of a regression equation. This example represents a paired-associate task, in which the subject is asked to respond with a B item when prompted with an A item. In this case, both A and B items are numbers. The first stimulus is 1 and the correct response is 2.9; the second stimulus is 2 and the correct response is 3.1; the final pair is 10 and 24. The black squares show perfect performance. To do well, a subject must learn all ten pairs. However, a schema for these relationships would reduce the memory load to just one item, the schema itself. In this case, the general relationship can be summarized as:

Response = (2 × stimulus) + 1

If a schema is thought of as an equation that relates two (or more) pieces of information, the concept is now precise, unambiguous, and testable. Furthermore, it exhibits all the properties listed above. A subject using this schema would be quite accurate on most pairs; for example, on item 1, the correct response is 2.9 and the subject gives 3.0. One reason for using schemas is that they work well enough most of the time. However, on some pairs the answer will be much less accurate: on item 4, it will be 9 instead of 11.5; on item 10, it will be 21 instead of 24. The increase in efficiency (having to remember only one schema rather than ten pairs) results in a loss of accuracy. A schema has another advantage: If a new stimulus is given (for example, 40), the subject can give a plausible response (in this case, 81). The person may not know whether this response is correct or not, but the schema allows expectations to be generated. If only the ten pairs were stored, then it would be far more difficult, if not impossible, to extrapolate to novel situations.

This simple example illustrates the kind of model developed by Rumelhart et al. (1986). In fact, they derived a set of equations that represented room schemas—connections between items that might be found in different sorts of rooms. Thus, bathtub has a strong link with sink (as in a bathroom), and sink has a strong link with stove (as in a kitchen), but bathtub and stove are not linked. The schema, then, is the pattern of activation over all the elements within the network. This model can be questioned in much the same way as a person might be. For example, what kind of room would have a telephone? There are several possibilities (probably more now that portable phones are more common), but one common answer is the kitchen; in most houses in the United States, the kitchen has a phone. In general, the responses given by the model were much the same as those given by people (see Rumelhart et al., 1986, for more details). This is not the only way to refine the concept of a schema so that it becomes more precise and able to make predictions, but it does illustrate one successful way.

Malleability of Generic Memory

So far we have examined reconstructive processes in autobiographical memory. Generic memory is also quite malleable, even for such well-known information as that George Washington was the first president of the United States or that the Eiffel Tower is in Paris (Gerrig, 1989). The initial motivation behind the experiments that demonstrate this malleability was trying to understand how a person could see a movie or read a book for the second or third time and still have a sense of uncertainty or suspense about the outcome. Gerrig (1989) presented subjects with two different versions of a short story, one that contained no suspense and one that created suspense. The no-suspense version of one story went like this:

> George Washington was a famous figure after the Revolutionary War. Washington was a popular choice to lead the new country. Few people had thought that the British could be defeated. The success of the Revolutionary War was attributed largely to Washington. His friends worked to convince him to go on serving his country. Washington agreed that he had abundant experience as a leader.

The suspense version was slightly different:

> George Washington was a famous figure after the Revolutionary War. Washington was a popular choice to lead the new country. Washington, however, wanted to retire after the war. The long years as general had left him tired and frail. Washington wrote that he would be unable to accept the nomination. Attention turned to John Adams as the next most qualified candidate.

In both cases, the key target sentence was identical: "George Washington was elected first president of the United States." The results are shown in Figure 12.2: Subjects were slower to verify this sentence following a suspenseful passage than after a passage with no suspense. Perhaps more surprising, this difference is quite long-lasting; subjects in the delayed condition showed a similar effect when the target sentence was presented 10 minutes after the passage.

Gerrig (1989) argued that this experiment reflects the memory processes that occur when watching a movie or reading a book for the second time. You have knowledge about the outcome, but this knowledge interferes with enjoyment of the movie: Why watch *Terminator* again if you cannot recreate the suspense of seeing it the first time? What happens is that the viewer does not access all the relevant knowledge, or even the key parts of the

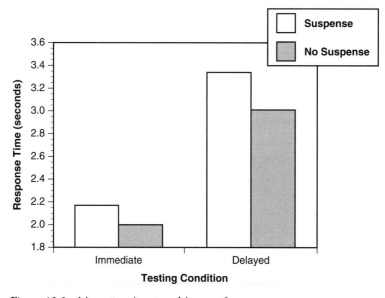

Figure 12.2 Mean time (in seconds) to verify a target sentence, either immediately after reading a passage or approximately 10 minutes after reading the passage.   SOURCE: Data from Experiments 1 and 3 of Gerrig (1989).

relevant knowledge, if that information would destroy the suspense. It is as though subjects were able to ignore the information that would interfere with pleasure, and this leads to the surprisingly long-lasting effect shown in Figure 12.2. Even well-learned information is potentially subject to modification.

Eyewitness Memory

Perhaps the most disturbing area in which reconstructive processes occur is in the memories of eyewitnesses. One summary has proved profoundly prophetic: Writing about memory changes to accommodate new information added after the original experience, Spiro (1980) suggested that, in general, (1) the chance of such changes increases with time, (2) the confidence the subject has that the memory is accurate will be as high as or higher than for "accurate" memories, and (3) there is no way to distinguish inaccurate memories from accurate memories without some objective external evidence.

One line of research supporting these statements was initiated by Elizabeth Loftus and her colleagues. The basic experiment begins with the subjects' seeing a series of slides or a film depicting an event such as a robbery, car accident, or other naturalistic eyewitness event. The experimenters then ask the subjects a series of questions. Typically, Loftus and her colleagues change the way one question is asked to determine its effects on subsequent recall.

In one study, Loftus and Palmer (1974) asked subjects the following question: "How fast were the cars going when they —— each other?" The researchers varied the intensity of the verb that described the collision, using *smashed, collided, bumped, hit,* and *contacted.*

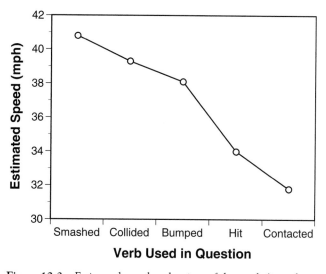

Figure 12.3   Estimated speed at the time of the crash (in miles per hour) as a function of the verb used in the question.   SOURCE: Data from Loftus & Palmer (1974).

When the verb was *smashed*, the estimates averaged 41 mph; when the verb was *contacted*, the estimates averaged 32 mph (see Figure 12.3). A follow-up question asked whether there was broken glass. Nearly one-third of the subjects who had the verb *smashed* said yes, but only one-tenth of those who had the verb *contacted* said there was broken glass. There was actually no broken glass. Clearly, the verb used led to a recon-struction of the memory consistent with the speed implied by the verb.

Several other studies have shown that the words used in questions can change an-swers that are presumed to be based on memory. For example, subjects will say yes more often to the question "Did you see *the* broken headlight?" than "Did you see *a* broken headlight?" (Loftus & Zanni, 1975). When asked "Do you get headaches frequently, and if so how often?" one sample of subjects gave an estimate of 2.2 headaches per week. When the word *frequently* was replaced by *occasionally*, the estimate dropped to 0.71 head-aches per week (Loftus, 1975).

Perhaps the most famous of these studies is the so-called "Red Datsun" study (Loftus, Miller, & Burns, 1978). Subjects saw a sequence of 30 slides that followed a red Datsun as the car made a turn and hit a pedestrian. Half of the subjects saw a stop sign at the inter-section, and the other half saw a yield sign. Buried among the questions was one that con-tained either consistent or misleading information: "Did another car pass the red Datsun while it was stopped at the ——— sign?" Half the subjects received consistent information (saw a stop sign and the question mentioned a stop sign, or saw a yield sign and the ques-tion mentioned a yield sign), and half received misleading information. Twenty minutes later, the subjects received a recognition test in which they were shown two photographs, one with a stop sign and one with a yield sign, and were asked which one they had seen.

Subjects who had received consistent information were accurate about 75% of the time, but those who had received misleading information were accurate only about 40% of the time. When tested after 2 weeks rather than 20 minutes, the effect was even larger:

Subjects who received the misleading information were accurate only about 20% of the time. The subjects in the misleading condition were far more likely to recall the planted information than the original information. Similar findings have been reported when changing other details, such as the color of the car (Loftus, 1979a). Note that this paradigm is very similar to the paired-associate learning discussed in Chapter 6, and is an interference paradigm.

Subjects who are misled and who recall the misleading rather than the original information respond just as quickly (Cole & Loftus, 1979) and express just as much confidence (Loftus, Donders, Hoffman, & Schooler, 1989) as do their counterparts who remember accurately. Furthermore, even when told of the experimental design, nearly 90% of the misled subjects believe they received consistent information which they reported accurately (Loftus, Miller, & Burns, 1978). Even offering a financial incentive does not improve accuracy (Loftus, 1979b).

One controversy concerns whether the original information is completely and permanently lost (Loftus & Loftus, 1980) or is retained but has become inaccessible (Capaldi & Neath, 1995). The biased guessing account (McCloskey & Zaragoza, 1985; Zaragoza & Koshmider, 1989) emphasizes the fact that the misleading information is more recent than the original information. In its simplest form, a *misleading information experiment* compares performance between a control group, which receives consistent information, and an experimental group, which receives inconsistent (misleading) information. At test, the subjects are forced to make a choice between the original and the misleading information. The typical finding is that the control subjects identify the original information far more accurately than the experimental subjects do.

In this situation, McCloskey and Zaragoza's argument goes like this: Assume that half the control subjects recall the event perfectly and the other half have forgotten. If this is the case, 50% of the subjects will get the answer correct because they remember it, and 25% will get the answer correct by chance (they guess and there are two possibilities). This gives an average of 75% correct for the control group. Assume further that the experimental subjects remember as accurately as the control subjects do; 50% of them will recall the original information and thus get the answer correct. The key to the biased guessing explanation lies in the other half of the experimental subjects. Unlike the control subjects who cannot remember, some of the experimental subjects will have something else to remember—the misleading information. If 30% of the subjects recall this information, which is more recent than the original, then that leaves only 20% who do not remember either. This remaining portion will be split evenly between the two options. Adding this up, the control group will be 75% accurate and the experimental group only 60% accurate (see Table 12.2). These numbers were picked for simplicity; if we assume some retroactive interference from the misleading information (the A-D pair) on the original information (the A-B pair), then the percent of experimental subjects correctly recalling the original will be lower and overall performance will be lower.

McCloskey and Zaragoza (1985) designed an experiment to distinguish between these accounts. Rather than presenting the subjects with a forced choice between the original and the misleading item, they used the original and a novel item. According to the impairment account (Loftus & Loftus, 1980), the control subjects should be more accurate than the experimental subjects because their memory for the original item was not overwritten. According to the biased guessing account, performance should be nearly equivalent for the two groups: With the other responding option (remember and pick the

Table 12.2   An example of how the biased guessing account explains the misleading information effect

| | Percentage of Subjects Who | | | | |
| | Remember and Pick | | Forget and Guess | | |
	Original	Misleading	Original	Misleading	Total Correct
Control	50%	—	25%	25%	75%
Experimental	50%	30%	10%	10%	60%

NOTE: The same number of people remember the original information, and when they remember nothing, half will pick the original and half will pick the misleading. The key is that some of the experimental group will remember only the misleading information, whereas none of the control group can. This reduces the number of subjects who remember nothing and reduces overall performance.

misleading item) removed, all the experimental subjects who do not remember the original item should guess in exactly the same way as the control subjects do. In fact, performance by the control and experimental groups did not differ (McCloskey & Zaragoza, 1985; Loftus et al., 1989).

The biased guessing account can explain more data than the overwriting account, but only a few experiments have been done to test it. Regardless of the outcome of the controversy, it is important to emphasize that no one doubts the basic effect: People are very likely to incorporate into their memories and subsequently report extraneous information (Weingardt, Loftus, & Lindsay, 1995). In most practical situations, we do not have the luxury of wondering whether the effect is due to overwriting or biased guessing; the inaccuracy will be what is important.

One criticism of some of this research is that the events are not as emotionally intense or arousing as real events. Even if this criticism were correct, research has shown similar results from situations that are undeniably emotionally intense; even very intense, very traumatic, and very long-lasting events do not guarantee accurate memory. For example, Wagenaar and Groeneweg (1990) studied the memory of concentration camp survivors. The researchers had access to films, photographs, and interviews that took place right after the camp was liberated. Some 40 years later, they questioned some of the survivors about conditions in the camp, guards, fellow prisoners, and other issues. Although some prisoners could recall a lot of information accurately with great detail, they also made many mistakes, including failing to remember whether they were housed in tents or wooden barracks or misremembering a prisoner as a guard. The general conclusion was that "the intensity of the emotion at the encoding of information is no guarantee for accurate eyewitness testimony" (p. 87). Memories of more brutal events were no more accurate than were memories of more ordinary events.

So far, we have presented cases in which the errors are mostly content errors—recalling a sign that was not present or being housed in a tent rather than a wooden hut. Many times, the content of the eyewitness memory may be accurate, but there is an attribution error. Baddeley (1990) relates one such case. Donald Thomson, an Australian psychologist who, ironically, has studied eyewitness memory, was picked up by police and identified by a woman as the man who had raped her. His alibi was that he had been on a television talk show at the time and that he had an assistant police commissioner as a witness. The police interrogator reportedly responded with "Yes, and I suppose you've got Jesus Christ and the

Queen of England too!" (Baddeley, 1990, p. 27). Later released and exonerated, Thomson found out that the woman had been watching TV when she was raped and had attributed the face she remembered (Thomson's) as the face of her attacker.

Attribution errors can be very common. We have seen them operate in the reality-monitoring paradigm, in which an item is attributed to either an external or an internal source, and they also play a large role in the false fame paradigm discussed later in this chapter. The larger point is that when a memory is recollected, the source of the memory can be attributed either accurately (I participated in the event, I read about the event, or I imagined the event) or inaccurately. Even if all the details are correct, an attribution error can result in a fundamentally inaccurate memory.

Researchers in this area have concluded that there is no way to assess whether a memory is accurate or not without objective corroborative evidence (Kihlstrom, 1994; Loftus, 1993a). Neither vividness, nor speed of recall, nor intensity of the experience, nor emotionality is correlated with accuracy. The subject may be accurately reporting the contents of memory, and thus not lying or trying to be deceitful. Nonetheless, the contents of memory can include information from other sources. Furthermore, as we saw when discussing reality monitoring, it is often difficult to distinguish between events that were experienced and those that were imagined (Anderson, 1984). If the only evidence is from an eyewitness and there is no other objective or corroborative evidence, then there is no way to assess the accuracy of the memory.

Flashbulb Memories

Brown and Kulik (1977) coined the term *flashbulb memory* to refer to a particular kind of memory, such as for where you were when John F. Kennedy was assassinated (or, more recently, when O. J. Simpson was acquitted). They suggested that these memories, which form only for highly surprising and highly consequential events, are "very like a photograph that indiscriminately preserves the scene" (p. 74). The metaphor refers to the scene captured when the flash on a camera goes off: The event is permanently chronicled in a highly detailed manner. Flashbulb memories are "fixed for a very long time, and conceivably permanently" (p. 85) and have other unique qualities because of a special neurological mechanism. Brown and Kulik's findings were similar to those of Colegrove (1899), who reported that a majority of subjects tested could recall where they were when Abraham Lincoln was assassinated, including details of what they were doing.

There have been numerous studies on flashbulb memories, and even several books on the topic (Conway, 1995; Winograd & Neisser, 1992). For events that are highly surprising and personally relevant, people do report especially vivid memories and do provide lots of details, particularly about where they were when the event happened, who told them, who was with them, and what their emotional reaction was. The main question of interest is whether there is sufficient evidence to support the claim for a special process.

One of the key claims that flashbulb memories are qualitatively different from other memories is that they remain fixed in memory. To substantiate this claim, researchers have examined the consistency of responses between the initial assessment of an event and subsequent recollection several months or years later.

On January 28, 1986, at 11:38 EST, the Space Shuttle *Challenger* exploded. One day later, Neisser and Harsch (1992) had 106 people fill out a questionnaire. The subjects answered questions to indicate what they were doing, who they were with, when they learned of the disaster, and so forth. Just under 3 years later, 44 subjects were asked again to recall this information. Their responses were coded in terms of accuracy of various attributes they had reported immediately after the event, including location, activity, informant, time, and others present. The mean score was only 2.95 attributes out of 7 correct. Twenty-five percent of the subjects were wrong about every attribute and received a score of 0; only 3 subjects received perfect scores. Being wrong means that, for example, they originally reported hearing about the event in their dorm room by themselves and 3 years later reported they were in a cafeteria surrounded by friends. Despite the poor overall performance, subjects rated their confidence very highly (4.17 out of 5). Of the 220 attributes tested, 93 were completely wrong, 60 were partially wrong, and 67 were correct. Although the subjects expressed a lot of confidence in the accuracy of their memories, and although they produced detailed and highly vivid recollections, their memories were not necessarily accurate and did not necessarily remain unchanged over time (see also Neisser, 1982).

Neisser and Harsch (1992) found little evidence that flashbulb memories of the *Challenger* tragedy were different from other memories. Instead, they suggest that flashbulb memories are subject to the same reconstructive processes as other memories. Compounding the problem for flashbulb memories is that because these events make for a good story (Bell & Loftus, 1989), many people are tempted to add details. Indeed, these flashbulb memories are the kind of stories that people—including memory researchers (Loftus & Kaufman, 1992)—love to tell and retell. If the "initial" memory is not assessed immediately, then it is likely that these constructed details get incorporated into the memory and are subsequently recalled, giving the illusion of accurate retention. When one compares a flashbulb memory to a non-flashbulb memory, there are likely to be huge differences in terms of rehearsal. Furthermore, asking people about how often they thought of the event is likely to produce highly inaccurate results (Arnold & Lindsay, 2002). In one sense, this is accurate retention, but it is accurate retention of constructed details.

This account leads to two testable predictions. First, subjects should be more consistent in their recollections when the initial assessment occurs after some delay than when the initial assessment occurs immediately after the event. Second, except for subjective measures of memory such as confidence and vividness, there should be no qualitative difference in objective measures of memory.

Winningham, Hyman, and Dinnel (2000) tested the first prediction. If people use the same reconstructive processes on flashbulb memories as on other memories, then one should expect the memory to change systematically over time. Crucially, one would expect the most changes early on as the subjects tell and retell the experience and make it into a coherent narrative. They had two groups of subjects answer standard questions (who told them, when did they find out, where were they, and what were they doing) after the O. J. Simpson murder acquittal verdict was announced. One group answered these initial questions 5 hours after the verdict, and the other answered the questions 1 week after the verdict. Both groups were retested 8 weeks after the event. Winningham et al. computed consistency scores for each group. This score measures the degree to which each subject's memory remained consistent from the initial assessment to the second assessment. A score of 8 meant that all details were the same; a score of 0 meant that no details were the same. Approximately 22% of subjects in the immediate condition had consistency scores of 7 or 8, compared to 53% of subjects in the delayed group. In other

Table 12.3   Sample studies of flashbulb memory: delay between the event and the initial assessment of subjects' memory of the event

Study	Delay	Event
Christianson (1989)	6 weeks	Assassination of Swedish Prime Minister Olof Palme
Curci et al. (2001)	1–2 months	Death of former French President Mitterand
Pillemer (1984)	1 month	Attempted assassination of Ronald Reagan
Bohannon (1988)	2 weeks	*Challenger* explosion
Conway et al. (1994)	Within 14 days	Resignation of Margaret Thatcher
Cohen et al. (1994)	Within 14 days	Resignation of Margaret Thatcher
McCloskey et al. (1988)	Within 1 week	*Challenger* explosion
Schmolck et al. (2000)	3 days	O. J. Simpson acquittal
Christianson & Engelberg (1999)	2 days	The MS *Estonia* ferry disaster
Wright (1993)	2 days	Hillsborough football tragedy
Weaver (1993)	2 days	Gulf War
Neisser & Harsch (1992)	Within 24 hours	*Challenger* explosion
Winningham et al. (2000)	5 hours	O. J. Simpson acquittal

words, more change was apparent in the group that was assessed only 5 hours after the event than for the group that was assessed 1 week after the event. This result is consistent with the reconstructive account of flashbulb memories and is problematic for the Brown and Kulik special mechanism account: If there is a special mechanism, why is there such a large difference between 5 hours after the event and 1 week after the event?

One methodological difficulty with studying flashbulb memories is that most events of this type are unpredictable. Because of this unpredictability, researchers might not be fully prepared to begin a flashbulb memory study until several days after the event. Table 12.3 shows that the delay between the event and the initial assessment in published studies has been as short as 5 hours and as long as 6 weeks. The results of the Winningham et al. (2000) study suggest that studies with delays of more than a day or so are likely to find that the flashbulb memories are very consistent. This is due not to a special mechanism, however, but rather to the fact that most of the reconstruction took place *before* the assessment. Because the event is so remarkable, people are likely to have constructed a coherent narrative as a result of numerous retellings. Only studies with very short delays between the event and the initial assessment are likely to be informative.

The second prediction—that except for subjective measures of memory such as confidence and vividness, there should be no qualitative difference in objective measures of memory—was assessed by Weaver (1993). Unlike most flashbulb memory studies, Weaver's included a control group so that he could directly compare memory of the flashbulb event to memory for a mundane event. He asked students to complete a typical flashbulb memory questionnaire after meeting a roommate (or other friend). Coincidentally, later that evening, the first President Bush ordered bombing attacks on Iraq, and 2 days later the same students received a questionnaire about that event. Weaver assessed their memories again 3 months later and 1 year later. In general, the accuracy of the memories decreased according to Ebbinghaus's forgetting function (see Chapter 1). For both types of events, there was a large drop in accuracy over the first interval and almost no change between 3 months and 1 year after the event. The most notable difference was that subjects expressed far greater confidence in their memories for the Iraq bombing than for the roommate meeting, even though this elevated confidence did not reflect better accuracy.

Weaver (1993) suggests that flashbulb memories are distinguished from other memories by two characteristics: (1) elevated confidence and (2) a compulsion or intent to remember the event. This latter characteristic appears to arise spontaneously in flashbulb memories and is often missing for more prosaic events. However, as Weaver's study shows, if one tries to remember a prosaic event, then accuracy can be as good as for a flashbulb event.

Other studies with very brief delays between the event and the initial assessment also conclude that there does not seem to be empirical support for the special mechanism account of flashbulb memories. For example, Christianson and Engelberg (1999) found that the proportion of correct responses dropped from essentially perfect to approximately 50% correct in 1 year. Moreover, their results "argue against a putative emotion mechanism for [flashbulb memories] such as the one hypothesized by Brown and Kulik (1977) and Bohannon (1988)" (pp. 480–481). Similarly, Wright (1993, p. 137) concluded that "the results show that recall of the Hillsborough disaster varies over time in terms of both subjective characteristics and recalled circumstances, thus favouring a reconstructionist explanation as opposed to Brown and Kulik's special mechanism hypothesis."

In addition to the methodological problems already noted (delay between the event and the initial assessment, the likelihood that the memory is told and retold, and the lack of control groups), two other problems remain. One concerns what type of event is a good candidate for a flashbulb event. Some researchers have suggested that the space shuttle *Challenger* disaster is such an event (Neisser & Harsch, 1992), whereas others have disagreed (Conway, 1995). Part of the argument is that different events are treated differently by different people, but this leads to some circularity. Flashbulb memories are those that produce excellent recall that does not change over time; we know that event X was not a flashbulb memory because it did not produce excellent results over time. A final problem is that the effects of emotion and arousal are rarely separated from other effects on memory for a unique event.

Most of these problems are due to the nature of the events that cause flashbulb memories. The event is so surprising that the initial memory questionnaire cannot be administered until days, weeks, or even months after the event. There is usually no control group, because it is highly unlikely that there will be a cotemporaneous event that is also unique but that is not surprising or does not involve the subject emotionally. Given these problems, the vast majority of researchers have concluded that flashbulb memories are no more accurate and do not have special mechanisms. As McCloskey (1992) puts it, "Given that flashbulb memories may not be all that good, and the performance expected from ordinary memory mechanisms may not be all that bad, motivation for postulating a special flashbulb memory mechanism may not be easy to come by" (p. 234). Most researchers agree that there is no special mechanism (see Winograd & Neisser, 1992). Although some researchers make a case for the specialness of flashbulb memories (Conway, 1995), most think that the results can be explained with regular principles of memory (Rubin & Kozin, 1984; Neisser & Harsch, 1992).

Hypnosis and Memory

Many people believe that hypnosis can increase the accuracy of eyewitness memory (Daglish & Wright, 1991; Wagstaff, Vella, & Perfect, 1992). Even therapists trained in hypnosis report widespread belief that hypnosis can unlock previously hidden memories and that memories obtained through hypnosis are more likely to be accurate than those that are simply recalled (Yapko, 1994).

Mingay (1987) reviewed two different areas that have explored the effects of hypnosis on memory. Studies from experimental psychology generally show that hypnosis in and of itself does not lead to better recall (see also Orne, 1979; Roediger, 1996; Smith, 1983). If you cannot recall something when not under hypnosis, this research suggests, you will not be able to recall it under hypnosis. This finding also applies when the material is presented under incidental learning conditions (Mingay, 1986; Murray-Smith, Kinoshita, & McConkey, 1990). However, the forensic literature cites many case studies in which a person recalls additional information when under hypnosis. Which of these claims is more accurate, and why is there a difference?

The problem with most case and forensic studies is that they lack objective evidence that can be compared with the memory produced under hypnosis. Although a person may produce new information and may express great confidence, the validity of this information usually cannot be assessed. There is no way of assessing the accuracy of the information without objective corroborative evidence.

Hypnotically obtained testimony was first used in a U.S. court of law in an 1846 murder trial (Gravitz, 1995). One controversial issue is whether it should be allowed today. The consensus, at least of researchers, is that the possibility of producing an inaccurate memory is too high to warrant the risk (Orne, 1979). Hypnotized subjects are also more easy to mislead than are nonhypnotized subjects (Sanders & Simmons, 1983), and they have great difficulty distinguishing between events that happened prior to the hypnotic session and those that happened during the session (Dywan & Bowers, 1983; Whitehouse, Orne, Orne, & Dinges, 1991). The question of concern is whether hypnosis per se facilitates retrieval from memory. This is a separate issue from whether hypnosis is a useful therapeutic process, where the distorting effects on memory can sometimes be beneficial (Gravitz, 1994). The general conclusion is that hypnosis per se does not facilitate recall (Dinges et al., 1992).

Yet another problem with hypnotically enhanced memories is the potential increase in confidence the subject reports. For example, Sheehan and Tilden (1983) presented subjects with a 24-slide sequence that depicted a wallet-snatching incident, after which questions were administered to determine how accurate the subjects' memories were. Half of the subjects were hypnotized and half were not, and within each of these groups, half of the subjects were characterized as being highly suggestible and half were low suggestible. The data of interest are shown in Table 12.4. First, there was very little effect of suggestibility on overall accuracy; second, the nonhypnotized subjects were slightly more accurate. Sheehan and Tilden also had each subject rate his or her confidence in having answered the questions

Table 12.4 Accuracy (percent correct) and confidence levels (percent of answers given the highest confidence rating) for hypnotized and control subjects

	Suggestibility	% Correct	% "Certain"
Hypnotic	High	79.5	64.5
	Low	79.5	57.2
Control	High	86.1	46.7
	Low	84.5	51.7

SOURCE: Sheehan & Tilden (1983).

correctly. The final column in Table 12.4 shows the percentage of answers to which subjects gave the highest confidence rating. Not only were the hypnotized subjects more confident, but of the hypnotized subjects, the more suggestible were even more confident. Thus, relative to a nonhypnotized control group, hypnotized subjects expressed more confidence in their memories, even though those memories were less accurate.

In the few studies that do suggest an increase in accuracy with hypnosis, a large proportion of the results can be attributed to processes other than hypnosis itself. *Hypermnesia* (the opposite of amnesia) is the finding that memory can improve with repeated tests. Erdelyi (1994) suggests that the repeated retrieval efforts made during the typical hypnotic session are what produce the enhanced memory, and that this result is no different from hypermnesia studies that do not use hypnosis (Payne, 1987).

The majority of studies do not find that hypnosis allows recollection of information that could not otherwise be recalled. When hypnosis does lead to enhanced recollection, it is almost always the case that some other principle, such as hypermnesia, is producing the benefit. Furthermore, hypnosis can lead to enhanced confidence in the produced memories, even though those memories may not be more accurate. In the next section, we look at another way of facilitating recall of information from eyewitnesses, this time based on principles of cognitive psychology.

The Cognitive Interview

Developed by Geiselman and his colleagues (Fisher, Geiselman, Raymond, & Jurkeich, 1987; Geiselman, Fisher, MacKinnon, & Holland, 1985), the *cognitive interview* is based on well-established principles of retrieval. It is best described by comparing it to standard interviewing techniques. Traditionally, police interviews of eyewitnesses began by requesting a narrative of the event, which proceeds uninterrupted. Following this is a question period in which additional information is sought. Little or no guidance is offered to help in the retrieval process. In contrast, in the cognitive interview, the interviewer use a number of memory-jogging techniques to maximize the completeness of the report. Rather than asking questions repeatedly, the cognitive interview involves using techniques designed to access memory in different ways from a variety of perspectives (Geiselman & Fisher, 1997).

The basic principles underlying the cognitive interview are (1) that memories are composed of multiple features (Underwood, 1969) and (2) that memories that might not be retrievable under one set of conditions may be recallable under a different set (Tulving, 1974). We have seen both of these principles in action many times, including the release from proactive interference paradigm (Gardiner, Craik, & Birtwistle, 1972; see Chapter 6).

The cognitive interview consists of four general retrieval methods (see Geiselman & Fisher, 1997). The first is mentally reconstructing the environmental and emotional context, to take advantage of context- and state-dependent memory (see Chapter 5). The second is reporting everything, including partial or incomplete information, regardless of the eyewitness's perceived importance of the information. Asking eyewitnesses to recall everything is a good way to help reinstate the original context, and is an attempt to overcome any criterion (as in signal detection theory; see Chapter 9) that might lead them to omit information they deem unimportant. The third is recounting the events in a variety of orders. When people recall events in order, they often reconstruct what is likely. When events are recounted backward, gaps or suppositions are often highlighted. The fourth is recounting the events from a variety of different perspectives. People often adopt a static perspective that focuses them on one particular aspect of the event, and asking them to recall from other perspectives can overcome this. These general techniques are supplemented by more specific techniques that are appropriate for retrieving specific kinds of information such as numbers. The enhanced cognitive interview (Fisher & Geiselman, 1992) adds procedures to facilitate communication between the interviewer and the eyewitness.

Evaluations of the original and enhanced versions of the cognitive interview have used both laboratory experiments with simulated events and field studies of real police and eyewitnesses. Overall, the cognitive interview leads to more correct information recalled than the standard interview. In a recent meta-analysis of 42 studies that reported 55 comparisons, only 4 did not find a significant advantage for the cognitive interview (Köhnken, Milne, Memon, & Bull, 1999).

The evidence is clear that the first basic component, reinstating the context, leads to substantial increases in the amount of information recalled (Memon & Higham, 1999). The second component, recalling everything, also increases the amount of information recalled (although perhaps not as much as context reinstatement) and has the added benefit of yielding information that is often valuable in putting together details from different witnesses to the same crime (Memon & Bull, 1991). Recalling in different orders, the third component, has also been shown to increase the amount of information. For example, Geiselman and Callot (1990) found that more information was recalled if eyewitnesses recalled in forward order once followed by reverse order than if they recalled in forward order twice. The fourth component has shown the least benefit (Boon & Noon, 1994; Memon & Higham, 1999).

Although the cognitive interview is clearly better than that standard interview (Geiselman & Fisher, 1997; Memon & Higham, 1999), it is not perfect. Its main advantage is that it is based on memory principles that are supported by empirical research. As the principles are refined and new discoveries are made, these will undoubtedly be incorporated into the cognitive interview, increasing its efficacy. The principles used in the cognitive interview, especially context reinstatement, are sometimes used with other techniques. Indeed, Geiselman and his colleagues suggest that on those occasions when hypnosis does help, it is likely that the hypnotist has stumbled onto the techniques proposed for the cognitive interview.

Implanting Memories

A growing literature has show that memories can be easily created (Loftus, 1993b; Roediger & McDermott, 1995); that is, after an experimental manipulation, a person "remembers" something that did not happen. One note on terminology is important here: These kinds of memories have unfortunately been termed *false memories*, leading to an implied dichotomy between those memories that are true and those that are false. This is unfortunate for several reasons. First, as the evidence reviewed in this chapter shows, almost all memories are a combination of episodic details and information from generic memory or from other sources. Thus, at least part of your memory for everything you have experienced is a false memory. To divide memory up as either true or false masks the fact that all memories are constructed and that the construction process draws on many types of information. Second, the term *false memory* suggests that the memory system has *stored* false information. This obscures the important point that the memory system is dynamic and continuously changing. A particular inaccurate memory may be accurate in all respects except one (as in the case with Donald Thomson, described earlier). What is important are the processes that lead to this result, not the simpleminded assertion that a memory is true or false.

Memory for items that were not presented has been demonstrated by Roediger and McDermott (1995). They describe a paradigm first used by Deese (1959a, 1959b) in which he used lists of 12 words, such as *thread, pin, eye, sewing, sharp, point, pricked, thimble, haystack, pain, hurt,* and *injection.* All these words are related to *needle,* which does not appear in the list. Deese found that many subjects would recall *needle* as one of the list items, and Roediger and McDermott (1995) replicated this result: The critical omitted word was recalled approximately 40% of the time. Following recall, the subjects were given a recognition test and were asked to indicate on a scale of 1 to 4 whether each item was from one of the lists or not. A 4 meant Sure Old, a 3 meant Probably Old, and 2 meant Probably New, and 1 meant Sure New. Along with the studied items, there were three types of lures. Some were unrelated, some were weakly related, and some were the strongly related critical lure. The results are shown in Table 12.5.

CogLab Experiment

http://coglab.wadsworth.com/experiments/FalseMemory/

Subjects treated the critical lures (mean rating 3.3) more as a studied item (mean rating 3.6) than as a nonstudied item (mean ratings 1.2 and 1.8). Similar results have been reported by Read (1996) and Payne et al. (1996). Note that both spreading activation and compound cue models (see Chapter 10) can explain this finding. In a second experiment, Roediger and McDermott (1995) had subjects make a remember/know judgment (see Chapter 9). Surprisingly, the proportion of studied items that received a remember judgment (0.79) was almost identical to the proportion of critical lures that received a remember judgment (0.73). This underscores one of the main findings from the misleading information paradigm (Weingardt et al., 1995): People can be very confident

Table 12.5 The proportion of items rated as Sure Old (4), Probably Old (3), Probably New (2), and Sure New (1), and the overall mean rating for studied items and three types of lures in a recognition test

	Old		New		
	4	3	2	1	Mean Rating
Studied	.75	.11	.09	.05	3.6
Unrelated Lure	.00	.02	.18	.80	1.2
Weakly Related	.04	.17	.35	.44	1.8
Critical Lure	.58	.26	.08	.08	3.3

SOURCE: From "Creating False Memories," by H. L. Roediger, III, and K. B. McDermott, 1995, *Journal of Experimental Psychology: Learning, Memory, and Cognition, 21,* 803–814. Copyright © 1995 American Psychological Association. Reprinted with permission.

Experiment   *Memory for Words Not Presented*

Purpose: To demonstrate recall of words that were not present on the list

Subjects: Thirty subjects are recommended.

Materials: Table J in the Appendix contains six lists of 15 words each. Each list has a critical word associated with it that you do not present to the subject. You will also need an answer sheet.

Procedure: Inform the subjects that in this experiment they will be hearing a list of words. Read the words at a rate of 1 word every 2 seconds. Before beginning each list, say "List 1," etc. Allow 2 minutes for free recall, and then ask the subjects to rate their confidence for each word on a scale from 1 to 4.

Instructions: "In this experiment, you will hear a list of words and will then be asked to recall as many words as you can. You may write down the words in any order you like. Then, I will ask you to judge your confidence in your responses using a scale of 1 to 4. A 1 means you are not very sure and a 4 means you are absolutely sure that the word was on the list. Then the next list will start. Any questions?"

Scoring and Analysis: For each subject, calculate the mean proportion of items recalled. Count up the number of words recalled and divide by the total number of words. Then, count up the number of times each critical item was recalled and also divide by 6. Also calculate the average confidence for the studied words and compare with the average confidence on the critical lure. Even though your data come from a free recall experiment, the results should be similar to those shown in Table 12.5, which come from a recognition experiment.

Optional Enhancements: Add a recognition test after presenting all six lists. Prepare some distractor words by including some unrelated words as well as the critical lures. Have the subjects respond using the same scale described in Table 12.5.

Source: Adapted from "Creating False Memories," by H. L. Roediger, III, and K. B. McDermott, 1995, *Journal of Experimental Psychology: Learning, Memory, and Cognition, 21*, 803–814.

---

that information they recall is accurate despite the fact that the information is completely wrong.

Once again, it may be objected that these memories are different from ones in which real-life events happened, but a recent study illustrates that this objection is not well founded. Loftus and Coan (cited in Loftus, 1993b) developed a way of implanting a specific memory—getting lost at age 5. Using a trusted family member, the procedure involves the subject in a game of "Remember when . . . ?" in which all but one of the events described is genuine. The subject of the study was a 14-year-old boy named Chris whose older brother convinced him that Chris had been lost in a shopping mall at age 5. The brother told the story, including details of the parents' panic and of finding Chris being led through the mall by an old man. Within 2 days of hearing the story, Chris began supplying details on how he felt. After about 2 weeks, Chris produced the following report (Loftus, 1993b):

> I was with you guys for a second and I think I went over to look at the toy store, the Kay-bee toy and uh, we got lost and I was looking around and I thought, "Uh-oh. I'm in trouble now." You know. And then I . . . I thought I was never going to see my family again. I was really scared you know. And then this old man, I think he was wearing a blue flannel, came up to me . . . he was kind of old. He was kind of bald on top . . . he had like a ring of gray hair . . . and he had glasses. (p. 532)

According to both the older brother and Chris's mother, this event never happened. Chris, however, described the memory as being reasonably clear and vivid. Being lost at the mall was the implanted memory, and all the other memories were of genuine episodes that Chris had experienced. When debriefed and asked to pick out the planted memory, Chris picked a genuine one. It is unlikely that such an elaborate procedure is even necessary for planting memories. Garry, Manning, Loftus, and Sherman (1996) have shown that simply imagining that some childhood event occurred can elevate confidence ratings that the event actually did occur (see also Hyman & Pentland, 1996).

Hyman and Billings (1998) demonstrated that simply asking college students to recall an event that had not occurred led to 27% recalling that event. Their procedure was simple. First, they asked the subjects to recall as much information as they could about events from their early childhood. Each subject was asked about two to four events that had actually occurred (according to the subjects' parents) and one event that had not occurred. This event, which supposedly happened when the subject was 5, involved going to a wedding and knocking over the punch bowl, spilling some punch on the bride's parents. For each event, if the subject could recall nothing, the experimenter "encouraged (but did not require) the student to visualise how the event would have appeared to him/her" (p. 6). At the end of the first interview, the subjects were asked to continue thinking about the events and told that there would be another interview approximately 2 days later. At the second interview, the subjects were again asked to recall as much as they could, visualizing the event to help them. In the first interview, subjects recalled 73% of the events that had occurred compared to only 3% of the events that had not occurred. In the second interview, they recalled 85% of the events that had occurred, and 27% of the events that had not occurred (see also Hyman, Husband, & Billings, 1995). Subjects were also asked to rate their confidence in the accuracy of their memory. There was no difference in the confidence ratings for real or made-up events.

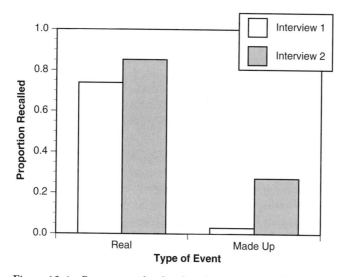

Figure 12.4   Proportion of real and made-up events recalled in the first interview and in the second interview.   SOURCE: Data reported by Hyman & Billings (1998).

One well-known example of a memory of an entire sequence that never happened concerns the famous Swiss psychologist Jean Piaget (see Loftus & Ketchum, 1991, p. 19). He had a memory of being kidnapped when he was an infant and found out later that his nanny had made up the story. It is likely that you have memories of events that did not happen. A student in one of my memory classes had a memory of a favorite pet golden retriever. After hearing my lecture on this topic, she checked with her parents: The dog had died 2 years before she was born. Apparently, she had heard stories and seen slides, and was attributing memory for these as memory for real events. Along similar lines, I received a nasty email from a journal editor asking where was my review of an article that he had sent some months previously. It was all too easy to imagine receiving the manuscript, placing it somewhere in my office, and then having it disappear under a mountain of papers. A couple of days later, I received an apologetic email from the editor saying that an overzealous automated warning system had fired off the missive and that he had not actually sent the manuscript. For those two days, however, I was so convinced that I had lost the paper that I conducted a frantic search of home and office.

Recovered Memories

The ease with which people can be led to recall events that did not occur and believe that these memories are of real events has led to a controversy that cuts across experimental and clinical psychology, known as the recovered memory debate (chapters representing many sides of the debate can be found in Conway, 1997). One problem with the term *recovered memories* is that it implies that the memory is of a real event. A better term, which we will use throughout the rest of this discussion is Schooler, Bendiksen, and Ambadar's (1997) *discovered memories*, which is neutral on whether the memory is of a real event or not.

The central question concerns the validity of memories about past sexual abuse that are discovered during psychotherapy. It is important to note than in the cases under question, there is a substantial time period (up to 20 years or more) during which the person had no memory of the event. Some clinicians (e.g., Bass & Davis, 1988) have concluded that such memories are generally valid, whereas some experimental psychologists (e.g., Loftus & Ketcham, 1994) argue that these memories may be the product of therapists' suggestions, much like the implanting of memories discussed in the previous section.

Part of the problem is that people trained as experimental psychologists rely on solid experimental evidence from (primarily) the laboratory. Based on such findings, Holmes (1990, p. 97) has concluded that "there is no controlled laboratory evidence for repression." Clinicians, on the other hand, see individuals who produce memories of traumatic past events and, with no objective evidence available, are faced with the task of deciding whether the memory is accurate or not. The debate not only has important theoretical and scientific implications, but also raises serious legal issues: Can a jury rely on a discovered memory to convict a person of sexual abuse that occurred 20 years ago?

Schooler, Bendiksen, and Ambadar (1997) provide a reasoned analysis that defines precisely what is meant by "recovered memories of sexual abuse." They note that this phenomenon entails three distinct claims. First is the reality of the original event. There must be evidence that the memory corresponds to an actual event. Second is the reality of the forgetting. It must be shown that there was a period of time during which the person did not remember the event. Third is the reality of the discovery experience, when the person becomes aware of remembering the sexual abuse. Schooler et al. point out that these three elements are independent. For example, the event could be real, and the memory could be accurate, but there might not have been a period during which the person was unaware of the event.

Schooler et al. (1997) document four cases in which they can demonstrate objectively that (1) the original event occurred, (2) there was a period of time during which the person did not remember the event, and (3) the memory was discovered. What this demonstrates is not that all discovered memories are of real events—there are cases too numerous to cite in which the memory turned out to be inaccurate—but rather that in at least some cases, a person can experience an event, can fail to remember that event, and then later can recall the event. The findings of Schooler et al. (1997) do not provide support for the idea of repression; rather, they provide empirical evidence that a person who did experience a highly traumatic event can suddenly discover memories of the event.

Of the three claims, the most interesting from a memory theorist's standpoint is the finding that someone can fail to remember an event at one time and then successfully remember the event at another. More precisely, at the time of discovery, the person has the experience of currently remembering the event but also believing that he or she had not previously remembered the event. In at least two cases, however, Schooler et al. (1997) demonstrate that the person had remembered the event previously.

CogLab Experiment

http://coglab.wadsworth.com/experiments/ForgotItAllAlong/

One explanation of this failure to remember that they had remembered has been termed the "forgot-it-all-along" effect (Schooler et al., 1997). (The name is based on the "knew-it-all-along" effect [Fischhoff, 1977], in which subjects who were told of a particular outcome overestimated what they would have known.) The basic idea is that during the discovered memory experience, the person thinks about the episode in a different way.

Arnold and Lindsay (2002) developed a laboratory analog of this phenomenon. The desired result was to show, in Phase 1, that subjects remembered a particular item and then, in Phase 2, have subjects determine whether or not they had remembered the item in Phase 1. In Phase 1, subjects saw homographic target words paired with disambiguating context words. For example, some subjects might see the word *palm* presented with the word *hand*. This biases subjects to think of *palm* in the sense of part of the hand rather than as a type of tree. At test, subjects were cued with either the same context item or with a different context item. For example, they might see *hand-p _ _ m* or *tree-p _ _ m*. In Phase 2, the test was slightly different. After being given another cued recall test, this time using the context from the study phase, subjects were asked to judge whether they remembered recalling the target in Phase 1. A second experiment manipulated context differently. The target words were embedded in two different sentences, such as "He swatted the fly with the palm of his hand" and "The fortune teller traced the lifeline on the palm of his hand." The key data are for words that were recalled at both Phase 1 and Phase 2. Figure 12.5 summarizes the results for both manipulations of context.

The proportion of words judged as "recalled" in Phase 1 when the context was the same for both the Phase 1 and Phase 2 test was 0.81 for the word context manipulation

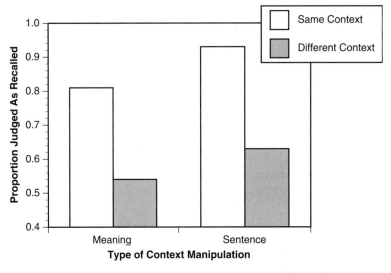

Figure 12.5   The proportion of items judged at Phase 2 as having been recalled in Phase 1 as a function of the type of context manipulation (meaning versus sentence) and whether the context at Phase 1 and 2 was the same or different.   SOURCE: Data reported by Arnold & Lindsay (2002).

and 0.93 for the sentence context manipulation. All of these items were recalled in both phases, so performance is not perfect. However, when the context was changed between Phase 1 and Phase 2, the proportion of recalled words judged as recalled in Phase 1 substantially decreased, to 0.54 and 0.63. In other words, the subjects in Arnold and Lindsay's (2002) study were failing to remember that they had remembered the information at an earlier time because of a change in how they were thinking about the target item.

Arnold and Lindsay (2002) are not claiming that this is exactly the same effect as when people say they had not remembered being abused earlier but now they do. Rather, their study demonstrates that people can forget that they remembered. It remains an empirical question whether this explanation is related to the discovered memory phenomenon, but it does have the advantage of explaining it using well-understood general principles of memory.

Memory Illusions

As Roediger (1996) points out, although there are hundreds if not thousands of studies on perceptual illusions, there are relatively few that deal specifically with memory illusions. One reason may be that with a perceptual illusion, such as those shown in Figures 12.6 and 12.7, both the objective and subjective versions can be continually experienced. With a memory illusion, only the subjective version remains. An additional reason may be that memory illusions are often referred to by other names and are not specifically identified as illusions. A recent issue of the *Journal of Memory and Language* is devoted to the topic of memory illusions (Murphy, 1996) and illustrates many effects. Here, we follow Roediger's terminology and describe some of these illusions.

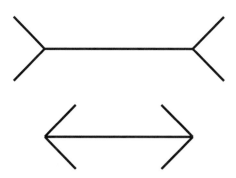

Figure 12.6   The Müller-Lyer illusion: Most people report that the top horizontal line looks longer than the bottom horizontal line even though they are the same length.

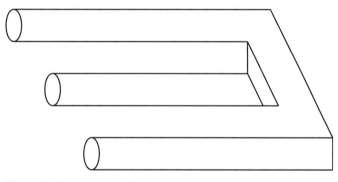

Figure 12.7   An impossible object.

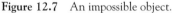

Verbal Overshadowing   Carmichael, Hogan, and Walter (1932; see also Moore, 1910) demonstrated that memory for simple line drawings is affected by the verbal label (see Chapter 6). Two circles connected by a line can be remembered as either a pair of glasses or as a set of dumbbells, depending on the label. Melcher and Schooler (1996) showed that novice wine drinkers could not recognize wines when they engaged in verbal description because their descriptions were not accurate. Experienced wine drinkers, on the other hand, showed no impairment because their verbal labels were accurate. As Roediger (1996) put it, "people remember the events as they described them to themselves, not as they actually happened" (p. 87).

Reality Monitoring   As reviewed in Chapter 11, the reality monitoring paradigm (Johnson & Raye, 1981) is fundamentally concerned with distinguishing memories of perceived events from memories of imagined events. Like research begun almost a century ago (Perky, 1910), this line of research has shown that it is often difficult for people to recall the source of a memory. Memories for events are often attributed to an incorrect source rather than to the actual one.

Misattributions of Memory   Many memory illusions are due to a misattribution. Jacoby, Woloshyn, and Kelley (1989) presented subjects with a list of nonfamous names and told the subjects that all the names were nonfamous. Subjects were then shown a list of mixed famous and nonfamous names and were asked to indicate which were famous. Some of the nonfamous names were new (they had not been seen before by the subject), and some were from the previous phase. The typical finding was that many of the nonfamous old names were judged as famous. The idea is that if subjects can recall seeing a name from the first phase, they know the name is nonfamous. If, however, they cannot recall this but instead are relying on overall familiarity, they will be more likely to say the old nonfamous name is famous. In many situations, ease of processing is taken as an indication that the information is well known (Begg, Duft, Lalonde, Melnick, & Sanvito, 1989; Kelley & Jacoby, 1996).

Remembering More Than Is Seen   When people see a moving picture through a small aperture, they remember more of the object than was actually seen (McCloskey & Watkins, 1978; see Figure 12.8). Motion is not necessary for this effect: When people see a still photograph, their memories include additional information that was not seen, relating to both the object and the background (Intraub & Richardson, 1989). The explanation is the use of schemas: If the picture is of two-thirds of a car, the remaining one-third can be filled in by knowledge contained in a schema.

This is by no means an exhaustive list of memory illusions; indeed, many others are described throughout this text. For example, we will see in Chapter 14 that self-reports of memory problems are usually unrelated to the actual number and severity of memory problems. The important point to remember is that most illusions will go unnoticed because, unlike perceptual illusions, there is nothing objective to compare with your internal representation.

Chapter Summary

Memories are not like books stored on a shelf. Memories are highly malleable and continually change. One reason is that recollection is often driven by general knowledge structures know as schemas. Memories can often change to be more consistent with the schema, or details associated with the schema can be remembered as if they were from the original event itself. Although this is most obvious for autobiographical memory, generic memory is also malleable.

Much research has been done on the accuracy of eyewitness recollections. In general, the chance of changes in memory increase with time, the confidence the eyewitness has that an inaccurate memory is accurate is usually as high or higher than for "accurate" memories, and there is no way to distinguish inaccurate memories from accurate memories without some objective external evidence.

Flashbulb memories are now seen as generally more similar than nonemotional, nonsurprising events. One key variable has been the delay between the event and the original assessment of memory. Studies with very short delays (24 hours or less) find that flashbulb memories are subject to substantial change and reconstructive effects. Studies with longer delays find fewer changes, because the majority of changes have already occurred.

Target Figures

Representative Reproductions

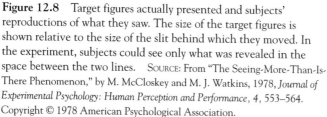

Figure 12.8   Target figures actually presented and subjects'
reproductions of what they saw. The size of the target figures is
shown relative to the size of the slit behind which they moved. In
the experiment, subjects could see only what was revealed in the
space between the two lines.   SOURCE: From "The Seeing-More-Than-Is-
There Phenomenon," by M. McCloskey and M. J. Watkins, 1978, *Journal of
Experimental Psychology: Human Perception and Performance, 4*, 553–564.
Copyright © 1978 American Psychological Association.

Hypnosis does not help in increasing the accuracy of memory or in facilitating retrieval
of forgotten information. If anything, hypnosis is likely to lead to increased confidence even
when the information is inaccurate. When hypnosis does lead to enhanced recollection, it
is almost always the case that some other factor is the cause. These other factors are typically well-established principles of retrieval that do not require hypnosis in order to be effective. Indeed, these principles form the foundation of the cognitive interview, an interviewing technique designed to increase the amount of correct information recalled.

A variety of techniques can lead people to recall events that did not occur. Unfortunately, these types of memories are often referred to as false memories. This is a misleading term because it implies a dichotomy—true versus false. In one sense, all memories are
false, because they are constantly changing and are likely to include information from
sources other than the original episode. The term "recovered memories" is similarly prob-
lematical, as it implies such memories are genuine. A better term is "discovered memories," where the discovery could be of an event that occurred or one that did not. The

phenomenon of discovered memories is real; in such cases a person becomes aware of a memory that he or she was not aware of earlier. The question of whether the event actually occurred is separate from demonstrating that discovery occurs.

In one sense, this entire chapter has been about memory illusions. With a perceptual illusion, both the objective and subjective versions can be continually experienced. With a memory illusion, usually only the subjective version remains. Thus, memory illusions, though common, are very difficult to notice.

Memory for When

Interviewer: "How many words did you have to say as King Lear?"

Actor: "Ah, well, I don't want you to get the impression that it's just the number of words. I mean, getting them in the right order is just as important."

—Monty Python

Many types of memory questions require a person to recall when something happened. When trying to recall where you parked your car, you are concerned not only with a spatial location (the "where") but also a temporal location (where you parked *today* rather than where you parked yesterday). In this chapter, we will be concerned with how people do this, what kinds of errors they make, and how general the findings are. We begin with an example of typical performance on a dating task and then refine the ideas through laboratory studies of memory for order.

An earthquake occurred on Friday, January 31, 1986, at 11:50 EST in Ohio, where earthquakes are extremely rare. Friedman (1987) had subjects complete a survey during September 1986 to assess memory for when the event occurred. Recall of the day of the week and date were at guessing levels, and the month was inaccurate by an average of 2 months. Memory for the time of occurrence was far better than chance, being accurate to within an hour. This study illustrates several common findings that theories of *memory for when* must take into account. First, time is represented cyclically, not linearly. Thus, subjects can be accurate on certain cycles (hours) and wildly inaccurate on other cycles (weeks). Second, subjects are often significantly more accurate than chance but seldom exactly right. Estimated time is often highly correlated with actual time, but people rarely locate an event in time exactly. Third, people use whatever useful knowledge or fixed points they can to figure out the time of occurrence. One reason that time of day was accurate in the earthquake study was that it occurred around lunchtime, a common reference point.

Data to Be Accounted For

Any theory of memory for time must take into account not only the general characteristics just outlined but also several types of results frequently observed in both laboratory and environmental studies.

Recency and Primacy Effects   One ubiquitous finding is that temporal accuracy is better for events that happened toward the end of the sequence than for items in the middle of the sequence (Zimmerman & Underwood, 1968). This is true not only for lab studies (Hintzman, Block, & Summers, 1973) but also for autobiographical events (Baddeley, Lewis, & Nimmo-Smith, 1978). A similar finding is that subjects are more accurate in judging when the first item in a series occurred than in judging when later items occurred (Zimmerman & Underwood, 1968). For example, Hintzman, Block, and Summers (1973) presented two lists of 40 words each to subjects. At test, the subjects were asked to indicate which third of each list contained the target word. Judgments were most accurate for items from the beginning of list 1 and the end of list 2; the least accurate were from the middle of list 1 and middle of list 2.

Telescoping   There are two kinds of telescoping: forward and backward (Rubin & Baddeley, 1989). *Forward telescoping* refers to the finding that people often give estimates of time of occurrence that are too recent. For example, Thompson, Skowronski, and Lee (1988) had students keep diaries of events for 12 weeks. At test, the experimenter would name an event, and the subject was asked to say when the event occurred. The measure of telescoping is the signed error: The number of weeks since the actual date is subtracted from the number of weeks since the estimated date. A negative number, meaning that the estimated date is more recent than the actual date, indicates telescoping. The results from four studies are summarized in Figure 13.1, showing that substantial telescoping occurred.

One consequence of telescoping is that people often inflate their estimates of the frequency of certain events (Bradburn, Rips, & Shevell, 1987). For example, if asked how many times you have been to see a physician in the past 6 months, you are likely to include visits that occurred more than 6 months ago.

A related phenomenon is *backward telescoping* (Hinrichs & Buschke, 1968). Here, events that occurred more recently than a specified time are included, as if they were judged to be older than they really are.

Better Accuracy with Longer Intervals Between Events   Many studies find that accuracy in judging when something occurred increases with the length of time between events (Underwood, 1977; Yntema & Trask, 1963). For example, Tzeng and Cotton (1980) presented a list of 50 words at a rate of 2 seconds per word with a 3-second interval between words. At test, the subject saw two words and was asked to indicate which had appeared more recently. Subjects were correct about 50% of the time when fewer than 9 items sepa-

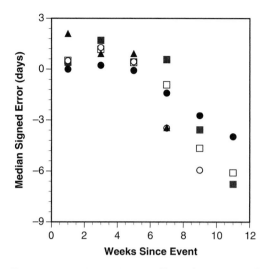

Figure 13.1   Accuracy in recalling when a naturally occurring event happened. Negative values indicate telescoping.
SOURCE: Data from "Telescoping in Dating Naturally Occurring Events," by C. P. Thompson, J. J. Skowronski, and D. J. Lee, 1988, *Memory & Cognition*, *16*, 461–468. Copyright © 1988. Reprinted by permission of Psychonomic Society Inc.

rated the two test items, but they were correct more than 80% of the time when 30 items or more separated the two test items.

Independent Time Scales   Many times, subjects may report an accurate date on one scale but an inaccurate date on another. For example, Hintzman, Block, and Summers (1973) found that subjects might recall an item on the wrong list but in the correct position; accuracy on one scale (position) can be better than on another, coarser scale (list). Friedman and Wilkins (1985) showed that memory for day of the week, date of the month, month, and year were essentially independent; that is, accurate memory for one was unrelated to accuracy on others.

Boundaries   Within each scale, there are anchor points. For example, Shannon (1979) asked subjects to name the day of week as quickly as they could. As Figure 13.2 shows, they were fastest for Sunday and Saturday, and slowest for Wednesday. Furthermore, the data differed depending on the culture and on whether Saturday or Sunday was the Sabbath.

One final characteristic should be discussed before considering theories of time. Sometimes, people directly encode the specific time, day, and date of an event (such as their marriage ceremony or the birth of a child). Direct recall of the time of occurrence can occur, but it is so rare (Friedman, 1993) that it should be viewed as the exception rather than the rule. Friedman (1990) concluded that "time memory seems more of a makeshift affair, requiring a patchwork of processes and considerable effort—and usually ending in imprecision" (p. 43).

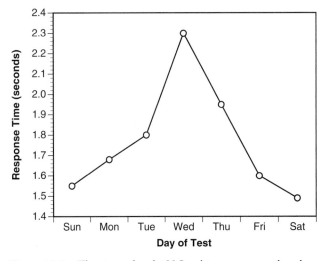

Figure 13.2   The time taken by U.S. subjects to respond to the question "What day is today?" as a function of the actual day of week.   SOURCE: Reprinted from "Yesterday, Today, and Tomorrow," by B. Shannon, 1979, *Acta Psychologica, 43,* 469–476, copyright © 1979 with kind permission from Elsevier Science-NL, Sara Burgerhartstraat 25, 1055 KV Amsterdam, The Netherlands.

Models That Don't Work

Friedman (1993) has identified eight theories of time and divided them into three major classes (see Table 13.1). Although all of these theories have been proposed at one time or another, some are better developed than others. In this section, we discuss six of the eight

Table 13.1   Eight theories of memory for time, the class of theory to which they belong, and the main source of temporal information

Theory	*Class*	*Source of Temporal Information*
Strength	Distance	Trace strength, accessibility, elaborateness
Chronological organization	Distance	Position in memory
Contextual overlap	Distance	Amount of context shared with the present
Time tagging	Location	Specific temporal tags
Perturbation	Location	Associations with control elements during encoding
Reconstruction	Location	Associations with contextual information and general knowledge
Associative chaining	Relative time	Links between events and immediate successors
Order code	Relative time	Pointers linking events to specific prior events

SOURCE: From "Memory for the Time of Past Events," by W. J. Friedman, 1993, *Psychological Bulletin, 113,* 44–66. Copyright © 1993 American Psychological Association. Reprinted with permission of the author.

theories identified by Friedman and illustrate why he concluded that they are not viable candidates for a general theory of memory for time.

Distance theories (Hinrichs, 1970) are based on some process correlated with the passage of time. For example, *strength theories* suggest that people make judgments about when an event occurred by assessing the strength of the memory trace or some other measure related to strength, such as the accessibility of the trace or the elaborateness of the information. Strength theories have trouble explaining the primacy effect, where accuracy is not correlated with the passage of time, and the finding that people evaluate time on independent scales.

Chronological organization theories (Koffka, 1935) suggest that temporal information is reflected in the way memories are stored. For example, Koffka assumed that as events are perceived, their traces are laid down by a continuously moving process. The result, which he called the *trace column*, is not unlike a tape recording, where time becomes spatialized. The traces in the column are assumed to be subject to the same spatial grouping principles that determine visual phenomena: The most recent items temporally would be the most distinct, just as in visual perception the closest items spatially would be the most distinct. This view has difficulty explaining primacy effects, telescoping, and independent multiple scales.

The final distance theory is the *contextual overlap view* (Glenberg, Bradley, Kraus, & Renzaglia, 1983). According to this view, temporal judgments are based on the degree to which the contextual information encoded at study overlaps with current context: The larger the change, the older the time judgment. Like the other distance theories, this view has difficulty with both primacy effects and independent time scales.

Three types of theories are based on location rather than distance. The earliest uses *time tagging* as its basic mechanism (Yntema & Trask, 1963). Essentially, this view maintains that the time of occurrence is stored with the memory for each event as it happens. Judgments of time are made by inspecting the tag, which can become dislodged from the item. The key claim is that time is encoded automatically (Hasher & Zacks, 1979). One major problem with this view is that time tagging theories are generally not sufficiently detailed to make accurate predictions (see Friedman, 1993, for a review). In addition, the evidence suggests that direct retrieval of the date is rare, and although accuracy on judgments is usually better than chance, exact times are rarely given. Finally, studies find only a weak relation between the amount remembered about an event and the date assigned to it. For example, Brown, Rips, and Shevell (1985) had subjects judge which of two news events from a 5-year period was the most recent. Subjects were very accurate in dating the events, even though they often could recall very little information about them.

We will postpone discussion of the two other location-based views—reconstruction and perturbation—because these two account best for the data. The final two theories we address here both rely on relative time and, to be fair, were designed to explain only relative order judgments (which of two items occurred first). TODAM (Lewandowsky & Murdock, 1989; see the optional chapter at the end of this book) is an *associative chaining theory* that was developed primarily as a model of serial order; nonetheless, Lewandowsky and Murdock (p. 25) suggest that similar principles apply when determining, for example, which of two Canadian prime ministers came first. TODAM accomplishes this by the formation of links between successive events. This view, however, has difficulty explaining how the memory system knows the time scale of links to form prior to the retrieval attempt.

Order code theories were also designed primarily to explain relative recency judgments. Unlike associative chaining views, order code theories (Tzeng & Cotton, 1980) allow for links to be established at any time. For example, hearing about one plane crash reminds you of earlier crashes, and thus an order link is formed. These views were not designed to explain time judgments of unrelated events.

We are left with two theories as viable candidates for a general theory of memory for time. We first examine perturbation theory and then describe the reconstructive view. To anticipate, although both can explain much of the data, perturbation theory makes more precise predictions, whereas the reconstructive view has the edge in intuitive appeal.

Perturbation Theory

Estes (1972) proposed the initial version of *perturbation theory*. The key idea is that associations are formed between items and control elements; thus, item and order information are separate. For example, if I want to remember my office phone number, I take advantage of the fact that phone numbers in the United States are divided into a group of 3 and a group of 4. One control element, C_1, is associated with two lower-level units (see Figure 13.3). The subscript 1 indicates that it is on the first level of the hierarchy. The two control elements that are associated with C_1 are called $C_{2,1}$ and $C_{2,2}$. The first subscripts here indicate they are second-level control elements, and the second subscripts indicate their order. The prefix 494 is associated with control element $C_{2,1}$ and the remaining four digits, 4607, are associated with the second control element, $C_{2,2}$. In an immediate test, recall begins with the highest-level control element. From there, the hierarchical structure is decoded, so that $C_{2,1}$ leads to the prefix and "494" is produced. Then, $C_{2,2}$ is accessed, and the rest of the number is reported. With this kind of structure, one might expect a slight pause between recall of the two units.

If recall is required after a delay, rehearsal is necessary to keep the items in order. This is accomplished by a reverberatory loop: The association between a particular item and its corresponding control element is refreshed, with each association being refreshed slightly after the preceding one. Thus, the sequential activation preserves the order. Errors happen when variations occur in the timing of the reverberatory loop. This means that one loop, say between 6 and $C_{2,2}$, might be activated after the 0 and $C_{2,2}$ loop. The order of

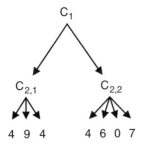

Figure 13.3   The representation of a phone number using Estes' (1972) perturbation model. Each C represents a control element. The first subscript indicates the level within the hierarchy, and the second subscript indicates the group within that level.

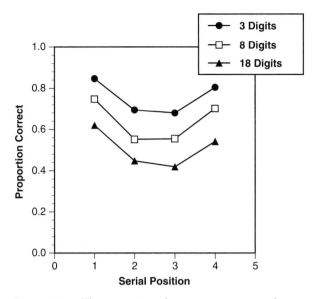

Figure 13.4   The proportion of correct responses as a function of input serial position when ordered recall follows shadowing of 3, 8, or 18 digits.   SOURCE: From "Separating Item from Order Information in Short-Term Memory," by A. F. Healy, 1974, *Journal of Verbal Learning and Verbal Behavior, 13,* 644–645. Copyright © 1974 Academic Press, Inc. Reprinted with permission.

the digits 6 and 0 has now been swapped, or perturbed (hence the name *perturbation theory*), and my phone number is now recalled as 494 4067. Because perturbations are due to random variations in timing, there will be more order errors, on average, with longer delays. Items cannot perturb between groups: The "9" will never swap places with the last four items, because it is associated with a different control element.

An experiment reported by Healy (1974) illustrates the basic phenomenon. She had subjects read aloud a list of four consonants, after which either 3, 8, or 18 digits were also read aloud. The purpose of the digits was to prevent rehearsal and to delay recall. At the end of the sequence, the subject was given 16 seconds to write down the four consonants in four boxes so that the first consonant was in the first box, the second consonant in the second box, and so forth. The results are shown in Figure 13.4. It is clear that the curves are bowed and that the loss of information about position is gradual.

These results are consistent with what Estes's (1972) perturbation theory would predict. The more digits that need to be shadowed, the longer the delay between presentation and test, and so the more opportunities there are for perturbations to occur. Overall performance decreases as the retention interval increases. In perturbation theory, the end items can perturb in only one direction, and so they are more likely to remain in the correct timing sequence. Because interior items can perturb in either direction, performance is better for the end items than for interior items.

This simple model also describes the loss of order information over far longer delays. Nairne (1992) performed an experiment similar to Healy's (1974) but varied the retention interval from 30 seconds to 24 hours. He presented five lists of five words, each of

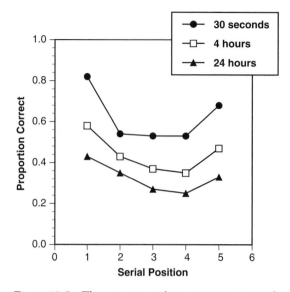

Figure 13.5   The proportion of correct responses as a function of
input serial position when the surprise reconstruction of order task
occurred after delays of 30 seconds, 4 hours, or 24 hours.
SOURCE: Based on data from Nairne (1992).

which was a common noun. As each word was presented, the subject was asked to give it
a pleasantness rating on a scale from 1 (unpleasant) to 3 (pleasant). The words were presented by a tape recorder, and subjects had 2.5 seconds to make their judgment. Each list
began with the word *ready*, and lists were separated by a 5-second pause. Subjects in the
2-, 4-, 6-, 8-, and 24-hour retention interval conditions were then excused and asked to
return at the appropriate time. Subjects in the 30-second retention interval condition
were asked to count backward for 30 seconds.

After the retention interval, subjects were handed a new response sheet that contained five rows of blank lines. Above each blank line was a word from the original list,
but the words were presented in a new random order. Everyone was told that the words
were in the correct list and was asked to indicate the original presentation order. Note
that this is a direct test, but one that follows incidental learning: Subjects were not intentionally trying to learn the items, because they were unaware that a test would follow. The
results for three of the conditions are shown in Figure 13.5.

Note how similar these data are to those collected by Healy (1974), shown in Figure
13.4. Nairne (1992) offered an interpretation of perturbation theory that differed from
Estes's (1972) original version, which had suggested that additional mechanisms and processes were needed to explain memory for order over the long term. Nairne argued that
the same principles applied regardless of the time scale. These data also suggest that rehearsal is not necessary for perturbations to occur, because the subjects had no reason to
rehearse during the retention interval.

Let's examine the perturbation model in more detail. The presentation of an event
(such as a word in a list) leads to an initial representation of values on a number of different dimensions (Lee & Estes, 1977, 1981), at least one of which is serial order (Fuchs,

Experiment *Memory for Position*

Purpose: To demonstrate the similar results obtained when memory for position is tested after 30 seconds or after 24 hours

Subjects: Twenty-four subjects are recommended; 12 should be assigned to the immediate group, and 12 to the delayed group. Subject 1 should be in the immediate group, Subject 2 in the delayed group, Subject 3 in the immediate group, and so on.

Materials: Table E in the Appendix lists 25 common two-syllable nouns. Create five lists of five words each by randomly assigning the words to a list. Each subject should get a different random ordering of items. Also, make two response sheets for each subject. The first answer sheet should have five rows of five boxes for the pleasantness ratings. The second answer sheet should show the words that the subject rated, but in a new random order. Below each list should be five boxes in which subjects will indicate the original presentation order.

Design: Because each subject experiences only one condition, delay is a between-subjects factor.

Procedure: Inform the subjects that in this experiment they will be rating lists of words for pleasantness. Read each word clearly, and give equal emphasis to each item. Subjects should have 2 seconds in which to make their rating. At the end of each list, wait 2 seconds and then say, "That's the end of list 1. Here's list 2." After reading all of the lists, dismiss the delayed group, requesting them to return in 24 hours. For the immediate group, tell them the next part will begin as soon as you get all the papers together. Spend 30 seconds shuffling papers, then pass out the second answer sheet. Ask the subjects to indicate the original presentation order. Give the delay group the second answer sheet when they return.

Instructions for the Immediate Group: "This experiment has two phases. In the first phase, you will be asked to rate five lists of words on how pleasant or unpleasant each word is. If you think a word has pleasant connotations, give it a 4 or 5. If you think it has neutral connotations, give it a 3. If you think it has unpleasant connotations, give it a 1 or a 2. You will have 2 seconds in which to make your judgment and write down your answer. Any questions?" (When you have finished reading all the items, spend 30 seconds shuffling papers, then pass out the second answer sheet.) "For the second phase, please indicate the original presentation order for the lists of words you just heard. The answer sheets give you all the items in the correct lists, but in a different order. Below each word, indicate what position in the list it occupied. It is better to guess than to leave a box blank."

Instructions for the Delayed Group: "This experiment has two phases; the second phase will take place tomorrow. In the first phase, you will be asked to rate five lists of words on how pleasant or unpleasant each word is. If you think a word has pleasant connotations, give it a 4 or 5. If you think it has neutral connotations, give it a 3. If you think it has unpleasant connotations, give it a 1 or a 2. You will have 2 seconds in which to make your judgment and write down your answer. Any questions?" (When you have finished reading all the items, collect the answer sheet and dismiss the subjects, reminding them to return tomorrow.) "For the second phase, please indicate the original presentation order for the lists of words you heard yesterday. The answer sheets give you all of the items in the correct lists, but in a different order. Below each word, indicate what position in the list it occupied. It is better to guess than to leave a box blank."

Scoring and Analysis: For each subject, count the number of times the first word was correctly placed in the first slot. This number will range from 0 to 5. Do the same for each serial position. Construct two serial position functions, one for the immediate subjects and one for the delay subjects. To do this, add up the individual subject data and divide by the number of subjects. The graph should resemble Figure 13.5.

Optional Enhancements: Include more intermediate delay conditions and perhaps an even longer delay. Plot the position error gradients (see Figure 13.7), and try to fit the perturbation model.

Source: Based on an experiment by Nairne (1992).

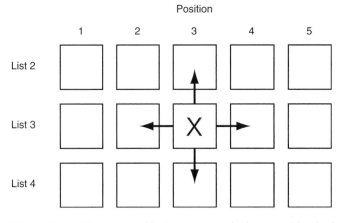

Figure 13.6   The four possible directions in which item *x* (the third item on the third list) can perturb. For example, it can perturb from S[3][3] to S[3][4] by perturbing to the right, or from S[3][3] to S[2][3] by perturbing to the previous list.

1969; Schulz, 1955). For example, in a typical serial recall test, there might be two relevant levels: list number and position within the list. This can be conveniently represented as a two-dimensional array, S[*i*][*j*], where the variable *i* counts the lists and variable *j* counts the items within a list. If *greyhound* were the fourth word on the third list, then it could be represented as S[3][4].

During forgetting, each of the originally encoded values loses precision. This process, known as *perturbation*, occurs when two encoded values swap positions with neighboring values (see Figure 13.6). For example, if a perturbation occurred for item S[3][4] along the dimension that represented position within a list, it might now be represented by S[3][3] or S[3][5]. If a perturbation occurred for item S[3][4] along the dimension that represented the list number, it might now be represented by S[2][4] or S[4][4].

There are three constraints on the perturbation process. First, the range of permissible values is constrained by the experiment. If the study uses nine-item lists, then the values for the dimension that represents position within a list must be between 1 and 9. Second, each dimension can have its own perturbation rate. If list 1 of an experiment contained bird names, list 2 contained dog names, and list 3 contained fish names, there would be very little movement along the list dimension. This rate is typically expressed as a probability that a perturbation will occur during a particular time interval. Third, most versions assume that movement is equally likely in either direction, but this need not always be the case. With this assumption, the end points of a particular dimension will always move more slowly than the middle points because half the time the direction of movement will be constrained (for example, an item in position 1 cannot have the value of its representation perturb to position 0, only to position 2). It is this factor that produces primacy and recency effects: Memory is better for the first few and last few items because the boundaries prevent them from perturbing as far as middle items.

This theory has the advantage of being described by a simple equation. Assume that we are dealing with perturbations along only one dimension. We can calculate the probability that an item, *S*, will occupy a particular position, *n*, during the next time slice,

$t + 1$, by taking into account where the item is at time t and what the probability of a perturbation is. Typically, the probability that an item will undergo a perturbation is represented by the Greek letter theta, θ. The probability that an item will be represented as being in serial position 3 at time $t + 1$ will be equal to (a) the probability that it was at position 3 at time t and no perturbation occurred $(1 - q)$, plus (b) the probability that it was at position 2 at time t and a forward perturbation occurred $(\theta/2)$, plus (c) the probability that it was at position 4 at time t and a backward perturbation occurred $(\theta/2)$. Put together, the whole equation is:

$$S_{n,t+1} = (1 - \theta)S_{n,t} + \left(\frac{\theta}{2}\right)S_{n-1,t} + \left(\frac{\theta}{2}\right)S_{n+1,t} \tag{13.1}$$

This equation assumes that movement in either direction is equally likely. Because this assumption is not valid for the end points, the equation is changed slightly:

$$S_{1,t+1} = \left(1 - \left(\frac{\theta}{2}\right)\right)S_{1,t} + \left(\frac{\theta}{2}\right)S_{2,t} \tag{13.2}$$

The probability that an item will leave the end point is $\theta/2$ because it can move in only one direction. Similarly, there is only one position in the list, position 2, from which an item can perturb into the first position.

These equations allow one to calculate, as a function of elapsed time, the likelihood that an encoded item will occupy a particular value along a particular dimension (Lee & Estes, 1977). Figure 13.7 shows the results of one such calculation. Each panel shows a *positional uncertainty gradient*—the probability that a particular item (item 1 in the first panel, item 2 in the second panel) will be recalled as having occurred in a particular position. The original serial position is typically most likely, with farther positions becoming increasingly less likely.

It is important to note that the perturbation model is *not* a decay model of memory. The model assumes that as time passes there will be more opportunities for perturbations

Figure 13.7   Predictions of the perturbation model for order judgments of a five-item list. The graph shows the distribution of probabilities that an item presented at the indicated position (e.g., item 1) would be assigned by the subject to each possible serial position at the time of recall. Thus, 76% of the time the subject is likely to indicate that item 1 was presented at position 1; 21% of the time it will be recalled incorrectly at position 2; 2.6% of the time it will be recalled incorrectly at position 3; 0.2% of the time it will be recalled incorrectly at position 4; and it will almost never be incorrectly recalled at position 5. For this simulation, $\theta = 0.12$, the equations were applied five times, and perturbations in either direction were equally likely.

to take place. This does not, however, mean that memory will always be worse after longer periods. The model allows for an item to perturb out of its original position, but it also allows for the item to perturb back to its original position. Thus, it is possible to recall the position of an item correctly at time t, to recall it incorrectly at time $t+1$, and to recall it correctly again at time $t+2$.

CogLab Experiment

http://coglab.wadsworth.com/experiments/PositionError/

Although there are more complex versions of perturbation theory (Cunningham, Healy, & Williams, 1984; Lee & Estes, 1981; Healy, Fendrich, Cunningham, & Till, 1987), the simple version seems to account for both Healy's (1974) and Nairne's (1992) data remarkably well. The positional uncertainty gradients can be calculated for each retention interval, and simulations of the perturbation model can then be compared with the data. Nairne (1992) was able to fit his data by setting θ to 0.12 and applying the equations 5 times to fit the 30-second group, then applying the equations an additional 5 times for every additional 2 hours in the retention interval. For example, the equations were applied 15 times for the 4-hour retention interval group. The results are shown in Figure 13.8.

In accordance with the model, subjects are more likely to correctly position the end items than the interior items; and when an error is made, it is likely to be close to the original position. As the duration of the retention interval increases, the gradients flatten and errors are more likely to include more distant positions.

The chapter began with a list of data to be explained; perturbation theory can explain all five types. Recency and primacy effects in temporal judgments arise because the end items have less opportunity to perturb than middle items do. The second result was telescoping—the finding that people think temporally remote events occurred more recently than they actually did. (The name comes from the metaphor of looking at distant objects through a telescope and having them appear closer than they really are.) Telescoping is accounted for by the same principle that explains primacy and recency effects. When an old item perturbs, it moves closer to the end of the list because of the boundary at position 1, and this produces forward telescoping. When a more recent item perturbs, it moves closer to the beginning of the list, and this produces backward telescoping. Nairne (1992) includes a fit of perturbation theory to both forward and backward telescoping phenomena.

The third result was better accuracy with longer intervals between items. This is readily understood within perturbation theory because an item is thought of as being encoded as a point in multidimensional space. Figure 13.6 showed an item represented as a point in two-dimensional space, where the two dimensions were list and position. It would be easy to add a third dimension (e.g., block), a fourth (experimental session), and so on. Multidimensional space, then, simply includes all possible dimensions that represent order information. If perturbation is considered as drifting along one of these dimensions (as opposed to the earlier idea of swapping control elements), then the longer the distance to drift, the more time it will take.

According to perturbation theory, people can be accurate on one time scale and inaccurate on another, because the rates of perturbation can be independent. Thus, in the

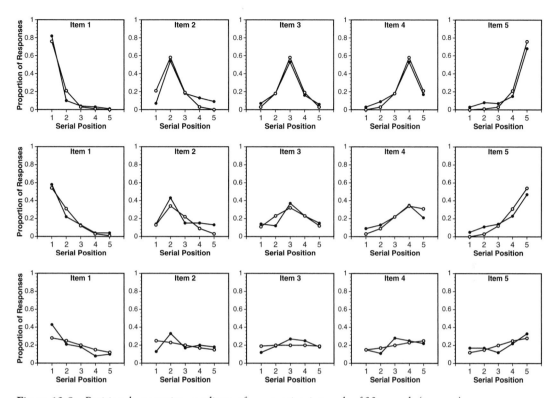

Figure 13.8 Positional uncertainty gradients after retention intervals of 30 seconds (top row), 4 hours (middle row), and 24 hours (bottom row). Each row shows the positional uncertainty gradient for serial positions 1 through 5. Lines with black circles represent the data, and lines with open circles are the predictions of the model. SOURCE: From "The Loss of Positional Certainty in Long-Term Memory," by J. S. Nairne, 1992, *Psychological Science, 3*, 199–202. Reprinted with permission of Blackwell Publishing Ltd.

laboratory, position information might be lost more quickly than list information (Nairne, 1991), just as in dating studies, people can remember hour information better than month information. Finally, the boundary effects are a fundamental part of the model.

Although most of the illustrations involving perturbation theory have been used to model data from laboratory studies, these data are also found in studies of naturally occurring events. For example, Huttenlocher, Hedges, and Prohaska (1992) asked subjects to recall the day on which they participated in a telephone survey. The survey took place between 1 and 10 weeks prior to the dating question. The data from weeks 1 through 5 are shown as black circles in Figure 13.9, along with the predictions of the perturbation model (open circles). Theta was set to 0.05, and the number of applications of the equations was 80 for Monday through Friday, and 10 each on Saturday and Sunday. Monday and Friday are considered boundary points of a five-item range, and Saturday and Sunday are boundary points of a two-item range. Because many subjects indicated that they were unsure of their response, a correction-for-guessing procedure was added to the model. The panel labeled "guessing" is the pattern of responses that would be predicted by chance. Most people do not like to respond with end items, and this inflates the number of guesses

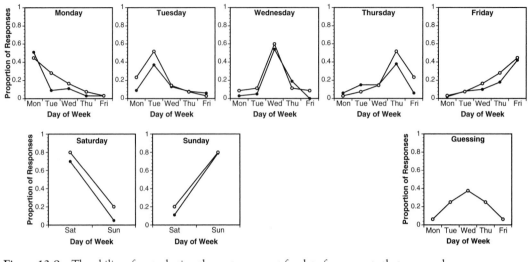

Figure 13.9   The ability of perturbation theory to account for data from events that occurred between 1 and 5 weeks ago.   SOURCE: Based on data from Huttenlocher, Hedges, & Prohaska (1992).

for Wednesday; these guesses are simply added to the values predicted by perturbation theory. As Figure 13.9 shows, the model captures the important aspects of the data. Perturbation theory fits these everyday data as well as it fit the laboratory data.

The main advantages of perturbation theory are its ability (1) to account for all five main results described above; (2) to describe memory for spatial order as well as temporal and positional order (Nairne & Dutta, 1992); and (3) to make precise, quantitative predictions. The main disadvantage of perturbation theory is that it is rather vague on the psychological processes underlying dimensional drift. Although the early versions (Estes, 1972) offered a very precise and detailed description of the psychological processes, the more recent versions (Nairne, 1992) lack this detail. This weakness is the major advantage of the other main theory of memory for when. Before considering the reconstruction account, however, it is useful to pause and consider the relation between memory for item information and memory for order information in more detail.

Item Versus Order Information

In the typical memory experiment, the subject has to remember when a particular item occurred: Was the word *greyhound* presented on list 3 or on list 4? Within the list, was the word *greyhound* the fourth item or the fifth item? When subjects forget a particular item, they do not forget the word itself; they are perfectly capable of producing the word *greyhound* at some time in the future. Indeed, the subjects usually "know" all of the item information prior to the experiment as well as after the experiment. What they do forget is the precise temporal occurrence of the word. This difference between item and order information is just another way of looking at when and how people date the occurrence of events, but it affords the possibility of separating these two factors.

One long-standing theoretical bone of contention has been the relationship between item and order information. Many researchers have offered theories that are centrally concerned with the relationship between item and order information (Brown, 1958; Crossman, 1960; Wickelgren, 1966). There is good evidence that the two are related, but there is also considerable evidence of dissociations between them (Bjork & Healy, 1974; Healy, 1974, 1982; Murdock, 1976; Murdock & Vom Saal, 1967). Some models, such as those of Murdock (1976), Shiffrin and Cook (1978), and Drewnowski (1980), include separate and distinct representations of item and order information, but the loss of one type of information can affect the other. The original version of the perturbation model (Estes, 1972; Lee & Estes, 1977) postulates only a single way of losing information—when a perturbation alters order information. Conrad's (1965) slot model also proposes only a single mechanism for forgetting, but in this model order errors are completely dependent on item errors.

Crowder (1979) argued that there is no fundamental difference between item and order information because each type of information is really a point on a scale. As discussed above, most memory judgments concern whether a particular item occurred at a particular time (Was the word *greyhound* on list 2 or list 3? Did we have apple pie last Thanksgiving or the one before?). According to Crowder, item information is simply order information at a coarser level. If the subject decides that an item occurred during a particular interval, the subject will report that item. If incorrect, the experimenter may interpret this as an item error, whereas Crowder argued it could simply be an order error: The subject mistakenly believed the item occurred in list 6, whereas it actually occurred in list 7.

Even though it seems plausible to think of item and order information as being related, there do seem to be important differences. Some manipulations seem to enhance one type of information at the expense of the other. The *generation effect* refers to the finding that memory is often better for items that are generated than for those that are merely read (Heller, 1956; Slamecka & Graf, 1978; see also Chapter 6). Nairne, Riegler, and Serra (1991) suggested that generation effects are not seen when the test emphasizes order information rather than item information. Serra and Nairne (1993) tested the idea that generation disrupts order information but enhances item information by comparing performance on pure lists (a pure list contains only one condition, read or generate) and mixed lists (a mixed list contains both read and generated items). Using a reconstruction of order task, Serra and Nairne found a negative generation effect: better memory for pure read lists than for pure generated lists. Approximately 68% of the read items were ordered correctly, whereas only 58% of the generated items were ordered correctly. There was no difference in performance for read items versus generated items in the mixed lists. Serra and Nairne replicated these results in a second experiment in which the subjects were not expecting a memory test.

A third experiment used free recall of pure and mixed lists. This time, there was a generation effect for generated items versus read items in mixed lists. Free recall of pure read lists was still better than recall of pure generated lists. In this experiment, Serra and Nairne also had subjects perform the reconstruction of order test *after* performing the free recall test. Even though they found a generation effect for generated items in the mixed list with free recall, there was no generation effect for these items on the subsequent reconstruction test.

Serra and Nairne (1993) argued that the act of generating an item disrupts order information but enhances item information. It disrupts order information by inducing item-specific processing; subjects focus more on the individual item than on relating the item to others in the list (Hunt & Einstein, 1981; see Chapter 6). When item but not order information is important at test—as in standard recognition tests—there will be a generation effect because the act of generation enhances memory for individual items. When order but not item information is important at test—as in the reconstruction of order test—there will be a negative generation effect because the act of generation disrupts memory for order. When both sources of information are required at test—as in a free recall test—the magnitude of the generation or negative generation effect will depend on the design. For example, in a pure generated list, the act of generation will enhance item information, but the output strategy, which typically relies heavily on order information, can mask the advantage. In a pure read list, there is no item information enhancement, but there is also no output strategy disadvantage. One prediction of this view is that if a different output strategy is induced, there should be a generation effect for pure generated items in free recall. This prediction has been confirmed: If category cues are used as aids in free recall, a generation effect can be seen with free recall of a pure generated list (McDaniel, Waddill, & Einstein, 1988).

One complication to this view arises from examining how item and order information interact within a specific model. In particular, it allows us to examine the causes of order errors (recalling an item in the incorrect position) and item errors (recalling an incorrect item). In the feature model (Nairne, 1990; Neath, 1999; see Chapter 4), item and order information are modeled separately. Order information is represented through the perturbation process described earlier. Item information is represented through features. Retrieval begins with the cue in primary memory that, according to perturbation theory, has the highest probability of originally being in the first serial position. That cue is then matched with an item in secondary memory; the item selected is then recalled. An order error can occur due to the loss of order information: The perturbation process can cause an item to be recalled out of order. An item error can occur due to the loss of item information: If there are many missing features, the matching process can fail and an incorrect item can be recalled.

The problem for an analysis of item and order errors is that order errors can be caused by a loss of item information and item errors can be caused by a loss of order information. For example, the cue for item 1 could be accurately provided by the perturbation process, so in the model there is no loss of order information. However, due to the relative matching process, the cue for item 1 might be matched with the secondary memory representation of item 3. Item 3 would then be recalled in position 1. This would look like an order error—an item in the list was recalled in the wrong position—but the cause is a loss of time information. A loss of order information can similarly result in an item error.

This analysis suggests that simply examining item and order errors does not allow us to specify whether the cause is a loss of item information or a loss of order information. Within the context of the feature model, either error can be caused by both types of information loss. It is only within the context of a model, then, that we can confidently apportion the relative contributions of item and order information in causing particular errors.

Although the concepts of item and order information appear simple, it is difficult to tease apart the effects of each. Finding manipulations, such as generation, that differentially affect each kind of information holds the promise of shedding light on the larger issue of how people remember when things happened and how people remember the order in which actions should be performed.

Pure Tests of Order Information

Given the difficulty of establishing whether an error is due to the loss of item information or order information, is there test that provides a pure measure of order information? The short answer is that if there is such a test, it has not yet been identified. Many researchers have suggested that a reconstruction of order test is a pure measure of order information. In this type of test, a series of items is presented and at test the same items are presented again, usually in a new random order. Typically, subjects are free to reconstruct the order in any manner they choose; for example, a subject might choose to indicate first which item occurred in position 5, then which item occurred in position 1, and so forth. This *free reconstruction of order test* may be contrasted with a *serial reconstruction of order test*, which requires the subject to indicate first which item occurred in position 1, then which item occurred in position 2, and so on. Because all of the items are given to the subject at the time of test, the reconstruction of order task "is typically seen as a pure test of position or order memory" (Whiteman, Nairne, & Serra, 1994, p. 276).

Arguing that presenting an item reinstates all relevant item information is the same as saying that the item itself, a so-called copy cue, is the best retrieval cue. The problem with this argument, as Tulving (1983) noted, is that it is simply incorrect. The recognition failure of recallable words phenomenon (Watkins & Tulving, 1975; see Chapter 9) is clear evidence of this: Subjects can fail to recognize an item when the only cue is the item itself. However, when a different item is used as the retrieval cue, the item is readily recalled. Further evidence that reconstruction of order tests are not pure tests of order information has been provided by Neath (1997).

Models of Serial Order

The perturbation model is only one of nearly a dozen current models of memory for serial order. It is useful to compare the models briefly to see what commonalities there are in how order information is formalized. Table 13.2 lists the models, along with the primary mechanism that each uses to model order information.

Table 13.2   Ten current models of serial order and the mechanism/process that governs order information

Model	Sample Reference	Mechanism
TODAM	Lewandowsky & Murdock (1989)	Item-item associations
Primacy model	Page & Norris (1998)	Single gradient
Brain state in a box model	Lewandowsky (1999)	Single gradient
Serial order in a box model	Farrell & Lewandowsky (in press)	Single gradient
OSCAR	Brown, Preece, & Hulme (2000)	Gradient + temporal context
Phonological loop model	Burgess & Hitch (1999)	Gradient + temporal context
Start-end model	Henson (1998)	Double gradient
ACT-R partial matching model	Anderson & Matessa (1997)	Position information
Perturbation model	Estes (1997)	Dimensional drift
Feature model	Neath (1999)	Perturbation

TODAM (Lewandowsky & Murdock, 1989) uses associations between items to retain the order; this scheme is usually referred to as chaining. That is, item 1 is associated with item 2, and item 2 is associated with item 3. As described in more detail in the optional chapter, the problem with this view is what happens if the chain is broken: When item 3 cannot be recalled, how can one get to item 4? One thing that separates TODAM from other chaining models is that it offers a solution. After recalling item 2, the person tries to recall item 3, but fails. What TODAM does, essentially, is to use the item that was recalled instead of item 3. It turns out that more often than not, this will successfully lead to recall of item 4.

Three models—the primacy model (Page & Norris, 1998), the brain state in a box model (Lewandowsky, 1999), and the serial order in a box model (Farrell & Lewandowsky, in press)—all use a simple gradient to retain order or item information. The gradient decreases over list positions in a nonlinear manner, and the probability of recalling a given item in a particular position is related to the magnitude of activation. By comparing the level of activation between two positions, it is possible to determine the order of the items, because earlier items will always have more activation than later items.

The primacy model (Page & Norris, 1998) assumes that the strength of the activation of successive list items decreases over list positions. The result is a primacy gradient in which activation is the mechanism retaining order information. Recall proceeds by choosing the most active item and then suppressing that item once it has been recalled. Thus, item 1 will typically be output first because it has the highest activation. The gradient decays over time, but the process is such that the early list items retain more activation than the later list items. Errors occur because of noise in the process.

The brain state in a box model (Lewandowsky, 1999) is a dynamic auto-associative network based on the model developed by Anderson, Silverstein, Ritz, and Jones (1988). At study, each item is associated with itself, and the result is added to a weight matrix that stores all of the studied items. The quality of information available in this associative stage decreases over serial positions, a form of gradient. Specifically, encoding strength decreases according to a power function. Items are retrieved by iteratively cueing the weight matrix until a stable state (known as an attractor) is reached. Recalled items are suppressed via anti-learning to prevent repetition. The quality gradient is the mechanism that produces fill-in errors: The higher the quality of information available, the larger the basin of attraction. The serial order in a box model (Farrell & Lewandowsky, in press) is a direct successor to the brain state in a box model. The major difference is the removal of several free parameters and the combining of the redintegrative and retrieval stages.

One major problem with simple gradient models is that they cannot account for data such as that reported by Cowan, Saults, Elliott, and Moreno (2002), discussed in Chapter 2. They found that the primacy effect is better explained by output interference than by a primary gradient. A second problem is the lack of motivation for such a gradient.

Two models of order include both a gradient and also a more sophisticated process for retaining order information. Both OSCAR (Brown et al., 2000) and the phonological loop model of Burgess and Hitch (1999) rely more on temporal/contextual information than on the gradient to determine order information. In OSCAR, successive list items become associated with successive states of a dynamic context signal. An activation gradient is produced by reducing the learning rate. Retrieval involves reinstatement of the original learning context, which then generates successive learning contexts. The item that is most highly activated by a particular context is then selected for output. OS-CAR produces fill-in errors as a result of the attentional gradient. The learning rate is typically set to 1.0 for the initial item but decreases over items to incorporate attentional decline.

The phonological loop model (Burgess & Hitch, 1999) is similar to OSCAR in that there is a context/timing signal in addition to a gradient. At presentation, item nodes, input phoneme nodes, and output phoneme nodes are activated. A competitive queueing process determines one winner, whose associations with the context/timing signal and with the input/output phoneme nodes are strengthened. The winner is then suppressed. The gradient is produced by having the suppression decay over time. At test, the context/timing signal is repeated, and the item nodes are activated. The item with the highest activation is then output.

The start-end model (Henson, 1998) is a positional theory of order memory that relies on two gradients, one associated with the start of the list and one associated with the end of the list. The model stores the order of events by associating each to-be-remembered event with its position in a sequence. The model assumes that when an event is encoded, an episodic token is created in short-term memory. Each token contains components that represent item information and position information. An item's position is defined relative to the start and end of the sequence. Retrieval in the model is driven by positional cues. The positional codes for each recall position are compared to the positional codes for each token in short-term memory, and the best-matching tokens are selected for recall. The major problem for this model involves the use of an end marker. As Murdock (2001) has noted, the problem is how to explain recall when the end of the list is unknown, either because it is the first trial or because the experimenter changes the list length from trial to trial. Crowder (1969) showed that recall of the last few items, where the end marker should dominate, was identical in two conditions: when the list length was known and when the list length was unknown.

The ACT-R partial matching model (Anderson & Matessa, 1997) is a positional model of order memory. Each element (item in a list) is indexed by its position. Forgetting is due to decay of activation. If an item cannot be retrieved, its position cannot be retrieved either, so the model must guess. The probability of confusing two items depends on the difference between the position indices. Crucially, the probability of positional confusion does *not* depend on the level of activation, so one can focus just on the difference between the position indices. The problem for this model is that it uses only position information, which is encoded on an ordinal scale. This means that position 2 is equally as different from position 3 as is position 4. This produces symmetrical effects, whereas the serial position curve is asymmetrical.

Rounding out the table are perturbation theory (Estes, 1997) and the feature model, which uses perturbation theory as its order mechanism. Both of these models have already been discussed, in this chapter and in Chapter 4.

This brief overview illustrates the renewed current interest in how people retain order information. Each of these accounts is instantiated in a quantitative model that makes unambiguous predictions about the full pattern of order data. The models vary in their account, but none can yet explain the full data set from even a seemingly simple task such as immediate serial recall.

The Inference Model of Memory for When

Examination of the perturbation model provided a detailed, quantitative account of memory for when and also offered the opportunity to examine the relation between item and order information in a detailed way. The other major account of memory for when, the inference or reconstructive model of memory for time, could hardly be more different. Rather than providing a detailed analysis of primarily laboratory-based phenomena, this approach gives a much more general account.

According to the *inference* or *reconstructive model* of memory for time (Friedman, 1993; see also Underwood, 1977), people use "general time knowledge and inferential processes at the time of recall" (Friedman, 1993, p. 47) to infer or reconstruct likely temporal sequences. (Reconstructive processes are covered in more detail in Chapter 12.) For example, many related memories provide clues to the likely time on one of many scales. Snow on the footpath may indicate winter, heading to lunch may indicate the hour, and wearing new mittens may indicate after Christmas rather than before.

This view predicts recency effects by assuming that less information is available for older than for more recent events. Primacy effects are explained in a way similar to perturbation theory. Whenever there is a landmark event (such as the first time you drove a car), there will be more information available and more chance of accurately inferring the correct time.

The third result to be accounted for is better accuracy when a long rather than a short interval separates two items. This can be seen as an example of a general principle of cognition: The larger the difference between two items, the easier is the discrimination. Temporal separation functions just as differences in size, frequency, or any other dimension do.

Telescoping is accounted for in a manner similar to recency effects. Older events have less other information available, so there is more uncertainty about these events. As a result, events that occurred earlier than the cutoff date will be included, producing telescoping. For many events, subjects will have so little information that they may guess, producing both forward and backward telescoping. The finding of accuracy on some scales with inaccuracy on other scales is also readily handled. As the examples above show, different sources of information will be available for the different scales.

The major strength of the inference model is that it accords with intuitions of how people date events and with studies showing that subjects make more accurate judgments when told to remember information about the event itself. This process seems more plausible and more sensible than having temporal information drift along multiple dimensions. The major weakness of the inference model is its imprecision. Although it can account for the major results, it does not provide enough detail to say how much primacy will be observed or how much better memory will be with an interval of 60 seconds than with an interval of 10 seconds. It is also harder to test: With its lack of detail, it is easy to accommodate a wide range of results.

It is likely that the inference model and perturbation theory can be combined in some fashion. The perturbation theory does include some knowledge (such as the boundaries), and it seems relatively straightforward to add more top-down information. For example, Huttenlocher, Hedges, and Bradburn (1990) identify two commonly used processes that give rise to telescoping. First are bounding processes, much like those described above and already included in the perturbation model. The second is rounding. When there is some indecision about a date, subjects prefer to use a number that corresponds to some meaningful time. Huttenlocher, Hedges, and Bradburn (1990) identify 14, 21, 30, and 60 days as typical values. It is easy to see how these values could be used as boundaries within a revised perturbation model.

Whether this combined approach is successful or not, it is clear that memory for time is not based simply on memory of a linear code and that it is not an automatic process. It is based on inference and reconstruction and includes memory for item information and memory for order. The last section of this chapter examines the relation between memory for when and the more general issue of autobiographical memory.

Self-Memory System and Autobiographical Memory

We have been concerned so far with memory for when something happened. This type of memory is often intimately related to autobiographical memory—memory for events that have happened to you—and also to your sense of self. We focus here on a recent account of autobiographical memory that not only proposes that these memories are fundamentally constructive, but also tries to develop a framework for relating autobiographical memories to memory processing in general. This is not a formal, quantitative model, but rather a framework for guiding further research.

Conway and Pleydell-Pearce (2000) propose that autobiographical memories are transitory, dynamic mental constructions that are generated from an underlying knowledge base. There are three main types of knowledge: lifetime periods, general events, and event-specific knowledge (see Figure 13.10). Lifetime periods represent such times of life as *when I was in college*, *when the children were small*, and *when I lived in Houston*. These represent distinct periods of time, although the start and end points may be either discrete or fuzzy, and are often organized thematically. These periods may overlap, but the thematic aspects are related to different parts of the autobiographical database.

General events are more specific than lifetime periods, and can include both unique (*when I went on vacation to Hawaii*) and repeated (*when I go to New York on the train*) events. These are often grouped in clusters, in which the memories are often causally related, temporally proximate, and similar in content (Brown & Schopflocher, 1998a). Although general events are often organized temporally, the organization is not necessarily chronological; the events that are clustered may be close in time or quite distant (Brown & Schopflocher, 1998b).

The third component is event-specific knowledge. As the name suggests, this type of information is concerned with the specifics of particular events. According to Conway and Pleydell-Pearce's (2000) framework, event-specific knowledge is linked to a general event initially, but unless these links are rehearsed (such as by telling and retelling the story), they are quickly lost. For example, Ross (1984) found that people learning to use a word processor often recalled the exact words they had edited in an earlier session. These "remindings" provide support for category learning, and Conway and Pleydell-Pearce suggest they may provide the basis for generalizations about the self and others. It is thought that event-specific knowledge is not stored in an organized way, but rather is organized "on the fly" depending on the particular cues used at retrieval (Conway, 1996). When the event-specific knowledge is sensory-perceptual in nature, it is often used in decisions about whether an event actually occurred or was imagined (Johnson, Foley, Suengas, & Raye, 1988; see Chapter 11).

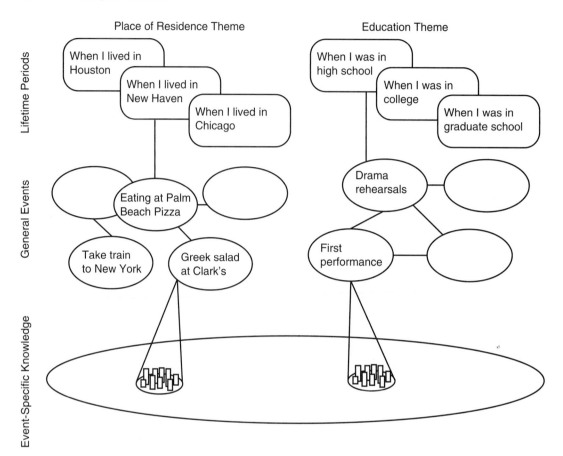

Figure 13.10 The three components of the autobiographical memory knowledge base. Lifetime periods are linked thematically. Event-specific knowledge is an undifferentiated pool of features, some of which are activated by cues originating at the general event level.   SOURCE: Adapted from Conway (1996).

Conway and Pleydell-Pearce (2000) go beyond other accounts of autobiographical memory by explicitly adding into their framework what they term the self-memory system. This is the conjunction of the working self with the autobiographical knowledge base, described above. The term *working self* is used to describe the self in the same way that the term *working memory* is used to describe memory. Thus, Conway and Pleydell-Pearce (p. 265) view working memory as "a set of control processes that coordinate and modulate other computationally separate systems" and the working self as "a subset of working-memory control processes organized into interconnected goal hierarchies that function to constrain cognition, and ultimately behavior." The concept of goals is of critical importance; they constrain both encoding and retrieval of autobiographical knowledge.

This view of autobiographical memory emphasizes both the constructive and the dynamic nature of memories. Autobiographical memories are transitory and are shaped by the interaction of the working self and the knowledge database. The combination of cognitive and motivational factors allows for the construction of both relatively accurate and

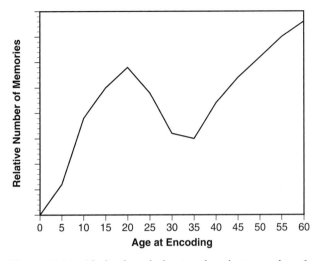

Figure 13.11   Idealized graph showing the relative number of
memories produced as a function of the age at which the event
occurred. Infantile amnesia is followed by a reminiscence bump.
SOURCE: Adapted from Conway & Pleydell-Pearce (2000).

relatively inaccurate memories, and also provides an explicit reason why memories for
both general and specific events change over the course of a lifetime. The particular information recalled will vary depending on the retrieval conditions. Sometimes recall of one
event will cue a second, whereas at other times the same event will cue a different event,
because the general events are organized in multiple ways, including causal, temporal, and
thematic. It is also because the self-memory system is involved in the elaboration of the
cue that is provided and the setting of a verification criterion.

This view is obviously incomplete, and largely speculative. Nonetheless, it illustrates
how reconstructive processes can be integrated within a larger framework that involves
the self, goals, and other noncognitive factors. It also offers an intriguing account of the
life-span retrieval curve. In general, when people are asked to recall events from their life,
they typically recall very few memories from infancy and early childhood. There is an increase, known as the *reminiscence bump*, for events that occurred between the ages of
about 10 and 30. Fewer events are recalled from middle age, and then there is an increase
for events from later in life (see Figure 13.11).

Conway and Pleydell-Pearce (2000) argue that infantile amnesia—the finding that
adults recall very few memories of events that occurred before age 4 or 5—is due to two
factors. First, the goals of an infant are likely to be very different from those of an older
child or adult. Second, an infant is unlikely to have a well-developed self system. Given
the importance of both of these for the encoding and retrieval of events, the lack of
memories from infancy is a strong prediction of this view.

The reminiscence bump, generally found in adults over the age of 35 or 40, is found
for a wide variety of types of material (Rubin, Rahhal, & Poon, 1998). Rubin et al. note
that many first-time experiences occur between the ages of 10 and 30, making these
events more distinctive. After this period, people's lives tends to be more stable, with

fewer distinctive events. Although this observation is probably correct, Conway and Pleydell-Pearce (2000) suggest that a more important factor is that ages 10–30 represent a critical period of self-development. It is during this time that people determine their personal identity, their social identity, and their long-term goals. Consistent with this account are findings that more of the memories contained in the reminiscence bump have to do with goals and sense of self than with first-time experiences (Fitzgerald, 1988; Holmes & Conway, 1999).

Memory for events over the life span varies dramatically with the age of the individual and the age at which the event occurred. In the next chapter, we consider the development of memory in greater detail.

Chapter Summary

When people try to remember when an event occurred, their recollections are more accurate for events at the beginning (primacy effect) and end (recency effect) of the sequence. People telescope, giving time of occurrences that are too recent, but their judgments are more accurate when more events separate the items. People often report an accurate time of occurrence on one scale (for example, day of the week) but not on another (for example, month).

Many models have been proposed that cannot explain these data; these include models based on the strength of the memory, those based on some underlying chronological organization, ones based on contextual overlap, and schemes based on direct temporal tagging of events. The two most accurate models are perturbation theory, which says events are encoded along multiple dimensions, and the inference or reconstruction model, which says people use whatever information they can to infer or reconstruct likely temporal sequences. Whereas the perturbation model is precise, the reconstruction model accords nicely with intuitions of how people date events.

Perturbation theory is just one of many current models of memory for order. The models can be roughly classified based on the mechanism or process that governs order information. Many models posit a single gradient, although some invoke a double gradient or a gradient plus context. Other models have suggested item-item associations as the fundamental process.

Recently, researchers have tried to integrate memory for when within the larger framework of autobiographical memory and memory processing in general. The self-memory system, it is proposed, has three main types of knowledge: lifetime knowledge, knowledge of general events, and event-specific knowledge. This view emphasizes both the constructive and the dynamic nature of memories and also provides an explicit reason why memories for both general and specific events change over the course of a lifetime. The particular information recalled will vary depending on the retrieval conditions. Also, sometimes recall of one event will cue a second, whereas other times memory of the same event will cue a different event, because the general events are organized in multiple ways, including causal, temporal, and thematic.

CHAPTER FOURTEEN

Memory Development

The phenomenon of Self and that of memory, are two sides of the same fact, or two different modes of viewing the same fact. We may, as psychologists, set out from either of them, and refer the other to it. We may in treating of memory, say it is the idea of a past sensation associated with the idea of myself as having it. Or we may say, in treating of Identity, that the meaning of Self is the memory of certain past sensations.

—John Stuart Mill

Throughout this book so far, most of the research has focused on how memory works in people who are between the ages of 18 and 25. However, the study of how these people developed their memory and what is likely to happen to their memory as they age can give us insights into memory from a more dynamic perspective. Both cognitive and developmental psychologists study memory and how it changes throughout the life span.

Memory in Infancy

Although the memories of infants seem to be quite different from those of the average 20-year-old, some basic processes and phenomena can still be observed. This is a difficult area to study, not only because infants do not yet have language, do not understand instructions,

315

and cannot write or say answers, but also because younger infants lack the skills to produce anything more than fairly simple motor responses. Therefore, memory studies of infants are more like those of rats and pigeons than of older humans. Memory in infants is often assessed by using learning techniques such as *habituation* and *novelty preference*.

Habituation involves repeated presentation of a stimulus (visual, auditory, tactile) until the infant's attention starts to wander. Immediately thereafter, a novel stimulus is presented. If the infant shows increased interest in this new stimulus, we assume that the infant can discriminate between it and the originally presented stimulus and that the infant has remembered the original stimulus at least long enough to compare it to the new one. Friedman (1972) used such an habituation procedure to see whether newborn infants (around 1 day old) could remember which objects they had seen. He presented the infants with various checkerboard patterns, which are sufficiently discriminable that even a 1-day-old child with 20/400 vision has the visual acuity to see differences among them. The more times a pattern was displayed, the less time the infant spent looking at it (habituation). However, when a novel pattern was shown, the infant spent a greater amount of time looking at it (dishabituation). This suggests that even newborn infants can form memories of complex visual forms and can remember which of these forms they have seen before, at least for a brief period of time.

Other experiments, using a novelty preference technique, have shown that very young infants can show some surprisingly enduring memory effects. These studies begin by habituating the infant to an object. Then, after a delay ranging from seconds to weeks, two objects—the one the infant was habituated to and a new object—are presented to the infant. Memory for the object is inferred when the infant prefers the novel object over the one previously seen. Using this technique, Bahrick and Pickens (1995) demonstrated that infants as young as 3 months old can remember objects for as long as 3 months.

Another popular method is to place a mobile over an infant's crib and to tie a ribbon from the infant's leg to the mobile. Most infants quickly learn that when they kick their foot the mobile moves, providing very interesting novel stimulation. After a delay, the ribbon is again attached to the infant's leg, but is not attached to the mobile. If the infant kicks at a greater rate than when the ribbon was not attached, it implies that the infant remembers the relationship between kicking and movement of the mobile. This procedure has been used to investigate a variety of different aspects of infant memory. For example, Rovee-Collier and her colleagues have shown that 2-month-olds retain the response for up to 3 days (Greco, Rovee-Collier, Hayne, Griesler, & Earley, 1986) but by age 6 months retention has increased to up to 6 weeks (Hill, Borovsky, & Rovee-Collier, 1988; Rovee-Collier, Schechter, Shyi, & Shields, 1992).

Even infants as young as 3 months encode and retain contextual information (see Rovee-Collier & Shyi, 1992, for a review). For example, Butler and Rovee-Collier (1989) tested infants in a crib in the mobile-kicking paradigm. The crib liner, which was very distinctive, could be either the same or different at test as it had been during acquisition, and the mobile could be the same or different. A group of 3-month-olds were tested 5 days after acquisition, but only those subjects with the same crib liner and the same mobile showed evidence of retention. That is, the same mobile was not itself a sufficiently useful retrieval cue unless accompanied by the same context. Infants as young as 3 months also show a misinformation effect (see Chapter 12; also Rovee-Collier, Borza, Adler, & Boller, 1993).

Even when 3-month-olds no longer show memory for the relationship between the ribbon and the mobile—the memory is not accessible—it is likely that they still do remember something, that the memory is potentially available (Tulving & Pearlstone, 1966). Sullivan (1982) used a procedure known as *reinstatement*, in which a cue is given to the infant prior to the memory test. It is important that the cue not allow new learning, because then nothing could be claimed about the old memory. A number of 3-month-olds were trained on a ribbon-mobile apparatus. When tested after 2 weeks, one group showed little evidence of memory. Another group received a reminder the day before the test, which consisted of having the infants watch the experimenter pull the ribbon. The next day, the infants' memory for the relationship was demonstrated when they immediately began kicking. Rovee-Collier and Fagen (1981) have shown reinstatement after a delay of 28 days.

Although we can infer a lot about memory in infants by studying leg kicking, a different method yields information about memory for sequences. Bauer and her colleagues (see Bauer, 1996, for a review) have developed a procedure for assessing memory for a specific sequence of actions. She first shows the infants a series of events using props. At recall, the props are again available, but the subject has to put them together in the correct temporal sequence to recreate the activity. For example, one event is to use a goalpost-shaped base, a bar, a hooked metal plate, and a mallet to make a gong. The child would be told the following (Bauer, 1996): "Let's make a gong. Put on the bar [placing the bar across the base to form a crosspiece]. Hang up the bell [hanging the metal plate from the crosspiece]. Ring the bell [hitting the metal plate with the mallet]" (p. 32).

The important claim is that performance on these tasks engages the same cognitive processes as verbal recall does. Results consistent with this claim come from studies with amnesics, who cannot perform verbal recall and also cannot perform this event sequence task (McDonough, Mandler, McKee, & Squire, 1995). Children as young as 11 months can recall novel event sequences when tested immediately, and the number of steps recalled in order systematically increases as they get older (see Figure 14.1). Bauer, Hertsgaard, and

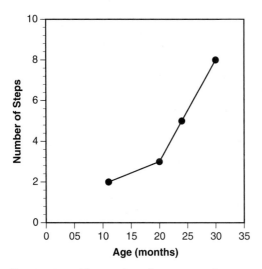

Figure 14.1   The number of steps in novel event sequences that children can immediately reproduce in order, as a function of the child's age.   Source: From data summarized in Bauer (1996).

Dow (1994) tested 21-month-olds, 24-month-olds, and 29-month-olds for sequences they had learned 8 months previously. All three age groups performed better than a control group, indicating retention of the specific sequences after an 8-month interval. As with memory in adults, memory in infants benefits from repetition and from the presence of appropriate retrieval cues at test (Bauer, 1996).

Rovee-Collier (1999) argues that the same basic memory processes are at work in both infants and adults. She shows that even very young infants can retain memories for long periods of time (perhaps forever) if they are periodically reminded. She has also shown dissociations between implicit and explicit memory in young infants similar to those found in adults. Whether one attributes implicit and explicit memory to different systems or to different processing (see Chapter 7), both are available and functional in infants, albeit at a lower level than in adults (Rovee-Collier, 1997).

Infantile Amnesia

One topic of much speculation is *infantile amnesia*—the finding that as adults, most people cannot recall events that happened to them before the age of about 3 or 4 years (Waldfogel, 1948). For example, Sheingold and Tenney (1982) asked college students to recall events surrounding the birth of a sibling. Subjects who were younger than 3 at the time of their sibling's birth recalled almost no information, whereas those older than 3 had quite good recollection. Winograd and Killinger (1983) found that few people who were younger than 3 years old at the time could recall where they were when John F. Kennedy was assassinated.

One problem with this type of research is determining the extent to which the memories are of the actual event rather than of some external source. Just over 90% of the subjects in the study by Usher and Neisser (1993) indicated that external sources of information (such as photographs and family stories) had been available to them. A second potential problem is determining the accuracy of these memories. When people recall events from this early part of their lives, it is difficult to distinguish between recollection of specific episodes and reconstruction from generic memory (Loftus, 1993a; see Chapter 12).

A report by Pillemer, Picariello, and Pruett (1994) is noteworthy because they had objective information about the event recollected. They tested children of two different ages—3 years, 8 months and 4 years, 7 months—for their memory of an emergency evacuation of their school after a fire alarm. Although all the children could answer some questions 2 weeks after the event, only those children in the older age group demonstrated memory for the event 7 years later. This result supports the general conclusion that infantile amnesia can last until age 3 or so; once a child is older than about 3, relatively little information about earlier experiences can be remembered (Kihlstrom & Harackiewicz, 1982).

It is important to note that before the age of 3 or 4, children can recall information about events that occurred much earlier in their lives. For example, Fivush and Hamond (1990) found that 2½-year-old children could readily recall events that had taken place 6 months earlier, and Myers, Clifton, and Clarkson (1987) found that almost all 3-year-olds could remember a visit to the psychology laboratory 2 years previously. Perris, Myers, and Clifton (1990) found that 2½-year-olds could remember a laboratory task learned at age 6½ months. Given successful recollection of early events prior to age 3, why is recollection so poor or even nonexistent after age 3?

The general consensus is that no theory of infantile amnesia accounts for all the data, although there is hardly a shortage of theories (Howe & Courage, 1993; Perner & Ruffman, 1995). Some theories emphasize the development of language, consciousness, and sense of self. As these become more available to the child, information begins to be processed differently than previously. To use a computer analogy, this change in operating system renders earlier memories incompatible and inaccessible. One weakness of this view is that it cannot account for infantile amnesia observed in nonhuman animals. For example, rats demonstrate infantile amnesia, but guinea pigs do not (Campbell, Misanin, White, & Lytle, 1974). Guinea pigs that learn an avoidance response in infancy retain it when tested as adults, whereas rats do not. One important difference between rats and guinea pigs is that, compared to rats, guinea pigs undergo very little brain growth after birth.

Another explanation emphasizes biological factors. To the extent that an animal is relatively well developed in infancy (as are guinea pigs), there will be little or no infantile amnesia. Whenever there is substantial biological development between infancy and adulthood, there will be infantile amnesia. One weakness with this approach is that infantile amnesia, in both humans and other animals, is not an all-or-none phenomenon. For example, recollection need not necessarily be completely absent. Newcombe and Fox (1994) found poor but above chance performance when 9- and 10-year-old children were asked to recognize the faces of preschool classmates. In addition, both rats and infants show evidence of memory when additional retrieval cues are used (Richardson, Riccio, & Axiotis, 1986; Rovee-Collier, 1993). The problem for the biological view is how to explain that the apparent loss can be reinstated.

A third explanation emphasizes the effects of multiple retrievals on the specificity of a memory. Given that inactive or forgotten memories can be reactivated and memory can be prolonged through exposure to reminders, early experiences accumulate and the original form gets lost. Thus, the infant (just like an adult) updates and changes memory for a previous experience every time it is retrieved. Over multiple retrievals, the memory incorporates the internal and external cues that were present at each retrieval and thus loses the sense of when the memory was originally formed, although not the memory itself (Rovee-Collier & Gerhardstein, 1997).

One other suggestion, which is consistent with the previous explanation, is that infantile amnesia is due to telescoping (see Chapter 13), which is observed when people think that an event occurred more recently than it really did. Rubin and Baddeley (1989) suggest that people may "telescope" memories of events from before age 4 and report them as occurring later than they did. This explanation might also be applied to animals, because they show similar patterns of temporal compression (Spetch & Rusak, 1992).

Memory in Older Children

The majority of studies on memory in children have been carried out on older children, between the ages of 5 and 12 years. The average memory span of a child increases gradually from about two items for a 2-year-old to about six items for a 9-year-old (Dempster, 1981). Explanations of the rapid increases in memory performance have focused on changes in basic capabilities, memory strategies, and domain knowledge (Schneider, 2000). We will discuss each in turn.

Basic Capabilities

Two types of capabilities have been studied extensively: speed of processing and immediate memory capacity. Speed of overall processing of information has been used as a basic factor explaining some of the differences in memory between children and adults. Younger children perform more slowly on any number of cognitive tasks (Kail & Salthouse, 1994), which has important consequences for memory. Faster processing allows the individual to make better use of the limited time available in most memory tasks for rehearsal or elaboration. For example, increases in memory span have been linked to the speed at which subjects can articulate. Hulme, Thomson, Muir, and Lawrence (1984) found that as children mature, their speech rate increases. Figure 14.2 shows the relationship they observed between increasing speech rate with age and increasing memory span. Note that it is not age per se that is driving this effect: Some adults fall in the 7-year-old range. The word-length effect, better recall of short compared to long items, is present from about age 4 if the to-be-remembered items are spoken (Hulme & Tordoff, 1989). If the items are either read silently or are the names of objects presented as pictures, the word-length effect is not observed until later (Hitch, Halliday, Dodd, & Littler, 1989).

In 5-year-olds, recall of the names of pictures does not show a word-length effect; but by age 11, there is a clear word-length effect and, furthermore, this effect is eliminated by articulatory suppression (Halliday, Hitch, Lennon, & Pettipher, 1990). The phonological similarity effect—worse recall for lists of items that sound similar—is evident with pictorial stimuli by about age 7 (R. Conrad, 1972), and with auditory stimuli by age 5 (Hulme & Tordoff, 1989).

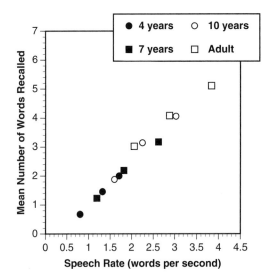

Figure 14.2   Mean number of words recalled as a function of speech rate (in words per second) and age of subject.   Source: From "Speech Rate and the Development of Short-Term Memory Span," by C. Hulme et al., 1984, *Journal of Experimental Child Psychology, 38,* 241–253. Copyright © 1984 Academic Press, Inc. Reprinted with permission.

Although average performance for groups of different ages is correlated with speed of rehearsal, when each individual's performance is correlated with his or her own memory span, the correlation disappears for younger children, but not for older children (older than about 8) and adults (Cowan et al., 1994; Gathercole, Adams, & Hitch, 1994). Thus, it is possible that speaking rate is related to something else that predicts memory span. Cowan (1992; Cowan, Wood, & Borne, 1994) showed that the spoken duration of each word when the child was correctly recalling a list of words did not differ between older and younger children, but the *pauses* between words were significantly longer in the younger children. Cowan (1992, 1997) argues that the pauses reflect the search through memory of the available items. This search speed might plausibly change as the child ages. Cowan (1997) concludes that two sources of speed of processing, rehearsal rate and memory search, both contribute to memory span and both increase as the child grows older.

An increase in speech rate and memory search are not the only factors contributing to increased memory performance. Samuel (1978) tested first- (mean age 6.4 years), third- (8.3 years), and sixth- (11.4 years) grade children and compared their performance on a modified digit span task to that of college students (19.1 years). Of most interest is an analysis of output order. Here, the experimenter calculates the percentage of correct responses on the first response, the second response, and so on. Usually, researchers report only input serial position curves, which show the percent correct as a function of input position; the output serial position curve shows the percent correct as a function of output position. To achieve optimal performance, a subject should recall the item most likely to be correct first, the second most likely item second, and so on. This would result in a correlation of 1.0 between accuracy and output position. The idea is that it is not useful to delay recall of an item that is likely to be correct because it may be forgotten or interfered with before it can be recalled. Samuel found that the correlation between output position and accuracy was 0.481 for the first-graders, 0.698 for the third-graders, 0.715 for the sixth-graders, and 0.884 for the college students. Samuel interpreted this result as showing that as children get older, they are more likely to use more effective or appropriate retrieval strategies.

The second type of basic capability that has been extensively explored is the number of things that can be held in memory at the same time or, loosely, the capacity of immediate memory. Cowan and colleagues (Cowan, Nugent, Elliott, Ponomarev, & Saults, 1999; Cowan, Nugent, Elliott, & Saults, 2000) asked 7-year-olds, 10-year-olds, and adults to perform a visual task while lists of digits were played in the background. Occasionally, there was a cue that indicated that the subject should recall the background digits. Cowan and colleagues presumed that these digits were held in a passive store and were not subject to mnemonic strategies such as rehearsal. They reported that although the pattern of performance was similar across the age groups, level of performance on both the attended and unattended digits increased with age. Cowan et al. (1999, p. 1093) argued that this showed a "short-term memory capacity that increases with development in childhood."

Memory Strategies

One of the major differences between memory in infants and memory in older children is the development of strategies, including rehearsal. Although not well developed until later, some precursors of these strategies can be seen in children as young as 2 years. DeLoache, Cassidy, and Brown (1985) observed children between the ages of 18 and 24 months use a variety of strategies to help keep alive information that had to be remembered. For example, the experimenter might hide a doll under a pillow and then distract the children with tempting toys before giving permission to retrieve the doll. During this time, the children frequently looked where the doll was hidden, pointed at it, or repeated its name. To demonstrate that this was a memory effect rather than, for example, a simple desire to get the toy, DeLoache et al. repeated the study, this time putting the doll on top of the pillow. In this case, very few orienting behaviors occurred.

With more complex tasks, the frequency of using self-generated strategies increases with age. For example, Ritter (1978) hid some candy under 6 cups on a turntable. Gold stars and paper clips available that could potentially be used to mark the cup that covered the candy, and the children were aware that they would have to close their eyes while the turntable was being spun. Third-graders placed the retrieval cues spontaneously, but preschoolers required prompting. Even with prompting, nearly one-third of the youngest preschoolers (ages 3 to 4½ years) failed to use the retrieval cues. It is clear, though, that preschoolers do consciously try to memorize information in certain situations (Baker-Ward, Ornstein, & Holden, 1984; Hudson & Fivush, 1983).

Researchers have taken advantage of the relative lack of sophisticated strategies in 3-year-olds to test hypotheses about adult memory. For example, the *spacing effect* refers to the finding that although repeated presentations of an item in a list can aid memory, the repetitions must be spaced. This finding is robust, occurring for both recall and recognition tests (Hintzman, 1974b) and with large variations in presentation rate (Melton, 1970). One explanation is that the effect in free recall is due to automatic rather than strategic processes (Greene, 1989). Toppino (1991) reasoned that if this view is correct, then even children as young as 3 and 4 should show a spacing effect. To test this hypothesis, children were shown a 22-item list; some items were presented only once, some were repeated adjacent to the first occurrence, and some were repeated 3 items after the first occurrence. As Figure 14.3 shows, both age groups performed better with distributed than with massed repetitions, and massed repetitions were no better than no repetition. Children as young as 3 show a spacing effect, suggesting that this effect is not due to complex strategies.

An enormous amount of research has been done on the development of rehearsal. Flavell, Beach, and Chinsky (1966) examined list learning in children ages 5, 7, and 10 years. The experimenter watched the child's mouth to see whether the child was rehearsing. Using this measure, the researchers found that only a few of the 5-year-olds displayed multiple-item rehearsal, compared to almost all of the older children. Most of the early work on this topic asked subjects to rehearse out loud, and the typical instructions were to tell the children that if they thought about a word, they should say it out loud. Ornstein, Naus, and Liberty (1975) compared overt rehearsal in third-, sixth-, and eighth-graders. The overall amount of rehearsal was equal for all three age groups, and total rehearsal correlated weakly with amount recalled, which did increase with age. The differences turned out to be in the size of the rehearsal set—the number of items rehearsed together. The youngest subjects rehearsed only one item at a time; as the age of the subjects increased, so did the number of items in the rehearsal set. Kunzinger (1985) has demonstrated an average increase from 1.7 items in 7-year-olds to 2.6 items in the same subjects 2 years later.

Children can have very good memory for events that happened earlier in their lives if the retrieval cues are appropriate. For example, Fivush, Hudson, and Nelson (1984) interviewed 15 first-graders about a museum trip. When given a general prompt such as

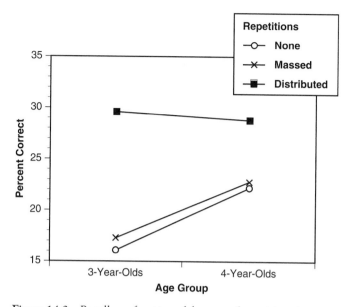

Figure 14.3   Recall as a function of the type of repetitions (none, massed, or distributed) and age. Both 3- and 4-year-olds show benefits of distributed repetitions.   SOURCE: Data from Toppino (1991).

"What happened when you went to the museum?" only 7% of the children recalled it. When given a more specific prompt such as "Do you remember, you learned about archaeology?" nearly 60% recalled the event. In a follow-up study 6 years later, Hudson and Fivush (1991) asked similar questions. With a general prompt, only 1 child reported remembering the information; when more specific prompts were used, including pictures, 13 children provided accurate information.

Lehman, Mikesell, and Doherty (1985) compared memory for various contextual features in children (third- and fourth-graders) and adults (college students). A list of 200 words was presented for continuous recognition judgments; that is, the subject sees or hears a word and is asked to decide whether the word is old or new. In this particular experiment, the subjects then also indicated, for words judged old, whether the presentation modality was the same or different. On the immediate test, there were no differences in accuracy of modality identification, and even on the delayed test, the young children forgot modality information no more quickly than adults did. Given these results, showing good retention of contextual information, it should not be surprising that children show the same context- and state-dependent memory effects as adults do (Bartlett & Santrock, 1979).

It seems from the above research that use of memory strategies and recall performance gradually increase as children grow older. However, research using longitudinal studies, which repeatedly test the same children at different points in time, has called this finding into question. Over multiple testing sessions, Schneider and Sodian (1997; Sodian & Schneider, 1999) found that the majority of their subjects made sudden jumps in performance from chance levels to near perfection. Only about 8% of the children showed gradual, instead of abrupt, increases. There was a great deal of individual variation in the use of strategies, and many children used a strategy in one session and then seemed forget it, only to rediscover it at a later point. By combining performance across children within an age group, as is done in most cross-sectional studies, researchers may be averaging together children who are performing at vastly different levels of competence and may be obscuring a great deal of information. These sudden changes in memory performance within an individual child could be used to argue against some of the theories of memory development that claim there are gradual increases in rehearsal speed or capacity of immediate memory. Due in part to these longitudinal studies, it has become increasingly clear that children's use of strategies and performance on memory tasks is most strongly related to their knowledge of how their memory works (metamemory) and their knowledge of the information they are trying to remember (domain knowledge).

Domain Knowledge and Metamemory

As children age, they acquire more knowledge. There is a large body of literature showing that the amount recalled is positively related to the amount known about the subject matter. (In many of these studies, it is impossible to separate the effects of knowledge from the effects of interest; see Schneider & Pressley, 1989, for a discussion.) One particularly interesting study was reported by Lindberg (1980), who compared recall of 30-item lists by 9-year-old third-graders and 20-year-old college students. One list was constructed using items the third-graders supplied during interviews, including names of cartoon characters, games they played, and the names of characters from *Charlie's Angels*, a late-1970s television show that was apparently popular with young children. A second list was constructed from category norms obtained from college students (Battig & Montague, 1969) that were conceptually similar to the third-graders' categories, such as natural earth formations, types of reading material, and female first names. The lists were presented to both groups of subjects at a rate of 1 item every 3 seconds. The results are shown in Figure 14.4: Each group recalled more information from the list that they knew more about. It was not the case that the college students outperformed the third-graders on every task; rather, the third-graders recalled more information from the list that they knew more about.

Knowledge can also affect strategy use and metamemory. Young children show surprisingly poor knowledge of how their memory works and how much information they can remember, even when they are confronted with memory failures. Increased knowledge about strategies is related to increased use of a strategy, which in turn is related to increases in memory performance (Schneider, 1999). Domain knowledge can also explain some of the other changes in memory. For example, people process known information faster and more efficiently, thus increasing basic processes such as rehearsal rate and memory capacity. Thus, domain knowledge is a powerful explanation of the increases in memory performance seen as children grow older.

Implicit Memory

Even though implicit memory is a very important aspect of learning about the world (Anooshian, 1998), relatively few studies have examined developmental changes in implicit memory from early to late childhood. However, this is a critical area because it can provide data for some of the core arguments in memory theory—in particular, the multiple memory systems debate. Proponents of the multiple systems view argue that there are at least two functionally distinct memory systems, sometimes called explicit and implicit memory (see Chapter 7 for other terms that are commonly used).

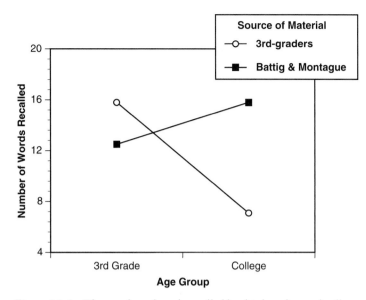

Figure 14.4   The number of words recalled by third-graders and college students as a function of the source of material: third-graders' versus Battig and Montague's (1969) norms.   SOURCE: From "Is Knowledge Base Development a Necessary and Sufficient Condition for Memory Development?" by M. A. Lindberg, 1980, *Journal of Experimental Child Psychology, 30*, 401–410. Copyright © 1980 Academic Press, Inc. Reprinted with permission.

Among researchers who argue for separate systems, implicit memory is thought to be the more primitive system, present in nonhuman animals as well as infants. Explicit memory, which requires awareness and conscious recollection, has been thought to be absent in nonhuman animals and infants and only partially developed in older children. It has been hypothesized that the two different systems mature at different rates, with implicit memory being fully functional by the end of the first year of life and explicit memory gradually maturing throughout childhood to adulthood. This supposition has been widely accepted in the literature (Bachevalier & Mishkin, 1984; McKee & Squire, 1993; Schacter & Moscovitch, 1984; Tulving & Schacter, 1990). However, Rovee-Collier (1997) argues that there are no empirical data from the human developmental literature to support this belief. She makes the case that the only evidence for this distinction comes from the fact that explicit memory can be virtually destroyed in amnesics and Alzheimer's patients while implicit memory is left intact (see Chapter 8). She points out that the main citation used to illustrate differences in the development of implicit and explicit memory is an article titled "The Development of Procedural Memory" by McKee and Squire (1993). The subjects in this study, however, ranged in age from 49 to 77 years. Rovee-Collier (1997) cites numerous studies showing dissociations between explicit and implicit memory in infants, using retention interval, interference, exposure time, number of trials, spacing effects, number of studied items, level of processing, and other variables. All of the results effectively mirror those found in adult populations. Rovee-Collier (1997) does not argue that memory does not develop—all those studies show large age-related changes in performance—merely that there is no evidence that implicit and explicit memory develop separately and not simultaneously.

Empirical data from older children also shows changes in implicit memory throughout childhood. Maybery, Taylor, and O'Brien-Malone (1995) compared performance on an implicit learning task by young children (mean age 6 years, 6 months) and older children (mean age 11 years, 1 month). The task, adapted from Lewicki (1986, Experiment 5.2), consisted of three phases: learning, indirect test, and direct test. The children were told: "In this game I will bring over a board that has lots of pictures on it. When I take the cover off, all that I want you to do is look closely at all of the pictures and point to the one of the house" (Maybery et al., 1995, p. 11). There were 16 pictures in a 4×4 matrix. When the apparatus was blue, the house was in the left half; when the apparatus was red, the house was in the right half. Furthermore, when the experimenter approached from the right, the house was in the upper half, and when the experimenter approached from the left, the house was in the lower half. These two cues indicated the correct quadrant, but the subject still needed to search for the exact location.

During the test phase, the pictures were covered; the child responded by lifting a cover, and if unsuccessful, lifting a second cover. Children were awarded 1 point for the correct quadrant, with a maximum possible score of 16 (2 attempts on 8 trials). Chance accuracy is 4 points. The younger group did not perform better than chance (mean score 3.63), but the older group was significantly better than chance (mean score 5.37). The researchers also tested both groups on an explicit learning task and found typical age-related differences. Contrary to the predictions of the multiple memory systems theory, then, this study found age-related changes in implicit learning tasks, as well as in explicit memory, in young children.

Similarly, Cycowicz, Friedman, Snodgrass, and Rothstein (2000) found age-related increases in implicit memory for pictures. They showed 5- to 7-year-olds, 9- to 11-year-olds, 14- to 16-year-olds, and 22- to 28-year-olds fragmented pictures of common objects. In the testing phase, subjects were asked to name the pictures. The dependent measure was the level of fragmentation necessary for correct identification of "old" pictures compared to "new" pictures. This task has been used extensively in adults to demonstrate implicit picture priming (Snodgrass & Vanderwart, 1980). The results showed significant improvement over the age groups, even when differences in explicit memory for the pictures was partialed out.

The literature on indirect tests of implicit memory in children (such as picture naming or word production) is both small and mixed. Several studies report no age-related differences (Carrol, Byrne, & Kirsner, 1985; Ellis, Ellis, & Hosie, 1993; Greenbaum & Graf, 1989; Russo, Nichelli, Gibertoni, & Cornia, 1995); others do report age-related differences (Drummey & Newcombe, 1995; Naito, 1990); and still others show no clear pattern (Parkin & Streete, 1988, and the reanalysis by Parkin, 1993b.

Instead of resorting to a multiple memory systems account, the results on the development of implicit and explicit memory might be explained by differences in types of processing, difficulty of the task, or the amount of environmental support given by the task itself (see Craik, 1983, 1986). Processing explanations have the advantage of being able to handle intermediate results. With a processing or task-specific view, it becomes crucial to examine performance on each task at various levels of difficulty rather than looking at dichotomous distinctions. However, dichotomies and simple interactions are easier to consider than systems that predict large numbers of interactions. It is likely that computational models will be necessary for the next step of theory development. These arguments are echoed in the literature on aging and memory, which we consider next.

Table 14.1 Percent correct as a function of the age group of the subjects

Age Group	20–25	26–40	41–55	56–55	65–86
% Correct	54.7%	47.9%	48.1%	41.6%	34.8%

SOURCE: Data from Delbecq-Derouesné & Beauvois (1989).

Memory and Aging

The typical view is that the older we get, the worse our memories become. For example, Delbecq-Derouesné and Beauvois (1989) measured immediate free recall of 15 words in several different age groups. The results, shown in Table 14.1, were that performance dropped by 20% over 40 years. However, it is not always the case that all forms of memory decline as we age. Indeed, numerous studies find no age-related decrement, and some even find an advantage for older subjects. For the remainder of this chapter, we examine memory in healthy older people, focusing on where memory deficits occur and where they do not.

There are two basic ways of conducting research on developmental changes in older adults, and both are fraught with difficulties. One is a *cross-sectional design*, in which the researcher compares memory performance in people of different ages. For example, a researcher might give the Brown-Peterson task to four groups: one group of 20-year-olds, another of 40-year-olds, a third of 60-year-olds, and a final group of 80-year-olds. Performance will most likely decline with age. This kind of research has four main problems. First, there is usually a larger proportion of nonhealthy individuals in the older age groups, and these health problems and the medications taken for them can adversely affect memory. Second, there are likely to be differences in educational levels. Today's average college undergraduate is likely to be very different from the average college student of 60 years ago, epecially in socioeconomic status. Third, current college students, having taken the PSAT, the SAT, the GRE, and similar assessments, are likely to be more practiced at taking timed tests with apparently arbitrary instructions. Finally, there are likely to be cohort effects. A *cohort* is the name given to a group of subjects of similar age and experiences. Today's 80-year-olds experienced the Great Depression, World War II, the Korean War, and the Vietnam War; today's 20-year-olds did not. These differences could affect responding, as, for example, could improved nutrition and prenatal care in the younger samples.

The alternative to cross-sectional research is a *longitudinal design*. Here, a group of subjects is followed for a long time, so that changes in performance of the same individuals can be tracked. Although this design controls for many of the weaknesses inherent in cross-sectional designs, it has its own set of problems. First, over the course of the study, many subjects will drop out, whether because of health problems, relocation, or lack of interest. Subjects who drop out for lack of interest are typically those who score lower on the test. Second, there are practice effects: Repeatedly taking the same test can increase scores, possibly masking any decrements in performance. Third, because these studies are very expensive, they tend to have a small sample size. In general, the smaller the sample size, the greater is the possibility that the results do not generalize. Finally, because longitudinal studies take so long to conduct, the researcher can leave (or die), and studies started 40 or 50 years earlier may continue to use methods that are no longer appropriate. Salthouse (1991, 2000) provides excellent discussions of both types of methodologies and also reviews statistical and methodological issues in cognitive aging research.

Fortunately, researchers have been able to overcome or work around these difficulties. For example, many studies use a cross-sectional design but use several different kinds of older subject groups. Other studies use a design in which a critical variable has two possible values: At one level, the researchers predict no age-related difference, but at another level, a large age-related difference is predicted. When these patterns occur, it is difficult to argue that they are due to the problems with cross-sectional design noted above.

In the sections that follow, we will first review the data regarding what areas of memory are or are not affected by normal aging and then discuss a number of theoretical frameworks that have been proposed to account for those data.

Immediate Memory

Immediate memory tests generally show smaller decrements than delayed memory tests; furthermore, the more complex the task, the more likely it is that age decrements will be found. For example, measures of memory span decline only slightly with age, from 6.4 to 5.8 (Parkinson, 1982). Span is less affected by age when the stimuli are digits than when they are words (Salthouse & Babcock, 1991). A task developed by Daneman and Carpenter (1980), called *working memory span,* involves having subjects read and comprehend a series of sentences while also remembering the final word of each. Working memory span is defined as the largest set of sentences for which the subject can comprehend the sentences and recall the final word of each. Although age differences in these tasks are generally small, when the results of many experiments are combined there is a clear decline as a function of age (Verhaeghen, Marcoen, Salthouse, & Goosens, 1993).

In span tasks, recall is assessed immediately, whereas in a Brown-Peterson task, recall is assessed after varying delays. Parkinson, Inman, and Dannenbaum (1985) found that young adults (mean age 19.2 years) performed more accurately on a Brown-Peterson task than did older adults (mean age 74.2 years), and that the difference in performance between young and old was larger with longer delays between study and test. In their second experiment, however, the researchers equated performance on the immediate test. Each subject was pretested to determine the number of repetitions of each to-be-remembered item such that the subject was approximately 90% correct on the immediate serial recall test. The young group needed an average of 2.25 repetitions, compared to 2.8 for the old group. With performance equated on the immediate test, performance on the delayed test was also equivalent. Because forgetting in Brown-Peterson is attributable to the role of proactive interference (see Chapter 6), these studies show that when performance is equated, older subjects are not differentially affected by proactive interference (although the authors interpreted the data in terms of equivalent forgetting rates).

Both verbal and spatial immediate memory can be shown to decline as a function of age. Salthouse, Kausler, and Saults (1988) used a matrix memory task to measure age differences in verbal and spatial memory. The task involved showing a 5 × 5 matrix of letters. On each trial, seven of the letters were highlighted. Subjects were asked either to remember the identity of the target letters in any order or to indicate where in the matrix the highlighted letters appeared, regardless of the identity of the letters. Thus, the stimulus was exactly the same in the two conditions. Subjects ranged in age from 20 to 79 years

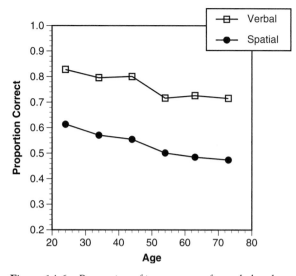

Figure 14.6   Proportion of items correct for verbal and spatial tasks as a function of age.   SOURCE: Data from Salthouse, Kausler, & Saults (1988), reported in Salthouse (1994).

old. Figure 14.6 shows the data for the verbal and the spatial conditions as a function of age. Although performance was substantially worse in the spatial than in the verbal condition, both declined as a function of age at roughly the same rate.

Encoding

One question of enduring interest has been whether older subjects differ from younger subjects in terms of encoding ability. Simon (1979) found that older adults do not seem to be able to use contextual information that usually leads to deeper encoding. She presented sentences with the to-be-remembered word underlined (for example, "The farmer drove his <u>truck</u>") to young (mean age 24), middle-aged (mean age 43), and old (mean age 66) subjects. At recall, the subjects were given either a free recall test or a cued recall test. In the free recall test, the subjects were asked to recall the words in any order. In the cued recall test, the subjects were also asked to recall the words, but they were given the sentence frame as a cue. As can be seen in Table 14.2, the young adults performed better than the middle-aged adults, who in turn performed better than the old adults. However,

Table 14.2   Percent correct as a function of age group and recall condition

	Free Recall	*Cued Recall*
Young	50%	70%
Middle-aged	35%	50%
Old	25%	25%

SOURCE: Data from Simon (1979).

both young and middle-aged subjects were better when a cue was given (cued recall) than when there was no cue (free recall), whereas the oldest group did not benefit at all from the cue.

This lack of a benefit when given a retrieval cue has been interpreted as showing that the poorer memory performance of older adults is due to a difficulty in encoding. This "encoding deficit" hypothesis predicts that if we train older adults in the use of deep encoding, or if we provide them with more specific cues, performance should improve. The data on this point, however, are extremely unclear. Craik and Jennings (1992, p. 75) summarized the situation this way: "What are we to make of the situation in which there are good data to support the conclusions that (a) older people benefit more than do their younger counterparts from more supportive encoding conditions, (b) older and younger subjects profit to the same extent, and (c) younger subjects profit to a greater extent." Compounding the problems with this research is the fact that many studies examine only one variable at a time, rather than examining several levels of several tasks.

There is some evidence that older subjects tend to remember fewer specific features than younger subjects do. For example, Kausler and Puckett (1980, 1981) found that older subjects had more difficulty remembering whether visually presented words were shown in upper- or lowercase or which voice spoke the words. Although older subjects perform worse on tests that require knowledge of contextual information, their performance can improve if specifically asked to study this information. Naveh-Benjamin and Craik (1995) had two groups of older (mean age 72 and 73 years) and younger (mean age 21 and 20 years) subjects listen to a list of words, which were spoken by two different male speakers. The test of interest was the voice memory test, in which subjects judged whether the word had been spoken by Voice A or by Voice B. In one experiment, the subjects were asked to rate the voice in terms of pitch, whereas in the second they were asked to rate the word in terms of pleasantness. The proportion of hits (correctly identifying Voice A and Voice B words) was the same for both old (.55) and young (.56) subjects when subjects rated the voice for pitch. When subjects rated the words for pleasantness, younger subjects were reliably better (.55) than older subjects (.51). Although this latter result looks small, it is reliable and replicable; a second study found that younger subjects again outperformed older subjects, this time .61 to .53.

Given this result, the reality monitoring framework (Johnson & Raye, 1981; see Chapter 11) predicts that older subjects should have more difficulty determining whether a word was perceived or imagined or whether an action was intended or performed. Results tend to confirm this. For example, Hashtroudi, Johnson, and Chrosniak (1989) found that although older subjects were almost as good as younger ones at distinguishing between whether they had generated an item or whether it had been spoken by an experimenter, the older subjects were worse at discriminating between items they had spoken and items they had imagined speaking. Older subjects are also typically worse at discriminating which of two speakers spoke a word (Johnson, De Leonardis, Hashtroudi, & Ferguson, 1995). Hashtroudi, Johnson, and Chrosniak (1990) found that older subjects had more difficulty determining whether complex events (such as packing a picnic basket) had been seen or imagined 3 weeks previously.

Cohen and Faulkner (1989) found that older subjects (mean age 70.4) were more likely to be influenced by misleading information than younger subjects were, and they also had more confidence in their errors than younger subjects did. The older subjects gave a rating of "very sure" to more than one-third of their incorrect responses, compared to less than 10% for the younger group. In addition, in the Deese-Roediger-McDermott paradigm older adults are more susceptible to falsely recognizing the critical lure as having occurred (see Chapter 12; Balota et al., 1999).

Micco and Masson (1992) compared the ability of younger (mean age 21.1) and older (mean age 70.2) subjects to generate and use cues. In Phase 1, both groups were asked to provide cues that would help another person generate a given target word. In Phase 2, a second group of young and old subjects were given the cues and asked to generate the target word. Cues generated by the first group of old subjects were less effective for both the old and young subjects in Phase 2. Furthermore, even when using the cues provided by the first group of young subjects, the older subjects still performed worse.

Consistent with the results of Micco and Masson (1992) is the finding that whenever the task offers reduced retrieval cues, performance will be impaired for elderly compared to younger subjects (Craik, 1983, 1994). The typical recall test offers fewer retrieval cues than does the typical recognition test. Craik and McDowd (1987) compared the performance of young and old subjects on both a recall test and a recognition test. As shown in Figure 14.6, the older subjects were impaired on the free recall task but not on the recognition task. This demonstration is important because Craik and McDowd's study obviates objections to previous work. Typically, recognition scores are very high—so high, in fact, that a difference between old and young subjects might be hidden by a ceiling effect. For example, if old and young subjects were presented with a two-item list for immediate free recall, there would probably be no difference in performance; both groups would recall perfectly, and the measure would not be sensitive enough to detect a difference. In the Craik and McDowd study, recognition performance was nowhere near ceiling, and so we can be far more confident of the result.

Craik, Byrd, and Swanson (1987) showed that performance on a cued recall test falls in between performance on free recall and recognition tests; more important, however,

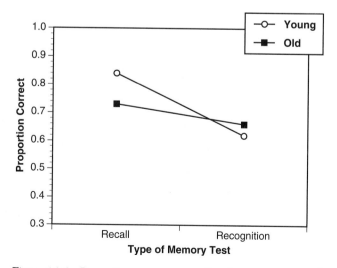

Figure 14.6   Proportion correct on recall and recognition tests for younger and older subjects.   SOURCE: Data from Craik & McDowd (1987).

Table 14.3   Characteristics of the four groups of subjects in Craik, Byrd, & Swanson (1987)

Characteristic	Group			
	Old 1	Old 2	Old 3	Young
Mean Age	76.2	73.5	73.3	19.7
Socioeconomic Status	Low	Low	High	Moderate
Vocabulary Score	31.2	35.0	52.2	48.1
Activity Level	Low	High	High	High

SOURCE: From "Memory Changes in Normal Aging," by F. I. M. Craik, 1994, *Current Directions in Psychological Science, 3*, 155–158. Reprinted with permission of Blackwell Publishing Ltd.

they included three different groups of old subjects. All old subjects were around age 74, but they differed in various other ways (see Table 14.3). Old 1 had relatively low socioeconomic status, had a relatively low vocabulary score on the Wechsler Adult Intelligence Scale–Revised (WAIS-R), and were not very active. Old 2 were similar except that they were active in the community—for example, volunteering for a local Foster Grandparents program. Old 3 were affluent, had high verbal scores, and were socially active. The young group were college undergraduates to whom Craik, Byrd, and Swanson assigned a socioeconomic status of moderate. This design enabled the researchers to explore differences between different elderly populations.

Craik, Byrd, and Swanson manipulated both study and test conditions. In the free learning/free recall test, a list of ten words was presented and the subjects attempted to recall the words without cues. In the cued learning/cued recall test, a list of ten words was again presented, but this time each word was accompanied by a cue. At learning, the cue might be "A type of bird—*lark*"; at test, the cue might be "What was the type of bird?" Two other conditions had the cue either at learning only or at test only. The results are shown in Table 14.4.

All groups did better with cued learning/cued recall, but the Old 2, Old 3, and young groups did better than Old 1 did. In fact, Old 1 did worse on all tests than Old 2, which differed only in terms of activity level. Old 3 and the young group were comparable on all tests except free learning and free recall, in which the young group performed better. Less

Table 14.4   Recall scores for the four groups of subjects in Craik, Byrd, & Swanson (1987)

Condition	Group			
	Old 1	Old 2	Old 3	Young
Cued Learning/Cued Recall	5.5	7.3	8.1	7.8
Cued Learning/Free Recall	2.2	5.4	5.8	5.6
Free Learning/Cued Recall	2.2	4.5	5.3	5.8
Free Learning/Free Recall	2.4	4.6	4.7	6.0

NOTE: Scores within the same shaded area can be considered equivalent.

SOURCE: From "Memory Changes in Normal Aging," by F. I. M. Craik, 1994, *Current Directions in Psychological Science, 3*, 155–158. Reprinted with permission of Blackwell Publishing Ltd.

active older subjects were significantly worse on all the tests, but even the more active older subjects were impaired relative to the college students when the task relied on internally generated cues.

Prospective Memory

Einstein and McDaniel (1990) compared prospective memory in younger and older subjects. *Prospective memory* refers to remembering to perform some action at some point in the future. Older (60- to 78-year-old) and younger (17- to 24-year-old) subjects were given the vocabulary test of the WAIS-R, a free recall test, and a recognition test. The subjects were also asked to press a particular key whenever a specified target word was shown. These target words could be familiar (*rake*, *method*) or unfamiliar (*sone*, *monad*). The data were then scored in terms of the proportion of times the subject responded when the target word was shown. The results are shown in Table 14.5.

There were no age differences on the WAIS-R vocabulary score, although the elderly did do worse on the free recall tests. On the prospective measure, however, there were no differences; if anything, the elderly subjects performed slightly better. Both groups performed better when the target word was unfamiliar than when it was familiar.

This lack of an age-related difference was explored further in a second study (Einstein, McDaniel, Richardson, Guynn, & Cunfer, 1995). Prospective memory tasks can be signaled in two different ways. In a time-based task, the subject must perform some activity at a certain time; in an event-based task, the subject must perform the activity when a certain event occurs. Examples are remembering to take a pill every 8 hours versus remembering to give Bob a message when you see him. Using a similar pool of subjects as in the previous study, Einstein et al. (1995) again found no age-related differences on an event-based prospective memory task, but they did find age-related differences with a time-based task.

One difference between event-based and time-based prospective memory is whether the retrieval cue is present in the environment or is internally generated. When it is internally generated or self-initiated (time-based), there are age-related differences. More recent research has qualified that result and shown that there are actually age-related deficits even when the task is event-based, although they are smaller than the deficit in time-based tasks (Maylor, 1998; West & Craik, 1999). Interestingly, older adults are often better than younger adults in remembering to perform real-life tasks, perhaps because of

Table 14.5 Performance on a retrospective memory task (free recall) and a prospective memory task (remembering to press a key when a target word was shown) for two different age groups with the same WAIS-R score

	Young		Elderly	
Measure	Familiar	Unfamiliar	Familiar	Unfamiliar
WAIS-R	53.33	50.50	57.42	56.42
Free Recall	.58	.51	.41	.47
Prospective Memory	.28	.83	.36	.94

NOTE: The older subjects show impairment on the retrospective memory task but no impairment on the prospective memory task.

SOURCE: Data from Einstein & McDaniel (1990).

greater motivation (Rendell & Thomson, 1999). Anderson and Craik (2000) argue that the self-initiated activities that show a large decline with aging in the prospective memory literature are the same as those that show a decline in recall and context; both are sensitive to the amount of environmental support available in the situation.

Neuropsychological Changes

It has been suggested that the frontal lobes are particularly affected in the course of aging (West, 1996; Raz, 2000; Anderson & Craik, 2000). As discussed in Chapter 8, the frontal lobes have been associated with a great many memory functions. There seem to be some similarities between the deficits found in the memory performance of older adults and patients with frontal lobe damage, although to a much lesser extent. Imaging data (PET, fMRI) show that areas of the prefrontal cortex are less active in older than in younger adults when performing some tasks, but more active with other tasks. For example, a common finding in younger adults is increased activity in the left prefrontal cortex during encoding and in the right during retrieval. In contrast, older adults often show less activation in the left prefrontal cortex during encoding but both left and right activation during retrieval (Cabeza et al., 1997; Bäckman et al., 1997).

Anderson et al. (2000) measured brain activity in both younger and older adults when they were performing a paired-associate task under conditions of full or divided attention. They found reduced activity in the left frontal lobe during encoding in the older adults as well as in the younger adults, but only when were performing the primary task while doing a secondary task. They suggest that older adults might be operating with reduced attentional resources all the time, which would affect memory processing. This fits in with the hypothesis that the frontal lobes are involved in strategic, self-initiated aspects of memory (Kapur et al., 1995) and that the difficulty that older adults have retrieving context may be due to a difficulty in the encoding and retrieval of associative information—the "associative deficit hypothesis" (Naveh-Benjamin, 2000).

The Victoria Longitudinal Study

The Victoria Longitudinal Study (VLS; Hultsch, Hertzog, Dixon, & Small, 1998) is a longitudinal study testing 487 individuals, ranging in age from 55 to 86 years, over a period of 6 years. Each of the older participants was tested a minimum of 3 times (the study has since been expanded to include new samples of participants added at 6-year intervals—those data are not yet published). A control group of 100 adults between 19 and 36 years of age was tested only once. This study is one of the few longitudinal studies to focus on how memory changes as a function of age. The goal was to separate out individual differences in the aging of memory from preexisting differences between individuals. Participants were given a battery of tests in three categories: memory variables, including tests of episodic, semantic, and implicit memory; cognitive variables, including measures of verbal fluency, reading comprehension, and vocabulary; and health variables, including physical and mental health, activity, and personality measures. To minimize practice effects on the memory measures, there were actually six alternate forms of the episodic and semantic memory measures. The order of these tests was partially counterbalanced across participants.

This study was a massive undertaking, and we will only touch on its major conclusions; the study is described fully in Hultsch et al. (1998). The authors first conclude that there are real differences in memory performance between older and younger adults; the differences that have been found in cross-sectional studies were not due to cohort or sample differences. For every variable, age by itself must be considered in order to explain the data. In addition, they found substantial declines on most of the cognitive variables, and these declines accelerated around age 75. Consistent with the multiple memory systems account of aging, which predicts that the more specialized episodic memory tasks will decline first and implicit tasks last, they found a decline on the episodic word recall task but no significant changes on the implicit memory tasks. However, text recall, another measure of episodic memory, did not decline in their sample, and fact recall, which should be a measure of semantic memory, did decline significantly. This pattern does not fit the multiple memory systems account but does dovetail nicely with Craik's (1994) reduced resources and self-initiated processing view, discussed below.

It is possible that as people grow older, everything gets worse because of a common underlying cause; as Rabbitt (1993) put it, "Does it all go together when it goes?" In the VLS, the factor for a general decline accounted for about half of the change, but the actual amount varied depending on the task. More than 75% of the change in some of the variables (fact recall, working memory, comprehension speed) was accounted for by a general decline, whereas only 25% of the change in other variables (verbal fluency, reading comprehension, semantic speed) was attributable to the general factor. The authors of the VLS conclude that the large amount of variance that is independent of a general factor makes it unlikely that a single cause or factor underlies the changes in memory that occur as we age. Measures of working memory seemed to be the best predictor of episodic memory performance, leading Hultsch et al. (1998, p. 276) to suggest that "a better answer to Rabbitt's (1993) question might be 'When working memory goes, a lot goes with it.'"

Self-Report Data

One final finding relevant to evaluating memory deficits in the elderly is the accuracy of self-reports. Rabbitt and Abson (1991) found that older subjects' estimates of their own performance were uncorrelated with their actual performance on recognition, memory span, recall, and cumulative learning tasks. However, there were significant correlations between estimated memory ability and reports of depression. Thus, although the elderly may report many more memory problems than younger adults do, and although this perceived loss may contribute to depression, self-reported memory problems may not be related to actual memory problems. Memory tasks that require self-generated cues are likely to suffer, but as we shall see in the next section, there are many tasks on which the elderly are not impaired.

Indirect Tests

Light and Singh (1987) compared memory performance on both direct and indirect tests of memory. A group of young subjects (mean age 23.1) and a group of old subjects (mean age 68.3) saw a list of words and were asked to rate each word's pleasantness. After the list had been presented, half of the subjects received a word completion test and half received a cued recall test. The only difference between the tests was the instructions. In the word stem completion test, the subjects were asked to write the first word that came to mind for each word stem. In the cued recall test, the subjects were told that some of the stems

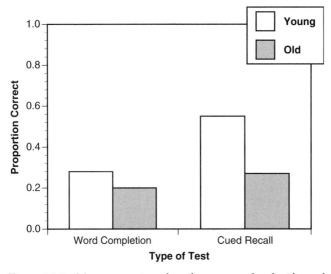

Figure 14.7   Mean proportion of word stems completed with words from the studied list. The only difference between the word completion and cued recall tests was the instructions.   SOURCE: Data from Light & Singh (1987).

came from the list they had just rated, and they were asked to treat the stems as clues for recall. Note that this is a test of incidental learning, using either an indirect test or a direct test. The results are shown in Figure 14.7. There was a large difference when the test asked the subjects to refer back to the learning episode (cued recall), but there was no reliable difference when the task did not refer back (word completion).

Many other studies have found reduced or absent age-related differences on indirect tests (Chiarello & Hoyer, 1988; Craik & Jennings, 1992; Graf, 1990; Light & Burke, 1988). For example, Java and Gardiner (1991) found that older subjects (ages 62 to 87) showed a reliable decrement in free recall, but found almost no influence of age on a word-stem completion task.

Parkin and Walter (1992) examined performance on a recognition test using the remember/know procedure (see Chapter 9) with subjects in three age groups—old (mean age 81.6 years), middle-old (mean age 67.7), and young (mean age 21.5)—all of whom performed equivalently on three different assessments of cognitive functioning. Subjects saw a list of 36 words printed on index cards for 2 seconds each and were asked to remember the words. At the end of the list, the subjects were engaged in "genial conversation" for about 10 minutes. Then the subjects saw 72 words and were asked to indicate which words were from the list and to mark whether they remembered the item or simply knew the item was on the list. The results are shown in Figure 14.8.

Although overall accuracy did not differ substantially between the groups, with increasing age, subjects were more likely to give a "know" response and less likely to give a "remember" response. This result has also been found in other studies (Mäntylä, 1993; Maylor, 1995). A second study showed equivalent confidence ratings between older and younger subjects, indicating that they were not basing their remember/know decisions on their level of confidence (see also Rajaram, 1993).

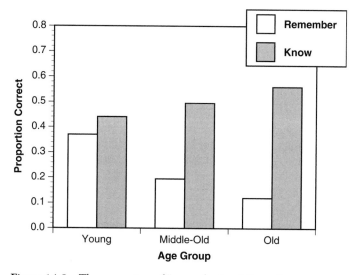

Figure 14.8 The proportion of "remember" and "know" responses given by young, middle-old, and old subjects. Older subjects were more likely to give fewer "remember" responses and more "know" responses than younger subjects, even though overall accuracy did not differ.
Source: From "Recollective Experience, Normal Aging, and Frontal Dysfunction," by A. J. Parkin and B. M. Walter, 1992, *Psychology and Aging, 7*, 290–298. Copyright © 1992 American Psychological Association. Reprinted with permission.

Larry Jacoby (Hay & Jacoby, 1999, p. 122) is fond of relating the following anecdote:

Consider the story of an aging math professor in Winnipeg who went to a conference in Chicago and was unable to find his airline ticket when he was ready to return home. After an extensive search for his ticket failed, he bought another and, on arriving in Winnipeg, called his wife to pick him up at the airport. She responded that she would be unable to do so because he had driven the car to Chicago.

Jacoby uses this story to illustrate the influence of automatic behavior or habit when recollection fails. The math professor's mistake was likely due to the fact that he usually flew to conferences (habit). However, a failure in recollection was also necessary for this mix-up to occur. In that particular situation, habit and recollection were in conflict. If conscious recollection is impaired but automatic or implicit processing is intact in older adults, we should be able to observe a decline using the process dissociation procedure discussed in Chapter 5. Hay and Jacoby (1999) did just this and found that older adults were more likely than younger adults to experience failures in recollection but showed the same pattern when automatic processes were measured.

One interesting parallel is that older subjects' performance is often like that of subjects with human amnesic syndrome (see Chapter 8), although with far less impairment. Both groups of subjects show relatively unimpaired performance on indirect tests and impairment on direct tests. When recognition performance is broken down into conscious recollection versus just knowing, then differences emerge. Consistent with this idea is an experiment by Dywan and Jacoby (1990), who compared performance of younger (mean age 19.5 years) and older (mean age 71.2 years) subjects in the false fame paradigm. Subjects see a list of nonfamous names and are told they are nonfamous; they then see a list of mixed famous and nonfamous names and are asked to indicate which are famous. Some of the nonfamous names have not been seen before by the subject, and some are from the previous phase. If subjects recall seeing a name from the previous phase, they know the name is nonfamous. If, on the other hand, they cannot recall that the name was from the old nonfamous list but instead rely on overall familiarity, they will be more likely to say the old nonfamous name is famous. Dywan and Jacoby found that the probability of saying an old nonfamous name was famous was higher for the older subjects (.20) than for younger subjects (.14). They argued that although both old and young subjects have similar feelings of familiarity, younger subjects are better able to recall the source of the familiarity and attribute it to seeing the name in the earlier phase of the experiment. Older subjects, on the other hand, are more likely to attribute the familiarity to the name's being famous.

Incidental learning (see Chapter 7) also seems relatively unimpaired, at least when assessed by indirect tests. Howard and Howard (1992) compared performances by a young group (mean age 19.4 years) and an old group (mean age 73.4 years) who were similar in their WAIS-R Vocabulary scores and WAIS Digits Backward scores. The task was implicit serial pattern learning, in which subjects were asked to press one of four keys as quickly as they could when an asterisk appeared in one of four locations. With A indicating the left-most location, there were two patterns—DBCACBDCBA and BCACDCDBADADACAD—but we will focus on only the short pattern. The first two blocks had trials that followed the pattern, the third block had a random pattern, and the fourth block again had the repeating pattern.

The older subjects' response times were consistently slower than those of the younger group, a standard finding (Salthouse, 1991). The older subjects were slightly more accurate than the young, with accuracy of .97, .97, .95, and .96 for blocks 1 through 4 for the young subjects, compared to .98, .98, .97, and .97 for the old subjects. The indirect test of pattern learning was to see if the median response times on block 3 were reliably greater than on block 2. Both groups were slower on the random patterns—the young group by 108 ms and the old group by 85 ms, which is not a reliable difference. Thus, on an indirect test of incidental learning, there was no age-related impairment. The direct test occurred in the fifth block. Here, subjects were asked to predict the next location prior to the appearance of the asterisk, and the measure was simply proportion correct. The young subjects were more accurate (.76) than the old subjects (.53). Thus, on indirect tests of incidental learning, there are no age-related differences; on direct tests of incidental learning, there are age-related differences. One qualification could be that this lack of impairment for indirect tests of incidental learning applies only for high-functioning elderly adults (Cherry & Stadler, 1995).

Theoretical Explanations of Aging and Memory

Of the many explanations for the effects of normal aging on memory, three main accounts are easily distinguishable: the disuse view, the multiple systems view, and the processing view. This last view encompasses several differing approaches, including a transfer appropriate processing account and one based on reduced resources or processing speed.

The Disuse View

One explanation for age-related declines has been termed the "use it or lose it" view. The analogy is to muscles, where exercise increases performance and lack of exercise induces atrophy, and can be traced back to at least Vives in 1523 (see Chapter 1). Some support for this view comes from numerous studies showing that rats raised in enriched environments show significantly better performance and more complex brain organization and functioning than do rats raised in sterile environments (Greenough, Black, & Wallace, 1987; Rosenzweig, 1984). Thus, given that use promotes brain functioning, the idea is that disuse depresses brain functioning. Many memory tasks require processing that may be unfamiliar to elderly subjects; because of their long-standing removal from academic environments, they may not have performed similar tasks for several decades, if ever. According to this view, then, tasks that tap processes still used by elderly subjects will reveal no deficits, whereas tasks that require less frequently used processes will show deficits.

Some support for this idea comes from a study of aging university professors (Shimamura, Berry, Mangels, Rusting, & Jurica, 1995). The reason for using this group of subjects is that all (both young and elderly) are cognitively active; have similar levels of academic training; and have similar cultural, economic, and social environments. The young professors had a mean age of 38.4 years, the middle-aged professors had a mean age of 52.2 years, and the senior professors had a mean age of 64.7 years. Although the older professors were impaired relative to the younger on tests of response time and paired-associate learning, there was no difference on measures of proactive interference and prose recall. These latter two results differ from those of most aging studies. Shimamura et al. (1995) suggested that one possibility was that "mental activity reduces the changes that typically occur as a result of aging" (p. 276). An alternative, however, could be that the "professors' preserved performance on behavioral measures is the result of an enhanced ability to compensate for decrements" (p. 276).

Although an intriguing idea, the disuse view has three main problems. First, Salthouse (1991, pp. 134–136) lists about 40 tasks on which researchers have found an age-related impairment. All of these tasks are described as meaningful or ecologically valid and are ones that the elderly subjects are likely to be still performing. Examples include memory for bridge hands by bridge players, memory for conversations, memory for faces, memory for songs, and memory for what one previously said or wrote. These results are a problem for the disuse view because all the tasks in this list are ones that the subjects are still performing. Even though they are still using these processes, the elderly subjects show age-related decrements.

A second problem is that the disuse view is potentially circular. Although older people with good memories may have good memories because they used them more, it could be the case that only those people with good memories are able to still use them. This is related to the third problem: The disuse view is rarely spelled out in enough detail to make predictions or to overcome the circularity problem. To quote Salthouse (1991), "Despite the attractiveness of this simple idea, it seems to have little convincing empirical support at the present time" (p. 351).

Multiple Memory Systems

The multiple memory systems view (reviewed in Chapter 7) states that memory can be broken down into a number of functionally different memory systems, including episodic, semantic, and procedural memory (Tulving, 1983). Tulving argues that episodic memory should be the last system to develop and the first system to be impaired. Craik (Craik & Jennings, 1992; Craik, 1994) makes the case that this view has not fared well in explaining age-related memory changes. In the elderly, the multiple memory systems view predicts that age differences will be small or nonexistent for tasks that tap semantic memory, but substantial for tasks that tap episodic memory. Although age differences are indeed relatively small on some tasks thought to tap semantic memory, there can be substantial age differences on other tasks that are also thought to tap semantic memory. For example, age differences are apparent when subjects are asked to retrieve words in response to definitions (Bowles & Poon, 1985) and in the time that inhibition of priming remains (Bowles, 1994). This type of result, Craik argues, suggests that it is a process that is affected, rather than a system. Similar problems arise when considering impairments on episodic tasks. Although the systems view says that these tasks should show substantial impairment, the actual impairment can be either minimal (as with cued recall or recognition) or large (as with free recall).

Processing Views

Speed of Processing   One of the main reduced resources views is that declines in performance that accompany normal aging are due to a general slowing down of processing speed (Birren, 1956; Salthouse, 1985). For example, Chapter 10 discussed associative priming, where seeing the word *doctor* facilitates processing the word *nurse*. Howard, Shaw, and Heisey (1986) found that whereas younger subjects showed priming when the prime and target were separated by as little as 150 ms, older subjects required about 500 ms between prime and target before priming was seen. According to a spreading activation view of priming, this can be interpreted as a reduction in the speed at which activation spreads. According to a compound cue view of priming, the search of memory takes longer to perform. More generally, this view holds that age-related decrements are due to a reduced capacity caused by a reduction in speed of processing. Although there is much evidence that at least some age differences are due to differences in speed of processing, this view is incomplete by itself and requires other factors to provide a more general explanation (Salthouse, 1991). In addition, the account is somewhat vague; no specific mechanisms are identified (Craik & Anderson, 1999).

Impaired Inhibition   The impaired inhibition view (Hasher & Zacks, 1988) is in some ways similar to the reduced speed of processing view. Both focus on processing differences between younger and older subjects, and both posit a general reduction in one particular area. According to the inhibitory view, deficits seen in memory performance by elderly subjects are due to an impairment in inhibiting irrelevant information (see also Rabbitt, 1965), one consequence of which is increased interference. In this sense, the inhibitory view is much like the interference view of amnesia discussed in Chapter 8.

The difficulty in inhibiting information could come in a variety of forms. Hasher, Zacks, and May (1999) have suggested that inhibitory processes could decline at three points: (1) inhibiting access of information to immediate memory; (2) deleting information from immediate memory; and (3) inhibiting output of irrelevant responses. Although separating out these possibilities is difficult, there is some evidence for deficits in each of those functions. The inhibitory view predicts not only worse performance on a variety of memory tasks but also an improvement under certain circumstances. For example, one major prediction is that older adults will have more difficulty eliminating information from working memory when it is activated but irrelevant. Thus, they should show better memory for irrelevant information than younger adults. Contrary to this prediction, Dywan and Murphy (1996) reported that when younger and older adults were given a surprise recognition test on irrelevant information, the younger adults actually remembered more of the distracting information than did the older adults. One interpretation is that both older and younger adults process irrelevant information, but the younger adults are better at assigning the source of the irrelevant information and can inhibit these responses at output. A summary of this approach is offered by Stoltzfus, Hasher, and Zacks (1996; see also Hasher et al., 1999).

Transfer Appropriate Processing   The transfer appropriate processing framework differs from the other processing views in that it offers an explanation of memory performance in both the young and the elderly. According to this view, "Encoding is simply the set of processes involved in the perception and interpretation of the original event . . . and retrieval is the attempted recapitulation of the original pattern of encoding activity" (Craik, 1994, p. 156). Recollection will be successful when the cues available at test, either internally or externally, allow recapitulation of the results of processing at study. Age-related declines are typically less when good external cues are available, and differences increase to the extent that internally generated cues must be relied on. Performance on most indirect tasks is well preserved because the task itself affords good cues.

Reduced Resources and Self-Initiated Processing   This view suggests that one of the effects of aging is a reduction in the resources available to do the memory task (Craik, 1986; Craik & Byrd, 1982; Craik, Anderson, Kerr, & Li, 1995). This is supported by studies showing that dividing attention in younger adults seems to simulate the effects of aging. In addition, aging and divided attention both result in reduced frontal lobe activity when measured by PET or fMRI. Attention is needed to initiate a strategy and to make use of elaborate, deep encoding. Thus, older adults are at a disadvantage in using context or identifying the source of the information. This viewpoint incorporates aspects of the transfer appropriate processing view in that environmental support provided at retrieval can interact with internal cues to make up for the deficit, which is why cued recall is better than free recall and recognition is better than cued recall (Craik, 1986; Craik & Anderson, 1999). This view suggests that a combination of all three elements—the person, the task, and the environment—is needed to explain age-related changes in memory.

The processing views outlined above are by no means mutually exclusive; they can be (and are) combined in a variety of ways to form a more complete theory of age-related declines. It is clear that no single process or resource view accounts for all the data, but the processing views seem to do a better job than the structural or multiple memory systems views (Craik, 1994).

Summary of Theoretical Explanations

Age-related decrements are slight when measured by simple span tasks, recognition memory tasks, and implicit memory tasks. In contrast, age-related losses are sizable when measured by tasks such as free or cued recall, those involving memory for context, and prospective memory tasks. The latter tasks generally require the manipulation of information or the coordination of multiple tasks. Performance on tasks that offer sufficient retrieval cues and performance on indirect tasks frequently show no age-related impairment. In sum, to the extent that self-initiated retrieval processes are important, there will probably be age-related differences; to the extent that the task provides sufficient retrieval cues, there will probably be few or no age-related differences.

The multiple systems view cannot readily explain this pattern of results. For example, it is unclear why some tasks from the episodic memory system are relatively unimpaired, whereas others are grossly impaired. Similarly, it is unclear why some semantic tasks are unimpaired and others are impaired. The current delineation of systems does not allow one to predict where the memory deficits will be observed. In contrast, a processing account that acknowledges the need to consider the person, the task, and the degree of environmental support fare far better.

Chapter Summary

By studying how memory changes and develops throughout the life span, we can look at memory from a dynamic perspective. Even in infancy, humans demonstrate surprisingly enduring memory effects. Infant memories seem to be more context-dependent than those of older children and adults, but that may be due to infants' lack of experience in multiple contexts. Older children from the ages of 5 to 12 years show smaller memory spans than adults, which may be due to rehearsal speed or overall capacity. One of the major differences between memory in children and memory in adults is in the use of memory strategies, which increases along with recall performance as children grow older. Finally, as children age, they acquire more knowledge. Given that knowledge in a domain helps a person organize and remember the material, domain knowledge is a powerful explanation of the increases in memory performance that we see as children grow older. It was originally thought that children's capabilities in implicit memory were essentially intact from birth. Although the conclusion remains controversial, there is a growing body of evidence suggesting that implicit memory develops as well.

What happens to our memories as we grow into late adulthood? The consensus seems to be that the more complex the task, the more likely that age-related decrements will be observed. In addition, whenever the task offers reduced retrieval cues, performance will be impaired for the elderly as compared to younger subjects. Performance on tasks that offer sufficient retrieval cues and performance on indirect tasks frequently show no age-related impairment. Incidental learning also seems relatively unimpaired, at least when assessed by indirect tests. Of the many explanations for the effects of normal aging on memory, three main accounts are easily distinguishable: the disuse view, the multiple systems view, and the processing view. The latter view contains several differing approaches, including a transfer appropriate processing account and one based on reduced resources. Although there is no consensus on which view is preferred, it seems at this point that some sort of processing view best explains the current data.

Mnemonics

The "secret of a good memory" is thus the secret of forming diverse and multiple associations with every fact we care to retain.

—William James

Can I Improve My Memory?

When people find out that I am a cognitive psychologist who studies memory, they invariably tell me that their memory is terrible and ask how they can improve it. The answer usually does not satisfy them because it is rather prosaic and the methods often involve a moderate amount of effort. They also do not appreciate it when I point out that they appear to have an excellent memory because they can remember every time their memory failed them. Indeed, the correlation between actual memory ability and perceived memory ability is typically very low (Hertzog, 1992).

Memory improvement books can be divided into two kinds: popular and scholarly. Typically, the popular books are written by people with no formal training in memory; they are either professional entertainers who have discovered techniques for memorizing a large amount of novel information for a brief period of time, or they are promoters of seminars and training sessions that, among other things, are designed to improve memory. Indeed, on the covers of many of these books are phrases such as "More Money! Higher Grades! More Friends!" Most of the popular books report the same techniques, and almost none offer much by way of explanation of how or why these methods work. The good news is that most of the methods do lead to substantial improvements in memory performance. The bad news, however, is that because many of these authors are removed from the scientific literature, these books often contain many errors, omissions, or statements that are simply meaningless. Furthermore, there is no easy or magical way to develop a perfect memory overnight. To anticipate the end of this chapter, the best way to improve your memory is to practice retrieving the desired information.

The Bad News

One common theme in popular memory improvement books is that "one only uses 10 percent of the potential of the brain" (Lapp, 1992, pp. 19–20) or "we use only a small percentage of our brain power" (Lorayne, 1957, p. 10). Other books quote figures as low as 1% (Herold, 1982), but in no case are references cited, nor is there any indication of what this means or how it was determined. In fact, this type of statement, although widely believed, is entirely meaningless. Consider the brain from an evolutionary perspective: Why would humans develop such a large brain but use only 10% of it? An analogous situation would be if we evolved with 20 legs but used only 2 of them. Although it would be nice to believe that we all have an enormous untapped potential (90% of our brains are in permanent idle), we can still believe in potential without resorting to meaningless statements. Given the frequency of this belief, where might it have come from?

One possible source is Lashley's (1950) report concerning rats trained to run in a maze. After the rats had learned where to go to reach food, Lashley destroyed parts of the rat's visual cortex. The animals were still able to find their way through the maze when 90% of their visual cortex had been destroyed, although their performance was diminished. Lashley's conclusion was not that rats use only 10% of their brain, but rather that brain function is not localized: Many different parts of the brain are involved in any given activity (see Chapter 8).

Calvin and Ojemann (1994, p. 15) speculate that this myth of untapped potential originally came from the observation that a slow-growing tumor has to destroy approximately 80% of the cells in a particular area within the motor strip of the brain before movement and control are lost. They also point out, however, that in skilled situations, such as finger movements by a pianist, some loss of control would be easily detectable far earlier. Moreover, if a sudden loss of as few as 30% of the neurons in the motor strip occurred (through a stroke, for example), complete paralysis could occur.

A third possible source comes from a misunderstanding about the results of a famous series of studies by Wilder Penfield (1969). Before performing brain surgery, surgeons must map out areas of the brain to ensure that areas responsible for functions such as speech and language are not damaged during the operation. This process of mapping out areas involves using a mild electrical current to stimulate a particular area. Because the patient is usually awake, the neurosurgeon can observe the patient's response and can locate motor areas, speech areas, and so forth. Penfield (1969) reported that he triggered long-forgotten memories when stimulating various regions in the cortex and argued that "it is clear that the neuronal action that accompanies each succeeding state of consciousness leaves its permanent imprint on the brain. The imprint, or record, is a trail of facilitation of neuronal connections that can be followed again by an electric current many years later with no loss of detail, as though a tape recorder had been receiving it all" (p. 165). Many memory improvement books (Buzan, 1984) follow this interpretation. They assume that the brain automatically records everything but that very little is actually recallable. The unused potential lies in trying to gain access to these memories, as Penfield's patients did. The problem is that fewer than 3% of all patients Penfield tested produced any response—that is, 97% of the patients produced no responses—and even in those cases, each recovered memory was highly generic and appeared to be an inference or a likely happening rather than a specific memory (Loftus & Loftus, 1980; Neisser, 1967; Squire, 1987).

Many books (Buzan, 1984; Herold, 1982) claim that one reason many people have poor memories is that they do not use the right brain and depend too much on the left brain. The left side of the brain is the seat of language in almost all right-handed people and in approximately 70% of left-handed people (Corballis, 1980). The left hemisphere is concerned with logic and reason, whereas the right hemisphere is the artistic, intuitive, holistic side. Although many popular books have been aimed at right-brain education, there is little scientific evidence to support these claims (Hellige, 1990; Springer & Deutsch, 1989).

Other statements in the popular memory improvement books do not accurately reflect the facts about memory. For example, Lapp (1992, p. 9) reasserts the common idea that elderly people have trouble remembering recent events and are particularly good at recalling older events. Research has consistently failed to support the idea that healthy older adults remember the past more clearly than they remember the present (Squire, 1974; Warrington & Sanders, 1971; see also Chapter 14). Most studies do show a memory loss for older subjects relative to younger subjects, but the loss is uniform rather than concentrated on recent events. Lapp (1992) also claims that "recognition memory is easy, whereas free recall is not" (p. 110). If this really were the case, then there should not be the phenomenon of recognition failure of recallable words. People can recall words they cannot recognize when the cues presented as part of the recall test are better than the cues presented as part of the recognition test (Watkins & Tulving, 1975; see Chapter 9). Lorayne (1957, p. 42) claims that creating bizarre (or to use his word, ridiculous) images leads to better memory. As discussed later, it is the interacting nature of the image that affords mnemonic staying power, not its bizarreness or ridiculousness (Wollen, Weber, & Lowry, 1972). The reason that many people believe bizarre images do increase retention is that bizarre images are typically interactive images. As a final example, Lorayne (1957) states, "Things that we see register upon our brains with much more emphasis than what we hear" (p. 121). This depends on the type of material and the type of test. The modality effect (Chapter 2) contradicts this statement when serial recall is the test, and Roediger, Weldon, and Challis (1989; see Chapter 7) document other situations in which auditory presentation leads to better performance.

Another method of improving memory that is often invoked is playing tapes containing subliminal messages while asleep. Greenwald, Spangenberg, Pratkanis, and Eskenazi (1991) tested whether subliminal audiotapes could improve memory. When played, these tapes appear to contain only relaxing sounds, such as music or waterfalls, but also recorded on them—according to manufacturers—is material that will improve memory. Greenwald et al. (1991) had four important features in their experimental design. First, a double-blind method was used, so that neither the subject nor the experimenter knew the actual content of the tape. Second, the tape was used according to the instructions provided by the manufacturer. Third, the study (actually, three separate replications) used subjects who were highly motivated and who expressed a desire to improve their memory. Fourth, the research used both pretest and posttest measures to determine whether any change had occurred as a result of using the tapes. Two types of tapes were tested: self-esteem and memory. One of the manipulations was whether the tape was labeled cor-

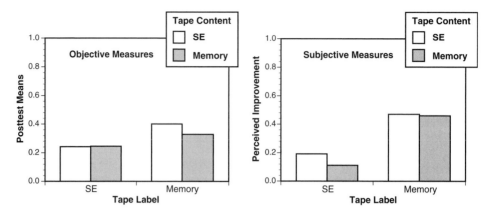

Figure 15.1 The left panel shows the average posttest score on the memory scale (in the form of a standardized score) as a function of audiotape subliminal content and tape label. The mean of the pretest scores was zero. The right panel shows the percentage of subjects perceiving improvement in memory as a function of audiotape subliminal content and tape label.   SOURCE: From "Double-Blind Tests of Subliminal Self-Help Audiotapes," by A. G. Greenwald et al., 1991, *Psychological Science, 2*, 119–122. Reprinted with permission of Blackwell Publishing Ltd.

rectly; thus, half the subjects listened to a tape that was labeled correctly (the tape was designed by the manufacturers to improve memory and was labeled as a memory improvement tape), and half listened to a tape that was labeled incorrectly (the memory tape was labeled as a self-esteem tape). The results are shown in Figure 15.1.

Although approximately 50% of the subjects reported an improvement in the domain listed on the tape label, a comparison of pre- and posttest scores on objective measures of memory performance led the researchers to conclude that "there was no trace of a subliminal content effect" (Greenwald et al., 1991, p. 121). Basically, if the tape said it improved memory, then the content was irrelevant: Subjects perceived an improvement in memory, even though there was no increase in memory performance on objective tests. Greenwald et al. termed this an illusory placebo effect.

The Good News

The good news is that many of the suggestions for improving memory offered in the popular books do work, although these methods are neither new nor particularly surprising. The good news is also somewhat qualified by the fact that most popular books fail to mention some of the easiest but nonetheless most potent strategies. One such overlooked contribution is the difference in acquisition and retention as a result of distributed rather than massed rehearsal. This omission is surprising because it offers an easy way to greatly increase retention. Studies demonstrating its advantage were reported by Ebbinghaus (1885, Section 34) and have been systematically explored ever since (see Underwood, 1961, for a review).

When trying to learn a motor skill, such as typing, playing a computer game, or any other such activity, people become better faster when they take a short break between each trial (*distributed practice*) than when no such break occurs (*massed practice*). An early study by Lorge (1930) examined performance on a mirror drawing task in which a chan-

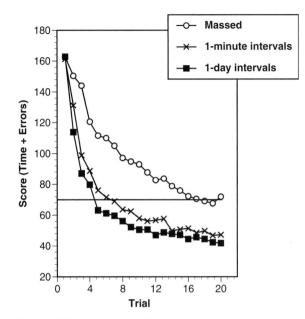

Figure 15.2   Performance learning in a mirror maze task as a function of interpolated activity. The massed group had no interval. The horizontal line shows that by the end of 20 sessions, the massed group was performing at the level achieved by the two distributed groups after 5 trials with 1-day intervals or 6 trials with 1-minute intervals.   SOURCE: Data from Table V of Lorge (1930).

nel in the shape of a six-pointed star was cut out of brass. The subject's task was to move a stylus around the channel without touching the sides, but the subject could not see the channel directly, only through a mirror. The score was simply the time taken to complete a circuit plus the number of times the stylus touched either edge of the channel. Subjects either had a 1-day interval between trials, a 1-minute interval between trials, or no interval between trials (massed). Performance after 20 trials with massed practice was the same as performance after only 5–6 trials with distributed practice (see Figure 15.2).

There does not seem to be any difference in the rate of acquisition when verbal material is learned using massed compared to distributed rehearsal (Underwood, 1961). The difference for verbal material shows up in measures of retention (Cain & Willey, 1939), particularly when the interval between practice sessions is longer than 24 hours (Underwood & Schulz, 1961).

For example, Keppel (1964, 1967) conducted two experiments that examined retention after 1 day or 8 days when practice was massed (4-second interval) versus distributed (24-hour interval). The difference between the two experiments was the degree of proactive interference: Subjects in the single list experiment learned only one list, and subjects in the multiple list experiment learned a total of four lists but were tested for just the final list. The results are shown in Figure 15.3. There was little difference after a 1-day retention interval except for the multiple list groups. However, by 8 days after studying, both of the massed groups had lost a substantial portion of the information, whereas the distributed groups showed relatively little loss. These results generalize to a whole host of tasks,

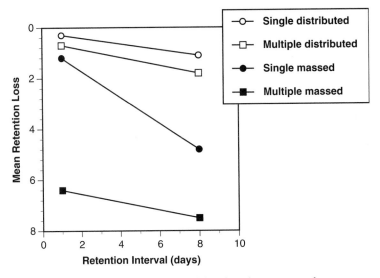

Figure 15.3   The effects of massed and distributed practice on the retention of verbal information. Distributed practice has only a small effect after a short delay but has a substantial effect after longer delays.
SOURCE: From "A Reconsideration of the Extinction-Recovery Theory," by G. Keppel, 1967, *Journal of Verbal Learning and Verbal Behavior, 6*, 476–486. Copyright © 1967 Academic Press, Inc. Reprinted with permission.

including multiplication tables, spelling, lecture material, foreign language vocabulary, and information from textbooks (Rea & Modigliani, 1988).

It should be emphasized that distributed rehearsal takes no more time than massed rehearsal; the only difference is that 2 hours of massed study might be broken up into four 30-minute sessions distributed over 4 days. The advantage of distributed over massed is so great, and the results are so reliable, that it is one of the most often mentioned techniques for improving memory in the more scholarly memory improvement books (Herrmann, Weingartner, Searleman, & McEvoy, 1992). It is also a technique most people do not believe works (Zechmeister & Shaughnessy, 1980). One reason students may not believe there is a difference is that massed practice does work, but only for the short run. Cramming the night before an exam is fine for performance on that exam, because the retention interval is less than 1 day. However, if you have a cumulative final at the end of the semester and you used massed practice, you will recall very little. If you want to retain the information so that you will remember it for the final, then distributed practice is the way to go (Bahrick, Bahrick, Bahrick, & Bahrick, 1993).

If you take breaks to distribute your study, what should you do during the interval? One easy thing is to sleep. As described in Chapter 6, Jenkins and Dallenbach (1924) showed that subjects were able to recall more of the items following a period of sleep than following a period of wakefulness. Of course, it is not sleep in and of itself that helps memory retention; rather, it is the absence of (or reduction in) potentially interfering material.

During the intervals created by using distributed processing, you should avoid performing tasks that can interfere. For example, if you are learning Spanish and Italian concurrently, you can easily become confused about which word means what in which lan-

Table 15.1 The two main sources of interference when learning Spanish vocabulary

	Study First	Study Second	Tested On	Interference
Experimental	Spanish	Italian	Spanish	RI
Control	Spanish	Math	Spanish	
Experimental	Italian	Spanish	Spanish	PI
Control	Math	Spanish	Spanish	

NOTE: Studying Italian vocabulary after the Spanish can result in retroactive interference, but studying Italian before studying the Spanish can result in proactive interference. Interference occurs because Spanish is similar to Italian.

guage. Let's say you have a test on Spanish vocabulary on Wednesday, and you study on Monday night. If you study Spanish vocabulary first and then Italian vocabulary, you will suffer from retroactive interference when you take the test: Studying the Italian interferes with the material you learned earlier. What happens if you reverse the order of studying to avoid retroactive interference? Your memory for the Spanish will be interfered with by the material you learned earlier, the Italian. This is proactive interference (see Table 15.1). To avoid retroactive interference, you should study something quite different (such as math). Or you can take a nap.

Most scholarly books suggest that, when studying, we should use processing that elaborates on the to-be-remembered information. One of the most influential papers on memory in the past 30 years formally introduced the idea of levels of processing (Craik & Lockhart, 1972; see Chapter 5). Depending on the type of material and the type of test, different elaborative processes can help in retaining the information.

For factual information, such as that conveyed by many textbooks, one of the best ways of performing elaborative processing is to ask yourself "Why?" Several studies (Woloshyn, Willoughby, Wood, & Pressley, 1990; Wood, Pressley, & Winne, 1990) have investigated the effects of using this elaborative interrogation. The technique involves asking people to think beyond the facts as stated and to construct reasons that explain why the factual relationships hold. The advantage presumably lies in getting people to make use of prior knowledge when they process new information. This research has shown beneficial effects for college students, adults, and even for young children (grades 4 through 8).

For certain types of tests, a shallow level of processing can lead to better performance than a deep level. As described in Chapter 5, Morris, Bransford, and Franks (1977) found that when the test required semantic processing, a deep level produced better performance; however, when the test required shallow processing, a shallow level produced better performance. This transfer appropriate processing approach retains much of the levels of processing view, but includes the processing done at test. The key is to ensure that the cues available at retrieval are effective for identifying the to-be-remembered material.

Many of the techniques that the less scholarly memory improvement books offer do work. The most common first suggestion is to pay attention during encoding. For example, a common problem many people report is an inability to remember people's names. A technique that works well begins with repeating the name out loud when introduced to a person for the first time to ensure that you have the correct basic information. Many failures to remember a person's name can be attributed to a failure to encode the material in the first place. If the name is unusual, do not hesitate to ask for spelling. Then, make sure you use the name in a sentence within a few minutes of meeting the person. Repeating the name in a distributed way will help. Finally, to remember the name permanently, associate the name with a distinctive feature of the person. The idea is that when you see the person again, the distinctive feature will stand out and will serve as a good retrieval cue.

Technical Mnemonics

Most books agree with William James (1890) on the basic method for improving memory: forming meaningful associations. For example, to remember the names of the Great Lakes, simply remember the acronym HOMES: Huron, Ontario, Michigan, Erie, Superior. Many biology and physiology students know the phrase "On old Olympus' towering top, a Finn and German viewed some hops." The first letters here give you the first letters of the 12 cranial nerves (olfactory, optic, oculomotor, trochlear, trigeminal, abducens, facial, auditory, glossopharyngeal, vagus, spinal accessory, and hypoglossal). ROY G. BIV is the formal name of the spectrum of colors: red, orange, yellow, green, blue, indigo, and violet. These techniques are useful for providing cues: The mnemonic provides you with the number of targets and the initial letter; all you need to do is search for a word that begins with that letter.

This is also a good way to remember computer passwords. To be secure, a computer password should not be a valid word. Numerous studies have shown that not only do most people use words as passwords, many people use the name of a pet or other loved one as their password. Some even use "password" as their password! The reason is that these are easier to remember than passwords such as It$4M | !a. However, if this is rephrased as "Is that money for me or not, eh?" it is easy to remember. In computer use, | is used for "or" and ! is used for "not"; $ is obvious; the capitalization comes from the emphasis in the sentence; and "a" poses the question.

Other mnemonic techniques require a preliminary learning stage before they can be applied. Almost all books mention what is variously referred to as the phonetic alphabet, the phonetic numeral code, or the major system. Attributed originally to Stanislaus Mink von Wennsshein around 1650 and subsequently modified by Richard Grey in 1730, this system has been mentioned by most writers on memory, including William James (1890, p. 629). Its main goal is to help with memory for numbers. One problem with trying to remember numbers is that they are relatively abstract and have very little that can be readily associated with them. The phonetic alphabet links a sound with each digit. To recall the number, just remember the sounds that are associated with that number.

First, each of the digits from 0 to 9 is associated with the sound of a particular consonant (see Table 15.2). Because it is the sound that is important, sometimes more than one letter is associated with a given digit. There is even a mnemonic to help remember the ten basic associations. The letter is typically chosen based on visual similarity with a handwritten form of the letter, on acoustic similarity, or on some other relatively simple facet. The key, though, is using the sound that is represented by the letters. The vowels (a, e, i, o, and u) and the letters w, h, and y (easy to remember because they spell "why") are not used; these letters are ignored for mnemonic purposes and are used in the second stage to form words using the consonant sounds.

Table 15.2   The phonetic alphabet, in which each number is associated with the sound of a particular consonant

0 = z or s, because these letters can sound like the first letter of "zero"
1 = t or d, because "t" looks like a 1 and "d" has one downstroke, like 1
2 = n, because "n" has two downstrokes
3 = m, because "m" has three downstrokes
4 = r, because "r" is the last letter in four
5 = L, because L is the Roman numeral for 50
6 = j, soft g, ch, sh, because 6 looks like an uppercase G
7 = k, hard c, hard g, because you can see two rotated 7s in uppercase K
8 = f or v, because a cursive "f" can look like an 8
9 = p or b, because "p" is a mirror image of 9

NOTE: Two or more consonant sounds are sometimes listed when the sounds are very similar.

The second step is to associate the sounds (and thus the numbers) with words. Note that only the key sound is important; the remaining letters fill out the word but do not provide any extra information. Among the most popular suggestions are

0 = zoo
1 = tie
2 = new
3 = ma
4 = rye
5 = law
6 = shoe
7 = cow
8 = foe
9 = bee

Other numbers use combinations of these basic sounds. For example, the number 10 might be associated with the word *toes*. Notice that the first consonant sound (t) is used for first digit (1) and the second consonant sound (z) is used for the second digit (0). The number 100 might be associated with the word *disease*. Buzan (1984) lists words for the first 1000 numbers (0–999) using the phonetic alphabet. Edward Pick (1888, p. 7) provides an illustration of how to use this method:

> To briefly show its use, suppose it is desired to fix 1142 feet in a second as the velocity of sound: t, t, r, n, are the letters and order required. Fill up with vowels forming a phrase, like "tight run," and connect it by some such flight of the imagination as that if a man tried to keep up with the velocity of sound, he would have a tight run. When you recall this a few days later great care must be taken not to get confused with the velocity of light, nor to think he had a hard run, which would be 3000 feet too fast.

The phonetic alphabet depends on imagery for the final stage, as illustrated in the example just quoted. As with all techniques, the key is having a cue at test that will trigger the appropriate response. When trying to recall the speed of sound, a natural image is of running, and that easily translates into a man running. The hardest part is moving on to a man racing sound and having a "tight run."

It is perfectly fine to use idiosyncratic associations. Some may be straightforward, as noting that 1066 is when the Battle of Hastings occurred, whereas others may simply be odd, as when people recall that the number 42 is crucially important in metaphysics (see Adams, 1981, p. 180). This technique can work quite dramatically as long as the cue is easy to generate. Empirical support for this was provided by Mäntylä (1986, Experiment 2). He presented subjects with 504 words, and each subject generated three properties of the word. At test, the experimenter presented the properties, and the subject had to respond with the original word. When tested immediately, subjects recalled approximately 91% of the words. Compare this figure with the 88% obtained by Shepard (1967) for recognition of 540 words. Recall without such cues was terrible.

One might object that getting any three properties would let a person guess the target word. Mäntylä included an important control condition. If subjects were simply generating the target item based on the properties, performance should not get worse over time. If, on the other hand, the properties were serving only as a cue to memory, then one might well expect performance to decrease. When the retention interval was 1 week, recall had dropped to about 65% correct. This is still an impressive feat, however: After 1 week, these subjects could recall nearly 330 words correctly!

The method of loci is a similar but far older method. Yates (1966) provides a superb history of this particular technique. According to Cicero (as translated by Sutton, 1942, pp. 465–467), it was invented by Simonides:

> There is a story that Simonides was dining at the house of a wealthy nobleman named Scopas at Crannon in Thessaly, and chanted a lyric poem which he had composed in honour of his host, in which he followed the custom of the poets by including for decorative purposes a long passage referring to Castor and Pollux; whereupon Scopas with excessive meanness told him he would pay him half the fee agreed on for the poem, and if he liked he might apply for the balance to his sons of Tyndareus, as they had gone halves in the panegyric. The story runs that a little later a message was brought to Simonides to go outside, as two young men were standing at the door who earnestly requested him to come out; so he rose from his seat and went out, and could not see anybody; but in the interval of his absence the roof of the hall where Scopas was giving the banquet fell in, crushing Scopas himself and his relations underneath the ruins and killing them; and when their friends wanted to bury them but were altogether unable to know them apart as they had been completely crushed, the story goes that Simonides was enabled by his recollection of the place in which each of them had been reclining at table to identify them for separate interment; and that this circumstance suggested to him the discovery of the truth that the best aid to clearness of memory consists in orderly arrangement. He inferred that persons desiring to train this faculty must select localities and form mental images of the facts they wish to remember and store those images in the localities, with the result that the arrangement of the localities will preserve the order of the facts, and the images of the facts will designate the facts themselves.

There are three steps to this system. First, you choose a well-known series of locations; for example, your route from your dorm room or apartment to class is well known to you and has many different locations along the way. You can even use imaginary locations; the importance of the locations is to provide a structure to retain the order information. The second step involves creating a mental image of the item you want to remember interacting with a specific location along your route. The most common use of this technique in the Roman world was as an aid for remembering speeches. Each point to be made would be represented by an image in a particular location. For example, if you are delivering a speech on the imminent demise of civilization and your third point concerns the

---

Experiment   *Imagery and Mnemonics*

Purpose: To demonstrate the use of visual imagery as a mnemonic device

Subjects: Thirty-two subjects are recommended; 16 should be assigned to the control group, and 16 to the imagery group.

Materials: Table I in the Appendix lists 80 concrete nouns. Create 20 random pairings of the nouns. The test list consists of the first item in a pair, and the target list consists of the second item in a pair. Write each word in large, clear form on a notecard. Each subject should get a different random ordering and pairing of items. Each subject should also get an answer sheet.

Design: Because each subject experiences only one condition, rehearsal instruction is a between-subjects factor.

Procedure: Inform the subjects that in this experiment they will be asked to learn an association between two words, so that when they are given the first word, they will be able to produce the second word. The control group is given no special instructions on how to do this. The imagery group is asked to form an interacting visual image. Each word pair should be shown for 5 seconds. At test, present the first word of each pair for 5 seconds, during which time the subject should try to write down the second word.

Instructions for Control Group: "In this experiment, I would like you to try to learn a list of word pairs. You will see each pair for 5 seconds. Please study the pair so that when you see the first word again, you will be able to produce the second word. For example, if you see the pair *dog-bicycle*, at test you will see just *dog* and you will be asked to produce *bicycle*. Any questions?"

Instructions for Experimental Group: "In this experiment, I would like you to try to learn a list of word pairs. You will see each pair for 5 seconds. Please study the pair so that when you see the first word again, you will be able to produce the second word. Try to visualize the two members interacting in some way. For example, if you see the pair *dog-bicycle*, you might visualize a dog riding a bicycle. At test you will see just *dog* and you will be asked to produce *bicycle*. Any questions?"

Test Instructions for Both Groups: "I will show you the first word from each pair that you just studied. Please write down the second word from the pair on your answer sheet. Any questions?"

Scoring and Analysis: The dependent variable is the number of words recalled correctly. Calculate this for each group, and then use a *t* test for independent groups to see whether the mean number of words recalled differs. You should find that the imagery group recalled significantly more words than the control group did.

Optional Enhancements: Change the experiment to test three groups: control, interactive imagery, and noninteractive imagery. The group that receives instructions to create interacting images should recall more than the group that creates noninteracting images.

Source: Based on an experiment by Bower (1972).

---

fact that the amount of graffiti is rising, you could imagine seeing a person spray-painting the word *graffiti* on the side of the fountain, the third notable location you walk by on your way to class. The final step is simply to mentally "walk" from one location to the next, recalling the images and reconstructing the desired memory.

Although it may seem to require a lot of effort, the method of loci does in fact work and is particularly useful for remembering order information. For example, Ross and Lawrence (1968) reported that with no more than two practice trials, subjects could recall a list of 40 or 50 items in order close to perfectly. One subject, after only two trials, could recall 52 items in backward order. Another study, by De Beni and Cornoldi (1985), showed that the benefits of this method were observable in both free recall and recognition tests that were delayed 1 week after study. The key to the method of loci lies in two components: Interactive imagery affords better memory than noninteractive imagery, and the known locations provide an organizational structure.

Is it important, as many popular books suggest, that the images be bizarre? Wollen, Weber, and Lowry (1972) compared memory when subjects used bizarre interactive images, bizarre images that were not interactive, common interactive images, and common images that were not interactive. Bizarreness neither helped nor hurt; memory was better with interactive images than with noninteractive images. Neisser and Kerr (1973) found similar results. Einstein and McDaniel (1987) reviewed 44 studies of normal versus bizarre imagery. For tests after very short delays, an advantage for bizarre items is found only (1) when both bizarre and normal images are used, (2) when used with free recall, and (3) when imagery instructions are emphasized. For tests after longer delays, they concluded that "the conflicting results within the four categories make these experiments difficult to summarize" (p. 86). Given these at best weak results, and the fact that no bizarre imagery effects are seen when only bizarre imagery is used, bizarreness should not be the prime criterion in creating an image.

When learning complex material, the mnemonics most often mentioned in popular books are not very good. Technical mnemonics are best for remembering a particular series of items, but writing down a shopping list can be far easier than using the method of loci. Indeed, such external means of remembering are used far more often, even by people familiar with and trained in using the mnemonic techniques (Bellezza, 1983; Park, Smith, & Cavanaugh, 1990). One reason is that unless you keep changing the locations or the keywords, an enormous amount of proactive interference can build up. For example, most books mention the peg-word method: Each digit is associated with a word that sounds like the number, so 1 is a bun, 2 is a shoe, 3 is a tree, and so on. For each item you want to remember, you associate the word with the appropriate item. When going to the grocery store, you may need milk, pretzels, cheese, and so on; you would imagine a bun being dunked in the milk, a shoe stomping on the pretzels, a tree oozing cheese, and so on. The limit occurs the next time you go to the store: Does bun still go with milk, or does it now go with lettuce?

For the type of material a typical college student must master, the technical mnemonics offer very little. The suggestions from the scientific literature—avoiding interference, distributed practice, interactive imagery, transfer appropriate processing—however, are exactly what you need.

CogLab Experiment

http://coglab.wadsworth.com/experiments/LinkWord/

As an example of how all this is put together, consider the link word method of foreign vocabulary learning (Gruneberg, 1994, 1998; http://www.unforgettablelanguages.com/; see also Atkinson & Raugh, 1975). The purpose is to learn a working vocabulary and basic grammar of a foreign language as quickly as possible; conversational fluency will be achieved only by extended study and practice in the foreign country. The link word method will get you going faster than rote learning and will complement formal instruction.

The key to Gruneberg's (1994) system is to form an interactive image made up of one object that corresponds to the English word and one that corresponds to the French. For example, the French for rabbit is *lapin* (roughly, "LaPaHn"). So, imagine a rabbit lapping at a bowl of water. Carefully study this image for about 10 seconds or so. The French for goat is *chèvre* ("shevr"). Imagine driving your Chevy with a goat in the back. After studying about 10 words or so, a quick test is given. This ensures distributed practice of generating the French word. Then a bit of grammar is introduced. French words are either masculine or feminine. To remember the gender of a word, you create an interactive image with either a boxer (to convey masculine) or a bottle of French perfume (to convey feminine). For example, you imagine a boxer punching a rabbit. Or you imagine pouring a bottle of perfume over a goat to stop the bad smell. You learn the gender of the words you previously learned, and then are tested again (that is, you are asked to come up with *le lapin* and *la chèvre*).

You would then learn another dozen animals, be tested, then learn their genders, and then be tested again. The next stage is to learn about a dozen useful words, such as adjectives (which are then tested), followed by learning the French present tense of *to be*. Finally, you put all this together, and produce sentences such as *Le lapin est petit*. You can go through an entire book in about 12 hours or so, and end up with a vocabulary of 500 or more words. Ellis and Beaton (1993) confirm that it is the combination of repetition and effective keywords (imageable nouns) that is important. This method works not only for college students, but also for elderly (Gruneberg & Pascoe, 1996) and low-achieving students (Gruneberg & Ellis, 1995).

Memory Strategies and Older Adults

Older adults often report a variety of everyday memory complaints, including forgetting names, losing objects, forgetting an appointment, or forgetting to do routine tasks. These difficulties are pervasive enough that a new term has been coined to describe them; they are now called senior moments. Is there anything we can do to reduce the occurrence of such senior moments?

First, it is actually the case that self-reports of memory problems are often not correlated with actual memory problems. Older adults seem to focus on and assign disproportionate importance to their memory failures and may merely be acting on their own stereotypes about older adults' memory (Kahn, Zarit, Hilbert, & Niederehe, 1975).

Second, the typical laboratory tests of memory include things like digit span or memorizing lists—tasks that are not very common in everyday life. Most of the memory skills training programs for older adults also focus on such little-used skills. One exception is a program developed by McEvoy and Moon (1988), who trained elderly adults (mean age 68 years) in six everyday skills—recalling names and faces, appointments, routine tasks, spatial orientation, locating objects, and concentration—using many of the imagery and mnemonic techniques described in this chapter. The program consisted of more than 11 hours of training, spread over a number of weeks, and used some of the following internal and external aids:

Internal Aids
- Attention: attending to what you're trying to remember (looking back at where you left your car)
- Repetition: immediately, then at gradually increasing intervals (expanding rehearsal)

- Elaboration: thinking about the meaning or generating a mental image
- Practicing a routine: always carrying out a task at the same time, linking it with a particular event (always taking medication after breakfast, watering the plants after the weekly gardening show)

External Aids
- Memos, notes, checklists
- Diaries, calendars
- Putting something in a special place
- Alarms, prompts

The dependent measure was a questionnaire on how often the participants experienced particular types of memory failure. McEvoy and Moon (1988) found a small but significant improvement in four of the six problem areas they targeted. In contrast, four control tasks not taught in the program showed no improvement. At least in this program, then, there is no general improvement in self-reports of memory problems with training, but there does seem to be some benefit for training specific areas.

Exceptional Memories

Although many people bewail their bad memory, there are quite a few people who have exceptional memory. Perhaps the most famous case of an exceptional memory was reported by Luria (1968). The English version is called *The Mind of a Mnemonist* and documents the remarkable memory of a Russian man named S., who appeared to have a limitless memory. All the following information and quotations come from that source.

S. was a reporter who took no notes during meetings, even though his assignments involved complex instructions on where to go to meet people or what information to seek out. His editor, thinking that S. was not paying attention, told him to repeat the assignment just given. S. did so perfectly. It was this editor who directed S. to Luria's laboratory. It is of interest that S. apparently did not think himself unusual; he believed everybody else's memory worked this way also.

Luria gave S. a standard battery of tests and quickly concluded that "there was no limit either to the capacity of S.'s memory or to the durability of the traces he retained" (p. 11). As long as there was a pause of approximately 3–4 seconds between each piece of information, S. could retain the information indefinitely. For example, when Luria presented S. with a table of 50 numbers, S. needed 3 minutes to learn the table and 40 seconds to recall it. However, he could recall the table by rows (as if reading across), by columns (as if reading down), or by diagonals or zig-zag patterns, and his performance did not decrease even after an interval of several months.

On June 11, 1936, S. learned a lengthy table composed only of the syllables *ma, na, sa,* and *va*. For example, the first two rows could have been *ma, va, na, sa, na, va* and *na, sa, na, ma, va, sa*. On April 6, 1944, S. recalled the table perfectly.

S. appeared to owe his exceptional memory to a process called *synesthesia*—perceiving one sensory modality with a different sensory modality. In S.'s case, when he heard a sound, he would also see lights and colors: "There was no distinct line, as there is for others of us, separating vision from hearing, or hearing from a sense of touch or taste" (p. 27). He reportedly told Vygotsky, the influential Russian developmental psychologist, "what a crumbly yellow voice you have" (p. 24). He said of a fence, "it has such a salty taste and feels so rough; furthermore, it has such a sharp, piercing sound" (p. 38).

The few errors of memory that S. did make tended to be errors of omission (failing to report an item) rather than recalling a different item. In one case, S. forgot to recall the word *pencil*. He explains why: "I put the image of pencil near a fence . . . the one down the street, you know. But what happened was that the image fused with that of the fence and I walked right on past without noticing it" (p. 36).

S. quit his job at the newspaper and became a professional mnemonist. Because he would often perform several shows a night, he became more economical in using his synesthesia and a variation of the method of loci, but the processes were essentially the same. His major problem was forgetting: He would sometimes recall a lengthy series of unrelated items perfectly, only to realize that it was the list from last week rather than the list for the current performance. He tried several ways of forgetting. He would imagine writing down the items he wished to forget on paper and then setting the paper on fire. The problem was that he could still see, in the charred remains, the writing on the paper. It is unclear exactly how he solved his problem. He told Luria only that one day, when trying desperately to forget a chart of numbers he had previously memorized, he looked to see if the chart was still there: "The chart of numbers isn't turning up now and it's clear why—it's because I don't want it to! Aha! That means if I don't want the chart to show up it won't. And all it took was for me to realize this" (p. 71).

Having a perfect memory, particularly one that depended on synesthesia, caused S. severe emotional and mental problems; in fact, he ended up in a Soviet asylum for the mentally ill. The primary reason was his inability to distinguish between reality and fantasy. An examination of various accounts of mnemonists, however, shows that S. was the exception rather than the rule. Most mnemonists seem to be otherwise normal people who have extensive practice with a limited range of material.

Susukita (1933, 1934) described a 26-year-old mnemonist named Sigeyuki Ishihara whose memory abilities appear to be as remarkable as those of S. Unlike S., however, Ishihara seemed to use more conventional mnemonic techniques and, according to the reports, did not suffer any of the emotional problems that made S.'s life so tragic.

Ishihara became interested in memory while at school, and he became a professional mnemonist. Because of his genuine interest, however, he participated in experiments in Susukita's laboratory and freely gave away his performance secrets. Typically, he was tested on random orders of digits, on male and female names, on Roman consonants, and on Japanese nonsense syllables. His memory for other materials, such as color names, for example, was no better than average. One difference between Ishihara and other noted mnemonists was that Ishihara could learn a list of digits much more quickly. For example, he could learn a series of 204 digits in approximately 5 minutes, 23 seconds and recall them in order in 3 minutes, 20 seconds. He learned the names of all 124 emperors of Japan in order in only 22 minutes, 38 seconds. For many of the lists of items learned, Ishihara organized the information with markers for every fifth item. Once learned, he could instantly give the name of the appropriate emperor when cued using the number; to name the 22nd emperor, for example, he would first find the 20th and from there retrieve the 22nd.

Perhaps most surprisingly, Ishihara required the same amount of time to learn any given item in a list regardless of the length of the list to be learned. Figure 15.4 shows the average amount of time needed to learn lists of names (left panel) and digits (right panel)

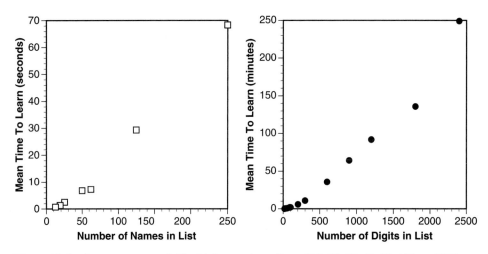

Figure 15.4   Average time needed by Ishihara to learn lists of 10, 15, 20, 40, 50, 100, and 200 names (in seconds) and lists of 20, 42, 60, 90, 102, 204, 300, 600, 900, 1200, 1800, and 2400 digits (in minutes).   SOURCE: From data reported in Susukita (1934).

of various lengths. Susukita determined that the mathematical relationship between the amount of material to be learned, x, and the learning rate, y, was approximately linear. That gives the equation $y = kx$, where k is a proportionality constant. The main difference in the data for Ishihara compared to other mnemonists was that k was smaller.

The technique Ishihara used was superficially similar to the method of loci but had important differences. Each digit automatically conjured up in his mind a specific visual image, such as the field behind his house, a rice paddy, or an elbow. These images could be combined, so that in the field behind his house there might also be a pear tree and a pile of wheat in front of the barn. In this way, he made random strings of numbers more meaningful, and from the image he could determine what the numbers were. Using eight basic images, he could combine them in different ways to learn a list of up to 2500 digits in about 3½ hours. The more frequently a basic image was used, however, the greater was the chance of an error.

Some images, such as a room for the number 163, led to errors; at recall, it was not clear what was important because the code word used meant "breadth" or "width." Similarly, sometimes the image did not convey the order. For example, the basic image for 47 is China, and that for 32 is spoon; the association for 4732 was therefore a Chinese man selling spoons. At retrieval, this combined image was interpreted as a "'spoon-selling Chinese man," and the number recalled was 3247.

Ishihara learned a list of 600 digits, and 31 days later he could report 357; his forgetting curve resembled that of Ebbinghaus. Susukita emphasized that when Ishihara "forgot" something, this was not a permanent loss but rather an inability to find the appropriate image. This image could be reported later on, sometimes with repeated testing, or hypermnesia. For example, at the first attempt to recall a list of 900 numbers, Ishihara failed to recall 12. A second retrieval attempt, immediately after the first, yielded 4 of the missing 12. A test 10 minutes later produced an additional 2. An hour later, 2 more were retrieved, and the next day, 2 of the remaining 4 items were produced. A more extreme example came from a test conducted 27 weeks after learning a list of 600 items. Although Ishihara could recall only 88, 9 of these were items he had failed to recall on the original test. If distributed rehearsal took place, such as 1, 3, 7, 14, 21, and 31 days after learning, then he could recall about 75% of the items 27 weeks later.

Ishihara was not easily distracted except by visual stimuli. For example, when he requested moving to a darker lab to reduce the interference, the loud noises that came from an adjacent room did not bother him and did not affect his performance. However, one factor that was referred to as "disadvantageous" for memory was earthquakes. The laboratory was on the second floor, and during the middle of one testing session in which Ishihara was learning a list of 200 female names, an earthquake hit, shaking the building quite violently. Ishihara learned some of the material prior to the earthquake, when presumably he was in a calm state, and learned some after the earthquake, when Ishihara was presumably in a state of shock. Furthermore, his memory was tested after the earthquake, when in a state of shock, but also later, when he returned to a calm state. His recall was better when the moods were consistent than when they differed, consistent with other experiments on mood-dependent memory.

Unlike S.'s memory, then, Ishihara's was not qualitatively different from normal memories; rather, it was the result of practice with a particular process for a limited range of stimuli. Other mnemonists are very much like Ishihara. For example, Hunter (1962) described a professor of mathematics, A. C. Aitken, who could recall 25 unrelated words in order 27 years after learning them; Rajan (Thompson, Cowan, & Frieman, 1991) has memorized pi to 31,811 places. Like Ishihara, both of these mnemonists were limited in the type of material that could be remembered. Rajan, for example, has exceptional memory only for digits.

V. P., a mnemonist studied by Hunt and Love (1972), also had an exceptional memory but claimed not to use the method of loci or synesthetic processes. Rather, he used idiosyncratic verbal associations to provide a far richer encoding format than most people use. His ability to do this was fostered by his knowledge of foreign languages (he could speak English, French, German, and Spanish, as well as Russian, Latvian, and Estonian) and the fact that his early schooling stressed rote memorization, giving him lots of practice (see below). His most noted memory feat was retaining the text of Bartlett's *War of the Ghosts* for more than a year with very little distortion.

One question that has concerned researchers on exceptional memory is the degree to which it can be acquired versus the degree to which you are (or are not) born with it. K. Anders Ericsson takes perhaps the most extreme position—that exceptional memory abilities are learned rather than innate—but he also offers a remarkable array of data to support the idea that exceptional memory abilities can be learned. He and his colleagues (Chase & Ericsson, 1981, 1982; Ericsson, 1985; Ericsson, Chase, & Faloon, 1980) have produced two exceptional mnemonists, both of whom began as typical college students.

Most people's memory span for a random series of digits is approximately 7, and this was S. F.'s span prior to practice. After 2 years of practice, however, it had increased to 84 and showed no signs of reaching asymptote (see Figure 15.5). S. F. accomplished this feat using his already extensive knowledge of long-distance running. For various distances, certain times have important meanings to a distance runner. For example, 2942 can be seen as 29 minutes and 42 seconds, a time associated with a 10K race (if you are a very good runner). This strategy posed a couple of problems. First, although all three-digit numbers from 100 to 959 can be made into times, any number with a 6, 7, 8, or 9 as the

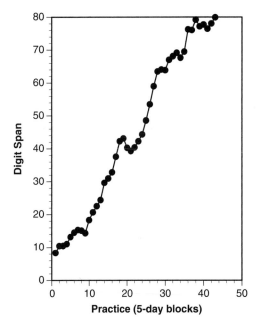

Figure 15.5   Average digit span as a function of practice for subject S. F. Each training session lasted approximately 1 hour, and each point is based on five training sessions.   SOURCE: Adapted from Ericsson & Faivre (1988).

middle digit creates an invalid time. At one point in training, S. F. was given a list entirely of numbers like this, and his digit span was severely reduced. A second problem is that this strategy works only for numbers. His ability to remember a random list of letters was no better than that of any other average college student: a memory span of 6. D. D., another distance runner, was trained using S. F.'s techniques, and his digit span has reached 106 (Ericsson & Staszewski, 1989).

Ericsson and Faivre (1988) suggest that exceptional abilities are not necessarily beyond the reach of nonexceptional people: "There is no reason to believe that exceptional memory performance is possible only for a small number of special individuals" (p. 450). Although practice in and of itself is not sufficient to develop an exceptional memory, it is certainly necessary. Practice in a variety of different areas can result in processes that are quite different from processes used when there is little or no practice (Ericsson, Krampe, & Tesch-Römer, 1993). There appears to be relatively little difference in performance between subjects who claim exceptional abilities and subjects who have acquired exceptional abilities through practice. For example, Ericsson and Staszewski (1989) found that their two trained experts (S. F. and D. D.) learned and recalled a matrix of 25 digits as fast or even faster than did others with exceptional memories (for example, Luria's S.). This was also true when recall was backward or by diagonals. Furthermore, with the exception of S., most acclaimed mnemonists use techniques and show patterns of responding similar to those of laboratory-trained subjects. As Ericsson and Faivre (1988) state, "The pattern of memory performance is so similar between subjects alleging exceptional abilities and subjects with acquired memory skill that the same basic mechanisms in both cases can be inferred" (p. 449).

Skilled memory theory, developed by Ericsson and his colleagues, summarizes what has been said above about memory improvement in general. First, the to-be-remembered material must be encoded in a meaningful manner. Most mnemonists use associations that are meaningful to them (Ericsson & Faivre, 1988; Hunt & Love, 1972; Hunter, 1962; Susukita, 1933): S. F. and D. D. used running times, and V. P. used his extensive knowledge of languages. The second key is to have useful retrieval cues available at test that will identify the target material. It seems likely, when trying to recall the speed of sound, that running against sound would produce a "tight run." Finally, the processes must be practiced. Although spending 500 hours practicing some task may seem unduly long and burdensome, it is little more than an hour a day for a little more than a year. For example, it might seem impossible for someone to learn to take dictation while simultaneously reading a novel. Even if it were possible, there must surely be some loss of speed or accuracy on the dictation task and a loss of speed or comprehension on the reading task. Spelke, Hirst, and Neisser (1976) showed that people can in fact learn to do this after sufficient practice; their two subjects could read a novel and take dictation at the same time. Compared to their original performance on these tasks separately, after extended practice there was no loss of comprehension of the novel and no increase in errors or decrease in speed when both tasks were performed simultaneously.

Wenger and Payne (1995) conducted a series of experiments to test some of the ideas of skilled memory theory. What makes their study unique is both the number of subjects and the highly controlled design. Subject S. F. was able to recall approximately 80 digits in order after 2 years of sessions (see Figure 15.5). Wenger and Payne had subjects use similar conditions of practice (with no explicit instruction on mnemonic techniques) but substituted words for the digits, and the results were even more remarkable. In less than 15 weeks, three subjects were able to recall more than 80 items in order, and an additional five subjects reached performance levels that were 4 to 5 times higher than their baseline performance. All subjects showed the type of organization in encoding and recall that S. F. showed: Just as S. F. made use of his running knowledge to guide encoding and retrieval, the subjects in Wenger and Payne's study used their verbal knowledge, particularly the ability to generate associations as the lists were being presented. The results were all well described by skilled memory theory.

Ericsson is aware that this explanation of exceptional memory performance may remove something mysterious or some magical quality and turn it into something more prosaic. But this is entirely in accord with two of the main goals of memory research: to explain how and why memory works, and to offer guidance for improving memory. If all we could say was that some people are mysteriously better than others, we would fail to achieve both of these goals.

With the exception of S., the vast majority of people exhibiting exceptional memories are otherwise normal, and the type of material they can retain is limited. The keys to developing an exceptional memory are neither mysterious nor difficult to master, and they echo the advice presented in this chapter and throughout the book for improving your own. First, associate the to-be-remembered material with something you already know, to take advantage of already existing structures and organizations. Second, process the material in a way that is appropriate for the test. Third, distribute your rehearsals over time. The old joke is almost right: How do you get to Carnegie Hall? Practice, wait a while, practice, wait a while, practice.

Chapter Summary

In many memory improvement books, it is often difficult to distinguish between suggestions that work and those that do not. Many books claim that people use only a small proportion of the brain, that they need to learn how to use the right hemisphere, or that they can improve memory while sleeping. None of this is true.

Substantial memory improvement will occur if you use distributed rather than massed studying, if you avoid situations that cause proactive or retroactive interference, if you use processing at study that is appropriate given the retrieval cues you will have at test, and if you pay attention so that you process the information in the first place. The link word method of foreign vocabulary learning is a good example of combining these tips. First, an interactive image is formed of an object that corresponds to the foreign word. Then, after studying 10 or so of these, you are given a test, forcing distributed practice. Then you learn genders using the same technique, followed by another test.

With one exception, most people with extraordinary memories use conventional techniques. Using these strategies, typical college students have increased their digit span from 7 to 80. These conventional techniques are: First, associate the material to be remembered with something that you already know so that you can take advantage of already existing structures and organizations. Second, process the material in a way that is appropriate for the test. Third, distribute your rehearsals over time.

Models of Memory

SAM	*Experiment: Recognition Failure*
Compound Cue Theory	*of Recallable Words*
The Diffusion Model	**TODAM**
MINERVA2	**Connectionist Models**
CogLab Experiment: Prototypes	**The Feature Model**

As far as the laws of mathematics refer to reality, they are not certain; and as far as they are certain, they do not refer to reality.

—Albert Einstein

Formal models are increasing in both popularity and sophistication in the study of human memory and in experimental psychology as a whole. Although mathematical descriptions have many potential problems, they also have many advantages (Lewandowsky, 1994; Neath, 1999b). Perhaps the most compelling advantage is that they provide an excellent check on human reasoning, particularly in situations involving complex interactions among several variables. Hintzman (1991) offers the following example of when a formal model might have prevented an embarrassing claim:

> A recent textbook on learning has a chapter on sociobiology, which contains the following claim regarding sexual promiscuity: "While adultery rates for men and women may be equalizing, men still have more partners than women do, and they are more likely to have one-night stands." . . . It is clear from the context that this does not hinge on the slight plurality of women to men (which would make it trivial), and that homosexual partners do not count. I challenge anyone to set up a formal model consistent with the claim—that is, there must be equal numbers of men and women, but men must have more heterosexual partners than women do. (While you are at it, derive the prediction about one-night stands.) An effort to set up such a model could have helped the authors avoid making a mathematically impossible claim. (p. 41)

Of course, formal models can make other errors that people do not, such as those due to programming errors, but to the extent that human reasoning and mathematical reasoning converge on the same answer, we can be more certain that we have not made an error of the type that Hintzman describes.

Several models of memory are usually referred to as *umbrella models*. They attempt to model, in a formal, quantitative fashion, human memory in a variety of different tasks, including both recall and recognition. When models are applied to many different experimental paradigms, they cannot be tailored to fit a particular finding. The same process that simulates recall of abstract words is also used to simulate recognition with differing proportions of distractor items. One advantage is that models will often uncover relationships between different paradigms or will suggest different explanations that may have been overlooked.

In this chapter, we present a variety of models. The three most prominent global memory models are SAM, which stands for "search of associative memory" (Raaijmakers & Shiffrin, 1981; Gillund & Shiffrin, 1984; Mensink & Raaijmakers, 1988) and focuses on modeling free recall and recognition; MINERVA2, the second version of a model named after the Roman goddess of wisdom (Hintzman, 1984b, 1986, 1987, 1988), which focuses on categorization, cued recall, and recognition; and TODAM, which stands for theory of distributed associative memory (Murdock, 1983, 1984; Lewandowsky & Murdock, 1989) and focuses on serial recall and recognition. The other model commonly grouped with these global memory models is Anderson's ACT series of models (Anderson & Lebiere, 1998). It is not included here because it is well described in an excellent Web site (http://act.psy.cmu.edu/).

In the context of discussing SAM, we cover both compound cue theory (Dosher & Rosedale, 1989; Ratcliff & McKoon, 1988) and the diffusion model (Ratcliff, 1978). The former enables SAM and other models to account for semantic priming, and the latter is a general model of response times. We also discuss a class of models known as nonlinear back-propagation connectionist models. Finally, we present the feature model (Nairne, 1988, 1990), an account of immediate memory.

Each model will be used to illustrate different advantages and disadvantages of using simulation models as a tool for analyzing human memory. For a review of other influential simulation models, see Raaijmakers and Shiffrin (1992).

SAM

Because Richard Shiffrin was a principal architect of SAM (Raaijmakers & Shiffrin, 1981; Gillund & Shiffrin, 1984), it should come as no surprise that SAM retains many properties of the highly successful dual-store model (Atkinson & Shiffrin, 1968; see Chapter 3). Short-term memory is viewed as a limited-capacity buffer that serves two roles: It affects which items will get stored in long-term memory, and it is used to assemble retrieval cues that access information in long-term memory. Long-term memory is assumed to be an (almost) unlimited set of interconnected (or associated) concepts. Information in long-term memory is assumed to be permanent; there is no erasing, decaying, or forgetting of information in long-term memory. All instances of apparent forgetting are retrieval failures. Successful retrieval depends on the cue that is used, with context playing a particularly important role.

A key concept in the SAM model is the image. An image is an interconnected feature set that contains information about the context in which the item was learned, the item itself (its meaning, its name, and so on), and its relation with other images. When trying to recall something, a person assembles a set of cues in short-term memory and then uses these to activate various images in long-term memory. Sampling refers to the selection of an image, and recovery refers to the process of getting information out of the image. Just because an item is sampled does not necessarily mean that the information within that image is recovered. Although this might sound odd, consider what can happen when you search for a book in the library. You might be interested in how people recognize faces, and so you assemble a cue, the index number for the human memory section of the Purdue psychology library (153.1). You next go to that section of the library and sample from the set of books whose call numbers begin with 153.1. Simply sampling these books, however, does not mean that you will find something about face recognition. Many of the memory books will discuss this process, and to the extent that they do, you will recover some basic information about face recognition. However, more information can be found with a slightly different cue (152.1), where you will find entire books that discuss research on face perception.

The associative retrieval structure is created by processes that occur in the storage buffer. The buffer has a fixed size, r, and once this capacity is exceeded, a replacement rule determines which items are lost. The first version of SAM (Raaijmakers & Shiffrin, 1981) assumed that each item in the buffer had an equal probability of being replaced ($1/r$). Later versions (Gillund & Shiffrin, 1984) used a different rule: The oldest item in the buffer was replaced. Rehearsal, the basis for incrementing the strength of three types of associations, is shared over all items currently in the buffer. Thus, if only a few items are in the buffer, associative strengths will increase more than if the buffer is full.

The time spent in the buffer determines context strength—the degree of association between the item and its context. Interitem strengths—associations between two items—are determined by the amount of time the two items spend in the buffer together. The strength of the association between an item and itself is also determined by the time spent in the buffer. Although this may sound like an odd sort of association, it will become important during the sampling phase, when this strength will determine whether a cue will sample the appropriate image. Four parameters are involved here, including a for context associations, b for interitem strengths, and c for associations between the word and itself. The fourth association is between two items from the same list that did not share time in the buffer; this residual associative strength is represented by a parameter called d. This last parameter is not calculated directly, but any two items in the retrieval structure that were not rehearsed together can have some associative strength. Thus, d is similar to b but is typically much smaller.

The strength of the association between the context, C, and a particular item, W_i, is given by Equation O.01. The parameter n refers to the number of items that are simultaneously maintained in the buffer, t_i is the length of time that item W_i spends in the buffer, and a is the context association parameter. The strength of the association between a particular item, W_i, and another item, W_j, is given by Equation O.02. It is almost identical to O.01 except that t_{ij} is the amount of time word i and word j spend in the buffer together, and b is the interitem associative strength parameter. Finally, the strength of the association between an item, W_i, and itself is given by Equation O.03. This equation is exactly the same as Equation O.01, except that a is replaced by the self-association parameter c.

$$S\left(C, W_i\right) = \frac{at_i}{n} \tag{O.01}$$

$$S(W_j, W_i) = \frac{bt_{ij}}{n} \tag{O.02}$$

$$S(W_i, W_i) = \frac{ct_i}{n} \tag{O.03}$$

One more storage assumption adds variability to the strengths discussed above. This variability is needed primarily for recognition. Basically, there is a ⅓ probability that a starting strength x will remain unchanged, a ⅓ probability that the strength will be increased, and a ⅓ probability that the strength will be decreased. The parameter that controls this is called v, and the resulting stored strength is called y. Equation O.04 describes this process.

$$y = \begin{cases} (1-v)x \\ x \\ (1+v)x \end{cases} \tag{O.04}$$

Once an item—or more accurately, an image—is stored, the free recall retrieval cycle can begin. The first step is assembling a retrieval cue in the short-term buffer. For most applications, sampling begins with just a context cue, followed by the context cue plus whatever item was just recalled. This cue is used to probe for images in long-term memory, and the images sampled and recovered can then be used as cues for the remaining items. This process continues until some ending criterion is reached.

The general course of the free recall retrieval process can be thought of as a flow-chart, as shown in Figure O.1. This particular chart illustrates the retrieval cycle, described in more detail by Gillund and Shiffrin (1984). In the flowchart, the retrieval cycle begins by using context as the cue. The process continues until there have been *kmax* total failures; these failures are counted using the variable k. A failure occurs if the sampled item is not recovered, or if the chosen item has been sampled on an earlier cycle (even if, on the earlier cycle, the item was not recovered). The other failure criterion, *lmax*, determines how long the model will use the just-recalled item, W_j, as a probe. Failures of this type are counted with the variable l. After *lmax* successive failures with a particular cue, the model shifts to the default cue, using just the context alone.

Formally, the probability of sampling (P_s) a particular item in the recall set (W_i) when the context (C) is used as a cue depends on the strength of the association between the item and the context, divided by the sum of the strengths of the association between the context and the other n items in the recall set. Mathematically, this can be expressed as

$$P_s(W_i \mid C) = \frac{S(C, W_i)}{\sum_{k=1}^{n} S(C, W_k)} \tag{O.05}$$

where n is the number of items in the recall set (usually the number of items in the list). The associative strength between the context and the word depends on how long the item was in the temporary buffer and how many other items were present simultaneously. The strength can also be modified by altering the value of the parameter a. When an

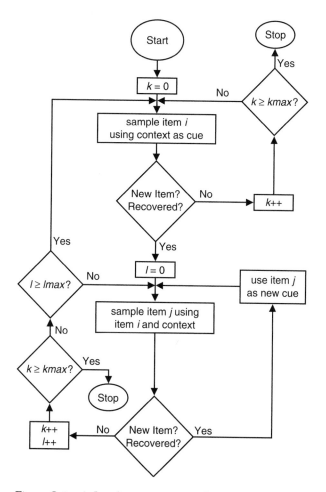

Figure O.1 A flowchart representing the Gillund and Shiffrin (1984) SAM retrieval cycle for free recall.
SOURCE: Gillund & Shiffrin (1984).

item, W_j, has been recalled, the model shifts to using context plus the item as a cue. Thus, two more terms are added to Equation O.05, reflecting (1) the associative strength between the item desired and the item used as a cue, and (2) the associative strength between the item used as a cue and all the other items in the recall set. Mathematically, Equation O.05 becomes

$$P_s\left(W_i \mid CW_j\right) = \frac{S\left(C, W_i\right)S\left(W_j W_i\right)}{\sum\limits_{k=1}^{n} S\left(C, W_k\right)S\left(W_j W_k\right)} \tag{O.06}$$

Once an item has been sampled, it still needs to be recovered. Recovery can be thought of as the process by which information is extracted from the image, and this process may or may not be successful. Just as there are two sampling equations (O.05 and O.06), there are also two recovery equations (O.07 and O.08), depending on whether the cue was just the context or the context plus an item.

$$P_R\left(W_i \mid C\right) = 1 - e^{-S\left(C, W_i\right)} \tag{O.07}$$

$$P_R\left(W_i \mid CW_j\right) = 1 - e^{-S\left(C, W_i\right)S\left(W_j, W_i\right)} \tag{O.08}$$

For a yes/no recognition test, it is assumed that recognition is determined by a direct-access familiarity process; there is no search. The subject probes memory with two cues, the context and the tested item. The total activation of long-term store in response to the probe is a measure of the familiarity not only of that particular item, but also of all other images in memory. For this reason, Gillund and Shiffrin (1984) termed this a measure of *global familiarity*. The subject makes a yes or no decision based on the global familiarity; if the value reaches some criterion, the subject responds "yes." In the typical case, the main recognition equation is very similar to the main sampling equation above. The familiarity of an item, when probing using context and the item itself, is given by the sum, over all the items in the recall set, of the product of the associative strength of the context with each item and the associative strength between the target and each item.

$$F\left(C, W_i\right) = \sum_{k=1}^{n} S\left(C, W_k\right)S\left(W_i, W_k\right) \tag{O.09}$$

Once the familiarity is determined, a criterion must be set; this value, indicated by Cr, is a free parameter of the model. Typically, it is set so that it is close to the crossing points for the familiarity values of the target and distractor distributions. The idea is based on signal detection theory, described in Chapter 9. (In fact, for the sake of convenience, the performance of the model on recognition tasks is often described in terms of d'.) For the simulations reported in Gillund and Shiffrin (1984), the appropriate formula was specified in terms of the mean value of the distractor distribution and the mean value of the target distribution:

$$Cr = 0.455\left(M_d + M_t\right) \tag{O.10}$$

It should be clear by now that SAM is complex and that it is most useful if incorporated into a computer simulation. This is exactly how most of the simulation modeling has been conducted. However, given the verbal description and the equations presented here, several properties of SAM should be evident. For example, SAM accounts for the serial position curve in free recall in much the same way as the dual-store model does. The recency effect is attributed to output from the buffer at the time of recall. The primacy effect is attributed to the more beneficial rehearsal received by the first few items, because they do not share processing with other items, yielding stronger associations. The probability of recalling or recognizing a particular item decreases as the length of the list of to-be-remembered items increases (Murdock, 1962; Strong, 1912). According to SAM, list length affects memory performance in the two tests differently. In free recall, increasing the list length reduces the probability of sampling a particular item. In recognition, the variance of both the target and distractor distributions increases, resulting in more overlap between the two and hence a decrease in d'.

Table O.1 The main parameters and their default values in SAM

Parameter	Value	Function
a	0.250	Context associations
b	0.200	Interitem associations
c	0.150	Self associations
d	0.075	Residual associations
v	0.500	Variability in association
t	2.000	Presentation rate (seconds per item)
r	4	Capacity of buffer
Cr	1.000	Criterion
ll	20	List length
$kmax$	30	Number of attempts using just context as a cue
$lmax$	8	Number of attempts using context plus a previously recalled item as a cue

Table O.1 lists the main parameters in SAM, but most of SAM's properties depend on the setting of just four parameters: a, b, c, and d. The effect of each of these parameters on recall and recognition performance is shown in Figure O.2.

The context parameter a acts only as a scale factor for recognition and so does not affect performance. In free recall tasks, an increase in a will increase the probability of recovering an item (but has no effect on sampling probability), so free recall performance will improve.

Increases in the interitem associative parameter b will improve recognition performance by raising the familiarity of the target distribution (but not of the distractor distribution). This parameter has a similar beneficial effect on free recall, improving recovery and also, in a less apparent way, decreasing self-sampling. *Self-sampling* is the tendency for an item, when used as a cue, to sample itself rather than other items.

Parameter c is the self-coding parameter. Increasing associations between the item and itself improves recognition performance because the familiarity of the target distribution is increased, with no change in the distractor distribution. In free recall, on the other hand, an increase in c reduces performance because self-sampling is increased. (Recall that self-sampling decreases performance because, when an item is used as a cue, it samples itself rather than another item in the list.)

Increases in the residual parameter d decrease recognition performance by increasing the familiarity of the distractors more than the familiarity of the targets and by increasing the overall variance of both distributions. Increases in d benefit free recall by increasing recovery probabilities and also by decreasing self-sampling.

Using only these four parameters, SAM is able to simulate many of the empirical results seen with both recall and recognition. In particular, it offers an explanation for the differential effects of intentionality and word frequency on recall and recognition, and it can also address the recognition failure of recallable words.

Intentionality Subjects tend to recall more items under intentional learning instructions than under incidental instructions, but subjects can often recognize more items under incidental instructions (Eagle & Leiter, 1964; Estes & Da Polito, 1967). According to SAM, increased intentionality leads to increased interitem coding because if subjects know a test is forthcoming, their usual strategy is to relate the words to each other.

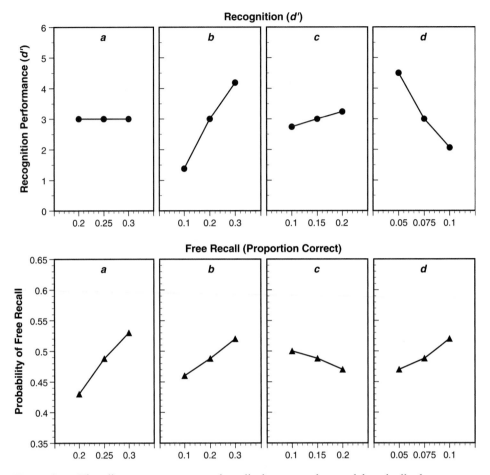

Figure O.2   The effects on recognition and recall of varying *a*, *b*, *c*, and *d*, with all other parameters held constant.   Source: Gillund & Shiffrin (1984).

Increased interitem coding is modeled by increasing parameter *b*, which, as can be seen in Figure O.2, leads to an increase in performance in both recall and recognition. However, increased interitem coding is usually associated with decreased self-coding. This is modeled by decreasing parameter *c*, which, as can be seen in Figure O.2, helps recall but hurts recognition. Simulation results are shown in Table O.2: As *b* increases and *c* decreases, recognition decreases and free recall increases.

Word Frequency Effect   The typical finding is that high-frequency words are recalled better than low-frequency words, but low-frequency words are recognized better than high-frequency words in pure lists of high- or low-frequency words; in mixed lists, recall of high- and low-frequency words is often equal (Gregg, 1976). The residual association between any two items not rehearsed together, or between any distractor and any list item, is assumed to be frequency-dependent. The parameter *d* is assumed to be larger for high-frequency words than for low-frequency words. For words that are rehearsed together, it is

Table O.2   Simulation results using the Gillund and Shiffrin (1984) version of SAM for recognition and recall of a 20-item list presented at a rate of 1 item every 2 seconds

Condition	Hit Rate	False Alarm	d′	Recall	b	c	d
Intentional	0.935	0.056	3.097	0.503	.22	.10	.075
Incidental	0.940	0.042	3.287	0.451	.18	.25	.075
High Freq	0.921	0.044	3.118	0.479	.20	.15	.075
Low Freq	0.954	0.012	3.931	0.424	.10	.15	.035

NOTE: For recognition, the hit rate, false alarm rate, and d′ are shown; for recall, the proportion correct is shown. The criterion, Cr, was calculated according to Equation O.10 and was approximately 1.0 for the first three simulations and approximately 0.5 for the last simulation. Parameters not shown were identical in all simulations and were those listed in Table O.1.

assumed that high-frequency cues are stronger than low-frequency cues—that b for high-frequency words is larger than b for low-frequency words. The parameters a and c are not frequency-dependent. Finally, the criterion will be different in the recognition phase for high- and low-frequency words. Although three parameters are changed (b, d, and Cr), this results in the appropriate pattern for pure and mixed lists (see Table O.2).

There is a pure-list advantage for high-frequency words in recall for a combination of two reasons. Any item sampled by a high-frequency word has a greater probability of being recovered because of the higher strength values. In pure high-frequency lists, only high-frequency cues are used, and in pure low-frequency lists, only low-frequency cues are used. In a mixed list, a high-frequency word is just as likely to sample a low-frequency word as a high-frequency word, and then both types are equally likely to be recovered. There is a consistent recognition advantage for low-frequency words regardless of the list composition. The residual parameter d has a smaller value for low-frequency words, and lower values increase recognition performance.

Recognition Failure of Recallable Words   SAM can also explain the other major problem facing a model of both recall and recognition: recognition failure of recallable words. Although the storage assumptions are the same for both recall and recognition, the retrieval assumptions are quite different. In SAM, recall requires a search, and a successful search means that an item was both sampled and recovered. Recognition, on the other hand, is based on a measure of global familiarity. Under certain circumstances, some searches will succeed in sampling and recovering an item even though the item may not reach the recognition familiarity criterion. One reason that an item may not reach the recognition familiarity criterion is a change in context, and SAM can easily model context effects: When the context changes, both a and c will change, and when the meaning of an item changes, changes in b will occur (see Gillund & Shiffrin, 1984, for details).

Summary   SAM has been an enormously successful and influential model of recall and recognition. With only a few parameters, all of them related to psychologically plausible concepts, SAM is able to explain memory performance in a wide variety of situations and different paradigms. It is also currently being used in conjunction with compound cue theory (see Chapter 10) to explain associative priming effects in generic memory. It is not without problems, however. First, because of the way the associative structure is set up,

SAM suffers many of the same problems as the dual-store model does (see Chapter 3). Second, although Table O.2 shows that SAM can simulate the mirror effect seen with word frequency, SAM cannot account for all aspects of the mirror effect (see Chapter 9).

Compound Cue Theory

One relatively recent competitor to spreading activation theories is a class of models known as *compound cue models* (Dosher & Rosedale, 1989; Ratcliff & McKoon, 1988). The basic idea is that instead of selecting items that have been activated by spreading activation, generic memory functions more the way other forms of memory function. Ratcliff and McKoon's (1988; McKoon & Ratcliff, 1992) model, for example, is based on a process similar to that used by SAM (Gillund & Shiffrin, 1984; see above).

The first change needed to add compound cue theory to SAM is the assumption that the item that preceded the target—the prime—can form a compound cue. This just adds another term to Equation O.09 for calculating the global familiarity of an item. Adding another cue, X, turns this into Equation O.11:

$$F(C, W_i, X) = \sum_{k=1}^{n} S(C, W_k) S(W_i, W_k) S(X, W_k) \qquad (O.11)$$

Or, rewriting to make it clearer which is the prime and which is the target,

$$F(C, T, P) = \sum_{k=1}^{n} S(C, W_k) S(T, W_k) S(P, W_k) \qquad (O.12)$$

Finally, a weighting parameter, ω, is introduced to give the current item (the target) more weight than preceding items (the prime):

$$F(C, T, P) = \sum_{k=1}^{n} S(C, W_k) S(T, W_k)^{1-\omega} S(P, W_k)^{\omega} \qquad (O.13)$$

One way of seeing how this accounts for the basic priming data is to consider that when two numbers close to 0 are multiplied, the result is a number even closer to 0. On the other hand, if two numbers near 1 are multiplied, the result is a number that remains close to 1. Imagine three items, P, T, and X. P stands for prime, and T stands for target. If the strength of the association between P and X is large (say, 0.90) and the strength of the association between T and X is large (say, 0.90), then when both of these values are multiplied together, the result is still quite large (0.80). On the other hand, if the strength of the association between P and X is large (0.90) but the strength of the association between T and X is small (0.10), then when both of these values are multiplied together, the result is small (0.09).

Adding the compound cue mechanism to SAM leaves one final problem: how to transform a measure of familiarity into a response time. Ratcliff and McKoon (1988) used Ratcliff's (1978) diffusion model, which converts high values of familiarity into fast and accurate positive response times, low values of familiarity into fast and accurate negative response times, and intermediate values of familiarity into slower and less accurate positive and negative response times.

The Diffusion Model

One common problem with models of memory is how to transform some measure related to accuracy, such as strength or familiarity, into response time. The issue is complex (Luce, 1986). Here, we focus on Ratcliff's (1978, 1981, 1985, 1988; Ratcliff, Van Zandt, & McKoon, 1999) diffusion model.

The diffusion model is one of a class of random walk models (Laming, 1968; Link & Heath, 1975; Stone, 1960). The basic idea behind these models is very simple: A decision is made on the basis of information that accumulates over time. The major difference between the diffusion model and other random walk models is that in the diffusion model, the information that drives the decision process accumulates continuously rather than in discrete steps. There are two decision boundaries, one for a positive choice and one for a negative choice. A decision is made as soon as the accumulated information crosses a boundary. The time to make a decision is the time needed to accumulate enough information to cross a boundary, plus response execution time (see Figure O.3).

The model has seven parameters. The upper boundary is marked by a, and the lower boundary is marked by 0. The starting point, z, is often set at $a/2$, and so is often not a free parameter. The mean drift rate, v, is set for each condition. The two variability parameters are s, the standard deviation within a trial, and η, the standard deviation across different trials. T_{er} reflects nondecision components, such as response execution time. In practice, s is often set to a fixed value, such as 0.1, and so is not a free parameter.

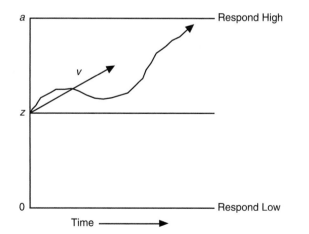

Figure O.3   The diffusion model. Evidence accumulates over time until either the Respond High or Respond Low boundary is crossed. Three parameters are shown: a = boundary position; z = starting point; v = mean drift rate (one for each condition). The other parameters are s = standard deviation in drift within a trial; T_{er} = encoding and response time; η = standard deviation in mean drift rate from trial to trial; and s_z = standard deviation in starting point.   SOURCE: Adapted from Ratcliff, Van Zandt, & McKoon (1999).

Details of fitting the diffusion model are given in Ratcliff (1978) and Ratcliff, Van Zandt, and McKoon (1999). Here, we highlight how the model accounts for a number of standard phenomena observed with response times.

Speed/Accuracy Trade-off   In general, the faster people respond, the more errors they make. In the diffusion model, this is accounted for by varying the boundary positions. For example, if a is set to a lower value (see Figure O.3), then it will take less time for the accumulation process to reach the boundary. Thus, response time will be faster. However, when the boundaries are closer to the starting point, it is more likely that variation in drift will lead to hitting the wrong boundary. Small variations will have a larger effect on the outcome when the boundaries are closer together. When the boundaries are farther apart, response time is slower, but there is less chance that variation in the drift will lead to an incorrect outcome.

Skewed Response Time Distributions   Response time distributions are skewed to the right. This means that the right tail extends farther than the left. The diffusion model produces this result because of variation in drift. For fast processes, there will be less time for variation to affect where they cross the boundary. Thus, fast processes are more likely to cross the boundary very close to each other. For slow processes, there is more opportunity for the variation to have large effects, and so these processes will cross the boundary over a widely distributed region.

Faster "No" Than "Yes" Responses   In many item recognition studies, response times for "no" responses can be almost as fast as for "yes" responses. It is also possible to have some "no" responses be faster than some "yes" responses (for example, Rips, Shoben, & Smith, 1973). This can happen in the diffusion model when the separation between one boundary and the starting point ($|0\text{-}z|$) is less than the separation between the other boundary and the starting point ($|a\text{-}z|$).

Information Effects   Informing subjects of what is likely to occur on a block of trials can affect response times. For example, if subjects are told that one outcome is quite unlikely, that will lead to slower response times in that condition and also to a change in the shape of the response time distribution. In the diffusion model, this can be explained by having the boundaries change.

The major advantages of the diffusion model over other models of response time are that (1) it predicts the shape of the response time distribution; (2) it includes variability in the parameters; and (3) it can explain response time data from many different paradigms, ranging from the simplest detection studies to recognition to priming.

One issue often raised in conjunction with the diffusion model is whether it can, in principle, be falsified. Given the use of variability in drift rate and the setting of different rates for each condition, can it produce all possible outcomes?

The diffusion model must predict that response time distributions are skewed to the right. If a response time distribution were observed that was bimodal or skewed to the left, the diffusion model could not produce that result. The model also places very tight restrictions on the difference in response times seen for correct and incorrect responses when the basic response time is very fast. That is, for the fastest conditions, the difference between the fast correct and fast incorrect times will be very small.

MINERVA2

One of the main goals in developing MINERVA2 was to explain memory for individual experiences (episodic memory) and memory for abstract concepts (generic or semantic memory) within a single system (Hintzman, 1984b). Primary memory plays a very minor role, either sending a retrieval cue or probe to secondary memory or receiving the reply, termed the *echo*.

The model assumes "(1) that only episodic traces are stored in memory, (2) that repetition produces multiple traces of an item, (3) that a retrieval cue contacts all memory traces simultaneously, (4) that each trace is activated according to its similarity to the retrieval cue, and (5) that all traces respond in parallel, the retrieved information reflecting their summed output" (Hintzman, 1984b, p. 96). It is clear how this might capture episodic memory phenomena. Generic memory follows from the assumption that although a separate trace of each episode is stored, the traces are activated in parallel by a retrieval cue, and abstractions can be constructed through the summed responses of those traces that are most strongly activated by the cue.

The repetition of an item improves memory performance not by strengthening a trace but rather by redundancy, creating multiple copies. When a probe is presented to secondary memory, it is simultaneously matched with every memory trace. Each trace is activated according to its similarity to the probe, and the echo that is returned to primary memory represents the summed reactions of all traces to the probe. Because a trace contributes to the echo only to the extent that it is activated, only similar traces will make substantive contributions. There is no process by which a particular memory trace can be isolated and further examined.

Information about an event or experience is represented as a vector, an ordered list of feature values. Each feature can take a value of 1, –1, or 0. Each feature of an event or experience in primary memory is encoded in secondary memory with a probability L, a learning parameter. In a secondary memory trace description, a 0 means either that the feature is irrelevant or that it was never stored.

Let P_j be the value of feature j in the probe, let $T_{i,j}$ be the value of feature j in trace i, and let N_r be the number of relevant features—the number of features that are not 0 in either the probe or the trace. The similarity of a particular trace, i, to the probe is

$$S_i = \sum_{j=1}^{n} P_j T_{i,j} \frac{1}{N_r} \qquad (O.14)$$

In this equation, S_i acts as a correlation coefficient. When the probe and trace are identical, it takes a value of 1; when the probe and trace are orthogonal, it takes a value of 0. Although values close to –1 are mathematically possible, they rarely occur in simulations. Imagine a probe item with a vector of feature values [1, –1, –1, 1, –1]. Using Equation O.14, the similarity between this probe item and a trace vector [1, –1, 1, 1, –1] is calculated as follows:

$$S_i = \frac{(1 \times 1) + (-1 \times -1) + (-1 \times 1) + (1 \times 1) + (-1 \times -1)}{5}$$

$$S_i = \frac{1 + 1 - 1 + 1 + 1}{5}$$

$$S_i = 0.60$$

A trace will be activated to the extent that it is similar to the probe. The activation level, A_i, is the cube of the similarity value:

$$A_i = S_i^3 \tag{O.15}$$

Because a cube is taken, the activation will preserve the sign of similarity measure. In addition, if there is little similarity between the trace and the probe, the activation will be close to zero. For the example given above, the activation would be $0.6 \times 0.6 \times 0.6 = .216$. An item that is less similar (such as $S_i = 0.4$) would have much less activation (0.064).

The echo that is returned has two properties, intensity and content. The intensity, I, of an echo is found by summing the activation levels of all the traces, M. It can be thought of as a measure of familiarity, and it is used when modeling recognition and frequency judgments.

$$I = \sum_{i=1}^{M} A_i \tag{O.16}$$

The content of the echo, C_j, is the activation pattern across features. The activation of a particular feature, j, in the echo is given by

$$C_j = \sum_{i=1}^{M} A_i T_{i,j} \tag{O.17}$$

Traces activated by the probe can contain information that was not originally in the probe. For example, an experience might be learning to associate a name with a face. Features 1 to 10 might represent information about the face, whereas features 11 to 20 might represent information about the name. Recalling a name upon presentation of the face could involve assembling a probe with features 1–10 containing information about the face and features 11–20 set to 0, and focusing on the content of features 11–20 in the returning echo (for example, examining C_{11} through C_{20}).

The resemblance between the original and the retrieved information is usually not perfect. One attractive feature of MINERVA2 is that it offers an elegant way of sharpening, or *deblurring*, the returned echo. The echo can be used as a second probe, the second echo can be used as a third probe, and so forth. After a few iterations, the resultant echo is more like an acceptable response than the first echo, and it is often an almost perfect copy of the original (see Hintzman, 1986). Recognition (hit rate) depends on the intensity of the echo and thus depends, in part, on the degree to which the target probe matches the subset of target features probed for. In addition, the learning rate will affect performance: The more features there are, the higher the intensity of the echo.

We will focus on just two aspects of MINERVA2. First, it demonstrates that both episodic and semantic memory processes can be accounted for within a single memory system; second, it sheds more light on recognition failure of recallable words. In both cases, MINERVA2 has served as an analysis tool to demonstrate that alternate conceptions to the standard view can predict and account for the same pattern of results.

Although there is wide acceptance of the distinction between episodic and semantic memory systems (Tulving, 1983), many researchers have documented both empirical and logical problems with the distinction (McKoon, Ratcliff, & Dell, 1986; Neely, 1989; see also Chapter 7). One purpose of MINERVA2 was to see if it could produce the appropriate pattern of results in both an episodic task and a semantic task. If it could, MINERVA2 would stand as an existence proof: It is possible to produce the correct results without postulating separate systems.

Hintzman (1986) applied MINERVA2 to the question of how abstract knowledge is related to specific experience. According to multiple systems theorists, repeated exposure to individual examples produces traces in episodic memory and also an abstract representation of the category in semantic memory (Tulving, 1983). In contrast, Hintzman took the view that only traces of individual episodes are stored and that abstract representations are simply a product of the way these individual traces are activated at retrieval. In this conception, there is no need for a semantic memory system. To see if this view was plausible, Hintzman simulated many findings from a research paradigm known as a *schema abstraction task* (Posner & Keele, 1968).

In the typical experiment, subjects may be trained to classify random dot patterns into three categories (Homa, Cross, Cornell, Goldman, & Schwartz, 1973). Each category has a different number of members, called exemplars—in this case, 3, 6, and 9. All exemplars are distortions of the prototype, but the subjects never see the actual prototype and are not told that such a prototype exists. During learning, a pattern is shown, and the subject classifies it as belonging to category A, B, or C. Subsequent feedback informs the subject what the correct response should have been. After learning to classify these 18 patterns, the subjects are then tested on their ability to classify five other patterns: (1) the training exemplars, which are now called "old" exemplars; (2) the three prototypes, none of which has been seen previously; (3) new exemplars that are relatively low-level distortions of the prototypes; (4) new exemplars that are relatively high-level distortions of the prototypes; and (5) random arrangements of dots. Figure O.4 illustrates the relationship of a low-level and a high-level distortion to the category prototype.

Among the results of interest are the following: (1) Subjects tend to classify the old exemplars more accurately than prototypes on an immediate test, but classification is either equal or slightly worse for old exemplars than for prototypes on a delayed test. (2) Old exemplars are classified more accurately than new exemplars on both immediate and delayed tests. (3) New exemplars that are low-level distortions of the prototypes are classified more accurately than new high-level distortions on both immediate and delayed tests. (4) Classification of new patterns is better for large categories (categories with more instances) than small categories. (5) Random patterns are more likely to be assigned to a large category than to a small category.

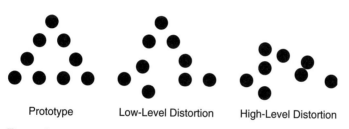

Prototype   Low-Level Distortion   High-Level Distortion

Figure O.4   Examples of a prototype, a low-level distortion exemplar, and a high-level distortion exemplar.   SOURCE: Based on stimuli used by Posner, Goldsmith, & Welton (1967).

CogLab Experiment

http://coglab.wadsworth.com/experiments/Prototypes/

MINERVA2 can simulate all five key results (Hintzman, 1986). For this simulation, each memory trace has 23 features ($n = 23$), with the first 10 coding the category name and the last 13 coding the stimulus pattern. The model is told of the appropriate category, just as the subjects were. Three prototypes were generated randomly, and exemplars were generated by multiplying a random 2 (low-level distortion) or 4 (high-level distortion) features from the last 13 by –1. Storage occurred as described above, and testing consisted of presenting the stimulus pattern as a cue (feature values 1 through 10 were set to 0 on the probe) and examining the category name portion of the echo content. To simulate a delayed test, each stored feature was set to 0 with a probability of 0.75 and then was retested. Figure O.5 shows some of the results from one simulation for the category with six items.

First, MINERVA2 correctly simulates differential forgetting rates for the prototype and old exemplars, with best performance on the immediate test for old exemplars but best performance on the delayed test for prototypes. Second, old exemplars are consistently categorized better than are new exemplars. Third, new exemplars of low distortion are categorized better than are new exemplars of high distortion. Not shown is the fourth finding: Performance for the 9-item category was better than for the 6-item category, which in turn was better than performance in the 3-item category. The fifth result described above—that random patterns are more likely to be assigned to a large category

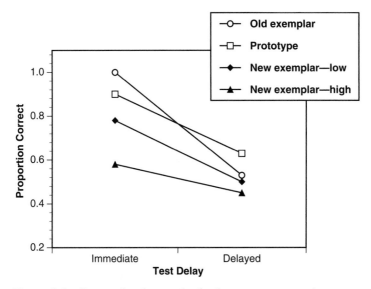

Figure O.5   Correct classification for the 6-item category as a function of probe type (old exemplar, prototype, low-distortion new exemplar, and high-distortion new exemplar) and test delay (immediate and delayed).
SOURCE: Adapted from "'Schema Abstraction' in a Multiple-Trace Memory Model," by D. L. Hintzman, 1986, *Psychological Review, 4*, 411–428. Copyright © 1986 American Psychological Association. Adapted with permission.

than to a small category—was also simulated by MINERVA2. Of the random patterns tested, 22% were assigned to the 3-item category, 31% to the 6-item category, and 34% to the 9-item category. The remaining items were assigned to a "junk" category, meaning that no clear response was given. These simulation results are not dependent on particular parameter settings; Hintzman (1986) replicated the results with different settings, in addition to reporting several other simulations.

The important point for our purposes is that MINERVA2, which simply stores every item experienced, can reproduce the key findings from the schema abstraction paradigm. Although it is possible to account for the results by postulating a separate semantic memory system, MINERVA2 illustrates that it is also possible to account for the data without such a separate system.

The second topic of interest for MINERVA2 is recognition failure of recallable words. As described in more detail in Chapter 9, it is possible to set up a situation in which an item can be recalled but cannot be recognized (Watkins & Tulving, 1975). Because this result seems counterintuitive, numerous studies have explored many different factors. When the proportion of words recognized is plotted against the proportion of words recognized that were also recalled, a regular pattern emerges; this pattern, known as the Tulving-Wiseman law (Tulving & Wiseman, 1975; Flexser & Tulving, 1978), looks like Figure O.6. The diagonal (dotted) line represents what should happen if there is no correlation between recall and recognition. The actual data, replotted from dozens of studies, fall on the curved (solid) line but always above the dotted line. This indicates that there is a positive correlation between the two scores.

There is an ongoing controversy about how to interpret this result (for example, compare Hintzman, 1992, with Tulving & Flexser, 1992). The key for our purposes is that the diagonal is supposed to mean that recognition and recall are independent processes. In MINERVA2, recall and recognition use the same memory trace, and so performance

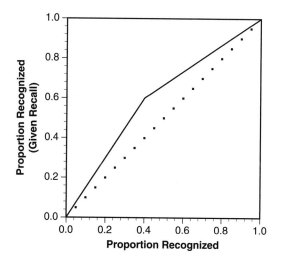

Figure O.6   A representation of the Tulving-Wiseman law. If recall and recognition are uncorrelated, performance should fall on the diagonal (dotted) line. Data plotted from many studies fall above the diagonal, in the region shown by the curved (solid) line.

Experiment   *Recognition Failure of Recallable Words*

Purpose: To demonstrate that some words cannot be recognized even though they can be recalled

Subjects: Sixteen subjects are recommended.

Materials: Table K in the Appendix contains two sets of target words and associated weak and strong cues. Create two lists of word pairs, with the weak cue word written in lowercase and the target written in uppercase, and put them on standard notecards. Half the subjects should get List A, and half should get List B. Also, make two response sheets giving just the cue word, with a blank space for the target. The order of the cue words should be random. Prepare a sheet for each list with the strong cue followed by four spaces; this is for the free association segment. Finally, make a list of all the target words from both lists, with the order of the words scrambled; this is for the recognition segment.

Design: This is a completely within-subjects design because each subject receives both a recognition test and a recall test.

Procedure, Step 1:   Inform the subjects that they will be performing a number of tasks. First, present the list to the subject, showing each notecard for 3 seconds.

Instructions, Step 1:   "I show you a notecard containing two words, one in lowercase and one in uppercase. Later on in the experiment, you will be given the lowercase word and asked to recall the uppercase word. Any questions?"

Procedure, Step 2:   The second step is the free association test. Distribute the free association answer sheet.

Instructions, Step 2:   "The next task is a free association test. I will read out a word, and you should write down the first four words that pop into your head. Any questions?"

Procedure, Step 3:   The third step is the recognition test. Collect the free association answer sheet, and pass out the recognition test sheet.

Instructions, Step 3:   "The next task is a recognition test. On this sheet of paper, please circle any words that you recognize as being one of the uppercase words in the first part of the experiment. For each circled word, please also rate your confidence in your judgment. A 3 means that you are certain the word was on the initial list, a 2 means the word probably was on the list, and a 1 means you are guessing. Any questions?"

Procedure, Step 4:   The fourth and final step is the recall test. Collect the recognition test sheet, and pass out the recall test sheet.

Instructions, Step 3:   "The final test is the cued recall test. For each cue, please write the uppercase word that was paired with it in the first phase of this experiment. Any questions?"

Scoring and Analysis: For each subject, count the number of target words that were recognized correctly in Step 3. Then, count the number of target words that were recalled correctly in Step 4. Finally, compute the proportion of target words that were recalled but were not recognized.

SOURCE: Adapted from an experiment by Watkins & Tulving (1975).

---

on the two tests should be correlated. In other words, if MINERVA2 were used to simulate recognition failure of recallable words, the simulation results should show a positive correlation and fall in the area where data from human subjects fall. Curiously enough, this is *not* what happens when the simulations are actually run.

Hintzman (1987) ran simulations of recognition failure of recallable words in which the model learned a list of cue-target pairs. Each pair had 20 elements; the cue was represented by the first 10 features, and the target by the second 10 features. For the cued recall test, only the cue was used as a probe, and the model's answer was the last 10 features of the echo. For the recognition test, just the target was used as a probe. If the target had been previously recalled, the resulting echo was added to the distribution of recalled echoes. If the target had not been recalled, the echo was added to the distribution of nonrecalled echoes. The new distributions were obtained by probing with new, random vectors. Remember that in a recognition test MINERVA2 uses the echo intensity; it is these intensities that are collected together to generate the distributions. With the distributions assembled, a signal detection analysis can be performed (see Chapter 9).

With standard parameters ($L = 0.45$ and list lengths of between 8 and 32), the data from MINERVA2 fell *exactly* on the diagonal. Mathematically, this can be interpreted as stochastic independence: Recall and recognition are independent. However, because we know that recall and recognition in MINERVA2 are not independent, something else must be going on.

According to this analysis, there are two ways of obtaining independence. First, recall and recognition might be truly independent. Second, there could be one or more variables that are positively correlated with both measures and one or more variables that are negatively correlated with both measures. For example, both recall and recognition benefit when more target features are stored (through the parameter L). The second variable could be variation in intralist similarity. High similarity is known to decrease the probability of correctly recalling an item on a cued recall test (due to interference) but to increase the probability of responding "old." However, it is not similarity per se, but variation in similarity, that could produce the negative correlation. Simulations reported by Hintzman (1987) confirmed this analysis. By varying the number of features encoded and the variation in similarity, he was able to move the data points either above the diagonal or below the diagonal.

What does this imply about recognition failure of recallable words? Because MINERVA2 usually produces results that indicate independence and it is known that MINERVA2's processes are not independent, it suggests that the Tulving-Wiseman law may be an artifact of as yet unexplored factors. One possibility is that variation in intralist similarity and degree of encoding might be affecting the results. Notice that the simulations from MINERVA2 do not prove this interpretation; rather, they again serve as an existence proof. Hintzman's argument is presented in more detail in Hintzman (1992); Tulving (Tulving & Flexser, 1992) offers an alternate explanation.

Summary   MINERVA2 was designed to account for recognition and cued recall. It has successfully shown that a model that does not distinguish between episodic and semantic memory can nonetheless produce the appropriate pattern of results, as seen in the schema abstraction results shown in Figure O.5. Furthermore, it can explain not only recognition data but also frequency data; that is, it can simulate the results of tests that ask people to judge how many times they have seen a particular item. Perhaps its most important feature is the ability to deblur an ambiguous echo without recourse to an external memory source. (We will discuss this issue in more detail in conjunction with TODAM.) As was the case with SAM, MINERVA2 is not perfect. It cannot explain the mirror effect (see Chapter 9), and because there are so few parameters, it cannot address other aspects of memory. Nonetheless, MINERVA2 is perhaps the most impressive model, if only because it can do so much with so few assumptions and parameters.

TODAM

Murdock's (1982, 1983, 1993, 1995; Lewandowsky & Murdock, 1989) theory of distributed associative memory (TODAM) is a very different kind of model from the two considered previously. It was designed to explain memory for serial order and recognition. Individual memories are stored in a distributed fashion; in other words, one memory storage system is involved with every memory. The simulation version has a common memory vector, **M**. Just as in connectionist models, each element in this vector is involved with storing every memory. TODAM can also be seen as an existence proof—that it is possible to store and retrieve information from a common memory vector.

In TODAM, vectors are centered at 0, meaning that the middle location is location 0, with an equal number of features to the left and to the right of this middle position. Each vector has N features, where N is theoretically a large number but in practice is on the order of 200 or so. The features in the vector are randomly drawn from a normal distribution with a mean of 0 and a standard deviation of $1/N$. This means that the vectors will have certain properties; for example, if a vector is multiplied by itself, the product is 1.

Two mathematical procedures make TODAM tick. The first is called *convolution* and is represented by the symbol *, and the second is *correlation*, represented by the symbol #. (This type of correlation is unrelated to Pearson's correlation, with the symbol r.) TODAM assumes that there is a main memory vector that stores two kinds of information: item information, which lets the system recall which information was presented, and associations between items, which lets the system recall in the appropriate order. Information is entered into the main memory vector by convolution and is retrieved via correlation.

At the time when item j is encoded, the state of memory vector **M** can be represented as

$$\mathbf{M}_j = \alpha \mathbf{M}_{j-1} + \gamma f_j + \omega_j f_j * f_{j-1} \qquad (O.18)$$

$\mathbf{M}_{j-1}$ is the state of the memory vector prior to learning the current item, item j. The parameter α is a noise or forgetting parameter that can vary between 0 and 1. The vector that represents item j is represented by f_j. The parameter γ is a weighting factor that increases or decreases the relative importance of item information. The parameter ω_j is a weighting factor that increases or decreases the relative importance of associative information. Finally, $f_j * f_{j-1}$ is a representation of associative information—in particular, the convolution of the current item with the previous item. Thus, the state of the memory vector after learning item j is the prior state altered by a little noise plus item j plus an association between item j and the item that preceded item j.

Convolution is a relatively straightforward procedure; the only trick is in keeping track of which elements are involved in each step. Eich (1982) gives a good description of convolution in a memory model and illustrates the procedure step by step. If L is $(N-1)/2$, and x ranges from $-L$ to L, then to convolve two vectors, **A** and **B**,

$$\left(\mathbf{A} * \mathbf{B}\right)_x = \sum_{i=-L}^{L} \left(\mathbf{A}_i \cdot \mathbf{B}_{x-i}\right) \qquad (O.19)$$

Serial recall is cue driven, and the first cue used is a context cue. When the subject is told to recall a list of items that was just presented, this is the cue to initiate retrieval. Retrieval is done through the process of correlation, an approximate inverse of convolution. If two vectors, **A** and **B**, are correlated, then

$$\left(\mathbf{A} \# \mathbf{B}\right)_x = \sum_{i=-L}^{L} \left(\mathbf{A}_i \cdot \mathbf{B}_{x+i}\right) \tag{O.20}$$

Because of the way that associative information is encoded, the cue for item j is item $j - 1$. The result will be a noisy, blurry, but potentially interpretable vector known as f'. Thus,

$$f_{j-1} \# \mathbf{M} = f'_j \tag{O.21}$$

Context, then, is the cue for f_1, f_1 is the cue for f_2, f_2 is the cue for f_3, and so on. This procedure is known as *chaining*, and it works well until one of the items is not recalled. The result of correlation is a blurry but potentially interpretable vector, and the model interprets this vector by computing the dot product between the recovered vector and the possible candidates. If this value is within acceptable limits, then the item is interpreted and produced. (The dot product of two vectors, a and b, is also a vector; the first element is the product of the first elements of a and b, the second element is the product of the second elements of a and b, and so on.) If an item is not recalled, a link in the chain is missing; in the typical chain model of memory, recall must necessarily stop at this point. This problem has limited the development of models of serial order for years (see Young, 1968), and one of the contributions of TODAM is a way around this problem. Regardless of its interpretation, f'_j will be used as the cue for the next item. Because the memory vector $\mathbf{M}$ contains both item and associative information, it turns out that f'_j can be a useful cue even if it is uninterpretable itself.

One intriguing aspect of TODAM's behavior is that several items can be stored in the common memory vector and then retrieved, and the simulation results closely resemble what subjects do. For example, Drewnowski and Murdock (1980) presented subjects with lists of 3, 4, 5, 6, and 7 items for immediate serial recall. The left panel of Figure O.7 shows some of their data. A response was scored as correct only if it was reported

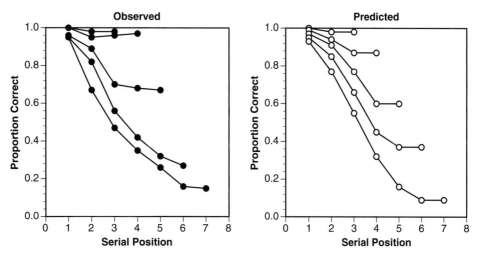

Figure O.7 Proportion correctly recalled in order as a function of various list lengths. As soon as one item was incorrectly recalled, no further items in the list were scored as correct. SOURCE: Adapted from "Memory for Serial Order," by S. Lewandowsky and B. B. Murdock, 1989, *Psychological Review*, 96, 25–57. Copyright © 1989 American Psychological Association. Adapted with permission.

in the correct order; thus, as soon as one error was made, no other responses were counted as correct. The predictions of TODAM, shown in the right panel, are clearly capturing the important aspects of the data.

TODAM has also been applied to recognition (Murdock, 1982). As with SAM and MINERVA2, recognition is based on a measure of familiarity. In TODAM's case, familiarity is defined as the dot product of the probe, f, and the main memory vector, $\mathbf{M}$:

$$f \cdot \mathbf{M} = \sum_{i=-L}^{L} \left(f_i \cdot \mathbf{M}_i \right) \tag{O.22}$$

If this value is greater than some criterion, then the response is "old"; if it is less than the criterion, then the response is "new." Hockley and Murdock (1987) have developed a sophisticated decision mechanism for interpreting the familiarity value that can predict both accuracy and latency. Their decision model is outlined in Figure O.8.

The memory comparison stage reflects the result of Equation O.22, a measure of familiarity. One of the key assumptions is that there is always some noise present in the memory system. Each time through the decision cycle, random noise is added to the original output of the memory system. The combined value is then compared to two criteria, a and b. If the value is less than a, a "new" decision is made; if it is greater than b, an "old" decision is made. If the value falls in between, then a wait interval occurs. A different random noise value is added to the output of the model, and a and b are moved closer together. The more wait intervals there are, the longer the time until (usually) the value falls either below a or above b and a response is made. Formally, the time to make a decision, T, is given by

$$T_k = \left(k^2 + k + 2 \right) BCT \tag{O.23}$$

where k is the number of previous cycles and BCT is the base cycle time—the time to complete one cycle. Typically, a value of 17.5 ms is used for BCT. This means that the fastest possible decision time is 35 ms, which would occur when an immediate "old" or "new" response is given. With an immediate response, k would be 0, so that $T_0 = 2 \times BCT$.

Figure O.9 shows an application of this decision model. The data come from an experiment reported by Hockley (1982) in which 80 words were presented once and 80 words were presented three times. Each time a word was presented, the subject was asked to decide whether the word had already appeared in the list. The lag between the first and second presentation of an item and the second and third presentation of an item could vary between 0 (the items appeared successively) and 40 (40 items intervened). The mean correct response times (in milliseconds), as well as the proportion correct, are shown for the second (2P) and third (3P) presentations. The best fit of the decision model is shown by the solid lines, with the original data shown as data points. The model produces an impressive fit (see Hockley & Murdock, 1987, for more details).

Although TODAM has successfully predicted many serial order phenomena, it has at least one important problem that is of central importance not only in TODAM but in any simulation model that produces a result that needs to be interpreted. This process is often referred to as *deblurring*. TODAM uses the concept of a competitor set—a set of items that the subject thinks is likely to have occurred on the trial—to aid in this process. For example, many experiments use numbers, letters, or some other relatively small set. In TODAM, f_j' is compared to the items in the competitor set, and whichever item is most

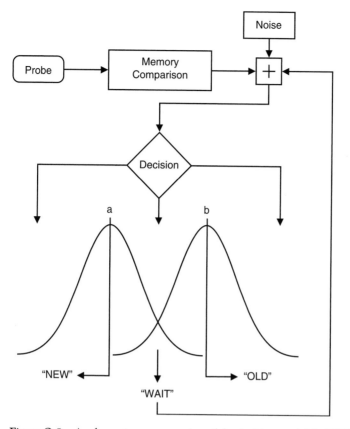

Figure O.8   A schematic representation of the decision model for TODAM. The probe is the item presented for a recognition judgment, and the memory comparison stage is based on assessing familiarity via Equation O.22. Noise (in the form of random variability) is added, and this is the input to the decision system. If this input is less than *a* or greater than *b*, a decision of "new" or "old" (respectively) is made. If the input falls in between, then the system enters a wait interval, during which a new value of random noise is added to the familiarity value and *a* and *b* are moved slightly closer together. This cycle continues until a decision is made.   SOURCE: Adapted from "A Decision Model for Accuracy and Response Latency in Recognition Memory," by W. E. Hockley and B. B. Murdock, 1987, *Psychological Review*, 94, 341–358. Copyright © 1987 American Psychological Association. Adapted with permission.

similar is the interpretation of f'_j. If this is a correct match, then the model is judged to have recalled the appropriate item and the item is removed from the competitor set. The reason for this removal is that subjects rarely repeat an item. The recalled item is then convolved back into the main memory vector to implement the idea that the subjects re-member which items they have recalled.

The problem arises when f'_j is matched with an incorrect item. In this case, there are two options. One is to remove the best matching item from the competitor, but this will prevent the model from producing recency effects. The reason is straightforward (Nairne & Neath, 1994). If there is a pool of 8 items in the competitor set, the 8th item has the most chances of being mistakenly recalled. If it is matched inappropriately to f'_j and

Figure O.9   The data points show observed data, and the solid lines show the predictions for response times (top panel) and accuracy (bottom panel) as a function of test lag.   SOURCE: Adapted from "A Decision Model for Accuracy and Response Latency in Recognition Memory," by W. E. Hockley and B. B. Murdock, 1987, *Psychological Review, 94*, 341–358. Copyright © 1987 American Psychological Association. Adapted with permission.

removed, then the model cannot recall the 8th item when the appropriate time comes. Another way is to remove the correct item anyway (Lewandowsky & Murdock, 1989). If this method is adopted, then TODAM can produce recency effects (see Figure O.10). By the time the last item is ready to be recalled, it is also the only item left in the competitor set; so as long as things have not gone disastrously awry, f'_j will always be matched with the last item because there is no other possibility.

Removing the correct item solves the problem of a lack of recency, but it introduces another: If the system does not know that f'_j is really item 2, how does it know to remove item 2 from the competitor set? The solution to this problem is neither trivial nor obvious (Lewandowsky & Li, 1994), and it remains unclear whether the solution solves all of the related problems.

Figure O.10   Two ways of removing items from the pool of competitors. If the correct item is removed from the competitor set, then the model produces recency. If the item that was actually matched to f_j' is removed, then there is no recency.
SOURCE: Nairne & Neath (1994).

Summary   TODAM was designed to account for serial order and recognition. Its most impressive accomplishment is to demonstrate that a model that consists of a single main memory vector can store items and successfully recall or recognize them. As such, it illustrates that, in principle, distributed memory models can work. TODAM has also successfully fit a variety of serial order and recognition data. One problem is the manner in which an item is deblurred; the original system does not work, and it remains to be seen if the problem can be fixed. A major challenge facing theorists is to develop a psychologically plausible method of deblurring that simulates human data. Like the other models discussed, TODAM also cannot account for the mirror effect (see Chapter 9).

Connectionist Models

Connectionist networks, also known as neural networks or parallel distributed processing (PDP), can be seen as an attempt to model complex behavior with neuronlike components. Just as the nervous system (greatly simplified) is composed of neurons and connections between them, so connectionist models are composed of (1) simple processing units (or nodes) that can either fire or not, and (2) connections between the nodes. We review the basic operation of a simple network (see Figure O.11) from Rumelhart, Hinton, and Williams (1986).

A connectionist network has a few basic components. First, there are nodes or units that are neuronlike, in the sense that they either fire or do not fire. These nodes are of three types: Input units receive activation from other networks; output units pass on activation to other networks; and hidden units receive no activation from outside the local

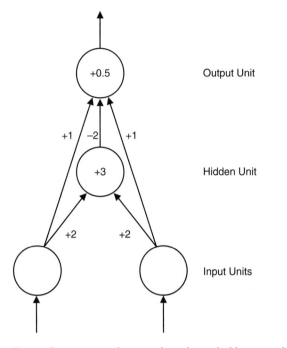

Figure O.11   A simple network, with one hidden unit, that can solve the XOR problem.   SOURCE: Adapted from "Learning Internal Representations by Error Propagation," by D. E. Rumelhart, G. E. Hinton and J. R. Williams. In D. E. Rumelhart and J. L. McClelland (Eds.), *Parallel Distributed Processing*, Vol. 1. Copyright © 1986 Massachusetts Institute of Technology Press. Adapted with permission.

network. Each node has an activation threshold (the number in the middle of each node), which is the amount of energy required to make it fire. In Figure O.11, the hidden node requires 3 or more units of activation before it will fire.

Second, there are connections between the nodes (hence the term *connectionist*). In the typical model, each node has multiple connections. These connections can be of two kinds, excitatory or inhibitory, depending on the weights. In Figure O.11, the connections between the input units and the hidden unit are excitatory because the weights have a positive value (in this case, 2). The connection between the hidden unit and the output unit is inhibitory because the weight is negative (−2). For simplicity, we assume that when a node fires, it sends 1 unit of activation along the connection. This value is modified by the weights on the connection.

The model shown in Figure O.11 was designed to solve the exclusive-or (XOR) problem. The XOR problem requires a specific solution: The output node should fire if and only if there is exactly one active input node. If both input nodes are active or if neither input node is active, then the output node should not fire. The actual operation is quite simple. If neither input unit fires, there is no energy in the system, and the output node will not fire. If just the left input node is active, it will send +1 unit of energy along each connection. The weight on the connection from the input unit to the hidden unit is 2, so the total amount of energy arriving at the hidden unit is 2×1, or 2. This value is less than the threshold of the hidden unit (3), so it does not fire. The weight on the connection from the input unit to the output unit is 1, so the total amount of energy arriving at the hidden unit is 1×1 or 1. This value is larger than the threshold, so the output unit fires. The same thing happens when just the right input unit fires.

When both input units fire, we do not want the output node to fire. Each input node sends 2 units to the hidden unit, so 4 units of energy arrive at the hidden unit. This value is greater than the threshold, and the hidden unit will fire. It sends 1×-2, or -2, units of energy to the output node. To see whether the output node fires, we need to calculate the total amount of energy arriving there. Each input node sends 1 unit. Thus, the output node receives 1 unit from the left input node, 1 unit from the right input node, and -2 units from the hidden node. The sum is a net activation of 0, which is less than the threshold; therefore, the output unit does not fire when both inputs are active.

The learning algorithm is what sets the weights on the connections. Typically, before a connectionist network has "learned" anything, the weights are set to randomly determined values. Notice that this incorporates the idea of a clean slate (tabula rasa) of Locke and Aristotle. As each stimulus is presented, the model produces some output. If the output is correct, the weights are altered to make that response more likely; if the output is incorrect, the weights are altered to make that response less likely. A specific type of algorithm, known as nonlinear back propagation, is discussed below.

As far as memory is concerned, the success of connectionist models has been less pronounced. As Ratcliff (1992) summarized it, "Few of the [neural network] models, however, have been seriously applied to the same range of experimental data in memory as the global memory models. It has been shown (McCloskey & Cohen, 1989; Ratcliff, 1990) that it is far from trivial to get models of this class to account for more than a few of the major trends in experimental data" (p. 431). The reason turns out to be rather straightforward: The very mechanism that allows these models to learn is also what causes them to forget.

One problem with studying connectionist models is the large number of possible variants. Most models can be instantiated in a three-layer architecture, and thus most models differ from others primarily in terms of the learning algorithm used. Ratcliff (1990) focused his attention on a class of connectionist models known as *nonlinear back propagation models*, a name that describes the learning mechanism. Most of Ratcliff's tests used a model like the one shown in Figure O.12. There are four input nodes, each of which is connected to three hidden units; the hidden units in turn are each connected to four output units. The basic paradigm was simulating studying a list of words and then being tested for recognition. Each "word" in the simulation was represented by a four-element vector of 0s and 1s (such as [1 0 0 1]), and the model was judged to have correctly recognized an old item if it reproduced a vector very similar to the input vector. For example, [0.94 0.04 0.04 0.96] would be judged as correct.

During study, a vector is presented to the input nodes. The activation that arrives at a particular hidden node i is simply the sum of all the activation that arrives over the four connections. For each connection, the value of the jth item in the vector (O_j) is multiplied by the weight on the connection between input node j and hidden node i (w_{ij}). The sum of all of these connections is the net activation (net_i):

$$net_i = \sum_j w_{ij} O_j \tag{O.25}$$

The hidden nodes are connected to the output nodes. The function that describes these connections is called a *logistic sigmoid function*, which converts numbers to a range

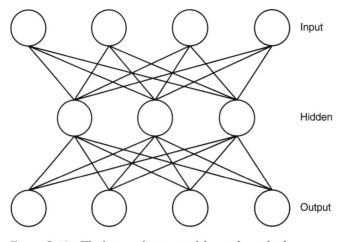

Figure O.12   The basic architecture of the nonlinear back propagation models tested in recognition judgments.   SOURCE: From "Connectionist Models of Recognition Memory: Constraints Imposed by Learning and Forgetting Functions," by R. Ratcliff, 1990, *Psychological Review*, 97, 285–308. Copyright © 1990 American Psychological Association. Adapted with permission.

from 0 to 1. It is useful to keep the activations in the range from 0 to 1 for easy interpretation and, more important, so that the values being used in the model do not become too large to work with. The logistic sigmoid function used to calculate the activation that arrives at output node i (O_i) is

$$O_i = \frac{1}{1 + \exp^{-net_i}} \tag{O.26}$$

Prior to training, the weights are set to random values to reflect the fact that the network does not yet know anything. The first time through, the output that the model gives will be quite different from the desired output. The difference between the actual output (O_i) and the desired output (t_i) is represented by δ_i and is calculated by

$$\delta_i = \left(t_i - O_i\right)O_i\left(1 - O_i\right) \tag{O.27}$$

The $t - O$ is the difference between teacher (desired) and output (actual) for a node. The $O(1 - O)$ represents a derivative of activation function with respect to the net input. Nonlinearity ensures that the greatest weight change occurs for those units that are uncommitted (closest to 0.5); units at 1 or 0 receive little change.

The error value, δ_i, is then used to change the weights on the connections so that the actual output on the next learning trial will be closer to the desired output. The change in weights between the output and hidden nodes (Δw_{ij}) is calculated by multiplying the error value by a learning rate parameter (η) and by the jth value of the original vector (O_j):

$$\Delta w_{ij} = \eta \delta_i O_j \tag{O.28}$$

The weights between the hidden nodes and the input nodes use a slightly different error value, which is calculated by

Table O.3   Results of recognition simulations with a three-layer nonlinear back propagation network when the four to-be-remembered stimuli are trained using simultaneous presentation

Study				Test				Response			
1	0	0	0	1	0	0	0	0.94	0.04	0.05	0.02
0	1	0	0	0	1	0	0	0.05	0.94	0.04	0.02
0	0	1	0	0	0	1	0	0.04	0.05	0.94	0.02
0	0	0	1	0	0	0	1	0.03	0.04	0.04	0.95

$$\delta_j = O_i(1 - O_i)\sum_k w_{ik}\delta_k \tag{O.29}$$

Then, the same equation as before (O.27) is used to calculate the actual change, but the new error value (δ_j) is used instead of the old (δ_i).

Ratcliff (1990) used two learning conditions. In the first, the model learned four words through what is known as *simultaneous presentation*, with the four words studied according to the following scheme: 1 2 3 4, 1 2 3 4, 1 2 3 4, 1 2 3 4, and so on. The results are shown in Table O.3.

So far, so good. The problem is that humans do not learn this way. They usually experience *sequential* presentation; that is, they study word 1 for a period of time, then word 2, and so on through the list, but once each item is finished with, it is not restudied before test. Ratcliff tried a version of sequential learning in which the network had the same number of learning trials, but the order of study was 1 2 3, 1 2 3, 1 2 3, . . . , 4 4 4, ... The results are shown in Table O.4.

Although the most recent item is well remembered, recognition performance of the first three items drops dramatically. As can be seen in Table O.4, the problem is that the last element of the vectors representing the first three items is contaminated by the last element in the vector representing the final item. Furthermore, the value of the other elements is greatly reduced. It turns out that this is a general problem: In several other simulations, Ratcliff tried various ways of minimizing this rapid forgetting, including (1) modifying only some of the weights, (2) adding more hidden units, (3) using longer vectors, (4) using bigger networks, and various combinations of these. None of these greatly changed performance of the model.

Our discussion of connectionist networks has emphasized that memory is distributed over every node and every connection; there is no one place where the information resides. Each weight is involved in memory for each item. When the items are learned using

Table O.4   Results of recognition simulations with a three-layer nonlinear back-propagation network when the four to-be-remembered stimuli are trained using simultaneous presentation for the first three items but sequential presentation for item 4

Study				Test				Response			
1	0	0	0	1	0	0	0	0.77	0.01	0.01	0.90
0	1	0	0	0	1	0	0	0.01	0.75	0.01	0.92
0	0	1	0	0	0	1	0	0.01	0.01	0.73	0.95
0	0	0	1	0	0	0	1	0.03	0.04	0.04	0.95

simultaneous presentation, the model is, in effect, finding one solution for all four problems. When the items are learned using sequential presentation, the model does not have to care about any item other than the one it is currently processing. Once the weights are established for this one item, the next item is presented. The model does not give a hoot about what it just learned; it adjusts the weights to learn the next problem. Therefore, the model is subject to catastrophic interference. Notice that it is the learning algorithm (changing the weights so that the actual output is more similar to the desired output) that also governs forgetting: Changing the weights will change the output of what was previously learned.

Summary   We have examined only one class of connectionist models but found an important limitation: Whenever a realistic training sequence is used, the models suffer from catastrophic interference. It remains to be seen whether this problem is inherent in models that use other learning algorithms. Although there are successful connectionist models of other cognitive phenomena, there is currently no connectionist model comparable to SAM, MINERVA2, or TODAM in terms of scope and accuracy of predictions.

The Feature Model

The feature model was designed to account for the major results seen in immediate memory, where the most common form of testing is immediate serial recall. Thus, recall begins with the cue in primary memory that has the highest probability of being the cue for the first item. This cue is used to sample from secondary memory. Any item sampled must be recovered prior to output. Recall then proceeds with the cue in primary memory that has the highest probability of being the cue for the second item.

In the feature model, order information is encoded as a point in multidimensional space and is stored with the cues in primary memory (see Neath, 1999a). For each cue, this point can drift (or perturb) along the relevant dimension in a way described by Estes (1972, 1997). The probability that a cue's encoded representation will perturb along the position dimension during a particular time interval is given by θ. This is held constant at .05 and is not considered a free parameter. It is assumed, for simplicity, that perturbations are equally likely in either direction and that an item cannot drift beyond the bounds imposed by the task. That is, an item cannot perturb to position 0 and cannot perturb beyond the last position. The probability that an item, I, will occupy a particular position, p, during the next time interval, $t + 1$, is given by the probability that no perturbation occurred $(1 - \theta)$ and the item was already in position p, plus the probability that a perturbation occurred and the item was one position away from position p.

$$I_{p,t+1} = \left(1 - \theta\right)I_{p,t} + \left(\frac{\theta}{2}\right)I_{p-1,t} + \left(\frac{\theta}{2}\right)I_{p+1,t} \tag{O.30}$$

For the first and last positions, a slightly different equation is used to reflect the assumption that an item cannot perturb to a position outside the list. For the first position,

$$I_{1,t+1} = \left(1 - \frac{\theta}{2}\right)I_{1,t} + \left(\frac{\theta}{2}\right)I_{2,t} \tag{O.31}$$

For the last position, n,

$$I_{n,t+1} = \left(1 - \frac{\theta}{2}\right)I_{n,t} + \left(\frac{\theta}{2}\right)I_{n-1,t} \qquad (O.32)$$

For each cue in primary memory, a positional uncertainty gradient is calculated. This gradient indicates the probability that the cue was originally encoded in each of the available serial positions. Recall begins by determining which cue was most likely in position 1 and then using that cue to sample. Order errors can occur as a result of (1) the perturbation process itself, in which a cue may be selected "out of order," and (2) the sampling procedure, in which even though the cue for a particular item in position n was used, it nonetheless sampled an item from a different position.

The probability of sampling, P_s, a particular secondary memory trace, SM_j, as a potential recall response for a primary memory trace, PM_i, is given by

$$P_s\left(SM_j \mid PM_i\right) = \frac{s(i,j)}{\sum\limits_{k=1}^{n} s(i,k)} \qquad (O.33)$$

The numerator is simply the similarity between primary memory trace i and secondary memory trace j. As this similarity increases, the probability of sampling the secondary memory trace *increases*. The denominator is the sum of the similarity between primary trace i and all secondary memory items in the search set. As this value increases, the probability of sampling the particular secondary memory trace *decreases*. The size of the search set is n, which in the case of recalling nine digits would be 9. The probability of sampling, then, is a ratio; the larger the denominator, the lower the sampling probability. This equation is a version of Luce's (1963) choice rule.

The similarity between items i and j, $s(i,j)$, is related to how different the two items are, $d(i,j)$:

$$s(i,j) = e^{-d(i,j)} \qquad (O.34)$$

By using the difference as a negative exponent for the mathematical constant e, we ensure that the similarity value is between 0 and 1.

The difference between two memory traces i and j, $d(i,j)$, is calculated by adding the number of mismatched features, M, and dividing by the number of compared features, N.

$$d(i,j) = \frac{a \sum\limits_{k=i}^{f} b_k M_k}{N} \qquad (O.35)$$

M_k is simply the number of times a particular feature position in item i does not equal the corresponding feature in item j. If the primary memory trace i has a 0 for feature 3, and the secondary memory trace has a 1, then this is counted as a mismatch. The parameter a is a scaling parameter; we adjust this value to raise or lower overall performance levels. The parameter b_k can be used to weight particular feature comparisons. For example, more attention might be given to certain modality-dependent features in a data-driven task than in a conceptually driven task (e.g., Roediger, Weldon, & Challis, 1989). In all simulations reported, b_k was set to 1.0 and so did not affect any of the results. Similarity is thus related to the proportion of mismatched features; the more mismatches there are, the larger $d(i,j)$ will be. The larger $d(i,j)$ is, the smaller $s(i,j)$ is.

If a subject selects as a response to a degraded primary memory trace an incorrect secondary memory trace, the subject will typically not choose that particular secondary memory trace again. The probability of recovering an item, $P(R)$, is related to the number of times it has already been recalled, r, and a parameter, c, known as the recovery constant. This latter parameter is the number of attempts that will be made to recover the item. Thus, the probability of recovering an item decreases the more times it has been previously recalled.

$$P(R) = e^{-cr} \tag{O.36}$$

A description of how the model operates, and how it accounts for much of the immediate memory data, is presented in Chapter 4.

Appendix

Table A Twenty-Four Nonsense Syllables (CVCs)

BAF	NUM	SAQ
BAP	PEC	SIM
BEF	PIM	SUC
GIF	QAW	TAY
HAB	QIR	VAM
JUV	QOG	VEN
KES	ROL	VEZ
NEM	SAH	VOT

SOURCE: Glaze (1928).

Table B   Random Arrangements of the Digits 1–9

```
5 1 3 9 7 2 4 6 8     5 7 2 3 6 8 9 1 4     9 4 2 6 7 5 3 1 8
8 4 9 1 2 7 3 5 6     1 9 3 2 5 7 6 4 8     1 7 3 9 8 4 5 2 6
1 6 3 9 5 4 7 8 2     2 1 3 5 7 8 4 9 6     9 1 8 6 4 7 3 5 2
4 7 2 3 8 6 9 1 5     8 4 5 1 6 7 2 9 3     2 5 4 7 9 3 1 6 8
5 3 1 7 4 9 6 2 8     6 2 5 1 3 9 4 8 7     8 4 1 7 2 6 9 3 5
8 5 1 6 2 4 3 7 9     9 6 2 7 3 5 1 4 8     3 9 2 1 4 8 6 7 5
3 2 1 7 5 8 6 9 4     4 3 8 6 9 1 5 7 2     8 7 2 9 6 1 3 5 4
6 1 4 2 8 5 9 7 3     5 1 3 2 9 7 6 8 4     5 2 4 7 1 6 8 9 3
9 6 3 1 8 7 4 5 2     2 4 9 6 3 8 5 1 7     5 1 3 8 9 6 7 2 4
7 1 9 2 4 8 3 6 5     3 6 4 5 9 7 2 8 1     6 9 2 7 4 1 5 8 3

6 3 7 8 9 4 2 5 1     6 3 1 7 8 4 9 5 2     3 1 2 4 7 5 8 6 9
7 9 6 4 2 3 8 1 5     7 2 3 9 1 4 8 6 5     1 5 4 2 6 9 8 7 3
2 9 3 4 1 6 7 5 8     6 4 8 1 5 9 7 2 3     5 2 9 7 6 3 8 4 1
5 2 6 7 1 9 4 8 3     9 3 6 2 5 8 7 4 1     4 6 7 3 1 5 9 8 2
3 6 1 9 5 2 7 8 4     4 6 5 1 3 9 8 2 7     7 8 1 5 9 4 3 2 6
4 5 9 3 7 2 1 6 8     7 1 8 3 6 2 4 9 5     2 4 8 5 7 1 6 3 9
9 2 7 3 1 6 4 8 5     2 8 7 3 6 5 9 1 4     7 1 5 6 8 3 9 4 2
3 1 7 6 2 9 8 5 4     8 2 9 4 5 7 3 6 1     4 1 2 7 6 5 9 8 3
3 4 6 2 7 5 1 9 8     6 4 2 1 7 5 8 3 9     5 3 7 9 6 1 4 8 2
5 7 9 4 8 2 1 3 6     3 1 9 8 7 5 2 6 4     4 5 9 7 2 3 8 1 6

8 3 9 1 7 5 2 6 4     2 6 5 1 3 9 4 8 7     5 4 6 8 1 9 2 7 3
2 6 3 8 1 7 4 5 9     6 4 1 9 2 5 8 7 3     3 7 6 1 2 8 6 4 5
1 4 2 3 5 9 6 7 8     1 8 3 7 4 9 6 2 5     2 9 4 1 7 6 8 5 3
9 2 8 5 7 4 3 6 1     8 2 5 4 7 6 3 1 9     3 5 1 6 9 4 2 8 7
8 7 9 3 1 4 2 6 5     2 3 8 1 7 5 6 4 9     5 8 3 2 9 7 1 4 6
7 6 8 9 1 4 5 2 3     7 4 1 9 6 8 3 5 2     6 2 7 9 5 3 4 1 8
6 3 4 2 7 9 1 5 8     8 4 2 3 7 5 9 1 6     4 1 9 5 7 2 3 6 8
7 3 2 4 9 6 8 5 1     3 5 8 2 4 6 9 7 1     1 4 6 7 5 8 9 2 3
9 3 5 6 4 8 1 2 7     2 1 8 9 5 6 3 4 7     7 6 1 3 9 4 5 2 8
8 6 4 2 5 3 7 1 9     4 1 6 2 9 5 3 8 7     8 5 1 9 4 3 6 2 7

5 9 1 2 7 3 8 6 4     6 2 4 8 5 9 1 7 3     9 3 7 4 5 1 2 4 6
3 6 2 4 9 8 1 7 5     2 1 6 5 4 8 7 9 3     5 7 3 4 8 2 9 6 1
7 9 3 8 6 4 5 1 2     3 9 5 2 1 6 8 4 7     7 6 5 8 3 9 4 1 2
6 2 9 3 7 4 1 5 8     5 1 8 4 3 2 6 7 9     3 4 8 7 6 1 5 9 2
1 8 3 2 5 6 9 4 7     4 9 8 1 7 6 3 2 5     6 1 4 8 7 9 2 5 3
2 4 9 6 7 1 3 8 5     2 6 1 7 5 3 8 9 4     2 9 6 1 4 7 3 5 8
4 5 8 2 1 9 6 3 7     9 3 7 4 2 5 6 8 1     1 7 2 9 3 5 4 8 6
3 5 7 9 8 4 2 1 6     9 5 1 7 3 6 8 4 2     4 1 9 2 3 6 7 5 8
2 6 3 9 1 7 4 8 5     6 7 4 1 8 3 9 5 2     9 3 1 7 4 6 2 8 5
2 6 8 1 3 4 9 7 5     4 7 1 6 2 9 5 8 3     9 4 8 3 5 2 7 1 6
```

Table C   Ninety-Six Two-Syllable Words

able	confirm	enter	herself	open	service
achieve	confuse	every	honest	oppose	shallow
although	control	explain	humble	pointed	shortly
amuse	correct	faithful	impulse	possess	sincere
anger	costly	farewell	include	prefer	slowly
approve	deadly	firmly	lightly	present	slumber
attain	decay	forward	linger	prevent	softly
away	degree	friendly	lively	proceed	suggest
awhile	depart	frighten	locate	proclaim	suppose
backward	describe	function	loyal	proper	survive
began	destroy	funny	lucky	protect	thinking
betray	dispose	future	meaning	publish	travel
beyond	dispute	gallant	method	punish	trifle
chosen	dissolve	going	mighty	really	trouble
climate	elect	gravely	modern	relief	within
command	enough	happy	obtain	resign	writing

SOURCE: Selected from Friendly, Franklin, Hoffman, & Rubin (1982).

Table D   Eight Short and Eight Long Words

beast	alcohol
bronze	amplifier
dirt	gallery
golf	mosquito
inn	musician
lump	officer
star	orchestra
wife	property

SOURCE: LaPointe & Engle (1990).

Table E   Twenty-Five Common Two-Syllable Nouns

Noun	Imageability	Concreteness	Frequency
ankle	6.77	7.00	21
apple	6.73	7.00	9
arrow	6.57	7.00	37
barrel	6.57	6.94	32
butter	6.57	6.96	27
cabin	6.47	6.96	23
candy	6.63	6.56	32
cellar	6.27	6.83	32
coffee	6.73	6.89	78
cottage	6.50	6.90	46
elbow	6.30	6.94	26
engine	6.33	6.76	50
fireplace	6.83	6.96	19
flower	6.57	6.96	21
hammer	6.73	6.96	34
hotel	6.40	6.83	126
infant	6.33	6.76	22
lemon	6.83	6.96	27
meadow	6.43	6.69	47
mountain	6.77	7.00	33
oven	6.40	6.96	29
palace	6.50	6.73	38
salad	6.53	6.83	28
slipper	6.47	6.94	20
sugar	6.57	6.96	34

SOURCE: From "Concreteness, Imagery, and Meaningfulness Values for 925 Nouns," by A. Paivio, J. C. Yuille, and S. A. Madigan, 1968, *Journal of Experimental Psychology Monograph Supplement*, 76, 1–25. Copyright © 1968 American Psychological Association. Reprinted with permission.

Table F   Thirty-Two Consonant Trigrams

BMZ	GKW	MQH	RJX
BPF	GJX	NWB	SGC
CGW	HFP	NZK	SJF
CJX	HZP	PNB	TJQ
DJF	JBW	PXZ	TZJ
DLH	JMC	QCF	XNZ
FQD	KFH	QKB	ZFK
FZH	LRB	RJP	ZSB

SOURCE: Witmer (1935).

Table G Fifty-Six Category Names

Precious Stone	Country	Type of Vehicle
Unit of Time	Crime	Area of Science
Relative	Carpenter's Tool	Toy
Unit of Distance	Member of the Clergy	Type of Dance
Metal	Substance for Flavoring Food	Vegetable
Type of Reading Material	Type of Fuel	Type of Footgear
Military Title	Occupation	Insect
Four-Footed Animal	Natural Earth Formation	Girl's First Name
Kind of Cloth	Sport	Boy's First Name
Kitchen Utensil	Weather Phenomenon	Flower
Religious Building	Article of Clothing	Disease
Part of Speech	Part of a Building	Tree
Article of Furniture	Chemical Element	Type of Ship
Human Body Part	Musical Instrument	Fish
Fruit	Kind of Money	Snake
Weapon	Type of Music	City
Elective Office	Bird	State
Type of Dwelling	Nonalcoholic Beverage	College or University
Alcoholic Beverage		

SOURCE: Battig & Montague (1969).

Table H Sixty Word Fragments

AARDVARK	ESPRESSO	PHARAOH
ABATTOIR	FLANNEL	PIGMENT
AGNOSTIC	GAZETTE	PLANKTON
ALMANAC	GRANARY	QUARTET
ANATOMY	HEXAGON	RAINBOW
ANYBODY	HORIZON	RHUBARB
APPROVAL	HYDRANT	ROTUNDA
BACHELOR	IDEOLOGY	RUFFIAN
BANDANNA	ISTHMUS	SAPPHIRE
BASSOON	KEROSENE	SHERIFF
BEHAVIOR	LAGGARD	SILICON
BOROUGH	LETTUCE	SPATULA
BROCCOLI	LITHIUM	THEOREM
CABARET	MIGRAINE	TOBOGGAN
CHIMNEY	MONOGRAM	TRICYCLE
CLARINET	MYSTERY	UNIVERSE
COCONUT	NOCTURNE	VERANDAH
CUPCAKE	ORATION	WARRANTY
DINOSAUR	OUTSIDER	YOGHURT
ELLIPSE	PENDULUM	ZEPPELIN

NOTE: The letters that should be missing from the fragment are underlined. For example, the target word AARDVARK should be tested with _AR_VA__.

SOURCE: From "Priming Effects in Word-Fragment Completion Are Independent of Recognition Memory," by E. Tulving, D. L. Schacter, and H. Stark, 1982, *Journal of Experimental Psychology: Human Learning and Memory, 8*, 336–342. Copyright © 1982 American Psychological Association. Reprinted with permission.

Table I   Eighty Concrete and Eighty Abstract Words

Concrete Words

accordion	child	hotel	pepper	stagecoach
acrobat	coffee	hurricane	photograph	storm
alligator	diamond	lake	physician	strawberry
ambulance	doctor	lemonade	piano	student
arrow	dollar	letter	potato	sugar
automobile	dress	library	prairie	swamp
avalanche	elbow	magazine	pudding	tablespoon
bagpipe	factory	meadow	railroad	thorn
barrel	forehead	meat	rattle	tree
book	forest	microscope	refrigerator	truck
bottle	garden	missile	restaurant	trumpet
butcher	girl	mother	river	umbrella
cabin	gold	newspaper	salad	valley
caterpillar	grandmother	ocean	seat	village
cellar	hammer	paper	slipper	window
chair	hospital	peach	spinach	woods

Abstract Words

adversity	economy	hope	mind	reaction
amount	effort	hour	moment	reminder
animosity	encore	idea	mood	sensation
aptitude	episode	idiom	moral	session
atrocity	equity	illusion	namesake	style
attitude	event	impulse	nonsense	tendency
boredom	exclusion	incident	obedience	theory
capacity	facility	irony	occasion	thought
chance	fantasy	jeopardy	ownership	tribute
cost	fault	justice	pact	trouble
crisis	folly	law	pledge	truth
custom	franchise	length	position	upkeep
deduction	gender	magnitude	prestige	vanity
democracy	greed	malady	quality	vigilance
distinction	hearing	malice	quantity	violation
duty	hint	method	rating	vocation

	Concreteness	Imagability	Frequency	Length
Concrete	6.51	6.82	50.26	6.73
Abstract	3.18	2.58	50.66	6.74

SOURCE: From "Concreteness, Imagery, and Meaningfulness Values for 925 Nouns," by A. Paivio, J. C. Yuille, and S. A. Madigan, 1968, *Journal of Experimental Psychology Monograph Supplement, 76,* 1–25. Copyright © 1968 American Psychological Association. Reprinted with permission.

Table J Six Lists of Words Related to a Critical Item

CHAIR	NEEDLE	MOUNTAIN
table	thread	hill
sit	pin	valley
legs	eye	climb
seat	sewing	summit
couch	sharp	top
desk	point	molehill
recliner	prick	peak
sofa	thimble	plain
wood	haystack	glacier
cushion	thorn	goat
swivel	hurt	bike
stool	injection	climber
sitting	syringe	range
rocking	cloth	steep
bench	knitting	ski

ROUGH	SLEEP	SWEET
smooth	bed	sour
bumpy	rest	candy
road	awake	sugar
tough	tired	bitter
sandpaper	dream	good
jagged	wake	taste
ready	snooze	tooth
coarse	blanket	nice
uneven	doze	honey
riders	slumber	soda
rugged	snore	chocolate
sand	nap	heart
boards	peace	cake
ground	yawn	tart
gravel	drowsy	pie

NOTE: The words in uppercase are the predicted intrusion errors for each list.

SOURCE: From "Creating False Memories," by H. L. Roediger, III, and K. B. McDermott, 1995, *Journal of Experimental Psychology: Learning, Memory, and Cognition, 21*, 803–814. Copyright © 1995 American Psychological Association. Reprinted with permission.

Table K   Forty-Eight Weak and Strong Cues

List A			List B		
Weak Cue	Strong Cue	Target	Weak Cue	Strong Cue	Target
ground	hot	COLD	hope	low	HIGH
head	dark	LIGHT	stem	long	SHORT
bath	want	NEED	whiskey	lake	WATER
cheese	grass	GREEN	moth	eat	FOOD
stomach	small	LARGE	cabbage	square	ROUND
sun	night	DAY	glass	soft	HARD
pretty	sky	BLUE	country	closed	OPEN
cave	dry	WET	tool	finger	HAND
whistle	tennis	BALL	memory	fast	SLOW
noise	blow	WIND	covering	lining	COAT
glue	table	CHAIR	barn	clean	DIRTY
command	woman	MAN	spider	eagle	BIRD
fruit	bloom	FLOWER	crust	bake	CAKE
home	bitter	SWEET	deep	bed	SLEEP
grasp	infant	BABY	train	white	BLACK
butter	rough	SMOOTH	mountain	leaf	TREE
drink	tobacco	SMOKE	cottage	hate	LOVE
beat	ache	PAIN	art	boy	GIRL
cloth	lamb	SHEEP	adult	labor	WORK
swift	stop	GO	brave	strong	WEAK
lady	king	QUEEN	door	color	RED
blade	scissors	CUT	roll	carpet	RUG
plant	insect	BUG	think	dumb	STUPID
wish	soap	WASH	exist	human	BEING

SOURCE: Watkins & Tulving (1975).

References

Abernathy, E. M. (1940). The effect of changed environmental conditions upon the results of college examinations. *Journal of Psychology, 10,* 293–301.

Adams, D. (1981). *The hitchhiker's guide to the galaxy.* New York: Pocket Books.

Algom, D., & Cain, W. S. (1991). Remembered odors and mental mixtures: Tapping reservoirs of olfactory knowledge. *Journal of Experimental Psychology: Human Perception and Performance, 17,* 1104–1119.

Algom, D., Wolf, Y., & Bergman, B. (1985). Integration of stimulus dimensions in perception and memory: Composition rules and psychophysical relations. *Journal of Experimental Psychology: General, 114,* 451–471.

Anderson, J. A., Silverstein, J. W., Ritz, S. A., & Jones, R. S. (1988). Distinctive features, categorical perception, and probability learning: Some applications of a neural model. In J. A. Anderson & E. Rosenfeld (Eds.), *Neurocomputing: Foundations of research.* Cambridge, MA: MIT Press.

Anderson, J. R. (1974). Retrieval of propositional information from long-term memory. *Cognitive Psychology, 6,* 451–474.

Anderson, J. R. (1976). *Language, memory, and thought.* Hillsdale, NJ: Erlbaum.

Anderson, J. R. (1978). Arguments concerning representations for mental imagery. *Psychological Review, 85,* 249–277.

Anderson, J. R. (1983a). *The architecture of cognition.* Cambridge, MA: Harvard University Press.

Anderson, J. R. (1983b). A spreading activation theory of memory. *Journal of Verbal Learning and Verbal Behavior, 22,* 261–295.

Anderson, J. R., & Bower, G. H. (1972). Recognition and retrieval processes in free recall. *Psychological Review, 79,* 97–123.

Anderson, J. R., & Bower, G. H. (1973). *Human associative memory.* Washington, DC: Winston.

Anderson, J. R., & Lebiere, C. (1998). *The atomic components of thought.* Mahwah, NJ: Erlbaum.

Anderson, J. R., & Matessa, M. P. (1997). A production system theory of serial memory. *Psychological Review, 104,* 728–748.

Anderson, N. D., & Craik, F. I. M. (2000). Memory in the aging brain. In E. Tulving & F. I. M. Craik (Eds.), *The Oxford handbook of memory.* Oxford, UK: Oxford University Press.

Anderson, N. D., Iidaka, T., Cabeza, R., Kapur, S., McIntosh, A. R., & Craik, F. I. M. (2000). The effects of divided attention on encoding- and retrieval-related brain activity: A PET study of younger and older adults. *Journal of Cognitive Neuroscience, 12,* 775–792.

Anderson, R. C., & Pichert, J. W. (1978). Recall of previously unrecallable information following a shift in perspective. *Journal of Verbal Learning and Verbal Behavior, 17,* 1–12.

Anderson, R. E. (1984). Did I do it or did I only imagine doing it? *Journal of Experimental Psychology: General, 113,* 594–613.

Angell, J. R. (1907). The province of functional psychology. *Psychological Review, 14,* 61–91.

Anisfeld, M., & Knapp, M. (1968). Association, synonymity, and directionality in false recognition. *Journal of Experimental Psychology, 77,* 171–179.

Anooshian, L. J. (1998). Implicit and explicit memory in childhood: A review of relevant theory and research. *Child Study Journal, 28,* 17–52.

Arnold, M. M., & Lindsay, D. S. (2002). Remembering remembering. *Journal of Experimental Psychology: Learning, Memory, and Cognition, 28,* 521–529.

Ash, M. G. (1995). *Gestalt psychology in German culture, 1890–1967: Holism and the quest for objectivity.* New York: Cambridge University Press.

Ashcraft, M. H. (1976). Priming and property dominance effects in semantic memory. *Memory & Cognition, 4,* 490–500.

Asratian, E. A. (1965). *Compensatory adaptations, reflex activity and the brain.* New York: Pergamon Press.

Atkinson, R. C., & Juola, J. F. (1973). Factors influencing speed and accuracy of word recognition. In S. Kornblum (Ed.), *Attention and performance IV.* New York: Academic Press.

Atkinson, R. C., & Juola, J. F. (1974). Search and decision processes in recognition memory. In D. H. Krantz, R. C. Atkinson, R. D. Luce, & P. Suppes

(Eds.), *Contemporary developments in mathematical psychology* (Vol. 1). San Francisco: Freeman.

Atkinson, R. C., & Raugh, M. R. (1975). An application of the mnemonic keyword method to the acquisition of a Russian vocabulary. *Journal of Experimental Psychology: Human Learning and Memory, 104,* 126–133.

Atkinson, R. C., & Shiffrin, R. M. (1968). Human memory: A proposed system and its control processes. In K. W. Spence & J. T. Spence (Eds.), *The psychology of learning and motivation* (Vol. 2). New York: Academic Press.

Attneave, F. (1959). *Applications of information theory to psychology.* New York: Holt, Rinehart & Winston.

Averbach, E. (1963). The span of apprehension as a function of exposure duration. *Journal of Verbal Learning and Verbal Behavior, 2,* 60–64.

Ayres, T. J., Jonides, J., Reitman, J. S., Egan, J. C., & Howard, D. A. (1979). Differing suffix effects for the same physical suffix. *Journal of Experimental Psychology: Human Learning and Memory, 5,* 315–321.

Bach, M. J., & Underwood, B. J. (1970). Developmental changes in memory attributes. *Journal of Educational Psychology, 61,* 292–296.

Bachevalier, J., & Mishkin, M. M. (1984). An early and a late developing system for learning and retention in infant monkeys. *Behavioral Neuroscience, 98,* 770–778.

Bäckman, L. (1991). Recognition memory across the adult life span: The role of prior knowledge. *Memory & Cognition, 19,* 63–71.

Bäckman, L., Almkvist, O., Andersson, J., Nordberg, A., Winblad, B., Reineck, R., & Langstrom, B. (1997). Brain activation in young and older adults during implicit and explicit retrieval. *Journal of Cognitive Neuroscience, 9,* 378–391.

Baddeley, A. D. (1966). Short-term memory for word sequences as a function of acoustic, semantic, and formal similarity. *Quarterly Journal of Experimental Psychology, 18,* 362–365.

Baddeley, A. D. (1976). *The psychology of memory.* New York: Basic Books.

Baddeley, A. D. (1986). *Working memory.* New York: Oxford University Press.

Baddeley, A. D. (1990). *Human memory.* Boston: Allyn & Bacon.

Baddeley, A. D. (1992a). Working memory. *Science, 255,* 556–559.

Baddeley, A. D. (1992b). Is working memory working? *Quarterly Journal of Experimental Psychology, 44A,* 1–31.

Baddeley, A. D. (1994). Working memory: The interface between memory and cognition. In D. L. Schacter & E. Tulving (Eds.), *Memory systems 1994.* Cambridge, MA: MIT Press.

Baddeley, A. D. (2000). The episodic buffer: A new component of working memory? *Trends in Cognitive Sciences, 4,* 417–423.

Baddeley, A. D., Baddeley, H. A., Bucks, K. S., & Wilcock, G. K. (2001). Attentional control in Alzheimer's disease. *Brain, 124,* 1492–1508.

Baddeley, A. D., Bressi, S., Della Sala, S., Logie, R., & Spinnler, H. (1991). The decline of working memory in Alzheimer's disease. *Brain, 114,* 2521–2542.

Baddeley, A. D., Della Sala, S., & Spinnler, H. (1991). The two component hypothesis of memory deficit in Alzheimer's disease. *Journal of Clinical and Experimental Neuropsychology, 13,* 372–380.

Baddeley, A. D., & Hitch, G. J. (1974). Working memory. In G. H. Bower (Ed.), *The psychology of learning and motivation* (Vol. 8). New York: Academic Press.

Baddeley, A. D., & Hitch, G. J. (1977). Recency reexamined. In S. Dornic (Ed.), *Attention and performance VI.* Hillsdale, NJ: Erlbaum.

Baddeley, A. D., Lewis, V. J., & Nimmo-Smith, I. (1978). When did you last . . . ? In M. M. Gruneberg & R. N. Sykes (Eds.), *Practical aspects of memory.* San Diego: Academic Press.

Baddeley, A. D., Lewis, V. J., & Vallar, G. (1984). Exploring the articulatory loop. *Quarterly Journal of Experimental Psychology, 36,* 233–252.

Baddeley, A. D., & Logie, R. H. (1999). Working memory: The multiple-component model. In A. Miyake & P. Shah (Eds.), *Models of working memory: Mechanisms of active maintenance and executive control.* New York: Cambridge University Press.

Baddeley, A. D., Logie, R., Bressi, S., Della Sala, S., & Spinnler, H. (1986). Dementia and working memory. *Quarterly Journal of Experimental Psychology, 38A,* 603–618.

Baddeley, A. D., & Scott, D. (1971). Short-term forgetting in the absence of proactive interference. *Quarterly Journal of Experimental Psychology, 23,* 275–283.

Baddeley, A. D., Thomson, N., & Buchanan, M. (1975). Word length and the structure of short-term memory. *Journal of Verbal Learning and Verbal Behavior, 14,* 575–589.

Baddeley, A. D., & Wilson, B. A. (1988). Frontal amnesia and the dysexecutive syndrome. *Brain and Cognition, 7,* 212–230.

Baddeley, A. D., & Woodhead, M. (1983). Improving face recognition ability. In S. M. A. Lloyd-Bostock & B. R. Clifford (Eds.), *Evaluating witness evidence.* Chichester, UK: Wiley.

Bahrick, H. P. (1970). Two-phase model for prompted recall. *Psychological Review, 77,* 215–222.

Bahrick, H. P. (1983). The cognitive map of a city—50 years of learning and memory. In G. H. Bower (Ed.), *The psychology of learning and motivation* (Vol. 17). New York: Academic Press.

Bahrick, H. P. (1984a). Semantic memory content in permastore: Fifty years of memory for Spanish learned in school. *Journal of Experimental Psychology: General, 113,* 1–29.

Bahrick, H. P. (1984b). Memory for people. In J. E. Harris & P. E. Morris (Eds.), *Everyday memory, actions and absentmindedness*. London: Academic Press.

Bahrick, H. P., Bahrick, L. E., Bahrick, A. S., & Bahrick, P. E. (1993). Maintenance of foreign language vocabulary and the spacing effect. *Psychological Science, 4,* 316–321.

Bahrick, H. P., Bahrick, P. C., & Wittlinger, R. P. (1975). Fifty years of memories for names and faces. *Journal of Experimental Psychology: General, 104,* 54–75.

Bahrick, H. P., & Hall, L. K. (1991). Lifetime maintenance of high school mathematics content. *Journal of Experimental Psychology: General, 120,* 20–33.

Bahrick, L. E., & Pickens, J. N. (1995). Infant memory for object motion across a period of three months: Implications for a four-phase attention function. *Journal of Experimental Child Psychology, 59,* 343–371.

Bain, A. (1855). *The senses and the intellect*. London: John W. Parker and Son.

Baker-Ward, L., Ornstein, P. A., & Holden, D. J. (1984). The expression of memorization in early childhood. *Journal of Experimental Child Psychology, 37,* 555–575.

Balota, D. A., Burgess, G. C., Cortese, M. J., & Adams, D. R. (2002). The word-frequency mirror effect in young, old, and early-stage Alzheimer's disease: Evidence for two processes in episodic recognition performance. *Journal of Memory and Language, 46,* 199–226.

Balota, D. A., & Chumbley, J. I. (1984). Are lexical decisions a good measure of lexical access: The role of word frequency in the neglected decision stage. *Journal of Experimental Psychology: Human Perception and Performance, 10,* 340–357.

Balota, D. A., Cortese, M., Duchek, J. M., Adams, D., Roediger, H. L. III, McDermott, K. B., & Yerys, B. (1999). Veridical and false memories in healthy older adults and in dementia of the Alzheimer type. *Cognitive Neuropsychology, 16,* 361–384.

Balota, D. A., & Engle, R. W. (1981). Structural and strategic factors in the stimulus suffix effect. *Journal of Verbal Learning and Verbal Behavior, 20,* 346–357.

Balota, D. A., & Neely, J. H. (1980). Test-expectancy and word-frequency effects in recall and recognition. *Journal of Experimental Psychology: Human Learning and Memory, 6,* 576–587.

Banaji, M. R., & Crowder, R. G. (1989). The bankruptcy of everyday memory. *American Psychologist, 44,* 1185–1193.

Banks, W. P., & Barber, G. (1977). Color information in iconic memory. *Psychological Review, 84,* 536–546.

Barry, H. (1978). Stimulus attributes of drugs. In H. Anisman & G. Bignami (Eds.), *Psychopharmacology of aversively motivated behavior*. New York: Plenum.

Bartlett, F. C. (1932). *Remembering: A study in experimental and social psychology*. Cambridge, UK: Cambridge University Press. (Reprinted 1977)

Bartlett, J. C., & Santrock, J. W. (1979). Affect-dependent episodic memory in young children. *Child Development, 50,* 513–518.

Bass, E., & Davis, L. (1988). *The courage to heal: A guide for women survivors of child sexual abuse*. New York: Perennial Library/Harper & Row.

Battig, W. F., & Montague, W. E. (1969). Category norms for verbal items in 56 categories: A replication and extension of the Connecticut category norms. *Journal of Experimental Psychology: Monograph, 80,* 1–46.

Bauer, P. J. (1996). What do infants recall of their lives? *American Psychologist, 51,* 29–41.

Bauer, P. J., Hertsgaard, L. A., & Dow, G. A. (1994). After 8 months have passed: Long-term recall of events by 1- to 2-year-old children. *Memory, 2,* 353–382.

Beauregard, M., Chertkow, H., Gold, D., & Bergman, S. (2001). The impact of semantic impairment on word stem completion in Alzheimer's disease. *Neuropsychologia, 39,* 302–314.

Begg, I., Duft, S., Lalonde, P., Melnick, R., & Sanvito, J. (1989). Memory predictions are based on ease of processing. *Journal of Memory and Language, 28,* 610–632.

Bell, B. E., & Loftus, E. F. (1989). Trivial persuasion in the courtroom: The power of (a few) minor details. *Journal of Personality and Social Psychology, 56,* 669–679.

Bellezza, F. S. (1983). Mnemonic-device instruction with adults. In M. Pressley & J. R. Levin (Eds.), *Cognitive strategy research: Psychological foundations*. New York: Springer-Verlag.

Birren, J. E. (1956). The significance of age changes in speed of perception and psychomotor response. In J. E. Anderson (Ed.), *Psychological aspects of aging*. Washington, DC: American Psychological Association.

Bisiach, E. (1999). Unilateral neglect and related disorders. In G. Denes & L. Pizzamiglio (Eds.), *Handbook of clinical and experimental neuropsychology*. Hove, UK: Psychology Press.

Bisiach, E., & Luzzatti, C. (1978). Unilateral neglect of representational space. *Cortex, 14,* 129–133.

Bisiach, E., Luzzatti, C., & Perani, D. (1979). Unilateral neglect, representational schema and consciousness. *Brain, 102,* 609–618.

Bjork, E. L., & Healy, A. F. (1974). Short-term order and item retention. *Journal of Verbal Learning and Verbal Behavior, 13,* 80–97.

Bjork, R. A. (2001). Recency and recovery in human memory. In H. L. Roediger III, J. S. Nairne, I. Neath, & A. M. Surprenant (Eds.), *The nature of remembering: Essays in honor of Robert G. Crowder*. Washington, DC: American Psychological Association.

Bjork, R. A., & Whitten, W. B. (1974). Recency-sensitive retrieval processes in long-term free recall. *Cognitive Psychology, 6,* 173–189.

Blaney, P. H. (1986). Affect and memory: A review. *Psychological Bulletin, 99,* 229–246.

Blaxton, T. A. (1989). Investigating dissociations among memory measures: Support for a transfer-appropriate processing framework. *Journal of Experimental Psychology: Learning, Memory, and Cognition, 15*, 657–668.

Blodgett, H. C. (1929). The effect of the introduction of reward upon the maze performance of rats. *University of California Publications in Psychology, 4*, 113–134.

Bloom, L. C., & Watkins, M. J. (1999). Two-component theory of the suffix effect: Contrary findings. *Journal of Experimental Psychology: Learning, Memory and Cognition, 25*, 1452–1475.

Blumenthal, G. B., & Robbins, D. (1977). Delayed release from proactive interference with meaningful material: How much do we remember after reading brief prose passages? *Journal of Experimental Psychology: Human Learning and Memory, 3*, 754–761.

Bohannon, J. N. (1988). Flashbulb memories of the space shuttle disaster: A tale of two theories. *Cognition, 29*, 179–196.

Boon, J., & Noon, E. (1994). Changing perspectives in cognitive interviewing. *Psychology, Crime, & Law, 1*, 59–69.

Boring, E. G. (1930). A new ambiguous figure. *American Journal of Psychology, 42*, 444–445.

Boring, E. G. (1950). *A history of experimental psychology* (2nd ed.). New York: Appleton-Century-Crofts.

Botwinick, J. (1961). Husband and father-in-law: A reversible figure. *American Journal of Psychology, 74*, 312–113.

Bousfield, W. A. (1953). The occurrence of clustering in the recall of randomly arranged associates. *Journal of General Psychology, 49*, 229–240.

Bouton, M. E. (1993). Context, time, and memory retrieval in the interference paradigms of Pavlovian learning. *Psychological Bulletin, 114*, 80–99.

Bowen, R., Pola, J., & Matin, L. (1974). Visual persistence: Effects of flash luminance, duration and energy. *Vision Research, 14*, 295–303.

Bower, G. H. (1972). Mental imagery and associative learning. In L. W. Gregg (Ed.), *Cognition in learning and memory*. New York: Wiley.

Bower, G. H. (1978). Interference paradigms for meaningful propositional memory. *American Journal of Psychology, 91*, 575–585.

Bower, G. H. (1981). Mood and memory. *American Psychologist, 36*, 129–148.

Bower, G. H., Black, J. B., & Turner, T. J. (1979). Scripts in memory for text. *Cognitive Psychology, 11*, 177–220.

Bower, G. H., & Clapper, J. P. (1989). Experimental methods in cognitive science. In M. I. Posner (Ed.), *Foundations of cognitive science*. Cambridge, MA: MIT Press.

Bowles, N. L. (1994). Age and rate of activation in semantic memory. *Psychology and Aging, 9*, 414–429.

Bowles, N. L., & Poon, L. W. (1985). Aging and retrieval of words in semantic memory. *Journal of Gerontology, 40*, 71–77.

Bradburn, N. M., Rips, L. J., & Shevell, S. K. (1987). Answering autobiographical questions: The impact of memory and inference on surveys. *Science, 236*, 157–161.

Brandt, J., & Rich, J. B. (1995). Memory disorders in the dementias. In A. D. Baddeley, B. A. Wilson, & F. N. Watts (Eds.), *Handbook of memory disorders*. New York: Wiley.

Bransford, J. D., Barclay, J. R., & Franks, J. J. (1972). Sentence memory: A constructive versus interpretive approach. *Cognitive Psychology, 3*, 193–209.

Bransford, J. D., & Johnson, M. K. (1972). Contextual prerequisites for understanding: Some investigations of comprehension and recall. *Journal of Verbal Learning and Verbal Behavior, 11*, 717–726.

Broadbent, D. E. (1958). *Perception and communication*. New York: Pergamon.

Broca, P. (1861). Remarques sur le siège de la faculté du langage articulé, suivies d'une observation d'aphemie. *Bulletin et Mémoires de la Société Anatomique de Paris, 2*, 330–357.

Brooks, L. R. (1968). Spatial and verbal components of the act of recall. *Canadian Journal of Psychology, 22*, 349–368.

Brown, G. D. A., & Hulme, C. (1992). Cognitive psychology and second language processing: The role of short-term memory. In R. J. Harris (Ed.), *Cognitive approaches to bilingualism*. Amsterdam: Elsevier.

Brown, G. D. A., & Hulme, C. (1995). Modeling item length effects in memory span: No rehearsal needed? *Journal of Memory and Language, 34*, 594–621.

Brown, G. D. A., Neath, I., & Chater, N. (2002). *A ratio model of scale-invariant memory and identification*. Manuscript submitted for publication.

Brown, G. D. A., Preece, T., & Hulme, C. (2000). Oscillator-based memory for serial order. *Psychological Review, 107*, 127–181.

Brown, J. (1958). Some tests of the decay theory of immediate memory. *Quarterly Journal of Experimental Psychology, 10*, 12–21.

Brown, J., Lewis, V. J., & Monk, A. F. (1977). Memorability, word frequency and negative recognition. *Quarterly Journal of Experimental Psychology, 29*, 461–473.

Brown, N. R., Rips, L. J., & Shevell, S. K. (1985). The subjective dates of natural events in very-long-term memory. *Cognitive Psychology, 17*, 139–177.

Brown, N. R., & Schopflocher, D. (1998a). Event clusters: An organization of personal events in autobiographical memory. *Psychological Science, 9*, 470–475.

Brown, N. R., & Schopflocher, D. (1998b). Event cueing, event clusters, and the temporal distribution of autobiographical memories. *Applied Cognitive Psychology, 12*, 305–319.

Brown, R., & Kulik, J. (1977). Flashbulb memories. *Cognition, 5*, 73–99.

Brown, R., & McNeill, D. (1966). The "tip of the tongue" phenomenon. *Journal of Verbal Learning and Verbal Behavior, 5*, 325–337.

Bruce, V., & Valentine, T. (1986). Semantic priming of familiar faces. *Quarterly Journal of Experimental Psychology, 38A*, 125–150.

Bub, D. N. (2000). Methodological issues confronting PET and fMRI studies of cognitive function. *Cognitive Neuropsychology, 17*, 467–484.

Buckner, R. L., Kelley, W. M., & Petersen, S. E. (1999). Frontal cortex contributes to human memory formation. *Nature Neuroscience, 2*, 311–314.

Buckner, R. L., Koutstaal, W., Schacter, D. L., Wagner, A. D., & Rosen, B. R. (1998). Functional-anatomic study of episodic retrieval using fMRI: I. Retrieval effort versus retrieval success. *Neuroimage, 7*, 151–162.

Buckner, R. L., & Wheeler, M. E. (2001). The cognitive neuroscience of remembering. *Nature Reviews Neuroscience, 2*, 624–634.

Burgess, N., & Hitch, G. (1999). Memory for serial order: A network model of the phonological loop and its timing. *Psychological Review, 106*, 551–581.

Burnham, W. H. (1888). Memory, historically and experimentally considered. *American Journal of Psychology, 2*, 39–90, 255–270, 431–464, 566–622.

Butler, J., & Rovee-Collier, C. (1989). Contextual gating of memory retrieval. *Developmental Psychobiology, 22*, 533–552.

Butters, N., & Cermak, L. S. (1980). *Alcoholic Korsakoff's syndrome: An information processing approach to amnesia.* New York: Academic Press.

Buzan, T. (1984). *Use your perfect memory: A complete program of new techniques for remembering.* New York: Dutton.

Byrne, J. H., & Berry, W. O. (1989). (Eds.). *Neural models of plasticity: Experimental and theoretical approaches.* San Diego: Academic Press.

Cabeza, R. (2000). Functional neuroimaging of episodic memory retrieval. In E. Tulving (Ed.), *Memory, consciousness, and the brain: The Talinn Conference.* Philadelphia: Psychology Press.

Cabeza, R., Grady, C. L., Nyberg, L., McIntosh, A. R., Tulving, E., Kapur, S., Jennings, J. M., Houle, S., & Craik, F. I. M. (1997). Age-related differences in neural activity during memory encoding and retrieval: A positron emission tomography study. *Journal of Neuroscience, 17*, 391–400.

Cabeza, R., Kapur, S., Craik, F. I. M., McIntosh, A. R., Houle, S., & Tulving, E. (1997). Functional neuroanatomy of recall and recognition: A PET study of episodic memory. *Journal of Cognitive Neuroscience, 9*, 277–288.

Cain, L. F., & Willey, R. de V. (1939). The effect of spaced learning on the curve of retention. *Journal of Experimental Psychology, 25*, 209–214.

Calkins, M. W. (1896). Association: An essay analytic and experimental. *Psychological Review Monograph Supplements* (No. 2).

Calvin, W. H., & Ojemann, G. A. (1994). *Conversations with Neil's brain: The neural nature of thought and language.* Reading, MA: Addison-Wesley.

Campbell, B. A., Misanin, J. R., White, B. C., & Lytle, L. D. (1974). Species difference in ontogeny of memory: Indirect support for neural maturation as a determinant of forgetting. *Journal of Comparative and Physiological Psychology, 87*, 193–202.

Campbell, R., & Dodd, B. (1980). Hearing by eye. *Quarterly Journal of Experimental Psychology, 32*, 85–99.

Campbell, R., & Dodd, B. (Eds.). (1987). *Hearing by eye: The psychology of lip-reading.* London: Erlbaum.

Capaldi, E. J., & Neath, I. (1995). Remembering and forgetting as context discrimination. *Learning & Memory, 2*, 107–132.

Caplan, D., Rochon, E., & Waters, G. S. (1992). Articulatory and phonological determinants of word-length effects in span tasks. *Quarterly Journal of Experimental Psychology, 45A*, 177–192.

Caramazza, A., Hillis, A., Leek, E. C., & Miozzo, M. (1994). The organization of lexical knowledge in the brain: Evidence from category- and modality-specific deficits. In L. A. Hirschfeld & S. A. Gelman (Eds.), *Mapping the mind: Domain specificity in cognition and culture.* New York: Cambridge University Press.

Carey, S., & Diamond, R. (1980). Maturational determination of the developmental course of face encoding. In D. Caplan (Ed.), *Biological studies of mental processes.* Cambridge, MA: MIT Press.

Carlesimo, G. A., Fadda, L., Sabbadini, M., & Caltagirone, C. (1996). Recency effect in Alzheimer's disease: A reappraisal. *Quarterly Journal of Experimental Psychology, 49A*, 315–325.

Carlesimo, G. A., Sabbadini, M., & Fadda, L. (1995). Forgetting from long-term memory in dementia and pure amnesia: Role of task, delay of assessment and aetiology of cerebral damage. *Cortex, 31*, 285–300.

Carmichael, L., Hogan, H. P., & Walter, A. A. (1932). An experimental study of the effect of language on the reproductions of visually perceived forms. *Journal of Experimental Psychology, 15*, 73–86.

Carr, H. A. (1925). *Psychology: A study of mental activity.* New York: Longmans, Green.

Carr, H. A. (1930). Functionalism. In C. Murchison (Ed.), *Psychologies of 1930.* Worcester, MA: Clark University Press.

Carrol, M., Byrne, B., & Kirsner, K. (1985). Autobiographical memory and perceptual learning: A developmental study using picture recognition, naming latency, and perceptual identification. *Memory & Cognition, 13*, 273–279.

Carruthers, M. (1990). *The book of memory: A study of memory in medieval culture.* New York: Cambridge University Press.

Cermak, L. S. (1982). The long and short of it in amnesia. In L. S. Cermak (Ed.), *Human memory and amnesia.* Hillsdale, NJ: Erlbaum.

Cermak, L. S., & Reale, L. (1978). Depth of processing and retention of words by alcoholic Korsakoff patients. *Journal of Experimental Psychology: Human Learning and Memory, 4*, 165–174.

Cermak, L. S., Talbot, N., Chandler, K., & Wolbarst, L. R. (1985). The perceptual priming phenomenon in amnesia. *Neuropsychologia, 23,* 615–622.

Cermak, L. S., Verfaellie, M., & Chase, K. A. (1995). Implicit and explicit memory in amnesia: An analysis of data-driven and conceptually driven processes. *Neuropsychology, 9,* 281–290.

Chan, A. S., Butters, N., Paulsen, J. S., Salmon, D. P., Swenson, M. R., & Maloney, L. T. (1993). An assessment of the semantic network in patients with Alzheimer's disease. *Journal of Cognitive Neuroscience, 5,* 254–261.

Chang, T. M. (1986). Semantic memory: Facts and models. *Psychological Bulletin, 99,* 199–220.

Chase, W. G., & Ericsson, K. A. (1981). Skilled memory. In J. R. Anderson (Ed.), *Cognitive skills and their acquisition.* Hillsdale, NJ: Erlbaum.

Chase, W. G., & Ericsson, K. A. (1982). Skill and working memory. In G. H. Bower (Ed.), *The psychology of learning and motivation* (Vol. 16). New York: Academic Press.

Chase, W. G., & Simon, H. A. (1973). The mind's eye in chess. In W. G. Chase (Ed.), *Visual information processing.* New York: Academic Press.

Cherry, K. E., & Stadler, M. A. (1995). Implicit learning of a nonverbal sequence in younger and older adults. *Psychology and Aging, 10,* 379–394.

Chertkow, H., Bub, D., & Caplan, D. (1992). Constraining theories of semantic memory processing: Evidence from dementia. *Cognitive Neuropsychology, 9,* 327–365.

Chiarello, C., & Hoyer, W. J. (1988). Adult age differences in implicit and explicit memory: Time course and encoding effects. *Psychology and Aging, 3,* 358–366.

Chiesi, H. L., Spilich, G. J., & Voss, J. F. (1979). Acquisition of domain-related information in relation to high- and low-domain knowledge. *Journal of Verbal Learning and Verbal Behavior, 18,* 257–273.

Chorover, S. L., & Schiller, P. H. (1965). Short-term retrograde amnesia in rats. *Journal of Comparative and Physiological Psychology, 59,* 73–78.

Christianson, S.-A. (1989). Flashbulb memories: Special, but not so special. *Memory & Cognition, 17,* 435–443.

Christianson, S.-A., & Engelberg, E. (1999). Memory and emotional consistency: The MS *Estonia* ferry disaster. *Memory, 7,* 471–482.

Cicero. (1942). *De oratore* (E. W. Sutton, Trans.). Loeb Classical Library. London: William Heinemann.

Claparède, E. (1951). Reconnaissance et moiité. In D. Rapaport (Ed.), *Organization and pathology of thought.* New York: Columbia University Press.

Cleeremans, A., & McClelland, J. L. (1991). Learning the structure of event sequences. *Journal of Experimental Psychology: General, 120,* 235–253.

Cocude, M., Charlot, V., & Denis, M. (1997). Latency and duration of visual mental images in normal and depressed subjects. *Journal of Mental Imagery, 21,* 127–142.

Cofer, C. N., & Davidson, E. H. (1968). Proactive interference in STM for consonant units of two sizes. *Journal of Verbal Learning and Verbal Behavior, 7,* 268–270.

Cohen, G., Conway, M. A., & Maylor, E. A. (1994). Flashbulb memories in older adults. *Psychology & Aging, 9,* 454–463.

Cohen, G., & Faulkner, D. (1989). Age differences in source forgetting: Effects on reality monitoring and on eyewitness testimony. *Psychology and Aging, 4,* 10–17.

Cohen, N. J., & Eichenbaum, H. (1993). *Memory, amnesia, and the hippocampal system.* Cambridge, MA: MIT Press.

Cohen, N. J., Eichenbaum, H., Deacedo, B. S., & Corkin, S. (1985). Different memory systems underlying acquisition of procedural and declarative knowledge. In D. S. Olton, E. Gamzu, & S. Corkin (Eds.), *Memory dysfunctions: An integration of animal and human research from preclinical and clinical perspectives.* New York: New York Academy of Sciences.

Cole, W. G., & Loftus, E. F. (1979). Incorporating new information into memory. *American Journal of Psychology, 92,* 413–425.

Colegrove, F. W. (1899). Individual memories. *American Journal of Psychology, 10,* 228–255.

Colle, H. A., & Welsh, A. (1976). Acoustic masking in primary memory. *Journal of Verbal Learning and Verbal Behavior, 15,* 17–32.

Collins, A. M., & Loftus, E. F. (1975). A spreading-activation theory of semantic processing. *Psychological Review, 82,* 407–428.

Collins, A. M., & Quillian, M. R. (1969). Retrieval time from semantic memory. *Journal of Verbal Learning and Verbal Behavior, 8,* 240–247.

Collins, A. M., & Quillian, M. R. (1970). Does category size affect categorization time? *Journal of Verbal Learning and Verbal Behavior, 9,* 432–438.

Coltheart, M. (1980). Iconic memory and visible persistence. *Perception & Psychophysics, 27,* 183–228.

Coltheart, M., & Glick, M. J. (1974). Visual imagery: A case study. *Quarterly Journal of Experimental Psychology, 26,* 438–453.

Conrad, C. (1972). Cognitive economy in semantic memory. *Journal of Experimental Psychology, 92,* 149–154.

Conrad, R. (1964). Acoustic confusions in immediate memory. *British Journal of Psychology, 55,* 75–84.

Conrad, R. (1965). Order error in immediate recall of sequences. *Journal of Verbal Learning and Verbal Behavior, 4,* 161–169.

Conrad, R. (1972). Speech and reading. In J. F. Kavanagh & I. G. Mattingly (Eds.), *Language by ear and by eye: The relationships between speech and reading.* Cambridge, MA: MIT Press.

Conrad, R., & Hille, B. A. (1958). The decay theory of immediate memory and paced recall. *Canadian Journal of Psychology, 12,* 1–6.

Conrad, R., & Hull, A. J. (1968). Input modality and the serial position curve in short-term memory. *Psychonomic Science, 10,* 135–136.

Conway, A. R. A., Cowan, N., & Bunting, M. F. (2001). The cocktail party phenomenon revisited: The importance of working memory capacity. *Psychonomic Bulletin & Review, 8,* 331–335.

Conway, A. R. A., & Engle, R. W. (1996). Individual differences in working memory capacity: More evidence for a general capacity theory. *Memory, 4,* 577–590.

Conway, M. A. (1995). *Flashbulb memories.* Hove, UK: Erlbaum.

Conway, M. A. (1996). Autobiographical memories and autobiographical knowledge. In D. C. Rubin (Ed.), *Remembering our past: Studies in autobiographical memory.* Cambridge, UK: Cambridge University Press.

Conway, M. A. (Ed.). (1997). *Recovered memories and false memories.* Oxford, UK: Oxford University Press.

Conway, M. A., Anderson, S. J., Larsen, S. F., Donnelly, C. M., McDaniel, M. A., McClelland, A. G. R., Rawles, R. E., & Logie, R. H. (1994). The formation of flashbulb memories. *Memory & Cognition, 22,* 326–343.

Conway, M. A., & Gathercole, S. E. (1987). Modality and long-term memory. *Journal of Memory and Language, 26,* 341–346.

Conway, M. A., & Pleydell-Pearce, C. W. (2000). The construction of autobiographical memories in the self-memory system. *Psychological Review, 107,* 261–288.

Conway, M. A., & Rubin, D. C. (1993). The structure of autobiographical memory. In A. F. Collins, S. E. Gathercole, M. A. Conway, & P. E. Morris (Eds.), *Theories of memory.* Hillsdale, NJ: Erlbaum.

Cooper, L. A., & Shepard, R. N. (1973). Chronometric studies of the rotation of mental images. In W. G. Chase (Ed.), *Visual information processing.* New York: Academic Press.

Copleston, F. (1985). *A history of philosophy* (Vol. 9). Garden City, NY: Image.

Corballis, M. C. (1966). Rehearsal and decay in immediate recall of visually and aurally presented items. *Canadian Journal of Psychology, 20,* 43–51.

Corballis, M. C. (1980). Laterality and myth. *American Psychologist, 35,* 284–295.

Corkin, S., Cohen, N. J., Sullivan, E. V., Clegg, R. A., Rosen, R. J., & Ackerman, R. H. (1985). Analysis of global memory impairments of different etiologies. *Annals of the New York Academy of Sciences, 444,* 10–40.

Cowan, N. (1984). On short and long auditory stores. *Psychological Bulletin, 96,* 341–370.

Cowan, N. (1988). Evolving conceptions of memory storage, selective attention, and their mutual constraints within the human information processing system. *Psychological Bulletin, 104,* 163–191.

Cowan, N. (1992). Verbal memory span and the timing of spoken recall. *Journal of Memory and Language, 31,* 668–684.

Cowan, N. (1993). Activation, attention, and short-term memory. *Memory & Cognition, 21,* 162–168.

Cowan, N. (1995). *Attention and memory: An integrated framework.* New York: Oxford University Press.

Cowan, N. (1997). The development of working memory. In N. Cowan (Ed.), *The development of memory in childhood.* Hove, UK: Psychology Press.

Cowan, N. (1999). An embedded-processes model of working memory. In A. Miyake & P. Shah (Eds.), *Models of working memory: Mechanisms of active maintenance and executive control.* New York: Cambridge University Press.

Cowan, N. (2001). The magical number 4 in short-term memory: A reconsideration of mental storage capacity. *Behavioral and Brain Sciences, 24,* 87–185.

Cowan, N., Cartwright, C., Winterowd, C., & Sherk, M. (1987). An adult model of preschool children's speech memory. *Memory & Cognition, 15,* 511–517.

Cowan, N., Day, L., Saults, J. S., Keller, T. A., Johnson, T., & Flores, L. (1992). The role of verbal output time in the effects of word length on immediate memory. *Journal of Memory and Language, 31,* 1–17.

Cowan, N., Keller, T., Hulme, C., Roodenrys, S., McDougall, S., & Rack, J. (1994). Verbal memory span in children: Speech timing clues to the mechanisms underlying age and word length effects. *Journal of Memory and Language, 33,* 243–250.

Cowan, N., Nugent, L. D., Elliott, E. M., Ponomarev, I., & Saults, J. S. (1999). The role of attention in the development of short-term memory: Age differences in the verbal span of apprehension. *Child Development, 70,* 1082–1097.

Cowan, N., Nugent, L. D., Elliott, E. M., & Saults, J. S. (2000). Persistence of memory for ignored lists of digits: Areas of developmental constancy and change. *Journal of Experimental Child Psychology, 76,* 151–172.

Cowan, N., Saults, J. S., Elliott, E. M., & Moreno, M. V. (2002). Deconfounding serial recall. *Journal of Memory and Language, 46,* 153–177.

Cowan, N., Saults, S., & Nugent, L. (1997). The role of absolute and relative amounts of time in forgetting within immediate memory: The case of tone pitch comparisons. *Psychonomic Bulletin & Review, 4,* 393–397.

Cowan, N., Saults, S., & Nugent, L. (2001). The ravages of absolute and relative time. In H. L. Roediger III, J. S. Nairne, I. Neath, & A. M. Surprenant (Eds.), *The nature of remembering: Essays in honor of Robert G. Crowder.* Washington, DC: American Psychological Association.

Cowan, N., Wood, N. L., & Borne, D. N. (1994). Reconfirmation of the short-term storage concept. *Psychological Science, 5,* 103–106.

Cowan, N., Wood, N. L., Wood, P. K., Keller, T. A., Nugent, L. D., & Keller, C. V. (1998). Two separate verbal processing rates contributing to short-term memory span. *Journal of Experimental Psychology: General, 127,* 141–160.

Craik, F. I. M. (1983). On the transfer of information from temporary to permanent memory. *Philosophical Transactions of the Royal Society of London B, 302*, 341–359.

Craik, F. I. M. (1986). A functional account of age differences in memory. In F. Klix & H. Hagendorf (Eds.), *Human memory and cognitive capabilities, mechanisms, and performances.* Amsterdam: Elsevier.

Craik, F. I. M. (1994). Memory changes in normal aging. *Current Directions in Psychological Science, 3*, 155–158.

Craik, F. I. M., & Anderson, N. D. (1999). Applying cognitive research to problems of aging. In D. Gopher & A. Koriat (Eds.), *Attention and performance XVII.* Cambridge, MA: MIT Press.

Craik, F. I. M., Anderson, N. D., Kerr, S. A., & Li, K. Z. H. (1995). Memory changes in normal ageing. In A. D. Baddeley, B. A. Wilson, & F. N. Watts (Eds.), *Handbook of memory disorders.* New York: Wiley.

Craik, F. I. M., & Byrd, M. (1982). Aging and cognitive deficits: The role of attentional resources. In F. I. M. Craik & S. Trehub (Eds.), *Aging and cognitive processes.* New York: Plenum.

Craik, F. I. M., Byrd, M., & Swanson, J. M. (1987). Patterns of memory loss in three elderly samples. *Psychology and Aging, 2*, 79–86.

Craik, F. I. M., Govoni, R., Naveh-Benjamin, M., & Anderson, N. D. (1996). The effects of divided attention on encoding and retrieval processes in human memory. *Journal of Experimental Psychology: General, 125*, 159–180.

Craik, F. I. M., & Jennings, J. M. (1992). Human memory. In F. I. M. Craik & T. A. Salthouse (Eds.), *The handbook of aging and cognition.* Hillsdale, NJ: Erlbaum.

Craik, F. I. M., & Lockhart, R. S. (1972). Levels of processing: A framework for memory research. *Journal of Verbal Learning and Verbal Behavior, 11*, 671–684.

Craik, F. I. M., & McDowd, J. M. (1987). Age differences in recall and recognition. *Journal of Experimental Psychology: Learning, Memory, and Cognition, 13*, 474–479.

Craik, F. I. M., & Tulving, E. (1975). Depth of processing and the retention of words in episodic memory. *Journal of Experimental Psychology: General, 104*, 268–294.

Craik, F. I. M., & Watkins, M. J. (1973). The role of rehearsal in short-term memory. *Journal of Verbal Learning and Verbal Behavior, 12*, 599–607.

Crossman, W. R. F. W. (1960). Information and serial order in human immediate memory. In C. Cherry (Ed.), *Information theory.* London: Butterworth.

Crowder, R. G. (1967). Prefix effects in immediate memory. *Canadian Journal of Psychology, 21*, 450–461.

Crowder, R. G. (1969). Behavioral strategies in immediate memory. *Journal of Verbal Learning and Verbal Behavior, 8*, 524–528.

Crowder, R. G. (1970). The role of one's own voice in immediate memory. *Cognitive Psychology, 1*, 157–178.

Crowder, R. G. (1971). Waiting for the stimulus suffix: Decay, delay, rhythm, and readout in immediate memory. *Quarterly Journal of Experimental Psychology, 23*, 324–340.

Crowder, R. G. (1972). Visual and auditory memory. In J. F. Kavanagh & I. G. Mattingly (Eds.), *Language by ear and by eye: The relation between speech and learning to read.* Cambridge, MA: MIT Press.

Crowder, R. G. (1973a). The representation of speech sounds in precategorical acoustic storage. *Journal of Experimental Psychology, 98*, 14–24.

Crowder, R. G. (1973b). Precategorical acoustic storage for vowels of short and long duration. *Perception & Psychophysics, 13*, 502–506.

Crowder, R. G. (1973c). The delayed stimulus suffix effect following arhythmic stimulus presentation. *Quarterly Journal of Experimental Psychology, 25*, 433–439.

Crowder, R. G. (1975). Inferential problems in echoic memory. In P. M. A. Rabbitt & S. Dornic (Eds.), *Attention and performance V.* London and New York: Academic Press.

Crowder, R. G. (1976). *Principles of learning and memory.* Hillsdale, NJ: Erlbaum.

Crowder, R. G. (1978a). Memory for phonologically uniform lists. *Journal of Verbal Learning and Verbal Behavior, 17*, 73–89.

Crowder, R. G. (1978b). Mechanisms of auditory backward masking in the stimulus suffix effect. *Psychological Review, 85*, 502–524.

Crowder, R. G. (1979). Similarity and order in memory. In G. H. Bower (Ed.), *The psychology of learning and memory* (Vol. 13). New York: Academic Press.

Crowder, R. G. (1982a). The demise of short-term memory. *Acta Psychologica, 5*, 291–323.

Crowder, R. G. (1982b). General forgetting theory and the locus of amnesia. In L. S. Cermak (Ed.), *Human memory and amnesia.* Hillsdale, NJ: Erlbaum.

Crowder, R. G. (1986). Auditory and temporal factors in the modality effect. *Journal of Experimental Psychology: Learning, Memory, and Cognition, 12*, 268–275.

Crowder, R. G. (1989a). Modularity and dissociations of memory systems. In H. L. Roediger III & F. I. M. Craik (Eds.), *Varieties of memory and consciousness: Essays in honour of Endel Tulving.* Hillsdale, NJ: Erlbaum.

Crowder, R. G. (1989b). Imagery for musical timbre. *Journal of Experimental Psychology: Human Perception and Performance, 15*, 472–478.

Crowder, R. G. (1992a). John A. McGeoch. In L. R. Squire (Ed.), *Encyclopedia of learning and memory.* New York: Macmillan.

Crowder, R. G. (1992b). Eidetic imagery. In L. R. Squire (Ed.), *Encyclopedia of learning and memory.* New York: Macmillan.

Crowder, R. G. (1993a). Systems and principles in memory theory: Another critique of pure memory. In A. F. Collins, S. E. Gathercole, M. A. Conway, & P. E.

Morris (Eds.), *Theories of memory*. Hove, UK: Erlbaum.

Crowder, R. G. (1993b). Short-term memory: Where do we stand? *Memory & Cognition, 21*, 142–145.

Crowder, R. G., & Morton, J. (1969). Precategorical acoustic storage (PAS). *Perception & Psychophysics, 5*, 365–373.

Crowder, R. G., & Schab, F. R. (1995). Imagery for odors. In F. R. Schab & R. G. Crowder (Eds.), *Memory for odors*. Mahwah, NJ: Erlbaum.

Crowder, R. G., & Surprenant, A. M. (2000). Sensory memory. In A. E. Kazdin (Ed.), *Encyclopedia of psychology*. New York: Oxford University Press and American Psychological Association.

Cunningham, T. F., Healy, A. F., & Williams, D. M. (1984). Effects of repetition on short-term retention of order information. *Journal of Experimental Psychology: Learning, Memory, and Cognition, 10*, 575–597.

Curci, A., Luminet, O., Finkenauer, C., & Gisle, L. (2001). Flashbulb memories in social groups: A comparative test-retest study of the memory of French President Mitterrand's death in a French and a Belgian group. *Memory, 9*, 81–101.

Curran, T., & Hintzman, D. L. (1997). Consequences and causes of correlations in process dissociation. *Journal of Experimental Psychology: Learning Memory, and Cognition, 23*, 496–504.

Curran, T., & Keele, S. W. (1993). Attentional and nonattentional forms of sequence learning. *Journal of Experimental Psychology: Learning, Memory, and Cognition, 19*, 189–202.

Cycowicz, Y. M., Friedman, D., Snodgrass, J. G., & Rothstein, M. (2000). A developmental trajectory in implicit memory is revealed by picture fragment completion. *Memory, 8*, 19–35.

D'Esposito, M., Zarahn, E., & Aguirre, G. K. (1999). Event-related functional MRI: Implications for cognitive psychology. *Psychological Bulletin, 125*, 155–164.

Daglish, M. R., & Wright, P. (1991). Opinions about hypnosis among medical and psychology students. *Contemporary Hypnosis, 8*, 51–55.

Dale, H. C. A., & McGlaughlin, A. (1971). Evidence of acoustic coding in long-term memory. *Quarterly Journal of Experimental Psychology, 23*, 1–7.

Dalla-Barba, G., & Wong, C. (1995). Encoding specificity and intrusion in Alzheimer's disease and amnesia. *Brain and Cognition, 27*, 1–16.

Dallett, K. (1965). "Primary memory": The effects of redundancy upon digit repetition. *Psychonomic Science, 3*, 237–238.

Daneman, M., & Carpenter, P. A. (1980). Individual differences in working memory and reading. *Journal of Verbal Learning and Verbal Behavior, 19*, 450–466.

Darwin, C. J., Turvey, M. T., & Crowder, R. G. (1972). An auditory analogue of the Sperling partial-report procedure. *Cognitive Psychology, 3*, 255–267.

Davidson, T. L., McKernan, M. G., & Jarrard, L. E. (1993). Hippocampal lesions do not impair negative patterning: A challenge to configural association theory. *Behavioral Neuroscience, 108*, 227–243.

De Beni, R., & Cornoldi, C. (1985). Effects of the mnemotechnique of loci in the memorization of concrete words. *Acta Psychologica, 60*, 11–24.

De Beni, R., & Cornoldi, C. (1988). Imagery limitations in totally congenitally blind subjects. *Journal of Experimental Psychology: Learning, Memory, and Cognition, 14*, 650–655.

De Renzi, E. (1982). Memory disorders following focal neocortical damage. *Philosophical Transactions of the Royal Society of London B, 298*, 73–83.

De Renzi, E., & Lucchelli, F. (1994). Are semantic systems separately represented in the brain? The case of living category impairment. *Cortex, 30*, 3–25.

De Vreese, L. P., Neri, M., Fioravanti, M., Belloi, L., & Zanetti, O. (2001). Memory rehabilitation in Alzheimer's disease: A review of progress. *International Journal of Geriatric Psychiatry, 16*, 794–809.

Deese, J. (1959a). Influence of inter-item associative strength upon immediate free recall. *Psychological Reports, 5*, 305–312.

Deese, J. (1959b). On the prediction of occurrence of particular verbal intrusions in immediate recall. *Journal of Experimental Psychology, 58*, 17–22.

Deese, J. (1961). From the isolated verbal unit to connected discourse. In C. N. Cofer (Ed.), *Verbal learning and verbal behavior*. New York: McGraw-Hill.

Delbecq-Derouesné, J., & Beauvois, M. F. (1989). Memory processes and aging: A defect of automatic rather than controlled processes? *Archives of Gerontology and Geriatrics: Supplement, 1*, 121–150.

Dell, G. S. (1986). A spreading-activation theory of retrieval in sentence production. *Psychological Review, 93*, 283–321.

Della Sala, S., & Logie, R. H. (2001). Theoretical and practical implications of dual-task performance in Alzheimer's disease. *Brain, 124*, 1479–1481.

DeLoache, J. S., Cassidy, D. J., & Brown, A. L. (1985). Precursors of mnemonic strategies in very young children's memory. *Child Development, 56*, 125–137.

Dempster, F. N. (1981). Memory span: Sources of individual and developmental differences. *Psychological Bulletin, 89*, 63–100.

Dempster, F. N. (1985). Proactive interference in sentence recall: Topic-similarity effects and individual differences. *Memory & Cognition, 13*, 81–89.

den Heyer, K., & Barrett, B. (1971). Selective loss of visual and verbal information in STM by means of visual and verbal interpolated tasks. *Psychonomic Science, 25*, 100–102.

Destrebecqz, A., & Cleeremans, A. (2001). Can sequence learning be implicit? New evidence with the process dissociation procedure. *Psychonomic Bulletin & Review, 8*, 343–350.

Di Lollo, V. (1980). Temporal integration in visual memory. *Journal of Experimental Psychology: General, 109,* 75–97.

Di Lollo, V., Hogben, J. H., & Dixon, P. (1994). Temporal integration and segregation of brief visual stimuli: Patterns of correlation in time. *Perception & Psychophysics, 55,* 373–386.

Diamond, R., & Carey, S. (1986). Why faces are and are not special: An effect of expertise. *Journal of Experimental Psychology: General, 115,* 107–117.

Diamond, S. (Ed.). (1974). *The roots of psychology: A sourcebook in the history of ideas.* New York: Basic Books.

Dick, A. O. (1971). On the problem of selection in short-term visual (iconic) memory. *Canadian Journal of Psychology, 25,* 250–263.

Dinges, D. F., Whitehouse, W. G., Orne, E. C., Powell, J. W., Orne, M. T., & Erdelyi, M. (1992). Evaluating hypnotic memory enhancement (hypermnesia and reminiscence) using multitrial forced recall. *Journal of Experimental Psychology: Learning, Memory and Cognition, 18,* 1139–1147.

Donaldson, W. (1992). Measuring recognition memory. *Journal of Experimental Psychology: General, 121,* 275–278.

Donaldson, W. (1996). The role of decision processes in remembering and knowing. *Memory & Cognition, 24,* 523–533.

Donegan, N. H., Gluck, M. A., & Thompson, R. F. (1989). Integrating behavioral and biological models of classical conditioning. In R. D. Hawkins & G. H. Bower (Eds.), *Computational models of learning in simple neural systems.* San Diego: Academic Press.

Doob, L. W. (1966). Eidetic imagery: A cross-cultural will-o'-the-wisp? *Journal of Psychology, 63,* 13–34.

Doody, R. S., Stevens, J. C., Beck, C., Dubinsky, R. M., Kaye, J. A., Gwyther, L., Mohs, R. C., Thal, L. J., Whitehouse, P. J., DeKosky, S. T., & Cummings, J. L. (2001). Practice parameter: Management of dementia (an evidence-based review). Report of the Quality Standards Subcommittee of the American Academy of Neurology. *Neurology, 56,* 1154–1166.

Dosher, B. A. (1999). Item interference and time delays in working memory: Immediate serial recall. *International Journal of Psychology, 34,* 276–284.

Dosher, B. A., & Ma, J.-J. (1998). Output loss or rehearsal loop? Output-time versus pronunciation-time limits in immediate recall for forgetting-matched materials. *Journal of Experimental Psychology: Learning, Memory, and Cognition, 24,* 316–335.

Dosher, B. A., & Rosedale, G. (1989). Integrated retrieval cues as a mechanism for priming in retrieval from memory. *Journal of Experimental Psychology: General, 118,* 191–211.

Drewnowski, A. (1980). Attributes and priorities in short-term recall: A new model of memory span. *Journal of Experimental Psychology: General, 109,* 208–250.

Drewnowski, A., & Murdock, B. B., Jr. (1980). The role of auditory features in memory span for words. *Journal of Experimental Psychology: Human Learning and Memory, 6,* 319–332.

Drummey, A. B., & Newcombe, N. (1995). Remembering versus knowing the past: Children's explicit and implicit memories for pictures. *Journal of Experimental Child Psychology, 59,* 549–565.

Duncan, C. P. (1949). The retroactive effect of electroshock on learning. *Journal of Comparative and Physiological Psychology, 42,* 32–44.

Dunn, R. (1845). Case of suspension of the mental faculties. *Lancet, 2,* 588–590.

Durlach, N. I., & Braida, L. D. (1969). Intensity perception: I. Preliminary theory of intensity resolution. *Journal of the Acoustical Society of America, 46,* 372–383.

Dywan, J., & Bowers, K. (1983). The use of hypnosis to enhance recall. *Science, 222,* 184–185.

Dywan, J., & Jacoby, L. L. (1990). Effects of aging on source monitoring: Differences in susceptibility to false fame. *Psychology and Aging, 5,* 379–387.

Dywan, J., & Murphy, W. E. (1996). Aging and inhibitory control in text comprehension. *Psychology & Aging, 11,* 199–206.

Eagle, M., & Leiter, E. (1964). Recall and recognition in intentional and incidental learning. *Journal of Experimental Psychology, 68,* 58–63.

Ebbinghaus, H. (1885). *Über das Gedächtnis: Untersuchungen zur experimentellen Psychologie.* Leipzig: Duncker and Humboldt. [Reprinted as H. E. Ebbinghaus. (1964). *Memory: A contribution to experimental psychology* (H. A. Ruger, Trans.). New York: Dover.]

Efron, R. (1970a). The relationship between the duration of a stimulus and the duration of a perception. *Neuropsychologia, 8,* 37–55.

Efron, R. (1970b). The minimum duration of a perception. *Neuropsychologia, 8,* 57–63.

Eich, E. (1989). Theoretical issues in state dependent memory. In H. L. Roediger III & F. I. M. Craik (Eds.), *Varieties of memory and consciousness: Essays in honour of Endel Tulving.* Hillsdale, NJ: Erlbaum.

Eich, E. (1995). Searching for mood dependent memory. *Psychological Science, 6,* 67–75.

Eich, E., & Birnbaum, I. M. (1982). Repetition, cueing, and state dependent memory. *Memory & Cognition, 10,* 103–114.

Eich, E., & Metcalfe, J. (1989). Mood-dependent memory for internal versus external events. *Journal of Experimental Psychology: Learning, Memory, and Cognition, 15,* 443–455.

Eich, J. E. (1980). The cue-dependent nature of state-dependent retrieval. *Memory & Cognition, 8,* 157–173.

Eich, J. E., Weingartner, H., Stillman, R. C., & Gillin, J. C. (1975). State-dependent accessibility of retrieval cues in the retention of a categorized list. *Journal of Verbal Learning and Verbal Behavior, 14,* 408–417.

Eich, J. M. (1982). A composite holographic associative recall model. *Psychological Review, 89*, 627–661.

Einstein, G. O., & McDaniel, M. A. (1987). Distinctiveness and the mnemonic benefits of bizarre imagery. In M. A. McDaniel & M. Pressley (Eds.), *Imagery and related mnemonic processes: Theories, individual differences, and applications*. New York: Springer-Verlag.

Einstein, G. O., & McDaniel, M. A. (1990). Normal aging and prospective memory. *Journal of Experimental Psychology: Learning, Memory, and Cognition, 16*, 717–726.

Einstein, G. O., McDaniel, M. A., Richardson, S. L., Guynn, M. J., & Cunfer, A. R. (1995). Aging and prospective memory: Examining the influences of self-initiated retrieval processes. *Journal of Experimental Psychology: Learning, Memory, and Cognition, 21*, 996–1007.

Einstein, G. O., Pellegrino, J. W., Mondani, M. S., & Battig, W. F. (1974). Free recall performance as a function of overt rehearsal frequency. *Journal of Experimental Psychology, 103*, 440–449.

Ellis, H. D. (1975). Recognising faces. *British Journal of Psychology, 66*, 29–37.

Ellis, H. D., Ellis, D. M., & Hosie, J. A. (1993). Priming effects in children's face recognition. *British Journal of Psychology, 84*, 101–110.

Ellis, H. D., & Young, A. W. (1989). Are faces special? In A. W. Young & H. D. Ellis (Eds.), *Handbook of research on face processing*. Amsterdam: North-Holland.

Ellis, N., & Beaton, A. (1993). Factors affecting the learning of foreign language vocabulary: Imagery keyword mediators and phonological short-term memory. *Quarterly Journal of Experimental Psychology, 46A*, 533–558.

Ellis, N. C., & Hennelly, R. A. (1980). A bilingual word-length effect: Implications for intelligence testing and the relative ease of mental calculations in Welsh and English. *British Journal of Psychology, 71*, 43–52.

Engen, T., Kuisma, J. E., & Eimas, P. D. (1973). Short-term memory of odors. *Journal of Experimental Psychology, 99*, 222–225.

Engle, R. W. (2001). What is working memory capacity? In H. L. Roediger III, J. S. Nairne, I. Neath, & A. M. Surprenant (Eds.), *The nature of remembering: Essays in honor of Robert G. Crowder*. Washington, DC: American Psychological Association.

Engle, R. W., Kane, M. J., & Tuholski, S. W. (1999). Individual differences in working memory capacity and what they tell us about controlled attention, general fluid intelligences, and functions of the prefrontal cortex. In A. Miyake & P. Shah (Eds.), *Models of working memory: Mechanisms of active maintenance and executive control*. New York: Cambridge University Press.

Engle, R. W., Tuholski, S. W., Laughlin, J. E., & Conway, A. R. A. (1999). Working memory, short-term memory, and general fluid intelligence: A latent variable approach. *Journal of Experimental Psychology: General, 128*, 309–331.

Erdelyi, M. H. (1994). Hypnotic hypermnesia: The empty set of hypermnesia. *International Journal of Clinical and Experimental Hypnosis, 42*, 379–390.

Ericsson, K. A. (1985). Memory skill. *Canadian Journal of Psychology, 39*, 188–231.

Ericsson, K. A., Chase, W. G., & Faloon, S. F. (1980). Acquisition of a memory skill. *Science, 208*, 1181–1182.

Ericsson, K. A., & Faivre, I. A. (1988). What's exceptional about exceptional abilities? In L. K. Obler & D. Fein (Eds.), *The exceptional brain: Neuropsychology of talent and special abilities*. New York: Guilford.

Ericsson, K. A., Krampe, R. T., & Tesch-Römer, C. (1993). The role of deliberate practice in the acquisition of expert performance. *Psychological Review, 100*, 363–406.

Ericsson, K. A., & Staszewski, J. (1989). Skilled memory and expertise: Mechanisms of exceptional performance. In D. Klahr & K. Kotovsky (Eds.), *Complex information processing: The impact of Herbert A. Simon*. Hillsdale, NJ: Erlbaum.

Estes, W. K. (1972). An associative basis for coding and organization in memory. In A. W. Melton & E. Martin (Eds.), *Coding processes in human memory*. Washington, DC: Winston.

Estes, W. K. (1973). Phonemic coding and rehearsal in short-term memory for letter strings. *Journal of Verbal Learning and Verbal Behavior, 12*, 360–372.

Estes, W. K. (1997). Processes of memory loss, recovery, and distortion. *Psychological Review, 104*, 148–169.

Estes, W. K., & Da Polito, F. (1967). Independent variation of information storage and retrieval processes in paired-associate learning. *Journal of Experimental Psychology, 75*, 18–26.

Farah, M. J. (1988). Is visual imagery really visual? Overlooked evidence from neuropsychology. *Psychological Review, 95*, 307–317.

Farah, M. J. (1989). Mechanisms of imagery-perception interaction. *Journal of Experimental Psychology: Human Perception and Performance, 15*, 203–211.

Farah, M. J., Hammond, K. M., Levine, D. N., & Calvanio, R. (1988). Visual and spatial mental imagery: Dissociable systems of representation. *Cognitive Psychology, 20*, 439–462.

Farah, M. J., & McClelland, J. L. (1991). A computational model of semantic memory impairment: Modality specificity and emergent category specificity. *Journal of Experimental Psychology: General, 120*, 339–357.

Farah, M. J., McMullen, P. A., & Meyer, M. M. (1991). Can recognition of living things be selectively impaired? *Neuropsychologia, 29*, 185–193.

Farah, M. J., Wilson, K. D., Drain, M., & Tanaka, J. M. (1998). What is "special" about face perception? *Psychological Review, 105*, 482–498.

Farrell, S., & Lewandowsky, S. (in press). An endogenous distributed model of ordering in serial recall. *Psychonomic Bulletin & Review*.

Feenan, K., & Snodgrass, J. G. (1990). The effect of context on discrimination and bias in recognition memory for pictures and words. *Memory & Cognition, 18*, 517–527.

Feigenbaum, E. A., & Simon, H. (1962). A theory of the serial position effect. *British Journal of Psychology, 53*, 307–320.

Finke, R. A. (1989). *Principles of mental imagery*. Cambridge, MA: MIT Press.

Finke, R. A., & Pinker, S. (1982). Spontaneous imagery scanning in mental extrapolation. *Journal of Experimental Psychology: Learning, Memory, and Cognition, 8*, 142–147.

Fischhoff, B. (1977). Perceived informativeness of facts. *Journal of Experimental Psychology: Human Perception and Performance, 3*, 349–358.

Fisher, R. P., & Craik, F. I. M. (1977). Interaction between encoding and retrieval operations in cued recall. *Journal of Experimental Psychology: Human Learning and Memory, 3*, 701–711.

Fisher, R. P., & Geiselman, R. E. (1992). *Memory enhancing techniques for investigative interviewing*. Springfield, IL: Thomas.

Fisher, R. P., Geiselman, R. E., Raymond, D. S., & Jurkeich, L. M. (1987). Enhancing enhanced eyewitness memory: Refining the cognitive interview. *Journal of Police Science and Administration, 15*, 291–297.

Fitzgerald, J. M. (1988). Vivid memories and the reminiscence phenomenon: The role of self-narrative. *Human Development, 31*, 261–273.

Fivush, R., & Hamond, N. (1990). Autobiographical memory across the preschool years: Towards reconceptualizing childhood amnesia. In R. Fivush & J. A. Hudson (Eds.), *Knowing and remembering in young children*. Cambridge, UK: Cambridge University Press.

Fivush, R., Hudson, J. A., & Nelson, K. (1984). Children's long-term memory for a novel event: An exploratory study. *Merrill-Palmer Quarterly, 30*, 303–316.

Flavell, J. H., Beach, D. H., & Chinsky, J. M. (1966). Spontaneous verbal rehearsal in a memory task as a function of age. *Child Development, 37*, 283–299.

Fleischman, D. A., Gabrieli, J. D. E., Rinaldi, J. A., Reminger, S. L., Grinnell, E. R., Lange, K.L., & Shapiro, R. (1997). Word-stem completion priming for perceptually and conceptually encoded words in patients with Alzheimer's disease. *Neuropsychologia, 35*, 25–35.

Flexser, A. J., & Tulving, E. (1978). Retrieval independence in recognition and recall. *Psychological Review, 85*, 153–171.

Foley, M. A., Johnson, M. K., & Raye, C. L. (1983). Age-related changes in confusion between memories for thoughts and memories for speech. *Child Development, 54*, 51–60.

Foster, J. K., & Jelicic, M. (Eds.) (1999). *Memory: Systems, process, or function?* New York: Oxford University Press.

Francis, G. (1999). Spatial frequency and visual persistence: Cortical reset. *Spatial Vision, 12*, 31–50.

Frankish, C. (1985). Modality-specific grouping effects in short-term memory. *Journal of Memory and Language, 24*, 200–209.

Franzen, J. (2001, September 10). My father's brain: What Alzheimer's takes away. *The New Yorker*, pp. 80–91.

Friedman, S. (1972). Newborn visual attention to repeated exposure of redundant vs. "novel" targets. *Perception & Psychophysics, 12*, 291–294.

Friedman, W. J. (1987). A follow-up to "Scale effects in memory for the time of events": The earthquake study. *Memory & Cognition, 15*, 518–520.

Friedman, W. J. (1990). *About time: Inventing the fourth dimension*. Cambridge, MA: MIT Press.

Friedman, W. J. (1993). Memory for the time of past events. *Psychological Bulletin, 113*, 44–66.

Friedman, W. J., & Wilkins, A. J. (1985). Scale effects in memory for the time of events. *Memory & Cognition, 13*, 168–175.

Friendly, M., Franklin, P. E., Hoffman, D., & Rubin, D. C. (1982). The Toronto word pool: Norms for imagery, concreteness, orthographic variables, and grammatical usage for 1080 words. *Behavior Research Methods & Instruments, 14*, 375–399.

Fromholt, P. & Larsen, S. F. (1991). Autobiographical memory in normal ageing and primary degenerative dementia (dementia of the Alzheimer type). *Journal of Gerontology: Psychological Sciences, 46*, 85–91.

Fromholt, P., & Larsen, S. F. (1992). Autobiographical memory and life-history narratives in ageing and dementia (Alzheimer type). In M. A. Conway, D. C. Rubin, H. Spinnler, & W. A. Wagenaar (Eds.), *Theoretical perspectives on autobiographical memory*. Dordrecht, The Netherlands: Kluwer Academic Publishers.

Fuchs, A. H. (1969). Recall for order and content of serial word lists in short-term memory. *Journal of Experimental Psychology, 82*, 14–21.

Fuchs, A. H., & Melton, A. W. (1974). Effects of frequency of presentation and stimulus length on retention in the Brown-Peterson paradigm. *Journal of Experimental Psychology, 103*, 629–637.

Fujisaki, H., & Kawashima, T. (1970). Some experiments on speech perception and a model for the perceptual mechanism. *Annual Report of the Engineering Research Institute, Faculty of Engineering, University of Tokyo, 29*, 207–214.

Funahashi, S., Bruce, C. J., & Goldman-Rakic, P. S. (1989). Mnemonic coding of visual space in the monkey's dorsolateral prefrontal cortex. *Journal of Neurophysiology, 61*, 331–349.

Fuster, J. M. (1995). Gradients of cortical plasticity. In J. L. McGaugh, N. M. Weinberger, & G. Lynch (Eds.), *Brain and memory: Modulation and mediation of neuroplasticity*. New York: Oxford University Press.

Fuster, J. M., & Jervey, J. P. (1981). Inferotemporal neurons distinguish and retain behaviorally relevant features of visual stimuli. *Science, 212,* 952–955.

Galton, F. (1883). *Inquiries into human faculty and its development*. London: Dent.

Gardiner, J. M. (1988). Functional aspects of recollective experience. *Memory & Cognition, 16,* 309–313.

Gardiner, J. M., Craik, F. I. M., & Birtwistle, J. (1972). Retrieval cues and release from proactive inhibition. *Journal of Verbal Learning and Verbal Behavior, 11,* 778–783.

Gardiner, J. M., & Gregg, V. H. (1979). When auditory memory is not overwritten. *Journal of Verbal Learning and Verbal Behavior, 18,* 705–719.

Gardiner, J. M., & Java, R. I. (1990). Recollective experience in word and nonword recognition. *Memory & Cognition, 18,* 23–30.

Gardiner, J. M., & Java, R. I. (1991). Forgetting in recognition memory with and without recollective experience. *Memory & Cognition, 19,* 617–623.

Gardiner, J. M., & Java, R. I. (1993). Recognition memory and awareness: An experiential approach. *European Journal of Cognitive Psychology, 5,* 337–346.

Gardiner, J. M., & Parkin, A. J. (1990). Attention and recollective experience in recognition memory. *Memory & Cognition, 18,* 579–583.

Gardner, H. (1985). *The mind's new science: A history of the cognitive revolution*. New York: Basic Books.

Garner, W. R. (1974). *The processing of information and structure*. Hillsdale, NJ: Erlbaum.

Garner, W. R., Hake, H. W., & Ericksen, C. W. (1956). Operationism and the concept of perception. *Psychological Review, 63,* 149–159.

Garry, M., Manning, C. G., Loftus, E. F., & Sherman, S. J. (1996). Imagination inflation: Imagining a childhood event inflates confidence that it occurred. *Psychonomic Bulletin & Review, 3,* 208–214.

Gathercole, S. E., Adams, A.-M., Hitch, G. J. (1994). Do young children rehearse? An individual-differences analysis. *Memory & Cognition, 22,* 201–207.

Gathercole, S. E., & Baddeley, A. D. (1993). *Working memory and language*. Hove, UK: Erlbaum.

Gauld, A., & Stephenson, G. M. (1967). Some experiments related to Bartlett's theory of remembering. *British Journal of Psychology, 58,* 39–49.

Geiselman, R. E., & Bjork, R. A. (1980). Primary versus secondary rehearsal in imagined voices: Differential effects on recognition. *Cognitive Psychology, 12,* 188–205.

Geiselman, R. E., & Callot, R. (1990) Reverse versus forward order recall of script based texts. *Applied Cognitive Psychology, 4,* 141–144.

Geiselman, R. E., & Fisher, R. P. (1997). Ten years of cognitive interviewing. In D. G. Payne & F. G. Conrad (Eds.), *Intersections in basic and applied memory research*. Mahwah, NJ: Erlbaum.

Geiselman, R. E., Fisher, R. P., MacKinnon, D. P., & Holland, H. L. (1985). Eyewitness memory enhancement in the police interview: Cognitive retrieval mnemonics versus hypnosis. *Journal of Applied Psychology, 70,* 401–412.

Geiselman, R. E., & Glenny, J. (1977). Effects of imagining speakers' voices on the retention of words presented visually. *Memory & Cognition, 5,* 499–504.

Gerrig, R. J. (1989). Suspense in the absence of uncertainty. *Journal of Memory and Language, 28,* 633–648.

Gillund, G., & Shiffrin, R. M. (1984). A retrieval model for both recognition and recall. *Psychological Review, 91,* 1–65.

Giray, E. F., Altkin, W. M., Vaught, G. M., & Roodin, P. A. (1985). A life span approach to the study of eidetic imagery. *Journal of Mental Imagery, 9,* 21–32.

Glanzer, M. (1972). Storage mechanisms in recall. In G. H. Bower & J. T. Spence (Eds.), *The psychology of learning and motivation* (Vol. 5). New York: Academic Press.

Glanzer, M., & Adams, J. K. (1985). The mirror effect in recognition memory. *Memory & Cognition, 13,* 8–20.

Glanzer, M., & Adams, J. K. (1990). The mirror effect in recognition memory: Data and theory. *Journal of Experimental Psychology: Learning, Memory, and Cognition, 16,* 5–16.

Glanzer, M., Adams, J. K., & Iverson, G. J. (1991). Forgetting and the mirror effect in recognition memory: Concentering of underlying distributions. *Journal of Experimental Psychology: Learning, Memory, and Cognition, 17,* 81–93.

Glanzer, M., Adams, J. K., Iverson, G. J., & Kim, K. (1993). The regularities of recognition memory. *Psychological Review, 100,* 546–567.

Glanzer, M., & Cunitz, A. R. (1966). Two storage mechanisms in free recall. *Journal of Verbal Learning and Verbal Behavior, 5,* 351–360.

Glaze, J. A. (1928). The association value of nonsense syllables. *Journal of Genetic Psychology, 35,* 255–269.

Glenberg, A. M., Bradley, M. M., Kraus, T. A., & Renzaglia, G. J. (1983). Studies of the long-term recency effect: Support for the contextually guided retrieval hypothesis. *Journal of Experimental Psychology: Learning, Memory and Cognition, 9,* 231–255.

Glisky, G. L., & Schacter, D. L. (1987). Acquisition of domain-specific knowledge in organic amnesia: Training for computer-related work. *Neuropsychologia, 25,* 893–906.

Glucksberg, S., & McCloskey, M. (1981). Decisions about ignorance: Knowing that you don't know. *Journal of Experimental Psychology: Human Learning and Memory, 7,* 311–325.

Godden, D. R., & Baddeley, A. D. (1975). Context-dependent memory in two natural environments: On land and underwater. *British Journal of Psychology, 66*, 325–331.

Godden, D. R., & Baddeley, A. D. (1980). When does context influence recognition memory? *British Journal of Psychology, 71*, 99–104.

Goldstein, A. G., & Chance, J. E. (1970). Visual recognition memory for complex configurations. *Perception & Psychophysics, 9*, 237–241.

Goodwin, D. W., Powell, B., Bremer, D., Hoine, H., & Stern, J. (1969). Alcohol and recall: State dependent effects in man. *Science, 163*, 1358.

Gorfein, D. S. (1987). Explaining context effects on short-term memory. In D. S. Gorfein & R. R. Hoffman (Eds.), *Memory and learning: The Ebbinghaus Centennial Conference.* Hillsdale, NJ: Erlbaum.

Graf, P. (1990). Life-span changes in implicit and explicit memory. *Bulletin of the Psychonomic Society, 28*, 353–358.

Graf, P., & Mandler, G. (1984). Activation makes words more accessible, but not necessarily more retrievable. *Journal of Verbal Learning and Verbal Behavior, 23*, 553–568.

Graf, P., & Schacter, D. L. (1985). Implicit and explicit memory for new associations in normal and amnesic subjects. *Journal of Experimental Psychology: Learning, Memory, and Cognition, 11*, 501–518.

Graf, P., & Schacter, D. L. (1987). Selective effects of interference on implicit and explicit memory for new associations. *Journal of Experimental Psychology: Learning, Memory, and Cognition, 13*, 45–53.

Gravitz, M. A. (1994). Memory reconstruction by hypnosis as a therapeutic technique. *Psychotherapy, 31*, 687–691.

Gravitz, M. A. (1995). First admission (1846) of hypnotic testimony in court. *American Journal of Clinical Hypnosis, 37*, 326–330.

Gray, C. R., & Gummerman, K. (1975). The enigmatic eidetic image: A critical examination of methods, data, and theory. *Psychological Bulletin, 82*, 383–407.

Greco, C., Rovee-Collier, C., Hayne, H., Griesler, P., & Earley, L. (1986). Ontogeny of early event memory: I. Forgetting and retrieval by 2- and 3-month-olds. *Infant Behavior and Development, 9*, 441–460.

Green, D. M., & Swets, J. A. (1966). *Signal detection theory and psychophysics.* New York: Wiley.

Greenbaum, J. L., & Graf, P. (1989). Preschool period development of implicit and explicit remembering. *Bulletin of the Psychonomic Society, 27*, 417–420.

Greene, R. L. (1986). A common basis for recency effects in immediate and delayed recall. *Journal of Experimental Psychology: Learning, Memory and Cognition, 12*, 413–418.

Greene, R. L. (1989). Spacing effects in memory: Evidence for a two-process account. *Journal of Experimental Psychology: Learning, Memory, and Cognition, 15*, 371–377.

Greene, R. L. (1992). *Human memory: Paradigms and paradoxes.* Hillsdale, NJ: Erlbaum.

Greene, R. L. (1996). Mirror effect in order and associative information: Role of response strategies. *Journal of Experimental Psychology: Learning, Memory, and Cognition, 22*, 687–695.

Greene, R. L., & Crowder, R. G. (1984). Modality and suffix effects in the absence of auditory stimulation. *Journal of Verbal Learning and Verbal Behavior, 23*, 371–382.

Greene, R. L., & Thapar, A. (1994). Mirror effect in frequency discrimination. *Journal of Experimental Psychology: Learning, Memory, and Cognition, 20*, 946–952.

Greenough, W. T., Black, J. E., & Wallace, C. S. (1987). Experience and brain development. *Child Development, 58*, 539–559.

Greenwald, A. G., Spangenberg, E. R., Pratkanis, A. R., & Eskenazi, J. (1991). Double-blind tests of subliminal self-help audiotapes. *Psychological Science, 2*, 119–122.

Gregg, V. H. (1976). Word frequency, recognition and recall. In J. Brown (Ed.), *Recall and recognition.* London: Wiley.

Gruneberg, M. M. (1994). *French by association.* Lincolnwood, IL: Passport Books.

Gruneberg, M. M. (1998). A commentary on criticism of the keyword method of learning foreign languages. *Applied Cognitive Psychology, 12*, 529–532.

Gruneberg, M. M., & Ellis, N. (1995). Retention of foreign language vocabulary using the keyword method: A ten year follow-up. *Second Language Research, 11*, 112–120.

Gruneberg, M. M., & Pascoe, K. (1996). The effectiveness of the keyword method for receptive and productive foreign vocabulary learning in the elderly. *Contemporary Educational Psychology, 21*, 102–109.

Gunter, B., Berry, C., & Clifford, B. R. (1981). Proactive interference effects with television news items: Further evidence. *Journal of Experimental Psychology: Learning, Memory, and Cognition, 7*, 480–487.

Haber, R. N. (1979). Twenty years of haunting eidetic imagery: Where's the ghost? *Behavioral and Brain Sciences, 2*, 583–629.

Haber, R. N. (1983). The impending demise of the icon: A critique of the concept of iconic storage in visual information processing. *Behavioral and Brain Sciences, 6*, 1–54.

Haber, R. N., & Haber, R. B. (1964). Eidetic imagery: I. Frequency. *Perceptual & Motor Skills, 19*, 131–138.

Haber, R. N., & Hershenson, M. (1973). *The psychology of visual perception.* New York: Holt, Rinehart & Winston.

Haber, R. N., & Standing, L. G. (1969). Direct measures of short-term visual storage. *Quarterly Journal of Experimental Psychology, 21*, 43–54.

Hall, J. F. (1954). Learning as a function of word frequency. *American Journal of Psychology, 67*, 138–140.

Halliday, M. S., Hitch, G. J., Lennon, B., & Pettipher, C. (1990). Verbal short-term memory in children: The role of the articulatory loop. *European Journal of Cognitive Psychology, 2*, 23–38.

Hanawalt, N. G., & Demarest, I. H. (1939). The effect of verbal suggestion in the recall period upon the reproduction of visually perceived forms. *Journal of Experimental Psychology, 25*, 159–174.

Hart, J., Berndt, R. S., & Caramazza, A. (1985). Category-specific naming deficit following cerebral infarction. *Nature, 316*, 439–440.

Hasher, L., & Chromiak, W. (1977). The processing of frequency information: An automatic mechanism? *Journal of Verbal Learning and Verbal Behavior, 16*, 173–184.

Hasher, L., & Griffin, M. (1978). Reconstructive and reproductive processes in memory. *Journal of Experimental Psychology: Human Learning and Memory, 4*, 318–330.

Hasher, L., & Zacks, R. T. (1979). Automatic and effortful processes in memory. *Journal of Experimental Psychology: General, 108*, 356–388.

Hasher, L., & Zacks, R. T. (1988). Working memory, comprehension, and aging: A review and a new view. In G. H. Bower (Ed.), *The psychology of learning and motivation* (Vol. 22). San Diego: Academic Press.

Hasher, L., Zacks, R. T., & May, C. P. (1999). Inhibitory control, circadian arousal, and age. In D. Gopher & A. Koriat (Eds.), *Attention and performance XVII.* Cambridge, MA: MIT Press.

Hashtroudi, S., Johnson, M. K., & Chrosniak, L. D. (1989). Aging and source monitoring. *Psychology and Aging, 4*, 106–112.

Hashtroudi, S., Johnson, M. K., & Chrosniak, L. D. (1990). Aging and qualitative characteristics of memories for perceived and imagined complex events. *Psychology and Aging, 5*, 119–126.

Hay, J. F., & Jacoby, L. L. (1999). Separating habit and recollection in young and older adults: Effects of elaborative processing and distinctiveness. *Psychology and Aging, 14*, 122–134.

Healy, A. F. (1974). Separating item from order information in short-term memory. *Journal of Verbal Learning and Verbal Behavior, 13*, 644–655.

Healy, A. F. (1982). Short-term memory for order information. In G. H. Bower (Ed.), *The psychology of learning and motivation* (Vol. 16). New York: Academic Press.

Healy, A. F., Fendrich, D. W., Cunningham, T. F., & Till, R. E. (1987). Effects of cueing on short-term retention of order information. *Journal of Experimental Psychology: Learning, Memory, and Cognition, 13*, 413–425.

Hebb, D. O. (1949). *The organization of behavior: A neuropsychological theory.* New York: Wiley.

Hebb, D. O. (1961). Distinctive features of learning in the higher animal. In J. F. Delafresnaye (Ed.), *Brain mechanisms and learning: A symposium.* Oxford, UK: Blackwell Scientific Publications.

Hebb, D. O. (1968). Concerning imagery. *Psychological Review, 75*, 466–467.

Heller, N. (1956). An application of psychological learning theory. *Journal of Marketing, 20*, 248–254.

Hellige, J. B. (1975). Hemispheric processing differences revealed by differential conditioning and reaction time performance. *Journal of Experimental Psychology: General, 104*, 309–326.

Hellige, J. B. (1990). Hemispheric asymmetry. *Annual Review of Psychology, 41*, 55–80.

Hellyer, S. (1962). Frequency of stimulus presentation and short-term decrement in recall. *Journal of Experimental Psychology, 64*, 650.

Helson, H. (1964). *Adaptation-level theory.* New York: Harper & Row.

Henson, R. N. A. (1998). Short-term memory for serial order: The start–end model. *Cognitive Psychology, 36*, 73–137.

Herold, M. (1982). *You can have a near-perfect memory.* Chicago: Contemporary Books.

Herrmann, D. J., & Chaffin, R. (Eds.). (1988). *Memory in historical perspective: The literature before Ebbinghaus.* New York: Springer-Verlag.

Herrmann, D. J., Weingartner, H., Searleman, A., & McEvoy, C. (Eds.). (1992). *Memory improvement: Implications for memory theory.* New York: Springer-Verlag.

Herrnstein, R. J., & Boring, E. G. (Eds.). (1965). *A source book in the history of psychology.* Cambridge, MA: Harvard University Press.

Hertel, P. (1992). Emotion, mood, and memory. In L. R. Squire (Ed.), *Encyclopedia of learning and memory.* New York: Macmillan.

Hertzog, C. (1992). Improving memory: The possible roles of metamemory. In D. J. Herrmann, H. Weingartner, A. Searleman, & C. McEvoy (Eds.), *Memory improvement: Implications for memory theory.* New York: Springer-Verlag.

Herz, R. S., & Eich, E. (1995). Commentary and envoi. In F. R. Schab & R. G. Crowder (Eds.), *Memory for odors.* Mahwah, NJ: Erlbaum.

Hill, W. L., Borovsky, D., & Rovee-Collier, C. (1988). Continuities in infant memory development. *Developmental Psychobiology, 21*, 43–62.

Hillis, A. E., & Caramazza, A. (1991). Category-specific naming and comprehension impairment: A double dissociation. *Brain, 114*, 2081–2094.

Hinrichs, J. V. (1970). A two-process memory-strength theory for judgment of recency. *Psychological Review, 77*, 223–233.

Hinrichs, J. V., & Buschke, H. (1968). Judgment of recency under steady-state conditions. *Journal of Experimental Psychology, 78*, 574–579.

Hinrichs, J. V., Mewaldt, S. P., & Redding, J. (1973). The Ranschburg effect: Repetition and guessing factors in short-term memory. *Journal of Verbal Learning and Verbal Behavior, 12,* 64–75.

Hintzman, D. L. (1967). Articulatory coding in short-term memory. *Journal of Verbal Learning and Verbal Behavior, 6,* 312–316.

Hintzman, D. L. (1974a). Psychology and the cow's belly. *The Worm Runner's Digest, 16,* 84–85.

Hintzman, D. L. (1974b). Theoretical implications of the spacing effect. In R. L. Solso (Ed.), *Theories of cognitive psychology: The Loyola symposium.* Hillsdale, NJ: Erlbaum.

Hintzman, D. L. (1978). *The psychology of learning and memory.* San Francisco: Freeman.

Hintzman, D. L. (1984a). Episodic versus semantic memory: A distinction whose time has come—and gone? *Behavioral and Brain Sciences, 7,* 240–241.

Hintzman, D. L. (1984b). MINERVA 2: A simulation model of human memory. *Behavior Research Methods, Instruments, & Computers, 16,* 96–101.

Hintzman, D. L. (1986). "Schema abstraction" in a multiple-trace memory model. *Psychological Review, 93,* 411–428.

Hintzman, D. L. (1987). Recognition and recall in MINERVA 2: Analysis of the "recognition-failure" paradigm. In P. E. Morris (Ed.), *Modeling cognition.* Chichester, UK: Wiley.

Hintzman, D. L. (1988). Judgments of frequency and recognition memory in a multiple-trace memory model. *Psychological Review, 95,* 528–551.

Hintzman, D. L. (1991). Why are formal models useful in psychology? In W. E. Hockley & S. Lewandowsky (Eds.), *Relating theory and data: Essays on human memory in honor of Bennet B. Murdock.* Hillsdale, NJ: Erlbaum.

Hintzman, D. L. (1992). Mathematical constraints on the Tulving-Wiseman law. *Psychological Review, 99,* 536–542.

Hintzman, D. L., Block, R. A., & Summers, J. J. (1973). Contextual associations and memory for serial position. *Journal of Experimental Psychology, 97,* 220–229.

Hintzman, D. L., Caulton, D. A., & Curran, T. (1994). Retrieval constraints and the mirror effect. *Journal of Experimental Psychology: Learning, Memory, and Cognition, 20,* 275–289.

Hintzman, D. L., & Curran, T. (1997). More than one way to violate independence: Reply to Jacoby and Shrout (1997). *Journal of Experimental Psychology: Learning, Memory, and Cognition, 23,* 511–513.

Hirst, W., Johnson, M. K., Phelps, E. A., & Volpe, B. T. (1988). More on recognition and recall in amnesics. *Journal of Experimental Psychology: Learning, Memory, and Cognition, 14,* 758–763.

Hitch, G. J., Halliday, M. S., Dodd, A., & Littler, J. E. (1989). Development of rehearsal in short-term memory: Differences between pictorial and spoken stimuli. *British Journal of Developmental Psychology, 7,* 347–362.

Hockley, W. E. (1982). Retrieval processes in continuous recognition. *Journal of Experimental Psychology: Learning, Memory, and Cognition, 8,* 497–512.

Hockley, W. E. (1994). Reflections of the mirror effect for item and associative recognition. *Memory & Cognition, 22,* 713–722.

Hockley, W. E., & Murdock, B. B., Jr. (1987). A decision model for accuracy and response latency in recognition memory. *Psychological Review, 94,* 341–358.

Hollingworth, H. C. (1913). Characteristic differences between recall and recognition. *American Journal of Psychology, 24,* 532–544.

Holmes, A., & Conway, M. A. (1999). Generation identity and the reminiscence bump: Memories for public and private events. *Journal of Adult Development, 6,* 21–34.

Holmes, D. (1990). The evidence for repression: An examination of sixty years of research. In J. Singer (Ed.), *Repression and dissociation: Implications for personality theory, psychotherapy, and health.* Chicago: University of Chicago Press.

Homa, D., Cross, J., Cornell, D., Goldman, D., & Schwartz, S. (1973). Prototype abstraction and classification of new instances as a function of number of instances defining the prototype. *Journal of Experimental Psychology, 101,* 116–122.

Honeck, R. P. (1986). A serendipitous finding in face recognition. *Bulletin of the Psychonomic Society, 24,* 369–371.

Horel, J. A. (1994). Some comments on the special cognitive functions claimed for the hippocampus. *Cortex, 30,* 269–280.

Howard, D. V., & Howard, J. H. (1992). Adult age differences in the rate of learning serial patterns: Evidence from direct and indirect tests. *Psychology and Aging, 7,* 232–241.

Howard, D. V., Shaw, R. J., & Heisey, J. G. (1986). Aging and the time course of semantic activation. *Journal of Gerontology, 41,* 195–203.

Howe, M. L., & Courage, M. L. (1993). On resolving the enigma of infantile amnesia. *Psychological Bulletin, 113,* 305–326.

Hudson, J. A., & Fivush, R. (1983). Categorical and schematic organization and the development of retrieval strategies. *Journal of Experimental Child Psychology, 36,* 32–42.

Hudson, J. A., & Fivush, R. (1991). As time goes by: Sixth graders remember a kindergarten experience. *Applied Cognitive Psychology, 5,* 346–360.

Hull, C. L. (1943). *Principles of behavior.* New York: Appleton-Century-Crofts.

Hulme, C., Lee, G., & Brown, G. D. A. (1993). Short-term memory impairment in Alzheimer-type dementia: Evidence for separable impairments of articulatory rehearsal and long-term memory. *Neuropsychologica*, 34, 161–172.

Hulme, C., Maughan, S., & Brown, G. D. A. (1991). Memory for familiar and unfamiliar words: Evidence for a long-term memory contribution to short-term memory span. *Journal of Memory and Language*, 6, 685–701.

Hulme, C., Roodenrys, S., Brown, G. D. A., & Mercer, R. (1995). The role of long-term memory mechanisms in memory span. *British Journal of Psychology*, 86, 527–536.

Hulme, C., Thomson, N., Muir, C., & Lawrence, A. (1984). Speech rate and the development of short-term memory span. *Journal of Experimental Child Psychology*, 38, 241–253.

Hulme, C., & Tordoff, V. (1989). Working memory development: The effects of speech rate, word length, and acoustic similarity on serial recall. *Journal of Experimental Child Psychology*, 47, 72–87.

Hultsch, D. F., Hertzog, C., Dixon, R. A., & Small, B. J. (1998). *Memory change in the aged*. Cambridge, UK: Cambridge University Press.

Humphreys, G. W., & Bruce, V. (1989). *Visual cognition: Computational, experimental, and neuropsychological perspectives*. Hove, UK: Erlbaum.

Hunt, E., & Love, T. (1972). How good can memory be? In A. W. Melton & E. Martin (Eds.), *Coding processes in human memory*. Washington, DC: Winston.

Hunt, R. R. (1995). The subtlety of distinctiveness: What von Restorff really did. *Psychonomic Bulletin & Review*, 2, 105–112.

Hunt, R. R., & Einstein, G. O. (1981). Relational and item-specific information in memory. *Journal of Verbal Learning and Verbal Behavior*, 20, 497–514.

Hunt, R. R., & McDaniel, M. A. (1993). The enigma of organization and distinctiveness. *Journal of Memory and Language*, 32, 421–445.

Hunter, I. M. L. (1962). An exceptional talent for calculative thinking. *British Journal of Psychology*, 53, 243–258.

Huppert, F. A., & Piercy, M. (1978a). Dissociation between learning and remembering in organic amnesia. *Nature*, 275, 317–318.

Huppert, F. A., & Piercy, M. (1978b). The role of trace strength in recency and frequency judgments by amnesic and control subjects. *Quarterly Journal of Experimental Psychology*, 30, 347–354.

Huttenlocher, J., Hedges, L. V., & Bradburn, N. M. (1990). Reports of elapsed time: Bounding and rounding processes in estimation. *Journal of Experimental Psychology: Learning, Memory, and Cognition*, 16, 196–213.

Huttenlocher, J., Hedges, L. V., & Prohaska, V. (1992). Memory for day of the week: A 5+2 day cycle. *Journal of Experimental Psychology: General*, 121, 313–326.

Hyde, T. S., & Jenkins, J. J. (1973). Recall of words as a function of semantic, graphic, and syntactic orienting tasks. *Journal of Verbal Learning and Verbal Behavior*, 12, 471–480.

Hyman, I. E., Jr., & Billings, F. J. (1998). Individual differences and the creation of false childhood memories. *Memory*, 1–20.

Hyman, I. E., Jr., Husband, T. H., & Billings, F. J. (1995). False memories of childhood experiences. *Applied Cognition Psychology*, 9, 181–197.

Hyman, I. E., Jr., & Pentland, J. (1996). The role of mental imagery in the creation of false childhood memories. *Journal of Memory and Language*, 35, 101–117.

Intons-Peterson, M. J. (1983). Imagery paradigms: How vulnerable are they to experimenters' expectations? *Journal of Experimental Psychology: Human Perception and Performance*, 9, 394–412.

Intons-Peterson, M. J. (1992). Components of auditory imagery. In D. Reisberg (Ed.), *Auditory imagery*. Hillsdale, NJ: Erlbaum.

Intraub, H., & Richardson, M. (1989). Wide-angle memories of close-up scenes. *Journal of Experimental Psychology: Learning, Memory, and Cognition*, 15, 179–187.

Jacobs, J. (1887). Experiments on "prehension." *Mind*, 12, 75–79.

Jacoby, L. L. (1983). Remembering the data: Analyzing interactive processes in reading. *Journal of Verbal Learning and Verbal Behavior*, 22, 485–508.

Jacoby, L. L. (1984). Incidental versus intentional retrieval: Remembering and awareness as separate issues. In L. R. Squire & N. Butters (Eds.), *The neuropsychology of memory*. New York: Guilford.

Jacoby, L. L. (1991). A process dissociation framework: Separating automatic from intentional uses of memory. *Journal of Memory and Language*, 30, 513–541.

Jacoby, L. L., Begg, I. M., & Toth, J. P. (1997). In defense of functional independence: Violations of assumptions underlying the process-dissociation procedure? *Journal of Experimental Psychology: Learning, Memory, and Cognition*, 23, 484–495.

Jacoby, L. L., & Dallas, M. (1981). On the relationship between autobiographical memory and perceptual learning. *Journal of Experimental Psychology: General*, 110, 306–340.

Jacoby, L. L., & Hollingshead, A. (1990). Toward a generate/recognize model of performance on direct and indirect tests of memory. *Journal of Memory and Language*, 29, 433–454.

Jacoby, L. L., & Shrout, P. E. (1997). Toward a psychometric analysis of violations of the independence assumption in process dissociation. *Journal of Experimental Psychology: Learning, Memory, and Cognition*, 23, 505–510.

Jacoby, L. L., Toth, J. P., & Yonelinas, A. P. (1993). Separating conscious and unconscious influences of memory: Measuring recollection. *Journal of Experimental Psychology: General, 122,* 139–154.

Jacoby, L. L., Woloshyn, V., & Kelley, C. (1989). Becoming famous without being recognized: Unconscious influences of memory produced by dividing attention. *Journal of Experimental Psychology: General, 118,* 115–125.

James, W. (1890). *The principles of psychology.* New York: Henry Holt. [Reprinted as W. James. (1983). *The principles of psychology.* Cambridge, MA: Harvard University Press.]

Jarrard L. E. (1989). On the use of ibotenic acid to lesion selectively different components of the hippocampal formation. *Journal of Neuroscience Methods, 29,* 251–259.

Java, R. I., & Gardiner, J. M. (1991). Priming and aging: Further evidence of preserved memory function. *American Journal of Psychology, 104,* 89–100.

Jenkins, J. G., & Dallenbach, K. M. (1924). Obliviscence during sleep and waking. *American Journal of Psychology, 35,* 605–612.

Jennings, J. M., & Jacoby, L. L. (1993). Automatic versus intentional uses of memory: Aging, attention, and control. *Psychology and Aging, 8,* 283–293.

Jevons, W. S. (1871). The power of numerical discrimination. *Nature, 3,* 281–282.

Johnson, G. J. (1991). A distinctiveness model of serial learning. *Psychological Review, 98,* 204–217.

Johnson, M. K. (1985). The origin of memories. In P. C. Kendall (Ed.), *Advances in cognitive behavioral research and therapy* (Vol. 4). New York: Academic Press.

Johnson, M. K., Bransford, J. D., & Solomon, S. K. (1973). Memory for tacit implications of sentences. *Journal of Experimental Psychology, 98,* 203–205.

Johnson, M. K., & Chalfonte, B. L. (1994). Binding complex memories: The role of reactivation and the hippocampus. In D. L. Schacter & E. Tulving (Eds.), *Memory systems 1994.* Cambridge, MA: MIT Press.

Johnson, M. K., De Leonardis, D. M., Hashtroudi, S., & Ferguson, S. A. (1995). Aging and single versus multiple cues in source monitoring. *Psychology and Aging, 10,* 507–517.

Johnson, M. K., Foley, M. A., Suengas, A. G., & Raye, C. L. (1988). Phenomenal charactersistics of memories for perceived and imagined autobiographical events. *Journal of Experimental Psychology: General, 117,* 371–376.

Johnson, M. K., & Hasher, L. (1987). Human learning and memory. *Annual Review of Psychology, 38,* 631–668.

Johnson, M. K., Kahan, T. L., & Raye, C. L. (1984). Dreams and reality monitoring. *Journal of Experimental Psychology: General, 113,* 329–344.

Johnson, M. K., Kounios, J., & Reeder, J. A. (1994). Time-course studies of reality monitoring and recognition. *Journal of Experimental Psychology: Learning, Memory, and Cognition, 20,* 1409–1419.

Johnson, M. K., & Raye, C. L. (1981). Reality monitoring. *Psychological Review, 88,* 67–85.

Johnson, M. K., Raye, C. L., Wang, A. Y., & Taylor, T. H. (1979). Fact and fantasy: The roles of accuracy and variability in confusing imaginations with perceptual experiences. *Journal of Experimental Psychology: Learning, Memory, and Cognition, 5,* 229–240.

Jolicoeur, P., & Kosslyn, S. M. (1985). Is time to scan visual images due to demand characteristics? *Memory & Cognition, 13,* 320–332.

Jones, D. M., & Macken, W. J. (1993). Irrelevant tones produce an irrelevant speech effect: Implications for phonological coding in working memory. *Journal of Experimental Psychology: Learning, Memory, and Cognition, 19,* 369–381.

Jones, D. M., & Macken, W. J. (1995). Phonological similarity in the irrelevant speech effect: Within- or between-stream similarity? *Journal of Experimental Psychology: Learning, Memory, and Cognition, 21,* 103–115.

Jones, G. V. (1988). Images, predicates, and retrieval cues. In M. Denis, J. Englekamp, & J. T. E. Richardson (Eds.), *Cognitive and neuropsychological approaches to mental imagery.* Dordrecht, The Netherlands: Nijhoff.

Joordens, S., & Hockley, W. E. (2000). Recollection and familiarity through the looking glass: When old does not mirror new. *Journal of Experimental Psychology: Learning, Memory, and Cognition, 26,* 1534–1555.

Kaas, J. H. (1995). The plasticity of sensory representations in adult primates. In J. L. McGaugh, N. M. Weinberger, & G. Lynch (Eds.), *Brain and memory: Modulation and mediation of neuroplasticity.* New York: Oxford University Press.

Kahn, R. L., Zarit, S. H., Hilbert, N. M., & Niederehe, G. A. (1975). Memory complaint and impairment in the aged: The effect of depression and altered brain function. *Archives of General Psychiatry, 32,* 1560–1573.

Kail, R. V., & Salthouse, T. A. (1994). Processing speed as a mental capacity. *Acta Psychologica, 86,* 199–225.

Kallman, H. J., & Massaro, D. W. (1983). Backward masking, the suffix effect, and perceptual storage. *Journal of Experimental Psychology: Learning, Memory, & Cognition, 9,* 312–327.

Kandel, E. R. (1977). Neuronal plasticity and the modification of behavior. In J. M. Brookhart & V. B. Mountcastle (Eds.), *Handbook of physiology: The nervous system* (Vol. 1). Bethesda, MD: American Physiological Society.

Kapur, S., Craik, F. I. M., Jones, C., Brown, G. M., Houle, S., & Tulving, E. (1995). Functional role of the prefrontal cortex in retrieval of memories: A PET study. *Neuroreport, 6,* 1880–1884.

Katona, G. (1940). *Organizing and memorizing: Studies in the psychology of learning and teaching.* New York: Columbia University Press.

Kausler, D. H., & Puckett, J. M. (1980). Adult age differences in recognition memory for a non-semantic attribute. *Experimental Aging Research, 6,* 349–355.

Kausler, D. H., & Puckett, J. M. (1981). Adult age differences in memory for modality attributes. *Experimental Aging Research, 7,* 117–125.

Kelley, C. M., & Jacoby, L. L. (1996). Adult egocentrism: Subjective experience versus analytic bases for judgment. *Journal of Memory and Language, 35,* 157–175.

Kendrick, K. M., & Baldwin, B. A. (1987). Cells in temporal cortex of conscious sheep can respond preferentially to the sight of faces. *Science, 236,* 448–450.

Keppel, G. (1964). Facilitation in short- and long-term retention of paired-associates following distributed practice in learning. *Journal of Verbal Learning and Verbal Behavior, 3,* 91–111.

Keppel, G. (1967). A reconsideration of the extinction–recovery theory. *Journal of Verbal Learning and Verbal Behavior, 6,* 476–486.

Keppel, G. (1984). Consolidation and forgetting theory. In H. Weingartner & E. S. Parker (Eds.), *Memory consolidation: Psychobiology of cognition.* Hillsdale, NJ: Erlbaum.

Keppel, G., & Underwood, B. J. (1962). Proactive inhibition in short-term retention of single items. *Journal of Verbal Learning and Verbal Behavior, 1,* 153–161.

Kerr, N. H. (1983). The role of vision in "visual imagery" experiments: Evidence from the congenitally blind. *Journal of Experimental Psychology: General, 112,* 265–277.

Kerst, S. M., & Howard, J. H. (1978). Memory psychophysics for visual area and length. *Memory & Cognition, 6,* 327–335.

Kihlstrom, J. F. (1994). Hypnosis, delayed recall, and the principles of memory. *International Journal of Clinical and Experimental Hypnosis, 42,* 337–345.

Kihlstrom, J. F., & Harackiewicz, J. M. (1982). The earliest recollection: A new survey. *Journal of Personality, 50,* 134–138.

Kinsbourne, M., & Cook, J. (1971). Generalized and lateralized effects of concurrent verbalization on a unimanual skill. *Quarterly Journal of Experimental Psychology, 23,* 341–345.

Kinsbourne, M., & George, J. (1974). The mechanism of the word-frequency effect on recognition memory. *Journal of Verbal Learning & Verbal Behavior, 13,* 63–69.

Kintsch, W. (1970). Models for free recall and recognition. In D. A. Norman (Ed.), *Models of human memory.* New York: Academic Press.

Kintsch, W. (1977). *Memory and cognition.* New York: Wiley.

Kintsch, W., & Buschke, H. (1969). Homophones and synonyms in short-term memory. *Journal of Experimental Psychology, 80,* 403–407.

Kintsch, W., Healy, A. F., Hegarty, M., Pennington, B. F., & Salthouse, T. A. (1999). Models of working memory: Eight questions and some general issues. In A. Miyake & P. Shah (Eds.), *Models of working memory: Mechanisms of active maintenance and executive control.* New York: Cambridge University Press.

Kirkpatrick, E. A. (1894). An experimental study of memory. *Psychological Review, 1,* 602–609.

Klatzky, R. L. (1984). *Memory and awareness: An information-processing perspective.* New York: Freeman.

Klatzky, R. L., & Atkinson, R. C. (1971). Specialization of the cerebral hemispheres in scanning for information in short-term memory. *Perception & Psychophysics, 10,* 335–338.

Knoedler, A. J. (1996). *Discrimination, response bias, and context: An explanation for elusive environmental context effects in recognition memory.* Unpublished doctoral dissertation, Purdue University.

Knoedler, A. J., Hellwig, K. A., & Neath, I. (1999). The shift from recency to primacy with increasing delay. *Journal of Experimental Psychology: Learning, Memory and Cognition, 25,* 474–487.

Koechlin, E., Basso, G., Pietrini, P., Panzer, S., & Grafman, J. (1999). The role of the anterior prefrontal cortex in human cognition. *Nature, 399,* 148–151.

Koenig, O., Wetzel, C., & Caramazza, A. (1992). Evidence for different types of lexical representations in the cerebral hemispheres. *Cognitive Neuropsychology, 9,* 33–45.

Koffka, K. (1935). *Principles of Gestalt psychology.* London: Routledge & Kegan Paul.

Köhnken, G., Milne, R., Memon, A., & Bull, R. (1999). The cognitive interview: A meta-analysis. *Psychology Crime & Law, 5,* 3–27.

Kolb, B., & Whishaw, I. Q. (1996). *Fundamentals of human neuropsychology* (4th ed.). New York: Freeman.

Kolers, P. A. (1973). Remembering operations. *Memory & Cognition, 1,* 347–355.

Kolers, P. A. (1979). A pattern-analyzing basis of recognition. In L. S. Cermak & F. I. M. Craik (Eds.), *Levels of processing in human memory.* Hillsdale, NJ: Erlbaum.

Kolers, P. A., & Roediger, H. L., III. (1984). Procedures of mind. *Journal of Verbal Learning and Verbal Behavior, 23,* 425–449.

Konorski, J. (1948). *Conditioned reflexes and neuron organization.* Cambridge, UK: Cambridge University Press.

Kopelman, M. D. (1985). Rates of forgetting in Alzheimer-type dementia and Korsakoff's syndrome. *Neuropsychologia, 15,* 527–541.

Koppenaal, L., & Glanzer, M. (1990). An examination of the continuous distractor task and the long-term recency effect. *Memory & Cognition, 18,* 183–195.

Korsakoff, S. S. (1889). Etude médico-psychologique sur une forme des maladies de la mémoire. *Revue Philosophique, 28,* 501–530.

Kosslyn, S. M. (1976). Can imagery be distinguished from other forms of internal representation? Evidence from studies of information retrieval times. *Memory & Cognition, 4,* 291–297.

Kosslyn, S. M. (1980). *Image and mind.* Cambridge, MA: Harvard University Press.

Kosslyn, S. M. (1994). *Image and brain.* Cambridge, MA: MIT Press.

Kosslyn, S. M., Ball, T., & Reiser, B. J. (1978). Visual images preserve metric spatial information: Evidence from studies of image scanning. *Journal of Experimental Psychology: Human Perception and Performance, 4,* 47–60.

Kunzinger, E. L. (1985). A short-term longitudinal study of memorial development during early grade school. *Developmental Psychology, 21,* 642–646.

Laming, D. R. J. (1968). *Information theory of choice reaction time.* New York: Wiley.

LaPointe, L. B., & Engle, R. W. (1990). Simple and complex word spans as measures of working memory capacity. *Journal of Experimental Psychology: Learning, Memory and Cognition, 16,* 1118–1133.

Lapp, D. C. (1992). *(Nearly) total recall: A guide to better memory at any age.* Stanford, CA: Stanford Alumni Association.

Lashley, K. S. (1929). *Brain mechanisms and intelligence: A quantitative study of injuries to the brain.* Chicago: University of Chicago Press.

Lashley, K. S. (1950). In search of the engram. In *Symposium of the Society for Experimental Biology* (Vol. 4). New York: Cambridge University Press.

Lawless, H. T., & Engen, T. (1977). Associations to odors: Interference, mnemonics, and verbal labeling. *Journal of Experimental Psychology: Human Learning and Memory, 3,* 52–59.

LeCompte, D. C. (1992). In search of a strong visual recency effect. *Memory & Cognition, 20,* 563–572.

LeCompte, D. C., Neely, C. B., & Wilson, J. R. (1997). Irrelevant speech and irrelevant tones: The relative importance of speech to the irrelevant speech effect. *Journal of Experimental Psychology: Learning, Memory, and Cognition, 23,* 472–483.

LeCompte, D. C., & Shaibe, D. M. (1997). On the irrelevance of phonology to the irrelevant speech effect. *Quarterly Journal of Experimental Psychology, 50A,* 100–118.

Lee, C. L., & Estes, W. K. (1977). Order and position in primary memory for letter strings. *Journal of Verbal Learning and Verbal Behavior, 16,* 395–418.

Lee, C. L., & Estes, W. K. (1981). Item and order information in short-term memory: Evidence for multilevel perturbation processes. *Journal of Experimental Psychology: Human Learning and Memory, 7,* 149–169.

Leeper, R. (1935). A study of a neglected portion of the field of learning: The development of sensory organization. *Journal of Genetic Psychology, 46,* 41–75.

Lehman, E. B., Mikesell, J. W., & Doherty, S. C. (1985). Long term retention of information about presentation modality by children and adults. *Memory & Cognition, 13,* 21–28.

Levine, D. N., Warach, J., & Farah, M. J. (1985). Two visual systems in mental imagery: Dissociation of "what" and "where" in imagery disorders due to bilateral posterior cerebral lesions. *Neurology, 35,* 1010–1018.

Levine, S. C. (1989). The question of faces: Special is in the brain of the beholder. In A. W. Young & H. D. Ellis (Eds.), *Handbook of research on face processing.* Amsterdam: North-Holland.

Levine, S. C., Banich, M. T., & Koch-Weser, M. P. (1988). Face recognition: A general or specific right hemisphere capacity? *Brain and Cognition, 8,* 303–325.

Levy, B. A. (1971). Role of articulation in auditory and visual short-term memory. *Journal of Verbal Learning and Verbal Behavior, 10,* 123–132.

Lewandowsky, S. (1994). The rewards and hazards of computer simulations. *Psychological Science, 4,* 236–243.

Lewandowsky, S. (1999). Redintegration and response suppression in serial recall: A dynamic network model. *International Journal of Psychology, 34,* 434–446.

Lewandowsky, S., & Li, S. C. (1994). Memory for serial order revisited. *Psychological Review, 101,* 539–543.

Lewandowsky, S., & Murdock, B. B., Jr. (1989). Memory for serial order. *Psychological Review, 96,* 25–57.

Lewicki, P. (1986). *Nonconscious social information processing.* Orlando, FL: Academic Press.

Light, L. L., & Burke, D. M. (1988). Patterns of language and memory in old age. In L. L. Light & D. M. Burke (Eds.), *Language, memory, and aging.* New York: Cambridge University Press.

Light, L. L., & Carter-Sobell, L. (1970). Effects of changed semantic context on recognition memory. *Journal of Verbal Learning and Verbal Behavior, 9,* 1–11.

Light, L. L., & Singh, A. (1987). Implicit and explicit memory in young and older adults. *Journal of Experimental Psychology: Learning, Memory, and Cognition, 13,* 531–541.

Lindberg, M. A. (1980). Is knowledge base development a necessary and sufficient condition for memory development? *Journal of Experimental Child Psychology, 30,* 401–410.

Link, S. W., & Heath, R. A. (1975). A sequential theory of psychological discrimination. *Psychometrika, 40,* 77–105.

Locke, J. L., & Fehr, F. S. (1970). Young children's use of the speech code in a recall task. *Journal of Experimental Child Psychology, 10,* 367–373.

Loess, H., & Waugh, N. C. (1967). Short-term memory and inter-trial interval. *Journal of Verbal Learning and Verbal Behavior, 6,* 455–460.

Loftus, E. F. (1973). Category dominance, instance dominance, and categorization time. *Journal of Experimental Psychology, 97,* 70–74.

Loftus, E. F. (1975). Leading questions and the eyewitness report. *Cognitive Psychology, 7,* 560–572.

Loftus, E. F. (1979a). Shifting human color memory. *Memory & Cognition, 5,* 696–699.

Loftus, E. F. (1979b). *Eyewitness testimony.* Cambridge, MA: Harvard University Press.

Loftus, E. F. (1993a). Desperately seeking memories of the first few years of childhood: The reality of early memories. *Journal of Experimental Psychology: General, 122,* 274–277.

Loftus, E. F. (1993b). The reality of repressed memories. *American Psychologist, 48,* 518–537.

Loftus, E. F., Donders, K., Hoffman, H. G., & Schooler, J. W. (1989). Creating new memories that are quickly accessed and confidently held. *Memory & Cognition, 17,* 607–616.

Loftus, E. F., & Hoffman, H. G. (1989). Misinformation and memory: The creation of new memories. *Journal of Experimental Psychology: General, 118,* 100–104.

Loftus, E. F., & Kaufman, L. (1992). Why do traumatic experiences sometimes produce good memory (flash-bulbs) and sometimes no memory (repression)? In E. Winograd & U. Neisser (Eds.), *Affect and accuracy in recall: Studies of "flashbulb" memories.* New York: Cambridge University Press.

Loftus, E. F., & Ketchum, K. (1991). *Witness for the defense.* New York: St. Martin's Press.

Loftus, E. F., & Ketchum, K. (1994). *The myth of repressed memory: False memories and allegations of sexual abuse.* New York: St Martin's Press.

Loftus, E. F., & Loftus, G. R. (1980). On the permanence of stored information in the human brain. *American Psychologist, 35,* 409–420.

Loftus, E. F., Miller, D. G., & Burns, H. J. (1978). Semantic integration of verbal information into a visual memory. *Journal of Experimental Psychology: Human Learning and Memory, 4,* 19–31.

Loftus, E. F., & Palmer, J. C. (1974). Reconstruction of automobile destruction: An example of the interaction between language and memory. *Journal of Verbal Learning and Verbal Behavior, 13,* 585–589.

Loftus, E. F., & Zanni, G. (1975). Eyewitness testimony: The influence of the wording of a question. *Bulletin of the Psychonomic Society, 5,* 86–88.

Loftus, G. R., & Irwin, D. E. (1998). On the relations among different measures of visible and informational persistence. *Cognitive Psychology, 35,* 135–199.

Logie, R. H. (1995). *Visuo-spatial working memory.* Hillsdale, NJ: Erlbaum.

Logie, R. H., & Marchetti, C. (1991). Visuo-spatial working memory: Visual, spatial or central executive? In R. H. Logie & M. Denis (Eds.), *Mental images in human cognition.* Amsterdam: Elsevier.

Logie, R. H., & Pearson, D. (1997). The inner eye and the inner scribe of visuo-spatial working memory: Evidence from developmental fractionation. *European Journal of Cognitive Psychology, 9,* 241–257.

Longoni, A. M., Richardson, J. T. E., & Aiello, A. (1993). Articulatory rehearsal and phonological storage in working memory. *Memory & Cognition, 21,* 11–22.

Lorayne, H. (1957). *How to develop a super power memory.* Hollywood, FL: Fell.

Lorge, I. (1930). Influence of regularly interpolated time intervals upon subsequent learning. *Contributions to Education*(Whole No. 438).

Lovatt, P., Avons, S. E., & Masterson, J. (2000). The word-length effect and disyllabic words. *Quarterly Journal of Experimental Psychology, 53A,* 1–22.

Lovatt, P., Avons, S. E., & Masterson, J. (2002). Output decay in immediate serial recall: Speech time revisited. *Journal of Memory and Language, 46,* 227–243.

Luce, R. D. (1963). Detection and recognition. In R. D. Luce, R. R. Bush, & E. Galanter (Eds.), *Handbook of mathematical psychology.* New York: Wiley.

Luce, R. D. (1986). *Response times.* New York: Oxford University Press.

Luria, A. R. (1968). *The mind of a mnemonist.* New York: Basic Books.

Lustig, C., & Hasher, L. (2001a). Implicit memory is not immune to interference. *Psychological Bulletin, 127,* 618–628.

Lustig, C., & Hasher, L. (2001b). Implicit memory is vulnerable to proactive interference. *Psychological Science, 12,* 408–412.

Lyman, B. J., & McDaniel, M. A. (1990). Memory for odors and odor names: Modalities of elaboration and imagery. *Journal of Experimental Psychology: Learning, Memory, and Cognition, 16,* 656–664.

MacKay, D. G. (1992). Constraints on theories of inner speech. In D. Reisberg (Ed.), *Auditory imagery.* Hillsdale, NJ: Erlbaum.

Mackworth, J. F. (1963). The duration of the visual image. *Canadian Journal of Psychology, 17,* 62–81.

MacLeod, C. M. (1975). Release from proactive interference: Insufficiency of an attentional account. *American Journal of Psychology, 88,* 459–465.

Madigan, S. A. (1971). Modality and recall order interactions in short-term memory for serial order. *Journal of Experimental Psychology, 87,* 294–296.

Madigan, S. A. (1983). Picture memory. In J. C. Yuille (Ed.), *Imagery, memory, and cognition: Essays in honour of Allan Paivio.* Hillsdale, NJ: Erlbaum.

Mair, R. G., Harrison, L. M., & Flint, D. L. (1995). The neuropsychology of odor memory. In F. R. Schab & R. G. Crowder (Eds.), *Memory for odors.* Mahwah, NJ: Erlbaum.

Mandler, G. (1967). Organization and memory. In K. W. Spence & J. T. Spence (Eds.), *The psychology of learning and motivation* (Vol. 1). New York: Academic Press.

Mandler, G. (1980). Recognizing: The judgment of previous occurrence. *Psychological Review, 87,* 252–271.

Mandler, G. (1991). Your face looks familiar but I can't remember your name. In W. E. Hockley & S. Lewandowsky (Eds.), *Relating theory and data: Essays on human memory in honour of Bennet B. Murdock.* Hillsdale, NJ: Erlbaum.

Manning, S. K., Koehler, L., & Hampton, S. (1990). The effects of recoding and presentation format on recency and suffix effects. *Memory & Cognition, 18,* 164–173.

Mäntylä, T. (1986). Optimizing cue effectiveness: Recall of 500 and 600 incidentally learned words. *Journal of Experimental Psychology: Learning, Memory, and Cognition, 12,* 66–71.

Mäntylä, T. (1993). Knowing but not remembering: Adult age differences in recollective experience. *Memory & Cognition, 21,* 379–388.

Marchant, B., & Malloy, T. E. (1984). Auditory, tactile, and visual imagery in PA learning by congenitally blind, deaf, and normal adults. *Journal of Mental Imagery, 8,* 19–32.

Marschark, M. (1992). Imagery. In L. R. Squire (Ed.), *Encyclopedia of learning and memory.* New York: Macmillan.

Martin, K. M., & Aggelton, J. P. (1993). Contextual effects on the ability of divers to use decompression tables. *Applied Cognitive Psychology, 7,* 311–316.

Martin, R. C. (1993). Short-term memory and sentence processing: Evidence from neuropsychology. *Memory & Cognition, 21,* 176–183.

Martin, R. C., Shelton, J. R., & Yaffee, L. S. (1994). Language processing and working memory: Neuropsychological evidence for separate phonological and semantic capacities. *Journal of Memory and Language, 33,* 83–111.

Martin, S. J., Grimwood, P. D., & Morris, R. G. M. (2000). Synaptic plasticity and memory: An evaluation of the hypothesis. *Annual Review of Neuroscience, 23,* 649–711.

Massaro, D. W. (1976). Perceptual processing in dichotic listening. *Journal of Experimental Psychology: Human Learning and Memory, 2,* 331–339.

Massaro, D. W., & Loftus, G. R. (1996). Sensory and perceptual store. In E. L. Bjork & R. A. Bjork (Eds.), *Memory.* San Diego: Academic Press.

Matarazzo, J. D. (1972). *Wechsler's measurement and appraisal of adult intelligence* (5th ed.). Baltimore: Williams & Wilkins.

Maurer, D. (1985). Infants' perception of facedness. In T. N. Field & N. Fox (Eds.), *Social perception in infants.* Norwood, NJ: Ablex.

Maybery, M., Taylor, M., & O'Brien-Malone, A. (1995). Implicit learning: Sensitive to age but not IQ. [Special Issue: Cognitive development.] *Australian Journal of Psychology, 47,* 8–17.

Maylor, E. A. (1995). Remembering versus knowing television theme tunes in middle-aged and elderly adults. *British Journal of Psychology, 86,* 21–25.

Maylor, E. A. (1998). Changes in event-based prospective memory across adulthood. *Aging, Neuropsychology and Cognition, 5,* 107–128.

McBride, D. M., Dosher, B. A., & Gage, N. M. (2001). A comparison of forgetting for conscious and automatic memory processes in word fragment completion tasks. *Journal of Memory and Language, 45,* 585–615.

McCarthy, R. A., & Warrington, E. K. (1990). *Cognitive neuropsychology: A clinical introduction.* San Diego: Academic Press.

McClelland, J. L., & Rumelhart, D. E. (1981). An interactive activation model of context effects in letter perception: Part 1. An account of basic findings. *Psychological Review, 88,* 375–407.

McCloskey, M. (1992). Special versus ordinary memory mechanisms in the genesis of flashbulb memories. In E. Winograd & U. Neisser (Eds.), *Affect and accuracy in recall: Studies of "flashbulb" memories.* New York: Cambridge University Press.

McCloskey, M., & Cohen, N. J. (1989). Catastrophic interference in connectionist networks: The sequential learning problem. In G. H. Bower (Ed.), *The psychology of learning and motivation* (Vol. 23). New York: Academic Press.

McCloskey, M., & Watkins, M. J. (1978). The seeing-more-than-is-there phenomenon: Implications for the locus of iconic storage. *Journal of Experimental Psychology: Human Perception and Performance, 4,* 553–564.

McCloskey, M., Wible, C. G., & Cohen, N. J. (1988). Is there a special flashbulb memory mechanism? *Journal of Experimental Psychology: General, 117,* 171–181.

McCloskey, M., & Zaragoza, M. S. (1985). Misleading postevent information and memory for events: Arguments and evidence against memory impairment hypotheses. *Journal of Experimental Psychology: General, 114,* 1–16.

McDaniel, M. A., Waddill, P. J., & Einstein, G. O. (1988). A contextual account of the generation effect: A three-factor theory. *Journal of Memory and Language, 27,* 521–536.

McDermott, K. B., & Roediger, H. L., III. (1996). Exact and conceptual repetition dissociate conceptual memory tests: Problems for transfer appropriate processing theory. *Canadian Journal of Psychology, 50,* 57–71.

McDonough, L., Mandler, J. M., McKee, R. D., & Squire, L. R. (1995). The deferred imitation task as a nonverbal measure of declarative memory. *Proceedings of the National Academy of Sciences, 92,* 7580–7584.

McEvoy, C. L., & Moon, J. R. (1988). Assessment and treatment of everyday memory problems in the elderly. In M. M. Gruneberg, P. E. Morris, & R. N. Sykes (Eds.), *Practical aspects of memory: Current research and issues* (Vol. 2). Chichester, UK: Wiley.

McGaugh, J. L., Weinberger, N. M., & Lynch, G. (Eds.). (1990). *Brain organization and memory: Cells, systems, and circuits.* New York: Oxford University Press.

McGeoch, J. A. (1932). Forgetting and the law of disuse. *Psychological Review, 39,* 352–370.

McGeoch, J. A. (1942). *The psychology of human learning: An introduction.* New York: Longmans Green.

McGeoch, J. A., & Irion, A. L. (1952). *The psychology of human learning* (2nd ed.). New York: Longmans Green.

McKee, R. D., & Squire, L. R. (1993). On the development of declarative memory. *Journal of Experimental Psychology: Learning, Memory, and Cognition, 19*, 397–404.

McKelvie, S. J. (1987). Learning and awareness in the Hebb digits task. *Journal of General Psychology, 114*, 75–88.

McKoon, G., & Ratcliff, R. (1992). Spreading activation versus compound cue accounts of priming: Mediated priming revisited. *Journal of Experimental Psychology: Learning, Memory, and Cognition, 18*, 1155–1172.

McKoon, G., Ratcliff, R., & Dell, G. S. (1986). A critical evaluation of the semantic/episodic distinction. *Journal of Experimental Psychology: Learning, Memory, and Cognition, 12*, 295–306.

McNamara, T. P. (1992a). Priming and constraints it places on theories of memory and retrieval. *Psychological Review, 99*, 650–662.

McNamara, T. P. (1992b). Theories of priming: I. Associative distance and lag. *Journal of Experimental Psychology: Learning, Memory, and Cognition, 18*, 1173–1190.

McNamara, T. P., & Altarriba, J. (1988). Depth of spreading activation revisited: Semantic mediated priming occurs in lexical decisions. *Journal of Memory and Language, 27*, 545–559.

McWeeny, K. H., Young, A. W., Hay, D. C., & Ellis, A. W. (1987). Putting names to faces. *British Journal of Psychology, 78*, 143–149.

Mechanic, A. (1964). The responses involved in the rote learning of verbal materials. *Journal of Verbal Learning and Verbal Behavior, 3*, 30–36.

Medin, D. L. (1989). Concepts and conceptual structure. *American Psychologist, 44*, 1469–1481.

Melcher, J. M., & Schooler, J. W. (1996). The misremembrance of wines past: Verbal and perceptual expertise differentially mediate verbal overshadowing of wine. *Journal of Memory and Language, 35*, 231–245.

Melton, A. W. (1963). Implications of short-term memory for a general theory of memory. *Journal of Verbal Learning and Verbal Behavior, 2*, 1–21.

Melton, A. W. (1970). The situation with respect to the spacing of repetitions and memory. *Journal of Verbal Learning and Verbal Behavior, 9*, 596–606.

Melton, A. W., & Irwin, J. M. (1940). The influence of degree of interpolated learning on retroactive inhibition and the overt transfer of specific responses. *American Journal of Psychology, 53*, 173–203.

Memon, A., & Bull, R. (1991). The cognitive interview: Its origins, empirical support, evaluation and practical implications. *Journal of Community and Applied Social Psychology, 1*, 291–307.

Memon, A., & Higham, P. A. (1999). A review of the cognitive interview. *Psychology Crime & Law, 5*, 177–196.

Mensink, G.-J., & Raaijmakers, J. G. W. (1988). A model for interference and forgetting. *Psychological Review, 95*, 434–455.

Merikle, P. M. (1980). Selection from visual persistence by perceptual groups and category membership. *Journal of Experimental Psychology: General, 109*, 279–295.

Merrit, J. O. (1979). None in a million: Results of mass screening for eidetic ability using objective tests published in newspapers and magazines. *Behavioral and Brain Sciences, 2*, 612.

Messier, C. (2001). Challenging the focal role of the hippocampus in memory processing. *Behavioural Brain Research, 127*, 1–4.

Meudell, P. R., Mayes, A. R., & Neary, D. (1980). Orienting task effects on the recognition of humorous material in amnesia and normal subjects. *Journal of Clinical Neuropsychology, 2*, 1–14.

Meudell, P. R., Mayes, A. R., Ostergaard, A., & Pickering, A. (1985). Recency and frequency judgments in alcoholic amnesics and normal people with poor memory. *Cortex, 21*, 487–511.

Mewhort, D. J. K., Campbell, A. J., Marchetti, F. M., & Campbell, J. I. D. (1981). Identification, localization, and "iconic" memory: An evaluation of the bar-probe task. *Memory & Cognition, 9*, 50–67.

Mewhort, D. J. K., & Leppman, K. P. (1985). Information persistence: Testing spatial and identity information with a voice probe. *Psychological Research, 47*, 51–58.

Meyer, D. E., & Schvaneveldt, R. W. (1971). Facilitation in recognizing pairs of words: Evidence of a dependence between retrieval operations. *Journal of Experimental Psychology, 90*, 227–234.

Micco, A., & Masson, M. E. J. (1992). Age-related differences in the specificity of verbal encoding. *Memory & Cognition, 20*, 244–253.

Miles, C., & Jenkins, R. (2000). Recency and suffix effects with immediate recall of olfactory stimuli. *Memory, 8*, 195–206.

Miller, G. A. (1956). The magical number seven plus or minus two: Some limits on our capacity for processing information. *Psychological Review, 63*, 81–97.

Miller, G. A., Galanter, E., & Pribram, K. (1960). *Plans and the structure of behavior.* New York: Holt, Rinehart & Winston.

Miller, R. R., & Grahame, N. J. (1991). Expression of learning. In L. Dachowski & C. F. Flaherty (Eds.), *Current topics in animal learning: Brain, emotion, and cognition.* Hillsdale, NJ: Erlbaum.

Miller, R. R., & Springer, A. D. (1972). Recovery from amnesia following transcorneal electroconvulsive shock. *Psychonomic Science, 28*, 7–8.

Milner, B., Corkin, S., & Teuber, H. L. (1968). Further analysis of the hippocampal amnesic syndrome: 14-year follow-up study of H. M. *Neuropsychologia, 6*, 215–234.

Minami, H., & Dallenbach, K. M. (1946). The effect of activity upon learning and retention in the cockroach. *American Journal of Psychology, 59*, 1–58.

Mingay, D. J. (1986). Hypnosis and memory for incidentally learned scenes. *British Journal of Experimental and Clinical Hypnosis, 3*, 173–183.

Mingay, D. J. (1987). The effect of hypnosis on eyewitness memory: Reconciling forensic claims and research findings. *Applied Psychology: An International Review, 36*, 163–183.

Mitchell, K. J., & Johnson, M. K. (2000). Source monitoring. In E. Tulving & F. I. M. Craik (Eds.), *The Oxford handbook of memory*. New York: Oxford University Press.

Miyake, A., & Shah, P. (Eds.). (1999). *Models of working memory: Mechanisms of active maintenance and executive control*. New York: Cambridge University Press.

Mohs, R. (1995). Neuropsychological assessment of patients with Alzheimer's disease. In F. E. Bloom & D. J. Kupfter (Eds.), *Psychopharmacology: The fourth generation of projects*. New York: Raven.

Moore, T. V. (1910). The process of abstraction: An experimental study. *California University Publications in Psychology, 1*, 73–197.

Moore, T. V. (1939). *Cognitive psychology*. Philadelphia: Lippincott.

Morris, C. D., Bransford, J. D., & Franks, J. J. (1977). Levels of processing versus transfer appropriate processing. *Journal of Verbal Learning and Verbal Behavior, 16*, 519–533.

Morris, R. G. (1992). Patterns of short-term memory impairment in Alzheimer's disease. In L. Backman (Ed.), *Memory functioning in dementia*. New York: Elsevier Science.

Morris, R. G. (1994a). Working memory in Alzheimer-type dementia. *Neuropsychology, 8*, 544–554.

Morris, R. G. (1994b). Recent developments in the neuropsychology of dementia. *International Review of Psychiatry, 6*, 85–107.

Morris, R. G. (Ed.). (1996). *The cognitive neuropsychology of Alzheimer-type dementia*. Oxford: Oxford University Press.

Morton, J., Crowder, R. G., & Prussin, H. A. (1971). Experiments with the stimulus suffix effect. *Journal of Experimental Psychology Monograph, 91*, 169–190.

Morton, J., & Holloway, C. M. (1970). Absence of a cross-modal "suffix effect" in short-term memory. *Quarterly Journal of Experimental Psychology, 22*, 167–176.

Morton, N., & Morris, R. G. (1995). Image transformation dissociated from visuospatial working memory. *Cognitive Neuropsychology, 12*, 767–791.

Moyer, R. S., Bradley, D. R., Sorensen, M. H., Whiting, J. D., & Mansfield, D. P. (1978). Psychophysical functions for perceived and remembered size. *Science, 200*, 330–332.

Müller, G. E., & Pilzecker, A. (1900). Experimentalle Beitrage zur Lehre vom Gedachtnis. *Zeitschrift für Psychologie, 1*, 1–300.

Murdock, B. B., Jr. (1960). The distinctiveness of stimuli. *Psychological Review, 67*, 16–31.

Murdock, B. B., Jr. (1961). The retention of individual items. *Journal of Experimental Psychology, 62*, 618–625.

Murdock, B. B., Jr. (1962). The serial position effect of free recall. *Journal of Experimental Psychology, 64*, 482–488.

Murdock, B. B., Jr. (1974). *Human memory: Theory and data*. Hillsdale, NJ: Erlbaum.

Murdock, B. B., Jr. (1976). Item and order information in short-term memory. *Journal of Experimental Psychology: General, 105*, 191–216.

Murdock, B. B., Jr. (1982). A theory for the storage and retrieval of item and associative information. *Psychological Review, 89*, 609–626.

Murdock, B. B., Jr. (1983). A distributed memory model for serial-order information. *Psychological Review, 90*, 316–338.

Murdock, B. B., Jr. (1993). TODAM2: A model for the storage and retrieval of item, associative, and serial-order information. *Psychological Review, 100*, 183–203.

Murdock, B. B., Jr. (1995). Developing TODAM: Three models for serial-order information. *Memory & Cognition, 23*, 631–645.

Murdock, B. B., Jr. (2001). Analysis of the serial position curve. In H. L. Roediger III, J. S. Nairne, I. Neath, & A. M. Surprenant (Eds.), *The nature of remembering: Essays in honor of Robert G. Crowder*. Washington, DC: American Psychological Association.

Murdock, B. B., Jr., & Metcalfe, J. (1978). Controlled rehearsal in single-trial free recall. *Journal of Verbal Learning and Verbal Behavior, 17*, 309–324.

Murdock, B. B., Jr., & Vom Saal, W. (1967). Transpositions in short-term memory. *Journal of Experimental Psychology, 74*, 137–143.

Murphy, G. L. (1996). Illusions of memory. *Journal of Memory and Language, 35*, 75.

Murphy, G. L., & Medin, D. L. (1985). The role of theories in conceptual coherence. *Psychological Review, 92*, 289–316.

Murray, D. J. (1966). Vocalization-at-presentation and immediate recall with varying recall methods. *Quarterly Journal of Experimental Psychology, 18*, 9–18.

Murray, D. J. (1967). The role of speech responses in short-term memory. *Canadian Journal of Psychology, 21*, 263–276.

Murray, D. J. (1968). Articulation and acoustic confusability in short-term memory. *Journal of Experimental Psychology, 78*, 679–684.

Murray, D. J. (1976). Research on human memory in the nineteenth century. *Canadian Journal of Psychology, 30*, 201–220.

Murray, D. J. (1988). *A history of western psychology* (2nd ed.) New York: Prentice Hall.

Murray, D. J. (1995). *Gestalt psychology and the cognitive revolution*. New York: Harvester Wheatsheaf.

Murray, D. J., Rowan, A. J., & Smith, K. H. (1988). The effect of articulatory suppression on short-term recognition. *Canadian Journal of Psychology, 42*, 424–436.

Murray-Smith, D., Kinoshita, S., & McConkey, K. M. (1990). Hypnotic memory and retrieval cues. *British Journal of Experimental and Clinical Hypnosis, 7,* 1–8.

Myers, N. A., Clifton, R. K., & Clarkson, M. G. (1987). When they were very young: Almost-threes remember two years ago. *Infant Behavior and Development, 10,* 123–132.

Näätänen, R. (1992). *Attention and brain function.* Hillsdale, NJ: Erlbaum.

Nairne, J. S. (1983). Associative processing during rote rehearsal. *Journal of Experimental Psychology: Learning, Memory, and Cognition, 9,* 3–20.

Nairne, J. S. (1988). A framework for interpreting recency effects in immediate serial recall. *Memory & Cognition, 16,* 343–352.

Nairne, J. S. (1990). A feature model of immediate memory. *Memory & Cognition, 18,* 251–269.

Nairne, J. S. (1991). Positional uncertainty in long-term memory. *Memory & Cognition, 19,* 332–340.

Nairne, J. S. (1992). The loss of positional certainty in long-term memory. *Psychological Science, 3,* 199–202.

Nairne, J. S. (1996). Short-term/working memory. In E. L. Bjork & R. A. Bjork (Eds.), *Memory.* New York: Academic Press.

Nairne, J. S. (2001). A functional analysis of memory. In H. L. Roediger III, J. S. Nairne, I. Neath, & A. M. Surprenant (Eds.), *The nature of remembering: Essays in honor of Robert G. Crowder.* Washington, DC: American Psychological Association.

Nairne, J. S. (2002). Remembering over the short-term: The case against the standard model. *Annual Review of Psychology, 53,* 53–81.

Nairne, J. S. (2003). Sensory and working memory. In A. H. Healy & R. W. Proctor (Eds.), *Comprehensive handbook of psychology: Vol. 4. Experimental psychology.* New York: Wiley.

Nairne, J. S., & Crowder, R. G. (1982). On the locus of the stimulus suffix effect. *Memory & Cognition, 10,* 350–357.

Nairne, J. S., & Dutta, A. (1992). Spatial and temporal uncertainty in long-term memory. *Journal of Memory and Language, 31,* 396–407.

Nairne, J. S., & McNabb, W. K. (1985). More modality effects in the absence of sound. *Journal of Experimental Psychology: Learning, Memory and Cognition, 11,* 596–604.

Nairne, J. S., & Neath, I. (1994). A critique of the retrieval/deblurring assumptions of TODAM. *Psychological Review, 101,* 528–533.

Nairne, J. S., & Neath, I. (2001). Long-term memory span. *Behavioral and Brain Sciences, 24,* 134–135.

Nairne, J. S., Neath, I., Serra, M., & Byun, E. (1997). Positional distinctiveness and the ratio rule in free recall. *Journal of Memory and Language, 37,* 155–166.

Nairne, J. S., & Pusen, C. (1984). Serial recall of imagined voices. *Journal of Verbal Learning & Verbal Behavior, 23,* 331–342.

Nairne, J. S., Riegler, G. L., & Serra, M. (1991). Dissociative effects of generation on item and order retention. *Journal of Experimental Psychology: Learning, Memory, and Cognition, 17,* 702–709.

Nairne, J. S., & Walters, V. L. (1983). Silent mouthing produces modality- and suffix-like effects. *Journal of Verbal Learning and Verbal Behavior, 22,* 475–483.

Naito, M. (1990). Repetition priming in children and adults: Age-related dissociation between implicit and explicit memory. *Journal of Experimental Child Psychology, 50,* 462–484.

Naveh-Benjamin, M. (2000). Adult age differences in memory performance: Tests of an associative deficit hypothesis. *Journal of Experimental Psychology: Learning, Memory, and Cognition, 26,* 1170–1187.

Naveh-Benjamin, M., & Ayres, T. J. (1986). Digit span, reading rate, and linguistic relativity. *Quarterly Journal of Experimental Psychology, 38A,* 739–751.

Naveh-Benjamin, M., & Craik, F. I. M. (1995). Memory for context and its use in item memory: Comparisons of younger and older persons. *Psychology and Aging, 10,* 284–293.

Neath, I. (1993a). Contextual and distinctive processes and the serial position function. *Journal of Memory and Language, 32,* 820–840.

Neath, I. (1993b). Distinctiveness and serial position effects in recognition. *Memory & Cognition, 21,* 689–698.

Neath, I. (1997). Modality, concreteness, and set-size effects in a free reconstruction of order task. *Memory & Cognition, 25,* 256–263.

Neath, I. (1999a). Modelling the disruptive effects of irrelevant speech on order information. *International Journal of Psychology, 34,* 410–418.

Neath, I. (1999b). Computer simulations of global memory models. *Behavior Research Methods, Instruments, & Computers, 31,* 74–80.

Neath, I. (2000). Modeling the effects of irrelevant speech on memory. *Psychonomic Bulletin & Review, 7,* 403–423.

Neath, I., Bireta, T. J., & Surprenant, A. M. (in press). The time-based word length effect and stimulus set specificity. *Psychonomic Bulletin & Review.*

Neath, I., & Crowder, R. G. (1990). Schedules of presentation and temporal distinctiveness in human memory. *Journal of Experimental Psychology: Learning, Memory and Cognition, 16,* 316–327.

Neath, I., & Crowder, R. G. (1996). Distinctiveness and very short-term serial position effects. *Memory, 4,* 225–242.

Neath, I., Farley, L. A., & Surprenant, A. M. (in press). Directly assessing the relationship between articulatory suppression and irrelevant speech. *Quarterly Journal of Experimental Psychology.*

Neath, I., & Knoedler, A. J. (1994). Distinctiveness and serial position effects in recognition and sentence processing. *Journal of Memory and Language, 33,* 776–795.

Neath, I., & Knoedler, A. J. (1997). *Dimensional distinctiveness and increasing primacy effects in perception, recognition and sentence processing.* Unpublished manuscript.

Neath, I., & Nairne, J. S. (1995). Word-length effects in immediate memory: Overwriting trace-decay theory. *Psychonomic Bulletin & Review, 2,* 429–441.

Neath, I., & Surprenant, A. M. (2003a). Mechanisms of memory. In K. Lamberts & R. Goldstone (Eds.), *Handbook of cognition.* London: Sage.

Neath, I., & Surprenant, A. M. (2003b). *Human memory: An introduction to research, data, and theory* (2nd ed.). Belmont, CA: Wadsworth.

Neath, I., Surprenant, A. M., & Crowder, R. G. (1993). The context-dependent stimulus-suffix effect. *Journal of Experimental Psychology: Learning, Memory and Cognition, 19,* 698–703.

Neely, J. H. (1977). Semantic priming and retrieval from lexical memory: Roles of inhibitionless spreading activation and limited-capacity attention. *Journal of Experimental Psychology: General, 106,* 226–254.

Neely, J. H. (1989). Experimental dissociations and the episodic/semantic memory distinction. In H. L. Roediger III & F. I. M. Craik (Eds.), *Varieties of memory and consciousness: Essays in honour of Endel Tulving.* Hillsdale, NJ: Erlbaum.

Neely, J. H., Keefe, D. E., & Ross, K. L. (1989). Semantic priming in the lexical decision task: Roles of prospective prime-generated expectancies and retrospective semantic matching. *Journal of Experimental Psychology: Learning, Memory, and Cognition, 15,* 1003–1019.

Neisser, U. (1967). *Cognitive psychology.* New York: Appleton-Century-Crofts.

Neisser, U. (1978). Memory: What are the important questions? In M. M. Gruneberg, P. Morris, & R. N. Sykes (Eds.), *Practical aspects of memory.* London: Academic Press.

Neisser, U. (1982). *Memory observed.* San Francisco: Freeman.

Neisser, U., & Harsch, N. (1992). Phantom flashbulbs: False recollections of hearing news about *Challenger.* In E. Winograd & U. Neisser (Eds.), *Affect and accuracy in recall: Studies of "flashbulb" memories.* New York: Cambridge University Press.

Neisser, U., & Kerr, N. (1973). Spatial and mnemonic properties of visual images. *Cognitive Psychology, 5,* 138–150.

Newcombe, N., & Fox, N. A. (1994). Infantile amnesia: Through a glass darkly. *Child Development, 65,* 31–40.

Nickerson, R. S. (1984). Retrieval inhibition from part-set cuing: A persisting enigma in memory research. *Memory & Cognition, 12,* 531–552.

Nickerson, R. S., & Adams, M. J. (1979). Long-term memory for a common object. *Cognitive Psychology, 11,* 287–307.

Nilsson, L.-G., & Gardiner, J. (1993). Identifying exceptions in a database of recognition failure studies from 1973 to 1992. *Memory & Cognition, 21,* 397–410.

Norman, D. A. (Ed.) (1970). *Models of human memory.* New York: Academic Press.

Nyberg, L., Cabeza, R., & Tulving, E. (1996). PET studies of encoding and retrieval: The HERA model. *Psychonomic Bulletin and Review, 3,* 135–148.

Nyberg, L., Tulving, E., Habib, R., Nilsson, L.-G., Kapur, S., Houle, S., Cabeza, R., & McIntosh, A. R. (1995). Functional brain maps of retrieval mode and recovery of episodic information. *Neuroreport, 7,* 249–252.

O'Reilly, R. C., & Rudy, J. W. (2001). Conjunctive representations in learning and memory: Principles of cortical and hippocampal function. *Psychological Review, 108,* 311–345.

Orne, M. T. (1979). The use and misuse of hypnosis in court. *International Journal of Clinical and Experimental Hypnosis, 27,* 311–341.

Ornstein, P. A., Naus, M. J., & Liberty, C. (1975). Rehearsal and organizational processes in children's memory. *Child Development, 46,* 818–830.

Osgood, C. E. (1953). *Method and theory in experimental psychology.* New York: Oxford University Press.

O'Toole, A. J., Deffenbacher, K. A., Valentin, D., & Abdi, H. (1994). Structural aspects of face recognition and the other-race effect. *Memory & Cognition, 22,* 208–224.

Overton, D. A. (1984). State dependent learning and drug discriminations. In L. L. Iverson, S. D. Iverson, & S. H. Snyder (Eds.), *Handbook of psychopharmacology* (Vol. 18). New York: Plenum.

Page, M. P. A., & Norris, D. (1998). The primacy model: A new model of immediate serial recall. *Psychological Review, 105,* 761–781.

Paivio, A. (1969). Mental imagery in associative learning and memory. *Psychological Review, 76,* 241–263.

Paivio, A. (1971). *Imagery and verbal processes.* New York: Holt, Rinehart & Winston.

Paivio, A. (1986). *Mental representations: A dual-coding approach.* Oxford, UK: Oxford University Press.

Paivio, A., & Cohen, M. (1979). Eidetic imagery and cognitive abilities. *Journal of Mental Imagery, 3,* 53–64.

Paivio, A., Yuille, J. C., & Madigan, S. A. (1968). Concreteness, imagery, and meaningfulness values for 925 nouns. *Journal of Experimental Psychology: Monographs, 76,* 1–25.

Paller, K. A., Kutas, M., & McIsaac, H. K. (1995). Monitoring conscious recollection via the electrical activity of the brain. *Psychological Science, 6,* 107–111.

Park, D. C., Smith, A. D., & Cavanaugh, J. C. (1990). Metamemories of memory researchers. *Memory & Cognition, 18,* 321–327.

Parkin, A. J. (1993a). *Memory: Phenomena, experiment, and theory.* Oxford, UK: Blackwell.

Parkin, A. J. (1993b). Implicit memory across the lifespan. In P. Graf & M. E. Masson (Eds.), *Implicit memory: New directions in cognition, development, and neuropsychology.* Hillsdale, NJ: Erlbaum.

Parkin, A. J. (1997). *Memory and amnesia* (2nd ed.). Oxford, UK: Blackwell.

Parkin, A. J. (1998). The central executive does not exist. *Journal of the International Neuropsychological Society, 45,* 518–522.

Parkin, A. J. (1999). Component processes versus systems: Is there really an important difference? In J. K. Foster & M. Jelicic (Eds.), *Memory: Systems, process, or function?* Oxford, UK: Oxford University Press.

Parkin, A. J., & Hunkin, N. M. (1993). Impaired temporal context memory on anterograde but not retrograde tests in the absence of frontal pathology. *Cortex, 29,* 267–280.

Parkin, A. J., Montaldi, D., Leng, N. R. C., & Hunkin, N. (1990). Contextual cueing effects in the remote memory of alcoholic Korsakoff patients. *Quarterly Journal of Experimental Psychology, 42A,* 585–596.

Parkin, A. J., & Streete, S. (1988). Implicit and explicit memory in young children and adults. *British Journal of Psychology, 79,* 361–369.

Parkin, A. J., & Walter, B. M. (1991). Aging, short-term memory and frontal dysfunction. *Psychobiology, 19,* 175–179.

Parkin, A. J., & Walter, B. M. (1992). Recollective experience, normal aging, and frontal dysfunction. *Psychology and Aging, 7,* 290–298.

Parkinson, S. R. (1982). Performance deficits in short-term memory tasks: A comparison of amnesic Korsakoff patients and the aged. In L. S. Cermak (Ed.), *Human memory and amnesia.* Hillsdale, NJ: Erlbaum.

Parkinson, S. R., Inman, V. W., & Dannenbaum, S. E. (1985). Adult age differences in short-term forgetting. *Acta Psychologica, 60,* 83–101.

Payne, D. G. (1987). Hypermnesia and reminiscence in recall: A historical and empirical review. *Psychological Bulletin, 101,* 5–27.

Payne, D. G., Elie, C. J., Blackwell, J. M., & Neuschatz, J. S. (1996). Memory illusions: Recalling, recognizing, and recollecting events that never occurred. *Journal of Memory and Language, 35,* 261–285.

Pazzaglia, F., & Cornoldi, C. (1999). The role of distinct components of visuospatial working memory in the processing of texts. *Memory, 7,* 19–41.

Pear, T. H. (1922). *Remembering and forgetting.* London: Methuen.

Pearson, D. G., De Beni, R., & Cornoldi, C. (2001). The generation, maintenance, and transformation of visuo-spatial mental images. In M. Denis, R. H. Logie, C. Cornoldi, M. de Vega, & J. Engelkamp (Eds.), *Imagery, language, and visuo-spatial thinking.* Hove, UK: Psychology Press.

Pearson, D. G., Logie, R. H., & Green, C. (1996). Mental manipulation, visual working memory, and executive processes. *Psychologische Beträge, 38,* 324–342.

Penfield, W. (1969). Consciousness, memory, and man's conditioned reflexes. In K. Pribram (Ed.), *On the biol-ogy of learning.* New York: Harcourt, Brace, and World.

Penney, C. G. (1989). Modality effects and the structure of short-term verbal memory. *Memory & Cognition, 17,* 398–422.

Perky, C. W. (1910). An experimental study of imagination. *American Journal of Psychology, 21,* 422–452.

Perner, J., & Ruffman, T. (1995). Episodic memory and autonoetic consciousness: Developmental evidence and a theory of childhood amnesia. *Journal of Experimental Child Psychology, 59,* 516–548.

Perris, E. E., Myers, N. A., & Clifton, R. K. (1990). Long-term memory for a single infancy experience. *Child Development, 61,* 1796–1807.

Peters, R., & McGee, R. (1982). Cigarette smoking and state-dependent memory. *Psychopharmacology, 76,* 232–235.

Petersen, R. C., Stevens, J. C., Ganguli, M., Tangalos, E. G., Cummings, J. L., & DeKosky, S. T. (2001). Practice parameter: Early detection of dementia: Mild cognitive impairment (an evidence-based review). Report of the Quality Standards Subcommittee of the American Academy of Neurology. *Neurology, 56,* 1133–1142.

Peterson, L. R., & Johnson, S. T. (1971). Some effects of minimizing articulation on short-term retention. *Journal of Verbal Learning and Verbal Behavior, 10,* 346–354.

Peterson, L. R., & Peterson, M. J. (1959). Short-term retention of individual items. *Journal of Experimental Psychology, 61,* 12–21.

Petros, T. V., Beckwith, B. E., & Anderson, M. (1990). Individual differences in the effects of time of day and passage difficulty on prose memory in adults. *British Journal of Psychology, 81,* 63–72.

Pick, E. (1888). *Memory and its doctors.* London: Trubner.

Pietrini, V., Nertimpi, T., Vaglia, A., Revello, M. G., Pinna, V., & Ferro-Milone, F. (1988). Recovery from herpes simplex encephalitis: Selective impairment of specific semantic categories with neuroradiological correlation. *Journal of Neurology, Neurosurgery, and Psychiatry, 51,* 1284–1293.

Pillemer, D. B. (1984). Flashbulb memories of the assassination attempt on President Reagan. *Cognition, 16,* 63–80.

Pillemer, D. B., Picariello, M. L., & Pruett, J. C. (1994). Very long-term memories of a salient preschool event. *Applied Cognitive Psychology, 8,* 95–106.

Pillsbury, W. B., & Raush, H. L. (1943). An extension of the Köhler-Restorff inhibition phenomenon. *American Journal of Psychology, 56,* 293–298.

Pinto, A. C., & Baddeley, A. D. (1991). Where did you park your car? Analysis of a naturalistic long-term recency effect. *European Journal of Cognitive Psychology, 3,* 297–313.

Pisoni, D. B. (1973). Auditory and phonetic memory codes in the discrimination of consonants and vowels. *Perception & Psychophysics, 13,* 253–260.

Pisoni, D. B. (1975). Auditory short-term memory and vowel perception. *Memory & Cognition, 3,* 7–18.

Pollack, I. (1952). The information of elementary auditory displays. *Journal of the Acoustical Society of America, 24,* 745–749.

Pollack, I. (1953). The information of elementary auditory displays: II. *Journal of the Acoustical Society of America, 25,* 765–769.

Pollack, I., & Norman, D. A. (1964). A nonparametric analysis of recognition experiments. *Psychonomic Science, 1,* 125–126.

Posner, M. I., Goldsmith, R., & Welton, K. E., Jr. (1967). Perceived distance and the classification of distorted patterns. *Journal of Experimental Psychology, 73,* 28–38.

Posner, M. I., & Keele, S. W. (1968). On the genesis of abstract ideas. *Journal of Experimental Psychology, 77,* 353–363.

Posner, M. I., & Raichle, M. E. (1994). *Images of mind.* New York: Scientific American Library.

Posner, M. I., Walker, J. A., Friedrich, F. J., & Rafal, R. D. (1984). Effects of parietal lobe injury on covert orienting of visual attention. *Journal of Neuroscience, 4,* 1863–1874.

Postman, L. (1961). The present status of interference theory. In C. N. Cofer (Ed.), *Verbal learning and verbal behavior.* New York: McGraw-Hill.

Postman, L. (1964). Short-term memory and incidental learning. In A. W. Melton (Ed.), *Categories of human learning.* New York: Academic Press.

Postman, L., & Keppel, G. (1970). *Norms of word association.* San Diego: Academic Press.

Postman, L., & Phillips, L. W. (1954). Studies in incidental learning: I. The effects of crowding and isolation. *Journal of Experimental Psychology, 48,* 48–56.

Postman, L., & Phillips, L. W. (1965). Short-term temporal changes in free recall. *Quarterly Journal of Experimental Psychology, 17,* 132–138.

Postman, L., Stark, K., & Fraser, J. (1968). Temporal changes in interference. *Journal of Verbal Learning and Verbal Behavior, 7,* 672–694.

Potter, M. C. (1979). Mundane symbolism: The relations among objects, names, and ideas. In N. R. Smith & M. B. Franklin (Eds.), *Symbolic functioning in childhood.* Hillsdale, NJ: Erlbaum.

Pratkanis, A. R. (1992). The cargo-cult science of subliminal persuasion. *Skeptical Inquirer, 16,* 260–272.

Prince, M. (1910). The mechanism and interpretation of dreams. *Journal of Abnormal Psychology, 5,* 139–195.

Propper, R. E., & Christman, S. (1999). A test of the HERA model II: Objects as stimuli. *Brain & Cognition, 40,* 227–229.

Pylyshyn, Z. W. (1973). What the mind's eye tells the mind's brain: A critique of mental imagery. *Psychological Bulletin, 80,* 1–24.

Pylyshyn, Z. W. (1979). The rate of "mental rotation" of images: A test of a holistic analog hypothesis. *Memory & Cognition, 7,* 19–28.

Pylyshyn, Z. W. (1981). The imagery debate: Analog media versus tacit knowledge. *Psychological Review, 88,* 16–45.

Quartermain, D., McEwen, B. S., & Azmitia, E. C., Jr. (1972). Recovery of memory following amnesia in the rat and mouse. *Journal of Comparative and Physiological Psychology, 76,* 521–529.

Quillian, M. R. (1967). Word concepts: A theory and simulation of some basic semantic capabilities. *Behavioral Science, 12,* 410–430.

Quillian, M. R. (1969). The teachable language comprehender: A simulation program and theory of language. *Communications of the ACM, 12,* 459–476.

Raaijmakers, J. G. W., & Shiffrin, R. M. (1981). Search of associative memory. *Psychological Review, 88,* 93–134.

Raaijmakers, J. G. W., & Shiffrin, R. M. (1992). Models for recall and recognition. *Annual Review of Psychology, 43,* 205–234.

Rabbitt, P. M. A. (1993). Does it all go together when it goes? The Nineteenth Bartlett Memorial Lecture. *Quarterly Journal of Experimental Psychology, 46A,* 385–434.

Rabbitt, P. M. A., & Abson, V. (1991). Do older people know how good they are? *British Journal of Psychology, 82,* 137–151.

Rabin, M. D., & Cain, W. S. (1984). Odor recognition: Familiarity, identifiability, and encoding consistency. *Journal of Experimental Psychology: Learning, Memory, and Cognition, 10,* 316–325.

Rabinowitz, J. C., Mandler, G., & Barsalou, L. W. (1977). Recognition failure: Another case of retrieval failure. *Journal of Verbal Learning and Verbal Behavior, 16,* 639–663.

Rajaram, S. (1993). Remembering and knowing: Two means of access to the personal past. *Memory & Cognition, 21,* 89–102.

Ramon y Cajal, S. (1894). La fine structure des centres nerveux. *Proceedings of the Royal Society of London, 55,* 444–468.

Rao, K. V., & Proctor, R. W. (1984). Study-phase processing and the word frequency effect in recognition memory. *Journal of Experimental Psychology: Learning, Memory, and Cognition, 10,* 386–394.

Ratcliff, R. (1978). A theory of memory retrieval. *Psychological Review, 85,* 59–108.

Ratcliff, R. (1981). A theory of order relations in perceptual matching. *Psychological Review, 88,* 552–572.

Ratcliff, R. (1985). Theretical interpretations of speed and accuracy of positive and negative responses. *Psychological Review, 92,* 212–225.

Ratcliff, R. (1988). Continuous versus discrete information processing: Modeling the accumulation of partial information. *Psychological Review, 95,* 238–255.

Ratcliff, R. (1990). Connectionist models of recognition memory: Constraints imposed by learning and forgetting functions. *Psychological Review, 97,* 285–308.

Ratcliff, R. (1992). Models of memory. In L. R. Squire (Ed.), *Encyclopedia of learning and memory*. New York: Macmillan.

Ratcliff, R., Allbritton, D. W., & McKoon, G. (1997). Bias in auditory priming. *Journal of Experimental Psychology: Learning, Memory, and Cognition, 23*, 143–152.

Ratcliff, R., & McKoon, G. (1981). Does activation really spread? *Psychological Review, 88*, 454–462.

Ratcliff, R., & McKoon, G. (1988). A retrieval theory of priming in memory. *Psychological Review, 95*, 385–408.

Ratcliff, R., & McKoon, G. (1994). Retrieving information from memory: Spreading-activation theories versus compound-cue theories. *Psychological Review, 101*, 177–184.

Ratcliff, R., & McKoon, G. (1995a). Bias in the priming of object decisions. *Journal of Experimental Psychology: Learning, Memory, and Cognition, 21*, 754–767.

Ratcliff, R., & McKoon, G. (1995b). Sequential effects in lexical decision: Tests of compound-cue retrieval theory. *Journal of Experimental Psychology: Learning, Memory, and Cognition, 21*, 1380–1388.

Ratcliff, R., & McKoon, G. (1996). Bias effects in implicit memory tasks. *Journal of Experimental Psychology: General, 125*, 403–421.

Ratcliff, R., & McKoon, G. (1997). A counter model for implicit priming in perceptual word identification. *Psychological Review, 104*, 319–343.

Ratcliff, R., Sheu, C.-F., & Gronlund, S. D. (1992). Testing global memory models using ROC curves. *Psychological Review, 99*, 518–535.

Ratcliff, R., Van Zandt, T., & McKoon, G. (1995). Process dissociation, single-process theories, and recognition memory. *Journal of Experimental Psychology: General, 124*, 352–374.

Ratcliff, R., Van Zandt, T., & McKoon, G. (1999). Connectionist and diffusion models of reaction time. *Psychological Review, 106*, 261–300.

Rea, C. P., & Modigliani, V. (1988). Educational implications of the spacing effect. In M. M. Gruneberg, P. E. Morris, & R. N. Sykes (Eds.), *Practical aspects of memory: Current research and issues: Vol. 1. Memory in everyday life*. Chichester, UK: Wiley.

Read, J. D. (1996). From a passing thought to a false memory in 2 minutes: Confusing real and illusory events. *Psychonomic Bulletin & Review, 3*, 105–111.

Reber, A. S. (1967). Implicit learning of artificial grammars. *Journal of Verbal Learning and Verbal Behavior, 6*, 317–325.

Reber, A. S. (1989). Implicit learning and tacit knowledge. *Journal of Experimental Psychology: General, 118*, 219–235.

Reber, A. S. (1993). *Implicit learning and tacit knowledge: An essay on the cognitive unconscious*. New York: Oxford University Press.

Reder, L. M., Angstadt, P., Cary, M., Erickson, M. A., & Ayers, M. S. (2002). A reexamination of stimulus-frequency effects in recognition: Two mirrors for low-

and high-frequency pseudowords. *Journal of Experimental Psychology: Learning, Memory, and Cognition, 28*, 138–152.

Reder, L. M., Nhouyvanisvong, A., Schunn, C. D., Ayers, M. S., Angstadt, P., & Hiraki, K. (2000). A mechanistic account of the mirror effect for word frequency: A computational model of remember/know judgments in a continuous recognition paradimg. *Journal of Experimental Psychology: Learning, Memory, & Cognition, 26*, 294–320.

Redish, A. D. (2001). The hippocampal debate: Are we asking the right questions? *Behavioural Brain Research, 127*, 81–98.

Reed, P. (2000). Serial position effects in recognition memory for odors. *Journal of Experimental Psychology: Learning, Memory, & Cognition, 26*, 411–422.

Reisberg, D. (1992). (Ed.). *Auditory imagery*. Hillsdale, NJ: Erlbaum.

Rendell, P. G., & Thomson, D. M. (1999). Aging and prospective memory: Differences between naturalistic and laboratory tasks. *Journals of Gerontology, Psychological Sciences and Social Sciences, 54B*, 256–269.

Rescorla, R. A., Durlach, P. J., & Grau, J. W. (1985). Contextual learning in Pavlovian conditioning. In P. D. Balsam & A. Tomie (Eds.), *Context and learning*. Hillsdale, NJ: Erlbaum.

Richardson, J. T. E. (Ed.). (1996). *Working memory and human cognition*. New York: Oxford University Press.

Richardson, R., Riccio, D. C., & Axiotis, R. (1986). Alleviation of infantile amnesia in rats by internal and external contextual cues. *Developmental Psychobiology, 19*, 453–462.

Richardson-Klavehn, A., & Bjork, R. A. (1988). Measures of memory. *Annual Review of Psychology, 39*, 475–543.

Richardson-Klavehn, A., Lee, M. G., & Joubran, R. (1994). Intention and awareness in perceptual identification priming. *Memory & Cognition, 22*, 293–312.

Riddoch, M. J., & Humphreys, G. W. (1987). A case of integrative visual agnosia. *Brain, 110*, 1431–1462.

Rips, L. J. (1975). Inductive judgments about natural categories. *Journal of Verbal Learning and Verbal Behavior, 14*, 665–681.

Rips, L. J., Shoben, E. J., & Smith, E. E. (1973). Semantic distance and the verification of semantic relations. *Journal of Verbal Learning and Verbal Behavior, 12*, 1–20.

Ritter, K. (1978). The development of knowledge of an external retrieval cue strategy. *Child Development, 49*, 1227–1230.

Robertson, J. M. (Ed.). (1905). *The philosophic works of Francis Bacon* (R. C Ellis & J. Spedding, Trans.). London: Routledge & Kegan Paul.

Roediger, H. L., III. (1980). Memory metaphors in cognitive psychology. *Memory & Cognition, 8*, 231–246.

Roediger, H. L., III. (1990a). Review of "Remembering reconsidered: Ecological and traditional approaches to the study of memory." *American Journal of Psychology*, *103*, 403–409.

Roediger, H. L., III. (1990b). Implicit memory: Retention without remembering. *American Psychologist*, *45*, 1043–1056.

Roediger, H. L., III. (1990c). Implicit memory: A commentary. *Bulletin of the Psychonomic Society*, *28*, 373–380.

Roediger, H. L., III. (1996). Memory illusions. *Journal of Memory and Language*, *35*, 76–100.

Roediger, H. L., III, Buckner, R. L., & McDermott, K. B. (1999). Components of processing. In J. K. Foster & M. Jelicic (Eds.), *Memory: Systems, process, or function?* Oxford, UK: Oxford University Press.

Roediger, H. L., III, & Crowder, R. G. (1976). A serial position effect in recall of United States presidents. *Bulletin of the Psychonomic Society*, *8*, 275–278.

Roediger, H. L., III, & McDermott, K. B. (1993). Implicit memory in normal human subjects. In H. Spinnler & F. Boller (Eds.), *Handbook of neuropsychology*. Amsterdam: Elsevier.

Roediger, H. L., III, & McDermott, K. B. (1995). Creating false memories: Remembering words not presented in lists. *Journal of Experimental Psychology: Learning, Memory, and Cognition*, *21*, 803–814.

Roediger, H. L., III, & Srinivas, K. (1993). Specificity of operations in perceptual priming. In P. Graf & M. E. J. Masson (Eds.), *Implicit memory: New directions in cognition, development and neuropsychology*. Hillsdale, NJ: Erlbaum.

Roediger, H. L., III, Weldon, M. S., & Challis, B. H. (1989). Explaining dissociations between implicit and explicit measures of retention: A processing account. In H. L. Roediger III & F. I. M. Craik (Eds.), *Varieties of memory and consciousness: Essays in honour of Endel Tulving*. Hillsdale, NJ: Erlbaum.

Roediger, H. L., III, Weldon, M. S., Stadler, M. L., & Riegler, G. L. (1992). Direct comparison of two implicit memory tests: Word fragment and word stem completion. *Journal of Experimental Psychology: Learning, Memory, and Cognition*, *18*, 1251–1269.

Roediger, H. L., III, Wheeler, M. A., & Rajaram, S. (1993). Remembering, knowing, and reconstructing the past. In D. L. Medin (Ed.), *The psychology of learning and motivation: Advances in research and theory*. San Diego, CA: Academic Press.

Rogers, S. (1993). How a publicity blitz created the myth of subliminal advertising. *Public Relations Quarterly*, *37*, 12–17.

Roodenrys, S., & Quinlan, P. T. (2000). The effects of stimulus set size and word frequency on verbal serial recall. *Memory*, *8*, 71–78.

Rosch, E., & Mervis, C. B. (1975). Family resemblances: Studies in the internal structure of categories. *Cognitive Psychology*, *7*, 573–605.

Rosch, E., Mervis, C. B., Gray, W. D., Johnson, D. M., & Bayes-Braem, P. (1976). Basic objects in natural categories. *Cognitive Psychology*, *8*, 382–439.

Rosenthal, R. (1966). *Experimenter effects in behavioral research*. New York: Appleton-Century-Crofts.

Rosenzweig, M. R. (1984). Experience, memory, and the brain. *American Psychologist*, *39*, 365–376.

Ross, B. H. (1984). Remindings and their effects in learning a cognitive skill. *Cognitive Psychology*, *16*, 371–416.

Ross, J., & Lawrence, K. A. (1968). Some observations on memory artifice. *Psychonomic Science*, *13*, 107–108.

Rovee-Collier, C. (1993). The capacity for long-term memory in infancy. *Current Directions in Psychological Science*, *2*, 130–135.

Rovee-Collier, C. (1997). Dissociations in infant memory: Rethinking the development of implicit and explicit memory. *Psychological Review*, *104*, 467–498.

Rovee-Collier, C. (1999). The development of infant memory. *Current Directions in Psychological Science*, *8*, 80–85.

Rovee-Collier, C., Borza, M. A., Adler, S. A., & Boller, K. (1993). Infants' eyewitness testimony: Effects of postevent information on a prior memory representation. *Memory & Cognition*, *21*, 267–279.

Rovee-Collier, C., & Fagen, J. W. (1981). The retrieval of memory in early infancy. In L. P. Lipsitt (Ed.), *Advances in infancy research* (Vol. 1). Norwood, NJ: Ablex.

Rovee-Collier, C., & Gerhardstein, P. (1997). The development of infant memory. In N. Cowan (Ed.), *The development of memory in children*. Hove, UK: Psychology Press.

Rovee-Collier, C., Schechter, A., Shyi, G. C., & Shields, P. J. (1992). Perceptual identification of contextual attributes and infant memory retrieval. *Developmental Psychology*, *28*, 307–318.

Rovee-Collier, C., & Shyi, C.-W. G. (1992). A functional and cognitive analysis of infant long-term retention. In M. L. Howe, C. J. Brainerd, & V. F. Reyna (Eds.), *Development of long-term retention*. New York: Springer-Verlag.

Rubin, D. C., & Baddeley, A. D. (1989). Telescoping is not time compression: A model of the dating of autobiographical events. *Memory & Cognition*, *17*, 653–661.

Rubin, D. C., & Kozin, M. (1984). Vivid memories. *Cognition*, *16*, 81–95.

Rubin, D. C., Rahhal, T. A., & Poon, L. W. (1998). Things learned in early adulthood are remembered best. *Memory & Cognition*, *26*, 3–19.

Rubin, D. C., & Wenzel, A. E. (1996). One hundred years of forgetting: A quantitative description of retention. *Psychological Review*, *103*, 734–760.

Rubin, D. C., Wetzler, S. E., & Nebes, R. D. (1986). Autobiographical memory across the adult lifespan. In D. C. Rubin (Ed.), *Autobiographical memory*. Cambridge, UK: Cambridge University Press.

Rudy, J. W., & Sutherland, R. J. (1989). The hippocampal formation is necessary for rats to learn and remember configural discriminations. *Behavioural and Brain Research*, 34, 97–109.

Rumelhart, D. E., Hinton, G. E., & Williams, J. R. (1986). Learning internal representations by error propagation. In D. E. Rumelhart & J. L. McClelland (Eds.), *Parallel distributed processing* (Vol. 1). Cambridge, MA: MIT Press.

Rumelhart, D. E., & McClelland, J. L. (1982). An interactive activation model of context effects in letter perception: Part 2. The contextual enhancement effect and some tests and extensions of the model. *Psychological Review*, 89, 60–94.

Rumelhart, D. E., & McClelland, J. L. (Eds.). (1986). *Parallel distributed processing* (Vol. 1). Cambridge, MA: MIT Press.

Rumelhart, D. E., & Norman, D. A. (1985). Representation of knowledge. In A. M. Aitkenhead & J. M. Slack (Eds.), *Issues in cognitive modelling*. London: Erlbaum.

Rumelhart, D. E., & Ortony, A. (1977). The representation of knowledge in memory. In R. C. Anderson, R. J. Spiro, & W. E. Montague (Eds.), *Schooling and the acquisition of knowledge*. Hillsdale, NJ: Erlbaum.

Rumelhart, D. E., Smolensky, P., McClelland, J. L., & Hinton, G. E. (1986). Schemata and sequential thought processes in PDP models. In J. L. McClelland & D. E. Rumelhart (Eds.), *Parallel distributed processing: Explorations in the microstructure of cognition* (Vol. 2). Cambridge, MA: MIT Press.

Rundus, D., & Atkinson, R. C. (1970). Rehearsal processes in free recall: A procedure for direct observation. *Journal of Verbal Learning and Verbal Behavior*, 9, 99–105.

Rushworth, M. F., Nixon, P. D., Eacott, M. J., & Passingham, R. E. (1997). Ventral prefrontal cortex is not essential for working memory. *Journal of Neuroscience*, 17, 4829–4838.

Russo, R., Nichelli, P., Gibertoni, M., & Cornia, C. (1995). Developmental trends in implicit and explicit memory: A picture completion study. *Journal of Experimental Child Psychology*, 59, 566–578.

Ryan, J. (1969). Grouping and short-term memory: Different means and patterns of groups. *Quarterly Journal of Experimental Psychology*, 21, 137–147.

Sakitt, B. (1976). Iconic memory. *Psychological Review*, 83, 257–276.

Sakitt, B., & Long, G. M. (1979). Spare the rod and spoil the icon. *Journal of Experimental Psychology: Human Perception and Performance*, 5, 19–30.

Salamé, P., & Baddeley, A. D. (1982). Disruption of short-term memory by unattended speech: Implications for the structure of working memory. *Journal of Verbal Learning and Verbal Behavior*, 21, 150–164.

Salthouse, T. A. (1985). *A theory of cognitive aging*. Amsterdam: North-Holland.

Salthouse, T. A. (1991). *Theoretical perspectives on cognitive aging*. Hillsdale, NJ: Erlbaum.

Salthouse, T. A. (1993). Influence of working memory on adult age differences in matrix reasoning. *British Journal of Psychology*, 84, 171–199.

Salthouse, T. A. (1994). The nature of the influence of speed on adult age differences in cognition. *Developmental Psychology*, 30, 240–259.

Salthouse, T. A. (2000). Methodological assumptions in cognitive aging research. In F. I. M. Craik & Salthouse, T. A. (Eds.), *The handbook of aging and cognition* (2nd ed.). Mahwah, NJ: Erlbaum.

Salthouse, T. A., & Babcock, R. L. (1991). Decomposing adult age differences in working memory. *Developmental Psychology*, 27, 763–776.

Salthouse, T. A., Kausler, D. H., & Saults, J. S. (1988). Investigation of student status, background variables, and the feasibility of standard tasks in cognitive aging research. *Psychology and Aging*, 3, 29–37.

Salway, A. F. S., & Logie, R. H. (1995). Visuo-spatial working memory, movement control and executive demands. *British Journal of Psychology*, 86, 253–269.

Samuel, A. G. (1978). Organizational vs. retrieval factors in the development of digit span. *Journal of Experimental Child Psychology*, 26, 308–319.

Sanders, G. S., & Simmons, W. L. (1983). Use of hypnosis to enhance eyewitness accuracy: Does it work? *Journal of Applied Psychology*, 68, 70–77.

Sartori, G., Miozzo, M., & Job, R. (1993). Category-specific naming impairment? Yes. *Quarterly Journal of Experimental Psychology*, 46A, 489–504.

Saufley, W. H., Jr., Otaka, S. R., & Bavaresco, J. L. (1985). Context effects: Classroom tests and context independence. *Memory & Cognition*, 13, 522–528.

Schab, F. R. (1990). Odors and the remembrance of things past. *Journal of Experimental Psychology: Learning, Memory and Cognition*, 16, 648–655.

Schab, F. R., & Crowder, R. G. (1995). Odor recognition memory. In F. R. Schab & R. G. Crowder (Eds.), *Memory for odors*. Mahwah, NJ: Erlbaum.

Schacter, D. L. (1982). *Stranger behind the engram*. Hillsdale, NJ: Erlbaum.

Schacter, D. L. (1985). Multiple forms of memory in humans and animal. In N. M. Weinberger, J. L. McGaugh, & G. Lynch (Eds.), *Memory systems of the brain*. New York: Guilford.

Schacter, D. L. (1987). Implicit memory: History and current status. *Journal of Experimental Psychology: Learning, Memory, and Cognition*, 13, 501–518.

Schacter, D. L. (1989). On the relation between memory and consciousness: Dissociable interactions and conscious experience. In H. L. Roediger III & F. I. M. Craik (Eds.), *Varieties of memory and consciousness: Essays in honour of Endel Tulving*. Hillsdale, NJ: Erlbaum.

Schacter, D. L. (1994). Priming and multiple memory systems: Perceptual mechanisms of implicit memory. In D. L. Schacter & E. Tulving (Eds.), *Memory systems 1994*. Cambridge, MA: MIT Press.

Schacter, D. L., Cooper, L. A., & Delaney, S. M. (1990). Implicit memory for unfamiliar objects depends on access to structural descriptions. *Journal of Experimental Psychology: General, 119*, 5–24.

Schacter, D. L., Cooper, L. A., Delaney, S. M., Peterson, M. A., & Tharan, M. (1991). Implicit memory for possible and impossible objects: Constraints on the construction of structural descriptions. *Journal of Experimental Psychology: Learning, Memory, and Cognition, 17*, 3–19.

Schacter, D. L., Eich, J. E., & Tulving, E. (1978). Richard Semon's theory of memory. *Journal of Verbal Learning and Verbal Behavior, 17*, 721–723.

Schacter, D. L., & Moscovitch, M. (1984). Infants, amnesics, and dissociable memory system. In M. Moscovitch (Ed.), *Advances in the study of communication and affect: Vol. 9. Infant memory.* New York: Plenum.

Schacter, D. L., & Tulving, E. (1994). What are the memory systems of 1994? In D. L. Schacter & E. Tulving (Eds.), *Memory systems 1994.* Cambridge, MA: MIT Press.

Schacter, D. L., Wagner, A. D., & Buckner, R. L. (2000). Memory systems of 1999. In E. Tulving & F. I. M. Craik (Eds.), *The Oxford handbook of memory.* New York: Oxford University Press

Schank, R. C., & Abelson, R. (1977). *Scripts, plans, goals and understanding.* Hillsdale, NJ: Erlbaum.

Schilling, R. F., & Weaver, G. E. (1983). Effect of extraneous verbal information on memory for telephone numbers. *Journal of Applied Psychology, 68*, 559–564.

Schmolck, H., Buffalo, E. A., & Squire, L. R. (2000). Memory distortions develop over time: Recollections of the O. J. Simpson trial verdict after 15 and 32 months. *Psychological Science, 11*, 39–45.

Schneider, W. (1999). The development of metamemory in children. In D. Gopher & A. Koriat (Eds.), *Attention and performance XVII.* Cambridge, MA: MIT Press.

Schneider, W. (2000). Research on memory development: Historical trends and current themes. *International Journal of Behavioral Development, 24*, 407–420.

Schneider, W., & Detweiler, M. (1987). A connectionist/control architecture for working memory. In G. H. Bower (Ed.), *The psychology of learning and motivation* (Vol. 21). New York: Academic Press.

Schneider, W., & Pressley, M. (1989). *Memory development between 2 and 20.* New York: Springer-Verlag.

Schneider, W., & Sodian, B. (1997). Memory strategy development: Lessons from longitudinal research. *Developmental Review, 17*, 442–461.

Schnorr, J. A., & Atkinson, R. C. (1969). Repetition versus imagery instructions in the short- and long-term retention of paired associates. *Psychonomic Science, 15*, 183–184.

Schooler, J. W., Bendiksen, M., & Ambadar, A. (1997). Taking the middle line: Can we accommodate both fabricated and recovered memories of sexual abuse? In M. A. Conway (Ed.), *Recovered memories and false memories.* Oxford, UK: Oxford University Press.

Schulz, R. (1955). Generalization of serial position in rote serial learning. *Journal of Experimental Psychology, 49*, 267–272.

Schweickert, R., & Boruff, B. (1986). Short-term memory capacity: Magic number or magic spell? *Journal of Experimental Psychology: Learning, Memory and Cognition, 12*, 419–425.

Schweickert, R., Guentert, L., & Hersberger, L. (1990). Phonological similarity, pronunciation rate, and memory span. *Psychological Science, 1*, 74–77.

Scoville, W. B., & Milner, B. (1957). Loss of recent memory after bilateral hippocampal lesions. *Journal of Neurological and Neurosurgical Psychiatry, 20*, 11–12.

Seashore, C. E. (1938). *Psychology of music.* New York: McGraw-Hill.

Segal, S. J., & Fusella, V. (1970). Influence of imagined pictures and sounds on detection of visual and auditory signals. *Journal of Experimental Psychology, 83*, 458–464.

Semon, R. (1904). *Die Mneme als erhaltendes Prinzip im Wechsel des organischen Geschehens.* Leipzig: Engelmann.

Serra, M., & Nairne, J. S. (1993). Design controversies and the generation effect: Support for an item-order hypothesis. *Memory & Cognition, 21*, 34–40.

Shallice, T. (1988). *From neuropsychology to mental structure.* Cambridge, UK: Cambridge University Press.

Shand, M. A., & Klima, E. S. (1981). Nonauditory suffix effects in congenitally deaf signers of American sign language. *Journal of Experimental Psychology: Human Learning and Memory, 7*, 464–474.

Shanks, D. R., & Johnstone, T. (1999). Evaluating the relationship between explicit and implicit knowledge in a serial reaction time task. *Journal of Experimental Psychology: Learning, Memory, and Cognition, 25*, 1435–1451.

Shannon, B. (1979). Yesterday, today, and tomorrow. *Acta Psychologica, 43*, 469–476.

Sheehan, P. W., & Tilden, J. (1983). Effects of suggestibility and hypnosis on accurate and distorted retrieval from memory. *Journal of Experimental Psychology: Learning, Memory, and Cognition, 9*, 283–293.

Sheingold, K., & Tenney, Y. J. (1982). Memory for a salient childhood event. In U. Neisser (Ed.), *Memory observed.* San Francisco: Freeman.

Shelton, J. R., & Martin, R. C. (1992). How semantic is automatic semantic priming? *Journal of Experimental Psychology: Learning, Memory, and Cognition, 18*, 1191–1210.

Shepard, G., & Koch, C. (1990). Introduction to synaptic circuits. In G. Shepard (Ed.), *The synaptic organization of the brain.* New York: Oxford University Press.

Shepard, R. N. (1967). Recognition memory for words, sentences, and pictures. *Journal of Verbal Learning and Verbal Behavior, 6*, 156–163.

Shepard, R. N. (1984). Ecological constraints in internal representation: Resonant kinematics of perceiving, imagining, thinking, and dreaming. *Psychological Review, 91,* 417–446.

Shepard, R. N., & Cooper, L. A. (1983). *Mental images and their transformations*. Cambridge, MA: MIT Press.

Shepard, R. N., & Metzler, J. (1971). Mental rotation of three-dimensional objects. *Science, 171,* 701–703.

Sherry, D. F., & Schacter, D. L. (1987). The evolution of multiple memory systems. *Psychological Review, 94,* 439–454.

Shiffrin, R. M. (1993). Short-term memory: A brief commentary. *Memory & Cognition, 21,* 193–197.

Shiffrin, R. M., & Cook, J. R. (1978). Short-term forgetting of item and order information. *Journal of Verbal Learning and Verbal Behavior, 17,* 189–218.

Shiffrin, R. M., & Nosofsky, R. M. (1993). Seven plus or minus two: A commentary on capacity limitations. *Psychological Review, 101,* 357–361.

Shiffrin, R. M., & Schneider, W. (1977). Controlled and automatic human information processing: II. Perceptual learning, automatic attending, and a general theory. *Psychological Review, 84,* 127–190.

Shimamura, A. P., Berry, J. M., Mangels, J. A., Rusting, C. L., & Jurica, P. J. (1995). Memory and cognitive abilities in university professors: Evidence for successful aging. *Psychological Science, 6,* 271–277.

Shimamura, A. P., Salmon, D. P., Squire, L. R., & Butters, N. (1987). Memory dysfunction and word priming in dementia and amnesia. *Behavioral Neuroscience, 101,* 347–351.

Shulman, H. G. (1970). Encoding and retention of semantic and phonemic information in short-term memory. *Journal of Verbal Learning and Verbal Behavior, 9,* 499–508.

Shulman, H. G. (1972). Semantic confusion errors in short-term memory. *Journal of Verbal Learning and Verbal Behavior, 11,* 221–227.

Simon, E. (1979). Depth and elaboration of processing in relation to age. *Journal of Experimental Psychology: Human Learning and Memory, 5,* 115–124.

Simon, H. A. (1974). How big is a chunk? *Science, 183,* 482–488.

Singh, S., Mishra, S., Bendapudi, N., & Linville, D. (1994). Enhancing memory of television commercials through message spacing. *Journal of Marketing Research, 31,* 384–329.

Slamecka, N. J. (1968). An examination of trace storage in free recall. *Journal of Experimental Psychology, 76,* 504–513.

Slamecka, N. J. (1985). Ebbinghaus: Some associations. *Journal of Experimental Psychology: Learning, Memory, and Cognition, 11,* 414–435.

Slamecka, N. J., & Graf, P. (1978). The generation effect: Delineation of a phenomenon. *Journal of Experimental Psychology: Human Learning and Memory, 4,* 592–604.

Slamecka, N. J., & McElree, B. (1983). Normal forgetting of verbal lists as a function of their degree of learning. *Journal of Experimental Psychology: Learning, Memory, and Cognition, 9,* 384–397.

Sloman, S. A., Hayman, C. A. G., Ohta, N., Law, J., & Tulving, E. (1988). Forgetting in primed fragment completion. *Journal of Experimental Psychology: Learning, Memory, and Cognition, 14,* 223–239.

Smith, E. E., Shoben, E. J., & Rips, L. J. (1974). Structure and process in semantic memory: A featural model for semantic decisions. *Psychological Review, 81,* 214–241.

Smith, J. A., & Knight, R. G. (2002). Memory processing in Alzheimer's disease. *Neuropsychologia, 40,* 666–682.

Smith, M. C. (1983). Hypnotic memory enhancement of witnesses: Does it work? *Psychological Bulletin, 94,* 387–407.

Smith, S. M. (1979). Remembering in and out of context. *Journal of Experimental Psychology: Human Learning and Memory, 5,* 460–471.

Smith, S. M., Glenberg, A. M., & Bjork, R. A. (1978). Environmental context and human memory. *Memory & Cognition, 6,* 342–353.

Smith, S. M., & Vela, E. (2001). Environmental context-dependent memory: A review and meta-analysis. *Psychonomic Bulletin & Review, 8,* 203–220.

Snodgrass, J. G., & Corwin, J. (1988). Pragmatics of measuring recognition memory: Applications to dementia and amnesia. *Journal of Experimental Psychology: General, 117,* 34–50.

Snodgrass, J. G., Levy-Berger, G., & Haydon, M. (1985). *Human experimental psychology*. New York: Oxford University Press.

Snodgrass, J. G., & Surprenant, A. (1989). Effect of retention interval on implicit and explicit memory for pictures. *Bulletin of the Psychonomic Society, 27,* 395–398.

Snodgrass, J. G., & Vanderwart, M. A. (1980). A standardized set of 260 pictures: Norms for name agreement, image agreement, familiarity, and visual complexity. *Journal of Experimental Psychology: Human Learning and Memory, 6,* 174–215.

Snodgrass, J. G., Volvovitz, R., & Walfish, E. R. (1972). Recognition memory for words, pictures, and words + pictures. *Psychonomic Science, 27,* 345–347.

Sodian, B., & Schneider, W. (1999). Memory strategy development: Gradual increase, sudden insight or roller coaster? In F. E. Weinert & W. Schneider (Eds.), *Individual development from 3 to 12: Findings from the Munich Longitudinal Study*. Cambridge, UK: Cambridge University Press.

Spear, N. E., & Riccio, D. C. (1994). *Memory: Phenomena and principles*. Boston: Allyn & Bacon.

Spector, A., Orrell, M., Davies, S., & Woods, B. (2001). Can reality orientation be rehabilitated? Development and piloting of an evidence-based programme of cognition-based therapies for people with dementia. *Neuropsychological Rehabilitation, 11,* 377–397.

Spelke, E., Hirst, W., & Neisser, U. (1976). Skills of divided attention. *Cognition, 4,* 215–230.

Sperling, G. (1960). The information available in brief visual presentations. *Psychological Monographs, 74*(Whole No. 11).

Sperling, G. (1967). Successive approximations to a model for short-term memory. *Acta Psychologica, 27,* 285–292.

Spetch, M. L., & Rusak, B. (1992). Time present and time past. In W. K. Honig & J. G. Fetterman (Eds.), *Cognitive aspects of stimulus control.* Hillsdale, NJ: Erlbaum.

Spilich, G. J., Vesonder, G. T., Chiesi, H. L., & Voss, J. F. (1979). Text processing of domain-related information for individuals with high- and low-domain knowledge. *Journal of Verbal Learning and Verbal Behavior, 18,* 275–290.

Spiro, R. J. (1980). Accommodative reconstruction in prose recall. *Journal of Verbal Learning and Verbal Behavior, 19,* 84–95.

Spoehr, K. T., & Corin, W. J. (1978). The stimulus-suffix effect as a memory coding phenomenon. *Memory & Cognition, 6,* 583–589.

Springer, S. P., & Deutsch, G. (1989). *Left brain, right brain* (3rd ed.). New York: Freeman.

Squire, L. R. (1987). *Memory and brain.* New York: Oxford University Press.

Squire, L. R. (1989). On the course of forgetting in very long-term memory. *Journal of Experimental Psychology: Learning, Memory, and Cognition, 15,* 241–245.

Squire, L. R. (1994). Declarative and nondeclarative memory: Multiple brain systems supporting learning and memory. In D. L. Schacter & E. Tulving (Eds.), *Memory systems 1994.* Cambridge, MA: MIT Press.

St. George-Hyslop, P. H. (2000). Piecing together Alzheimer's. *Scientific American, 283,* 76–83.

Stadler, M. A. (1995). Role of attention in implicit learning. *Journal of Experimental Psychology: Learning, Memory, and Cognition, 21,* 674–685.

Stadler, M. A., & Frensch, P. A. (Eds.). (1998). *Handbook of implicit learning.* Thousand Oaks, CA: Sage.

Stadler, M. A., & Roediger, H. L., III. (1998). The question of awareness in research on implicit learning. In M. A. Stadler & P. A. Frensch (Eds.), *Handbook of implicit learning.* Thousand Oaks, CA: Sage.

Sternberg, S. (1966). High speed scanning in human memory. *Science, 153,* 652–654.

Stoltzfus, E. R., Hasher, L., & Zacks, R. T. (1996). Working memory and aging: Current status of the inhibitory view. In J. T. E. Richardson (Ed.), *Working memory and human cognition.* New York: Oxford University Press.

Stone, M. (1960). Models for choice reaction time. *Psychometrika, 25,* 251–260.

Stromeyer, C. F., & Psotka, J. (1970). The detailed texture of eidetic images. *Nature, 225,* 346–349.

Strong, E. K. (1912). The effect of length of series upon recognition memory. *Psychological Review, 19,* 447–462.

Stuart, G., & Hulme, C. (2000). The effects of word co-occurance on short-term memory: Associative links in long-term memory affect short-term memory performance. *Journal of Experimental Psychology: Learning, Memory, and Cognition, 26,* 796–802.

Suengas, A. G., & Johnson, M. K. (1988). Qualitative effects of rehearsal on memories for perceived and imagined complex events. *Journal of Experimental Psychology: General, 117,* 377–389.

Sulin, R. A., & Dooling, D. J. (1974). Intrusion of a thematic idea in retention of prose. *Journal of Experimental Psychology, 103,* 255–262.

Sullivan, M. W. (1982). Reactivation: Priming forgotten memories in human infants. *Child Development, 57,* 100–104.

Surprenant, A. M. (1992). *The mind's ear: Imagery for vowels and consonants.* Unpublished doctoral dissertation, Yale University.

Surprenant, A. M. (2001). Distinctiveness and serial position effects in tonal sequences. *Perception & Psychophysics, 63,* 737–745.

Surprenant, A. M., LeCompte, D. C., & Neath, I. (2000). Manipulations of irrelevant information: Suffix effects with articulatory suppression and irrelevant speech. *Quarterly Journal of Experimental Psychology, 53A,* 325–348.

Surprenant, A. M., & Neath, I. (1996). The relation between discriminability and memory for vowels, consonants, and silent-center syllables. *Memory & Cognition, 24,* 356–366.

Surprenant, A. M., & Neath, I. (1997). T. V. Moore's (1939) *Cognitive psychology. Psychonomic Bulletin & Review, 4,* 342–349.

Susukita, T. (1933). Untersuchung eines ausserordentlichen Gedächtnisses in Japan (I). *Tohoku Psychologica Folia, 1,* 111–134.

Susukita, T. (1934). Untersuchung eines ausserordentlichen Gedächtnisses in Japan (II). *Tohoku Psychologica Folia, 2,* 15–42.

Swinney, D. (1979). Lexical access during sentence comprehension: (Re)consideration of context effects. *Journal of Verbal Learning and Verbal Behavior, 18,* 645–659.

Tan, L., & Ward, G. (2000). A recency-based account of the primacy effect in free recall. *Journal of Experimental Psychology: Learning, Memory, and Cognition, 26,* 1589–1625.

Teasdale, J. D., & Russell, M. L. (1983). Differential effects of induced mood on the recall of positive, negative, and neutral words. *British Journal of Clinical Psychology, 22,* 163–171.

Tehan, G., & Lalor, D. M. (2000). Individual differences in memory span: The contribution of rehearsal, access to lexical memory, and output speed. *Quarterly Journal of Experimental Psychology, 53A,* 1012–1038.

Tenpenny, P., & Shoben, E. J. (1992). Component processes and the utility of the conceptually-driven/data-driven distinction. *Journal of Experimental Psychology: Learning, Memory, and Cognition, 18,* 25–42.

Thapar, A., & Greene, R. L. (1993). Evidence against a short-term-store account of long-term recency effects. *Memory & Cognition, 21,* 329–337.

Thompson, C. P., Cowan, T., & Frieman, J. (1991). Rajan: A study of a memorist. *Journal of Memory and Language, 30,* 702–724.

Thompson, C. P., Skowronski, J. J., & Lee, D. J. (1988). Telescoping in dating naturally occurring events. *Memory & Cognition, 16,* 461–468.

Thomson, D. M., & Tulving, E. (1970). Associative encoding and retrieval: Weak and strong cues. *Journal of Experimental Psychology, 86,* 255–262.

Toppino, T. C. (1991). The spacing effect in young children's free recall: Support for automatic process explanations. *Memory & Cognition, 19,* 159–167.

Toth, J. P., & Hunt, R. R. (1999). Not one versus many, but zero versus any: Structure and function in the context of the multiple memory systems debate. In J. K. Foster and M. Jelicic (Eds.), *Memory: System, process, or function.* New York: Oxford University Press.

Tracy, A. L., Jarrard, L. E., & Davidson, T. L. (2001). The hippocampus and motivation revisited: Appetite and activity. *Behavioural Brain Research, 127,* 13–23.

Tulving, E. (1962). Subjective organization in free recall of "unrelated" words. *Psychological Review, 69,* 344–354.

Tulving, E. (1972). Episodic and semantic memory. In E. Tulving & W. Donaldson (Eds.), *Organization of memory.* New York: Academic Press.

Tulving, E. (1974). Cue-dependent forgetting. *American Scientist, 62,* 74–82.

Tulving, E. (1983). *Elements of episodic memory.* New York: Oxford University Press.

Tulving, E. (1985). Memory and consciousness. *Canadian Psychology, 26,* 1–12.

Tulving, E. (1986). What kind of a hypothesis is the distinction between episodic and semantic memory? *Journal of Experimental Psychology: Learning, Memory, and Cognition, 12,* 307–311.

Tulving, E. (1989). Remembering and knowing the past. *American Scientist, 77,* 361–367.

Tulving, E. (1998). Neurocognitive processes of human memory. In C. von Euler, I. Lundberg, & R. Llinas (Eds.), *Basic mechanisms in cognition and language.* Amsterdam: Elsevier.

Tulving, E., & Flexser, A. J. (1992). On the nature of the Tulving-Wiseman function. *Psychological Review, 99,* 543–546.

Tulving, E., Hayman, C. A. G., & MacDonald, C. A. (1991). Long-lasting perceptual priming and semantic learning in amnesia: A case experiment. *Journal of Experimental Psychology: Learning, Memory, and Cognition, 17,* 595–617.

Tulving, E., Kapur, S., Craik, F. I. M., Moscovitch, M., & Houle, S. (1994). Hemispheric encoding/retrieval asymmetry in episodic memory: Positron emission to-

mography findings. *Proceedings of the National Academy of Sciences, USA, 91,* 2016–2020.

Tulving, E., & Pearlstone, Z. (1966). Availability versus accessibility of information in memory for words. *Journal of Verbal Learning and Verbal Behavior, 5,* 381–391.

Tulving, E., & Schacter, D. L. (1990). Priming and human memory systems. *Science, 247,* 301–306.

Tulving, E., Schacter, D. L., & Stark, H. (1982). Priming effects in word-fragment completion are independent of recognition memory. *Journal of Experimental Psychology: Human Learning and Memory, 8,* 336–342.

Tulving, E., & Thomson, D. M. (1973). Encoding specificity and retrieval processes in episodic memory. *Psychological Review, 80,* 352–373.

Tulving, E., & Wiseman, S. (1975). Relation between recognition and recognition failure of recallable words. *Bulletin of the Psychonomic Society, 6,* 79–82.

Turner, M. L., & Engle, R. W. (1989). Is working memory capacity task dependent? *Journal of Memory and Language, 28,* 127–154.

Turvey, M. T. (1973). On peripheral and central processes in vision: Inferences from an information-processing analysis of masking with patterned stimuli. *Psychological Review, 22,* 142–147.

Turvey, M. T., Brick, P., & Osborn, J. (1970). Proactive interference in short-term memory as a function of prior-item retention interval. *Quarterly Journal of Experimental Psychology, 22,* 142–147.

Turvey, M. T., & Egan, J. F. (1970). Release from proactive interference in short-term memory as a function of change in visual and phonemic structure and retention interval. *Perception & Psychophysics, 7,* 169–172.

Tzeng, O. J. L. (1973). Positive recency effect in a delayed free recall. *Journal of Verbal Learning and Verbal Behavior, 12,* 436–439.

Tzeng, O. J. L., & Cotton, B. (1980). A study-phase retrieval model of temporal coding. *Journal of Experimental Psychology: Human Learning and Memory, 6,* 705–716.

Underwood, B. J. (1957). Interference and forgetting. *Psychological Review, 64,* 49–60.

Underwood, B. J. (1961). Ten years of massed practice on distributed practice. *Psychological Review, 68,* 229–247.

Underwood, B. J. (1969). Attributes of memory. *Psychological Review, 76,* 559–573.

Underwood, B. J. (1972). Are we overloading memory? In A. W. Melton & E. Martin (Eds.), *Coding processes in human memory.* New York: Wiley.

Underwood, B. J. (1977). *Temporal codes for memories: Issues and problems.* Hillsdale, NJ: Erlbaum.

Underwood, B. J., & Freund, J. S. (1968). Errors in recognition learning and retention. *Journal of Experimental Psychology, 78,* 55–63.

Underwood, B. J., & Schulz, R. W. (1961). Studies of distributed practice: XX. Sources of interference associated with differences in learning and retention. *Journal of Experimental Psychology, 61*, 228–235.

Urcuioli, P. J., Klein, R. M., & Day, J. (1981). Hemispheric differences in semantic processing: Category matching is not the same as category membership. *Perception & Psychophysics, 29*, 343–351.

Usher, J. A., & Neisser, U. (1993). Childhood amnesia and the beginnings of memory for four early life events. *Journal of Experimental Psychology: General, 122*, 155–165.

Valentine, T. (1988). Upside-down faces: A review of the effect of inversion upon face recognition. *British Journal of Psychology, 79*, 471–491.

Valentine, T., & Endo, M. (1992). Towards an exemplar model of face processing: The effects of race and distinctiveness. *Quarterly Journal of Experimental Psychology, 44A*, 671–204.

Van de Vijver, G. (1990). Schematism and schemata: Kant and the PDP. *Communication and Cognition, 23*, 223–233.

Van Zandt, T., & Townsend, J. T. (1993). Self-terminating versus exhaustive processes in rapid visual and memory search: An evaluative review. *Perception & Psychophysics, 53*, 563–580.

Verfaellie, M., & Treadwell, J. R. (1993). Status of recognition memory in amnesia. *Neuropsychology, 7*, 5–13.

Verhaeghen, P., Marcoen, A., & Goosens, L. (1993). Facts and fiction about memory aging: A quantitative integration of research findings. *Journal of Gerontology: Psychological Sciences, 48*, 157–171.

Vokey, J. R., & Read, J. D. (1992). Familiarity, memorability, and the effect of typicality on the recognition of faces. *Memory & Cognition, 20*, 291–302.

von Restorff, H. (1933). Analyse von Vorgangen in Spurenfeld: I. Über die Wirkung von Bereichsbildung im Spurenfeld. *Psychologische Forschung, 18*, 299–342.

Wagenaar, W. A., & Groeneweg, J. (1990). The memory of concentration camp survivors. *Applied Cognitive Psychology, 4*, 77–87.

Wagstaff, G. F., Vella, M., & Perfect, T. (1992). The effect of hypnotically elicited testimony on jurors' judgments of guilt and innocence. *Journal of Social Psychology, 132*, 591–595.

Waldfogel, S. (1948). The frequency and affective character of childhood memories. *Psychological Monographs, 62*(Whole No. 291).

Walker, I., & Hulme, C. (1999). Concrete words are easier to recall than abstract: Evidence for a semantic contribution to short-term serial recall. *Journal of Experimental Psychology: Learning, Memory, and Cognition, 25*, 1256–1271.

Wallace, W. P. (1965). Review of the historical, empirical, and theoretical status of the von Restorff phenomenon. *Psychological Bulletin, 63*, 410–424.

Warrington, E. K., & McCarthy, R. (1983). Category specific access dysphasia. *Brain, 106*, 859–878.

Warrington, E. K., & Sanders, H. J. (1971). The fate of old memories. *Quarterly Journal of Experimental Psychology, 23*, 432–442.

Warrington, E. K., & Shallice, T. (1984). Category specific semantic impairments. *Brain, 107*, 829–854.

Warrington, E. K., & Weiskrantz, L. (1968). New method of testing long-term retention with special reference to amnesia patients. *Nature, 217*, 972–974.

Warrington, E. K., & Weiskrantz, L. (1970). Amnesic syndrome: Consolidation or retrieval? *Nature, 228*, 628–630.

Warrington, E. K., & Weiskrantz, L. (1974). The effect of prior learning on subsequent retention in amnesia patients. *Neuropsychologia, 16*, 169–176.

Washburn, M. F. (1916). *Movement and mental imagery*. Boston: Houghton Mifflin.

Watkins, M. J. (1972). Locus of the modality effect in free recall. *Journal of Verbal Learning and Verbal Behavior, 11*, 644–648.

Watkins, M. J. (1977). The intricacy of memory span. *Memory & Cognition, 5*, 529–534.

Watkins, M. J. (1979). Engrams as cuegrams and forgetting as cue overload: A cueing approach to the structure of memory. In C. R. Puff (Ed.), *Memory organization and structure*. New York: Academic Press.

Watkins, M. J. (2001). The modality effect and the gentle law of speech ascendancy: Protesting the tyranny of reified memory. In H. L. Roediger III, J. S. Nairne, I. Neath, & A. M. Surprenant (Eds.), *The nature of remembering: Essays in honor of Robert G. Crowder*. Washington, DC: American Psychological Association.

Watkins, M. J., & Gardiner, J. M. (1979). An appreciation of generate–recognize theory of recall. *Journal of Verbal Learning and Verbal Behavior, 18*, 687–704.

Watkins, M. J., Neath, I., & Sechler, E. S. (1989). Recency effect in recall of a word list when an immediate memory task is performed after each word presentation. *American Journal of Psychology, 102*, 265–270.

Watkins, M. J., & Sechler, E. S. (1989). Adapting to an irrelevant item in an immediate recall task. *Memory & Cognition, 17*, 682–692.

Watkins, M. J., & Tulving, E. (1975). Episodic memory: When recognition fails. *Journal of Experimental Psychology: General, 104*, 5–29.

Watkins, M. J., & Watkins, O. C. (1973). The postcategorical status of the modality effect in serial recall. *Journal of Experimental Psychology, 99*, 226–230.

Watkins, M. J., & Watkins, O. C. (1974). A tactile suffix effect. *Memory & Cognition, 2*, 176–180.

Watkins, O. C., & Watkins, M. J. (1980). The modality effect and echoic persistence. *Journal of Experimental Psychology: General, 109*, 251–278.

Watson, F. (1915). The father of modern psychology. *Psychological Review, 22*, 333–353.

Watson, J. B. (1913). Psychology as the behaviorist views it. *Psychological Review, 20*, 158–177.

Watson, J. B. (1939). *Behaviorism* (2nd ed.). Chicago: University of Chicago Press.

Watson, R. I. (1968). *The great psychologists: From Aristotle to Freud* (2nd ed.). Philadelphia: Lippincott.

Waugh, N. C., & Norman, D. A. (1965). Primary memory. *Psychological Review, 72*, 89–104.

Weaver, C. A., III. (1993). Do you need a "flash" to form a flashbulb memory? *Journal of Experimental Psychology: General, 122*, 39–46.

Wechsler, D. B. (1963). Engrams, memory storage, and mnemonic coding. *American Psychologist, 18*, 149–153.

Weingardt, K. R., Loftus, E. F., & Lindsay, D. S. (1995). Misinformation revisited: New evidence on the suggestibility of memory. *Memory & Cognition, 23*, 72–82.

Weingartner, H., & Faillace, L. A. (1971). Alcohol state-dependent learning in man. *Journal of Nervous and Mental Disease, 153*, 395–406.

Weiskrantz, L. (1982). Comparative aspects of studies of amnesia. *Philosophical Transactions of the Royal Society of London B, 298*, 97–109.

Weiskrantz, L. (1985). On issues and theories of the human amnesic syndrome. In N. M. Weinberger, J. L. McGaugh, & G. Lynch (Eds.), *Memory systems of the brain*. New York: Guilford.

Welch, G. B., & Burnett, C. T. (1924). Is primacy a factor in association formation? *American Journal of Psychology, 35*, 396–401.

Wenger, M. J., & Ingvalson, E. M. (in press). A decisional component of holistic encoding. *Journal of Experimental Psychology: Learning, Memory, and Cognition*.

Wenger, M. J., & Payne, D. G. (1995). On the acquisition of mnemonic skill: Application of skilled memory theory. *Journal of Experimental Psychology: Applied, 1*, 194–215.

Wenger, M. J., & Townsend, J. T. (Eds.). (2001). *Computational, geometric, and process perspectives on facial cognition: Contexts and challenges*. Mahwah, NJ: Erlbaum.

West, R. (1996). An application of prefrontal cortex function theory to cognitive aging. *Psychological Bulletin, 120*, 272–292.

West, R., & Craik, F. I. M. (1999). Age-related decline in prospective memory: The roles of cue accessibility and cue sensitivity. *Psychology of Aging, 14*, 264–272.

Wheeler, M. A. (1995). Improvement in recall over time without repeated testing: Spontaneous recovery revisited. *Journal of Experimental Psychology: Learning, Memory, and Cognition, 21*, 173–184.

Wheeler, M. A., & Roediger, H. L., III. (1992). Disparate effects of repeated testing: Reconciling Ballard's (1913) and Bartlett's (1932) results. *Psychological Science, 3*, 240–245.

Whitehouse, P. J., Maurer, K., & Ballenger, J. F. (Eds.). (2000). *Concepts of Alzheimer disease: Biological, clinical, and cultural perspectives*. Baltimore, MD: Johns Hopkins University Press.

Whitehouse, W. G., Orne, E. C., Orne, M. T., & Dinges, D. F. (1991). Distinguishing the source of memories reported during prior waking and hypnotic recall attempts. *Applied Cognitive Psychology, 5*, 51–59.

Whiteman, H. L., Nairne, J. S., & Serra, M. (1994). Recognition and recall-like processes in the long-term reconstruction of order. *Memory, 2*, 275–295.

Wickelgren, W. A. (1965). Short-term memory for phonemically similar lists. *American Journal of Psychology, 78*, 567–74.

Wickelgren, W. A. (1966). Associative intrusions in short-term recall. *Journal of Experimental Psychology, 78*, 853–858.

Wickelgren, W. A. (1968). Sparing of short-term memory in an amnesic patient: Implications for a strength theory of memory. *Neuropsychologia, 6*, 235–244.

Wickelgren, W. A., & Norman, D. A. (1966). Strength models and serial position in short-term recognition memory. *Journal of Mathematical Psychology, 3*, 316–347.

Wickens, D. D. (1970). Encoding categories of words: An empirical approach to meaning. *Psychological Review, 77*, 1–15.

Wickens, D. D. (1972). Characteristics of word encoding. In A. W. Melton & E. Martin (Eds.), *Coding processes in human memory*. Washington, DC: Winston.

Wickens, D. D. (1987). The dual meanings of context: Implications for research, theory, and applications. In D. S. Gorfein & R. R. Hoffman (Eds.), *Memory and learning: The Ebbinghaus Centennial Conference*. Hillsdale, NJ: Erlbaum.

Wickens, D. D., Born, D. G., & Allen, C. K. (1963). Proactive inhibition and item similarity in short-term memory. *Journal of Verbal Learning and Verbal Behavior, 2*, 440–445.

Wilson, B. A. (1999). Memory rehabilitation in brain-injured people. In D. T. Suss, G. Winocur, & I. H. Robertson (Eds.), *Cognitive neurorehabilitation*. Cambridge, UK: Cambridge University Press.

Wilson, B. A., & Baddeley, A. D. (1988). Semantic, episodic, and autobiographical memory in a post-meningitic amnesic patient. *Brain and Cognition, 8*, 31–46.

Winningham, R. G. (2001, April). *Age-related differences in the accuracy of adults' eyewitness reports*. Paper presented at the 71st annual convention of the Rocky Mountain Psychology Association, Reno, NV.

Winningham, R. G., Hyman, I. E., Jr., & Dinnel, D. L. (2000). Flashbulb memories? The effects of when the initial memory report was obtained. *Memory, 8*, 209–216.

Winocur, G., & Weiskrantz, L. (1976). An investigation of paired-associate learning in amnesic patients. *Neuropsychologia, 14*, 97–110.

Winograd, E., & Killinger, W. A., Jr. (1983). Relating age at encoding in early childhood to adult recall: Development of flashbulb memories. *Journal of Experimental Psychology: General, 112,* 413–422.

Winograd, E., & Neisser, U. (Eds.). (1992). *Affect and accuracy in recall: Studies of "flashbulb" memories.* New York: Cambridge University Press.

Witherspoon, D., & Moscovitch, M. (1989). Stochastic independence between two implicit memory tasks. *Journal of Experimental Psychology: Learning, Memory, and Cognition, 15,* 22–30.

Witmer, L. R. (1935). The association value of three-place consonant syllables. *Journal of Genetic Psychology, 47,* 337–360.

Wittgenstein, L. (1953). *Philosophical investigations* (G. E. M. Anscombe, Trans.). Oxford, UK: Blackwell.

Wixted, J. T. (1992). Subjective memorability and the mirror effect. *Journal of Experimental Psychology: Learning, Memory, and Cognition, 18,* 681–690.

Wollen, K. A., Weber, A., & Lowry, D. H. (1972). Bizarreness versus interaction of mental images as determinants of learning. *Cognitive Psychology, 3,* 518–523.

Woloshyn, V. E., Willoughby, T., Wood, E., & Pressley, M. (1990). Elaborative interrogation facilitates adult learning of factual paragraphs. *Journal of Educational Psychology, 82,* 513–524.

Wood, E., Pressley, M., & Winne, P. H. (1990). Elaborative interrogation effects on children's learning of factual information. *Journal of Educational Psychology, 82,* 741–748.

Wood, N. L., & Cowan, N. (1995). The cocktail party phenomenon revisited: Attention and memory in the classic selective listening procedure of Cherry (1953). *Journal of Experimental Psychology: Learning, Memory, & Cognition, 21,* 255–260.

Woodworth, R. S. (1938). *Experimental psychology.* New York: Holt.

Wright, A. A., Santiago, H. C., Sands, S. F., Kendrick, D. F., & Cook, R. G. (1985). Memory processing of serial lists by pigeons, monkeys, and people. *Science, 229,* 287–289.

Wright, D. B. (1993). Recall of the Hillsborough disaster over time: Systematic biases of "flashbulb" memories. *Applied Cognitive Psychology, 7,* 129–138.

Wright, J. H. (1967). Effects of formal interitem similarity and length of retention interval on proactive inhibition in short-term memory. *Journal of Experimental Psychology, 75,* 366–395.

Yapko, M. D. (1994). Suggestibility and repressed memories of abuse: A survey of psychotherapists' beliefs. *American Journal of Clinical Hypnosis, 36,* 163–171.

Yates, F. A. (1966). *The art of memory.* Chicago: University of Chicago Press.

Yeomans, J. M., & Irwin, D. E. (1985). Stimulus duration and partial report performance. *Perception & Psychophysics, 37,* 163–169.

Yin, R. K. (1969). Looking at upside-down faces. *Journal of Experimental Psychology, 81,* 141–145.

Yntema, D. B., & Trask, F. P. (1963). Recall as a search process. *Journal of Verbal Learning & Verbal Behavior, 2,* 65–74.

Yonelinas, A. P. (2001). Consciousness, control, and confidence: The 3 Cs of recognition memory. *Journal of Experimental Psychology: General, 130,* 361–379.

Yonelinas, A. P. (2002). The nature of recollection and familiarity: A review of 30 years of research. *Journal of Memory and Language, 46,* 441–517.

Yonelinas, A. P., Kroll, N. E. A., Dobbins, I., Lazzara, M., & Knight, R. T. (1998). Recollection and familiarity deficits in amnesia: Convergence of remember–know, process dissociation, and receiver operating characteristic data. *Neuropsychology, 12,* 323–339.

Young, A. W., Hay, D. C., & Ellis, A. W. (1985). The faces that launched a thousand slips: Everyday difficulties and errors in recognising people. *British Journal of Psychology, 76,* 495–523.

Young, R. K. (1968). Serial learning. In T. R. Dixon & D. L. Horton (Eds.), *Verbal behavior and general behavior theory.* Englewood Cliffs, NJ: Prentice-Hall.

Zaragoza, M. S., & Koshmider, J. W., III. (1989). Misled subjects may know more than their performance implies. *Journal of Experimental Psychology: Learning, Memory, and Cognition, 15,* 246–255.

Zechmeister, E. B. (1972). Orthographic distinctiveness as a variable in word recognition. *American Journal of Psychology, 85,* 425–430.

Zechmeister, E. B., & Nyberg, S. E. (1982). *Human memory: An introduction to research and theory.* Pacific Grove, CA: Brooks/Cole.

Zechmeister, E. B., & Shaughnessy, J. J. (1980). When you know that you know and when you think that you know but you don't. *Bulletin of the Psychonomic Society, 15,* 41–44.

Zimmerman, J., & Underwood, B. J. (1968). Ordinal position knowledge within and across lists as a function of instructions. *Journal of General Psychology, 79,* 301–307.

Zusne, L. (1975). *Names in the history of psychology: A biographical sourcebook.* New York: Halsted Press.

Author Index

Glossary/Subject Index

Br   A measure of bias within the two-high-threshold model of analyzing recognition memory, 204

Brain, 163–197

Brain state in a box model   A model of serial order that uses an activation gradient as the mechanism for retaining order information, 307–308

Brightness masking   A flash of light that masks visual information in the eye, 25

Brown-Peterson paradigm   A memory task in which lists comprised of three randomly chosen letters (usually consonant trigrams) are presented for recall, which occurs after varying amounts of distractor activity, 48–49, 125–129, 187, 327–328
and aging, 327–328
and Alzheimer's disease, 187
interference versus decay in, 125–129

Broca's area   A part of the brain, located in the frontal lobe, that is believed to be responsible for speech or language planning and production, 192

C

C   A measure of bias within signal detection theory, 202–204

Candidate set. *See* Set

Capacity   Limitation on information processing, which constrains the amount of information that can be retained or resources that can be brought to bear on a cognitive task, 44, 46–48, 69, 77, 83–84, 85, 100, 243
of generic memory, 243
of iconic memory, 23–24
of long-term memory, 77, 100
of semantic memory, 243
of sensory memory, 23–24, 100
of short-term memory, 44, 46–48, 100
of working memory, 69, 83–84

Cartesian dualism   A philosophical theory, proposed by René Descartes, that separates the mind and body into separate aspects, only connected via the pineal gland, 11

CAT scan. *See* Computerized axial tomography (CT) scan

Catastrophic interference   In connectionist networks, the problem that new information causes complete disruption of old information when items are learned using sequential presentation, 391–392

Category   A group of concepts that are held together by a common theme, 240–242
basic level, 240
subordinate level, 240
superordinate level, 240
See also Concept

Ceiling effect   When performance on a task cannot be improved, 188, 331

Central executive   A process within working memory that is responsible for controlling and distributing resources among the various slave systems, 69. *See also* Working memory

Cerebral cortex   A part of the forebrain that is associated with complex thought and cognition, 166

Chaining   The idea that serial learning consists of forming associations between adjacent items, 294–295, 383

Changing distractor effect   The finding that the recency effect disappears when the distractor activity after the final item is different from the distractor task that followed every other list item, 59–66

Characteristic feature   A feature that is usually, but not necessarily, true of a concept, 227–231

Children, memory in, 315–326

Chunk   A meaningful piece of information, 47–48

Chunking   Process by which individual pieces of information are bound together into a meaningful whole, 47–48

Cicero, 9

Clustering   The term used to describe subjects being likely to recall items from the same category sequentially even though the items are separated in the list, 103

Coding   The transformation of information from one form (visual, auditory, etc.) into a different form or code, 45–47, 52, 67, 70, 245–246, 252–253

Cognitive economy   A principle in Collins and Quillian's hierarchical model of generic memory that assigns the properties of a category to the most general level possible, thus reducing redundancy, 225

Cognitive interview   A procedure in which the interviewer uses a number of memory-jogging techniques, such as guided imagery and context reinstatement, to maximize the completeness of the report, 279–280

Cognitive psychology   The branch of psychology primarily focused on thinking or cognition. Topics include perception, memory, language, decision making, reasoning, and problem solving, 18

Cohort   A group of subjects of similar age and experiences, 327

Collins and Quillian's hierarchical model   A model of generic memory in which concepts are arranged in a hierarchical fashion from the general to the specific, 224–227

Comparison set. *See* Set

Competitor set. *See* Set

F

Penfield, Wilder, 136, 344

Perceptual representation system (PRS)
A nondeclarative memory system, within the multiple memory systems view, that is responsible for many of the effects seen on indirect tests, 151, 153, 211. *See also* Implicit memory

Perky effect The finding that imagining a stimulus increases the threshold for detecting a similar physical stimulus, 249

Permastore A theoretical memory store that holds information permanently, 137

Perseveration The continued processing of an item after practice or rehearsal ends, 117–118

Perturbation As it pertains to memory, a process that occurs when two encoded values swap positions with neighboring values, 300

Perturbation theory A theory of serial memory in which items in a sequence perturb or swap positions, leading to order errors, 294–295, 296–304, 307

PET scan. *See* Positron emission tomography (PET)

Phonetic alphabet A mnemonic technique to improve memory for numbers that involves linking a particular sound with a particular digit, 350–351. *See also* Mnemonics

Phonetic numerical code. *See* Phonetic alphabet

Phonological loop A slave system in the working memory framework consisting of the phonological store and the articulatory control process, 69–76, 77, 79–80, 82, 94. *See also* Working memory

Phonological loop model A model of serial order that uses an activation gradient plus context as mechanisms for retaining order information, 307–309

Phonological similarity effect The finding that memory is worse for items that sound alike than for items that differ, 70–71, 76, 84, 90, 92, 94, 186–187, 320
and articulatory suppression, 70–71, 90, 92, 94
in children, 320
and feature model, 84, 90, 92
and working memory, 70–71, 76

Phonological store A memory store that can retain about 2 seconds of speech-based information for a short period of time. It is part of the phonological loop slave system within the working memory framework, 69, 71, 75, 78. *See also* Working memory

Photographic memory. *See* Eidetic imagery

PI. *See* Proactive interference

Piaget, Jean 284

Picture superiority effect The finding that pictures are often remembered better than words, 211, 249

Plasticity. *See* Neural plasticity

Plato, 2, 8, 267

Plotinus, 9

Positional uncertainty gradient The probability that a particular item will be recalled as having occurred in a particular position, 301, 303–304, 393

Positron emission tomography (PET) A non-invasive technique for measuring brain activity based on measuring blood flow in the brain, 171, 173, 184, 192–196, 334, 341

Postsynaptic potential (PSP) The change in the voltage in a neuron that occurs after neurotransmitters attach themselves to receptor sites on the dendrites, 165

Pr A discrimination measure within the two-high-threshold model of recognition, 204

Practice, massed versus distributed, 346–348

Precategorical Information preserved as an unanalyzed representation of the original physical stimulus, 31

Precategorical acoustic store (PAS) A theory of echoic memory that assumes that auditory to-be-remembered items are stored in a relatively uncategorized code for brief periods of time, 7, 31–37, 93. *See also* Echoic memory

Preterminal suffix effect A reduction in memory for items other than the final item in the list, caused by a stimulus suffix, 32

Primacy effect In serial or free recall, the finding that the first items in a sequence are recalled better than the middle items in the sequence, 38, 57–58, 60, 65, 189, 292, 302, 310, 368
and dating events, 292, 302, 310
and free recall, 57–60, 65
and recognition,
and rehearsal, 57–60
and sensory memory, 38

Primacy gradient An activation gradient that decreases over list positions in a nonlinear manner; the probability of recalling a given item in a particular position is related to the magnitude of activation, 308. *See also* Primacy model; Brain state in a box model; Serial order in a box model

Primacy model A model of serial order that uses an activation gradient as the mechanism for retaining order information, 307–308

Primary memory The contents of consciousness or the information that is the focus of attention at any one time. Sometimes called the "psychological present," 7, 43, 44, 46–48, 49, 67, 85–86, 88, 153
capacity, 46–48
See also Immediate memory; Short-term store

Priming The finding that a response to a target stimulus is faster when the same stimulus or a related stimulus has been presented just prior to the target stimulus, 234–236, 238–239. *See also* Association priming; Mediated priming; Repetition priming

Subliminal   Term used to describe the situation in which a stimulus is presented so quickly or so quietly that it is not consciously perceived, 141, 345–346

and memory improvement, 345–346

and perception, 141

Subordinate level category   A specific level of abstraction of a category, 240

Subvocal rehearsal, 72

Suffix effect. *See* Stimulus suffix effect

Superordinate level category   A very broad level of abstraction of a category, 240

Syllable-based word length effect   The finding that words with fewer syllables are recalled better than are equivalent words with more syllables, 72, 74–76, 91

Synapse   The gap between the end of the axon of one neuron and the dendrites of another, 164–165

Synaptic plasticity   The changes that occur at and around the synapse as a function of experience, 164

Synesthesia   The phenomenon of perceiving incoming sensations with an inappropriate sensory modality (e.g., "seeing sounds"), 356–357

Systems view. *See* Multiple memory systems

T

Tabula rasa   A clean or empty slate, 11, 389

Tacit knowledge   The information people possess that reflects their beliefs about how things should work but that might not be verbalizable, 253

Tactile imagery   Imagery for touch, 261

Tagging model   A single process model of recognition that assumes recognition is accomplished by finding metaphorical "tags" that were placed on items at encoding, 204

Task demands   The task or experimental situation causing a subject to behave in one way rather than another, 254

Task dissociation   Method that compares performance on two tasks that are thought to differ in their reliance on one process versus another. *See* Dissociation

Telescoping   The finding that people often give estimates of time of occurrence that are too recent (forward telescoping) or older than they really are (backward telescoping), 292, 302, 310, 319. *See also* Time, memory for

Temporal lobe   The lobe of the brain near the temples that contains primary auditory cortex, 168

Tests of memory

2 AFC, 199

4 AFC, 299

continuous recognition, 323

direct test, 140, 148–150, 155–156

fragment completion, 138, 145–150, 155, 180–181, 326

free recall, 56–57, 59–65, 72, 94, 97, 99, 101, 105, 110, 151, 155, 174, 180, 186, 205–206, 211, 212, 237, 249, 282, 305, 306, 322, 327, 329, 332–333, 336, 340–341, 345, 353–354, 364, 366–370

indirect test, 140, 144–150, 155–156, 326, 335–338

reconstruction of order, 307

serial recall, 30, 32, 38–40, 57, 72, 75, 76, 79, 81, 88, 93

yes-no recognition test, 199

Three-factor theory of forgetting   Theory of forgetting proposed by McGeoch in which forgetting is caused by interference. Interference can be caused by response competition, altered stimulus conditions, and set, 122–124

Thoth   The Egyptian god of learning, memory, and wisdom, 8

Time, memory for, 291–314

and boundaries, 293–294

inference model, 310–311

models of, 294–304, 307–311

perturbation theory, 296–304

and primacy effect, 292, 302, 310

and recency effect, 292, 302, 310

reconstruction model, 310–311

and spacing effect, 292–293

and telescoping, 292, 302, 310

Time-based word length effect   The finding that if one set of words takes less time to pronounce than another set, memory will be better for shorter items, 73, 76–77

Tip of the tongue phenomenon   A situation that occurs when a person cannot remember a specific piece of information but can provide information about that item and can accurately predict whether the answer will be recognized, 53

TODAM (theory of distributed associative memory)   A global memory model that focuses on serial recall and recognition, 210, 213, 216, 237, 295, 307–308, 382–387

and compound cue model, 237

context, 382–383

deblurring, 384

familiarity, 384

Tower of Hanoi problem   A puzzle in which the goal is to move disks of various sizes from one peg to another with the constraint that only one disk may be moved at a time and a larger disk cannot be placed on top of a smaller disk. It has been used to show intact procedural memory in amnesics, 179–180

Transfer-appropriate processing (TAP)   A memory framework that suggests that words will be remembered to the extent that the processing at encoding is appropriate for the particular test; no one type of processing is advantageous for all tests, 101–102, 154–156, 160–162, 338, 340–342, 349, 354
and aging, 338, 340–342
and implicit memory, 154–156, 160–162
and memory improvement, 349, 354

Tulving-Wiseman Law   A description of the relationship between recall and recognition that suggests that the two measures are uncorrelated, 379. *See also* Recognition failure of recallable words

Two-alternative forced choice. *See* 2AFC

Two-high-threshold model   A model of recognition that supposes that there is a threshold for old items and a threshold for new items and only items that exceed the threshold will be recognized, 204. *See also* Recognition; Signal detection theory

Two-stage models   A class of models that assume that recall is accomplished by using at least two processes, whereas recognition is accomplished by using a single process, 206–208. *See also* Generate-recognize models of recognition

Typicality effect   The finding that typical members of a category are verified faster than are atypical members, 229

U

Umbrella models   Memory models that attempt to model, in a formal, quantitative fashion, human memory in a variety of different tasks. *See* Global memory models

Unconstrained recall. *See* Free recall

Unilateral visual neglect   A neuropsychological impairment caused by damage to one side of the brain in which stimuli in one visual field are not detected even though the basic perceptual processing is intact, 255

V

Validity. *See* Ecological validity

Verbal learning   An atheoretical approach to studying the acquisition and retention of verbal material, 19

Verbal overshadowing   The finding that memory for perceptual stimulation can be affected by the verbal label it is given, particularly if the label is inaccurate, 286–287

Visual imagery   Imagery for visual information. *See* Imagery

Visual information storage. *See* Iconic memory

Visual persistence. *See* Perseveration

Visual scribe   The visual analog of the articulatory control process in the working memory framework, 69, 257. *See also* Working memory

Visuo-spatial sketch pad   A slave system in the working memory framework responsible for processing and manipulating visual-spatial information, 69, 79, 250, 257. *See also* Working memory

Vives, Juan Luis, 2, 10, 339

Von Restorff effect   The finding that if one item in a list differs from the others, it is better recalled, 130

W

Wada test   Also known as the intracarotid amobarbital perfusion test, in which a short-acting anesthetic is injected into one of the carotid arteries, resulting in a temporary paralysis in the front two-thirds of the cerebral hemisphere on the same side as the injection, 170–171

War of the Ghosts   A North American folk tale, used by Bartlett in his seminal studies on the reconstructive nature of memories, 267, 359

Watson, John B., 18

Weak cue   A word that elicits a target word only rarely, 104, 207–210, 307, 371, 379–381. *See also* Recognition failure of recallable words

Weber, Ernst Heinrich, 14

Weber's Law   For an increment in a stimulus to be just noticeably different, the size of the change is a certain proportion of the stimulus magnitude, 14

Wertheimer, Max, 18

Whole report technique   Method wherein participants are asked to report all of the items in an array, 24, 26, 29

Word fragment completion. *See* Fragment completion

Word frequency effect   The finding that high-frequency words are recalled better than low-frequency words, but low-frequency words are recognized better than high-frequency words, 73, 81–82, 146, 174, 205–206, 370–371
in recognition, 205–206, 214
and SAM, 370–371

Word length effect   The finding that memory is worse for lists of items composed of long (multisyllabic) words compared to short words, 70, 71–76, 91–92, 94, 320–321
and articulatory suppression, 75–76
in children, 320–321
and feature model, 91–92
and language, 74
negative word length effect, 76–77